Walking
A C R O S S

A Golden Years Odyssey

John P. Beam

ISBN-10: 1490425446
ISBN-13: 9781490425443

ACKNOWLEDGMENTS

Walking Across America could not have been written without the day-to-day encouragement (and forbearance) of my wife Helen, as I sat for hundreds of hours before the computer. More to the point, the walk itself would not have happened without her patience, enthusiasm, and support.

Ken Fenter, author and educator, gave appreciated encouragement early in the book's writing, and Barbara Friedman Schechter, professional editor and writer, was very helpful with her comments and editing skills. Valuable encouragement was also provided by Ernie and Jean Maier, as well as by the "Double Ringers" of the Silver Lakes RV Resort near Naples, Florida.

On the road and clear across America, Helen and I met dozens of pleasant people, most of whose names we would never know. A few, whose names we did learn and who are mentioned in this book, are Mike Babb, Dick Cain, Phyllis Johnson, Barbara Lumbaca, Sue McKee, Marvin Olson, and Daniel Rohrer Sr. and Jr.

In addition, there were many others whose kindnesses, smiles, friendly gestures, or shared life experiences remain cherished memories. These people have been given fictitious names, and their stories are modified or displaced in time and location in order to preserve their privacy.

CONTENTS

Acknowledgments...iii
Preface ix

Section I: From Home to the Hudson River 1

First Day on the Road 2
The "Off-Road Hop" 8
A Thumbnail Sketch of Our Lives.. 16
Reaching Middletown on the Connecticut River 28
The Issue of Carrying a Gun 36
The Nostalgia of an Antique Train 46
Northfield to Litchfield 53
Memorial for a Long Dead Soldier 58
Into New York State 67
We are Innocent of Trespassing.. 77
We Reach the Hudson and Quit for the Winter 80

Section II: From the Hudson River to El Paso, Illinois 87

Walking in the Spring of 1999.. 88
Collecting Aluminum Cans 96
Aluminum Can Idea a Bust.. 103
Helen Leaves Walking to Me.. 111
Walking in Western Pennsylvania... 122
We Move Lurch Too Far Ahead 133
Muscle Aches and Horse Liniment... 142
Horse Liniment Doesn't Work.. 151
I Meet a Rough Friendly Pup 164
An Uncommonly Courageous Person 174
Buying Leveling Jacks.. 181

About Spelling Potato 191
Listening While an Egotist Paints a Tractor 201
Our Morning Household Routine 209
"This Jacket Won't Leak!" 217
My Knee Gets Really Sore 225
But More Knee Trouble 234

Section III: El Paso, Illinois, to Hastings, Nebraska 243

Returning to Illinois 244
We Skip the Illinois River Bridge 252
Apple Dumplings and a Cornhusking Champ 260
Sightseeing Along the Mississippi 266
I Acquire a Bicycling Buddy 272
Did Todd Lincoln Live Near Here? 279
Two Very Different Brothers 286
New Tires and a Motel Invasion 292
The Loudest Cricket in Iowa 297
Battling Radio Problems 304
The Dangers of Blasphemy 308
The Transient Iowa Indians 312
Photographer or Carpenter? 317
The Prairie as it Once Was 320
Zigzags, Dust, and a Grim River Floodplain 323
The Vietnam Vet 327
"Foreign Hunters" 332
Who Lost the Picnic Cooler? 335
Winding Down 342
On the Way Home 345

Section IV: Hastings, Nebraska, to Teton Hole, Wyoming 351

An Impatient Winter in Florida 352
On the Road Again 359
The Noise of Nighttime Trains 367

A Roadside Crematorium 372
Likeable Do-Gooders and Welder's Art 378
A Too Professional Young Cop 386
Was The Old Rancher Lying? 392
Mountain Oysters and a Very Sore Leg 400
Convalescing and Touring Near Scottsbluff 408
Back on the Road 415
A Doomed Communication Tower 423
The Lonely Rancher 435
Prairie Dog Hunters 445
Brave Casper Collins and Poison Spider Road 460
Walking Indians and a Cheerful Swiss National 470
Lonely Teton Hole 482

Section V: Teton Hole, Wyoming, to the Pacific Ocean 491

Hosting Grandchildren at Yellowstone Park 492
We Return to Cross-Country Walking 503
Entering Idaho 511
One Woman's Views on Overeating 516
Panthera-Leos Dual and Quad 525
Wolfdogs? A Submarine in the Desert? 536
Once You Send 'Em Off To College 547
"Play Dumb," the Good Sheriff Advised 553
We Cross Into Oregon 558
The Indian Fisherman 568
Fuzzy-Minded Northeastern Environmentalists 575
Walking in Western Oregon 584
We Reach the Pacific 592
But There Was a Little More Walking to Do 600

PREFACE

In October 1998, my wife Helen and I set out from our home in Lebanon, Connecticut, to walk across America. We did well while walking together until we reached the mountains of Pennsylvania, where for health reasons Helen had to give up actual walking. After that, she would drop me off with the car at the end of the previous day's walk; I would hike by myself throughout the day, and she would pick me up at day's end.

Using that regimen, we accomplished the walk in five sections as shown in the above map. Section I, markers A to B, was from our home in Connecticut to the Hudson River at Rhinebeck, New York. Section II, markers B to C, was from the Hudson River to El Paso, Illinois. Section III, C to D, El Paso to Hastings, Nebraska. Section IV, D to E, Hastings to Teton Valley, Wyoming. Section V, E to F, Teton

Valley to the Pacific Ocean at Newport, Oregon, where we finished in September, 2000.

Walking Across America is both narrative and dialogue as it takes the reader through the industrial towns of Connecticut, across the Appalachians, across the Midlands, across the Rockies, and finally to the Oregon coast. It is a story of sun and sky and endless miles, of chance-met strangers with fascinating stories. Combining humor with the perspective of nearly eight decades, the book portrays the great walk as the defining feature of the couple's retirement years, a couple chronologically old but determinedly young in outlook.

John (Phil) Beam
Lebanon, Connecticut
September, 2012

SECTION I

From Home to the Hudson River

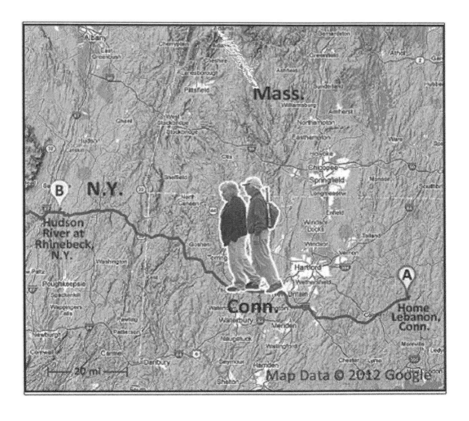

First Walk Segment: October 11 Until November 22, 1998

FIRST DAY ON THE ROAD

It was a bright Sunday morning in October 1998 when my wife Helen and I hurried out of our house and almost trotted to separate vehicles, I to my pickup truck and she to her car. Minutes later, we were en route to our town green in Lebanon, Connecticut, where, upon arriving, Helen pulled in and paused in the green's gravel parking lot. She left the motor running as she waited for me to park the truck and hurry over to join her. Then, wasting no time, she got back on the road and quickly drove us home. Once there, we did *not* go back into the house; instead, we immediately began walking down our long curved lane some seven hundred feet to the road. We were retired, in our late sixties, and a little bored with life; consequently, the evening before we had decided to fight the blahs by walking across America. Only a dozen hours had passed, but with a determined start we were already on our way.

Fifteen minutes later we were walking along Connecticut 207 and enjoying feelings of initial euphoria—maybe from the mere fact of having started the unlikely adventure. Such feelings soon faded, however, as morning traffic forced us against a guardrail along a narrow stretch of road. "If we're going to be crowded like this very much," I said, as an eighteen-wheeler roared past, "we'll have to learn to jump guard fences."

"It'll get better," Helen replied with typical optimism. "There'll be miles and miles where we'll see no guard fences at all."

We arrived at the green about forty minutes later, coincidentally in time to meet a neighbor who was beginning his morning jog. After five minutes of light conversation, he suddenly exclaimed, "Hey Phil! Helen! Where'd you people come from? You walk up here from home?"

Caught in the act and not an hour on the road! Nevertheless, we were not about to tell him that we had contracted a hare-brained idea to walk clear across the country. "Yep," I answered as breezily as I could, "doubt if we'll do it again though. Way too much traffic."

As neighbor resumed his run, Helen and I walked over and got into the truck. Neither of us said much during the short drive home, but we did agree that except for the traffic, walking had been unexpectedly easy. I was not tired, and Helen said she hardly felt a thing. Thus happy to be started, we resolved to continue the walk that very afternoon.

While Helen fixed lunch, I rummaged around the basement and found a small knapsack that had belonged to the children, who had used it years before on scouting trips. A bottle of water, a bag of cookies, a couple of apples—all went into the pack. Light jackets went in too, since summer was well past and it was getting cool in late afternoons.

After eating we sat down to rest—not for long though we told each other—then we would get on with the walk. Within minutes I was dozing and dreamily musing about my thoughts of the evening before, in particular the thoughts that had led to our beginning this cross-America odyssey. At the time neither Helen nor I had any inkling we would start the next day.

We had been taking an after-dinner walk on the green. Like many New England towns, Lebanon uses its green to host concerts, antique shows, parades, and other activities of rural life. Above all, however, Lebanon's green is a historic place where French soldiers once bivouacked, and where Jonathan Trumbull, Connecticut's Revolutionary War governor, provisioned troops and held secret meetings with other patriots, including Washington. The place once hummed with momentous activities, and though calm now, an ambience lingers that somehow suggests the transience of people and affairs, however once important. Be up and doing, my feelings seemed to prompt that evening—while you still have time.

An old footpath leads down the green toward a distant Baptist Church. Perhaps it was my mood, but as we walked along, the church became, for me, some place to the west, a vague place but nevertheless a place that could be walked to, and from there the path (now a road) continued to another place (now a town), beyond which was "farther west" and on and on.... With the sequencing images came a sense of excitement, of imminence; an idea was forming—something wild and crazy—and suddenly I blurted, "Helen, let's walk across the country!"

She was quiet for a moment; then she matter-of-factly said, "You're serious."

Was she asking if I was serious? — or acknowledging she knew I was. *Yes* would work either way, so I said it, adding, "I think we can do it."

It has never taken Helen long to commit to going anywhere, and she goes with all the enthusiasm of a kid. Once, she got so excited about a trip to Florida that she fell down the back porch steps and had to sit on her left bottom all the way to Georgia. And so it went that evening on the green. Only minutes after I mentioned the idea, she signed on without reservation. "Let's start planning right now," she said. "When shall we start? next spring?"

"No, we'll start tomorrow morning after breakfast."

"You're kidding!"

"Nope, by noon we'll be well on our way."

*   *   *   *

And indeed we *had* started, but now it was already past noon of the following day, and Helen was quietly dozing on a living room chair. Time to get back on the road. I gently roused her saying, "Let's get walking, Helen … before we wake up and find it's dinnertime."

The afternoon began just as the morning had, with me driving the truck and Helen the car. However, this time we drove several miles past the green and parked the truck in a grassy area just off the road. Then, bringing the pack, we returned to the green in the car. Forgetting the pack, leaving it in the truck, and then having to walk without it (or drive back to get it) were mistakes we would make several times in the days ahead. But that first afternoon we got it right, and after briefly resting we backtracked about twenty paces before about-facing to resume the walk. We would routinely use short back tracks in the weeks and months ahead, just to be sure there were no gaps in what we would sometimes call our "crazy walk project."

From the green we hiked a quarter mile south on Connecticut 87 and then west on Goshen Hill Road: past the pond by the corner, past the town garage, past the fire station where we vote on election days. All very familiar; we had seen it during a hundred drive-bys, yet it looked different that day. Moving slowly and not confined to a metal and glass car, we saw and appreciated the landscape from constantly changing perspectives. Houses we had hardly noticed before captured our interest with their differing sizes, styles, gardens, and out buildings—even their surrounding clutter.

The first dog we encountered was tied in the side yard of a house, and I made something of a fool of myself trying to make friends with him. "Rover" was not sure he even liked our walking by. A big shot, he seemed to see himself, what with his tail held high and many many barks. The trouble was that whenever he stopped barking, a foolish genialness came over his face, and he couldn't keep his tail still either. "He's probably frustrated," Helen said. "I doubt if he gets much respect."

Moments later Rover must have wondered, *Why's that skinny old man walking up here from the road? People are supposed to be terrified when I sound off, not just laugh between themselves and say things like,* I'll give the old mutt one of these cookies; they're gettin' stale anyway. *When he gets closer, I'll make a little lunge at him. Waiting, waiting, waiting ... NOW! Ah, more fun! Look at the geezer go; he tripped on the peonies and darn near went down!*

Panting slightly, I slowed to a walk and rejoined Helen, who clearly appreciated Rover's giving *her* a good laugh.

As we walked farther, the houses thinned into a countryside of wood plots and farms, which in that part of Connecticut can range from thirty to three hundred acres or occasionally more. These typically lie spread over low hills and broad intervening valleys, and many fields are bounded by stone fences piled up centuries ago when men cleared woodlands an acre at a time. Meat, dairy, and poultry production are active pursuits, and produce crops include a wide variety of fruits, vegetables, and orchard products.

We passed a field of stubble that were remnants of a corn harvest, and we marveled at a hundred crows that were landing and taking off and wheeling and cawing as they competed for corn still lying on the ground.

Ten minutes later, the road split with the left fork curving away toward the south and the right continuing toward the truck, which we could see in the distance. The truck was a welcome sight—not that either of us admitted to being tired. It was just that its appearance put something of a *period* to the end of the walk segment, a mark of intermediate completion before continuance of the adventure.

What a high we were on! During that second leg of the walk, we had covered three miles and had seen and taken note of roadside houses and farms we hadn't been aware of before. We had not expected to be bored, but neither had we expected the excitement and sense of well-being that both of us were feeling. Since we were not particularly tired, we would do a third leg, maybe only a couple of miles, but it would be that much more of the great journey behind us.

So we rode back to the green; then, with me again driving the truck and Helen the car, we moved forward, past the current walk's end and two miles still farther, parking the truck this time in a shallow valley near an old stone bridge. Finally, we returned to walk's end in the car. Getting out was slightly achy, but after a few groans, a few aspirin, and another short, overlapping back track, we were again walking west.

Before long we came to a dirt road that was damp and soft so that our heels sank slightly into the surface. No mud collected on our shoes though, and we quickly noticed that walking on the soft dirt was easier on our knees and ankles than walking on macadam had been. We would gradually learn many things about cross-country walking; this was just one of the first.

Sky colors became pastel, and soon the road led toward a wooded area where the upper parts of trees glowed strikingly in late afternoon sun. I wondered aloud how much of the beautiful sky colors came from "man-made additions" to the air—just a passing thought—but to lighten it, I quipped, "It's an ill wind that blows no good at all!"

Helen came quickly to the point: "Why euphemize, Phil? You're talking about pollution, but remember, the air's far cleaner now than it was fifty years ago."

"There's less soot," I allowed, then added, "there's more green-house gas, though."

But thoughts of environmental issues didn't linger because we were coming to the end of the woods, and here and there were houses with barns and outbuildings to divert and capture our attention. Presently, our spirits rose even more because close ahead was the truck, and by now we were definitely tired. It was time to call it a day.

Helen could hardly move when we got home a half hour later and she went to get out of the car. Stiffness had snuck up on her, and she walked as if she had a board down her back. I was hardly better off. My board might have been curved, for it had me bending forward at the waist. I groaned, forced myself upright, and enquired, "What's for dinner, m'Love?"

"TV fare," she said with a grin, "or you can take me out to a restaurant."

"Just what I wanted."

She tumbled to the ambiguity even as I pecked her cheek, but ambiguities aside, we would have been quick to go out if we hadn't been too tired to get back in the car.

So it was TV fare that first night, and afterward we sat down to watch the news. Ken Starr was badgering President Clinton again, probably about chasing Monica. However that was nothing new, and within minutes we were both asleep. When we awoke, cold, around nine-thirty, Helen declared she could hardly move and that we really ought to go to bed. We got up but soon sat down again, and for another hour we talked about our lives together, since we started dating back in 1950.

It seemed a good night for reminiscing.

THE "OFF-ROAD HOP"

The next day we were busy at volunteer hospital jobs in Willimantic, Connecticut, about eight miles north from where we live. Consequently, it was the following day before we got back on the road. We took care to park the car at walk's end in exactly the place where the truck *had* been; then, as was already becoming habit, we backtracked a short distance to insure a good overlap.

A half-mile uphill walk brought us to Connecticut 16, and near the southwest corner there was a grassy area that somebody, or possibly the state, kept rough-mowed during the summer. The grass was still low, and Helen pretended she was going to stay there and walk in circles rather than start for Colchester four miles farther on. She laughed and said that would be easier than walking route 16 which, though not really busy, was certainly carrying several cars per minute. Although we joked, we were concerned about traffic. We had got a taste of it the first day but only for a mile or two; today we would face it for a couple of hours, or at least until we reached Colchester. What would it be like?

We began walking and were soon passing through an area where the landscape was hills and hollows and steep ravines, where highs and lows were a quarter mile apart. One long down-hill slope had a nearly constant gradient thanks to cuts through local high spots and to fills where adjacent grounds were low. Guard fences promised to keep cars from careening into depressions, but that morning they were keeping Helen and me just a few feet from whizzing traffic. We had both become nervous when I finally said, "Practice, Helen; that's what we've got to do."

"Practice what?"

"Practice jumping guard fences, that's what."

"You're joking. We're not young, you know."

I told her we would get no older if some driver talking on his or her cell phone drifted off the road and plowed into us. I took care to say *his or her* rather than just *her* lest she cheerfully accuse me of belittling woman drivers. On the other hand, I avoided *his* lest she accuse me of being a dinosaur stuck in masculine usages nowadays under revision. How can a body win? Still, writing *her* where *him* used to be conventional often strikes me as jarring, while trying to work in *him or her* (or *her or him*) can easily over-tax my writing skills. So with due respect to all woman readers, I sometimes still use the masculine pronouns. Of course my *he's*, *his's*, and *him's* should be understood to tenderly, happily, indeed *"lovingly" embrace* their feminine counterparts—and certainly in a spirit of equality.(Gender frolic inspired by Isaac Asimov.)

But back to dodging cars.

If an oncoming car, I argued, going fifty miles per hour, were to drift toward us from say two hundred feet away, then we would have about three seconds to get out of the way. Not really a problem if we were alert. Even if a full second elapsed before we began to react, in the remaining two seconds we should be able to scramble a few feet to the left—far enough, probably, to be missed, unless the driver happened to swerve sharply at the last instant. But I left that unsaid.

"Hold on," Helen came back. "We'll never be able to stay alert all the time; we could easily miss that one car in a million that drifts toward us."

"Right you are. We'll do the best we can."

"Really, what could we possibly do if there's a guard fence?—like the one we're beside right now. You're joking about jumping fences."

"Nope, that's what I've got in mind. I'm telling you, we've got to dry-run how we'll do it."

Helen was sixty-eight at the time, and I didn't hear her say much more. I went on:"Now, if I yell *jump*, put your left hand on top the fence, use your arm like a pole, pivot on it, and throw yourself over."

That instruction didn't seem to take, so I loudly said, "Helen, when I yell *JUMP*, you *JUMP!*"

She heard that all right, and when the happy commotion died down, we became serious and agreed that staying alert and practicing jumps and quicksteps off the road were the best ways, maybe the only ways, to minimize our chances of being hit. Someday, somewhere, we might really need to dodge a car.

So we began practicing what we would soon be calling the "off-road hop." We would be walking along single file when suddenly I'd give out with "Practice … JUMP!" *Practice* I would say in a moderate tone, *jump* in a full-blown holler. We'd twist to the left, grab the guardrail, throw out our right legs, stop the vault before it began, and invariably end up laughing.

And so we went along.

The countryside became less wooded as we entered an area of occasional farms and many houses, some of them new, although others appeared to date from the early nineteen hundreds. Beautiful stone fences bordered the front yards of several properties.

We were still practicing the hop when we spotted a woman raking leaves across a broad front lawn. She glanced our way—a long glance—then she abruptly turned away and continued raking, raking, furiously raking. Moments later she looked again but again looked quickly away. We quit joking around and tried to make eye contact, just to say hello. Nothing doing. "Ms. Severe" stuck determinedly to her task and wouldn't look up at all. After we passed, though, we stole backward glances, and sure enough, she was standing full front toward us, ramrod straight, and stuffed full of disapproval. We could almost feel her stare.

"We'd better get serious," Helen whispered with a chuckle. "Somebody might think we're on the lam from somewhere—call the cops."

After that we walked quietly for a while, until Helen remarked how local road names change along state and U.S. highways. "Ever notice that?" she asked.

"No," I replied, "never paid much attention." Then, thinking for a moment, I added, "Well, those kinds of roads typically pass through many towns. Obviously they'll have different local names all along the way."

She laughed. "'Obvious' you say … now that I've mentioned it … you having rarely thought about it yourself. Come on, Dearie, you can do better than that!"

Truth was I had never paid much attention to road names, but Helen sensed she was on to something. She knew that Connecticut 16, which we were walking, had different names in Colchester, which was close up ahead, but she did not yet know how often 16's name changes. We would pay attention that day and be surprised at all the "aliases."

Where we got onto route 16, its name (besides 16) is Colchester Road. A mile farther west it becomes Peace Road, and it remains Peace Road for three miles, to the outskirts of Colchester itself. Four tenths of a mile from downtown, where Elm Street connects from the southeast, 16's name changes again, this time to Lebanon Avenue. That makes sense, because from downtown back the way we came the road leads eventually to Lebanon.

Continuing west into town center, 16 briefly shares Main Street with another state route before branching right to become Linwood Avenue. From there it follows downhill to a Connecticut 2 overpass just west of town. Beyond that, it's Middletown Road, leading eventually to the town of Middletown on the Connecticut River, eighteen miles away. We noted that overall, route 16 has six different names in less than five miles.

However, I'm getting ahead of myself.

We were entering Colchester. Houses, at first sparse, became more closely spaced, and here and there were small businesses: a hardware store, a dry cleaner, and, on Lebanon Avenue, a bakery. A bakery! Helen, never one to pass up a doughnut, immediately wanted to stop. "But we have cookies and apples," I protested. "I've been carrying them for the past hour and a half."

"We can eat them this afternoon," she replied. "They'll be as fresh then as they are now, but we'll get no chance to buy doughnuts this afternoon." And with that she started for the door.

Doughnuts sounded better than cookies, and besides, I knew the bakery had coffee. So I followed right in behind her, though mildly grumbling about what I was pleased to do anyway.

A young woman clerk saw my pack and pleasantly inquired, "Out walking? Not many walkers come in here."

I told her we had come over from Lebanon but that this was the second day we had walked, that we covered part of the distance two days before. Fascinated, the girl immediately asked where we were walking to. Helen told her we hoped to get as far as Middletown, which was about eighteen miles farther on. Neither she nor I mentioned going beyond that. We would be in New York State and close to the Hudson River before we would admit to anyone that we hoped to walk clear across America.

Although this was the second day of our walk, the bakery clerk was the first person we actually spoke to on the road. Of course we couldn't know it then, but her kind of pleasantness was something we would find in almost everyone we met. Also, she had a best-wishes attitude, and above all, she admired us for what we were doing. Nothing like admiration to inspire one to continue whatever evoked the admiration to begin with—especially when the admirer is forty years your junior.

We took coffee and doughnuts with us and continued down Lebanon Avenue, buoyed now by a sense of exhilaration that doubtless came from the coffee and the chill of the morning, but surely from the young clerk's friendliness as well. Life was good, and we congratulated ourselves that we were out walking our unlikely adventure and not sitting home wondering what to do with the rest of the day.

Lebanon Avenue soon became Main Street, which took us through the busiest part of town, but there were sidewalks so traffic was no problem. In addition, street-side businesses and the presence of people were welcome changes after the earlier miles of open-country walking. Eventually, a right turn onto Linwood Avenue started us downhill to the Connecticut 2 overpass, and we stopped there to look down on traffic racing by toward the north. We smiled and waved, and a few drivers *did* wave back. But did that one face show apprehension? Did she think we might drop something? You hear of it now and then, yet surely we old apparitions couldn't possibly look threatening. On the other hand, maybe we better move on; we might distract someone too much—maybe cause an accident.

So we continued past the bridge and on to the truck, which was parked in a nearby commuter lot.

At that point, Helen and I had not discussed taking pictures or keeping any record of the walk. After all, we knew the country thereabouts by heart, and although we were seeing it in an altogether different way, it was far off places—like Pennsylvania, Iowa, Oregon—where I thought we would want to take pictures and keep a journal. Nevertheless, as we were getting into the truck, Helen suggested we buy a camera and tape recorder, and that we begin keeping a journal right away. I disagreed, arguing that it was important *not* to become bogged down with that familiar, annoying compulsion to take a snapshot of this or that, or to write down every thought, or for that matter, to do much writing at all.

What in the world was I thinking?

I continued my pitch: Instead of worrying about cameras and journals, we should concentrate on organizing the clothes, shoes, and equipment we would need during a typical day on the road. For the two days we had already walked, we had worn everyday clothes and jackets, and our shoes had been everyday street shoes. (Helen's were just starting to give her trouble.) The problem, I said, was that we had already done too much agonizing about what to wear.

Therefore, to diminish the hassle and make things simpler, we should each maintain a good-sized suitcase of exclusively functional clothes: light clothes to heavy clothes to rain gear— clothes that could be worn in layers, depending on the weather. The trick would be to routinize our use of those suitcases—dress from them in the morning, keep them in the car during the day, and bring them into the house or motel or wherever each night. Before going to bed, I said, we should put our clothes, washed if necessary, right back into those suitcases. So much for the clothing problem. Nothing to it! Gonna get organized!

Helen didn't say much as I got further and further into my do-it-by-the-numbers idea. Finally, tongue in cheek, I wrapped it up:"What say we begin living out of suitcases tonight, just to get the knack of it."

"Well Philip, if that's what you want, you go right ahead and pack yourself a suitcase and start living out of it. I'm putting that off as long as I can."

Back I came:"It's a fifteen mile drive home already, and as the days pass, it's going to be steadily longer. Then it will really be important to have all the stuff we need, because it'll be too far to go home and get whatever *you've* forgotten."

She mumbled something like, Who'd you say might forget something?

Me again:"We'll have to pack especially good lunches too if we don't wanna eat in restaurants."

"Who's 'we'll'? You gonna pack 'em?"

I went on about how I don't like restaurants very much, except for a few favorites we regularly use near home. After that, Helen began to talk about how she thought things ought to go. She'll put up with only so much regimentation—however enthusiastically promoted—and as she talked, it became clear, although she didn't actually say it, that she thought she could do the logistics far better than I could. If I would just leave it to her, we would quickly develop efficient ways to keep ourselves in clean clothes and everything else we'd need, including food. She would see to that, and she sweetly implied that things would likely go both smoother and quieter if I would just "hang loose" (translation: relax and stay out of the way), just as I always had "whenever we've gone on vacation or moved the whole darn household from one part of the country to another—or out of it!" That's exactly what she said!

We sat in the truck and talked it over for another half hour; then I started the motor and pulled onto the highway. By then we had agreed it would probably be a good idea to buy a camera, a light one that would be compact and easy to carry, and maybe a recorder too. In addition, we would start a journal, and I agreed not to worry about organizing clothes or anything else too much; we'd play that by ear as we got further into the walk. Finally, although we would pack lunches, we wouldn't rule out using restaurants on occasion, maybe even that night.

It would turn out that throughout the long walk ahead, Helen would keep a journal of our days on the road, and I would take over a thousand pictures, and carry and often use a pocket tape recorder.

Helen's always been good about coming around to my way of thinking.

A THUMBNAIL SKETCH
OF OUR LIVES

Walking was rained out the next day, which was just as well because we needed to go shopping. It was already mid October, and the weather would be getting cooler in the days ahead. That meant we would be wearing extra clothes on chilly mornings, and consequently I would need a bigger knapsack to carry them in as it warmed up later in the day. In addition, we wanted to buy a bat or pepper spray or something as defense against dogs. The last day we'd walked, we were barked at by two German shepherds that a woman was exercising in her front yard. Though obedient to the woman's "stay" command, the big dogs seemed eager to race down toward us—probably just to do greetings, but who knows?

Another thing we needed was a computer mapping program, since it was time to address the issue of which roads to walk in the days ahead. So far, being near home, we had several times been able to use back roads we were already familiar with—one had even been dirt. However, the walk had progressed to where we no longer knew the back roads, so unless I could find them with computer maps, we would be forced to use the main roads one normally sees on standard road maps. Of course that would mean dealing with a lot more traffic.

At a local mall we easily found a bigger knapsack. In addition, as protection against dogs, I bought a short aluminum softball bat that could be holstered on the left side of the knapsack and quickly drawn by an overhead yank with my right hand. God forbid I should ever need it!—rather just meet friendly mutts, feed 'em Milk-Bones and be friends for life.

Selecting a map program turned out to be more difficult. We could not tell from the boxes they came in how useful they might be for what we wanted, so in the end we bought three, one of which was relatively inexpensive.

16

Upon trying them out that evening, we found the pricier programs to have many extra features that might be useful for planning ordinary car trips, but we immediately preferred the inexpensive one for the degree of local detail it provided. Its maps, though not perfect, would often help us find remote country roads as well as obscure back streets through congested towns.

Using the new program, I printed a map showing roads between Colchester and Middletown, the next sizeable town we would come to. Clearly, we would have to continue along busy route 16 for another six miles, to Salmon River State Park, but a half mile beyond the river, the map showed a Markham Road branching left to begin a sequence of connecting secondary roads. These appeared to parallel 16 for five or six miles before rejoining the highway east of Middletown. If we could find those back roads, they would be just what we hoped for. It would take longer to walk them, but the payoff should be much less traffic.

*   *   *   *

The following morning we positioned the truck in a gravel parking lot at Salmon River and then returned by car to Colchester, where we had finished walking two days before. After a spirited discussion about whether to carry raincoats, we struck west along route 16. We expected plenty of traffic and indeed there was; noise made it hard to talk as we trudged along single file. I soon noticed that going uphill was tiring Helen; she would slow down on steeper grades, and sometimes she had to stop. Nevertheless, we eventually came to a meadow on the left, beyond which lay Babcock Pond, and beyond that a stand of evergreens. It was a beautiful spot—perfect for whiling away an hour. We sat for a while, had mid-morning snacks, and eventually began talking about our family.

Helen and I have four children, two boys and two girls, and three have children of their own. Good citizens they are, each established in his or her separate life and completely independent of us. They lived through early childhood under a regimen of few rules, but those few were firmly, occasionally even strictly, enforced. Meanwhile, aside from school and Saturday morning chores, their leisure time was reserved for them so they could play dolls, read, build model airplanes, roam....

As they entered adolescence, we advised the children to avoid smoking, not only because we disapproved of it as an expensive, smelly habit, but especially because of the health hazard. One sees few heavy smokers over fifty who retain much vitality. At the same time, we opined that if they did smoke, it would probably have no lasting detrimental effects—provided they quit within a few years. However, before you start, we warned, realize that nicotine is extremely addictive and that the habit, once rooted, may be impossible to break.

As for drinking, our advice was as follows: Best of all *don't*; however, if you do, learn a lesson the first time you drink too much. You'll know when that happens—you'll wish you were dead the following morning! But if toward evening you find you crave more "hair of the dog that bit cha," then quit drinking right there and don't ever imbibe again. On the other hand, if for a week you can hardly stand a whiff of the stuff, then you probably have some built-in defense against alcohol. Even at that be careful. Oncoming alcoholism can be an insidious thing where one drinks a little more this year than last year, a little more next year than this year, and so on toward addiction.

Having no firsthand experience with narcotics beyond caffeine, nicotine, and alcohol, but going on the theory that nothing is free, we argued that a drug trip would have to be paid for in the same coin as an alcohol trip—but with more interest and greater liability to addiction. Helen and I had both seen human drug wrecks on the sidewalks of New York and San Francisco.

Whether it was our seat-of-the-pants parenting or simply good luck, the kids avoided drugs and tobacco altogether, and as adults, the heaviest drinker is a glass-of-wine-a-week man.

So there we sat, Helen and I. Twenty years had passed since the children left home, and we were marveling that we were embarked on this crazy walk project.

"But this walk's not really out of line with the way we've lived our lives," Helen said.

And that's probably true, but in any case, I'll devote the next several pages to our not extraordinary lives; then I will leave the subject for good and get on with the story of the cross-country walk.

Helen and I began our lives together in 1950, when I was an apprentice bricklayer for a Philadelphia construction company and she was a student nurse training in Delaware. Our future seemed exciting to us, for although our families were traditionally of the trades, a university education had been my personal goal for several years. With Helen in full support, a pleasant sense of anticipation filled our lives.

After four years of laying bricks and two years of army, I finally began college in 1956 and graduated in 1960. During those lean years, Helen's and my primary income was the GI bill, which we supplemented with her night nursing and my jobs moonlighting with the bricklayer's trowel. In addition, the last two of our children were born in 1959 and 1960. We were indeed busy!

College graduation was a special time because it marked the achievement of a goal we had worked toward for ten long years. Throughout that period I had known a heady sense of "becoming," that is, a feeling of expanding insights not only into the world of physics, my college major, but into personal relationships, into the construction business, into campus politics, and, from afar, into the mechanics of academia. I doubtless made the usual young-adult mistake of assuming that my own maturing outlooks were somehow unique to me.

After college, I took a research assistantship at a government ordnance lab hosted by Penn State University. The work was mundane (data analysis and manual preparation), but by 1964 I had finished a master's program, and thanks to the trowel and Helen's nursing, all debts from the education years were paid off. We were ready to move on, and that would require new employment.

Fortunately (for me at least) research and development jobs were plentiful in the mid-1960s, for it was a period of great military buildup. The most fearful years of the Cold War had ended with the Cuban Missile Crisis, but though the Soviets backed down during that debacle, they emerged from it resolved to build a blue-water navy second to none. In response, American defense spending soared, and since new weapons systems require new underlying research, there were many job opportunities at industrial and government research facilities nationwide.

Of five facilities offering jobs, I chose the U.S. Navy Underwater Sound Laboratory at New London, Connecticut, in February 1965. I could say that I chose the lab because it offered the best opportunity to participate in relatively basic research in underwater sound. Indeed that was true, but we were a family of six, and it didn't hurt that the lab's pay and benefit package was the best offered.

So we moved to New London, and "becoming" began anew as lab postings took us to live in Bermuda, then Pennsylvania, then back to Bermuda, and finally back to New London. The children adjusted well to the hopping about, and by the late seventies they were in adolescence or early adulthood and definitely outward bound. Helen had returned to nursing, and within nine months rose from floor nurse to charge nurse to assistant director and finally to director of a large nursing home. Meanwhile, for me, a final degree program led into years of varied and fascinating engineering and scientific work.

In the end, whatever is lasting in a scientist's reputation lies largely in the content of his writings. They contain an overview of the current state of his discipline, a record of his insights, the hypotheses that stem from the insights, the experiments that test the hypotheses and, finally, the newer insights that add to the global literature of the field. In all, they comprise another small step in the evolving body of *what is known*. The gratifications provided by the research endeavor are surely akin to those enjoyed by the artist or writer, and once experienced, they, and their required habit of intense concentration, become almost addictive.

For me, professionally, the middle years passed in a long sequence of successful scientific endeavors—all making for a fascinating and fulfilling career. Though modest by the standards of world-class science and engineering, my small achievements were recorded in a growing body of technical literature that brought appreciated recognition to one who in youth dreamed of greatness (I blush to admit it), and who in maturity was grateful to make perhaps a journeyman's contribution to his art.

It was about 1990 that I began using a prescribed eye drop for glaucoma. The conscientious doctor repeatedly warned me to watch out for slowly increasing fatigue that could come on unnoticed over time. Nevertheless, years passed before I was gradually overtaken by tiredness that I ascribed simply to growing older, and late one night, while working alone in the lab, I found myself leaning against a wall unable to continue. Retirement came three months later, in June 1994, from the U.S. Navy Underwater Sound Lab, now known as the U.S. Navy Undersea Warfare Center. Doing things together, as always, Helen retired the same day.

Then came a post-career letdown made worse by growing fatigue that was down deep, all over, and never ending. There was no excuse for it, but it was a long time before it finally dawned on me that the eye drops might be the problem. To check it out, I stopped taking them, and within days the result was like shedding twenty years. The threat of glaucoma, however, was still there, and presently the good doctor prescribed a different drop along with *fresh* and *firmer* warnings to watch out for side effects.

Alas, a year later chronic fatigue had overtaken me again, but accompanied now by pervasive physical weakness and a great deal of pain. Incredibly, I was again without a clue as to what could be causing it!

Helen was returning from Florida one April morning in 1996 when I drove to the airport to meet her. The pain was especially great by the time she arrived, and it was on our way home that I acknowledged to myself that I would probably soon be living in a wheel chair. That afternoon, as I lay in near despair on the bedroom floor, it finally dawned on me what the problem might be. The new eye drops! Could it be? Had I done it again?

Indeed I had. I had allowed a medication to gradually cripple me, simply because I had failed to be alert for side effects, had failed to remain aware of a doctor's repeated warnings. In this case it was "generalized muscular weakness," listed as a rare side effect in a brochure that came with the drops. Again I abruptly stopped taking them, and a week later the problem was gone. Subsequently, a third change of medication led to prolonged control of the glaucoma without serious side effects. Perhaps needless to say, I read drug brochures very carefully nowadays.

During my first year of retirement, although continually tired, I tutored at Centro de la Comunidad in New London, Connecticut. Students were Spanish-speaking immigrants who came to the center to learn English. And try their best they did. One woman told me that she and her husband had often made an English-only rule in their home, feeling it would be the quickest way for the entire family to become fluent in the new language. Then, in fractured English, she asked me in effect: *Can you imagine what it's like to try to talk in a half-learned language at the end of the day … when you're bent over the stove, the kids are bickering, and your husband's just finished ten hours driving taxi? Pretty soon the whole family's speaking Spanish again.*

I learned a great deal about culture shock during my nine months at Centro, and I developed a healthy appreciation for the courage it takes to leave everything behind, move to another country, and start all over in a new language.

During my second and third years of retirement, I was a member of the Brilliant Technical Committee, a volunteer group of retired scientists and engineers who donated their time to the study of sailboat dynamics. *Brilliant* is the name of a famous schooner based at Mystic Seaport in Mystic, Connecticut. The boat was used by the committee to gather at-sea test data, and for that reason alone the word *Brilliant* was used in the committee's official name. Looking back, it is debatable how appropriate *Brilliant* was, given that we failed even to try to develop a computer model of sailboat dynamics—dynamics being what we were supposedly studying.

After the "Brilliant" years I did various other volunteer jobs—hospital work, library work, museum work—until the winter of 1998 when I went to work for a large termite- and pest-control company in Florida. Helen and I were spending the winter there, and sheer boredom and nagging depression led me to take the seven-dollar-an-hour job. On the whole it was a help. My boss, the office manager, was a woman about fifty, and she was a pleasure to work for. So was her boss, the facility manager, who at thirty was far younger than any of my children. Only a chewing out by a quality control officer mars the memory of those happy months. It happened when I answered the phone one day with "Good afternoon. Gigantic Termite and Pest Control. May I help you please?" *Gigantic* was not the company's real name, but it will do for here.

"What's your name?" came a demand that was blunt, unfriendly, and authoritarian.

"John Beam, sir. How can I help you?"

"I'm head of quality control for this company, and it's company policy that whenever you answer the phone, you always give your name."

"Sorry … won't happen again. I'm pretty sure I've got it right in the past … well, almost always … obviously I slipped up this time." Was this really me pausing and groveling like this?

"You slipped up all right, but we're not finished. I'll talk to your facility manager now." The man was tough, unforgiving, menacing. There would be no amends accepted by this company lieutenant.

Held back, out of respect for co-workers, from quitting on the spot and telling the creep to futz off, I put him through. Afterward, the manager didn't even mention the matter, and I appreciated that for I would have quit over that too—even though I liked everybody at Gigantic and very much wanted to leave on a friendly note. Still, the question leapt to mind: *What in hell, John Beam, are you doing here?* I had always felt I was humble enough to work at anything or for anybody— well, within reason—but after this job there would be no way I would ever give another snotty underachieving pissant a chance to stroke his ego at my expense.

I stayed on at Gigantic for another few weeks; then, early in April, we went home to Connecticut to spend the spring and summer. By early October I was almost desperately searching for something to do. Nothing could replace my former career; I didn't expect that, but there had to be something more interesting than typical volunteer work—something with adventure to it, something even dangerous, something to be a hedge against nagging depression.

And that, of course, was how I was feeling when Helen and I began walking on Lebanon Green, the night we decided to walk west. Now back to Babcock Pond where we sat dreamily passing time—until Helen ended it with a *jolt.*

"Phil! Did you lock the house before we left?"

"Yep. What made you think of that? Let's get moving; we've been sitting here forty-five minutes, and reminiscing 'll never get us across the country."

Two more miles brought us to Salmon River, and when we arrived, a number of people were patronizing a vender who had his lunch truck parked in one corner of the lot. The truck was the kind of painted beauty you would expect to see at a carnival. Behind the cab its box-like body formed a galley with a customer window, awning, and foldout counter.

Sitting in our own truck, we watched several people queuing up to place their orders. But how, we wondered, could they possibly hear? Blaring music came from speakers mounted on the upper corners of the truck's body; the parking lot was bathed in a mind-numbing beat. "Does that guy think," I complained to Helen, "that everybody wants to listen to that stuff? Does he think about it at all? Does he think at all?"

Then, a little remorseful for badmouthing the man (or a little embarrassed for doing it out loud), I softened my tone: "No doubt he thinks, and he's probably a decent enough guy. Still, the world glows with noise without him adding to the racket. I'm convinced that some people can't stand quiet."

Partly to get away from the din and partly out of curiosity, we moseyed over to famous old Comstock Bridge, which crosses the river a hundred yards to the north. Comstock is one of only three covered bridges remaining in Connecticut. Originally built in 1791, it was rebuilt in the 1830s, and again in 1936 by Roosevelt's Civilian Conservation Core. It was refurbished completely in the 1970s, then given a final spruce-up in the 1990s. Like the other two bridges, one of which we would later cross at West Cornwall, Comstock has been preserved not only for its beauty but also for its historic interest. It was the main highway bridge between Colchester and Middletown in the 1800s, and today it remains a fascinating example of a last evolution in covered bridge technology.

"This bridge must have been a welcome shelter for old timers caught in showers," Helen said. Then she laughed and went on: "I bet it still collects plenty of bikers when the weather turns bad … characters like you."

"Sounds good to me," I answered. Truth was I had often sheltered under bridges while motorcycling, but I didn't like her use of *biker*. "*Biker* suggests gang," I told her. "I rode alone."

But time was passing and we were repeatedly putting off walking. We knew we were not far from where we hoped to turn onto Markham Road, which, according to our new computer map, was the first of those back roads that would get us away from route 16. The trouble was that we had often driven 16 to and from Middletown, but neither of us could remember seeing a road named Markham. Maybe it doesn't exist anymore, we speculated.

Another thing bothering us was that although it was only two in the afternoon, Helen was already tired and limping from a worsening bunion. So why hurry back to walking? We'd just loaf around and rest her foot a bit longer.

Eventually, after putting off doing anything for over an hour, we justified still more procrastination by agreeing that we really ought to drive ahead and reconnoiter the way we would walk—*if we ever got back to walking*. That agreement reached, we let another ten minutes drag by before we got into the truck and back on the road.

According to our map, we should have found the east end of Markham only a half mile from Comstock Bridge. However, when we got to where it *should* have been, we saw only power lines and a scattering of low trees that ranged up a moderate hill to thicker, taller woodlands. The direction toward the top of the hill seemed right for Markham, but there was no sign of the road. Uh-oh! Was this map program going to do us any good at all?

I grumbled a bit, but following our now suspect map, we drove a mile farther west before turning south onto narrow Tartia Road, which quickly brought us to an intersection with a road sign saying WEST MARKHAM. "You know," Helen ventured, "given this road has a west end, it's got to have an east end somewhere." Indeed, only minutes later we met an elderly woman who had lived in the area all her life. She told us that the eastern part of Markham, though an official road, had never been more than a gravel footpath. It once connected, she said, with route 16 at the present-day power lines, but was later abandoned.

With that clue we continued east as the road changed from two paved lanes, to one paved lane, to one unpaved lane, and finally to a dirt extension that petered out near the top of a tree-covered hill. Getting out of the truck, we peered down through the trees. Sure enough, we were standing at the top of the same hill we had looked up across from route 16 only twenty minutes before. Below, beyond the trees, lay the highway, and the power lines crossed nearby.

Well, we had wanted a map program that would show us many local roads, and evidently this one would show us both roads that were and roads that had been! By helping us find traces of a footpath that no longer existed, it had actually led us to a shortcut we would use the following day. Come morning, we would cut cross-country up the hill and through the trees, where we would join Markham at the crest and subsequently avoid several miles of busy highway.

But what would it be like in the future, we wondered, when our map program showed us nonexistent roads?

The answer would be small adventures, welcome shortcuts, and sometimes very frustrating dead ends.

REACHING MIDDLETOWN ON THE CONNECTICUT RIVER

The next morning we walked out of the parking lot at Salmon River, and soon left route 16 to climb the hill toward Markham Road. It was a rocky hike through scrubby trees, and there *were* traces of an old gravel footpath although it was obvious there had never been a road.

On the whole, Helen took the climb well. The night before I had cut a good-sized piece out of the side of her right shoe, so as to relieve pressure on her bunion. Nevertheless, I was sure she was minimizing when she said her foot was only slightly achy. We worried about her feet—half expected they would give more trouble as the walk progressed.

Reaching the crest of the hill, we continued west along Markham, which ran almost parallel to route 16. Good! Thus we were efficient as far as direction was concerned, but we were definitely going too slow. It took twenty minutes to cover three quarters of a mile, which amounted to only two and a quarter miles per hour. Still, walking was pleasant—it was sunny and crisp, and we met only one car. It came up from behind, so quietly that we hardly knew it was there until it stopped beside us. The driver, a middle-aged, well-dressed woman, asked if we were all right and if we needed a ride.

"We're fine," Helen answered with a grin. "No thanks on the ride. We're walking to Oregon." It was a jocular, toss-off comment—meant to be friendly, not to convince. And of course it didn't. The woman just grinned, waved dismissively, and drove on. "If she'd believed me," Helen said, "she'd probably have thought her 'all right?' better addressed to our brains than our bodies."

By eleven-thirty we had walked only a mile and a half. Helen said we would have to start earlier the next morning, and we were discussing just how early when we were distracted by a man up ahead raking leaves. He had a small dog with him, and nearby was another man whom we didn't see at first.

The dog saw us though and bounded up with woofs and yaps and racings all around. We could tell he'd be friendly as soon as he finished the obligatory racket, and sure enough, he soon sidled up, shyness waning, rear-end swinging in sync with his tail. I quietly told him I thought he was an impertinent little mutt, and that it looked as if somebody had slammed his tail in a door. (There was a definite crook in it.) He seemed to think those were the nicest words he had ever heard, but just as I bent over to pet him, the aluminum bat, which I had begun carrying the day before, came loose from the pack and fell over my left shoulder. It barely missed the poor dog before bouncing onto the ground with a diminishing sequence of clangs that must have been hearable for a quarter mile. "Fido" went flying as the men laughed. We just waved and smiled.

Very aware of the men's amusement, I strolled over to the bat, which had rolled about ten feet along a curved path to the middle of the road. Trouble was, when I bent over to pick it up, the knapsack fell forward on my back knocking my hat to the ground. This struck the men as hilarious, and the one pleasant *wise guy* yelled, "Could we be of assistance?"

"Maybe," Helen replied, "if this keeps up." She pulled the knapsack down, and slid the bat back in where it belonged as I put on my hat—but not before dropping it and having to pick it up a second time. Then, with backhanded waves to our delighted audience, we strolled away—pictures of dignified nonchalance, we hoped. If you can be dignified and nonchalant at the same time.

*   *   *   *

Only a short time later Helen fell. We had been walking down-hill when she scuffed a foot, probably the sore one, and down she thudded onto her knees, then forward, hands out, barely saving her face from the pavement.

Diffuse pain swept through my stomach and legs, then up through chest and arms and hands and face, only to fade and be followed by concern and a lingering clamminess. Relief came quickly, however, for as I helped her up she blurted "How dumb!" and actually began to laugh. Her knees were skinned, though not badly, and she had some road rash on her left hand. She had saved her face, though, and nothing was broken.

While she brushed cinders off her hands and knees, I wiped the scrapes with a wet handkerchief and checked and rechecked on her "okayness," until she finally said, "Phil, relax! I'm just fine."

Then we went on.

But her falling bothered me more than it did her. Not one to pamper herself, if Helen hurts, she keeps it to herself—minimizes it. I'm less that way, and her hitting the pavement was a wake-up call for me. This hiking across America would have its hazards, and as we walked along, I began tormenting myself with candidate misfortunes. For one of us to be bit by a dog, hit by a car, or, remotely, to be accosted, worse yet, assaulted by some predatory person—these and other specters paraded through my mind. How would I handle such a situation should one come along?

Eventually, of course, I began to relax. After all, I told myself, we've already practiced the off-road hop, and we're carrying Milk-Bones, pepper spray, and a softball bat to deal with any dog problems. Why worry yourself with *what-ifs* now, out here, when in everyday life you don't plague yourself with worries of this or that unlikely happening. Better just to be careful, put worry out of mind, and take it one mile at a time. Everything will be okay.

We covered just over five miles that day, all but a half mile on back roads parallel to Connecticut 16. That kept us pretty well away from traffic, but there was no avoiding it the following morning when we rejoined the highway east of Middletown. As cars swished by, I began to consider our progress in terms of average distance walked per day, and how long, at the rate we were going, it would take to cross the country.

Briefly, my thinking went as follows: Say we walk six miles per day for five days each week. That's thirty miles per week or about a hundred and thirty miles per month. Now, figuring three thousand miles across the country, that comes to about twenty-three months total walking time. If we walk about eight months per year, it will take three years to get to the West Coast!

But wait! We're not going to get much farther this year; it's already the third week of October. We'll be lucky to get another hundred miles before cold weather, and that means we'll have roughly twenty-nine hundred miles to walk in the summers of 1999, 2000, and 2001. Good Lord, 2001 is the year I'll turn seventy and Helen will be seventy-two!

"Helen, we gotta walk faster."

"Why?"

"Cause we're gettin' older faster than we're walkin' west."

We began to walk faster then, not that an occasional spurt of *faster* would make much difference. We both knew well that we were going to have to walk both faster and farther every day if we were really going to make it across the country. Nevertheless, it was still early in the game, and although we tried, we could not maintain a steady methodical pace. Before long we had again drifted back to a near saunter. It reminded me of when I was back in high school and knew a big test was coming, but teacher had not said just when it would be, just that it was coming—sometime—in the middle-distance future. So for me there would be no point getting all worked up about it—not too soon anyway.

Toward late morning we came to a wayside Christmas shop whose sign proclaimed GIFTS FROM THE HEART. Helen was bound to check it out, but being a bit concerned, I told her that if she bought anything she would have to carry the pack. I doubt the threat had anything to do with it; even so, all she bought was a Sprite from a vending machine on the front porch. The swigs she gave me hit the spot.

A half hour later we were approaching the most striking engineering structure we had come to so far: the Arrigoni Bridge, which in that area is the main highway bridge across the Connecticut River. Big milestone! Looking south from the bridge, we could see a miscellany of old buildings along the west bank on the other side of Connecticut 9. You can almost feel history here. Twenty-five miles downriver is Long Island Sound and the coastal town of Old Saybrook, where white men and Indians tortured and killed each other in the spring of 1636. Only months later came the first major White-Indian conflict in the Northeast, the Pequot War, and when it was over, the entire Pequot tribe had been annihilated, exiled to the West Indies, or dispersed as slaves to other New England tribes.

Beyond the western bridge approach lay Middletown, which was founded in 1650 where an Indian village had earlier stood. In its beginning years, the town was a trading port with the West Indies, and shipbuilding was important. Nowadays, aircraft parts are manufactured there, and so is hardware, computer equipment, and industrial machinery. Of course, this being Connecticut, there is also the insurance industry. Wesleyan University (1831) is on the southwest side below Washington Street, but the ambiance of the town seems

Helen Approaching the Arrigoni Bridge

more New-England manufacturing than collegiate. Maybe that is because the population is about forty-eight thousand—too big to be much influenced by a college of three thousand students.

We continued down off the bridge and entered town, where we quit for the day at the corner of Main and Spring Streets.

*   *   *   *

The following morning we resumed the walk from Main and Spring but avoided Middletown's downtown in favor of back streets through quiet residential areas. We were passing a house with holiday decorations when Helen suddenly came alive: "Good Lord, Phil, it's almost Halloween and we've got nothing in the house for trick-or-treaters!"

"Don't worry. I'll give 'em each five bucks instead of a treat. That'll keep 'em happy."

"You do that and they'll be coming from over in Rhode Island next year."

"Just kidding, just kidding."

It was near the north edge of town that we passed a house where a woman was arranging jack-o'-lanterns on the front steps. She returned our greetings and would have had us stop and talk, but a sense of urgency kept us walking quickly on. Autumn was well along, and talking it over the night before, Helen and I agreed that we should at least try to reach the Hudson River before cold weather. The Hudson was a hundred miles still farther west, thus seventeen days at six miles per day. We had our work cut out for us.

Nevertheless, only a half hour later our faster pace slowed to its usual crawl. A view to the east required a pause and look-see— just for a minute of course—but only ten minutes later we were stopped and looking again, this time across swamplands to the Connecticut River, and beyond to low hills that were spectacular in autumn gold. A few minutes after that it was time for a snack. Helen groped about for doughnuts in the knapsack, which was still on my back, and I lurched about, jerked this way and that by her rummagings. Unable to get hold of her quarry, she gave up—a minute longer and she would have had me on the ground! I took off the pack and got the doughnuts, squashed by then The bat came loose, fell with a clang and rolled five feet into the road....

However, it would be too awkward, we agreed, to eat and walk at the same time; better we just stand and talk—eat the doughnuts, drink the coffee. Then we'd really get moving.

Five minutes sped by. Ten. Then Helen again, and loud: "Good Grief, John Philip, we've got to stop dawdling and start walking!"

Helen uses *John Philip* when she means to be emphatic. Usually she calls me *Phil*, short for *Philip*, which is the middle name I was raised by. I was *Philip* to everybody until I went into the army, and that's when I learned I was *John P. Beam* according to the army's first-name, middle-initial, last-name formula. *And you'd better damned well never forget it, young soldier! If the army'd wanted you to have a middle name, it woulda give you one!*

I expected to go back to *Philip* when I got out of the army, but I would revert to *John P.* now and then—especially in the presence of authority, real or imagined. So I was *Philip* on my driver's license; *John P.* on GI Bill documents; *John,* no *P.,* as registered in college; and both *John* and *Philip,* believed to be two different people by a local bank. Lots of confusion! The easy way out was to go to *John P.* for everything, and thus I became *John* to everyone but the family. I didn't even try to bring them around. Can you imagine trying to get your wife, parents, or brother to call you by a name that is different from the one you grew up with? I mean your Christian name, not a nickname.

Anyway, I've digressed again, just as we kept digressing from walking that lazy autumn morning. "Here we go," I firmly said as I charged off at a good clip—only to realize that Helen could not even begin to keep up. At a much slower pace we eventually reached a bend in the road, where we stopped to look at a brick house that had a weird facade. The windows were of different sizes, and they were not symmetrically positioned. One that should have been directly over the front door was about a half window width to the left.

This was no artistic break from lockstep symmetry; it did to the eye what a sour note does to the ear. Expensive house too. We stood across the street and eyed the place with sidelong glances and whispered comments like "I bet it's nice inside" or "Let's hope it is" or "No doubt it is." Finally, with mock enthusiasm, I said, "Clearly, they sacrificed outside appearance for interior beauty and convenience."

To which Helen dryly replied, "Put it in everyday terms, Philip. They probably blew the inside too."

We started walking again—finally—but it was nearly one o'clock and we had covered only five miles. Soon we reached Connecticut 217 which took us north a half mile to route 372, and from there it was another quarter mile to a Wal-Mart in East Berlin, where the truck was waiting.

But this was hardly progress, and driving back to Middletown, we made ambitious plans for the afternoon. We would eat at a restaurant and then drive both car and truck back through East Berlin and on to Kensington, four miles farther west. Leaving the truck there, we would ride back to Wal-Mart's in the car, and then walk forward to the truck to get in another leg of the Great Beam Hike. We were all good intentions as we sat down for lunch, but good intentions or not, by the end of the meal we had again caved in to laziness and decided to quit for the day.

The drive home that afternoon was thirty-seven miles, and both Helen and I noticed not only the length of the trip, but also the heavy traffic. We were aware too that we had walked barely six miles. To be sure, we had had a pleasant time, but six-mile days would never do it. That night we agreed that more than one repositioning of the vehicles per day took too much time. Tomorrow, we would park the truck ten miles beyond East Berlin and do the whole distance as a single day's walk. In addition, we would start earlier. This starting at ten-thirty in the morning was two hours too late.

THE ISSUE OF CARRYING A GUN

West of Middletown but still in the Connecticut River Valley lie the old industrial towns of East Berlin, Berlin, Kensington, New Britain, Plainville, Bristol, and Terryville. Beyond Terryville the terrain rises, ultimately to an elevation of fourteen hundred feet before descending through New York State to the Hudson River. The old cities would introduce us to urban walking with its congested traffic and narrow streets, while the highlands would give us our first taste of walking anything more taxing than the gentle hills near home.

From East Berlin, we walked along heavily traveled two-lane thoroughfares, some with sidewalks, some without. The area was neither pretty nor easy to walk through, but it *was* interesting. Memories of the walk include car dealerships, strip malls, manufacturing sites, branch banks, busy intersections, occasional motels, highway underpasses—even a sports complex. Here and there were houses or groups of houses, not those of professionals but rather the small singles, doubles, or layer houses of unskilled or semiskilled workers. A few were wrecks tucked forlornly between small, grimy factories, but most were in better repair. And some, by their fresh paint and neat little gardens, told of occupants with pride, order, and a sense of beauty in their lives.

But there was constantly the noise: OSHA beepers, honking horns, truck brakes, car radios—the usual din of high volume traffic. A car pulled up at a red light, and sat there throbbing kaboom, kaboom, kaboom. Its man-child driver, billed hat on backwards, evidentially thought his racket a declaration of NO FEAR. A sticker on his back window said exactly that. I told Helen he was betraying a subconscious longing for the security of his mother's womb, for the comforting sounds of her beating heart. Helen thought this interpretation of youthful music hilarious—said I would make a good pop psychologist.

Soon afterward, we stopped at a place called the CUTTING EDGE. According to its sign and window displays, it sold all kinds of outdoor sporting equipment. On the front door was the word OCSHOECOUSA—obviously some shoe company. We went in because I was interested in buying another backpack, something still larger than the one I had bought only a week before. There's doubtless a principle here, and it is probably that no matter how big your pack is, you will always overfill it. Or your spouse will if yours is like mine, bless her heart.

A young clerk offered help, but it was soon clear that the store did not have what we wanted. Even so, we talked for a few minutes, and when Helen mentioned that we were out walking, he asked where we were headed.

"Oh, just a bit farther west," she replied, "probably over to New Britain." She was deliberately vague. We were weeks away from admitting our real goal.

"That's six or eight miles from here!" the young man exclaimed, and then he wanted to know where we were coming from.

"From over in Lebanon, about twenty miles east of the river."

"You didn't walk that far today!"— histrionic astonishment and us lapping it up.

"No," I told him, "this is the fifth day we've walked. Started from Wal-Mart's parking lot an hour ago, over in East Berlin."

"Great! Most people can't walk a mile, even young people."

He instantly caught his "even young people" slip, and he awkwardly tried to talk his way out of it. Helen and I grinned and did our best to help him dig himself in deeper, until Helen finally said, "Phil, let's see if us ancients can stagger on a few more miles, 'fore we get any older and collapse."

With that, the fellow recovered and came on with two or three rapid-fire quips that became progressively bolder and finally went over the top. "If I'd been a bit sharper," he said, "I would have realized you were octogenarians and wouldn't have been so gauche."

Gauche? Don't often hear that word. Anyway, he knew darn well we were not in our eighties; it was just that he could give as well as take, and he had to prove it. He was genuinely friendly though, and after a little more sparring, Helen and I left the store and returned to walking, warmed however by the fun we had had with the "yout." That night I looked up *gauche* in Merriam-Webster and found it to mean "lacking in social graces or ease, tact, and familiarity with polite usage." I didn't think the young fellow was *gauche*, although he could certainly put his foot in his mouth. But I can do that myself....

*   *   *   *

Ahead, an old man was walking down toward a roadside mailbox, and spotting Helen and me, he waited there, clearly wanting to talk. Frail and slightly tottery, he remarked on his poor health and then went on to say that his wife was not well either. They had lived in another state for most of their lives, and had only recently come to Connecticut to "buy that house to retire to." He gestured over his shoulder toward a small bungalow.

But why here? I immediately wondered. None of their friends are here, and even if he and his wife are outgoing enough to meet people, they won't live long enough for new acquaintances to become anything like a supportive circle of old friends. And where would they meet people anyway? Maybe church or someplace where they might do volunteer work. Either way, they would need to be able to drive, and this octogenarian (he really was an octogenarian) won't be driving much longer. The old man's chin sprouted an eighth inch of stubble.

"My daughter lives nearby," he volunteered. "That's why we retired here. We'll see 'em more now than we've ever seen 'em before, 'specially the kids."

Once started, he talked and talked, and with anxious hopes for the future. Nevertheless, it struck me that daughter and family would have busy lives of their own, and as well-meaning as they might be, these old people were in for an isolated, transplanted, and very lonely time. We talked a while longer about the importance of family and friends—he would have talked indefinitely. But Helen and I had miles to go, and as soon as we gently could, we excused ourselves and moved on.

Subdued by the old man's pathetic hopes, Helen said almost nothing for the next quarter hour, while for me the image of a tired, gray-haired bricklayer slowly came to mind. He was my father, aged sixty-two, and he and my mother had just bought a drafty farmhouse at a lonely crossroads in upstate Pennsylvania. They had moved there because seven miles to the southwest lay tiny Millville, the center of mother's extended family. The idea was that "my people" (her phrase for those folk) would be their social group for company and companionship during family gatherings and impromptu visits. They did that sort of thing in those parts. Maybe they still do.

However, the word *society* connotes a group of persons with a common culture, and the village culture of *her people* was certainly not that of a Philadelphia bricklayer. Tensions set in, and mother soon realized that her husband, who had barely been accepted by her people in youth and midlife, would not likely be accepted in his golden years.

Not that the fault lay entirely with his in-laws. Dad could carry himself with a calculated calmness that was as hard to pinpoint as it was exasperating. He was short on education but long on savvy— brutal experience too. Savvy came from a childhood on the unforgiving streets of West Philadelphia; brutal experience included the trenches of the War to End Wars, followed, in the nineteen-thirties, by Philadelphia's blood pits. That's what Philadelphia bricklayers, some of them ex-doughboys, called buildings under construction during the depression. The brick superintendent on a few of those jobs was "Dutch Henry," who in Dad's words was an "arrogant ex-Kraut-Army officer bossing doughboys he'd tried to kill twenty years before."

Anyway, the move upstate was a bad one, and my parents soon returned to suburban Philadelphia where they belonged. The only winner was a local man who had watched Dad laboriously improve his property and who was quick to step forward and buy it. To his credit, however, he willingly paid a fair price.

So much for leaving one's locality, occupation, and friends when advancing years hold the risk of isolation and vulnerability.

*   *   *   *

There is a place called Mother's Family Restaurant in New Britain, Connecticut, and lunch there was a nice break from our usual packed sandwiches. While we waited for food, Helen opened a "scroll map" on the booth table, and we discussed which roads to use on our way to Plainville, the next town over. The scroll map was simply several eight and a half by eleven inch computer maps which I had taped together to show an area five miles north to south and twenty miles east to west. The larger width of the map, compared to its height, often made it easy to find back roads or streets paralleling busier roads we preferred not to walk.

When the waitress brought our lunches, I rolled up the map and laid it aside at the far end of the table. And there, of course, is where we remembered it to be, an hour later, as we walked along Corbin Avenue near the west end of town. Helen waited with the pack while I hustled back to Mother's to get it. The manager, bless her heart, poked around in the pantry trash until she found it, slightly greasy but still useable. She was a good sport too—she even helped me wipe it off with napkins.

Mother's Family Restaurant

Five minutes later I was on my way back to rejoin Helen, and it was while I was walking along Myrtle Street that I became aware of how much more ground I could cover when Helen was not with me. Not that she was more to blame than I was for stopping and lollygagging every fifteen or twenty minutes. It was just that my natural pace was much faster than hers and I didn't tire as easily. Although we didn't realize it then, this would have much to do with how we would manage the walk when we encountered the mountains of Pennsylvania the following spring.

Later that afternoon we passed a deserted, shed-like building that sat maybe fifty feet from the street in a weedy, cluttered lot. There was a smudged sign over the front door saying *Al's* or *Albert's Scrap Yard*, or something like that, and while trying to decipher it we failed to notice a Doberman lying near the door. We noticed him seconds later, however, when he suddenly sprang up and raced toward us until stopped cold by a twenty-foot chain. We had planned for a possible dog attack, and as "Intimidator" lunged again, Helen quickly moved around me away from the dog, while I reached over my head and grabbed the bat handle.

We hardly slowed as we hurried past, staring at the beast just enough, we hoped, to make him think we were not afraid. I doubt he was fooled, but the chain held, even though he lunged again and carried on as if he would have liked to kill us.

"He'd tear us apart if he could," I remarked.

"You know"—Helen thoughtful now—"if that dog had got loose, your bat might not have been enough."

"Well, what do you suggest?" I flippantly inquired. "Maybe we should get you a bat too." I tried to play it light, but it didn't work. She was determined to be serious.

"Phil, that dog weighs seventy-five pounds if it weighs an ounce. It's savage and quick, and if there'd been another like it and they'd both got loose, you couldn't possibly have held them off."

She said no more and I thought the incident was behind us, but a half hour later she got around to it again: "You know, there was no cop with a gun back there to save our skins, and if we're ever really attacked, you can bet there'll be no cop to save us then either."

Helen does not scare easily, but she was right about our vulnerability to dog attack. She was hinting that I should begin carrying a gun, but I was in no mood even to consider the idea. I just said, "Hell-Helen, we'll probably get run over before the dogs get us."

"I'm not Hell-Helen!"

"Of course you're not. I meant to say 'Hell, Helen, we'll...' but I garbled it and accidentally ran *Hell* and *Helen* together. I didn't mean to call you '*Hell-Helen*.' Hell-Helen, you're still shook up about that Doberman."

"And you're Fulla-Bull-Philip," she said as she walked along—stalking a bit, I thought.

An hour later, we were sitting on an old railroad tie near an abandoned quarry. Nearby was a sign that proclaimed Plainville to be a town once *RENOWNED IN THE HISTORY OF CANALS-CARRIAGES AND RAILROADS.*

Plainville's Renown

"Well, there's your railroad," Helen said. She had spotted tracks across the road, and they followed a stream that looked too straight to be natural. "I bet that stream was dredged and straightened to be a canal," she continued. "Far's I'm concerned, it counts. I don't care if it's the Quinnipiac River!"

I didn't think it was wide enough to be a river, and I wasn't sure it had ever been a canal; nevertheless, "going with the flow," I said, "Well, you've spotted a railroad and a canal, but you'll never see a carriage."

"Oh, I see plenty of carriages, Philip, and so do you—all horseless."

And so the afternoon went, until sometime around four o'clock we came to the truck, where we had parked it near a Volkswagen dealership. Up until then, we had been averaging about six miles per day, but this day we managed nine and a half in a single walk segment. The trouble was that Helen was much too tired to appreciate it, and she was dreading the forty-five-mile drive home. It would be well after dark by the time we got there.

That night I looked into it with the computer-mapping program, and sure enough, the too-straight waterway we had wondered about was indeed the Quinnipiac River.

*   *   *   *

We didn't walk the following two days since Helen had grand-motherly babysitting to do; however, the day after that we made it from west Plainville through Bristol to Terryville, again a distance of nine and a half miles. Thanks to the mapping program, we were able to avoid busy state routes in favor of less-used local roads, which took us through several industrial areas and residential neighborhoods as well as through downtown Bristol.

In general, we were pleased with the increasing lengths of our daily walks, but we still felt we were stopping too often. For example, we became stuck in the New England Carousel Museum at Bristol. A visit there is a special treat. The museum features beautiful, refurbished, merry-go-round horses by different artists from different times. Different themes, finishes, and styles of carving are represented, and there are interactive, moving displays. While we were there, several enthralled and noisy children found them delightful.

We had extracted ourselves from the museum and were walking an otherwise quiet street when a motorcycle roared toward us making an almost painful racket. The biker, riding a straight-piped Harley, had a face the shape of an insolent mask with two dead, staring eyes. He up-shifted the bike with an ear-splitting roar prompting Helen to fuss and exclaim, "Why do they have to do that?"

"Couldn't tell you for sure," I replied, but then I sketched how I view the type:

Work history for him is a series of unemployments alternating with unskilled jobs, which he regularly quits or is fired from. Lumberyard worker, janitor, laborer—all worthy enough employments—but he lasts at none of them. He may start out all right, but before long he's calling in sick or just not showing up, and when he *is* on the job, he can't take an order without feeling he's losing face. He's bad tempered and so poorly motivated that he does nothing well; consequently, the boss invariably becomes fed up and eventually lets him go. Then he's out of work again until the next time. The roar of that motorcycle is really his scream of frustration, and when people look away, intimidated, he gets a rare nonchemical high: he's been noticed—even if people avoid looking at him. That's heady stuff for a born loser.

"They can't all be like that," Helen said, mildly bothered by my harshness.

"You're right," I agreed, softening slightly. "Probably even *he* is not that bad. Let's hope he's just another unestablished 'yout' who will eventually find himself and get over his loutish ways."

Beyond Bristol and approaching Terryville, we noticed that housing areas and business areas were thinning, and here and there were patches of deciduous woodlands. The land as a whole was beginning a gradual rise, in addition to the normal ups and downs of local hills and valleys. These were the beginnings of the Litchfield Hills and never again, in our entire walk across America, would we walk through industrial areas as extensive as those from East Berlin through Plainville to Bristol.

Near Terryville, we paused to rest near an old railroad right-of-way. We were just beginning to realize how many railroads have come and gone over the past 150 years. Aside from modern, active ones, many more lie abandoned, their remaining traces being perhaps a depot renovated for modern purposes, or an abandoned roadbed scarcely noticeable in encroaching vegetation. Some of these are being developed as walking trails.

The last few miles into town were so steep that we had to stop several times for Helen to rest. We would have stayed in Terryville that night rather than drive all the way home, but we saw no motels that appealed to us, and of the few we looked at near Bristol, none were inviting. One place confronted the would-be guest with a blank wall pierced by a barred window, in front of which he or she was supposed to stand during check-in. Turned off by the severity of that place, we drove to a motel we had seen still earlier—just to see if it looked any better a second time around.

It didn't. It was a generic two-story cellblock, and in its macadam parking lot some seedy looking people hung around an old pickup truck, listening to blasting music from a huge boom box. The racket must have been hearable a quarter mile away. As for the people, they were not "soiled" in the sense of clean grime acquired in the course of a day's manual labor; they were grungy in the sense of unwashed for days or weeks, or, who knows, maybe even months. We sat in the truck discussing whether to rent a cell or start for home, and all the while, on the front walls of a dozen rooms, air conditioners droned away, dominating the background during gaps in the thudding music. The whole place was alive with noise.

After ten minutes of acoustic pummeling, we abandoned the idea of staying near Terryville and instead headed home, stopping only for dinner in Middletown.

THE NOSTALGIA OF AN
ANTIQUE TRAIN

Our next walking day took us from Terryville to Northfield, Connecticut, but before beginning, we stopped at a gas station on Terryville's eastern edge. Upon pulling in, I asked an elderly man at the next pump if you had to pay first. "Yep," he said with noticeable annoyance, "but it wasn't like that in the old days. In them days, you just pulled in, filled 'er up, and told 'em to put it on your tab."

"Isn't that kind of what we do nowadays when we put it on a credit card?" I joked.

"Maybe you do but I don't," he growled. "Look, you pay twenty percent for credit-card money if you don't pay it off come the end of the month. Figure it out for yourself."

I wondered how stupid I looked to prompt that response; however, just like that, the old man smiled and said, "Before the war there wasn't no credit cards."

I hadn't heard "before the war" in years, yet from his age I knew he meant the Second World War.

Suddenly, unexpectedly, he said, "Ellen, my wife, died two years ago; we was married fifty-eight years."

Unable to think of anything else to say, I asked if they had been happy. If he had answered with the stock market average or told me to get lost, I wouldn't have been surprised.

Instead, he replied, "Yes we was. I spent four of the first five years we was married workin' away from home, but after that we had it pretty good." Then he brightened and said, "I worked in Philadelphia. Ever been there?"

I told him I had, years ago; then I went in and prepaid for gas. When I came out he was gone, which was a bit of relief since he was unpredictable and seemed liable to become belligerent about almost anything. I remarked to Helen that I hoped the next person I talked to was upbeat, young, and lovely.

"How 'bout me?" she came right back.

*   *   *   *

While walking through Terryville, we stopped too often to look at this or that. The first thing to grab our attention was a reconstructed waterwheel where Main Street passes over tiny Pequabuck River. This stream, though hardly noticeable now, must have been very important in the early eighteen hundreds. Much of the manufacturing in New England was done by waterpower, and you can stand by the wheel and easily envision pulleys and belts driving roomfuls of machinery.

There might have been an excuse for stopping at the waterwheel—it was historically interesting—but there was no excuse, a half hour later, for spending fifteen minutes browsing a modern hardware store. We did though, and it was almost noon when we approached Thomaston, having walked only four miles all morning.

Thomaston was the site of Seth Thomas's clock and watch factory through the first half of the nineteenth century, but in those days the town was called Plymouth. Thomas died in 1859, and to honor him the town's western part, the site of the clock factory, was renamed Thomaston; meanwhile, the smaller, eastern section retained the name Plymouth.

As we approached from the east, Thomaston first appeared as nestled in the Naugatuck River Valley against a backdrop of low mountains, and glancing south from an overpass, we could see an old passenger station of the Naugatuck Railroad. The roof and walls of that once important structure were sound, but a porch over the platform was in decay and the tracks had a coating of rust. On a siding beyond the station sat four old train cars, one a passenger coach from a bygone era.

Looking down over station, tracks and cars, my thoughts drifted back to an early childhood scene—a scene in which I am five years old and standing with my mother on a train platform in Philadelphia. The passenger coach has become part of a newly arrived train, and the picture livens with activity as people hurry about, some getting off the train, others waiting to board. A conductor standing on the platform tries to keep order, and nearby a young couple embrace, lost in each other as people walk around them. A man glares and nearly trips on their luggage.

Two cars forward and close to the locomotive, a porter (a redcap in those days) grumpily loads a dozen suitcases, while pointedly ignoring an elderly woman's constant buzzing in his ear. Several businessmen talk among themselves, and standing by the station door, a middle-aged woman, pale and drawn, keeps looking from car to car, searching faces—one by one.

Eventually, the baggage is loaded and a last few passengers hurry to board. I know what happens next. Soon the ticket agent will come to the station door and give a "go" sign to the conductor. He, in turn, will shout, "All Aboard!" and when he is sure that everyone still on the platform is clear of the train, he will give his signal to the engineer. Only then will the train leave.

Old Train Cars at Thomaston

I'm wary now as I stand near the frightening, throbbing locomotive, which seems alive with the sounds of water and rasping snorts inside. Finally the signal is given, and shortly afterward, almost imperceptibly, the train begins to move. For several moments there is a long, strange quiet which ends with an ear splitting blast of steam, then another, and another, and another in closer and closer succession. Now the cars are passing, ever more quickly, until soon, with high pitched squeals, the caboose, that tail end car of yesteryear, clears the platform and grows smaller and smaller in the distance....

My thoughts return to the present as station, tracks, and train fade back into modern decay. Helen nudges me and we continue down off the bridge. Ahead is town, and to the left a brass factory, to the right a lumberyard; there are cars too, on the bridge and parked by nearby buildings. We pass a woman who nods to us, and we both return the greeting. It's reassuring to be back among the things and people of the present. Helen squeezes my arm and says, "Glad you've returned, Honey. Now let's get something to eat."

*   *   *   *

That day we lunched on soup and sandwiches at a corner diner in Thomaston. I barely remember the food, but I clearly remember a cop who sat at the counter across from our table. He was middle-aged and outgoing, and he knew the locals well—he kidded with the waitresses and they happily kidded back. Nevertheless, his presence made me keenly aware that I had a gun in my pocket.

The gun issue had come up several times, and I had always put it off. However, the day before, while walking near Plainville, we had unexpectedly become aware of a Pit Bull and a Rottweiler not fifty feet away in a yard full of junk. One was chained to a tree, the other to several cinder blocks; and they both lay there staring— tethered malevolence. We fully expected them to jump up and lunge to the ends of their chains as the Doberman had the week before. But neither moved, and our brief alarm soon faded as we hurried on.

Yet the memory lingered. By now, we had met a rare mutt running loose, and we'd seen many more that were tied. Some of the latter barked a great deal, although you could tell they were not really hostile. On the other hand, there had been several times when we were sure that tied dogs would have charged had they got loose, and each time Helen had mentioned gun. It was the Rottweiler and Pit Bull, however, that settled the issue, and now, for the first time in my life I was carrying a thirty-eight revolver.

Guns are not new to me; I have always enjoyed target shooting, and I have had a permit to carry a pistol for many years. But I had never actually "packed" one before that morning near Thomaston, and carrying it, I felt self-conscious and silly. Besides, a gun is a clumsy lump to carry.

Anyway, the food was slow coming, and as we waited, I grew steadily more conscious of that "darn thing" in my right pants pocket. What if it fell out on the floor? Of course that couldn't happen because Helen had sewn Velcro around the pocket's lip just to guard against that possibility. Still, sitting there with nothing to do, my imagination had it fall out anyway, and right in front of the cop.

Eventually, the soup and sandwiches arrived and I stopped obsessing and began eating; nevertheless, for a day or two afterward the gun would remain a psychological nuisance. In a compulsive way, having it would keep me reviewing candidate interactions I might have with other people. It made me resolve to be civil with everyone I met, and regardless of circumstances, never to show irritation, speak a cross word, or allow a confrontation of any kind.

Interestingly, after a few days, those particular worries began to fade only to be replaced by others: What if I became so used to carrying the gun as to eventually forget it was there? What if I thoughtlessly walked through one of those detectors they have in stores to catch shoplifters? Would it set off an alarm?

In the end, I suppressed even those fears with the personal injunction: Quit worrying Beam. Just don't make some dumb mistake that will put you in the slammer!

*   *   *   *

A quarter mile west of Thomaston, U.S. 6 joins Connecticut 254, which was our intended route to Northfield. Approaching the intersection, we noticed that traffic was moving at unusually responsible speeds, and rounding the corner we quickly saw why. A police car sat with its side-mounted radar pointing up a long grade toward the north. Walking by, we exchanged nods with the cop and were soon a good distance farther up the road—to about where a speeding driver would first notice the cruiser. Sure enough, down the hill came a woman going maybe seventy miles an hour (the limit was fifty-five), and just then she spotted the trap. On went her brakes, upon which the front of the car dipped slightly as she hurriedly slowed down. It's odd how funny a scene like that can be if you don't happen to be the driver!

Our first reaction was pure delight, followed by brief suspense until the woman was safely past the law.

"You should be ashamed of yourself," Helen chided, "laughing at the poor soul like that."

"Don't bother me about laughing," I said. "You were laughing yourself. Even your 'poor soul' grinned as she hit the brakes, and she's probably laughing right now and looking for a doughnut shop downtown. But I knew the cop wouldn't stop her; I wouldn't either. She's way too pretty—at least at seventy mile an hour."

"You're all eyes, aren't you, when you think the lookin's good."

And that was all I heard from my happy bride for at least thirty seconds.

As we continued north, the road followed a slowly rising valley with a creek that we eventually found dammed to form Northfield Brook Lake. The lake was a striking landmark where we just had to stop, linger, take pictures. Consequently it was a full hour until we got back to walking, with our usual resolves to keep moving and not stop so often.

We noted few fields along the narrow valley, mostly just woods with the occasional house, always set well back from the road. A Christmas Shop beckoned, but at the moment we were still concerned about moving too slowly. We passed it up, determinedly avoiding even looking in the window, but soon we were dawdling again, this time near a small bridge. "Why can't we keep moving?" Helen wondered aloud. "We're forever wasting time."

Eventually we turned onto Main Street, Northfield, and a half-block walk got us to the truck which was parked near a general store, the only store in town.

General stores have always attracted Helen and me, and soon we were inside browsing. Meats, vegetables, groceries, canned goods—in short, the usual; however, any supermarket would doubtless have broader selections at lower prices, Still, there was a pleasant ambiance to the little store that contrasted with the typical impersonal supermarket, which I normally like to get *in to* and *out of* as quickly as possible. We lingered for a while and talked to a pleasant young clerk, who was happy to sell us soft drinks and a bag of cookies.

Afterwards, we walked out to the truck, whereupon I drove us back to Terryville, whereupon Helen transferred to the car, whereupon we drove car and truck seventy tedious miles home— tedious in the telling, even more so in the doing. In truth, it was time to consider exactly how we would handle this odyssey in the future. Obviously we wouldn't be driving home at the end of every day.

At that point we were about sixty miles from the Hudson River, which we had already made our goal for the year. We would cover that distance with three or four walk sessions where we would drive out from home, stay at a motel, walk a couple of days, and then drive home again. Easy enough. But we agreed that come next spring, when we would be walking beyond the Hudson and farther west, changing motels every few days and constantly eating in strange restaurants would be an unpleasant way to live. We would be better off with a motor home, which we could move from place to place as the walk progressed. It would become our home away from home, a familiar place to return to at the end of long days on the road.

Meanwhile, there would be no more walking for at least two weeks. The following morning we would leave for Franklin, Tennessee, to visit our younger daughter and her family. Four days of driving and three of visiting would account for a week. Upon returning, we would begin looking for a used motor home.

NORTHFIELD TO LITCHFIELD

On Friday, November 5, we returned to Northfield and parked the car for the next walk segment. It had been a long drive out from home, made even longer by a northwest detour to position the truck at Litchfield, six miles ahead. Maybe that was why I had trouble getting around to walking. Even after snacks and fifteen minutes of just sitting, I remained "inert" according to Helen, who began prodding me with blurbs like *We have to get moving, Phil, Litchfield's seven miles away,* or, *We need to strike while the iron's hot,* or, *Remember our resolution not to dawdle.* She said some other things too—partly in fun, but partly because she was getting "sick and tired" of my "torpor." "Torpor?" I inquired. "Helen, we've both been driving for hours, I'll grant you that. But that truck, with its he-man clutch and no power steering, is a lot harder to drive than your nice automatic sedan. If you'd been driving that rough-rider, you'd be in a torpor too!"

But I slowly perked up and was about to get out of the car when up the street came a couple of "mother hens" with a brood of twelve. The brood, however, were not chicks; rather they were kindergarten children with their teachers, but for all the world the women made me think of hens. It was not from the noises they made—they weren't clucking—it was just that whenever a child would stray from the group, one of the women would laughingly dart after it with forward-sloping body and quick small steps, and upon reaching the stray, she would spread her arms (wings?) and *shoo shoo* it back to the group. It was a game to the women and they grinned as they did it; the kids enjoyed it too, and so did Helen and I. It happened three times before they came abreast of us, parked on the other side of the street.

I should have kept my mouth shut, but I had to call over: "Are all those kids yours and hers?" This to the young woman who walked on the street side of the column, closest to us.

"Of course not, this is a kindergarten class," she replied, busy and not appreciating the distraction. "We're taking them to the library."

The library was a half block farther along on the other side of the street.

Her "of course not" should have warned me that teacher had enough to do without humoring a too mouthy old man; nevertheless I added, "Looks as if you've got things under control." I was trying to lighten her up, but she ignored me—severely I thought—although the other escort turned and laughed.

Soon they had passed, and Helen went back to nagging me about how we had better start walking or "the day will be over before we've covered a mile!" Meanwhile, I had become distracted by something else. A half block down the street, two men were busying about near the edge of the road, and I decided to go take a look. That brought an unvarnished, "Phil, if we don't get going we'll still be here in Northfield tonight!"

I replied that given it was already after eleven, we should relax and eat lunch right there in the car rather than take it with us, only to stop and eat an hour later along the road.

"Nothin' doing! Let's go now!" She didn't growl, but she had had enough procrastinations. Still, I couldn't get moving, and I really wanted to talk to the workers—find out what they were doing.

"I'll only be a minute," I promised, as I got out of the car and headed for the job site.

One fellow was helping, and the other, a bricklayer, was down in a hole building a beehive-shaped storm drain that was about three feet across at the bottom. The bricklayer said he would taper the structure to two feet at street level; then he and his helper would install a grate on top. Around the time they got the grate in place, the regular road-maintenance people were scheduled to arrive to backfill it with dirt and pave around it. The town had needed the drain for years, and within hours they would have it.

The men were fun to talk to, and soon one of them asked where I was going. When I said that Helen and I were about to walk to Litchfield, they were surprisingly curious. Right away they wanted to know how we were going to get back from Litchfield once we got there.

"We've parked a truck there," I said.

That led to further questions: "Where do you live?" "How far do you plan to walk past Litchfield?" and more. They were a curious pair, and like most others whom we'd meet, had plenty of questions. On the other hand, there would be an occasional person who would ask what we were doing and, when told, would have no questions at all. It would never be possible to predict by education, occupation, or anything else who would or would not be interested.

I could have hung around talking to the men for a while longer, but Helen came down from the car with the pack on her shoulder and a look in her eye that said we were about to leave, whether I was ready or not.

So we said good-bye to the workmen and started up Camp Hill Road on the way to Litchfield. "I was surprised," I said to Helen, "that they were so interested in what a couple like us would be doing walking to Litchfield."

"Phil, what do you mean, 'us' walking to Litchfield? I'm walking … three steps ahead of you.… You're still moseying and it's almost noon!"

From Northfield, the road passed through rounded, hundred-foot hills overlain by fields and woods that gave the countryside a varied look. The brilliant reds and yellows of a few weeks past were gone; only bronze oak leaves held on, as if challenging the approaching cold. A few times we saw gathering flocks of birds. I had read somewhere that by flocking, birds gained safety from predators and advantages for finding food. That didn't seem obvious to me. On the other hand, the article also said that by flocking, birds could preserve body heat by roosting closely together at night. That made more sense—but not much more.

We passed a tree farm on the left, a derelict barn on the right; there was the occasional small business, an infrequent old house. Near the outskirts of Litchfield, we went out of our way to visit a replica of Our Lady of Lourdes Shrine. It was off the road about a quarter mile, and in its stone grotto was a nativity scene with an alcove and a statue of the Virgin Mary. Looking at it, we found ourselves uneasy and a bit subdued. Helen said she could almost sense the momentum of a faith that inspires modern believers to Lourdes for healing, and earlier Christians to the Holy Land—to fight the infidel, of course. I found the ambiance old and faintly mysterious, even mildly depressing.

The Grotto (taken in winter after the walk)

Litchfield, which we soon entered, is pretty much a residential community and tourist town. Houses on the outskirts are not particularly fancy—more like the better homes we saw near industrialized Bristol, though maybe a notch higher and with broader lawns. Farther along, toward the center of town, are beautiful colonial homes set well back from the road on good-sized lots. Town center is an attractive square lined with restaurants, gift shops, and small furniture stores; in short, it is a pleasant place to visit on a Sunday afternoon.

On South Street we found historic Litchfield Law School (1784), the first such school founded in the United States. There must have been a day in 1784 when suspicious Eliza asked dubious Ebenezer, "Just what is a law school?"

"A place to spawn politicians, I fear!" might well have been the reply. But to be serious, in its early decades the school graduated dozens of men who went on to become representatives, senators, supreme court justices, and governors. There were even two vice presidents: John Calhoun and Aaron Burr.

It was five o'clock and the sun was low when we arrived at the truck, which we had left on Sedgewick Lane. What a welcome sight! Helen noted that counting the trip out from home, we had each driven seventy-five miles that day even though we walked only six. Driving more than walking had tired us. Nevertheless, we were in fine spirits for so late in the afternoon because we were not facing a long drive home. We had reservations for the night at the Yankee Pedlar Inn in Torrington, Connecticut, which was only a short drive from Litchfield. We would walk again the next day, Saturday, stay another night at the Pedlar, walk a half day Sunday, and then go home on Sunday afternoon. Two more weekends like that would bring us to the Hudson River, where we would finish for the winter.

The Yankee Pedlar (U.K. spelling of course) turned out to be a charming holdover from the nineteenth century. Entering from Main Street, we saw the front desk to our left, and to the right a great staircase which led to a landing before continuing to the second floor. The lobby had high ceilings, dark brown woodwork, and old rocking chairs. News clippings in shallow glass cabinets adorned plaster walls. Our room proved to be a refreshing change from the tedious sameness of modern motel rooms: it had wallpaper, a steam radiator, and a bathtub that rested on clawed feet gripping cannon balls!—things of another era. Happily, it also had a shower.

I don't know who said what, Helen or me, but somehow the desk clerk concluded that we were walking "clear across Connecticut!" We hadn't said anything of the kind, much less that we meant to walk clear across the U.S. However, just our walking the back roads of Connecticut made us minor celebrities to her, and when we got to the dining room, she had already passed the word so that restaurant staff greeted us with congratulations and many questions about the walk.

Dinner with wine and dessert was excellent, and we split a plate for a couple of dollars. Afterwards, we drew friendly smiles as we struggled up from the table, stiff and sore. Helen laughed and whispered, "Phil, them youngsters must think we're ninety years old!"

MEMORIAL FOR A LONG DEAD SOLDIER

Since it was only seven miles from the Pedlar to walk's end in Litchfield, we were on the road early the next morning. Our first mile took us through the center of town, and along the way we stopped at a supermarket deli to buy sandwiches. People in the market were neater and better dressed than the people we had seen in the industrial areas around Bristol and New Britain. It was obvious there is a lot more money around Litchfield. As Helen put it, "It's a place of high priced cars, three-letter license plates, and well groomed men in little French berets."

Inspired by the visible affluence, I decided to annoy Helen with freshman-dorm philosophy:

"Humans," I began, "are acquisitive by nature—acquisitive for money, property, status, power, even for eternal life...." Here I trailed off, becoming busy selecting the two best apples from a bin full of Cortlands. But eventually I got back on track. "The urge to acquire may be no stronger in the rich than in the poor, but served by greater measures of boldness and intelligence, it's doubtless more often satisfied. Couple boundless opportunity with a free-market economy, and the result, at least for the gifted, becomes unprecedented prosperity."

"Platitude City," Helen muttered; then brightly, "We've got sandwiches and apples. Let's go."

"I thought we were talking philosophy."

"OK, here's some more: It's a great time if you're as lucky as we've been—thank God. How's that for a truism? Come on, Mr. Phil Osopher, let's pay for these things and get moving."

"What you just said wasn't metaphilosophically profound."

"Phil, you can't put off walking forever."

"I can try."

*   *   *   *

From Litchfield we walked northwest toward Kellogg Corners, which is about nine miles as the crow flies but over twelve miles along the twisty, hilly roads we planned to walk. A drizzle was setting in, and although light, it came from a solid gray sky. Nevertheless, our spirits were high, and before long we paused to talk to an athletic young woman who had been raking leaves so fast she could have been racing somebody.

After smiles and nods, I ventured, "How come you're working so hard?"

"For the exercise," she replied. "It's better than working out in a gym—not as boring."

Helen quickly agreed.

We had been talking for maybe five minutes when the woman suddenly asked where we were walking to, and when we told her Kellogg Corners, she immediately assumed we lived in Litchfield. Her next question was, "Why pick a wet day like this for a ten-mile stroll?"

Why indeed? But rather than dancing around what we were really trying to do, I changed the subject. "I'm not one to tell somebody else how to manage a lawn," I began, "especially somebody I don't even know. But if it were me, I'd let those leaves lay where they are and give the whole place a good cleaning up next April."

She took that with pursed lips but twinkling eyes, so I kept on going. "After all, about ten percent of your leaves are still up there. They're all gonna come down right where you're raking, and besides, a lot of little branches'll break off this winter and litter all over the place. You're gonna have to redo the whole job. Aren't *you* just wasting time?"

I wouldn't have said *wasting time*, except that by now she was broadly smiling.

Back she came: "Why don't you just pitch in and help instead of telling me I'm wasting time?"—which was a good enough answer, but then a better one began forming in her head. I sensed what was coming, and as she began to chuckle, she said, "Why don't you just walk back to Litchfield, get in your car, and drive to Kellogg

Corners? You don't have to walk up there, you know. Aren't *you* just wasting time?"

I ignored the question, because the woman was lightning quick, and I was sure she'd have an unanswerable comeback for anything else I might try. I'd just change the subject and talk about the weather: how it had been, was, or would likely become; neither she nor Helen would notice the switch—I hoped. Of course it didn't work. Both women caught right on and joined forces in joshing me about the "verbal retreat."

After a few more pleasantries, Helen and I got back to walking. Leaf Raker's dog followed along for a hundred yards before her calling and our scolding persuaded him to go back.

The drizzle had slacked off a half hour later, and since it was warm, I took off my jacket and stashed it beside a tree behind an old stone wall. I tried to get Helen to put hers there too, figuring we would pick them up on our way back to Litchfield that afternoon. But she just stood there looking at the sky. Finally she said, "Nothing doing."

"Why not?"

"Because it's gonna rain again ... harder." And with that she took off her jacket and handed it to me to put in the pack—which was already stuffed with a water bottle, a thermos, a camera, two sweatshirts, two extra sweaters, two knit hats, and the apples and sandwiches we had bought at the supermarket.

"There's not enough room in the pack, and it won't rain anyway," I told her. Nevertheless, she wouldn't leave the jacket behind and instead tied it around her waist by its arms. It is a fairly long jacket and the bottom came to the middle of her calves, making for a funny sight on a sixty-eight-year-old grandmother with short legs.

*　　*　　*　　*

Somewhere north of Litchfield we came to an old stone wall, beyond which stood a small cottage in an overgrown lawn. The cottage was obviously long vacant, but from a weathered plaque low in the wall, we learned something of its history:

IN MEMORY OF
ALVIN H. WORDEN
WHO DIED IN ACTION
SERVING HIS COUNTRY
ON 30 JULY 1944.
HE WAS AWARDED
THE PURPLE HEART
BRONZE STAR MEDAL,
AND IS BURIED IN ST. LAURENT, FRANCE
THIS HOUSE WAS HIS BOYHOOD HOME

The sign was an amateur's job—wording clumsy, punctuation faulty—but surely put there by someone who cared. His father maybe? A brother? Friends?—did he have friends? Did his mother get over the sorrow of his death? Did he have a mother?

So we knew where Alvin spent his childhood, and we knew where he died, but what about his life in between? Standing there in stillness by the wall, I envisioned a life for the memory of Alvin Worden.

Earliest recollections begin the same for us all. After eternal oblivion and perhaps a year into life, a fire, a fall, maybe even a family quarrel impacts so vividly as to be retained as a first recallable memory. From there forward we learn the stuff of everyday life: how to make toilet, how to get dressed, how to avoid burns, how to practice good manners, how to live with siblings, how to read, how to do arithmetic, how to work, what girls are like, what boys are like…. And year by year, the developing mind, according to general human nature and its own individuality, receives all inputs and organizes them into steadily more mature streams of thoughts, feelings, and images.

We can guess at some of the images of Alvin's mental life. Surely they included images of the cottage from all directions within and without, images of the wall at the front of the yard, the hill to the north, the trees in the lawn, the view up the road toward Kellogg Corners. Surely he knew Litchfield and Torrington as they were in the early 1940s. It's fair to assume he would have gone to school nearby, and there would have remained in his mind images of classmates, both boys and girls, along with impressions of their developing yet still young personalities. Feelings of comradeship, affection—even hatred—would have attended those images. In short, he could have been much like anyone else.

Departing from my own safe experience of military induction and stateside duty, I mentally accompanied Alvin to war—to basic training, to troop ships, to embarkation, debarkation, and finally to deployment on the European front. I saw his brief life in France as an alternating sequence of periods of dreary inactivity mixed with intervals of horror. During quieter times he would have enjoyed images of homecomings, had yearnings for love; and he would have pictured in his mind his childhood friends, his cottage with sloping lawn, the quiet road to Litchfield. But I also saw him sick with boredom, then brave in combat, and finally in pain, followed by shock, despair, and a slow return to oblivion.

I left him there in St. Laurent, and flew forward through decades of maturity that he would never know. Was there ever such a man as Alvin Worden? In the everyday world the question made no sense. Of course there was; there was the bronze plaque attesting to his life. Nevertheless, standing there by that wall, I was not so sure. He had lived for a few minutes in my mind, and he could still be living in the memories of a few surviving contemporaries now grown old. But they too would soon be gone and so would I; and the house, the plaque, even the wall would disappear. In the end there would be neither physical evidence nor transient memory that there ever was an Alvin Worden.

Beam, I suddenly thought, you're being a bit too reflective for your own good. Of course there was an Alvin Worden and you've been standing here honoring his memory. Now come back to the moment and rejoin Helen—get on with this walk.

*   *   *   *

We were eating our deli sandwiches as we rested in a grassy lawn near an unharvested cornfield. It was a low valley area, but we knew that a few miles ahead the terrain would rise in a grade that was steeper than any we had walked so far. We worried about the coming climb; Helen had been getting out of breath on lower hills. And another thing annoying us was uncertainty about whether we were on the right road.

Not long after we resumed walking, we spotted two men up ahead who were standing just off the road near an up-scale house. My first impression was that they were not permanent residents of the area; they looked too urban, dressed as they were in elegant casuals instead of weekend work clothes. It was Saturday, and I guessed they were professionals of some sort—probably Hartford residents out for a country weekend. As we approached with smiles and cheerful hellos, they turned from their conversation and surprised us with inscrutable, almost challenging faces, while not responding at all to our greetings. Do they mean to appear so forbidding? I wondered. Do they practice such looks in front of mirrors?

Taken aback, I opened with "Excuse us folks; we're walking from Lickfield to Kellogg Corners. Can you tell us if we're on the right road?"

Awkward seconds passed as the pair continued to appraise us. Finally, the taller one said, "It's pronounced *Litch* not *Lick*." He didn't smile but his buddy smirked.

"Lickfield," I tried, getting it wrong again. Why didn't I just answer, *Whatever, you jerk!*

"Okay, you're coming from L-i-t-c-h-f-i-e-l-d"—he slowly spelled it out—"and you're going where?"

"Kellogg Corners," I coldly said. "If we stay on this road, will it get us there?" By then I was so annoyed I could hardly get the question out, and I'd be darned if I'd try to say Litchfield again.

"Several roads can get you to Kellogg Corners."

Nothing more. Blank stare.

This was too much. I turned to Helen to say, *Let's go,* but she had also had enough. "Let's get the h-e-c-k out of h-e-r-e," she growled, spelling *heck* and *here,* just as he'd spelled *Litchfield.*

However, as we turned to leave, the man suddenly relented and began to speak. Helen and I paused briefly, but then moved quickly on. We had had enough of his superior-to-you, or cat-and-mouse, or whatever ego-stroking game he was playing.

"You're on the right road," he called. "Just keep walking. Stay on Milton till you come to East Cornwall, which forks off to the north. Follow that. Kellogg Corners will be about five miles farther on."

Why he bothered I don't know, because he was talking to our departing backs.

We would meet little of such rudeness in the months and miles ahead. Maybe those particular denizens felt their territory was being violated; there were NO TRESPASSING signs complete with threats of prosecution on half the trees along the road. Nevertheless, it *was* a public road and we certainly were *not* trespassing. Probably what bugged us most was that although the men appeared to be successful middle-aged professionals, they acted like arrogant college fraternity boys. It had been a strange encounter, and we hoped there would be no more like it.

Two hours later, we came to the climb we'd been worrying about. Earlier, the hills had been relatively low with most extending only a quarter mile or so; now we faced a full mile of steady grade where inclines would be as much as four percent, meaning four feet up for every hundred feet forward.

About a half mile into the climb the rain returned in earnest, and there being no wind it came almost straight down. Helen was quick to put on her jacket, even as I wished I had not stashed mine by that tree back near Litchfield. Before long I was wet from rain along with soggy from perspiration.

But in spite of having her jacket, Helen was uncomfortable too. She took medicine daily for high blood pressure, but now, when she was walking uphill, the drug was slowing her pulse, holding down the pressure, and thus denying her body of needed greater blood flow. It was a classic Catch 22. Once, I suggested we quit for the day, but she gamely hung on although we often had to stop and she was noticeably pale.

The climb eventually brought us to the crest of a high ridge, from which the road descended a steep quarter mile before joining Tanner Brook and continuing on to Kellogg Corners. Standing up there we could hear the stream as distant background against the quiet patter of nearby raindrops. Beautiful vistas added to the gentle ambience, and we would have lingered to enjoy, except that we were both chilly and it was getting late in the afternoon.

Coming down off the ridge, my feet banged forward in my shoes with every step, and Helen was especially uncomfortable since not only did her feet bother her, but her shins were hurting as well. After what seemed like ages we reached flatter ground, where walking became easier and we began to feel better.

A mile farther on we came to the Mohawk Ski Resort which lies just east of the road, and looking up across the slopes, we were well aware of oncoming winter. There was snow up there, artificial to be sure, but it was there. In two more weeks the slopes would be covered with real snow.

Thirteen miles was our "score" for the day, and to say we were ready to quit would be understatement. Stiff as could be, we drove back to the hotel, where we felt like a hundred years old struggling up the great staircase. Thank goodness there were no people around, because we began laughing and doubtless would have looked silly to any onlookers.

Helen at
Mohawk Mountain

Dinner at the Pedlar's was again excellent, and later we both appreciated how much easier it was to walk up the staircase *after* dinner than it had been when we first returned from walking. We would often notice how quickly our bodies recovered from stiffness once they were fed!

That evening Helen kept dozing in the bathtub, and I would pop in now and then to wake her up. "Afraid you're gonna drown,"

I would tell her. She found that funny and told me not to worry, that a sleeping person couldn't simply slide under the water and drown; they would wake up choking every time. Eventually, she crawled out of the tub and began a half hour's ministration to her feet. The bunion had a blister now, and there was one on her other foot too. We worried about how well she would be able to walk the next day, especially since we faced another steep climb just out of West Cornwall. Still, when I suggested we call it off for the weekend, her reply was a quick "No way!"

INTO NEW YORK STATE

The next morning began with a slight upgrade near Kellogg Corners, after which it was three relatively flat miles to West Cornwall on the Housatonic River. We were familiar with the river sixty miles to the south where, broad and slow, it empties into Long Island Sound near Bridgeport. We expected it to be narrower with more current there in the highlands, and indeed it was. Flowing swiftly along a well-defined valley, it is bordered by six-hundred-foot ridges which have been set in relief by eons of erosion. For obvious reasons railroad tracks often follow the relatively constant slopes of river valleys, and the Housatonic Railroad, no exception, follows this valley to Danbury, Connecticut, forty miles downstream.

Upon arriving in West Cornwall, we crossed the tracks on a modern railroad bridge. However, just beyond the tracks the road crosses the river itself through an old covered bridge, a counterpart of the one we saw near Comstock on our third day out from home. This Cornwall bridge has only one lane, so cars coming from opposite directions are obliged to coordinate their entries or somebody has to back up. *Is there a protocol?* I wondered, *for who goes first when people arrive at opposite ends at the same time.*

I must have spoken the thought out loud, because Helen surprised me with "Probably an informal one, Phil, among the locals.... Outside of that I doubt there's much.... Wonder how often cars are stopped at both ends waiting for each other to go?"

"Not often," I answered, "but it's bound to happen. You can bet there are times when two people stop ... wave each other on ... both wait ... both go, stop, go.... Most

The Author at West Cornwall Bridge

people would grin, some would avoid eye contact, a few would snarl!" I was happily working into it: "I can see two rednecks acting like Robin Hood and Little John—neither willing to yield an inch."

Meanwhile, Helen was thinking about something far more dear to her heart than my halting chatter about who might go first across a one-lane bridge. "Let's get some doughnuts," she brightly said.

"Good idea, but where can we get any around here?"

"At that general store at Kellogg Corners, you know, where the car's parked." Then suddenly: "Phil! We've walked past the truck!"

Indeed we had, and we were almost to the bridge which seemed to invite us to enter, cross, and continue walking west. Of course we would eventually have caught our mistake and come back, but that kind of walking we definitely wanted to avoid. The cross-America hike would be long enough without increasing it by carelessness.

So we returned to the truck, which was still in sight, and drove back to Kellogg Corners—for lunch, it turned out, because it was already past noon. Afterward, we moved the truck two miles forward, toward Sharon near the New York border; then we returned to West Cornwall and parked the car exactly where the truck had been. In the process we contracted our usual "slows," so it was one-thirty by the time we'd got out of the car and were again walking toward the covered bridge.

And again we didn't quite get there.

A big, tail-wagging mongrel walked up, and Helen paused to make a fuss over her. Definitely a mistake! The dog liked that so much that she suddenly jumped up and planted an appreciative kiss right on Helen's mouth, which she took with smiles as I collared the dog and pulled her away. The embarrassed owners rushed forward with many apologies, which Helen said were unnecessary since she'd asked for it. By now she had knelt down and was rubbing the dog's ears. The owners said they had had the dog to obedience school but she flunked out. We would hear that story again, several times, in the next two years.

Ten minutes later we were finally across the bridge, but easy walking soon ended as we began the steep climb that had concerned us the night before. It started at the foot of Surdan Ridge, just west of the river, and it seemed to go straight up as it rose in a twelve percent grade. Every few hundred feet we would stop and rest, and in all the climb took nearly a half hour. Helen managed it surprisingly well, however, which was a big relief for both of us.

Beyond the ridge another mile brought us to the truck, where we became sidetracked into wandering around a small cemetery. Alas, a low, nondescript stone caught our attention: WW II, FRANCIS W. COLE, U.S. NAVY, DIED NOVEMBER 11, 1942, AGE 19, LOST AT SEA.

Cole had died exactly twenty-four years to the day after the end of World War I. I speculated that he was probably lost during one of the many naval actions near Guadalcanal during the fall of that year. "He gave his all," I said to Helen. "That stone should be eight feet tall."

But I refused to imagine a life and death for Francis Cole, as I had for Alvin Worden only a few days before. I was old enough to remember the Second World War, and we had had many wars since and had lost many thousands of young people—not one directly defending the political institutions or territorial integrity of the U.S. No use standing there dwelling on it; nevertheless, I couldn't help wincing upon recalling the Bible's stoic declaration that there would always be wars and rumors of wars. Defeatist, I thought; hopefully someday humanity will do better.

*　　*　　*　　*

It was the following Thursday that Helen and I bought a motor home. The dealership was forty miles from where we lived, and of course the only practical route home required a double lane-switch to exit from I-84 near Hartford—a maneuver not made easier by driving rain. We could have used back roads instead of the interstate, but as small as our motor home was by current standards, its eight-and-a-half-foot width and twenty-six-foot length seemed huge to me. Still, though insecure driving it that day, I learned one important fact: Other drivers give you plenty of room if you're driving something big and not very well.

Once home, the first thing I told Helen, after nearly hitting the garage overhang, was that I was going to put a sign on the back saying LEARNER. That should strike a "modicum" of fear in opposing drivers—get me even more room.

"Phil, you shouldn't speak of other drivers as if they're opponents."

"That's better than what my father used to call 'em," I told her. "To him they were always 'the enemy.'" That too probably came from his doughboy days in France.

Helen, the Author, and the new Motor Home

Although I would drive the motor home to Florida and back during the coming winter, I would still not feel completely comfortable behind its wheel. Nevertheless, beginning the following spring and beyond, it would serve us well during our continuing walk west. Meanwhile, for the remainder of 1998 and until we reached the Hudson River, we would leave it home and continue using motels.

The Saturday after we bought the motor home (RV as they are often called), we returned to western Connecticut where we rented a room in downtown Sharon. Leaving the truck at the motel and using the car, we drove to the little cemetery where we had finished up the Sunday before. Then, wasting no time, we quickly got back to walking.

By lunchtime we were sitting in a Sharon restaurant talking about the great milestone we would reach that very afternoon, namely, the Connecticut/New York border. It was Friday the thirteenth and the thirteenth day we had walked, so we joked about preserving our good luck by watching out for black cats, ladders, and broken mirrors. But the border was only a mile away, and we would reach it that afternoon if we had to crawl—or so we told each other.

In truth, nothing would happen to us over the next two years and 3400 miles that could seriously be called *bad luck*. When you are in your late sixties and healthy enough to walk across the country, you can easily think of yourself as *continuously* lucky. Minor mishaps like fender benders, frozen pipes, lost hats—things ordinarily considered bad luck—really amount to hardly more than minor inconveniences. I enthusiastically told all this to Helen and she readily agreed, but then she suggested that if I lost my wallet that afternoon, I should not count it as bad luck, just a minor inconvenience.

God bless her!

We were walking again by one o'clock, and in less than an hour we reached the border. There is a picture of Helen in her pink-red jacket standing beside a sign that says DUTCHESS COUNTY 1, SHARON STA. RD. Big milestone! While standing there, we began talking about soliciting charitable pledges for the miles we would walk beginning the following spring. However, nothing would come of that until the following autumn, when, growing confident that we would complete the long journey, we would finally go public. Through *Lebanon Life*, our hometown newspaper, we would invite readers to make pledges to favorite charities for the miles we would walk from Nebraska to the West Coast.

We lingered by the DUTCHESS sign for ten or fifteen minutes before anticlimax began to set in. Then suddenly Helen rallied: "Well, Philip, we've got only eleven more states to cross; then we'll be on the West Coast. Aren't you glad we're not almost there?" She was serious and at the same time excited, happy, eager to continue.

Helen at the New York Border

The day wore on as we passed through farming districts where autumn scene after autumn scene were treats to the eye. Once, for me, the scene was of Helen walking a few yards ahead as the road took us beneath leafless maples that followed a bordering fence line. The sun was low and golden, the shadows long and sharp, and off to the right was a farmhouse and near it towering evergreens, their darkness emphasized by blue sky and white clouds. Beyond a nearby barn were yellow and bronze fields which covered hollows and low knolls, and these, in turn, spread off to the north, each successively farther away, each less distinct, all ultimately merging near a low, distant ridge.

Later, I became reflective as we rested in a grassy area amid newly fallen leaves. "Helen," I said, "it always seems incredible to me, during late autumn, that these seemingly dying fields and trees can ever show life again."

"You've got to have faith, Phil."

"I know there'll be a next spring. But I can look past this apparently universal death to a spring of resurrection only because I've seen it happen before."

"That's not faith, that's like confidence in the sun's rising tomorrow, or that we'll still have our room when we get back to the motel."

"Okay, I'll grant you that's not faith. Faith, as I understand it, amounts to an ability to have continuous confidence in the truth of an unlikely proposition in the absence of supporting experience—or even in the face of experience to the contrary. This enables faith's possessor to rejoice in anticipation of wondrous but undefined things to come in a subsequent life. In the Christian tradition, in order to have faith in that eventuality, one must first have unquestioning belief in something else."

"What something else?" Helen asked, as if she didn't know.

"Unquestioning belief in a set of claims about the nature and omnipotence of Jesus as he relates to God; that's the something else. To the mind capable of confident belief without rational proof, Christianity promises not only nirvana after death but also a secure place among fellow religious followers during life. The appeals are obvious: the pleasures of social functions, a sense of belonging, support in time of need, a bright future beyond the grave."

"All sounds good to me." Helen thoughtful now.

"Yes it is," I continued, "*if* you can believe. The problem is that there is no provision in Christianity for persons not capable of faith, and to be capable or incapable seems inherent in an individual's nature. There's no free will there, no matter of choice. In that sense I believe in predestination—predestination by genetics."

"Phil, we are what we are. Let's get moving; it's getting chilly sitting here."

I wasn't sure by what she meant by "getting chilly," but soon we were back on the road.

An hour later we were passing a huge field that seemed alive with geese, literally hundreds of them. We were used to large flocks near home, but nothing like this. It was a noisy scene, yet beautiful, as groups of ten or twenty or more arrived and departed against a cloudless sky. Sometimes the incoming birds actually had trouble finding space to put down, and there were near misses in the air too. Several times we saw groups approaching to land, only to veer away as other geese rose in their path. This was invariably accompanied by a cacophony of angry honks. Helen said they needed air traffic control.

We reached the truck about five-thirty, and fifteen minutes later we were back at our motel in Sharon. There had been little traffic on the short drive, which was very different from the rush hour congestion we invariably faced when driving home to Lebanon. We took dinner at a restaurant across from the motel; then it was off to bed with resolves to get a good night's sleep. Trouble was, we began reading and stayed up till nearly midnight.

*   *   *   *

While positioning the vehicles, it was becoming our habit to drive forward over the same back roads we intended to walk, the idea being that if we were going to make wrong turns and have to backtrack, then better to do it early with the car and truck rather than later while walking.

In any case, that was our thinking when we set out to position the truck at Pine Plains, New York, the following morning. Helen was following in the car, and we had not gone far when I took a wrong turn and, minutes later, did it again. Both times Helen smiled politely, tooted the horn, and waved as I sheepishly glanced back through the rear view mirror. Trouble was, I was in one of my we've-got-all-day moods, and when I went astray a third time, her patience ran out. Smiles went, toots became honks, and polite waves became gestures with both hands raised palms up in frustration. We stopped and "agreed" that she would take the lead the rest of the way to Pine Plains. That worked, and we arrived twenty minutes later without further detours. But then....

"Phil, let's grab coffee and doughnuts."

"What do you mean?— grab coffee and doughnuts? Thought you were all fired up to get walking!"

"I am, but there's no use rushing things," she smilingly replied.

We quickly found an open diner; still, it was twenty minutes before we finished there, and twenty more by the time we arrived back at walk's end and began walking.

Now earlier, while driving to Pine Plains, we had both noticed a cow standing in a fenced enclosure beside a shed. We had thought little of it at the time, but now we were approaching the place and wondering if she would still be there. Sure enough, she was, but in the meantime she had given birth to a calf, which, though still wet, was on its feet and obviously trying to suckle. As it stretched forward, however, and craned its neck to take a nipple, its mother moved a half step away causing it to fall forward beneath her belly. Moments later it struggled to its feet and again set out to nurse. Same story. Mother moved too far and calf went down underneath. On try number three, mom stayed put and little one finally got what it wanted. To us it seemed clear that mother was deliberately using the calf's need for nourishment to get it to exercise its legs.

Fascinated, we watched for probably twenty minutes, during which the little one visibly strengthened. "What a far cry from the helplessness of human infants," Helen remarked, and I agreed, adding something about how quickly animals develop to full maturity compared to humans.

But it was another cold morning, and we were becoming thoroughly chilled watching this drama of early life. Helen

Into New York State

suddenly said, "We better get moving," and off she led at a brisk pace that quickly faltered until we slowed to a walk she could actually sustain. After that, it was slightly uphill for the next three miles, although not so uphill as to cause her problems. It was enough, however, to get our blood coursing and our bodies warm by the time we reached the crest of Silver Mountain.

"It must be a rare local who could tell you what this hardly-a-mountain is officially called," I remarked.

In fact, Silver Mountain was less a mountain than a low highland, from which the far view was slightly lower hills covered as usual by fields and small wooded areas. Most of the woodlands were deciduous, although a few were evergreen and a few mixed. We continued past the "summit" and down the northwestern side, which turned out to be slightly steeper than the south side we had just come up. Once I glanced around and caught Helen limping, but when I asked if her chest or feet or legs hurt, she denied that anything did, and even as I dropped back to walk beside her, the limping stopped. Later, when we were down on flat ground, she seemed okay.

For the rest of the day walking was relatively easy. Once, at a crossroads called Bethel, a young cop stopped and waved, and then drove on. After that it was just pick-'em-up, put-'em-down, pick-'em-up, put-'em-down. Even so, we were not bored; indeed we enjoyed a mild, continuing satisfaction that we were getting farther and farther from home while becoming steadily more enthused about continuing the adventure. "This is going to work!" Helen declared.

It was only when we arrived at Pine Plains about four o'clock that we remembered we had to find a place to stay for the night—preferably someplace less expensive than the touristy Sharon motel we had checked out of that morning.

I had tried to get the proprietor, a likeable young Indian, to drop the price twenty dollars, but he just smiled an inscrutable smile. Since that didn't work, I asked if he had a senior rate. That didn't work either, so I pointed out that it was off-season. Still no luck, and although by this time we were both enjoying the exchange,

I still had to give seventy dollars for the room. We vowed we would not pay that much tonight, so now we found ourselves tired out and in need of a place to stay.

Amenia, New York, which is ten miles south of Pine Plains, seemed like a good place to start looking. It was an easy drive and sure enough, luck was with us when we found a mom-and-pop motel on the west side of town, tended that night by Mom herself. The price was right too, being only two thirds of what we had paid the night before; and our room, though small, was warm and clean.

A question that had been on our minds for some time was, Where would we be able to park the motor home when we began using it the following spring? I asked Mom how she would feel if somebody offered to pay to park in her motel lot. She said it would be fine with her except on busy nights, when there might not be enough room. She was confident, however, that anyone could park in the vacant lot across the street, and that no one would bother them, even the police. I wasn't so sure about the last part, but Helen and I assured each other that if she was any indication, we could expect to find plenty of people who would let us park on their properties, provided we offered to pay and didn't leave a mess. Nevertheless, it would turn out that we would almost always park in private campgrounds just like other motor-home campers.

Later that evening, we made plans to quit walking at noon the following day and get an early start on the hundred-mile drive home. Five or six miles was all we would have time to walk, which meant we would be positioning the truck just once, and west of the Taconic State Parkway.

WE ARE INNOCENT OF TRESPASSING

To our surprise we had trouble finding a place to park the truck the following morning. West of the Parkway was mostly wooded remote country, but there were no turnouts along the narrow road we planned to walk, just overgrown ditches and occasional driveways. Finally we found a place where there was a house on the north side of the road, and on the south a pasture that sloped a quarter mile to a creek. A fence eight feet from the road bounded the north edge of the pasture, and the owner of this spread, or maybe a hired hand, kept the area between fence and road neatly mowed—as if it were private lawn.

We parked as far as we could from the house, at least two hundred yards, and near where the mowed area gave way to the brushy ditch of an adjacent property. Against Helen's advice and in a moment of naive goodwill, I left a note on the truck saying, "Gone for a hike, be back soon." Then we drove back to Pine Plains to begin the day's walk—after doughnuts, of course, at the Pine Plains diner.

Walking was at first along back roads with mostly low hills. There was one two-hundred-foot climb, but it stretched out a full mile and was not steep enough to cause Helen difficulties. The subsequent descent took us past several large houses and then an exclusive-looking golf course near the parkway. There was clearly wealth in the area, and we guessed it to be city wealth, come up via the parkway from New York or down from Albany to the north.

Things were going well, and we were in fine spirits until we reached the truck two hours later. That's when we found that my good intentioned courtesy note had received a shaky-handed addendum: YOU ARE TRESPASSING. KEEP OFF! No signature. No clue who left it.

"Who the hell does this clown think he is?" I exploded.

"He probably thought we were walking on his precious private estate," Helen replied. "Your note did say we were hiking."

I could tell from her tone that she too was irked, but she had a point. Even so, I heated up still more and growled, "The half-width of this road *is* public property, and it reaches from the road's edge to at least that fence. Somebody's mowing public land and trying to keep people from even parking for a few hours. Actually, this darned fence is on public property, and this truck is legally parked!" I bellowed the last in the direction of the house, just in case somebody was watching and could hear.

Driving back to Pine Plains, we chewed over ways of getting even with the phantom note writer, whom we assumed lived in the nearby house. "I'll learn to fly," I declared, "and we'll fly over and dump garbage on 'im."

"Easier than that," Helen enthused, "why don't we just drive by and dump a bushel of those Styrofoam peanuts they use for packing material?"

"You mean ghost turds?"

Helen winced. But just coming up with inventive things to do to the hit-and-run note writer was fun, and it kept us occupied until we came to where a dump truck had upset on a curve. Nobody was hurt, but the road was blocked as a huge wrecker cleared the mess. Cars were turning around and going back the way they came, and we would have done the same if we had known the area better or were not too lazy to find a different way to town. We'd just park and wait till they got the road opened.

Before long a trooper came along and asked why we were just sitting there. I told him, and trying to be helpful, he said there was an easy alternative way to Pine Plains. "You can't miss it. It's called Stissing Mountain Road, and you pick it up a mile back on your left. It'll take you straight into town."

I thanked him, but still thinking about the note on the windshield, I asked if it wasn't legal to park anywhere along a road—as long as there were no *official* NO PARKING signs.

"Sure, you can park wherever you want, just so you're not blocking traffic or anything."

Then I told him why I was asking, i.e., about the note. He listened and seemed to understand, but then he responded with, "Maybe it would be best just to park in town."

The cop was a well-meaning guy, but his answer didn't really follow from the first thing he said, and it certainly wasn't what we wanted to hear.

I thanked him and turned the car around, but irked all over again, we got onto another round of imaginative things we could do to the note writer if we just knew who it was. Eventually, that petered out as we found the Stissing Mountain shortcut, and sure enough, it took us directly back to Pine Plains.

WE REACH THE HUDSON AND QUIT FOR THE WINTER

It was almost noon on Friday, November 20, by the time we completed the long drive from home and began walking again. A wet, miserable weekend was predicted, but we were determined to make it to the Hudson River by Sunday afternoon. This would be our last weekend of walking in 1998; furthermore, it would be the last time we would drive out to walk's end, walk a few days, and then drive all the way home again. Come next spring, home would be our new RV, and we would park it and re-park it in step with the advancing walk west.

We repositioned the car and truck twice that afternoon, although I don't remember why. It may have been that Helen was not feeling well and did not want to commit to a single long segment. In any case, the first leg of the walk was only three and a half miles through an area west of the Taconic Parkway. There were thick forests and occasional houses, but we saw few farms, although the reason was not clear. "Maybe the soil's not rich enough," Helen murmured. "The terrain certainly isn't rough." She spoke so softly that I could hardly hear. *Wet and chilly* was her excuse for mumbling, but I was pretty sure she was not feeling well.

About two o'clock, we stopped and ate sandwiches we had brought from home. It was drizzling as I stood behind the car heating coffee on a butane stove, and moments later I took two pictures. One shows a leaf-strewn foreground and the stove with a saucepan on top. Helen stands to the side, dressed in her pink-red jacket, navy blue pants, and new white walking shoes. Behind her, the car's trunk lid is up, and you can see a suitcase with two cups sitting on it. The second picture shows a small patch of blue sky through a high dark overcast, and below and close overhead are round-bottomed storm clouds. In the middle-distance, bare trees reach skyward, and past them, along a turn in the road, stands a dark patch of evergreens.

"It's going to clear up," I optimistically said to Helen, and for a while it did. But eventually the rain set in in earnest, and we walked along for two more hours, quietly for the most part, except for our squishing footsteps.

That night we stayed at a Super 8 Motel outside of Kingston, New York, across the river from walk's end. I took a wrong turn en route to the motel and ended up in a hectic confusion of darkness, drizzle, and traffic. Some locals in a side-street bar gave me directions that eventually got us to our destination. There was hard rain later in the evening; big puddles formed in the parking lot and it turned raw and cold. Our room was warm though, and we had wine and good ham dinners at a nearby restaurant, which, we were glad to learn, would open at 6 a.m. for breakfast.

It was still raining the next morning, but we were not about to let that hold us back. At first our walk track took us through thin woods broken in places by one-, two-, and three-acre lots with houses. We presumed they were those of suburbanites who had come out from nearby towns for more room, better schools, or less danger from drugs for their kids. The towns, of course, would be Kingston, Red Hook, or Rhinebeck.

"Helen," I said, "do you ever wonder if it's really safer for people when they move from town out to places like this?"

"Never thought much about it…. Well, there shouldn't be much street crime."

"Maybe so. But everybody out here, young or old, gets into a car whenever they go anywhere. More time on the road means more chances for accidents—right?"

"Most city dwellers have it the same way," she replied. "Almost everywhere they go they have to use cars. There aren't many downtown shopping areas anymore, at least none that amount to anything…. And the malls are usually way out of the town."

I was tired of the subject already, but suddenly I thought of something really good to bug her with. "Let's talk," I began, "about how much time people actually spend in their cars. For starters, say the average suburbanite makes a thirty-mile commute, five days a week, fifty weeks a year. That's seventy-five hundred miles, and at an average of forty miles per hour, she'll be on the road almost a hundred and ninety hours in a given year. That's stressful driving, you know!"

Having heard something like this before, Helen pretended to put her fingers in her ears.

I kept going.

"Now say that commuter experiences, suffers, or enjoys—according as she's American, English, or French—sex with her partner three times a week, fifty-two weeks a year. Assume further that these 'events' last from two minutes to two hours with the average being forty minutes. Take two weeks out for headaches and other excuses, and you have six thousand minutes or only a hundred hours. That boils down to almost two hours of commuting for every hour of sex in the course—not to say intercourse—of an entire year. What I'm saying is that if people would stop and think about it, they'd probably opt to commute less and make more love. Furthermore—"

"There's somebody up ahead," Helen interrupted, as if she hadn't been listening to my views on commuting versus lovemaking. Then she mumbled some phrases like, You had it pretty good, Don't remember much complaining, Those were the good old days, Dried up old man, and even, Need some Vigoro. Can't imagine what she was talking about. Vigoro (not to be confused with Viagra) is a plant fertilizer that's been around as long as I can remember. People used it when I was a kid and raved about how it made things *grow*.

But in fact there was a man up ahead, and he was walking our way. Twice he stooped to pick up cans, which he put into a plastic garbage bag. Becoming uneasy as we drew closer, he twice glanced back, and we were still forty feet away when he stopped, turned toward us, and called a greeting, which we returned with smiles and waves.

"You live near here?" I asked when we paused upon reaching him.

"Weys Corners," he answered. "Just out collecting cans."

"Maybe we should start collecting cans," I said. "We've just walked over from Eighmyville and we've seen dozens of 'em."

He gave us a thoughtful look, then, "Where yuh walkin' to?"

"Rhinecliff Bridge ... over on the Hudson." I tossed it off as a trifling thing, but right away he wanted to know if we were going to walk back to Eighmyville after we reached the bridge. "No, we're going to drive back," I said. "We have a truck parked at the bridge."

"How'd the truck get there?"

"We put it there this morning."

"Ah, you live in Eighmyville and you drove to the bridge this morning and parked the truck. Then you walked home, and now you're walking back to the bridge to *get* the truck. Why didn't you just walk to the bridge and then back to Eighmyville? Save the gas. Why bother with the truck at all?"

Obviously, no evasive answer would satisfy this fellow, so with Helen joining in I proceeded to tell him our real goal and how far we had progressed since starting from home six weeks before. Genuinely interested but clearly skeptical, the old man put down his garbage bag, steadied himself, and backed up against the rusty guard fence. He politely interrupted two or three times as we talked. Questions would come to mind which he obviously needed answered before the rest of the story made sense to him.

When we finished, he ventured that our attempt to cross America on foot was a "commendable undertaking," but he thought we would never get there at the rate we were going. He quickly surmised that we were averaging about seven miles per day (very close), and he made the point that crossing the country at that rate would mean years of walking. There was nothing patronizing about the old man, but neither was he wearing rose-colored glasses.

Eventually he told us that he had been a florist and that since retiring he made a practice of walking every day and picking up cans. He regularly switched between a pair of heavily traveled roads where people tossed out lots of cans, and the money he made from them helped pay for occasional travels. He had collected enough over the years to pay for part of the costs of an extensive bus tour in the U.S. and another in Germany and Poland.

But time was flying so we began walking again, all three of us together. Minutes later, however, he had fallen behind to collect another can, so with waves and called good-byes, we parted for good.

No more than five minutes passed before Helen said, "Phil, why don't we start collecting cans?"

I was not surprised by the suggestion; actually I had begun thinking about it myself: *Let's see.... Say we start next year. If we pick up twenty-five cans every mile and walk ten miles every day, that's two hundred and fifty cans. At a nickel apiece, that comes to twelve-fifty per day—almost enough to pay for lunch on days when we buy it on the road.*

That screwy idea would keep us occupied for four days the following spring—days when I would walk left and right as much as straight ahead. While eagle-eyed Helen could and would spot cans as far as fifty feet from the road, it would be up to me to get them. The result, of course, would be wet feet, scratches from bushes, and one very close encounter with an SUV. But that would be the following year....

An hour later: "Helen, what are you doing?"

"Picking up money. Somebody dropped some change here."

We were in a parking lot three miles from Rhinecliff Bridge, and I had been taking pictures when Helen wandered off to look at graffiti on a nearby telephone pole. On the way, she spotted some coins lying on the ground and now she was picking them up. Moments later she had them all, a dollar and forty-nine cents worth, which together with what she'd already found along the way, amounted to almost three dollars. "Next year," she said, "between your collecting cans and my finding money, we'll be able to eat out every night."

Helen Finding a Bonanza in Coins

"I still like the meals you make better than any we'll likely find in restaurants," I grumbled, but she pretended not to hear.

We arrived at Rhinecliff Bridge about eleven o'clock, but with mixed feelings of satisfaction and letdown. We had expected satisfaction, since for weeks reaching the Hudson had been our big goal. Walking the last few miles, however, seemed ordinary. I waxed philosophical: "Is there not something fundamental here, m'Love?

Are not the journeys of life the things that provide the most fulfillment, while arrivals and what follows are often letdowns?"

Helen, down to earth as usual, said, "Phil, don't be airy; let's talk about how we're gonna to get across this bridge."

"You mean *aviatorial?*" I inquired. "Is that a word?"

At the time, Rhinecliff Bridge had two traffic lanes but no walkway, and a prominent sign said NO PEDESTRIANS OR BICYCLES. We retreated a quarter mile and milled around in a gravel parking lot trying to decide what to do next. I took some pictures and Helen looked for more coins, as we tossed suggestions back and forth. Finally, plan in mind, we sauntered onto the approach road and began walking quickly toward the bridge. If we could just get past the middle, a cop, in ordering us off, would logically send us ahead, not back, and—hurray!—we would soon be on the other side.

We had reached the bottom and were just starting up when a police car came along, slowed way down, and the cop frowned and firmly gestured for us to turn around. That squashed that, so we walked back to the parking lot to talk it over some more. Eventually, we convinced ourselves that not walking Rhinecliff Bridge did not matter much anyway; after all, what could missing one bridge mean in a three-thousand-mile walk? We'd just grit our teeth and not let it bother us. No problem.

In truth, it would bother us a great deal, and two years later I would cross the bridge with a 3 a.m. dash in the rain.

We hung around the parking lot for another ten or fifteen minutes before leaving to look for a motel. That morning we had checked out of the Super 8, which was too far from walk's end and which we used only because it was easily telephoned for reservations. The new place we found was near the western bridge approach, and Frau So-and-So, the clerk on duty, was friendly enough when we arrived that afternoon with car and truck. "Wot ehiclesv? On roblemp. Ustj eelf ta omeh!"

Pig-English notwithstanding, her welcome seemed genuine and we enjoyed our stay that night. Two years later we would find that Frau So-and-So could be plenty cranky when she had no vacancies and was busy watching television.

*   *   *   *

The next morning we set out by car to explore two candidate walk tracks leading west from the bridge. One led into the center of the Catskill Mountains north of huge Ashokan Reservoir, an important element in New York City's water supply system. From there it continued on to the town of Liberty, some forty miles to the west. The other route skirted the southern edge of the reservoir before likewise leading to Liberty.

We decided to check the northern route first, and that brought us to the town of Phoenicia near Woodstock—the Woodstock of rock festival fame. We spent an hour in Phoenicia and then continued west a few miles before making a wrong turn that brought us south to New York 28 on the northern shore of the reservoir. We had gone in a great big semicircle!

At that point we both had had enough. It was already noontime and again threatening rain. We pulled into a wayside parking area to discuss the situation, but we were finished for the year and we knew it. After some desultory talk about going back to the bridge and walking "one last short segment," we caved in and within minutes started home.

That night we talked about where we stood in our great walk west. Most important, we agreed, was our learning that we could walk all day in sun or rain or wind, and then get up the next morning enthused about doing it all over again. We joked about what that said about our sanity. But on a serious note, we knew that using the motor home the following spring would mean shorter drives to the walk track, and that, in turn, would mean more miles walked. Our average so far had been roughly seven miles per day, but we were sure that the following spring we would be able to double that. Were we to start in April and average fourteen miles per day for five days each week, then we should get half way across the country by mid October.

Actually, we *would* get that far the following year, but not using any regimen we imagined that night.

SECTION II

From the Hudson River to El Paso, Illinois

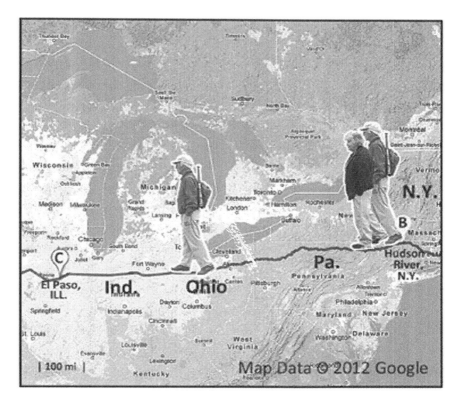

Second Walk Segment: April 11 Until July 2, 1999

WALKING IN THE SPRING OF 1999

During the winter of 1998/1999, Helen and I talked several times about the two walk routes we had tentatively identified leading west from Rhinecliff Bridge. We came to think of them as the southern route and the northern route, i.e., south of Ashokan Reservoir versus north of it, and almost thoughtlessly we began to think of the northern route as better. We imagined it as more quickly leaving the busy environs of Kingston as well as carrying less traffic in the Catskill Mountains toward Phoenicia, which we had visited the autumn before.

So Phoenicia was our destination when we set out from home with the car (Helen) and the truck (me) on the morning of April 11. We expected an arduous move. Upon arriving in Phoenicia, we would find a nearby campground and leave the truck there. Next, we would drive home together, and finally, I would drive the motor home back to the campground while Helen followed in the car. There would be lots of driving, but by the end of the day (albeit the second day), we would have all three vehicles near the walk track, and the new motor home would be our home on the road as we resumed the great walk west.

Pulling into Phoenicia about one o'clock, we toured Main Street in search of a sandwich shop or deli, but more importantly for information about where there might be a campground. We soon found lunch, but no one could help about a campground. After a number of fruitless inquiries, we eventually wandered into a general store on Ava Marie Drive, where a clerk told us that campgrounds in the area were not yet open. It was too early in the season.

Then came unexpected luck. Barbara Lumbaca, a local woman, was standing nearby, and upon overhearing our inquiries, she stepped forward and offered to let us park at nearby Sky Rise Apartments. She and her husband were resident managers there.

Of course it was a pleasant surprise, and we accepted the offer sight unseen.

Sky Rise turned out to be a quiet, park-like campus with a broad green that was itself encircled by a road fronted by rental properties. Barbara showed us where to park the truck, and she wished us luck as we began the 140-mile drive home.

The drive went well enough, but that night, as we picked at our TV dinners, we began to have second thoughts about walking north around Ashokan Reservoir. Would the northern route really be better than the southern?—we had not put much thought into which route to follow. No matter. We were committed; we had already parked the truck at Sky Rise, so that's where we would take the motor home the following day. Anyway, we told ourselves, one route couldn't be that much different from the other.

Next morning a steady rain added to the mild uneasiness I had been feeling about driving the RV first through Hartford and then over the narrow roads of western Connecticut. I was still not comfortable driving the behemoth even in the best of weather, though we had taken delivery of it the past fall and I had driven it to Florida during the winter. On the whole, that had been straightforward highway driving with few of the backups, turn-arounds, and so forth that accustom one to a new vehicle. In addition, I had learned early on that "Lurch," as we had come to call our barely roadworthy monster, didn't like crosswinds or sharp turns—didn't like going around corners for that matter.

Around eight o'clock we were hurtling through Hartford on rain-soaked I-84 as spray kicked up from speeding cars formed a thick, gray blanket above the road. I was in frozen concentration when the CB radio crackled and Helen, close behind in the car, said, "Honey, your turn signal's still on."

"Thanks," I answered. That explained why so few people were passing and why one person gave me a middle-finger salute as he swung back into line. Drivers were obviously afraid I would change lanes and run them into Jersey barriers that bordered the left lane. That was not the first mistake I had made with Lurch, and it wouldn't be the last. Still it bothered me, as it always does, when I make some mundane driving error.

South of Hartford we exited west onto Connecticut 4 and for the next three hours worked our way through countryside we had walked across the autumn before. Away from high-speed traffic, I relaxed a bit although the motor home's eight-and-a-half-foot width made the roads seem doubly narrow.

Arriving at Sky Rise, we met Carl Lumbaca, who proved to be just as helpful as his wife. He not only showed us where to park, but even offered a hose with which to connect Lurch to his home water supply. Although they would accept no money for letting us park on the property, we eventually learned that the Lumbacas were active in scouting. That gave us the opportunity, when we moved two days later, to leave a contribution with a neighbor to help them in that work. We would be the beneficiaries of many more kindnesses in the months ahead, but the Lumbacas' help, coming early in the trip, remains an especially pleasant memory.

That night Helen and I came back to the issue of which route would be better: the northern route which we had positioned ourselves to walk, or the southern route below Ashokan Reservoir. After fifteen minutes of useless speculation, I finally turned on the computer and we looked at detailed maps of the entire area. That settled the matter right away. The southern route was obviously less mountainous than the northern route, and there was really no reason to believe it would have more traffic. What's more, although the two routes began at Rhinecliff Bridge and joined at Liberty, sixty miles to the southwest, the northern route was eighteen miles longer! Suddenly the extra miles seemed a very long distance, and we wryly agreed that the southern route could easily have been chosen, if we had used the map program weeks before and had considered the "which route" issue more carefully.

But what to do? Stay put and walk the northern route?—the southern route?—or move south the next day and begin walking the day after that. In the end we decided to remain at Phoenicia and get started on the southern route the following morning. However, we had certainly put ourselves in an awkward spot.

Where we were camped was more than forty miles from where we would be walking, which would mean hour-long drives to and from the walk track. Still, we would accept the inconvenience for a day or two just to get back on the road. Later, we would move the RV south, closer to where we should have parked it to begin with.

So the next morning, April 13, we resumed the great trek from the western end of Rhinecliff Bridge. The first five miles went quickly along high-speed, limited-access U.S. 209. There were neither houses nor businesses along that stretch of road, and wide, concrete shoulders made walking easy. Turning west onto N.Y. 28, we passed several miles of businesses with the usual mix of fast food eateries, strip malls, and so on—interesting in places, but ugly nonetheless and typical of too many places around the country.

About one o'clock, we branched off of 28 and onto a road that followed the southern shore of Ashokan Reservoir, often only a hundred yards from the water. On the landward side small houses sat in broad lawns which contained old oak trees and their inevitable over-winter clutter of leaves and twigs. At one place a young man was busily cleaning up, and his little boy, maybe three years old, was helping—or at first glance it looked as if he were helping. Looking more carefully, though, we realized that as dad put leaves and twigs into a wheelbarrow, little guy would take a few out and scatter them back on the lawn.

"You've got a real helper there," I called from the road. "Maybe you could hire 'im out."

"I'd do it in an instant," the man answered with a grin. "But I think he'd rather work for me. At least he works cheap." Then he added, "Actually, I think he likes the leaves strewn around the yard better than raked up in piles or in the barrow."

"At least he works," I said, as the boy smiled from ear to ear and this time put some leaves *into* the wheelbarrow.

We talked to the man for several minutes—small talk about the weather and about how bad traffic was on route 28, which we had recently left. Then suddenly he asked if we would like some coffee. He had a thermos full on a nearby table, and he was obviously ready for a break and eager to continue the conversation. We declined however, knowing that if we hung around for coffee, we would probably be another twenty minutes getting back on the road. We were anxious to get as far as we could that first day back. This year, we resolved, different from last, we would keep moving and not stop so often.

It was nearing three o'clock when we came to the truck, where we had parked it off the road by the lake. Such a welcome sight! It had grown raw and cold, and already Helen was having trouble with her feet. We would quit for the day, and since neither of us felt like cooking, some restaurant on the way back to Phoenicia would have to do for dinner.

A half hour later, we thought we were in luck when we spotted a roadside diner near Kingston, but as we impulsively pulled in, we noticed there were no cars in the parking lot, just two old pickup trucks. That should have warned us that we would probably find ourselves sitting alone in an aging greasy spoon, and indeed, we soon were. After we had gone unacknowledged for at least three minutes, the only waitress stopped talking to a young man and came over to take our orders. She seemed agitated and preoccupied, and it was only when she called, indeed brayed, our orders back to the kitchen that we realized somebody besides her was on duty.

Our orders now with the cook, the girl returned to talking to the man in confidential and very passionate tones. Helen nagged me for eavesdropping their conversation, but I was not intentionally listening; it was more that you couldn't help overhearing bits and pieces of a very intense exchange. Helen was hearing it too although she too tried to ignore it.

The young woman had just told the fellow she thought she was pregnant. She was not certain, but it looked that way, and if she was, he was definitely the father. Far from being shocked or put off by the bombshell, he seemed genuinely pleased—he was reassuring and pledged that he was not simply trying to placate her, that they would "definitely work something out." Whatever he'd come to that diner for, it was surely not what he was getting, although he handled it commendably.

The girl visibly calmed as time went by and our food cooled off on the pass-through from the kitchen. Only the noisy arrival of four bikers brought her back to her waitressing job, whereupon she grabbed rolls on her way to bring our meals, which, Helen whispered, looked suspiciously like microwaved TV dinners "escaped" from their trays. One of the rolls had small spots of green mold; however, the young woman, God bless her, promptly though mechanically brought another. She was still out of it—still absorbed in her hopefully lessening crisis.

Helen and I joke that we leave restaurants not hungry for either of two reasons: the food is okay and we eat our fill, or it's so bad we use a few bites to kill our appetites. In this case we went the latter route. Even so, we left a six-dollar tip on a twenty-dollar check—not for the service, but rather on the theory that the poor girl would soon need all the cash she could get.

*   *   *   *

Although we had resolved to stay camped at Lumbaca's until we walked a few tens of miles, we now changed our minds and decided to immediately move closer to the walk track. Besides being too far from where we were walking, camping at Lumbaca's was proving inconvenient—much as we appreciated their hospitality. We were hooked up to their water supply and that was convenient, but we were using the motor home's batteries for light and its propane for heating. In addition, although the black-water tank (sewage tank) would be all right for a few more days, it would all too soon have to be emptied. We needed a commercial RV park with full-hookup service, where we could connect to the park's facilities for electricity, water, sewage disposal, and cable TV if available.

Consequently, the next day, instead of walking, we looked for a campground south of the reservoir. Glenwood Park near Ellenville, where we finally settled, charged sky-high rent, but it did have excellent campsites. Ours was in a beautiful, private section of the park with trees and open grassy areas toward the south. Local talk had it that bears were sometimes seen in the meadows, but we didn't see any. In fact, we would look for bears all the way across the United States and never see *one*, except in a private zoo near Yellowstone Park.

Our spirits sagged that night. Three days had passed since we brought the truck out from home, and we had managed to walk only twelve miles in all that time. It was as if we were simply marking time. We hashed and rehashed our dissatisfaction until around nine o'clock, when Helen said, "Phil, we should go back to where we branched west from 209 onto 28, and start walking south on 209. That'll bring us directly here to Ellenville where we're camped; then it'll be straight walking west to Liberty."

"Down to here and then west to Liberty," I replied, "might be less zigzaggy than our present route below the reservoir, but we won't walk any faster and the two routes are almost the same length. We won't save any time."

"Yes we will. We'll have much shorter drives to and from the walk track; that'll save maybe a half day. Besides being straighter, my way will be flatter and not as tiring."

"But we're already six miles west of where we turned off of 209. If we start over going your way, we'll be giving up those miles. We'll probably get beat up by traffic too."

Nevertheless, Helen's shorter "to and from" drives together with "straighter" and "flatter" carried the day—although later we would both wonder why.

So the next morning we started south on 209, and finally, it seemed, we were really on our way. Walking was easy at first since grassy areas along the highway and a dirt service road kept us fifty feet from heavy traffic. All too soon, however, the service road petered out and we found ourselves sharing the high-speed, two-lane, shoulderless artery with hundreds of cars en route to Kingston. A number of times we had to step off the macadam and wait for traffic to pass; then we would go on with minimum risk to life and limb—we hoped. The agony continued until eleven-thirty when we reached the town of Stone Ridge, only six miles from where we started four hours before.

Jittery and frustrated, we lunched at a small restaurant and agreed we would never again let ourselves in for that much traffic, if we could help it. Tomorrow, we would go back and continue the walk from up by the reservoir—from where we left off two days before. But for the time being we had had enough walking. During the afternoon we visited Camping World in Kingston, where Helen bought books listing RV parks all across the country, and I inquired about leveling jacks for the camper. Jacks would allow us to park the unit on uneven ground and then level it up, front to back and left to right. Maybe keep us from falling out of bed some night.

That evening we agreed that a difficult period was behind us. We had selected a roundabout walk route to begin with (the northern route), and had positioned Lurch close to it for convenience's sake. Then, even before starting that route, we changed our minds and began walking the more direct route south of the reservoir. After moving Lurch to be near that route, we had promptly turned to a third route, which proved so dangerous that now we were going back to route number two. As confused and disorganized as we had become, we were now confident we were on the right track. We would stick with the route along the south shore of the reservoir—and we would definitely plan better in the future!

About eight o'clock we began watching *My Cousin Vinny* on the motor home's VCR system. We were in need of some good laughs and that movie has lots of them. Helen awarded Marisa Tomei her ultimate accolade when she exclaimed, "That girl's no star, she's a genuine actress," and in a final burst of enthusiasm she said, "Let's go to bed right now, Honey, and go straight to sleep … so we can start real early in the morning."

COLLECTING ALUMINUM CANS

Surprise, surprise! Early the next morning the RV's pipes were frozen. Not bad though—just enough so that when Helen turned on the water only a drizzle came out. To our relief the ice cleared within minutes as normal flow followed hisses, gurgles, and burps.

An hour later, having written off the six miles on 209, we drove to the lakeside spot where we had finished walking two days before. It was surprisingly cool, even for April, and we shivered at first as we resumed walking along the reservoir's southern shore.

Toward midmorning, we met an elderly woman who was supervising a young man building a low stone wall. The wall ran along a brook that flowed beside the road, and the idea, according to her, was to keep the brook from flooding whenever there was a hard storm. I didn't see how there could be flooding problem; from the brook to her house was uphill ten feet. I questioned her about that, and in response she admitted—somewhat defiantly—that there had never been flooding and that she was really building the wall to improve the looks of things between the lawn and the road.

"Who's paying?" I asked, "you or the county?" I hoped the county wasn't, but I had seen some amazing uses of county money in Pennsylvania when we lived there years before.

"I'm paying," she snapped. "I've been trying to get 'em to pay for years. But do you think they'll cough up a dime?"

They and *'em* seemed to mean Greene County. But on she went: "They say the ditch works fine without the wall, and that you're not supposed to build on public property anyway. An improvement's an improvement far as I'm concerned. Why shouldn't they at least pay for the stones if I'm willing to give 'em the labor?" Her bored dog lay nearby, and I wondered if all of this sounded as absurd to him as it did to Helen and me.

We mumbled noncommittally, then I changed the subject: "You've got a beautiful view here. Do you know when Ashokan Reservoir was developed?" We were in sight of the water and I waved in that direction.

She didn't answer the question but instead launched into a monologue about the history of the area, and out of the past marched images of Confederate war prisoners indentured to local farmers but under pain of execution should they try to escape. She even knew, or thought she knew, some of their names, where and when they were captured, and whom they had worked for locally. Then she went still further back—back to revolutionary war times—and now the subject was colonial treasure, in particular gold. According to her, even as British soldiers were sacking and burning nearby Kingston, colonial New York's entire gold supply was being spirited out of town to be buried in the Catskills.

"What became of it?" I asked.

"Never recovered," she said. Her manner had become condescending, even patronizing, and it only grew more so the longer she talked. She was proud of her knowledge while disdainful of our ignorance, yet it pleased her that we should stand there and listen to her talk. Later, Helen said she came across like a bully who needed the society of others—even her victims. She reminded me of the man from whom we'd asked directions the previous fall—the one who tried to teach me how to pronounce *Litchfield*.

But we had had all of the woman we could take, interesting though her story was; still, Helen couldn't resist the final obvious question: "What became of the gold?"

"At the bottom of the reservoir," she said with a smug smile and a gesture toward the lake.

"How would *you* know that?" I asked.

"There's maps," she answered, her tone implying we were nervy even to ask—maybe nervy even to be addressing her exalted self.

"Well, nice talking to you," Helen said as we started to leave.

The woman didn't bother to answer—just turned away, climbed onto a motorized wheelbarrow, and started up the driveway toward the house. Her German shepherd leaped aboard. The young man continued working. He had never said a word, never even raised his head.

"I don't see how the poor dog puts up with her," Helen said.

"He has to," I answered. "His food and shelter depend on it, and boss-lady no doubt enjoys his dependence on her. She wouldn't want friends or companions, canine or human; her kind needs satellites. They must have caught hell at the county office when they wouldn't pay for the wall."

*   *   *   *

The next four days took us forty-five miles farther west, the first fourteen along the reservoir's shore to West Shokan. We stopped at town hall to ask about conditions on the road ahead, which, from our map, appeared to pass through fairly remote country. Town hall was a laid-back place. A fixture of the office was a black mongrel who lounged about, having been rescued by township workers from being lost—or more likely abandoned. One of the town employees told us that the road ahead was extremely steep in places, but she allowed it was walkable if you were "in good shape."

So on we went, good shape or not. At first there were a few houses, but after a quarter mile, all buildings were behind us as the narrowing road followed a tumbling stream up a tightening and ever wilder ravine. Eventually the road branched away toward the north, crested a steep hill, and entered the valley of Rondout Creek, which leads to another reservoir fifteen miles to the southwest.

By the time we entered the valley, we had been earnestly collecting aluminum cans for two days. Of course we got the idea the autumn before, from the retired florist we talked to on the other side of the Hudson. He had paid for some of his travels with money from redeemed cans, and we sensed a bonanza. "With all the cans lying along these roads," Helen enthused, "we should even be able to pay for our campground rents. All we have to do is pick 'em up and turn 'em in at redemption centers. They don't weigh anything, and we can cash them in every week or so."

"OK, so they don't weigh much, but who's going to carry them and what's *he* going to carry them in—his pockets?" I knew both answers: *He* was me, and I would be carrying them in black plastic garbage bags.

Now, everyone knows there are plenty of cans and bottles scattered almost everywhere along the roads. What I had not thought about was that those close to the road and easily reached are quickly collected by regular "can patrollers" like the old florist. The rest lie half buried in roadside ditches or barely visible in off-road brush. Those were the ones that Helen was great at spotting but no good at digging out or struggling through thickets to collect. That was my job, and every few minutes, as we walked along, I would hear, "Honey, there's one over here" or "Honey, there's one over there." Once in a while, she would just laugh and yell "Fetch!"

Well scratched up and en route to still another can, I was crossing the road for the thousandth time when an SUV came fast around a nearby bend. I jumped just in time as the driver swerved past and braked to a stop. He obviously meant to talk, and as I walked toward the car, I hoped he wasn't upset enough to tell me to stay the devil off the road. It had been my fault.

He smiled though and brushed off my apology, but then, surprisingly, he launched into a series of quick questions: "Where are you from? How long are you going to be here? Do you know this is private property?" When he mentioned private property, I pointed out that we were standing on a public, not private, road and that I didn't care if the land on either side was "public, private, or belonged to Uganda."

Coming right back, he told me that he was a friend of the property manager who was responsible for land extending about a mile along the road, including the roadside creek. He said it was part of the manager's job to keep squatters and trespassers off.

"So why are *you* telling *me* this?" I demanded. "My wife and I are walking through here on a public road. Your manager friend himself—let alone you—would be off base saying more than hello … unless we were actually trespassing or throwing trash onto his master's exalted property! Which we haven't been doing and don't intend to do!"

"Sorry, maybe I'm being a bit harsh.… But he's got a really tough job."

"How so?" I demanded, hardly satisfied with the half-apology, yet curious about what else he might say. And he definitely had more.

"Well, the problem is that during summer weekends people scatter litter of all kinds along the road. They even pitch tents in roadside clearings or in the woods—whole families, mind you. Sometimes there'll be clotheslines strung across the creek, and once in a while you see people doing their business in the woods. Disgusting! The manager's even got his fingers into pooped diapers trying to find letters or receipts with names and addresses that would let him track the S-O-Bs down."

The more the man talked the more intense he became, and my face must have turned beet red as an urge to laugh battled with annoyance. "Wait!" I finally said, "I can understand your friend's frustration, but not yours. Dealing with trespassers and litter is obviously part of a property manager's job; it comes with the territory. He must know that … *and you too!*"

"Yeah," he said, softening some, "but you just don't know how bad it gets. Anyway, that's the reason everybody around here is so sensitive about the whole business of trespassing, and that's why there's NO TRESPASSING signs on just about every other tree. Not only that—"

"Thanks for not running over my husband," Helen interrupted with a smile, "and tell your manager friend that you met two nice people who are helping out with his litter problem and not even charging for it. Tell him they're collecting tons of cans and they're gonna turn 'em in for a fortune, and maybe they'll share it with him … but probably not."

That gave us all a laugh, and after a few conciliatory remarks and a comment about the weather, the man drove on, but not before offering to shake hands. Both Helen and I accepted, of course. Then I was back under Helen's direction—"here Phil, there Phil"—picking up cans while zigzagging tens of feet right and left for every slow mile forward.

But the can episode had dented my mood, and before long I was brooding about the YOU ARE TRESPASSING note that somebody had left on the truck windshield the autumn before—back near the Taconic Parkway. From there I grouched my way to KEEP-OFF signs in general, to their obvious necessity for property owners but their predictable annoyance to passers-by. "Property owners do have understandable problems," I allowed for Helen's benefit, "but these KEEP-OFF signs are posted equivalents of animal warnings—you know, they essentially growl, 'Keep moving stranger, this territory is mine!'"

We even saw KEEP-OFF signs nailed to telephone poles, and I was tempted to ask the manager's friend if landowners got permission from the power companies to "decorate" poles that way. I didn't however; neither did I tell him that the day before I had thrown the remains of an apple at one of those signs. Helen and I had even seen NO PARKING signs hanging on private fences that people had built within a few feet of the road. Clearly the over-reaching owners were knowingly infringing on public property.

*   *   *   *

Friday, April 23, was driving rain and cold as walking took us from tiny Sundown along a narrow creek toward Rondout Reservoir. All along the road, and especially off the road, there was much too much litter. Seeing it made us more sympathetic to the property manager's problems, but we were delighted with all the cans we found. With far more than was carryable, we stashed a bagful behind a fallen tree, joking with each other that someone might find our trove and make off with it. Then we went back to walking and were still in lighthearted moods when Helen initiated the following:

"Philip, I've got a great idea for a new car."

"Why do we need a new car? We're two hundred miles from home and saddled with a car, a truck, and Lurch to worry about. Who needs another car?"

"I don't mean that we ourselves need a new car. I mean that the car manufacturers are missing a golden opportunity. They should design a sport car for forty- to sixty-year-olds."

"Don't getcha. Excellent opportunity? Who'd design a sport car for an age group that's more interested in sedans and hatchbacks? Sport cars are for *youts*, not baby boomers—sorry you don't like the phrase *baby boomer*, m'Love, but that's what forty- to sixty-year-olds are."

Anyway, what was she getting at?

"I'm serious, Phil. Design it for forty- to sixty-year-olds, but design it to be what they would have liked when they were, say, in their twenties. Make it the sportiest car in the world."

I still didn't get it. I knew there was a punch line coming and that she was trying to trick me into setting it up. To keep things going, I lazily agreed. "Yep, design it for the tastes of the twenty-somethings of nineteen seventy-five; then sell it to the same people now that they're middle-aged, overweight, and doctoring varicose veins. Sounds like a winner."

"Wanna know what I'd call it?"

I made her wait a minute, but curious, I soon caved in.

"OK, I'll bite. What *would* you call this sport car for boomers in crises?"

"Why, *Boomer Zoomer*, of course"

"Hell-Helen, I'd call it the *Midlife Rocket*."

Six more miles brought us to tiny Grahamsville near the western end of Rondout Reservoir. By that time we had walked for several days straight, and although we hadn't walked far each day, we were pleased enough with our progress to take a day's break.

ALUMINUM CAN IDEA A BUST

After our one-day recess, we resumed walking from Grahamsville with our immediate destination being Liberty, which was now only ten miles to the west. The countryside became more open as we left the Catskills and passed Neversink Reservoir—another element of New York City's water supply system. We saw many deer that day; possibly the population is greater there than in the mountains, since there are farm fields to supply more and better food. They were fairly tame too. Once, when we were riding in the car, three crossed the road just ahead. I stopped and they stopped—no more than thirty yards away. One, a small buck, looked back over his shoulder as the others began to browse. "Stay off the road," I yelled, "or you'll get run over!" Little Buck stared a moment longer before they all bounded off toward the woods.

Sometime, about half way through the day, can collecting came to an end. It had started out fun but had eventually grown tedious; also, it was proving to be a very inefficient way to walk across the country. Progress was slow enough along the winding back roads we were using, and picking up cans only made it slower. At that point we had little confidence we would ever get completely across, and we were both anxious to make better time. So we would give up the can idea, cash in those we had, and get more serious about covering ground. Resolved!

With that in mind, we found a supermarket in Liberty, New York, which had a redemption center with machines that beep out an accumulating credit slip as you feed in your cans. When finished, you take your slip to a cashier for cash, or you can use it against a grocery purchase.

A middle-aged man in grungy clothes stood by the door of the center and watched me carry two bags of cans up from the parking lot.

"Afternoon," he said, all smiles. Recalling his smile later, I would be reminded of a cat getting ready for its dinner.

"Afternoon."

"Gotta lotta cans there."

"Yeah, been picking 'em up along the highway the last couple days. How do you work these machines?"

"Show yuh," he quickly volunteered.

I opened one of the bags and pulled out a can, which he took from my hand and fed into a machine. A bang and a thump and a beep, and right away I had a nickel's worth of credit. That seemed easy enough, so I fed in a couple of cans which both went through okay. But the machine kicked my third one back uncounted. "It's bent too much," my new friend said.

"What'll I do with it?"

"I'll take it," came his reply, "so you won't have to throw it back out on the road." He had a sense of humor.

"What'll you do with it?"

"Put it in this machine over here. Sometimes when they won't go through one machine, they'll go through a different one."

I watched him massage the can, twist it straighter, tap it on a nearby doorjamb. Then he shoved it into the machine, and presto, he had a nickel's credit. From my can!

"That my credit slip too?" I wondered aloud, but he grinned and gestured toward his ear as if he couldn't hear.

After that, I got two or three more through my machine, but then another can came rattling back, and he took it and darned if he didn't get that one through his machine, and quick too. So I started trying to true them up some, but that didn't work very well. A few would go through just fine, but then one would come clattering back and he'd snap it right up.

The man was a real expert at getting bent cans through redemption machines, and he was good at sizing up people too, at least this person. Long before me, he knew he'd get most of the cans.

I held out until I had a dollar and ten cents worth (twenty-two cans), and I think that bugged him—he was pretty sure I'd give up before that. Ha! I finally caved in, though, and told him he could have the rest of the cans I'd brought up from the truck along with three more bags full that were still out there.

He grinned from ear to ear and said, "Ain't cha gonna carry 'em up from the lot for me?"

"Hell no! When'd you first figure you were gonna get all my cans?"

"About the time I saw you gettin' outta your truck," he replied, with a roguish wink and a click of his tongue.

I was grinning too, but in fact I was relieved to be spared what loomed as a frustrating, tedious job. Half my cans were bent or messed up somehow.

With that we shook hands and I went looking for Helen, who had disappeared somewhere among the back aisles of the supermarket. A half hour later, just as we were leaving, I spotted my can-buddy coming out of the redemption center with a credit slip three feet long. He gave me a toothy smile and said he'd enjoyed doing business with me.

*   *   *   *

The following day, a Monday, we drove home to Connecticut for doctor's appointments, after which we stayed in the area to visit relatives before returning to Ellenville on Wednesday. Then it was back to walking, the current segment taking us from Liberty to Jeffersonville, a distance of twelve and a half miles.

On the eastern edge of Jeffersonville, we were passing a service garage on the other side of the street when a youngish man called to ask if he hadn't seen us near Liberty that morning. We called back that he probably had, and with that we walked over, inclined as always to talk to anybody who seemed friendly.

Where have you come from? he immediately wanted to know, and when we told him, he called into the garage for four large teenage boys to come out and join the conversation—or more accurately, benign interrogation. "Where are you going?" "Why are you doing this?" and "How far will you get by tonight?" they asked, among a number of other questions. They were a curious if unlikely group, and we enjoyed talking to them; still, it seemed odd that boys that age would find interesting what people our age were doing.

Later, Helen said that if "those huge boys" hadn't been so courteous and if there hadn't been other people around, she might have become uneasy. I agreed but added that if we ever met dangerous people, we would almost certainly sense it right away. Of course *almost certainly* was the key phrase; we could conceivably misread somebody—to our hazard. But there was no point in dwelling on that; we would simply make sure to always stay alert, and especially to appear alert to others.

After leaving our "interviewers," we continued into downtown Jeffersonville, and there, for the first time, Helen felt so bad she had to stop. Her feet were sore and she was nauseated—as she had often been since we resumed walking from the Hudson two weeks before. The obvious thing was for her to wait there in town, while I walked the remaining distance to the truck and then returned to pick her up.

We found a cruel place for her to wait—a bench beside an ice cream stand. She was the one who picked it. I told her she was being masochistic, that is, taking pleasure in torturing herself with nearby ice cream while too sick to enjoy any. On the other hand, I made myself a silent bet that she would be well enough to indulge by the time I got back.

It took thirty-six minutes (I timed it) to walk to the truck, and while returning, I measured the distance with the truck's odometer. It was almost exactly two miles. Thus I had been walking close to three and a third miles per hour, which was much faster than when Helen and I walked together. In three quarters of an hour I was back and sitting beside her near the ice cream stand.

"How'd you make it back so soon?" she asked.

Of course we both knew the answer. It was obvious that walking alone I could make much better time than when she and I walked together. Before long we would have to ask ourselves if we were being realistic trying to walk across America while limited by her much slower pace. Meanwhile, just as expected, Helen was feeling better, and there was still ice cream nearby. She was sure a cone would help her feel even better yet. Would I get her one?

"Of course m'Love, and I'll get me one too."

In the ice cream line stood an attractive yet disheveled young woman with three children—two walking and one in a stroller. While the stroller kid howled, the others bickered and mom seemed to grow more haggard by the minute. When her turn came to order, the woman dipping ice cream complimented her by saying how pretty the children were, and on impulse I chimed in: "Naturally they're pretty, they've got a pretty mother!"

The young woman lit up with a beautiful smile, and turning toward me, she said, "Thanks so much, I really needed that."

The ice cream lady was pleased with her remark, and I was glad mine came out as well as it did. I'm apt to muff it when I sound off like that. Thankfully, I didn't say, "Mom's pretty too, spite a them beautiful bickerin' kids."

*   *   *   *

That night I cooked pork chops on a portable propane stove while Helen boiled potatoes and corn. Until then we had mostly used TV dinners, except when we ate out. But we were tiring of that routine, and this was the start of our making special dinners now and then just to break the monotony. Eventually, we would sometimes stew a chicken or do a pork roast, or even bake a pie or cake.

Overall, we were becoming quite used to motor-home life. An electric heater, which we had bought in Liberty a few days before, was making Lurch more comfortable at night. It eliminated the noise and drafts generated by the RV's propane furnace, thus allowing us to sleep better. Helen's nausea and soreness remained a concern, but apart from that, our walk project was going well and we were cheerfully aware that we were now over two hundred miles from home.

The next morning we left Jeffersonville to face a steep hill that I had climbed the afternoon before while Helen waited in town. In spite of how bad she felt then, she took the grade well, and continued to do well, so that we arrived in Callicoon on the Delaware River about noon.

The old Western Hotel is on Academy Street, Callicoon's main thoroughfare, and it stood dazzlingly bright in high-noon sunlight. Of course the hotel would stand out in any light. Its Victorian architecture features a wide entrance beneath a portico ringed by low railings and supported by stately white columns. Extending above both portico and second-floor windows is

The Western Hotel

the roof of a magnificent porch which stretches across the entire front of the building. The porch roof is also supported by pillars, and third floor windows are double hung with black shutters that contrast with yellow siding. Above these and completing the facade, shallow dormers project from concave wall lines, which in turn recede up and back to white roof cornices. It is an impressive and attractive building.

The Western used to host many social functions, but once, incongruously, it hosted a murder! More benignly, melodramas, concerts, and roller skating derbies were popular events, as were Chautauqua lectures. Chautauquas were originally religious, adult, summer-school programs that were first organized in Chautauqua County in western New York. Popular and successful in the late 1800s, the movement eventually evolved into the Chautauqua Circuit, a traveling commercial venture that provided forums for politicians and social reformers as late as the 1920s.

Besides the Western Hotel there is the Delaware House, which in olden times had both a ballroom and saloon. There a Judge Ward held court, fining those who disturbed the peace at a rate of five dollars and drinks for the house.

We wondered at first what such striking old buildings were doing in tiny Callicoon. Clearly, tourism is nowadays a significant industry; the Villa Roma, a fabulous resort hotel, is only eight miles away. However, Callicoon's history relates primarily to the nearby river, which, year after year during the nineteenth century, carried thousands of log rafts down to Trenton and Philadelphia. There the logs were used as raw material in the production of everything from bowling balls to industrial chemicals.

Thousands of men were involved in the rafting trade; they worked on the river during the day and stopped over in riverside towns at night. Sometimes several hundred rafters would be looking for accommodations on a given night, and by the mid-eighteen hundreds, Callicoon was catering to the trade with dozens of hotels and boarding houses. The town must have throbbed with action, and Judge Ward must have had a whopping caseload!

Gradually, rafting timber gave way to moving it by rail. Across Academy Street stands a depot of what is now the Norfolk and Southern Railroad. However, the original roadbed was laid by the Erie Railroad Company, which was chartered in 1832 by entrepreneurs at the very threshold of the railroad era. Their farsighted dream was to build a railroad from Buffalo on Lake Erie all the way down to New York City.

An early hitch in the railroad project was that its Buffalo organizers were reluctant to see construction start near New York City. They feared that if it began that far south, some glitch could come up and the road might never be completed to Buffalo. Conversely, New York City backers felt that if construction started near Buffalo, the railroad might never reach downstate to *them*. Compromising, the groups started roadwork in 1842 on the upper Delaware near Callicoon, of course, and the town quickly became a passenger stop and watering station for steam-powered locomotives.

Helen and I crossed the Delaware River on Joint Bridge Commission, NY-PA Bridge No. 7. Not an interesting name for a bridge with spectacular views both up- and down-river. There were no ghostly rafts of logs that afternoon; still, there were several islands in the stream, and in shallows near one, three deer stared at us as we stared back from the bridge. For long moments they stood frozen like statues; then, one lowered its head and began to drink while the others meandered toward green grass along an island shore. Obviously nervous, however, they soon moved away and back toward the eastern riverbank.

Two hours later we reached the truck, which was parked four miles into Pennsylvania near Abrahamsville. We had covered twelve and a half miles and were in the third state we had walked in since beginning our adventure the year before. Even better, Helen had felt well all day. Life seemed good that afternoon as we started back to the RV, our increasingly appreciated home on the road.

HELEN LEAVES WALKING TO ME

Our next move with the RV took us from Ellenville to a campground near Hop Bottom, Pennsylvania, twenty-five miles north of Scranton. This took a lot of driving since we had to move both car and truck to Hop Bottom, leave the truck, go back for the RV, and finally drive both RV and car back into Pennsylvania. Still, by evening we were ensconced in Shore Forest Campground, a private RV park with a much lower rate than we had paid at Ellenville.

We rested the following morning; then, in the afternoon, we explored by car our intended walk route from Abrahamsville west to Towanda on the Susquehanna River. That seventy-five-mile trek would be over zigzagging back roads—traffic-free and beautiful walking, but increasingly hilly. We had really only skirted the southern edge of the Catskills, and Helen and I wondered how she would fare as we left the Delaware River valley and entered the higher mountains of eastern Pennsylvania.

Only two days later we had our answer. It was an oppressive, wet morning, and during a particularly hard climb Helen became so sick she had to stop and sit down on a stone wall. It was the heart medicine again. It had several times interfered with her walking, always when going uphill, but this time the effect was so pronounced she could not continue. Clearly, this was dangerous business, and as I walked ahead to get the truck, I made up my mind that this kind of risk-taking was going to stop. I would suggest that she temporarily give up walking and begin a regimen of dropping me off with the car and picking me up farther along. I would do the walking myself. Later, in flatter country in the Midwest, we would go back to walking together if she could handle it. Meanwhile, if she would *not* agree to give up walking in the mountains, then I would refuse to continue this crazy walk and we would go straight home—arguments be darned.

As it turned out, no argument ensued. Helen is sensible, and that evening she announced that for the time being she would quit walking and devote herself to "support." By that she meant dropping me off each morning at the day-before walk's end, and then driving ahead a few miles to wait. I would walk to the car, upon which she would move ahead again and we would repeat the process—and repeat it and repeat it. We agreed that sometime in the future, when we were out of the mountains and if she could do it, we would go back to our old routine of walking together. We had enjoyed that, but if it was not to be, then my walking alone would have to be the next best thing.

That night we also acknowledged another long-ignored reality: seven, eight, even ten miles per day would never be enough. If we (now meaning me) could not do a lot better than that, then again, we would give up walking and go home.

So the following morning, Helen dropped me in front of the Pleasant Mountain State Fish Hatchery, where I had finished by myself the day before, and as she drove away, we were well aware that this was the crucial day. I would have to walk at least sixteen miles by day's end. Otherwise....

An hour and fifty minutes later I reached the car where she was waiting, and for both of us time had seemed to fly. Later, she wrote that she had eaten some Fig Newtons and begun reading a magazine, and suddenly I was there. She had driven ahead a carefully measured six miles, so a quick calculation showed my pace to be three and a third miles per hour. Not bad, if I could keep it up. I had a Fig Newton myself and a cup of coffee; then I began another six miles, which I again managed in less than two hours.

We grabbed lunch at a country store—wolfed down hamburgers. But why wasn't I more tired? We did two more walk segments that day for a total of just over twenty-four miles—far more than either of us had expected. Helen kept saying things like, Do you feel all right? Do you have pain anywhere? How are your feet?

112

We even found time to call the doctor I'd visited in Connecticut the week before. "Good news, John," the doctor was happy to report. "Your prostate's lookin' good. Keep walking." He had been treating me for prostatitis, a non-serious but miserable thing to have. I got it by lifting heavy stuff in the garage when my bladder was too full. Obviously there's a moral here....

Breakfast the next morning was a special treat of pancakes, hot cereal, and bacon and eggs. Helen was treating me like a king, and in turn she said she expected a twenty-five-mile day. We did it too, actually twenty-five point three by her reckoning. And no serious physical difficulties at all: no chest or stomach or muscle or joint problems. Only my feet were complaining. Over the past couple of weeks I had used old work boots, sneakers, sandals, and this day a pair of Thom McAn street shoes. By late afternoon they were a half size too small, my feet having swollen during the twenty-five mile hike (about 53,000 paces). I had several blisters too, big ones, so I was beginning to think about buying new shoes, maybe a pair specially designed for walking. Not too expensive though; I'd be wearing them out anyway.

Some distance west of Hop Bottom, we used a gravel shortcut that saved miles of walking, and it also treated us to spectacular vistas. It was a windy day, and occasional fluffy clouds hurried along beneath a high, thin overcast. Lower down were storm clouds with rounded gray undersides ringed by lighter borders, and the air still lower was entirely without haze—an almost surreal clarity. At the horizon, this unusual skyscape merged with the landscape colors of early May. Fields were lush dark greens while woodlands appeared in the lighter shades of small new leaves, set off in places by dark gray trunks. The beauty of Pennsylvania was in those skies and rolling hills, and here and there were small lakes where ducks and other wild birds lived in greater numbers than we had seen farther east.

We reached the Susquehanna River at Towanda, Pennsylvania, on May 7, and we finished the day a few miles to the west on U.S. 6. In three days, with me walking alone, we had covered over seventy-two miles—over three times the distance we had ever covered when Helen and I walked together. The reasons for the difference were obvious. Aside from my much faster pace, we were spending far less time positioning and repositioning car and truck. For the first time we sensed we might actually make it across the country and that we might do it in less than two years. It was disappointing, to be sure, that we could not walk together, but with Helen in the role of "general facilitator" and me functioning as "ground pounder," we would indeed see the project through.

*   *   *   *

Once, while we were still camped at Hop Bottom, we took off from walking and drove forty miles north to Binghamton, New York, to visit Horst and Polly Herrmann. Polly, a college friend of Helen's, went to Germany in the mid-fifties to teach in an army service school. She soon met Horst, and after marriage they settled in the U.S., eventually near Binghamton. When we were in our twenties and early thirties, we visited each other occasionally, but through the long, child-raising middle-years, contacts dropped off to Christmas cards and rare phone calls. Nevertheless, we had reconnected a few years back, and reciprocal visiting was as pleasant as ever.

We spent a relaxing day with the Herrmanns, and in late afternoon they took us to dinner at their daughter's home. That turned out to be an extended family get-together, and we felt privileged to be included. Then it was back to Hop Bottom for the night, but not before making plans to spend another day with the Herrmanns. There was shopping to do, good eats to be had, and pleasant hours of just socializing. In addition, I still needed to buy walking shoes.

Horst and Polly Herrmann

After breakfast the next morning, Helen did a wash while I house-cleaned the RV and drained the black-water tank. That event was always satisfying—like "enjoying an overdue constitutional" an earthy camper would later tell me.

About eight o'clock, our chores completed, we drove back up to Binghamton.

That afternoon Horst and I went shopping for walking shoes, and good natured, uninhibited German that he is, he told me just the kind I would need. According to Horst, when you walk long distances and your shoes are too loose, your feet will slip up and down and rub blisters on your heels. On the other hand, if they are too short, the blisters will show up on your toes. He told me all this, mind you, after I had walked seventy-some miles in the preceding three days and had blisters galore to show for it. As if I wasn't already an expert on getting blisters! Given a chance, Horst would instruct the Pope on how to conduct mass. He'll help you out, drive you nuts, make you mad, make you laugh. He's one of my favorite people.

I ended up with three pairs of Rockport walking shoes, sizes nine, nine and a half, and ten. If you're not sure what you need, then bracket the problem!

Meanwhile, as Horst helped me buy shoes, Helen and Polly did what they've always loved to do—shop. Nevertheless, that did not keep Polly from serving a wonderful dinner of sauerbraten that evening, straight from the land of beer and Volkswagens. After a pleasant evening, we stayed overnight with the Herrmanns.

The next morning we drove back to Hop Bottom, where I thought we should spend another day just relaxing. Helen, however, had other ideas, and we had hardly arrived when she declared we should "head for the field and hit the road."

I complained *but she prevailed*, so for the rest of the morning it was pick 'em up, put 'em down, pick 'em up, put 'em down.... As I walked and walked that morning, thoughts of Bill Gates' wealth kept going through my head. I had heard or read somewhere that his holdings were in the neighborhood of thirty billion dollars, and that got me thinking as follows: *Beam, the length of your pace is about two and a half feet, so if you figure five thousand feet per mile* (low, but close enough for rough computation), *you'll take about two thousand steps for every mile you walk. Assuming it's three thousand miles across the country, then you'll have walked six million steps when you wet your feet in the Pacific. So far so good. Now, watching out for zeros, divide thirty billion by six million.... You got it! ... Good Lord, Beam, it looks as if Bill's worth about five thousand bucks for every step you'll take on this seemingly endless journey! Well, if Melinda's thrifty about buying food and clothes, the Gates family should be okay.*

But on a serious note, the Bill and Melinda Gates Foundation surely represents one of the most worthy uses of private wealth in history.

*   *   *   *

According to its sign, the small business on U.S. 6 near Burlington, Pennsylvania, managed dairy herds, and as I passed the office on the north side of the road, I noticed a young man getting into a pickup truck. Assuming he worked for the business, I called over and asked what managing dairy herds meant.

"We track a herd, keep the paper work on it," he called back.

He seemed a pleasant person—pleasant enough that I didn't hesitate to cross the road and walk up to the truck. "What kind of records do you keep?" I asked. "Do you mean you manage herds that aren't your own?"

"You got it. We manage a number of herds in the area, all owned by different people."

I had never thought about the management of dairy herds, but hazy images of a dairy farm came to mind: farmhouse, barn, silo, and cows—cows in a pasture, cows in a barn, cows all over the place. All were impressionistic, those images, like vague parts of a bucolic painting. But then I thought about milking.

Presto! An image snapped clear and I was a ten-year-old kid in a rickety shed, and there were a dozen cows tethered in a row on a long concrete slab. The cows' rear ends were over an inclined narrow channel, where ejected pee and cow pies splashed and plopped and sloshed downslope then out onto the ground. You didn't stand near that channel if you knew better, which I did not the first time I went to Mabrey's farm. Got splattered all over. My mother had sent me there with an aluminum can to buy raw milk for seven cents a quart.

There were no milking machines on the Mabrey farm. In those days milking was done by hand, and sometimes Mr. Mabrey would put me to work milking Mabel, an uncommonly patient cow. "Never be afraid to put your hand on a teat," he would say with a grin, and every time he did, Mrs. Mabrey would glare at him for reasons that were years beyond me.

I would grab the poor beast's teat and clamp the upper part between my thumb and forefinger, not tight, mind you; she wouldn't stand for that. The clamping would close the duct between her milk-filled teat and the udder just above. Then in quick succession I would close my second, third, and fourth fingers against the heel of my hand thus forcing a jet of milk out of her nipple and into a bucket between my legs. I was clumsy and slow, but I would eventually worry some milk out of the long-suffering beast. Mr. Mabrey or his son Bud would usually finish the job.

Like learning to tie your shoes or floss your teeth, it takes time to master the milking technique, but a good milker can work with both hands at the same time and as quick as lightning. All you hear is *sssst, sssst, sssst* as squirts go into the bucket. Mr. Mabrey was really good, and once in a while he would aim a jet at Sidewinder, the barn cat, and hit him right in the face. That's why Sidewinder was there; he liked milk—would even open his mouth to catch a jet. He liked warm, sunny naps too, but he hated people and would bite if you tried to pet him. That's why they called him Sidewinder.

Mabrey's wife would sometimes help with the milking and so would Bud. Bud was a really good milker when he wasn't flying his Piper Cub airplane. Later he went off to war....

"Typically," the young businessman was saying, "we'll have a contract with a dairyman—keep a file on each of his animals."

"Huh?" I was miles and years away.

"We keep files on his animals so he knows what's going on with the herd."

"Sorry," I said, my reverie ending. "What do you keep track of? What's in the files?"

"The animal's age, health, and milk production history. We provide inoculations and artificial inseminations too. Beyond that, the records are a guide to the dairyman; they let him know when it's time to replace an animal."

Traffic was building, so it was getting hard to talk. In addition, it was obvious the man had to get on with his day's work. Still, it struck me that there must be an optimum average age for a herd of dairy cows, and I asked him about that.

"Yes," he said, "you gotta be sure a herd doesn't, little by little, become too old. Maintenance costs stay about the same, but milk production slowly drops off."

Finally, I asked what they did with cows that had passed their best milk production years.

"They're sold off for beef, nothing goes to waste."

"Just as I thought," I said. "And all that old-cow beef ends up where my wife grocery shops."

"Mine too," he laughingly replied, as he started the truck and began to ease away.

You're a lucky guy, was my parting thought. *You're busy with important things to do….*

Just as the young man was pulling onto the highway, an older man came out of the herd-management office and casually joined me as I began walking again.

"Hello," he said.

"Morning. You live near here?"

"About a half mile over the next hill. I walk here most mornings … now I'm retired."

"What'd you retire from?" I asked.

"Had my own accounting business. Graduated from Penn State in fifty-seven. After that I worked a couple of different places, including eight years in Pittsburgh. Finally came home here to Burlington in seventy-five and started my own business—been here ever since." He hesitated a moment and then remarked that he had grown children in the area. "A man," he said, "oughtta be grateful to have his children around in his old age."

A man. I hadn't heard that phrase since the beginning of the women's movement. But I live in the Northeast where people are possibly more "politically correct" than in other parts of the country, except maybe California. I dislike the phrase, *politically correct,* just slightly less than *a man,* which sounds back-woodsish, even redneck. I was surprised to hear it from an accountant, even an elderly one.

Since this fellow had graduated from Penn State in 1957 and I graduated in '60—fairly close—we began the alumnus-meets-alumnus game of searching for common acquaintances. Alas, we found a number of names we both recognized, but none of people we had both known well.

We walked along quietly after that until he suddenly asked me where I was from. My answer, Connecticut, drew the quick question: "Well, what are you doing in Pennsylvania with a pack on your back?"

"Walking across America," I told him, surprising myself as I said it, since I was still reluctant to acknowledge what we really intended to do. Helen's and my uncertainties had of late changed to cautious confidence. We knew now that walking alone, I could cover between twenty and thirty miles a day, and that meant the chances were good that we would get half way across the country by fall. If I could maintain the pace, then we should finish at the Pacific in autumn of the following year. I was on an optimistic high that morning. Fresh off of two days' rest, walking, blood coursing—I felt as if I could walk around the world.

Duly impressed, my fellow walker soon asked what would become a fairly common question. Smilingly, formally, he said, "It's none of my business, sir, but just out of curiosity, how old are you?" I told him, and was congratulated on my "adventurism and good health," but then he launched into a long story about his own endless battles with diabetes and emphysema. After maybe five minutes, he began to trail off—as if he were embarrassed and thought he had said too much. For my part, I had become uncomfortable in the presence of someone with problems I couldn't even imagine.

We walked slower then, in awkward near silence, until he suddenly brightened and said, "Why the baseball bat?"

The question caught me off guard. I didn't think the bat was noticeable, attached as it was to the side of the pack. Besides, I had taken pains to make it inconspicuous by keeping its upward pointed handle partially covered by a pulled-over sock. Evidently this fellow didn't miss much, and he laughed when I told him it was my second line of defense against "man-eating dogs."

"You'll meet no dogs to be afraid of around here," he assured me, "just a mutt or two now and then. What's your first line of defense?"

"Dog biscuits," I said, pulling one from my pocket to make the point. I didn't mention the pepper spray.

As sharp as the old man was, he knew less about dogs than I'd recently learned, and I would dispense more than dog biscuits before the walk was over.

At a woodsy crossroads my alumnus friend paused and offered his hand. "This is where I get off," he said. "Good luck with your hike. But watch yourself; this road is curvy and hilly clear across the state."

He was right about that. Ahead were a series of mountain ridges separated by broad valleys with rumpled local hills and confusing secondary roads. The only practical way through was to stay on U.S. 6; however, even if 6 were straight, it would not have been an easy walk. Although only two lanes, it was used not just by locals, but also by truckers whose runs were long yet not long enough to warrant detours either south to Interstate 80 or north to the Southern Tier Expressway. Consequently, traffic was sometimes heavy and noisy, and occasionally even frightening.

It didn't happen often, but it happened a couple of times along route 6. "It" is when you are walking a two-lane road and an abruptly increasing roar tells you that behind you a car has swung out to pass another car. By the time you hear it, it's too late to jump. Presumably the driver has seen you and will successfully slice through the narrow lane between you and whatever he or she is passing. I always felt I was in considerable danger during those events, but as it turned out, the only times I came close to being hit (once by the property manager's friend and once in Idaho), the near misses were my own fault.

WALKING IN WESTERN PENNSYLVANIA

Harmony Acres Campground lies five miles east of Port Allegany, Pennsylvania, which is more than half way across the state. We arrived there with Lurch during the second week of May, and were checked in by a personable young woman whom we thought was the park manager. Later we realized that Alice was just an uncommonly efficient employee. In any case, she invited us to drive through the park, look over the campsites, and take any one we wanted that wasn't occupied.

Ten minutes of reconnoitering brought us to the most inviting-looking spot in the whole park. It lay close by the Allegheny River, and it was shaded by a tall willow tree and had thick grass on soft, dry soil. (Aside: The town and river names are spelled differently, thus *Allegany* for the town but *Allegheny* for the river.) After leveling Lurch and connecting utilities, we were established only six feet from the water's edge. From inside we could hear the water as it flowed by and gently splashed against rocks a few yards downstream. How idyllic! We congratulated ourselves on having the best campsite in the whole park, even as we vaguely wondered why it had been vacant. "Them other campers don't know a good spot when they see one!" I told Helen.

Where were our brains?

Several people were fishing nearby, and one had been doing particularly well, having caught three good-sized trout while other anglers were coming up empty. He had worked his way along the creek and now stood on the bank beside Lurch. An architect from Pittsburgh, he was up on the Allegheny for a fishing vacation, and right now he was preoccupied with the hatch, meaning small flies that had just emerged from eggs and which the fish were feeding on. "When they're working a fresh hatch is when you wanna be fishing," he said, and then, "That's why I'm doing so well; there's really nothing to it."

That comment surprised me for it was obviously false modesty. The fellow knew how to fish while the other anglers were far less expert, and he was not a humble person—either in dress or demeanor. But neither was he unpleasant, and when I answered, "Yeah, I hear you talking," he grinned, bobbed his head, and held up his hands in a fake effacing gesture meaning, What can I say?— I'm just good!

Full of himself, he was; even so, I enjoyed talking to him.

We discussed the weather, especially how dry it was, and he told me the river was lower than he had ever seen it. And even as we talked, it never crossed my mind that if there was a rainstorm anything like what he and the locals were praying for, then our RV, perched a mere two feet above the water, would probably end up flooded or sunk to its axles in Harmony Acres mud. Sometimes ignorance really is bliss.

I had to break off talking when Alice came over from the office to connect us to the campground's TV system. Getting involved, I managed to crush a connector in the distribution-box door, but Alice said I could buy another at a Radio Shack in nearby Port Allegany. Not to worry, we needed a trip to town anyway; there were clothes to wash and groceries to buy. We'd put that off until tomorrow, however; it had been a long drive out from Hop Bottom.

Two days passed before we got back to walking.

*   *   *   *

Entries in Helen's log: Wednesday, May 12, Sylvania to Wellsboro, twenty-five miles; Thursday, Wellsboro to West Pike, twenty-eight miles; Friday, West Pike to Burtville, twenty-nine miles.

Friday's walk took us past an important milestone, the Appalachian Divide. Beyond West Pike, route 6 follows first Pine Creek and then Ninemile Run, climbing steadily for ten miles. Eventually the stream ends but the road climbs a little farther, to just past a small pond. From there it begins, just as gradually, to descend. The high point is the divide, and how impressed we were to have crossed it! Runoff to the east enters Ninemile Run, flows to Pine Creek at West Pike, then on to the Susquehanna River, and eventually to the Atlantic Ocean. To the west it enters Trout Run, flows to Mill Creek at Sweden Valley, then on to the Allegheny River, the Ohio, the Mississippi, and finally, of course, to the Gulf of Mexico.

That night we celebrated crossing the divide with extra glasses of wine, and Helen declared, "As far as I'm concerned, we're a third of the way across the country."

"How's that?"

"Well, think of the country as divided into three sections by the Appalachian Divide and the Continental Divide."

"I'm thinking."

"Then, since we've walked the entire section east of the Appalachians, we can say we're a third of the way across."

I don't remember my answer, but with that kind of rosy-eyed outlook, how can you help but keep walking? The truth was that we had come about 320 miles and were over 2100 from the West Coast as the crow flies, and over 2800 along the twisty roads I had yet to walk. Still, Helen would always be an inspiration. One night she tried to prep me for a longer day's walk the following day. "Honey," she said, "your step lacked spring today."

I was sixty-seven years old!

*   *   *   *

For some time Helen had been referring to the truck as "that albatross around our necks." We had not used it since she stopped walking in eastern Pennsylvania—except to move it from there to our present campsite at Harmony Acres. During that involved project, we had first driven the car and truck 130 miles from Hop Bottom to Harmony. Then, leaving the truck, we drove back to Hop Bottom in the car, only to turn around and drive both car and motor home back out to Harmony to complete the move. All told, it had taken two days, and amounted to 390 miles of driving for the car plus 130 each for truck and motor home. Obviously, if we had taken the truck home first, the whole move would have been a straightforward one-day job, with me driving the motor home and Helen the car.

The real question was, Would Helen do any more walking? If *yes*, then we would need the truck; if *no*, then there was no point in moving it from one campground to another, always farther west and at considerable expense in time, money, and energy. It was up to Helen, and it was she who decided we should take the truck home and give up the idea that she would eventually resume walking. "If I do," she said, "we probably won't average more than eight or ten miles a day, and that'll never get us across the country." She felt that with her continuing to drive support, we would cover just over a hundred miles a week—enough to put us in Nebraska by early fall. From there we should be able to finish the walk by the following September.

The decision made, we started home with car and truck the next morning, Saturday, May 15, and we arrived there about five in the afternoon. After going out to eat (there was no food in the house), we turned on the Weather Channel. There had been bad floods somewhere, not in the East but somewhere, and soon we were obsessing about where we left the RV. We had been smugly pleased to get the campsite nearest the Allegheny River—"Them other campers don't know a good spot when they see one!" Now we cringed at images of home-sweet-home lying miles downstream and wheels-up in mud. So much for hubris.

We should relax, we eventually agreed; the floods were not in western Pennsylvania. Nevertheless, we would hurry back to Harmony Acres the next morning and continue the walk, but more importantly to be with Lurch, in order, as Helen put it, "to rescue *him* from a flood if necessary." *Him!* That was one of the first times either Helen or I referred to Lurch in the masculine *him* instead of the neuter *it*. However, our clunky motor home did seem to have an animate, masculine personality—sometimes a malevolent one—so we would soon be referring to it regularly with *he's* and *him's*.

On our way back to Harmony, we stopped to visit an archeological dig along U.S. 6 in Pennsylvania. The site lay along a creek, and several graduate students were excavating an Indian campsite that had been used, they said, about eight thousand years ago. The earnest students showed us several pieces of stone they had found which they were sure showed marks of human tooling. They could not say, however, what they were or what ancient tool or implement they may have been part of. As for Helen and me, we could not convince ourselves the tiny objects were other than random pieces of stone that could easily have been scratched and marked by natural processes. Of course we said nothing like that to the pleasant young people, whose enthusiasm was almost contagious. Presumably their professor would know what the little stones were—or were not.

Three hours later we arrived at Harmony Acres and were happy to find Lurch just as we left him, i.e., high, dry, and six feet from the river. Luckily, there had been no rain.

* * * *

We should have taken it easy the next day since it had been a tiring trip back and forth to Connecticut. We were eager, however, to get on with the walk, so at eight the next morning Helen dropped me off on the outskirts of Port Allegany. I had walked only a short distance when I paused on a bridge over Lillibridge Creek, a small tributary of the Allegheny River, and gazing down, my attention idly *drifted* toward a surface-water pipe before *jumping* to a trout resting quietly nearby. I had crossed many bridges and seen many fish, but this fellow was the biggest so far.

Twenty minutes later, turning west off of Main Street (seems as if every town has a Main Street), I crossed another bridge, this one over the Allegheny itself. Along the bank about fifty feet to the north, two boys sat fishing. I called hello and inquired about their luck. "No luck," was the lethargic response of one kid; his buddy didn't bother to look up.

"Well, there's a big trout just off the bridge coming into town— saw 'im about twenty minutes ago."

That woke them up. "Where 'bouts?" This quickly from the boy who had ignored me a minute before.

"I just told you!" I yelled back laughing. He had heard the "big trout" part, but nothing after that.

"Ah, no foolin'," the first boy said. "You really see a trout?"

I was surprised the kids didn't know about the fish since it was obviously pretty tame. I had seen plenty of big fish like that when we lived in Bellefonte, Pennsylvania, years before. Spring Creek flows through Bellefonte along Water Street, and people traveled for miles to stand behind a dike-like wall and throw dough balls down to the fish. You could buy fish food across the street, and the lazy creatures never moved any more than they had to. Doubtless, most were escapees from Fisherman's Paradise, a private fishing park four miles upstream, and you would probably have got less jail time for bank robbery than for hooking one of those fish.

In any case, I convinced the boys that the fish really was in Lillibridge Creek, whereupon they sprang into action, pulling in their lines and grabbing their gear. They were dashing up the bank as I walked on. "Thank'ee you," one of them hollered. "We're gonna git 'im."

That day Helen and I logged the longest walk to date, thirty-three miles, but there would be few other days when I would walk that far. It was not that the distance was too tiring; it was rather that the day lasted too long. We left the RV at eight that morning, and except for chat stops and lunch, I was on the road till after seven that evening. By then we were forty miles from camp, and with the long drive back it was another hour until we got there. After showers and dinner, there was hardly time to relax before bedtime. Too much walking. Too long a day. We'd keep it shorter in the future.

*   *   *   *

We left U.S. 6 at Kane, Pennsylvania, and cut southwest through the Allegheny National Forest on state 66. Leaving 6, we thought we would see fewer trucks, but alas, for truckers en route still farther west, 66 is an easy choice. In just over forty miles it connects with I-80 which leads to Akron, Toledo, and on through the American heartland, all the way to the West Coast. Although there were few cars the day I walked 66, roaring trucks came by at a rate of about one per minute. In between I would hear birds singing and soft breezes in the trees—pristine, almost silent. Then from afar would come the thunder of a mighty eighteen-wheeler. Louder and louder the din would grow, until the huge machine would pass with a blast of wind and an ear-splitting crescendo, which, in turn, would slowly fade again to welcome, soft quiet.

It was a hot day and just off the road a creek veered away and up a ravine, tumbling and falling over small waterfalls and short stretches of rapids. How welcome a sight! I followed it for a hundred yards, to a shady bank where a large stone had waited for eons just for me to sit upon. Delicious! Within minutes I was dozing, only to wake with a start, doze again, wake with a start, doze again.... Presently, I determinedly roused myself, ate a granola bar, took off my shirt to splash water over chest and back and head. Then, soaking my shirt and hat too, I put them back on to enjoy still more pleasant cooling. Rid now of too much heat, and quite refreshed, I was ready to move on.

A shortcut out of the ravine and back toward the road brought me, surprisingly, to a small park with an inviting little spring. Hunched over the water, a burly trucker was cupping his hands to drink, and I knew, as I approached from behind, that it would be hard not to spook him. Stopping while still about forty feet away, I called a soft "Yo," upon which he dropped a cupped handful of water and, spinning around, stared as if a bear were about to get him. Then he grinned broadly, and as soon as he re-swallowed his heart, he blurted, "Hell'd you come from? You scared the shit outa me!"

"Sorry, knew I was gonna scare yuh. Couldn't think how not to."

He was a friendly fellow—a friendly giant. "Hey Good Buddy! You mean t' stand there and tell me you're walkin' across the United States? … clear to the West Coast?"

"Yep, all the way. And this is only the start of it."

"How old are you? Where do you sleep at night? Your pack's too small. You ain't got no tent."

Two questions and two statements before I could answer a single word. But when he paused I managed a comeback: "Sixty-seven. In a motor home. No it's not. You're right."

"Huh?" He was quiet for a moment before bursting into laughter. "You got me. My wife's always sayin' I rattle out questions and never wait for answers." Then, even before I could respond, he continued: "Your wife's waiting up ahead, ain't she?"

"Yeah," I said, continuing the game as best I could. "She's parked in a Toyota. Your wife's right. How far west is she?"

"Good Buddy, you got me again! We talkin' about your wife or mine? About four miles. But you guys are a long way from Connecticut. Right?"

Whose wife's whose? Helen four miles west? Us from Connecticut?—all three thoughts in one run-together sequence as if one followed the other, which was hardly the case as he well knew. He had been coming from the west and noticed the Toyota with its Connecticut license plate. It had been easy to connect me, Helen, the car, and his wife in this playful game of mix-up-what-you-say. But Good Lord, what a screwy exchange to have with a total stranger!

We rapped and bantered for another five minutes, until he announced he just had to get back on the road. Even so, more time passed as with several pauses we walked out of the tiny park and down toward his monster truck, which had been running the whole time. If we could have shouted over the racket, we would have kept talking there too, but it was impossible. As I turned and began walking, he climbed up into his cab, and with many a wave and a bellowed, "Good luck, good buddy," he headed east toward Towanda. Whoever that trucker was, he would always be a cherished memory.

*   *   *   *

Sometimes I would walk for long times in deep thought, almost oblivious to the world around me. I came to think of these times as "Musing Holidays," and one day, along state 66, my thoughts drifted to the causes leading up to the Civil War. Fragmented and incomplete the thinking was; nevertheless, an outline formed of the evolving nature of the country in the decades between 1790 and 1860. Dots connected and thoughts developed, the picture became something as follows:

The federal government was established in 1789 by the plantation aristocracy of the South and the commercial classes of the North. Its primary purpose was to create between the colonies-come-states an independent free trade environment that would further the economic interests of both sections of the country. Imports and exports, though always factors in the colonial economy, were not yet of great importance. This was because most manufactured goods were consumed within a few miles of where they were made, either by individual craftsmen or in small shops employing only a few workers.

In the North things changed quickly during the first half of the nineteenth century, primarily because of a fast-growing factory system made possible by the mechanical revolution. As immigrants flooded into the country and manufacturing output rapidly increased, the need to move materials to factories and products to markets impelled the North to build roads, canals, and eventually railroads. These, in turn, stimulated still further economic growth in a circular pattern that consistently favored development in the industrializing North over development in the relatively sedentary, agrarian South. In addition, roads and railroads built into the Midwest facilitated shipments of cattle and grain from those regions to the East, thereby insuring that the Midwest, though mostly agrarian like the South, would ultimately align politically with the industrializing North.

Protecting domestic markets from cheaper foreign imports increasingly forced northern industrialists to push for high tariffs, and consequently the South was eventually buying northern manufactured goods at higher prices than similar imported goods would have cost in the absence of such tariffs. To add insult to injury, the British, in retaliation for American sanctions against their products, tariffed American imports, even southern cotton! Cotton, of course, was the chief U.S. export, the main source of southern wealth, and hence the golden link that tied that region to the plantation system and its necessary institution, slavery.

Religion and idealistic declarations aside, a people's moral viewpoints usually reside where their economic needs put them, and slavery to the plantation owner was absolutely necessary for his economic survival. As he saw it, "that peculiar institution" was beneficial not only to himself but to the slave as well. After all, was not the black man provided access to the gospel, and did he not have a certain economic security that went hand in hand with his master's prosperity?

On the other hand, the northern abolitionist, his viewpoint detached from his wallet, enjoyed the idealistic high ground: slavery to him was morally wrong. Inspired to a great degree by *Uncle Tom's Cabin*, he demanded abolition in accordance with ambiguous biblical implications together with the Declaration of Independence's assertion that "all men are created equal." Anyway, the north needed those tariffs.

By the mid eighteen-fifties, patience and tolerance were running out on both sides. Over the preceding thirty-five years, as new territories applied for statehood, bitter disputes had broken out over whether they should be free or slave. No prospective employer of free men could afford to be in competition with a nearby counterpart using slave labor, and no southerner wanted additional Free States that would shift federal power still further toward the North. There was the Missouri Compromise of 1820, the Compromise of 1850, and finally the Kansas-Nebraska Act of

1854 which left it to those states-to-be to decide for themselves whether to be slave or free. The bloody pro- vs. anti-slavery skirmishes that followed in those regions were the real first battles of the Civil War....

Not gunfire but the roar of a truck suddenly brought me out of contemplations and back to real life. It was late afternoon and I was tired of walking, although it would be another hour before I would meet Helen at a crossroads called Marienville. That would be the end of traffic noise for a while, since during the following days, walking would be over remote back roads that would ultimately take us to the Ohio border.

WE MOVE LURCH TOO FAR AHEAD

From Marionville, I walked twenty-four miles through deciduous woodlands to Frills Corners, about twenty miles east of Oil City. The region is part of the Allegheny Plateau, and although the land as a whole is fifteen hundred feet above sea level, many local rolling hills are no more than a hundred feet higher than adjacent lowlands. Much of the region is designated state game lands, and aside from an abundance of deer (I saw probably ten) the low hills mean easy walking. This doubtless contributes to the area's popularity as hunting country.

Various smaller roads branched off the gravel connector I was walking, and small cottages and hunting cabins were all along the way. Typically, these were one-story affairs with wooden porches, tarpaper siding, and crude stone chimneys. Often, antlers hung over cabin doors, to vouch for the prowess of the hunter-owners. In some yards were remnants of old target setups that people had used to sight in rifles.

For me it was a day of recollections, because I was once a hunter myself. There is a thrill to hunting that carries through from prehistoric times, when primitive men either hunted successfully or their groups and families starved. Twenty-something and young, I enjoyed the hunt—the excitement, the camaraderie, the sense of adventure. Nevertheless, I eventually grew away from all of that, and nowadays I recall those times with little other than nostalgic memories—except for the depressing ends of successful hunts. I say to myself that I could never shoot an animal again, but down deep I know that that is not necessarily true. Let me be hungry, let my family be in need, let circumstance harden my heart with necessity. That would change my mind, and relieved of the luxury of modern moralizing, I would surely respond to the hunting imperative and no doubt kill again....

About ten miles west of Marionville I began to notice blue blazes of the North Country National Scenic Trail. The North Country Trail is part of the National Trail System, which includes, among others, the better known Appalachian Trail. However, while the Appalachian Trail essentially follows the spine of the Appalachian Mountains from Georgia to Main, the North Country Trail weaves its way across widely diverse countryside from Crown Point, New York to Sakakawea State Park in North Dakota. There is talk of rerouting short sections of one or both trails to create a common section in Pennsylvania, but this will require the approval of Congress.

Walking ended about five o'clock, after which it was a sixty-mile drive back to Harmony Acres.

*　　*　　*　　*

While still at Harmony, we took a day off from walking and drove a hundred miles southeast through beautiful, remote country to State College, Pennsylvania. We made the trip to visit Bob and Jeannette Eberhart, who, like the Herrmanns in Binghamton, were old friends. Jeannette and Helen grew up only a quarter mile apart, and they have known each other some sixty-five years.

We had a delightful time. Bob is retired Penn State faculty, and his updates on university goings-on are always of interest to me. Tractors, gardens, dogs, and reminiscences filled the day. There was even time for a brief tour of the Penn State campus. A new library wing that was under construction was especially interesting. Appropriately, it was to be named after the football coach, Joe Paterno, who contributed generously to the library over many years.

In the evening Helen and I returned to Harmony Campground. We could have stayed overnight with the Eberharts—they asked us to—but increasingly, we were eager to keep pushing west. We had become firmly convinced that our earlier casual attitude toward the coast-to-coast walk would surely lead to failure. Push hard, rest, push hard, rest, push hard, rest.… That was the approach we concluded would most likely get us to the Pacific someday. "Pace yourself" may be good advice for someone entering a footrace, but for this project, dawn till exhaustion hikes separated by unavoidable rests seemed most likely to succeed.

Driving back to Harmony was even more beautiful than driving down had been. For a while, the changing landscapes and skies were a sequence of studies in pastel. In scene after scene, the sun, now low in the west, cast warm light on the leaves and trunks of endless trees, and swaths of tall brown stalks, last year's growth, glowed orange against new green meadow grass. Above the landscape, white clouds against a pinkish-blue sky completed panoramas that were at once the same yet constantly changing, mile after mile after mile. Gradually, as the sun went down, daytime contrasts gave way to soft shadows and grays, and these in turn, almost imperceptibly, darkened with oncoming night.

Our moods grew thoughtful as the headlights led us through tunnels of trees, and though we were keenly aware of the utter remoteness of the country, there was the road and the car itself to mentally tie us to our modern times—hedges, perhaps, against ancient fears that may have assailed our souls in less enlightened times. Helen began to talk about what the earth might have been like before there were people, and I, being me, had to indulge in whimsical speculation.

"If there was no one here to behold it," I remarked, "does the question, What was the world like? have any meaning?"

"Ask the more general question," Helen came right back. "Does it make sense to assume there's a universe if there's no human to observe it? It's like the old paradox, you know—if a tree falls in the wilderness and no one's around to hear it, does it make a sound?"

"No comparison," I said. "The tree story assumes there really are people in the world, and that there might or might not be somebody present to hear it fall. The paradoxical part is nothing more than a play on possible meanings of the word *sound*. If *sound* means perceptions produced in the brain by air vibrating an eardrum, and no eardrum is around to vibrate, then there is no sound. On the other hand, if *sound* means the air vibrations themselves, then there is sound."

We were off to a good start. I assumed the nasal, high-pitched voice of a high school teacher we had both known fifty-five years before.

"Every person," I began, "has a model of things beyond him- or herself that resides in his or her mind. Call it the 'world-without.' This model, though nonexistent at birth, evolves over the years in response to the myriad sights and sounds and smells that come to him through his senses. The mind interprets these stimuli and integrates them into an evolving mental picture which the holder assumes is a reflection of the unique and 'real' world outside himself, i.e., a physical universe independent of the beholder or, for that matter, all humanity. A universe of atoms and energy, stars and time."

"And hot air," Helen sweetly added. "Honey, this sounds teenagey. Makes me feel like we're kids again. I love it."

I ignored her—just drew myself up and kept going.

"But when we assume we are thinking about the universe without, we're actually contemplating facets of those personal models of the universe that we have developed in our own minds. We may, at the time, be looking or hearing or smelling or tasting, but we don't have to be. An individual's personal internal world can be contemplated in a darkened room in the absence of all external stimuli—even as a prisoner in solitary confinement can think about the world outside, or even as Helen Keller did in spite of greatly reduced powers of vision, hearing, and speech."

"Keep going, Phil; you sound like Harvey." Harvey was a teenage friend of ours who used to talk about how many angels could stand on the head of a pin.

And keep going I did: "It's unimaginable that after death the dispersed atoms of a former person's brain retain a mental model of the universe, let alone that they should think about one. And before a human's conception, it's unthinkable that the scattered molecules that will someday *be* that person's brain are capable of collectively thinking. Furthermore, during life, a person cannot honestly imagine himself as conscious either before conception or after death, nor can he project himself to either of those temporal positions and from there think about anything. As soon as he tries, all thinking shuts down as some still small voice pipes up and says, 'Wait! You can't think. You don't even exist!'

"So, Helen, for any individual the universe exists only as a mental model and only during his or her lifetime; before or after such time, there is no world.… Did I hear you giggle?"

"Yes! No!… Phil, what do you want me to say?"

"Now, what I've said about a single human can just as well be said about humanity as a whole. Before our species came into existence, there were no thinking beings to harbor the notion of a universe, and therefore, for all practical purposes, there was no universe at all. By the same reasoning, there will be no universe when the last of our kind are gone."

"Honey, watch the road. There was a deer back there."

"So, the assumption of a universe without humans requires a ghost to envision it, and that, my dear, in any sense, is meaningless! Now back to the original issue: What was the world like before people were here?"

I answered myself with flourish and finality: "There wasn't any world; it didn't exist because nobody was around to think about it."

"What about dinosaur bones?" Helen mumbled, definitely beginning to get drowsy. "They're in museums all over the world, and they didn't come from nowhere, you know. Dinosaurs lived ninety million years ago, and there were no people around to see them. Don't you believe in dinosaurs?"

"It's fun to make up stories about great big lizards that lived in prehistoric times, especially ones that might gobble up an old nurse or an English teacher. But again, in a practical sense they exist only in the present as images in our and other people's minds—especially kids'. Which brings me to the business of paleontological history: It's all bunk!"

"Why's it all bunk? You sound like Henry Ford."

"Because there never *were* any dinosaurs. Those fossilized bones were made by the devil and put here on earth to fool gullible people like you—lead 'em astray."

Sleepily:"Keep talking, Phil. Somebody'll make you an honorary Creationist."

I expounded (gassed) a while longer, but Helen said nothing more. Eventually I switched on the dome light and glanced over. Sure enough, she'd gone to asleep.

*　　*　　*　　*

It was nearly midnight when we arrived back at Harmony Acres, and the next morning we were thoroughly groggy and suffering from nagging impatience. Granted I had walked ten of the preceding seventeen days and had averaged almost twenty-six miles per day. On the other hand, we used two days to visit the Herrmanns, two to move Lurch to Harmony Campground, two to take the truck back to Connecticut, and one to visit the Eberharts. Too many days not walking, we told each other; we'd have to do better if we really wanted to get across the country.

So in that frame of mind, we moved Lurch all the way to Sycamore Campground north of Warren, Ohio, which was ninety-five miles beyond walk's end and over meandering narrow roads at that! Upon arriving, we paid a week's rent in advance; then we stayed at the campground the next day and fidgeted constantly as we tried to relax.

Finally, the following morning, we drove all the way back to walk's end, and that torturous drive took nearly three hours. By the time Helen dropped me off and I took my first steps, it was already one in the afternoon. Worse yet, the weather had turned wet—not gentle showers but a violent storm of gusting winds and driven rain, complete with flying leaves and occasional downed branches. I was soaked before I walked a hundred yards. Meanwhile, Helen taxied alongside and tried to get me to quit for the day."Me? Quit? Not a chance, Dearie! We didn't come all the way back here for nothing."

"Your call," she replied, as she began easing away. "Far be it from me to tell *you* what to do."

"Beg your pardon ma'am, but that's exactly what you *are* trying to do. I'm not quitting till I get washed away!"

And on I went, and nearly *did* get washed away. At a sharp bend where the road had no shoulder, a passing car crowded me into the weeds. Stopping, I tried to put on a poncho since my jacket was already soaked. But the wind whipped the poncho around making it nearly impossible to fasten snaps that went down its back, and when I finally did get it on, it blew up around my chest and had to be unrolled with various expletives and more struggling against the wind.

As I resumed walking, the wind actually became dangerous. Twice it blew me a step or two toward the middle of the road, while its noise masked the sounds of cars approaching from behind.

I eventually met Helen at a place called Fryburg, a mere five miles from Frills Corners, where we had started from two hours before. It was already midafternoon, and facing a three hour drive back to Ohio, we called it quits. All told, we drove 180 miles that day and accomplished only five miles of walking.

It was still raining the next morning, at which point we were well aware that we had moved Lurch much too far ahead. As Helen put it, "Heck Phil, if we moved Lurch all the way to Indiana, it wouldn't mean that walk's end was anywhere near there. It would just mean a three-hundred-mile drive back to where we really are, namely, western Pennsylvania."

In fact, up until then, we had moved the RV only three times and had not yet concluded that an ideal repositioning would place it roughly forty-five miles beyond the current walk's end. In our impatience, we had moved twice that far. Consequently, instead of getting into the car and driving ninety miles east to begin what would doubtless be another short day's walk, we decided to cut our losses and move back into Pennsylvania.

Helen got out her campground guide and began looking for some place that was, as she put it, "a realistic distance from walk's soaking-wet end." What she found was Goddard Vacation Land

Park, about twenty miles east of the Pennsylvania border and a more reasonable thirty-some miles from where we had finished walking. Good enough! Goddard's was where we would head the following morning.

Breaking camp, that is, getting Lurch out of Sycamore Campground, proved to be fun—at least to look back on. When we had checked in, two days earlier, I noted that the inlet pipe, into which I'd be connecting our RV's waste hose, ran along the ground for several feet before disappearing into a low, flat dirt mound. I assumed the mound covered a small septic tank with a drainage field beyond a nearby footpath. The inlet pipe from a neighboring campsite also went into the mound beside a three-inch, upright vent pipe.

I asked office staff if there was anything special I needed to know before using the iffy-looking arrangement. "Oh no, Mr. Beam. Just connect to the input pipe, open your valve, and drain your black-water tank. Nothing to it."

So we got up early the morning of the move, and after breakfast I set out to drain the tank. Things went well at first. I shoved my waste hose into the inlet pipe, just as I'd been told. Then I opened the valve and heard the black water race by on its way, I thought, out of my life forever. Such a satisfying sound! Suddenly there was a thud followed by whoosh, and back the sewage came as a two-foot fountain gushing up from the vent pipe. At least a quart soaked my left ankle and foot before I could scramble out of the way, and thanks to a breeze (or no thanks), light mist "caressed" my face as I blundered back to close the valve.

That's when Helen laughed!

I got mad and noisy and hollered out my opinion of the "Rube Goldberg" responsible for such a miserable excuse of a septic system to begin with. A woman and two men were laughing and watching from nearby campsites, but they turned around and went inside when I glared.

I'm not squeamish, but I didn't enjoy picking up the bits and wads of paper, garbage, and scatological debris that were the residue of that debacle. I dropped the smelly mess down the vent pipe of a different campsite's sewage system, if you could call those things sewage systems. Actually, they were nothing more than holed fifty-five-gallon drums set in the ground and surrounded by gravel—no drainage fields at all.

The water hose was still connected, so I hosed my legs and feet and face, and rinsed my mouth a thousand times; then I went inside and took a shower. Helen was mostly done laughing by then. Minutes later, though, she looked away, put a hand over her face, and began snickering all over again. I pretended not to notice; besides, by then I was beginning to see it funny myself—at least a trifle.

I was going to complain to the park owner about our—make that my—misadventure with the sewage, but when you've paid for seven nights, stayed only two, and are hoping for a refund, well then, you have to be nice. Actually, the office people were pleasant when I asked for money back, but they said there wasn't enough cash on hand, it still being early in the morning. Would we come back in an hour or two, after somebody had been to the bank?

We passed an hour in a nearby restaurant, and when we returned, the owner had arrived. He cheerfully refunded our money, and we considered ourselves fortunate; nevertheless, at the time, we did not realize how fortunate we were. Several park owners, whom we would encounter later, would require advance payment while at the same time firmly declaring a strict no-refund policy. Helen called such places "Heads-I win-tails-you-lose parks."

By eleven o'clock we were on our way back to Pennsylvania and Goddard Vacation Land Park.

MUSCLE ACHES AND
HORSE LINIMENT

Our new base camp was now a reasonable distance from walk's end; consequently we were in the field and I was marching by seven the next morning. I caught up with Helen four hours later near a mountain prominence called Cream Hill, and somehow, over lunch, we began talking about how tired we had become of lunch-meat sandwiches washed down with soft drinks. The cookies or pieces of pie that we usually finished up with still went down okay, but something had to be done about the main course. Helen said she would begin packing course-sized servings of beef or pork or fried chicken packed in sandwich bags—they should go good when eaten with bread and butter. That was fine with me. But good intentions aside, we were still normalizing our morning routines to more efficiently support the daily walks, and bothering to pack fancier lunches would have to come later. For the time being, we would use roadside restaurants more often.

I arrived in Oil City, Pennsylvania, about one o'clock. The town lies on a bend of the Allegheny River where famous Oil Creek enters from the north. Sixteen miles upstream is the site of Drake's Oil Well, and nearby is Titusville. We were surprised to learn that Titusville was an old town when oil was discovered in 1859, while Oil City was only established the following year, as a refining and shipping center for the anticipated oil bonanza. In those days the region's main avenue to the outside world was the river, and at first both crude and refined oils were taken by boat to Pittsburgh, 120 miles downstream. By 1869, however, the newly completed Allegheny Railroad, now in competition with the riverboats, shipped over a million barrels of raw crude to Pittsburgh, which by then was itself becoming a major refining center. That reminded Helen and me of the how trains had taken over from rafting in shipping logs down the Delaware River to Trenton and Philadelphia. It was the second half of the nineteenth century, and railroads were quickly developing everywhere.

During the afternoon, walking was along the Allegheny to Franklin, and a few miles beyond toward the town of Nicklin. During the last mile I caught up with a fifteen-year-old bicyclist named Jack, who had dismounted in order to push his bike up a steep hill. He was an engaging young man, and as we walked and talked I almost forgot the encroaching fatigue.

Jack's ambition was to become an auto mechanic and, using his trade, to work his way through college to an engineering degree. That struck an understanding chord! Certainly his interest in mechanical things fit the appearance of his bike which, though old, was obviously in perfect condition. He told me that his family had always lived in Franklin (*always* seemed to mean about thirty years), and that several of the men had become mechanics, one going on to college to become a high school shop teacher.

Pleasant and straightforward, Jack was easily taken seriously; there was a reserve about him and a confidence that belied his years: he seemed pragmatic—not a common quality in people his age. My guess was that he would start out a mechanic, but seduced by success in that field, he would forgo engineering and move on to own an auto repair shop or body shop or eventually even a dealership.

We parted near the crest of the hill and within five minutes of starting down, I met a seventyish couple who were definitely on the opposite end of the personality curve. They were filling water bottles at a roadside spring and loading them into a raggedy station wagon. Still in a good mood from talking to the boy, I approached with a cheery, "Good afternoon."

"Murumpff" came as a grunt from the man's wooden face.

Too slow-witted to quit right there, I tried again, but this time with the woman. "Do you come far for water?" I asked.

She made some kind of smileless noise, never paused in what she was doing, never made eye contact. Nevertheless, as I passed by she whined something about just trying to get water. Her tone was peevish, indeed bitter, and when I glanced back, so was her stare. The old man also glared and then muttered something about having come up there to get water, not waste time "blathering." I was surprised to where I almost laughed.

Fifteen minutes later I met Helen, and it occurred to me what a contrast she was to "Mrs. Pickleface," as I had already begun to think of the woman. The old man was unlucky to have a shrew for a wife, but on the other hand they seemed to be much of a kind. "They deserve each other," I told Helen as we drove back to camp.

*　　*　　*　　*

Georgetown Road follows along the eastern shore of Lake Wilhelm, a long, narrow lake much like several others in Pennsylvania's northwest corner. With two lanes and hardly any shoulder, it is the kind of road you have to step off of, if two cars, coming from opposite directions, happen to pass you at the same time. Fortunately there was no wind, so I could hear traffic approaching from behind. Even so, walking was hard, and the fatigue I had noticed the afternoon before now seemed worse.

About ten o'clock, a car with four teenagers sped down from the north, and as they passed, one tossed a paper cup of water from the right rear window. The cup missed but water hit my right shoulder, leaving me fuming as they disappeared around a bend. Annoying as it was, the prank looked more like high jinx than meanness, and sure enough, minutes later, I heard a car approaching from behind and slowing, slowing, and finally drawing abreast. Sensing it was the youths, I held my stride, gripped the pepper spray in my left pants pocket, and turned to look straight at them.

"Sir?" Tentatively—the driver.

"So what do you guys want?"

"Well, sir, we're sorry about the water. Anyway, this jerk ain't got no cool." He gestured over his shoulder toward a kid in the back seat.

Lacking cool or not, "Jerk" came through with his own apology, albeit with obvious reluctance and considerable pressure from his car-mates.

"Forget it," I told the boy.

The apology offered and accepted, we began to talk, but not so much as I with them and they with me, but seemingly in opposite, parallel directions—as I past them and they past me. Maybe it was the great difference in age or maybe it was just the personalities.

"Anyway, how come you guys aren't in school?" I asked with a smile. "It's Thursday morning."

"How do you know school's not out for the summer? Anyway, where are you headed with a pack on your back?"

"Oregon. Anyway, do you guys even go to school?" If they went, I assumed it would be in Meadville, Franklin, or Greenville—all nearby towns.

Suddenly the kid in the left rear seat laughed and said, "Anyway, anyway, anyway. Everybody keeps saying *anyway*."

"Yeah, anyway, we hear your Oregon," chimed in the kid in the passenger seat. He grinned from ear to ear, but there was no answer from any of them about where or whether they went to school.

"Well, anyway, you're laughing," I said, ready to be done with the odd, competitive exchange.

They were boisterous young bucks; nevertheless their apology seemed genuine. Presently the driver and the kid behind him offered to shake hands, and since they reached their arms well out of the windows, I accepted. There was no way I would reach in, and even as I shook with my right hand, I clutched the pepper spray with my left. Then, with a roar and a screech of tires they were off and heading north, back in the direction they'd been coming from when the water flew.

I was glad they had returned and apologized, but glad too that they were gone; they made me a little uneasy although I was sure they were harmless. They're close to the end of their tax-free years, I told myself; real life will hit 'em pretty soon. But what would it hold for them? I wondered. The military? The trades? Probably not college—not those guys—although everybody seems to go to college these days.

An hour later I began looking forward to arriving at Goddard Campground, since this would be one of those rare days when I would eat lunch "at home." When we retreated from Ohio, we were only thinking about placing Lurch reasonably close to the current walk's end. It was pure luck that from there west the best route would take me right by the campground. In any case, I arrived about twelve noon, and eating at the table in the motor home was much pleasanter than eating in the car along the road.

After lunch Helen and I lazily reviewed our progress. (Actually, I was procrastinating—didn't feel good.) Helen declared that we had finished crossing the Appalachians, that we were entering a new phase of the walk, and that walking would be easier from there on. I had thought little about it except to note that six miles west of Nicklin the woods thinned and the mountains gave way to rolling hills that sloped down toward Lake Wilhelm. There were cornfields too, and when one to the south had caught my eye, I remembered an old farmer, years before, telling me that corn should be "knee high by Fourth of July." He would have loved those fields. The corn was waist high and it was only the end of May.

But Helen was right. The mountains were definitely behind us, and for the next twelve hundred miles we would have relatively flat walking.

That afternoon I fought a pervasive fatigue unlike anything I had felt before on the trip. Helen wondered if I was coming down with something, but I reminded her that I had walked the day before, and that during the three days before that we: one, had moved Lurch from Pennsylvania into Ohio, two, had driven a round trip of 180 miles to get in a measly five-mile walking day, and three, had returned Lurch from Ohio back into Pennsylvania to Goddard Park. Punchy and dragging though I was that afternoon, I still managed to finish at Leech's Corners, thus only a dozen miles from the Ohio border and twenty-seven miles from our starting place that morning. In truth, it felt more like fifty.

*   *   *   *

We had to move from Goddard on Friday, May 28, the reason being that all the campsites had been reserved for the upcoming Memorial Day weekend. Excitement filled the air, and by 8 a.m. there were kids all over the place. I told Helen that somebody around there had ten identical boys. I claimed I saw one kid in the office; then, minutes later, another identical squirt on a trash Dumpster. Still a third materialized on a jungle gym; a fourth ran between campsites, and a fifth came riding down a footpath on a bicycle. And all this, I said, in less than five minutes. In the next fifteen, I saw five more, all the same in dress, manner, and squeaky voice. Helen said it was the same kid and that he moved with the speed of light. I still say there were ten, all from the same litter, all with the same gappy teeth.

There were even more kids when we got to Willow Lake Park near Champion, Ohio, about noon. We were lucky to get a campsite, for here too campers were arriving from all over— from Warren, five miles away; Youngstown, fifteen; Akron, thirty-five; and even Cleveland, which was only forty-five miles to the north. Willow Lake boasts the largest concrete swimming pool in the world, and if it isn't, it looks as if it could be. It's shaped like a regular rectangular pool, yet it seems the size of a football field. I doubt it would seem crowded with three hundred people in it.

With the aid of a campground staffer we were parked and settled in by one o'clock, and it was a good thing we arrived when we did. An hour later, when Helen was in the office buying bread, the desk help were turning people away.

We had just finished setting up camp when our neighbors from the next campsite came over and introduced themselves. They were a group of four, which included a mother, a boy and girl (ten and twelve), and a man who was neither the woman's husband nor the children's father. He made that clear when he laughed and commented, "Them ain't my kids and she ain't my wife." Very funny, I thought—and said right in front of the kids.

Helen and I didn't like the sound of that. The kids took it impassively, but the woman flinched, forced a smile and said,

"Oh, pay no attention to him; he says things without thinking—happens all the time."

Yeah, and does things without thinking too, I thought, especially when he's drunk—like times when he got those wall-to-wall tattoos.

During the few days that we lived beside them, Sport (that's what she called him) acted more like an adolescent suitor than a candidate husband and stepfather for two children. Helen said, "That woman had better watch herself, she's headed for trouble." Truth was the poor woman seemed the personification of low self-esteem. She was almost tragically plain and seemed pathetically eager to please Sport, who received her ministrations as if they were birthrights. Although we would see more of that later, we caught only a glimpse that afternoon when we first arrived at Willow Lake. Then, for Helen and me, it was off to Mennonite country some twenty miles to the northwest, to the environs of the town of Burton.

At Burton we quickly found an old store that was staffed by young women wearing flowered print dresses and ribbons in their hair. They were obviously Mennonites, but of some less conservative subgroup than others we saw who dressed in blacks, purples, and dark blues. Homemade ice cream was a specialty of the house, and the trip from Willow Lake would have been worth it just for that.

We wandered out of the ice cream store and down a block to a park-like place where more conservative brethren parked their horse-and-buggy rigs. These men wore straw hats and beards, and their homespun clothes were fastened with hooks and eyes, as if they had just stepped out of the eighteenth century. Across the street was a storefront porch, where a vintage Ford was on display as the first delivery truck of some 1920s' business. Meanwhile, in the street itself were modern people with modern cars, modern clothes, and outwardly modern lifestyles. The ambience of the town was an intriguing mixture of old, less old, and very new.

Eventually we came to an emporium which had everything from shoes to lunch meat, along with a drug section with a special cabinet for veterinary medicines. I recalled the old farmer who told me that corn should be "knee high by the Fourth of July." He had also said that horse liniment was good for aches and pains. Well, my left knee had been aching of late and there was a bottle of horse liniment right there in the cabinet, although it was labeled *Veterinary Liniment*. Maybe I'd try some.

"I wouldn't put that stuff on my hide," the man who waited on us said.

"Why not?"

"Cause it'll eat your skin off."

Even so, I bought a bottle.

Then it was time to look for a restaurant, hopefully one offering Mennonite cuisine, which somebody told us was "scrumptious." But who ever heard of a Mennonite restaurant?—even the phrase seemed oxymoronic. Of course we found no such thing; however, we did find a good "English" restaurant that served excellent ham dinners and apple pie that Helen declared "out of this world."

A light drizzle was falling when we got back to Willow Lake that night, but it hardly dampened the holiday mood of the campers. Fires burned at a dozen campsites, and smoky haze lay just above the ground—especially in the low, flat, grassy area where our motor home was parked. We still had not learned that an ideal campsite should be high and dry, and ours was low and getting wetter by the hour.

Our neighbors, Sport, girlfriend, and kids, had a particularly smoky fire, and everybody laughed as the kids dodged smoke and roasted marshmallows that half the time caught fire. Sport was in a good mood and less macho than he seemed when we met him earlier in the day. "He's had the first of his beers," Helen whispered. "Let's see how he is about midnight."

In a nearby row of campsites, two boys played with a dog while several girls tossed a beach ball, which they had no doubt brought to play with in the pool. Suddenly the ball bounced away and the dog went after it, but it was far too big for "Ruff" to get his teeth around. Every time he snapped his jaws the ball would go bouncing still farther away. The girls screamed and the boys laughed and they all ran after the dog, who managed to bounce the ball into the fire of another group of campers who were roasting hotdogs.

Order was quickly restored by attending adults, and everybody laughed including Helen, me, and the dog—who kept his eyes glued on the ball, just waiting for another chance to go after it.

But the fun was not limited to our immediate area. As darkness fell and the drizzle became heavier, we donned hats and ponchos and walked along gravel roads among more distant campsites. The wet was dampening festivities to some extent, but people had come camping to sit around campfires, and light rain was not going to drive them in too quickly. At one fire a woman played an accordion; at another a man played a guitar; and from inside a motor home came the sounds of someone playing a violin—not well, but playing nonetheless.

People of all ages were in the park. There were many under-tens with their thirty-something parents, but there were plenty of seniors our age too. In addition, there were a few groups of late teenagers and twenty-somethings. These were the roisterers, and when we worked our way toward some particularly raucous music in a remote part of the campground, we found three groups of noisy young people who must have had their neighbors praying for a downpour.

Eventually we walked back to Lurch and settled into the coziness of our home-away-from-home, and by and by and all around, slowly increasing rain drove the diehards in for the night….

"They're fighting." Helen was shaking me awake at one in the morning. Sure enough, Sport and his girlfriend were arguing. We couldn't hear what was said, but the squabble waxed and waned until about two o'clock. Then a car door slammed, a motor started and Sport left. We hoped for the family's sake he was gone for good, but he was back the following afternoon when we returned from walking.

HORSE LINIMENT DOESN'T WORK

The rain had stopped by morning, but it looked as if it could start again any minute. Nevertheless, we had always made a point of loading up each morning and heading out to walk's end, even if the weather looked bad. The idea was that I would walk if conditions were anything short of prohibitive—any mile covered was one more behind us and one less ahead. So by nine o'clock I was on the road under still threatening skies, having agreed with Helen that we would meet in Greenville, Pennsylvania, about six miles short of the Ohio border.

A couple of hours later, I was on Greenville's main street looking for Helen but seeing no sign of her. An interesting antique store spilled onto the sidewalk and reminded me of a tag sale. I browsed for a few minutes (don't recall going in); then I crossed an intersection to a corner that gave a good view along the busy streets. I expected to spot Helen or the car somewhere—anywhere—but it didn't happen, and eventually I left town and continued west.

Excited about approaching the border, I almost trotted along thinking that any minute I would catch sight of the Toyota parked up ahead. It was not to be, however, and a half hour later it was clear we had finally really missed each other. She's probably messing around back in town somewhere, I thought to myself, feeling the first twinges of annoyance. No problem. We had always agreed that if we missed a rendezvous and became separated, Helen would just drive back to the campground and wait. I would walk or hitchhike or something, but eventually I would get there and we'd take it from there.

So on I went for another hour, all the while becoming hungrier by the minute and correspondingly frustrated—Helen would say ticked off—until eventually I heard a car approaching from behind and gradually slowing down. Even before I turned I was sure it was Helen, and after forty-six years of marriage, I knew we were about to have a fight.

"I've been looking for you for two hours," she growled across the road. "Where the *dickens* have you been?" This from her before I could even open my mouth!

"Well," I said, "during the last two minutes, I've been walking through the tenth of a mile you can see in your rear-view mirror. In the two minutes before that, I was in the tenth of a mile behind that tenth of a mile, and so on back through who knows how many tenths of miles to Greenville and finally to Leech's Corners where I last saw you three hours ago! Where the *dickens* have *you* been? You were supposed to be near that flea market back in town."

An oncoming driver, obviously puzzled at my gesturing toward the Toyota, slowed way down and carefully, almost diffidently, passed through between us.

"I *was* near that flea market," Helen came back, "and I waited a full hour. You weren't looking and walked right by."

"Why didn't you spot me? You were asleep or in a store somewhere—right?"

By then a car had pulled up behind her and had to wait as another car, approaching from the other direction, slowed way down before passing through. Meanwhile, we continued bickering back and forth across the lane. Finally, understandably, the driver behind Helen blew his horn. "Let 'im hold his water," I stage-whispered; then, "better pull over and let him by before he—"

It was another few seconds before she got partly off the road and the man could start around her. But he had heard my "hold his water," and as he came abreast he slowed down, smiled pleasantly, and then growled, no, snarled, "Why the hell don't you get in the damned car 'stead a walking along yakkin' and holdin' people up?"

Then he was gone!

It was the perfect squelch! The smile disarmed me; the snarl left me speechless. But I'd deserved it, and when I regained my voice, I called, "Helen, how 'bout movin' on ahead—find a place to park so we can eat lunch and finish this battle in peace."

She pulled away and was still in sight when she came to a place to pull off the road. When I got there, we wrangled some more as we got out sandwiches, but once eating, the food took hold and our rare spat tapered off.

Five minutes later I just had to say it: "Helen, you never know about an argument like this—you could be as right as me, or I could be as wrong as you." I should have kept my mouth shut, but I couldn't resist. That got her going for another minute or two, but her heart wasn't in it and before long, relieved to be together again, we drifted off the botched rendezvous and began talking about my left leg. It was normal for it to stiffen up at lunchtime, but it had hurt off and on for the past week, and this day it was aching more than usual. Oh well, not to worry, maybe the horse liniment would fix it; at least it should unstiffen the muscles. I had been looking forward to trying it anyway.

I opened the bottle (it smelled like Absorbine Jr.) and poured some into my right hand; then I sloshed it on my knee and leg, and vigorously rubbed it in. It did almost no good at all. I had hoped for something that would sting, burn, and instantly banish all aches and pains. No such luck. Even after two more douse-and-rubs, the muscles were as stiff as ever, albeit the skin was now plenty red. Helen said it was the color of a lobster with a sunburn.

I gave up and began walking, and before long the stiffness worked itself out just as it always did after a few minutes back walking, no thanks to the liniment. Nevertheless, the knee joint itself continued to ache, and I was pretty sure I would have trouble with it before the summer was over—could sense it coming.

An hour later, I spotted Helen up ahead standing under a big sign that said "OHIO *Welcomes You.*" We had forgotten we were approaching the border, maybe because of post-argument amnesia. Again however, we found arriving at a border anticlimactic—like when we arrived at the Connecticut-New York border the autumn before. We hung

Another Milestone

around only long enough for hugs, a few pictures, and for me to complain about the horse liniment: "The stuff's no good, Dearie. How's about you take it back and tell 'em your husband's still hurtin'. See if they'll refund the money. Then you can give it to me."

"Phil, the store's just gonna to say that horse liniment's for horses, not old men. Besides, if I get money back, I'll keep it."

And with that declaration and a happy smile, she got in her car and drove into Ohio.

Two miles farther on, there she was again, this time waiting at a causeway leading to a bridge over Pymatuning Creek. The problem was that the entrance to the causeway was barricaded, and there was a sign saying, BRIDGE UNDER CONSTRUCTION, DETOUR SOUTH. Our map showed that detouring would mean at least seven extra miles around a broad area of wetlands, and that got us wondering if it would be possible to walk the bridge in spite of its being under construction. There didn't appear to be anybody working up ahead, and there were no bridge sections out that we could see.

We ducked under the barricade and hurried down the causeway. Sure enough, the bridge's subsurface was continuous clear across to the other side; it was the road surface itself that was being broken up and replaced. New concrete had recently been poured, but it was dry and reinforcing mesh was in place for later pours. I could easily make my way across step by step, mesh by mesh. A little girl would be reminded of hopscotch.

The only problem would be if a cop showed up. But even if one did, he or she would have to move part of the barrier to drive down the approach, and by the time they got there, I'd be well on my way to the other side. Why waste the time?—a body could do better eating a doughnut. I told Helen that if a cop did get me, I'd pretend to be senile. To which she replied: "That shouldn't take much convincing," then sweetly, "but Honey, that wasn't a last-word quip about your missing the rendezvous."

So I would walk the bridge, and Helen would drive around the wetlands and meet me at Vernon on the other side. What could be simpler?—she would have seven miles to drive, but

I would have less than a mile to walk. We made especially sure we understood each other. After the busted Greenville meet-up, we were determined to get this one right.

And we did. Twenty minutes later we met in a school parking lot just east of town, and we rejoiced in the two and a half hours saved. Even as we stood there, however, the importance of two and a half hours seemed to fade in light of the hundreds of hours and thousands of miles that still lay ahead. Unexpectedly we became serious, almost somber for a few minutes; then we rallied and made up our minds to "snap out of it." "Come on Phil," Helen said. "We need food. Let's get back to Lurch and get something in our stomachs. A little wine and we'll be celebrating how far we've already come."

That evening we cut the Ohio, Indiana, and Illinois pages out of a road atlas and taped them together to form a big, cumbersome map of all three states. Using Magic Marker, we drew in a twenty-mile-wide corridor with northern boundary extending west from the Ohio-Pennsylvania border and passing south of Cleveland, Ohio; Fort Wayne, Indiana; and Kankakee and Kewanee, Illinois. The southern boundary passed north of Youngstown and Mansfield, Ohio; north of Indianapolis, Indiana; and north of Normal, Illinois. Finally, containing Peoria, it ended in the vicinity of Burlington, Iowa, on the Mississippi River. What the drawn-in corridor really amounted to was our decision as to the *approximate* track we would take through those three states.

Of course as small scale as the map was, it showed main roads but few of the local roads we would actually be walking. To determine these, I ran the computer mapping program, and staying within the corridor, I printed a series of page-size maps, each overlapping its predecessor and each showing an adjacent but more westward area. Trimmed and taped together, these formed an eleven by thirty-six-inch scroll similar to the one we had used in Connecticut. It showed great detail, and on it we highlighted a set of county roads and possible alternates as appropriate for the next seventy-five miles of walking. We would mark off our progress and plan rendezvous points as we progressed. Upon arriving at the end of this scroll, we would make another, and so on, until we reached the Mississippi.

Along with map making we resolved to avoid agonizing when arriving at places along the way where more than one candidate road appeared to lead west with equal efficiency or appeared equally interesting. We would simply pick a road and walk it—no further ado. But even as we resolved, we hedged and conceded that we would not require ourselves to be *invariably* locked into the corridor's limits—especially if the terrain suggested that a better east-west road might lay just to the north or south. We were trying to have our cake and eat it too.

*   *   *   *

The following morning took us around the southern end of Mosquito Lake just north of Warren. The lake's outflow is really the headwaters of Mosquito Creek, which flows sixty-one meandering miles south to the Ohio River. The terrain is flat near Warren, as it is all across northern Ohio except for some rumpling south of Cleveland. Wandering streams are slow and soupy with topsoil runoff, which is a serious concern for agriculture all across the heartland.

On the remote roads that I would be walking farther west, addressing nature's calls in privacy would be easy, but in this part of Ohio, five miles from the center of Warren, houses were everywhere and traffic was heavy. Lucky for me, I spotted a small building with public restrooms in Mosquito Creek Ravine. Thank God, just in time! It was brutally hot, and after relieving myself, I took off my shirt, soaked it in water, and went through the cool-off routine I had first used near Port Allegany, Pennsylvania—the day of the double-talking trucker. Then, soaked to the skin from hair to socks, I walked out of the hollow and onto the road again. Helen would be waiting up ahead—eight miles, ten miles—maybe more.

Ohio 82 was a busy, narrow, two-lane road with almost no shoulders and ugly ditches on both sides. Smelly, stagnate water lay in the ditches, and beyond were strips of road-front land that farmers had sold to developers who built houses on one- or two-acre plots. The houses were somewhat different in detail but still managed to look much the same overall.

Presently I spotted a man up ahead, still far away but busy doing something—wonder what? ... getting closer ... see 'im better now ... yes, he's digging, there by the road's shoulder near a driveway. But what's he digging?

When I got up to him and said hello, he paused, introduced himself as Bill, and started right in talking. "Digging a new mailbox hole," he volunteered. "Mailbox over there's not working out."

His old mailbox stood on the other side of the driveway, a bit crooked but it looked okay to me. "Why's it not working out?" I asked. "Doesn't matter—does it?—which side of the drive it's on."

"Problem isn't which side it's on. Problem is that dirt behind the post slopes toward the bottom of the ditch, and every couple months, the mailbox, mail and all, goes kerplunk right into the water."

In order to fix the problem, he was moving the mailbox across the drive to where the bank was less steep. His new hole, which was about half dug, would be deeper than the old one, and he planned to plant the post in concrete. The trouble was that even though the bank was less steep, dirt at the back of the new hole still kept breaking off and rolling down into the water even as he dug.

"Why won't the dirt keep falling away *after* you've poured your concrete? ... just the way it's doing right now?" I asked. "Maybe you oughtta just brace the old box with a two-by-four from the other side of the ditch. Be easier than movin' the whole thing over here."

The words were hardly out of my mouth before I thought, *Beam, how old are you going to be before you learn to keep your mouth shut?*

"This'll work," the man snapped, "and if it don't, I'm going to sell this damned house. Can't stand them barkin' dogs over there anyway."

I had been tactless to doubt his project out loud, but he was doubting it too. I've slogged through many a dreary task unsure of the outcome. Sometimes things work out, sometimes they don't, but usually it is best to stick with a plan and just keep working. Even so, it has never been easy for me to be gracious whenever anybody, even innocently, questions the good sense of something I'm doing—especially if I'm already questioning it myself.

Bill soon recovered from his momentary irritation; still, he seemed generally unhappy. He had moved out from Warren into what he considered the country, only to find that his new location was noisier than most places in the city. The noise background, as we stood there, was a steady din of ordinary car and truck traffic punctuated by a cacophony of popping compression brakes, throbbing car radios, and roaring motorcycles. Some of the bikers were scruffy looking creatures with offhand postures and sardonic faces. "Why the hell does society tolerate those deliberately intimidating bastards?" Bill wondered out loud. "Are we afraid of 'em?"

And all the while, four dogs kept barking from across the road. Bill said there were five all told, although I saw only four: two atop flat-roofed doghouses and two others on chains. The unhealthy-looking critters were randomly distributed around an uncut lot, which also contained various pieces of junk ranging from old stoves to dryers to the carcasses of several old cars. He said the other dog would be around there somewhere, either in a chicken-coop-like building or in the ramshackle house. As for people, he said a commune rather than a family lived there, and that it included several women, a couple of men, and two or three kids—always dirty and, as far as he could tell, rarely going to school. The dogs, he said, would bark whenever he or his wife ventured outside, and to work in the yard was impossible "because you just can't stand the racket."

I asked if the authorities couldn't do something about the dogs. "No," he said, "the warden came out here a couple of times, but as near as I can tell, he just told the people there'd been a complaint." He mimicked the dog warden with a spoken falsetto: "Won't you please try to keep your doggies quiet?" Then he went on to say how he had been to town hall with the problem, but the people there had referred him back to the dog warden.

"You see," Bill bitterly continued, "this is the era of the dog in this country. They're everywhere. And I bet you that for every ten darling puppies sold at any pet shop across the land, four are discarded by their owners and dead before they reach their second birthdays. It's a national disgrace."

I had heard enough and fled. I didn't know about his four-out-of-ten number for dogs got rid of and dead, but I had already walked past several dog pounds with their doomed inmates. It was invariably depressing.

* * * *

I caught up with Helen about a half hour after talking to "Mailbox Man." She had been to a Wal-Mart near Warren and was happy to show me her new pants and two new shirts. She had also bought a new watch. The clothes looked nice and I told her so, but I couldn't pass up the opening: "Now that you have a brand-new watch, you'll never miss another rendezvous … right?"

"Hear you m'Love, and just for that we'll go out for dinner tonight—to an expensive restaurant if we can find one. No fast food or TV dinners."

Expensive restaurants are favorite threats of Helen's.

And the morning continued.

Lunchtime found us under a shade tree on a grammar school lawn. It was pleasant there except for the noise which Helen took note of in her log: *The racket here is unbelievable. Between trucks, music from cars, and loud motorcycles there's no quiet anymore. No wonder people are forever stressed out!*

I wasn't the only one bothered by noise that day.

But apart from the noise lunch was good, and I was soon back on the road albeit under threatening skies. As the afternoon wore on, walking became a drudgery of heat, noise, traffic, and occasional showers—steamy and uncomfortable. Neither was the countryside any prettier than it had been in the morning. Although low and poorly drained, there were still more subdivisions of mundane housing, where countless acres of farmland had been turned to lawn, and weeds faced death by herbicide.

Toward five o'clock, I met Helen at an abandoned gas station in Southington, and lo and behold, after all my complaining about motorcyclists, a scruffy looking one had stopped and asked if she needed help.

"Helen," I said, "these people are causing me problems. Just when I'm satisfied that I can spot the ones that are congenital jerks, one comes along and contradicts the type. Why can't a man be left in peace once he's locked into a good, satisfying bias?"

"Don't worry," she replied. "The majority of bikers are okay, but a certain percentage do behave like vermin." I'd been joking, but she was more fed up with motorcycles than I was—especially Harleys and their noise.

"Let me tell you about the Harley Company," I said, beginning a mini-lecture. "Their notoriously undependable bike was on the ropes by the early nineteen eighties, threatened with extinction by reliable, heavy road bikes built by Honda, Yamaha, and Kawasaki. Harley was greatly helped in 1983, when the government placed tariffs on large, imported Japanese bikes. In addition, that year the protected company founded and sponsored the Harley Owner Group, which has vigorously promoted the bike and made it the centerpiece of the Harley-cult lifestyle. So Harley-Davidson survived along with many American jobs. No problem there. But the quiet, dependable, Japanese road bikes are pretty much gone, along with their similarly unobtrusive riders, and we're left with a nation-wide infestation of noisy Harleys, too many ridden by people who rejoice in 'collective individuality' and the racket they make.

"As for the noise, Harley uses an engine design that imparts a unique offbeat resonance to the exhaust, and that throaty beat has become the celebrated 'Harley sound.' Harley's promoted it right into modern Americana, and with many people it ranks up there with apple pie, motherhood, and Dodge trucks."

"Why don't they just quiet the bikes?" Helen said, "muffle 'em and reduce the noise. You've said yourself they're beautiful bikes, and the majority of riders *are* courteous and nonthreatening."

It was just then, as we stood grouching about Harleys, that a youngish man with a very loud car pulled up and asked if we needed help!

I forced a congenial smile and told him we were doing just fine. Thanks for stopping.

"Where yuh headed?"

"Just down the road a couple miles, down where route five thirty-four meets three-o-three."

"That's where interstate eighty goes through. Mind my asking why you're wearin' a pack?"

Actually I did mind; even so, I told him I was walking cross-country.

The next thing he wanted to know was my age. "Sixty-seven," I flatly told him—very flatly.

"Wow!" he exclaimed, "I don't get it. Why don't you walk in a park? They drive like hell around here."

By themselves, his comments and questions were too familiar—the kind that would put most strangers off. Long hair, white tee shirt, and designer stubble didn't help much either. Still, his smile and confident friendliness were hard to resist, and he was a far sharper character than a passing glance would hint.

It was hot and sticky, and I was anxious to get walking, but suddenly he said, "You're from Connecticut by your license plate. Visiting people out here?"

"We're walking across the United States," I replied, caving in. "We started at the Hudson River in April, and since then this is how far we've got. With luck we'll make it to Nebraska by fall."

He met these words with the usual interest. "Son of a gun, and you're sixty-seven years old! That's fantastic!" Then he asked many details about how we lived on the road, how far I walked in a day, how I took care of my feet.

By now, Helen and I were enjoying the attention and telling him everything he wanted to know, although he asked no really personal questions beyond my age. Eventually, the conversation drifted away from what we were doing as he began to talk about *his* parents. They were younger than Helen or I, but his mother had a bad heart and couldn't do much anymore. Taking care of her was exhausting his father, who was "totally unsuited for care-giving."

This scruffy man in his beat up car told us he was going to have to "make arrangements" for his parents. They were not well off, but he could help there. He modestly said that money was no problem; he could afford whatever it took. The real problem was how to pick an assisted-living community where mom and dad would be comfortable and happy.

Reluctant as I had been even to talk to the man, it was he who eventually brought the conversation to a close. "I have to get moving," he said, "need to get made up for tonight."

We talked for a few more minutes; then, after handshakes, we went our separate ways—he east toward Warren, Helen and I south toward the intersection of 534 and 303—her driving, of course, me walking, as usual. Meanwhile, the rain, which until then had been sporadic and too light to ground the bikers, finally began falling in earnest. I refused to quit, however, and managed to get in another three miles.

That night we conjectured about the odd man with the noisy car. To this day Helen laughs and says he was an undercover narc (narcotics cop) off for the holiday weekend. That would explain why this bright and articulate person looked unkempt and drove such a beat up car. Going by his "need to get made up for tonight," I said he was a character actor from some Cleveland playhouse, half made up for the coming night's performance.

We spent another hour talking about how limited people are in really knowing other people. Eventually I drifted into mild lament: "We're constantly reading and rereading others by their dress, or body language, or by what they say and how they say it. Usually however, beyond these superficial impressions, coworkers, neighbors, even family members remain psychologically apart from us. We can know other people only so well...."

"You're becoming pensive, Philip," Helen was saying. "The closest of people can share each other's thoughts only so far. Our minds aren't physically connected, not cerebrally interwoven; we share streams of awareness only by virtue of common experience and reciprocal verbal transactions, or by expressions of face or body. Even our most immediate loved ones are consigned by nature to remain apart from us in their own ultimate selves with their own unique 'withouts.'" For a moment tears came to her eyes and to mine as well. But we held each other close that night, and thanked, if not God, at least our lucky stars for all we *did* share, however briefly.

I MEET A ROUGH FRIENDLY PUP

One morning we arrived at walk's end only to find that I had left my pack at the motor home. Helen graciously solved the problem by driving thirteen miles back to get it and then *fifteen* return miles to catch up with me, since I had been walking west from my starting place. Helen would drive many miles that day. After she delivered the pack, she was off again, this time to the Wal-Mart near Warren where she had shopped a day or two before. Her new pants didn't fit and she needed to exchange them for a smaller pair. While at the Wal-Mart, she also had the car's oil changed; then it was back to meet me at Shalersville many hours later. By then the day was almost over, and she had driven ninety-six miles.

Helen's days were rarely that busy, but she would often do more than simply "escort me across the country," as she sometimes liked to put it. When possible, she would get the food shopping done, or do the wash, or hunt down some "whatever" that we suddenly thought we needed. She would attend to such things during the day while I was walking. That way we had more time to live like normal people, such as when we took what we called tourist days (sightseeing days) or when we moved Lurch farther west—if my driving Lurch and Helen following in the car could be considered normal. Normal people usually ride together in their motor homes and tow their cars.

*　　*　　*　　*

The flat countryside through which I had been walking eventually gave way to low hills near Hudson, Ohio, which I reached on a Tuesday afternoon about three o'clock. Entering town was a relieving change after miles of project housing along state 303.

Hudson was founded in 1799 by Connecticut pioneer David Hudson in what was then Connecticut's Western Reserve.

Twenty-seven years later it became the founding place of Western Reserve College, which then became Western Reserve University, which later merged with Case Institute of Technology, which finally became Case Western Reserve University in Cleveland. More later about the Western Reserve.

Hudson reminded Helen and me of an especially wealthy college town, although nowadays it is principally a bedroom community for the rich of Cleveland, Akron, and environs. Wealth seems manifest in attractive tree-lined avenues that obviously reflect the tastes of the people who live there. Houses along the main street are large and architecturally unique, although sometimes partially hidden behind well-kept hedges or walls.

In a convenience store, an old-time resident buttonholed me and told me what to him might have been the most important thing about the town. "Did you know," he asked, "that Dante Lavelli was born here?"

"No," I said in a tentative tone which quickly prompted, "Well, he was," then, "You don't even know about Lavelli, do you?"

Truth was I didn't, and all I really wanted was to walk the rest of the way from the ice cream cabinet to the cash register and pay for a Popsicle that was going soft in my hand. However, I had been stopped en route, and I could tell I was going to know who Lavelli was. "Pops" would see to that.

It took the old man two or three false starts and a few verbal back tracks, but when he finally stopped talking, I knew that Dante Lavelli had been a professional football player for the Cleveland Browns from 1946 to 1957. He was known as "Glue Fingers" for his great pass-catching prowess, and he played in four AAFC (All-America Football Conference) and six NFL (National Football League) championship games.

Now how 'bout that!

From my informant's pride, it was obvious that Lavelli was something of a hometown-boy-made-good, and in his own hometown at that—Cleveland being only twenty miles "up the road" from Hudson. He was certainly a hero to the octogenarian who was telling me the story. I should have asked the old man if he had known Dante as a boy; they would have been close to the same age if Lavelli was still living.

Ten minutes later I had finally paid the cashier and stepped out of the store to get back on the road. The chocolate coating was sliding off the Popsicle, but I caught most of it with my teeth as melting vanilla ran down my fingers. Then, two and a half miles of walking brought me to the intersection of Ohio routes 8 and 303. It was raining again, slightly, and I had a dull ache in my left knee. Helen was waiting.

We began the following day with a breakfast of French toast, which I always made outside on an electric griddle that doubled as a waffle iron. It had plates that were flat on one side and shaped for waffles on the other. Helen said she was proud of me for always getting them in right, according to whether I was making pancakes or French toast or waffles. Actually, we did most of our cooking outdoors using—besides the griddle—an electric oven, an electric fry pan, and a two-burner propane stove. That way we kept food odors out of Lurch and me out of Helen's way while she was doing the indoor part of meal getting.

After breakfast, Helen caught up on her notes while I swept out the RV, defrosted the refrigerator, and washed the car. Later, we were off to Wal-Mart for what I don't remember, but I do recall a huge parking lot, and across the street a Perkins restaurant where we split a club sandwich for lunch. It was in Perkins that we saw a memorably beautiful young Mennonite woman, paradoxically in a light pink dress! Later that afternoon we relaxed and watched TV movies, while outside the campground grew steadily quieter as the last holiday campers left for home.

*   *   *   *

On Wednesday, June 2, in spite of a late start, we covered twenty-four miles to Medina, Ohio. My route was still state 303, which passed over the Cuyahoga River only twenty-five miles south of Cleveland. Being so close to the city, it seemed odd, though gratifying, that much of the river valley had been set aside as the Cuyahoga National Recreation Area. The countryside for a number of miles both east and west was urban sprawl or just flat fields, but the recreation area was a green oasis of rolling low hills. Heavy traffic, however, made for difficult walking, but that would improve beyond Medina.

That evening, Helen worriedly referred to Willow Lake Park, our current campground, as "this place of endless rain." We planned to leave the following morning, and she wondered if the ground was getting ready to swallow our beloved Lurch—it had rained off and on the whole time we were there. I told her to stop worrying, that the thick turf on which we were parked felt reasonably firm, and Lurch was heavy and had good tires. Besides, on the day we arrived I had laid planks on the ground and gently drove up onto them; all four wheels were dry and off the grass. Even so, I now went outside and put a few remaining planks behind the rear tires in the direction of the service road, which was only thirty feet away. How could there be a problem?

The moment of truth came just after seven the next morning. I thought that if I held the rig with the brake, put it in reverse and gunned the motor slightly—not too much—then I should easily get back to the service road on the first try. Not to be. The instant I hit the gas the old bus kicked boards in every direction and sank four inches through the grass into the mud. One plank sailed out from under the right rear wheel and hit a picnic table with a crack they heard clear over in the office. A woman came out and claimed she heard a racing motor followed by a gunshot—asked if she ought to call the cops. Very funny.

A fellow from another campsite came over and began calling out advice: "Turn your wheel left! … Turn your wheel right! … Give 'er more gas! … Ah rats!" Eventually he went away and the park manager showed up with a tractor. Still, even with him pulling it took a lot of wheel spinning, yelling, hollering, and even some laughing to get Lurch back to the service road.

So much for my theory that a heavy RV should be good on mud. What we did get from the struggle was a keen awareness of how lucky we had been when we parked Lurch only six feet from the Allegheny River. Had it rained then, we might have lost the old lemon.

Twenty minutes after escaping the mud, we were on our way to another Willow Lake Park, this one near Brunswick, Ohio, fifty miles away. We didn't know if the two Willow Lakes were connected or if they had the same names by coincidence. It could have been coincidence; there were plenty of willow trees in that part of Ohio, all thriving in the often wet soil. In any case, we considered ourselves experienced now about mud and motor homes, so we vowed that in the future our most important requirement for a campsite would be a gravel parking place. At Brunswick we got exactly that. What we still didn't know was just how brutally hot a motor home can become under an all-day Midwest sun. We would learn that soon enough, and a shady campsite would soon seem almost as important as gravel.

*   *   *   *

Beyond Medina, Ohio, the land rises almost imperceptibly, a vast plain tipped upward a mere hundred feet in three miles. After that there is a descent of perhaps twice as much over five or six miles to the east branch of Black River, a sluggish mud-laden stream that slowly moves toward Lake Erie, twenty miles to the north. Another five miles of sloped pseudo plain—intuitively noticeable to a walker, invisible to a motorist—and the "big" hills are behind. There follow fifteen miles over which the steepest grades rise or fall no more than ten feet in a half mile. And all along the way the flat, flat land runs out to the horizon, field after field after field.

Many of the farm roads in the Midwest are organized into east-west by north-south grids, and in some places these grids are gapped or distorted by highlands, or river systems, or by compromises attendant to surveying straight lines onto the earth's spherical surface. In such areas, roads seldom run exactly east and west or north and south, and crossroads can be anywhere. Gravel for the most part, the roads are maintained by the successive townships or counties through which they pass, and typically they may have township, county, or state route numbers, in addition to descriptive names that tell where they go, or once went, or what local persons they honor.

Some of the roads I walked in that area were by name, length and direction as follows: Chatham Road, 1.5 miles west; Carsten Road, 0.75 miles south; Coon Club Road, 3.25 miles west; Avon Lake Road, 0.5 miles south; Old Mill Road, 7.7 miles west; Stewart Road, 8.2 miles west; Gore Orphanage Road, 1 mile south; and state route 162, three miles west.

State 162 brought us into New London, Ohio, which has a namesake—New London, Connecticut— and therein lies a story that goes clear back to 1662. That was the year King Charles II granted colonial Connecticut dominion over all lands in the west "from sea to sea." He was a giving king; later he gave the same lands to the colonies of New York and Pennsylvania! After the revolution, Connecticut refused to yield all of her land claims to the newly formed Confederation Government. After all, the federal Territory of Ohio was as yet not even organized. Instead, Connecticut retained a "Western Reserve" of about forty-five thousand square miles bounded on the north by Lake Erie, on the south by present-day Youngstown, on the west by Sandusky, and on the east by the nowadays Pennsylvania border.

In 1795, Connecticut gave eight hundred square miles of the northwestern part of the reserve to Connecticut townsmen who had suffered at the hands of the British during the Revolutionary War. The area is known to this day as the Sufferers' Lands or Fire Lands, and the townsmen did indeed suffer and burn. In the Fire Lands, within a circle of twenty miles, are four towns whose namesakes in Connecticut are New Haven (captured, 1779), Greenwich (burned, 1779), Norwalk (burned, 1779), and, of course, New London (burned, 1781). Ironically, New London was burned by Connecticut's own Benedict Arnold, who was himself from Norwich, only twelve miles to the north. Needless to say, there is no Norwich in the Fire Lands.

In 1800, Connecticut finally ceded her reserve to the by-then-organized Territory of Ohio, and in 1803 the Territory gained statehood. Today, what was once the reserve contains Sandusky, Cleveland, Akron, Warren and Youngstown, and more than one third of the population of Ohio lives there. The southwestern corner of the area is marked by a stone post, a schoolteacher told me, near the town of Willard.

*   *   *   *

It may be that my noting the flatness of the land and the names of roads walked, gives the impression that walking the Midwest was eternally boring. That however was not the case. Here and there I would come to groves of trees, usually near slow moving streams, and sometimes I would pause at such places to rest in the quiet and cool. And every so often there would be a farmhouse, and more often than not a dog, typically a mongrel, who would race down to the road and give loud notice that the farm and all about were his or her exclusive territory. Usually, having made his point, he would succumb to a dog biscuit and become my bosom pal. I always looked forward to meeting these characters, and almost always the encounters were fun.

Somewhere on the road west of New London, a startled mutt broke out of a cornfield to my left and skidded out of control down a low embankment, to land with a splash in the inevitable ditch. I couldn't tell what scared him or why he was in such a hurry, but the combination of being spooked from behind, dunking himself, and then coming face to face with a total stranger threw him to a panic. Barking wildly and with tail between legs, he raced up the road, stopping eventually about a quarter mile away. There, in front of a farmhouse, he raised his tail and took a stiff-legged stance that made it clear there would be no further retreat. He would do battle there—to the death if necessary. I continued walking and fished a Milk-Bone out of my pocket.

As I came nearer, his barking slowly changed from continuously ferocious to intermittently whiny, while his stiffly held tail moved from up behind him, to out behind him, to down behind him, and finally to between his legs. By then he was completely silent.

"Killer" stood his ground a minute longer—until I closed to maybe a hundred feet; then he broke into another wild dash that took him to the front porch of the house, where a woman stood who had come out to see what the fuss was all about.

She and I exchanged waves as Killer, wet and smelly as he must have been, backed right up between her legs and started haranguing all over again. He was still barking ten minutes later, but by that time I was a half mile away. It's amazing how far you can hear a dog on a quiet day.

Within a mile I met another dog, but there was nothing skittish about this fellow. Barely a year old and weighing at least eighty pounds, "Puppy" must never have met anybody he didn't like or anybody who didn't like him—except maybe people he accidentally knocked down. He spotted me while I was still a quarter mile away, and down the dusty road he came, tail flailing and mouth wide open in an ear-to-ear smile. I fed him three dog biscuits, one by one, and before each I made him promise to go home and not bother me anymore. No promise keeper, he pestered me till we were right in front of a farmhouse, whose manicured front yard was interspersed with a half dozen small, beautifully kept gardens. It was while I stood admiring these that he came up from behind and, rearing onto his hind legs, came down with both paws near the top of my pack.

Down I went onto hands and knees right into a mud puddle, and a split second later Puppy's tongue slurped the side of my head knocking my hat in too. I let out a loud growl just as a big woman came around the house yelling, "Bad Puppy. You come here right now. How many times do I have to tell you?" She hollered a couple more full sentences as if the dog could understand everything she said.

Puppy sat down on the far side of a flowerbed with his tongue lolling and tail wagging. But he never took his eyes off the woman.

Sending several apologies my way, she repeatedly tried to catch the dog, but he wouldn't let her get anywhere near. She would charge and he would sidestep—sometimes to the right, sometimes to the left, always behind a flowerbed.

"He just won't mind," she blurted as she lost her cool and then added, "Damn him, we've had him to obedience school twice, but it's done no good at all."

That was probably the third time people told me they'd had their dogs to obedience school.

"Obedience school's a bummer," I was dumb enough to say. "Everybody sends 'em, but from what I've seen, it's a waste of money. The dogs must think it's summer vacation."

"Let's hope not." She momentarily shifted her glare from the dog to me, and that released him. He began ripping and tearing all around the yard, back and forth and left and right—every which way; twice he jumped over flower beds. When he finally stopped running, the woman started the charge-and-dodge game all over again.

Feeling a bit responsible for all the excitement, I volunteered to help. "I'll catch him," I said, "watch this." Exuding confidence and eager to show off, I knelt, held out a Milk-Bone, and began to coax the big dog in. He was instantly suspicious, but unable to resist. Slowly, slower, slower yet, he worked his way closer, closer, as close as he thought he dared. Then, stretching his neck way out, he tried to snatch the bone from my out-stretched hand. "Gotcha," I blurted as I sprang forward and grabbed him by the collar.

Of course I couldn't hold him. He yanked me off balance and down I went again, this time with my left knee in a flowerbed and his rear end backed halfway through to the other side. I hung on long enough for the woman to get a vice grip on his collar from the far side of the flowers. He didn't even try to get away from her; she was big enough to hold him and me too if she'd wanted to.

Once Puppy was caught, the woman relaxed and was not at all upset about her crushed pansies. She and her husband expected the dog to settle down as he became older and "matured out." *Matured out at 120 pounds,* I thought to myself. That would make him only ten pounds lighter than me. The woman and I talked for a few more minutes during which she twice mentioned how much she and her husband liked the dog. Then, right out of the blue, she looked me in the eye and said, "You want him?"

Was she kidding or was she serious? Caught off guard, I hesitated, but only for a second before getting out an emphatic "No Thanks!" My next thought was, *Beam, you'd better get out of here!*

I gave the dog one last Milk-Bone; then I hurriedly got back on the road. Later, I found myself wondering if the woman was joking or if she really had tried to unload that monster pup on me. Images of him in the motor home crowding Helen whenever she moved were comical in the extreme.

"How'd you get mud all over you?" Helen asked when I got to the car a few hours later.

"Dog knocked me down. You won't believe it, but his owner gave him to us. He's ours. We've got to pick him up tonight."

"He's big enough to knock you down, and he's going to be living with us in that motor home? Phil, are you kidding?"

"Yep."

"Yep what?"

"Yep, he's coming to live with us."

I kept it up a few more minutes before telling her the truth.

In fact, the issue of adopting a dog had come up before. While still in Pennsylvania, I met a farmer who was well known in the area for being too soft to turn away a stray. People brought them in the daytime or dropped them off at night; either way, he would do his best to find them homes. When I talked to him, he had four cats and six dogs, and he tried hard to get me to take a dog. He said it would be more interesting "walkin' with a pooch," than it would be just walking alone.

I agreed that it would be enjoyable to have a four-legged companion, but Helen and I had already discussed the idea of adopting a dog. It would be a commitment, of course, for the life of the dog, and we did not know how we would be living in the years ahead. Thus we had decided not to take it on.

AN UNCOMMONLY
COURAGEOUS PERSON

I was small—a Lilliputian walking between earth and sky and dreaming, dreaming until gradually, reluctantly, I came awake: *Beam, there's something in the road up ahead … way ahead … a form … no … two forms? … different maybe? … different colors and shapes? … can't tell for sure, too distant yet…. Not cattle—too small and the shapes aren't right. Not deer either; wrong time of day. Be patient, you'll catch up soon enough.*

As I slowly drew nearer, the object (objects?) morphed into an upright figure and a squat brown blob, and the combination would move together briefly then separate, the blob remaining in the road, the person (person?) moving away, sometimes to the left, sometimes to the right, always to rejoin the thing left behind. Since they were moving west like me, it took ten full minutes of fast walking before my growing curiosity was finally satisfied.

What I had been seeing was a tall, elderly woman with a brown plastic bag, which she would move from place to place and into which she was putting collected fragments of litter. "To tidy up my little stretch of road," Dianne Fencer told me when I caught up to her. "My little stretch" amounted to a quarter mile on either side of the farmhouse where she lived.

Curious as I was about what she was doing, she was equally curious about me; in particular, she wanted to know exactly what this lone man was doing purposefully walking along an Ohio farm road with a pack on his back. Her early questions were crisply businesslike, but gradually they softened and presently she apologized, admitting they reflected an underlying concern: Farmers in the area had been suffering crop vandalism, something I had never heard of but would hear more about later on.

Once assured that I was no threat to the crops, Dianne seemed eager to talk about herself. Married in her early twenties, she had

174

lived through her young adult years on a nearby farm with her husband and his parents. Two boys had been born to the couple, and with fond pride she told how they had grown up, gone off to college, and passed out of their parents' lives in the best possible way—as self-sufficient adults. One had become an economics teacher; the other, if I remember right, an executive in the auto industry. Though far away, the boys, now men, maintained close yet nondependent relationships with their parents.

Dianne did not mention *her* parents, but her husband's father had died some years earlier, and his widow seems to have been not only Dianne's mother-in-law but her closest friend as well. She in turn had passed away three years before, and Dianne said it had taken her a long time to get over the old lady's death. But life goes on, and Dianne and her husband, now in their late sixties, had begun to expand their horizons. They had been to Europe and were planning a trip to Russia for the fall of 1997, when a routine mammogram showed lesions in her left breast.

There followed a radical mastectomy, radiation treatment, and finally chemotherapy—one side effect being hair loss which she hid with a bandana. She told me all this with no trace of self-pity, but concluded by remarking that brave as friends and acquaintances thought she was, deep down she was fighting a nagging fear.

I found it humbling to talk to this courageous woman, whose bearing as well as words bespoke *quality*. She had never worked outside of her home but had always been active in community affairs. Religious, but not overly so, she was also a reader, and when she asked if I had read Least Heat Moon's *Blue Highways*, we were able to share memories of a fascinating book. Of course, she asked about the book because I had already told her that I was, with Helen's help, walking across America.

We probably would have talked for another hour except that a neighbor came along and pulled up to say hello. Dianne introduced me to her; then, after a few minutes of three-way conversation, I left the women and got on with walking.

Later, I would marvel at how I had found myself listening to private matters in the life of a woman who would doubtless have said nothing had she thought we would ever meet again. Maybe, if circumstances are just right, a chance meeting with a stranger can give an ailing soul an opportunity to talk out their fears, and thus, for a short while, find some measure of relief. I like to think that my listening to Dianne Fencer that day was helpful to her and remains a pleasant memory.

*   *   *   *

We left Willow Lake Park on June 6. The staff had been accommodating and several campers were interesting to talk to. The only downside had been stifling heat. We still considered gravel to park on as our first priority, but a shady campsite increasingly seemed important.

Indian Trails Campground near Fitchville, Ohio, became our next home base, and while checking in we asked about the campground's name. A staff member told us it was inspired by the Native American history of the area. Nearby was a mound piled up by prehistoric Indians who, like peoples all around the world, built thousands of artificial hills over the interred remains of important people. As we walked over to see the mound up close, we were struck by how out of place it appeared. Tree covered and perhaps twenty feet high, it stood prominently above the otherwise flat landscape.

The question naturally came to mind: Could the tradition of building such monuments have independently occurred to the North American Indian without relating somehow to similar traditions in other parts of the world? Both Helen and I thought it unlikely that the notion could twice, by chance, have taken root in human imagination. Surely the Pharaoh's towering pyramid and the Chief's low hill share common origins somewhere in the distant past.

Later that evening I remarked to Helen how we moderns can hardly relate to the faiths and fears that could have motivated the building of such memorials. How could the memory of a leader, however venerated, remain so compelling as to move a people to complete monuments requiring so much labor? Helen felt that perhaps such leaders were not men at all; perhaps to their people they were gods, and that mound building to deities was ingrained in their culture.

"Well it's hard to appreciate a culture that would have its people building mounds for dead gods," I declared with self-conscious complacency. "On the other hand, I'd bet that ten percent of modern music fans would be *'far enough out'* to build a mound for John Lennon."

"Phil, I can think of plenty of things in modern cultures that are pretty far out."

"Like what?"

"Bullfights, dog fights, cock fights, cage fights."

"Yeah, but they're off-beat things; the majority of people don't watch 'em, don't condone 'em.

"But we tolerate them, and we shouldn't."

"Helen, we're getting into tricky territory. For the most part, precepts of right and wrong are fairly constant from one culture to another, but there're plenty of exceptions along the fringes. For example, in our culture it's okay for a woman to wear a bikini in public, and I think that's great; in Middle Eastern cultures it's wrong if she doesn't wear a burka. Dressing his woman in burkas must save a man plenty of money. Them Muslim guys don't have it all wrong."

"Philip, you better be kidding!"

And with that, I shut up and went to bed—my side of the bed.

*   *   *   *

A few days later I was about forty miles southwest of Cleveland and twenty miles south of Sandusky, which is near the western end of Lake Erie. Distances to the two cities were just enough that we were finally getting past their western-most patches of sprawl. The road was typical of the area—narrow with ditches on either side and the usual cornfields and beanfields beyond. But there was no car or truck traffic so walking was easy.

Suddenly voices growing louder behind me interrupted my thoughts and caused me to pause and quickly turn. It was a pair of young bicyclists, who returned my hello but pedaled by without breaking pace. "Where you headed?" I called after them.

"Spokane, Washington," the man threw back over his shoulder.

"Oregon," I yelled, loud and clear. They were already a hundred feet away and I didn't expect them to stop. But stop they did, and as they turned around, I heard the girl say, "Bet there's a story here."

I soon learned they were a pair of attorneys, recently out of law school and on their way to jobs in Spokane. Both Easterners, they had met in law school, were engaged to be married, and had just spent time with family and friends in Washington, D.C. Now it was off to new careers and a cross-country adventure besides.

"When do you have to be in Spokane?" I asked.

"September," the young man said. "We're in good time though, we're averaging sixty miles a day."

"You're way ahead of schedule, aren't you? It's only early June, so you've got almost three months."

Momentary silence. Then from him: "You know, we've always thought of it as three thousand miles across the country—"

"Honey," his partner broke in, "you keep thinking it's three thousand miles. It wasn't that far when we left D.C., and we're a third of the way out there now. Can't be even two thousand from here to Spokane. That's what I've been trying to tell you."

She was smiling, but the complaint she'd evidently been harboring for the last few days was definitely showing itself. There was a long pause. Somewhere a tractor started, a dog barked; there was a faraway thud toward the south—like blasting or a sonic boom. We all looked that way.

Honey himself finally broke the silence. "I guess we've been pushing it some, but—"

"You've been."

"I guess I've been pushing it," he continued, "but we gotta keep ahead of schedule. Don't wanna use up our time loafing along and then be rushed at the end."

"We've got loads of time," she quickly countered, but with a smile. She wanted no quarrel, but she was clearly tired of rush, rush, rush.

We began guesstimating how far it really was from where we were to Spokane, and what that meant in term of how many days they would have to ride, and how many miles each day. We came up with roughly eighteen hundred miles, and he conceded they could certainly get in twenty riding days each month during July, August, and what was left of June.

"That amounts to only sixty riding days in the next three months," the girl quickly said. "Let's see ... sixty into eighteen hundred equals thirty—that's only thirty miles per day on days when we actually ride. We can take it easy the other twenty or so days ... just tour. Honey, we really do need to stop early tonight!"

"Okay, okay," he said, in good humored concession. "We'll slow down, Mary Jane. Promise."

Mary Jane. Now there, I thought, is a name you seldom hear nowadays. And yes, from here on they'll probably do a lot more sightseeing. Still, I could appreciate the young man's eagerness to charge ahead, and even his failing to take account of where they were or how much of the ride still lay ahead. Helen and I had made our own planning mistakes, the latest the month before when we moved Lurch too far into Ohio.

Once the pair got past how they would handle the rest of their ride, they wanted to hear all about Helen's and my walk. They couldn't believe we had thought of it one day and begun walking the next.

I gave them the usual briefing; then, just as we were getting ready to part, the girl exclaimed, "Oh dear, we almost forgot to have him sign." She meant autograph her saddlebag, on which were already a half dozen signatures. She was getting people to sign and date it, and write the state they were in—just so their "case could be proven," if somebody were to doubt they actually bicycled across the country.

Did I mention they were lawyers?

I watched the young people recede into the distance; then it was back to walking. For a while I formalized my stride into something like a march. I would do that now and then just for a change. In general, it was less tiring to walk quickly and purposefully than it was to saunter along at that dawdling speed people sometimes use when shopping. I once met a man who called that *mall pace.* "It's the walk people use," he said, "when they're moseying around a shopping mall with a not quite maxed-out credit card. They're looking for something—they don't know what—but something which, once seen, will surely be something they can't live without. What they do when they spot that something is called *impulse buying.*"

"Yeah," I said, "I've heard it called *recreational shopping.*"

"*Patriotic purchasing*, too," he allowed for a finish....

An hour later I came to a stretch of road that had been trashed with graffiti. I had seen marked-up pavement in other places, but this was the worst yet. Bitter, vicious pictures and words, hateful of girls in particular but gays as well. References to schools, but mostly to individuals, with words like *kill, fuck* and *beat,* and obscene pictures strangely out of place in a countryside of prosperous farms and open skies. What convolved hatreds dwell in the minds of such "artists" one can hardly imagine. Maybe it takes a warped mind or a trained professional to make sense of such poison.

I walked slower after that—a bit subdued. The young lawyers had been a pleasant high, only to be followed by the muck on the pavement. The graffiti would wear off my mood in hours, but on that lightly traveled farm road it would surely be readable for years.

BUYING LEVELING JACKS

From Indian Trails Campground we moved Lurch some forty-five miles to Beech Tree Park, which is near Van Buren, Ohio. We slept late the morning of the move; nevertheless, things went so smoothly that we had arrived at the park and were set up by noon.

After lunch, Helen dropped me off for a half day's walk while she went grocery shopping; then we met toward four o'clock at a crossroads just north of the campground. We had planned to quit there, but it seemed so early that I continued on, getting in another hour's walking and finishing with a respectable twelve-mile day. Not bad, considering we had moved that morning.

Helen spent part of the next day knitting an afghan. She had already finished one and this was her second; there would be three more completed over the remainder of 1999, and five more the following year before we reached the Pacific. As for walk progress, we were on the road at five-thirty that morning, and things went so well that I finished up near Rice, Ohio, thirty-one miles farther on. That was about five o'clock. Obviously, this was one of our long-days, which, of course, was not only long in miles but long in hours as well. Typically, we would get in a long day when I was well rested after a few days off or when the morning drive from camper to starting place was short, as it had been that day.

So that was it for June 10, 1999 for the elderly adventurers, Phil and Helen Beam, who were increasingly entering a detached world of their own. Not that they were uninterested in the doings of family back home or for current events of the evening news, but all those things seemed to have less and less to do with them. Comfortable in their motor home at night, and with the world shut out, they found the little chores of evening especially pleasant to do. There were dishes to wash, the bed to open, lunches to pack, maps to make—small things, but comforting in their routineness after long days in the wide open.

Sometimes while walking along, I would imagine myself floating above my real self, and picturing in that person far below a "spot behind the eyes," where all the world was beheld and thought about, where the scenes and thoughts of life pass by. And the road and fields and fence and sky would seem a continuum of natural things including me, not as the consequence of some special creation, but lucky first cousin to all God's creatures and legitimate heir to a billion years of evolution.

At other times I could feel isolated and insignificant, a feeling brought on, no doubt, by the vastness of the countryside itself. Often there would be no trees nearby, although in the far distance would usually be a house or barn or silo. And always under that endless sky were the fields, and cutting through them the road, generally empty, endless, and narrow for mile after mile.

One day I was treated to a special sight. It happened when I was passing a wide cornfield in which the tassels on the cornstalks were uniformly bowed by a mild northeasterly breeze. Nothing unusual about that, but gradually I became aware of a strange whooshing noise—like gentle airs troubling leafy trees. I paused, and looking out across the field, I noticed a strange irregular area in which the tops of the corn were tossing about in agitated and random ways.

The noise and restless corn defined the forward motion of a near-ground patch of swirls and eddies that was moving as a whole with the breeze. As I continued along, the patch slowly approached the road and presently passed over me with a pleasant cooling effect. Then, all too soon, it was disappearing, fading out over a cornfield to the south but leaving me pleased to have experienced something new—at least to me. I suspected that it was a common enough phenomenon and that meteorologists would have a name for it. It reminded me of sea-surface ruffles caused by sudden, local breezes—*cat's-paws* in meteorological terms.

*   *   *   *

A few days later we broke off walking and moved from Beech Tree clear back to Willow Lake Park near Brunswick. We hated making a move that would take us ninety-five miles east rather than still farther west, but we had an appointment with an RV service center near Cleveland, ten miles north of Brunswick. They were to install leveling jacks on the motor home, which also needed an oil change and grease job. In any case, Helen and I were ready for a break; we had covered ninety-five miles in four consecutive days, and that was one too many days in a row. It would be relaxing, we told each other, to do some touring around Cleveland, and getting jacks installed shouldn't be a hassle. On that point we were wrong.…

"There are three grade levels of jacks, sir: good, better, and best. I recommend the best." This from the service manager at Hassle Free Camping Services, Inc.—obviously not the company's real name.

"That's what I want to talk about. It looks as if the only difference between the three systems is how fancy they are. The basic levelers come with a joystick mounted on the floor between the driver's seat and the driver's door. To level the coach, you stand outside with the door open and move the stick as indicated by guide lights. Looks good to me. Have I got that right?"

"Yes, but our next grade up is better. It lets you level up with something like a television remote from anywhere inside the coach. You don't have to stand outside in the rain and you don't have to worry about a joystick."

"OK. But the remote has electronics that are not in the joystick version. I like things simple."

Came his reply: "The remote's electronics won't let you down, but if that's your worry, then you'd do best with our top-of-the-line product. With that unit, all you do is press a button on the dashboard and it does the entire leveling job by itself—completely automatic. Perfect reliability too. Write you up for top of the line?"

He talked breezily, as if it were obvious I was a man who caught on quickly and was accustomed to the best—of course. Maybe twenty-eight years old, this guy.

"Hold on," I said. "Your top grade has even more electronics than your middle grade, and all the electronics do is ostensibly make leveling easier. But here's the thing: Unless you're parking on solid ground, you have to put wooden slabs under the jack's feet; otherwise the weight of the coach forces them into the ground when you go to level up. With the basic system, you stand *outside* and carefully watch as you lower the jacks till they're half way down; then you position your slabs and finish leveling with the joystick. Behold, you're done! In either up-scale system you're *inside* when you begin lowering the jacks; however, you can't see what you're doing so you have to *guess* when you've got 'em half way down. Then you go outside to position your slabs, but invariably Murphy's Law will have one or two jacks so far down the slabs won't fit under. So you go back inside and guess again. You could be in and out of the coach three or four times before you got the slabs right and could finish the job. Am I missing something?"

I was doing my best to see why anybody would pay six hundred dollars extra for the "better" system let alone twelve hundred extra for the "best." Nevertheless, I would get no help from this fellow. He didn't even try to answer my question. His non sequitur of an answer (the essential hogwash) went something like this: We address technical requirements of the RV and the needs of the owner in combination; in other words, our policy is to integrate to a best fit and recommend accordingly. I have to say that experienced RVers almost always purchase in accordance with their own matured-out perceptions of what's appropriate in their particular situation. We've had nothing but good feedback on our top-of-the-line system. That's what I'd recommend.

Finally I asked what system he would install if it were his motor home. He said he didn't have a motor home, but on mine he would definitely install one of the higher grades—it would put more value "in your rig for when you trade up from entry-level."

I walked out of the service department and into the sales room, where Helen was looking for who-knows-what. When I cooled off some, I went back in. There was a mechanic doing paperwork at a stand-up desk, and since the service manager was busy with another customer (potential fish?), I sidled up to the mechanic and asked which jacks he would install on his motor home. Back came his unhesitating answer: "The joystick rig." Then, after a furtive glance in the direction of the manager, he said the joystick was the cheapest, simplest, most reliable, and the easiest to use of the three systems. Then he added, "I guess I just cost the company some bucks."

I went and told the manager that I wanted the joystick system, and madder now than ever, I also told him that if his was a job that required straight answers, he wouldn't last a day. At that point I hardly cared if I got the jacks or not. Of course the insult rolled off the man as if he hadn't heard it; he only seemed pleased to have made the sale.

The mechanic I had just talked to ended up doing the installation, and afterward he took me out to the garage for an inspection of the job along with a demonstration of how the jacks worked. However sleazy his boss, the mechanic was a gentleman and a real professional. His work was well done—hydraulic lines well routed and wiring runs neatly secured. The system would work flawlessly for years. Later however, in a cynical moment, I told Helen I doubted he would be working for Hassle Free much longer. No way would that con-artist manager tolerate his combination of honesty and skill.

With the new jacks installed, we only needed the RV's oil changed; then we would be ready to return to Beech Tree Park and get on with the walk. The following morning we found a garage that would do the oil change, and while waiting, we "toured a mall" as Helen is fond of putting it. Actually, it was a good chance to get rid of one of the three pairs of walking shoes I had bought in Binghamton, New York, when we visited the Herrmanns. It was the size-ten pair, which turned out to be too big so I hadn't used them. I considered myself fortunate when an accommodating store manager let me trade them in on a new pair of street shoes.

Lurch was not ready by the time we finished malling and returned to the garage, so we resigned ourselves to sitting in the car for the rest of the wait. Now, it happened that between us and an adjacent building there was a small tree in which a pair of doves were building a nest. Moreover, each time they approached or left the site, they would fly right over us, as close as five or ten feet.

The female definitely had the easier job. Once in a while she would fly out and get a twig or a blade of grass, but usually she just worked into the developing nest whatever bit or piece of building material her mate brought in. She was actually doing the construction; still, she had plenty of time off. She would just sit there and rest while he was off scrounging for whatever. Once he brought the stump of an old cigar. Maybe he planned on a smoke if she ever gave him a break.

After watching for a few minutes, I turned to Helen and said, "I didn't know that even the birds were into role reversal. This poor guy's in big trouble; he's more gopher than bird."

She didn't respond at first; she'd got into a book and didn't want to be bothered. Eventually though, she just had to say something: "The trouble with you is that whenever you see things the way they oughtta be, you think it's a violation of male birthrights, yours and the bird's—especially yours."

Ah, now I was getting somewhere. I was starting to tell her to enter that in her "Trouble with Phil File," when Lady Dove flew out and with a solid thwack splattered the windshield right in front of her face!

I was delighted, she was indignant. She claimed she and the bird had been in symbiotic communication, that they had planned the attack together, and that the bomb was actually intended for me. "It was a fluke," she declared. "I've been hit by friendly fire." Then she went back to her book, and though tempted to pester her further, I opted for caution and shortly dozed off.

An hour later the oil change was finished, and our reasons for diverting from the walk and coming east to Brunswick were behind us. There would be no more delays. After a quick lunch at a nearby McDonald's, we headed back to Beech Tree Park, eager to get back to walking.

*　　*　　*　　*

That evening we battled campground showers. Each stall had a special control box into which you put a quarter for a few minutes of water. Of course, the first time Helen tried it, the box took her quarter but gave no water. She had to get out of the shower, get dressed, walk back to the RV, get more quarters, and try again in a different stall. The second shower worked okay, except she had hardly begun before she was feeling uncertain about how much time she had left. So it was hurry, hurry, hurry and twice feed the machine wet coins. Very annoying.

Being forewarned, I did better, although the first shower I tried wouldn't even take my money. "If we could go to the moon in nineteen sixty-nine," I grouched, "how come we can't have decent shower controls in the year of our Lord, nineteen ninety-nine?" Undoubtedly we were not the only people grumbling about the showers.

The following morning we were back on the road, having resolved never again to break from the walk and drive east for RV repairs or car repairs or anything else. Our next trip east would take us home to Connecticut.

So we settled into days of walking that were a steady succession of crossroads, fields, farmhouses, out-buildings, and flat flat landscapes as the miles and tens of miles went by. My left knee would occasionally kick up. It carried me well enough as long as it was not twisted, but let it be twisted ever so slightly and it would hurt so bad I would grunt and catch my breath. We worried more and more that it might eventually slow us down.

In addition, it was blazing hot.

I had got into the habit of wetting myself down whenever I met Helen in the afternoons. We carried plenty of extra water for just that purpose, and though I would be briefly sloppy afterward, it helped to avoid dehydration. Of course I didn't always have to wet *myself* down; occasionally nature would take care of that with a quick, cool shower. Toward early afternoon, little storms would congeal from the haze, slowly mature, and then disappear toward late evening. Sometimes I would see a half dozen at once, with their rounded bottoms and towering heights. Darker ones might have rain tendrils drifting down toward the fields below.

Once I idly estimated the size of the skyscape in which I could see storms, or at least thickenings in the atmosphere. Since it was a hazy day, I took the limiting distance for seeing a storm or thickening as ten miles—probably conservative. Approximating the area of a circle as three times the radius times the radius (forget about pi for rough calculations), I computed three hundred square miles for the circular area (me at the center), in which such storms should be visible. Pretty impressive, I thought to myself; no wonder I see so many. Obviously, most of the storms were well beyond the terrestrial horizon, which in that endless flat farmland was usually about three miles away.

Although I never minded rain—often looked forward to it— lightning was a different story. Along those wide open roads you stick up like a lightning rod, and if I worried a little about being hit, Helen worried a lot more. From where she was waiting far ahead, she would see flashes in my direction, and taking no chances, she would hurry back to pick me up, only, in many cases, to see the storm dissipate or veer away.

At other times she would be unaware of lightening near me and consequently would *not* come back. More than once I took cover near the mouths of under-road culverts or stooped low along muddy creeks, below the banks when possible. A few times I even sat under trees in small patches of woods. True or not, I assumed that lightning was less likely to strike a tree and flash down through me, than it was to hit me directly if I were standing in the open.

Late afternoons when lightning forced us into the car were always uncomfortable times. Helen would be tired but patient, and I would be some combination of tired, sweaty, and maybe a trifle glum. We would sit and swelter and yearn to quit for the day; nevertheless, we would normally wait out the lightning and I would return to walking, rain or not. Getting out of the car would invariably be a stiff struggle, and more often than not my knee would be hurting.

*   *   *   *

Helen's notes record a day when several people saw her sitting in the car and stopped to offer help. There was a farmer and a UPS driver, and later a mail-lady and a road-crew foreman. However, her most interesting "encounter" was with a young woman officer of a local police department. She had stopped ostensibly to ask if Helen was okay, but no doubt she was doing another duty as well, namely, finding out what that out-of-state car was doing parked near a bank in a western Ohio town. And was that woman in the driver's seat asleep?—or just sitting there with her eyes closed and up to no good. What the cop didn't know was that the woman had just finished her book and was indeed wide awake. Moreover, she was slightly bored and would be happy to talk to somebody—anybody.

At first the young cop was simply rude—much too crisply professional—but surprisingly, her manner gradually changed to almost diffident curiosity. And Helen, barely forgiving the rudeness, indulged her skill in capturing listeners as she told her about the walk—all about it—and the longer she kept the poor woman buttonholed, the more she devilishly enjoyed it. After two attempts to politely break away the cop eventually escaped, but the encounter remained for Helen an ironic memory.

"You were cruel," I told her that night, with a laugh.

"She'll be all right, but she's shy by nature, and she's overcompensating to play the tough cop. Hopefully she learned something." Helen is a forgiving type, but she was still irked by the woman's manner.

Not all of Helen's note taking had to do with the people she met. Referring to western Ohio, she wrote how well kept the houses appeared, being brick faced in many cases and built in ranch or French styles. Often in their front lawns would be a man-made pond, sometimes with a dock or diving platform and maybe a nearby gazebo.

A road-crew worker told me that the ponds sometimes do more than simply serve as decorative landscape features. Surface water that could lie stagnant around buildings, along with surplus water from the irrigation of fields, is often fed into them. There, fountains provide both pleasing esthetics as well as aeration. In this way the ponds become part of the area's water management regime and thus aid in draining the land, which is mostly served by slow moving streams and rivers en route to Lake Erie.

The Blanchard River in particular attracted Helen's attention, and she took a picture of it where it passes under the road near Glandorf. Dense trees line both banks of this muddy waterway, which is about forty feet wide. The water was hardly moving, yet its burden of soil particles was so fine that there was little sign of it settling out. Clearly the suspended material would eventually end up at the mouth of the Maumee River where it empties into Lake Erie northeast at Toledo. Of course farmers are well aware of this topsoil run-off problem; they worry about it and practice farming techniques intended to minimize it.

At least some do.

ABOUT SPELLING POTATO

It was mid June in western Ohio, and I was walking, walking, walking. A pair of ducks suddenly flew up from a roadside ditch, and though I didn't quite jump, I was, as usual, briefly startled. There were lots of ducks, and many patient hens had eight or ten chicks following along behind them. Other birds were also having their young. They appeared less often, but now and then one would fly very close beside or above me, invariably causing me to duck. I assumed they had nests with little ones in the weeds along the road or in the occasional patch of trees, and several times I searched for them by carefully parting stalks or pulling down low branches. Twice I found nests with chicks, but both times I was driven away by swooping, furious adults.

The killdeer in particular was fascinating. He is about nine inches head to tail, has a long beak, four- to five-inch legs, and yellow and brown plumage. I would be walking along, seemingly alone, when suddenly, in the air all around me, there would be a dozen or more of them wheeling and turning and screeching their high pitched calls.

Often the swirling birds would move past me and begin alighting and departing from the road twenty or thirty yards ahead. Several at a time would land and race along, their tiny legs a blur, their incessant calls like haunting pings from tiny sonars. None ever stayed for long. Once on the ground they would perform their busy act for a dozen or so feet and then take off again, presently to be replaced by others. In relays, it seemed, they would accept responsibility for leading me, an intruder, still farther from their threatened nests. Then, just as suddenly as they'd come, they would all fly away, yielding the road to the quiet and the heat.

One especially hot day lightning became a problem so soon after lunch that we broke off walking and drove west to the vicinity of Van Wert, Ohio. Our goal was to check out an RV park called Blue Water Campground.

As we entered Blue Water's approach road, we were taken aback at the sight of a World War II cannon. Yes, a cannon! Moreover, sometime, somewhere, the relic had been struck by a shell that tore a hole in the shield that was supposed to protect the gun crew.

"Do you think?" Helen wondered, "that that gun was damaged during the war, or was it used later for artillery practice at some stateside army base? When you were in the army, you used to talk about seeing old cars that had been used for artillery practice."

"Doubt if it was artillery practice. When I was in the army, old cars used that way were hit so many times you could hardly tell they'd ever been cars. That single hit on the crew shield suggests battle damage, but who knows?"

We inquired, but office staff knew nothing about the gun; it had been there, they thought, when the present owners bought the business. They weren't curious, but then our questions were doubtless routine to them. Probably everybody who came there asked about the gun.

Once past the defenses, everything at Blue Water seemed peaceful by contrast. Granted there was no blue water, but there was Middle Creek, a light brown stream that meandered through an attractive stand of trees where many of the campsites were. We had reconnoitered the place for only ten or fifteen minutes before we decided to move there. Then it was back to Beech Tree Park for the night.

After breakfast the next morning, I made a new scroll map to cover the next seventy miles. We had "walked off" the western edge of the old map, and the new one was especially important because we were in the process of changing our intended route. Until four days before, we had been thoughtlessly heading directly towards Fort Wayne, Indiana; then we had wakened up and begun modifying the route in order to pass as far as practical below the busy city. In the preceding two days we had managed to divert six or eight miles south in the course of thirty-five miles west. Now we wanted another four miles, and the new map showed we could get it by using any of a dozen north-south farm roads that lay just ahead.

With map-making completed by eight o'clock, we broke camp and headed for Blue Water, where we were assigned a campsite in the woods. It met both of our current requirements, namely, shade and gravel to park on.

All in all, things went so smoothly that morning that we had Lurch set up by twelve o'clock, and Helen, determined "not to see the afternoon wasted," managed to pester me back to the road by one. By four o'clock, after I had walked four miles south and six miles west, we were a mere day's walk from the Indiana border and already in good position with respect to Fort Wayne. Continuing due west, we would pass a dozen miles below the city—far enough, we were confident, to avoid most of the sprawl.

We spent our first evening at Blue Water exploring the campground. The young couple who were our next-door neighbors had a boy and two little girls, and we first met the family down by the creek fishing. They were not catching much, nor did they have to in order to remain in a perpetual state of excitement over, as far as we could see, nothing at all. The little boy would let out a high-pitched, nasal screech whenever his line so much as twitched, whereupon his mother would jump forward and let out a little screech of her own. It was not hard to hear where his voice came from. We talked to the family for five or ten minutes and then walked on, meeting and talking to a few other people who were also enjoying the evening.

Eventually, as dusk fell and the mosquitoes came out, the fishing family packed up, and almost everyone else disappeared, including Helen. She's a culinary delicacy to the insect world, judging by the slapping and fussing that goes on whenever they begin biting her. I held out a while longer looking for somebody else to talk to, but there was nobody around so I too eventually headed home.

We talked with our young neighbors several times after the first evening, and camping beside them was a pleasure. Helen got along well with mother and daughters while I found her husband knowledgeable and engaging. The boy, who had been so excited the first night, proved to be a quiet little guy when he wasn't fishing. We would laugh to watch him copy every gesture and movement of his father, who was forever showing him how to do this or how to do that. In fact, he stayed so close to dad that Helen and I began referring to him as "Shadow."

*　　*　　*　　*

Our only worry those days was my left knee, and it was threatening to become a serious problem. I had never had many aches and pains—other than occasional minor stiffness from exercise—but this knee pain was different. Helen suggested I use a muscle rub. However, it struck me that I more likely had a joint problem than a muscle problem, and consequently Helen's off-the-shelf remedy did not seem worth trying. Besides, I had already tried horse liniment to no avail.

In any case, the knee was hurting less than usual the next morning as I was walked due west along CR 214, a.k.a. Elm Sugar Road, and every hour brought us closer to the Indiana border. Indiana, I thought, will be the fifth state we pass through, and as the crow flies, we'll be 650 miles from home. It's starting to look as if this adventure might indeed take us to the Pacific.

Engrossed in such thinking, I was surprised when noisy activity erupted just ahead and down off the road. I had startled a mother duck and chicks as they were swimming in the usual roadside ditch, and now, panic stricken, she was shooing them into a culvert out of sight. Moments later, upon coming abreast of the place, I was amazed, as with a flopping waddle mother duck struggled up the bank directly toward me. It was as if both her wings were broken! She flopped by only feet away, and then continued her crippled-bird act along the road beside the ditch for a couple hundred feet. Finally, tumbling down into the water, she struggled along for another twenty feet before abandoning the sham as quickly as she'd begun it. I could see her swimming about, agitated but obviously unhurt.

Quickly crossing the road, I crouched down to see if she would return to her chicks. Sure enough, in just a few minutes, fast as a bullet, she came flying back along the ditch; then, suddenly seeing me, she swerved out across a bean field and began circling.

I hurried away feeling I had disturbed her enough, but when I was some distance off, she made a beautiful sweeping turn and glided back to the culvert where she had hidden her chicks. Presumably she was convinced that her ruse had saved the day.

I was glad to have seen something I had never seen before: a mother animal protecting her young. Of course we have all seen nature programs on TV, and I might have seen something similar to this. But this was the real thing—live and unedited—and I knew it was unlikely I would ever see anything like it again.

A half hour later I spotted the Toyota up ahead, and that blob in the road by the driver's door was, sure enough, a dog. Does he have Helen trapped in the car? I wondered. Coming closer, I soon realized that he was just keeping her company. Helen had got out of the car to take pictures of an old, one-room schoolhouse, and Rover had been sleeping in the garden of a nearby house. Grumbling softly and limping with age, he had wandered over to check her out. A dog biscuit had quickly made him her bosom pal—so much so that she got back in the car to escape his wet tongue and bad breath.

Helen and Friend for Life

The schoolhouse was an interesting example of western Ohio's public school buildings in the latter part of the nineteenth century. Built in 1891, it was a rectangular brick structure with granite quoin corners, forty-foot side walls, and thirty-foot end walls, the latter gabled to support sloped roof-halves.

The building's designers were probably under direction to make sure it conveyed an aura of no-nonsense authority. Three imposing inlaid panels dominated the front elevation, each recessed from the main wall by stepped-back courses of brick. The central feature was a double brick arch straddling a four-foot panel of wooden siding, beneath which was the front door. The door happened to be open while we were there, and for all the world, the overhead panel looked just like the raised front of a box trap. You got the feeling that if you went through that door, the panel would drop and you would never get out. It probably looked like that to school kids too, a century ago. Doubtless, many a kid got his or her jarring introduction to the "system" right there, as well as a basic grounding (grinding?) in the three R's.

"I bet those kids learned how to spell potato," Helen said.

"What are you talking about?" I asked, but before she could answer I caught on and added, "and quail too, spelled q-u-a-i-l, not Q-u-a-y-l-e, which is how the Vice President spells his name."

"Wasn't he from around here?"

"Huntington. It's about forty miles past the Indiana border. We'll reach the border by the end of the day."

"I bet Dan knows how to spell potato now," she said. Then, "I bet you don't."

She was making fun of my "challenged" spelling skills, but I'd be darned if I'd let her get the better of me so early in the day. So I spelled potato for her just the way the Vice President did: P-o-t-a-t-o-e. When she finished laughing, she got out of the car and we fed the dog two more biscuits while we fed ourselves slices of coffee cake. We took pictures too; in particular, I got a good one of Helen and Rover with the schoolhouse as background.

But it was time to move on, because the old building was starting to remind me of grade-school days sixty years before. Kindly Miss Yerkes would be in there, and so would Miss Kerns and Miss Chrysler—decent, exemplary people and uncommonly conscientious teachers. May you rest in peace gracious mentors, and thanks for the memories....

I began walking again but followed now by Rover, who had decided to tag along and see the world. Helen coaxed him back and kept him there at the expense of a few Milk-Bones, by which time I was a hundred yards down the road. Then she got in the car and slowly pulled away, leaving him sitting there with orders to stay put. Presently he got up and shook himself (I saw the dust fly), and wandered back toward his garden.

About four-thirty that afternoon we reached a crossroads where a tall sign labeled the east-west road FLATROCK and the north-south road the OHIO-INDIANA STATE LINE. Hooray for us! We hung around for five or ten minutes hoping somebody would come along in a car. If they would stop, we would get them to take our picture underneath the sign.

Although no cars came, we soon noticed two men standing near a barn a couple hundred yards away, and sure enough, they were aware of us. Every so often one or both, clearly curious,

At the Ohio-Indiana Border

would look our way; then they would go back to talking business, one fellow with much arm waving.

Helen said, "One of them'll come over here before long, mark my words, and I bet we get our picture." Five minutes passed, ten; then, even as they continued talking, one fellow began drifting away from the other and toward a nearby lawn tractor. "Here he comes! Here he comes!" Helen laughingly repeated, as he rode the tractor down the driveway and onto a grass apron along the road. Moments later he pulled up beside us, broad smile and all.

"You knew I'd come down here, dint-cha?"

Clearly, there would be no ice to break with this fellow.

"Yep, what took you so long?" Helen answered with a grin. Then we told him what we were doing and asked if he would take our picture.

As we were posing, I noticed beyond him a vast cornfield of maybe a hundred acres. The crop was only a couple of feet high, which I thought odd since in another nearby field the corn was at least twice as high and beginning to tassel. I asked the farmer why the difference, and he told us something about planting that Helen and I should already have known.

"All fields of any crop," the man began, "are not usually planted in the same day or sometimes even in the same week. So the plants in one field are often taller than those in another. Planting takes time, you see, and the important thing is to get your seeds in the ground *after* it's too early and *before* it's too late." He bore right down on *before* and *after* with a nod that suggested a farmer had better get it right or he'd be out of business in no time. He continued: "The same is true of harvest time; obviously that's not a day, it can be a week or two."

Obvious?—I asked myself. *Yes, of course; certainly it would be to him.* A bit sheepishly I recited the saying, "Learn something new every day."

He sensed my chagrin, however, and quickly replied, "Hell, I talk easy about it, but I'd never have thought of it if farmin' wasn't my business."

He was a let-'em-down-easy kind of guy.

After a few more pleasantries, our farmer friend mounted his lawn tractor and started back toward the barn. We got in a few more miles that day, but crossing the border had been another of those mild letdowns that were becoming routine as we passed from one state to another. Eventually, Helen would refer to them as *"post-parturient downers."* I would tell her she was *stretching* usage.

Anyway, the big thing that sunny afternoon was that we were finally in Indiana. Enough for the day, time to quit. Besides, my knee was hurting more than usual.

*　*　*　*

On occasional afternoons I would take a nap along the road if I was especially sleepy and could find a comfortable place to lay down. Such naps never lasted long—maybe twenty minutes—but drifting off was always bliss, and I would usually awake refreshed. I would tell myself that I would walk faster and farther having rested a few minutes, and true or not, that was what I would tell Helen whenever I was late for a rendezvous and she had come back to look for me.

I awoke slowly about two one afternoon, having dozed beside a fenced-in field that was really a small pasture. Surprise, surprise!

Thirteen eyes peered at me from a distance of maybe twenty feet. Their owners, thirteen white geese, stood quietly and motionlessly, and as I slowly turned to see them better, I was seized by stiffness that always came whenever I laid down along the road.

One goose, the largest, seemed to be the leader. Maybe it was on some soundless cue from him or her that all thirteen birds, in perfect unison, suddenly waddled a turnabout and surveyed me anew with thirteen other eyes, still in silence and never moving.

Whimsically I asked if they were studying me with one set of eyes while watching a nearby cow with the other set, but they gave me no answer to that. "I don't see how you can look in two directions at once," I declared, and then I wanted to know if they were ignoring images from half their eyes while concentrating on images from the other half. "Do you do that deliberately or is it all automatic?" I asked. Still they made no reply, but watched with rapt fascination this white-haired apparition lying there on the ground.

Feigning annoyance at their woodenness, I told them to watch out or a fox would "git 'em" from behind. That too left them unfazed, but presently the cow ambled over and the spell was broken. The geese, with soft murmurings, slowly waddled away.

Bossy stopped where the geese had been, and stared with an expression that has always been mildly disquieting. It's a mixture of curiosity, innocence, sweetness, a little fear, and finally trust— trust inevitably and necessarily betrayed, yet for a little while, hopefully, not misplaced in the humans who hold her fate. Ideally they'll provide green pastures and a stress-free life, right down to the moment she departs this world and leaves her remains for our sustenance. Perhaps we humans should divide our mealtime thanks and direct some portion to our fellow animals who with their very flesh sustain our lives.

I stood up then, and a long, long drink left my canteen nearly dry. Not to worry. Helen would be five or six miles ahead, and there I would drink my fill—and get ready for the next walk segment.

Late that afternoon I noticed that the second toenail on my left foot was starting to ache, and that a new blister was coming up on my right heel. I knew the toenail was doomed; it would be pinkish-purple by bedtime, and over the next few weeks it would turn steadily blacker before eventually coming off. But after that a new one would gradually grow in. No problem. The blister was no worry either. Once you've had a few, neither the idea of blisters nor blisters themselves are much bother. Treating one is just a matter of piercing the bubble, peeling off the skin, adding a dab of ointment, and applying a Band-Aid. Presto!—all taken care of. That may sound blasé, but with the miles I was walking, I would get a blister, it seemed, about every week, and I had become used to treating them.

On the other hand, a sore knee joint is a different matter, and mine had been getting sorer for some time. I should have kept my mouth shut, but that night I complained more than usual to Helen, and that got her going. For the first time she gingerly raised the possibility of our having to give up the walk.

I let out a loud "NO!"

For both of us, quitting now was almost unthinkable. We were thoroughly enjoying the ongoing adventure, and were guardedly optimistic about reaching the Pacific the following year— assuming no major health problems.

"But what if you ruin your knee?" she pressed.

I reminded her that we knew people who had had knee replacements that were working out just fine. Nevertheless, the idea of possibly wearing out a knee doing what I was doing brought Helen straight to the point: "Would the satisfaction of completing this cross-America walk be worth having to have your knee replaced?"

"Definitely," I was able to answer, because for me the preceding weeks had brought a sense of well-being that I had not felt since retirement, and which I doubted I would ever feel again.

LISTENING WHILE AN EGOTIST
PAINTS A TRACTOR

We had intended to move the following day, but instead we drove up to Saint Joseph Medical Center in Fort Wayne to have the knee looked at. After entering the center we found our way to the registration desk, where to my annoyance they immediately made me sit in a wheelchair! The fact that I had walked twenty-two miles the day before and had walked into the hospital on my own two feet—indeed without limping—made no difference at all. The receptionist laughed when she said I would absolutely have to take a ride: "Hospital regulations, sir, you know, it's all about insurance. Sorry, no exceptions!"

Before I knew it, a merry twenty-something was rolling me down a hospital corridor, she and Helen happy partners in their enjoyment of my grumblings.

It was not a long wait in the treatment room. Within minutes the doctor came in, a middle-aged gentleman who got right down to business. He carefully pulled, pushed and twisted my leg this way and that—spent a lot of time doing it. He kept saying things like, Does this hurt? Does that hurt? It doesn't? Are you sure? Then, "We gotta be right about this, you know"—as if he thought I might be minimizing symptoms. Nothing hurt, at least not to speak of, and I told him the essential truth. But he was already skeptical about my continuing the walk. He said he was going to order an X-ray, and if he saw any sign *whatsoever* of arthritis in *that* joint, he was going to *strongly* advise me to *quit* the walk *immediately*. If I didn't, he warned, I would *wear out* the joint and end up in *excruciating pain*. He was quite emphatic.

As it turned out, the X-ray showed no arthritis at all, and prescribing an anti-inflammatory, the good doctor left me with the admonition to "take it easy and play it by ear." He struck Helen and me as conscientious, conservative, indeed caring; and though not much for bedside manner, you didn't have to guess what he was thinking. We left the hospital relieved that nothing was *obviously* wrong with the knee, but puzzled nevertheless. Why was it hurting so much?

In any case, I was comfortable enough to walk the following morning, and presently I was passing through especially flat countryside, and contemplating the vast land and sky that had me feeling—as usual—very small. There was an overarching canopy of clouds beneath which the air was crystal clear, and as I focused on a building low on the horizon, I reminded myself that clouds appearing to either side of it were much farther away. But how much farther? I asked myself. And if that cloud layer were a thousand feet above me, then how many square miles of clouds was I seeing when I turned on my heel and scanned the sky full circle? In particular, how much of that vast canopy lay between me and the terrestrial horizon (marked by that not-so-distant building), and how much more lay beyond the horizon and out to the most distant low clouds?

That night I worked the problem with a model similar to the one I used when considering the visibility of atmospheric storms. I began with the earth a perfect sphere within a slightly larger bubble populated by imaginary clouds. I was six feet tall, the earth was 4000 miles to center, and the height of the clouds was 1000 feet. Ten minutes of computing showed that an imaginary line emanating from my eye would define the terrestrial horizon by grazing the earth only three miles away. After that, it would continue on, slowly rising, ultimately to strike the clouds at a distance of 40 miles. Using the three times radius times radius rule (same as for stormscapes), I computed a total visible sky area of about 5000 square miles, a mere 27 of which lay over ground between me and the nearby horizon. Expressed differently, only 0.5 percent of the sky lay above fields and trees and roads that I could actually see, while 99.5 percent lay beyond, i.e., over land invisible because of the curvature of the earth.

The result intrigued me and allowed me to appreciate why a clear sky tended to give a lesser impression of vast openness than one interspersed with clouds. Barring the sun and perhaps the moon, clear skies offer no deep-space references, and consequently one feels at the center of an overhead vault that is vast indeed but defined, seemingly, by buildings and fields only a few miles away. Conversely, clouds visible above the horizon but forty miles away, clouds stretching up and over and down the opposite sky; such clouds define a far greater heavenly vault and therefore impart a far greater sense of one's smallness.

No wonder I felt so miniature under those endless Midwestern skies!

*   *   *   *

Long Lake Resort at Laketon, Indiana, became our next home away from home, and once again we hit it lucky. Our new campsite had not only a gravel parking strip, but electricity, water, and very welcome shade.

I could have done some walking that afternoon; on the other hand, giving the knee a rest seemed a good idea, especially since the campground was another nice place to relax. They sold good ice cream in the office store—we checked it twice that afternoon. Otherwise, we lazed around and read till seven o'clock when I finally said, "Helen, why don't we go get some fast food? I'm full of ice cream, don't need much to eat—what about you?" I wanted to talk her out of fixing dinner at home, mainly because I didn't feel like helping but knew my conscience would bother me—slightly—if I just sat there reading.

But Helen was in a mood to cook, full of ice cream or not, and before long she was putting together a dinner of tossed salad, pork chops, mashed potatoes, gravy, baked beans, and fresh fruit for dessert. These are going to be first class eats, I thought to myself—just wish I was hungry.

She had been at it for maybe twenty minutes when I looked up and said, "Helen, I've been thinking about a rating system for dinners. Wanna hear about it?"

"Not particularly, unless you wanna to do the cooking."

"No, I'm serious. Obviously you always do a great job, but let's face it, some banquets are better than others."

"Keep it up, Dearie. You'll get cold shoulder for dinner tomorrow night."

Still, with her busy cooking and me busy resting, it seemed like a good time to tell her all about my brand-new Generic Dinner-Grading Scale (GDGS). It goes as follows:

There are eight dinner grades ranging from A double-plus to F, and most everyday dinners fall somewhere in the basic B category. Casserole fare makes for grin-and-bear-it meals that just barely struggle into class D. Sometimes Helen threatens to have one of those, and when she does, we usually go to a restaurant.

The best TV dinners squeak into grade B; the worst rate with casseroles. Egg dinners are solid C-plus. "Trouble is," I told Helen, "after an egg dinner, I usually find myself getting ready to go to work thinking I've just had breakfast."

Good leftovers from grade A meals score near the middle of grade C, while the best gust to the lower levels of B, especially after holidays.

"Helen," I said, when I'd finished, "I'm truly grateful you've made grade B dinners most of our married life. And on this trip too."

"Phil, get out the wine and make yourself useful. When do I make B-plus dinners?"

She instantly knew the question was a mistake, because she was cooking pork, which I like, though I've always preferred beef or chicken. But Helen has always done the food shopping, so we have had considerably more pork than beef or chicken over the past half century. She admits that. Anyway, she began to laugh as we both recalled a time when I'd been complaining of eating too much pork of late. Her answer had been, "Phil, I do the shoppin' so them's the breaks!"

Recalling all that, she expected a smart answer to her "When do I make B-plus dinners?" and I was happy to oblige. "Why Honey,"

I said, "what you're fixing right now is darn near a B-plusser. If them pork chops was just beef or chicken, you'd be smack in the middle of B-plus country."

I got out the wine and poured two glassfuls, making sure to get in her way as much as possible.

"If you're not gonna help, then go sit down." She gave me a shove toward where I'd been sitting and I grabbed her and planted a slurppy kiss on the back of her neck. Then I went back to reading.

Pretty soon she said, "When do I make grade A dinners?"

"Why, every holiday, Honey. You're the best cook in the whole world. If you weren't, we'd go out to eat a lot more often."

Helen's holiday dinners are always winners—roasts of turkey or beef, or sometimes she does a ham. She does party meals for guests from time to time, and these normally come in at high A-plus, although in recent years we have begun serving lighter fare and less liquor. Our older friends don't drink much anymore; their innards can't process it the way they used *to*. That's why people need to drink heavily while they're young and can still get away with it. *Not serious, of course.*

The A double-plus dinners that Helen has made over the years are so rated because they had flaming deserts. I can't remember their names, but bananas or cherries or strawberries were usually involved, and once in a while she would even do a baked Alaska. One of her Alaskas topped off a roast beef dinner with Yorkshire puddings, and the entire presentation was a spectacular success in both looks and taste. My job included flaming the Alaska with rum, and the only downside, as we enjoyed ice cream and scorched meringue, was the smell of burned hair from the back of my left hand.

Helen will laugh when she reads this and probably threaten to have a casserole for dinner. And if we don't go out, I'll no doubt do the dishes—just as I did that night in Indiana when I first revealed my dinner-grading scale.

*   *   *   *

The farms of eastern Indiana appeared less prosperous than those we had been seeing in Ohio. I was curious about that, but not curious enough to bring it up while talking to one particular Indiana farmer. I came upon him when he was hovering beside a John Deere tractor, getting ready to touch up its paint.

After a cordial enough hello, he held up a hand for me to wait until he finished reading the directions for applying Paint Land's Premium Protective Enamel. I told him I had better go, since he was busy and I didn't want to distract him. I wasn't sure I wanted to stay anyway—just in case he might get the way I get when confronted with lawyer-written paint-can directions.

"No, don't go," he said. "Hang around." It almost sounded like an order.

I stood awkwardly for a half minute before he muttered, "Soon as I figure out how to put this stuff on...." He trailed off, squinted at the can, and slowly turned red. Came the explosion: "Damn! I'm supposed to get all the oil, grease, and loose paint off this old horse and then wash 'er down with Paint Land's heavy-duty cleaner. Well, that makes sense, but after that it should have a coat of Paint Land's special primer. Not just any primer'll do, mind you. What do you think of that horseshit?"

"Huh?" was the best I could answer.

"But," he went on, "if I want a really good job, I should start with Paint Land's pre-primer—especially if there's any 'considerable exposure of bare metal.' Who ever heard of pre-primer?" He looked at me as if I might be a pre-primer salesman. On he went: "Stuff in this can's supposed to be primer, and it says it works on metal. Hell do I need pre-primer for?" By now he was thumping the can with a hand that was twice the size of mine and half as old.

I stooped over and tried to work a stone out of my shoe without actually taking it off.

He continued: "You go buy Paint Land's pre-primer and that there can, surer'n hell, will tell you that for the very best results you should start with Paint Land's pre-pre-primer. And by the way, make sure the temperature's above fifty degrees Fahrenheit. They tell you right here that's ten degrees Celsius, which people in the middle of Indiana, who never use Celsius, really need to know—don't you think?"

"Couldn't tell you." He obviously knew about temperature scales; there was nothing dumb about the man.

"Humidity has to be below eighty percent too. You got a humidistat?" He actually said *humidistat*.

Before I could answer, he began to read aloud and word for word how, if you wanted to thin the paint, you needed Paint Land's thinner, and you were supposed to apply everything with a Paint Land application system. He got even louder: "Hell did a paint brush become an 'application system'?"

I started to leave but paused when he growled, "Hang around, buddy, there's more. It tells you right here that ingesting this paint can be harmful or fatal. Why don't they just say fatal, that oughtta cover harmful. Here I'd planned to have a cupful with lunch. Also, you're not supposed to concentrate and inhale the stuff 'cause that'll give you a high—I thought that's why you inhaled stuff in the first place. And don't get any in your eyes or on your skin or on your clothes." He looked at me again and demanded, "You ever seen a painter who dint have paint all over 'em?"

"Only me," I half growled. "I've done plenty of painting, and I don't buy paint to smear all over myself. Sounds like you have as much trouble with a paint brush as you do with paint-can directions." That brought a half grin and something of a touché, but even at that he seemed patronizing.

By now I was annoyed myself. I appreciated, indeed shared, his contempt for paint-can directions, but he was coming through as an overbearing character just naturally inclined to intimidate others if he could. I started to leave but paused when he suddenly asked where I was headed. When I told him, he replied that his wife had recently read a book written by somebody who had "*really* walked across the country." Plowing ahead, he talked about experiences that person had had as if an exalted significance attached to them that couldn't possibly attach to anything anybody else would ever do. He spoke with great pride, as if he himself had done the walking. I asked if he had met the author-walker, and he said *no* but he would like to—"There was a man you could really admire." That came out as if somebody admired by him had much to be grateful for.

I had had all of the man I could take, but before I left, I asked him to read off all the Paint Land products he would supposedly need to touch up the tractor. Here is the list: Paint Land's Premium Protective Enamel, Paint Land's Heavy Duty Cleaner, Paint Land's Oil Base Primer, Paint Land's Pre-Primer, Paint Land's Thinner, and a Paint Land's Application System— a.k.a. paintbrush. If each item cost an average eight dollars, he would spend forty-eight dollars to touch up one square foot of bare metal and there would be about forty-five-dollars' worth of paint and what-have-you left over.

"Mr. Ego" concluded that if you really set out to meet all the requirements listed on the can's label, you never would get around to putting on the paint, but in case you did and it ever chipped off, you would have no claim whatever against the paint company. That, he said, was the real purpose of all those impossible-to-meet conditions printed on the backs of paint cans.

I wanted to tell him there was a definitely more to it than he was claiming, that if he wanted the paint to stay on, he really did need to get the grease off. Of course he knew that. Still, I couldn't argue with his claim that paint-can directions are obviously loaded to "cover the company's backside." He had that close enough for everyday use.

So I wrote off "Paint Man" with a perfunctory "see you," and left him there, in his mind, no doubt, at the center of the universe.

Back walking, it was not long before I found myself laughing at the paint company's use of 'application system' for paintbrush. The use of abstract or generic language where plain works better often sounds funny. Years before, I had heard some cub reporter's description of a Boston fire: "The conflagration communicated itself from one combustible chamber through a vertical boundary to an adjacent space subject to rapid oxidation." Translation: The fire spread to the next room.

OUR MORNING
HOUSEHOLD ROUTINE

Walking … walking … walking…. The sky became overcast, and toward noon I noticed the land becoming a bit less flat. There were low washboard-like hills with reliefs of twenty, thirty, or fifty feet that were separated, knoll to knoll, by maybe a third of a mile. Hardly hills except in comparison to the tens of miles of flat country I'd been crossing.

Presently the land as a whole began to tilt, barely noticeably at first but gradually steeper, eventually to become the shallow valley of Eight Mile Creek. Coming out of the valley, I crossed a low rise, thence to descend to the Little Wabash River northeast of Huntington, Indiana.

The corn was tall now, and young ducklings along roadside ditches were half grown. I had seen several groups lately, but usually there were only two or three chicks. A month before it had been common to see six or eight or more trailing behind their patient mothers. Attrition? Probably. Doubtless only a small percentage of hatchlings reach adulthood.

Late that afternoon, I passed through Bippus, a town of about seven hundred souls eight miles northwest of Huntington. Chris Shenkel, a well-known sportscaster, grew up there. I learned that from a local man in a convenience store where I was buying Chap Stick for my ever-sunburned lips. However, this local was a generation younger than the clerk at the Hudson, Ohio store, i.e., the octogenarian who told me about Danny Lavelli. He was also different in that he was in a hurry. "Got an appointment, gotta go," he said, as he turned from me to the cashier to pay for cigarettes. But appointment or not, he was waiting when I came out, for he had become curious and wanted to know why I was wearing a backpack.

So I told him about the Great Beam Odyssey and how, in the preceding days, it had been like walking through a sea of corn. "Right on," he enthused, "insuring those crops is my business." Then he told me about crop insurance. The concept was new to me, although I had learned about herd management services back in Pennsylvania and was well aware that many different kinds of businesses support farming per se. An exuberant fellow, he was soon expounding on everything from crop loans to banking to general farm-supply businesses. There were even heavy equipment dealerships that cater exclusively to the farm industry, he said, and veterinary services too. He talked farms and farm support for a good ten minutes, until I reminded him he was in a hurry. "Good Lord, I'm outta here," he exclaimed, and off he dashed, hopefully not late for his appointment.

I went back to walking and an hour later met Helen on county road 800 just east of Rock-Springs Pike. There ended another day's hike, and as always those days, my knee was hurting like a toothache.

*　　*　　*　　*

Came a morning when Helen shook me awake with "Happy Father's Day, Honey. You stay in bed, I'll do the chores."

I thanked her but mumbled we should both go back to sleep. Five minutes later, when I realized she *had* gone back to sleep and I was awake for good, I struggled out of bed to begin the day. By now, weeks of repetition had rendered the morning's prewalk routines perfected to where we could do them almost automatically.

First, I put two pans on the stove. One held water hot from the tap, to be rushed to a boil for jump-start coffee. The other contained cold water that would come to a boil at a more leisurely rate. It would be used to make coffee for the road. While the waters were heating, I attended bathroom duties.

Upon returning to the stove, I made two strong cups of instant and called Helen, who was beginning to stir again by herself. While she was in the bathroom, I got the day's drinking water ready.

Preparing the drinking water always started with putting two trays of ice cubes into the bottom of a round, insulated cooler. We bought drinking water in one-gallon jugs, and I got one of those out of the refrigerator and put it in the cooler on top of the ice. It fit perfectly; the cooler's lid screwed on easily without binding on the top of the jug. With this arrangement, the water would stay cold all day, the ice not fully melting until late afternoon.

Once the drinking water was ready, I made coffee for the road, which always included a struggle with the vacuum bottle's lid. The thread in that expensive, stainless steel bottle was a low, rounded ridge that extended only one-and-a-half revolutions around the interior of the bottle's mouth. The corresponding thread on the mating, too-soft plastic cap was interrupted, so that in principle coffee could be poured with only partially unscrewing the lid. Of course, before the bottle was used a half dozen times, the heat-softened plastic thread was slipping over its hot steel counterpart, and after that it was always a struggle to get the lid tight enough to keep the bottle from leaking. Undoubtedly the bottle's manufacturer had known about the problem for years. How could they not?

While I was grouching and finishing the battle of the vacuum bottle, Helen came out and began to cook breakfast. With her busy at that, I made sure that what I would need during the day's walk was in the backpack. Then I carted backpack, coffee, and water out to the car, and by the time I got back, Helen had the lunch cooler packed with sandwiches we had made the night before. I took that to the car too, and then we sat down for breakfast.

After breakfast I washed the dishes while she dried and put them away. We made sure the gas stove and electric heater were off, and we locked the windows and turned the water off outside where it connected to Lurch from the park's water supply. That way we could not possibly have a flooded camper when we got home at night.

On the way out of the park we stopped at the bathhouse for final necessities; then it was off to walk's end, which that Father's Day morning was only nine miles away.

An hour later I was hurrying along intrigued by beautiful near and middle distance views. The road was of shell-white pebbles bordered by spectacular arrays of wild flowers. Especially, there were low purple blooms growing in profusion between grassy ditches and cornfields forty feet beyond, and interspersed with the purple was Queen Anne's lace, and here and there were tall stalks of grass with tops that looked like little wheat spikes. I pulled a few, rolled them between my hands and gently blew away the chaff. The seeds were very small—a fraction the size of wheat grains. Idly I wondered if they were edible, but it seemed that even if they were they would be impractical to harvest.

The morning wore on....

Ahead, on the left, a house sat back among shade trees, and nearby was a farm wagon beneath which lay a dog. He looked my way but did not move, did not bark—just lay there watching. Or was he staring? *Just keep walking,* Beam, *as if you don't even see him. But get out a dog biscuit, just in case he comes down here with an attitude.*

Moments later he was indeed on his way, attitude and all. From lying prone to a dead run in one swift bound, out from under the wagon he charged and straightaway down the drive. I groped for the dog biscuit even as it dawned on me that this would be no dog-biscuit occasion. *This mutt definitely wants something else,* I thought. *He's a hundred feet away now and coming like a freight train. My God, he growls when he breaths in and growls when he breaths out—didn't know they could do that. And he's bigger than I thought, probably fifty pounds, maybe more. I can see him clearly now—pulled back lips, bared teeth, flattened ears. For God's sake, Beam, forget the dog biscuit! Grab the pepper spray! This thing's almost here!*

I struggled for the spray in my left shirt pocket, and holding it in my right hand, I scrambled backward while raising my left arm to fend off the brute should he leap for my chest. In the last few yards, he dropped to a running crouch before rising into a leap that took him full-face into my squirt of pepper spray. His right haunch banged the fronts of my legs as he hurtled past, but he'd been instantly silenced by the noxious mist and completely discouraged from continuing the attack.

I watched him run back up the drive making no sounds at all, and when he got to the lawn he began pushing his face across the grass, trying to rub pepper spray from nose and mouth and eyes.

He'll be all right, I assured myself; the effects won't last *that* long. At the moment, however, I would hardly have cared if he were dead. It was a close call, and the attack was totally unprovoked.

For an hour afterward I kept thinking about the dog attack and was bothered by feelings that I had not handled it well. Presenting my left side to the brute and extending my left arm to fend it off had been the right thing to do. But I had sprayed with my right hand held across my body, and to avoid spraying my left arm, I held the canister low—only about waist high. Had I missed and been knocked backwards, my right arm would have been in no position to break the fall. I could have ended up flat on my back with a slashing dog on top.

I began to rehearse a different tactic for dealing with a dog attack, should I be unlucky enough to face another. Next time, instead of holding the spray in my right hand and down by my waist, I would grab it early with my left hand and hold it out toward the oncoming dog. That way the spraying distance would be an arm's length less, and should I miss, my left arm would still be out there to stiff-arm the brute away. Meanwhile, early on, I would get my right hand on that thirty-eight in my right pants pocket, and if necessary, near the end of the dog's charge, I would draw, cock, and hold it low and away behind me. I promised myself I would hold on to that gun no matter how hard I was hit. That way I'd have it to blow the bastard's lungs out in case I ended up underneath.

That first serious dog encounter left me unnerved and it was surprisingly hard to put out of mind. Gradually however, as hours went by and the angst subsided, I thought less and less about it, and by the end of the day I had given three more biscuits to flop-eared mutts who were happy to become my pals. Nevertheless, that particular dog would not be the last to taste my pepper spray.

*   *   *   *

It being Father's Day, Helen wanted to take me out to dinner, except that we couldn't find a place that was open. So it was back to the camper, TV dinners, and a walk around the campground to end Father's Day, 1999—until eleven o'clock that night....

"Honey, there's something outside." Helen was prodding me out of a deep sleep.

I listened for a minute, and sure enough, the rustling was a dead giveaway. There had to be a raccoon in the trash bag that I had put outside to take to the Dumpster in the morning. If I could just go back to sleep, maybe it would go away. Helen too.

"Phil!"

But she was still there, wide awake now and telling me the raccoon would have "paper and stuff" strewn all over the campground by morning unless I got out there and "did something about it."

"Good Lord, it's not enough I walked twenty-six miles today and was nearly eaten by a dog; now I've gotta chase raccoons around the darn campground in the middle of the night."

By then she had got a flashlight out of a drawer and me out of bed. Next, she opened the camper door and stood back as I, still half asleep, charged out with a shout—and right at the raised tail of a skunk who, thank God, held his fire.

I did a quick about-face and hopped back inside as Helen clapped her hands. Next, she went to the kitchen window and shined the flashlight at "Mr. Odor," who didn't mind a bit and went calmly ahead rooting around the usual stuff you put in trash bags—stuff that was now pretty much scattered about. I opened the door a foot, and to satisfy Helen I asked the skunk if he wouldn't please go somewhere else. He instinctively knew what to do: he turned right around and raised his tail again. Clearly, he had been through all this before and knew exactly how to deal with campers dumb enough to leave their trash outside. I slammed the door and yielded him the night. I'd pick up the trash in the morning.

The following evening I got into a conversation with a couple of men who often spent weekends at the campground with their wives. We talked weather, we talked politics, we talked about different campgrounds. Everything was going fine until I mentioned skunks. Sure enough, they knew all about the skunk-in-the-trash routine. They said Mr. Odor (although they didn't call him that) was a well-known fixture around the campground, and nobody "messed with him if they knew what was good for 'em." They also let me know—not as tactfully as I should have liked—that they thought I was a little stupid for leaving the garbage bag out.

I'd have argued the point but didn't see how I could win.

After that, our talk drifted to the relative merits of different brands of cars, but gradually the two men were talking more and more to one another, me being left out. Trying to stay in the conversation, I submitted a few bland comments which brought no response until I praised Helen's indestructible Toyota. "It's already got over two hundred thousand miles on it," I enthused.

Big mistake! The men were retired Detroit autoworkers with Hummer-like personalities and black-belt loyalties to American cars. I gave up and walked back to Lurch, where Helen and I read for a while before going to bed. I had earlier taken the trash to the Dumpster, just in case Odor came back.

*　　*　　*　　*

Next morning, we were en route to the walk site when we stopped at Roann, Indiana, where a covered bridge spans the beautiful Eel River. The bridge is dated 1877, although a passerby told us it may be a reconstruction. In any case, it was painted barn red, and our view from the north framed it against adjacent trees along the river bank. It was a beautiful sight. We walked around the area for ten or fifteen minutes making a big thing of the scenery, but in truth, I was simply putting off walking. My knee was hurting again, more than ever,

At the Eel River

and that had the magic effect of causing this view or that view to need to be looked at from this angle or that angle, and thoughtful speculation was required about the history of the area, and so on—anything to put off walking.

Eventually, unable to delay any longer, we got back in the car and continued west to tiny Deedsville, where we had finished the day before and where I now resumed walking. It was just after seven o'clock.

The day must have been a pleasant dreamlike one for Helen as she wrote about swaying cornfields and vast beanfields and, as always, about the endless flatness of the land. She spoke of cornflowers along roadside ditches, and she hoped that anyone reading her scribblings (her word) would have an appreciative feel for the soft noises of birds and insects—sounds that were disturbed only rarely by the clatter of distant machinery. Most of all she wrote about the peacefulness of the land. For me walking and for her waiting, the separation between mind and land and sky often seemed indistinct—we felt "part of things" in a manner not experienced before in our nearly seven-decade lives. Of course, we had never lived that way before.

"THIS JACKET WON'T LEAK!"

I met Mike Babb one morning while he was adjusting a fertilizer spreader along the edge of a cornfield. Mike had not been a farmer by occupation, but after retirement he took it up on a small scale, more to keep busy than make money. We spent a pleasant half hour talking as he worked and I put off walking. Mike was interested in why Helen and I had embarked on our odyssey, and I, as usual, was happy to tell him all about it. When we parted around eleven o'clock, neither of us expected we'd meet again.

However, during lunch that day, Mike told his wife about meeting this walker from Connecticut. She immediately became interested and suggested the story might be grist for the *Milepost*, a small newspaper published monthly out of Twelve Mile, the next town over. Agreeing that it might indeed be worth pursuing, Mike called Phyllis Johnson, a friend of theirs and journalist for the paper, and about one that afternoon, using his truck, he and Phyllis began looking for me along the farm roads near Twelve Mile. After an hour and a half of driving first east on one road then west on another, they finally spotted a Connecticut license plate on an oncoming car. A quick U-turn followed by plenty of horn blowing, smiling, and waving eventually got Helen to pull over.

Conversation between Helen, Phyllis, and Mike at one point addressed the demise of a number of small towns that we had passed through in Ohio and Indiana. In many, the houses looked okay but the businesses had long since failed—victims of the automobile and the ease with which people can drive miles to supermarkets and department stores. Clearly, no small business can compete across the board with the giants, but the convenience of a hometown store should still be worth something. Helen said she would hate to have to drive thirty miles for a box of cough drops or, worse yet, for a suddenly needed bag of sugar. In many small towns you can't even buy a gallon of gas or a cup of coffee.

After getting directions from Helen, Phyllis and Mike had no trouble finding me. I saw them coming from far away, and I quickly recognized Mike as they pulled up with a cloud of dust and friendly greetings. Introductions complete, I answered many questions from Phyllis about what it was like to walk across America, and how Helen and I got started on the project to begin with. As usual, I enjoyed the attention, and after they drove away, I hoofed along thinking all sorts of modest thoughts, for example, *What intrepid souls Helen and I must be. We could take on just about anything!* By then I had almost forgotten about the dog that had come after me the week before.

Phyllis wrote up her interviews with Helen and me, and her well written article appeared in the July 1999 issue of *Milepost*. She sent a copy to our home in Connecticut, and Helen I enjoyed reading it. Nowadays, years later, it remains a pleasant memory.

$$* \quad * \quad * \quad *$$

On June 22 we moved Lurch for what seemed like the tenth time, although we were only a quarter of the way across the country. Decamping went smoothly, and by ten o'clock we were on the road and driving to Farmers Woods Campground, which is in White County, Indiana, about three miles west of Monon. It was only a fifty-mile drive and everything went smoothly—we easily found the campground and were parked and set up by eleven o'clock.

Not interested in "heading for the field" (our current phrase for getting out there and walking), we began the afternoon by driving into Monon. We were especially curious because we had heard the name in the movie *Hoosiers* where there was passing reference to a railroad. We enjoyed a half-hour reconnoiter of the town and later learned that it originated in 1852 along the newly laid tracks of the Louisville, New Albany and Chicago Railroad.

Along with supporting the local farming community, Monon quickly grew into a railroad support center with two large yards, a roundhouse, a machine shop, and an engine shed. The last of those facilities was still in use as late as the 1960s, although the depot itself had been destroyed by a train wreck a dozen years earlier. About three the afternoon of September 17, 1951, the *Thoroughbred*, a southbound train, jumped the track, killing the engineer and injuring three others as it plowed clear through the station.

Active as they once were, Monon's railroad yards are nowadays ghostly lots of spotty grass and scattered gravel. Even so, the modern CSX Railroad still junctions there with tracks leading northwest to Chicago, west to Peoria, southeast to Monticello, and due south to Lafayette, Indiana.

The following morning saw me back on the trail, starting at the intersection of White County Roads 1400 E and 900 N, and walking west of course, ever west. Throughout the morning I would pass a patch of forest here, another there—mere islands of deciduous woodlands dispersed through endless farmlands. Typical sizes for the patches ranged from forty to eighty to maybe three hundred acres; about ten percent of the countryside consisted of little woodlands like these. Locals told us that deer lived there, but I didn't see any although Helen saw three the next day.

Vast farmlands notwithstanding, it was intriguing to us that only 150 years before, extensive areas of the upper Midwest were marshy and unfit for agriculture. White County itself, an area of approximately 500 square miles, was at least one-quarter swampland. In 1873, in order to open the lands to cultivation, the state chartered "draining companies" to channel away the water and assess property owners for the benefits. The result was the extensive grid of artificial ditches and modified natural waterways that network the land today. So important is the drainage system that some natural streams have come to be referred to as ditches. Little Monon Creek, which passes through south Monon, is also known as McKillip Ditch.

That day turned out to be a particularly lucky one for Helen and me. Early in the afternoon and eight miles west of Monon, Marvin Olson, a farmer, stopped to ask Helen if she needed help. The two conversed easily, and in the short while they talked, Marvin answered Helen's questions about fields and crops in the area. Of course she told him who we were and what we were doing.

The Olson farm was about a quarter mile from where the two talked, and at the end of the day we had to drive past the farmhouse on our way back to camp. I was hoping for a chance to thank Marvin for checking on Helen, and as luck would have it, he was standing near a flowerbed in the front yard. I thanked him and appreciated his sincere "you're welcome." After that we talked for a few minutes, until Helen and I, eager to get back to camp, began taking our leave. However, Marvin gestured for us to hold up, and then he surprised us with, "How about coming in and having dinner with us?"

It was an invitation we were happy to accept.

Mrs. Olson put together a tasty dinner of soup, sandwiches, and salad, which was a delightful change for us. Afterward, we chatted on the patio behind their house, and later Marvin showed me his tractors and a fifth-wheel camper which they took to Florida in the winter. In passing, Marvin mentioned that he rented out hunting rights on his land, a practice that was new to me. When I was young and still hunting, most people hunted on state game lands. Hunting on private property was considered a privilege granted free by the owner to immediate family or very close friends.

Our evening with the Olsons sped quickly by, and it was nearing nine o'clock when Helen and I left to go home for a good night's sleep. I was determined to walk the following day, although my knee had been hurting most of the afternoon. In parting, we took with us spinach and lettuce from the Olson's garden, but especially we left with a warm appreciation for Hoosier hospitality.

*   *   *   *

"This jacket won't leak," the young clerk declared. "If it does, just bring it back." She seemed detached to the point of rudeness.

It was a muggy day, and thanks to intermittent rain we had called off walking about eleven o'clock and driven north to

Rensselaer, Indiana. We were looking for a reasonably waterproof jacket of some kind, something better than the vinyl poncho I had been using—which didn't leak but didn't breathe, and was hard to put on in gusty wind. The problem with buying a jacket had been that those we kept seeing were all marked "water repellent," and we thought that probably meant they would be okay in a light drizzle but leak aplenty in a hard rain. A couple of salespeople we talked to thought so too.

Finding nothing suitable in Rensselaer, we were returning south to resume the walk when we unexpectedly spotted this likely looking store in Collegeville.

So there we were, talking to a borderline-brusque salesgirl—or saleswoman—or salesperson—or whatever she was. She certainly wasn't a lady. "It says water repellent not waterproof," I mused. "I'm worried about *repellent*. They'd say waterproof, wouldn't they?—if they were sure it wouldn't leak at all."

"It won't leak," she repeated. "We've had no complaints at all about these jackets." Her tone was clipped, her smile nonexistent.

I was still unconvinced, but the seams were tightly sewn and the material was a little denser, a little more closely woven than any we had seen in other jackets. Finally I said I would take it. Then, trying to coax a smile from the dour woman, I grinned and said, "But you'll *cheerfully* refund my money, won't you?—if it rains and I get soakin' wet ... right?"

"You won't get wet!" she snapped in a voice that was slightly raised and tinged with sarcasm. Until then she had hardly looked at either Helen or me, but now she took a step back and with barely concealed hostility looked not in my eyes, but at some spot near my hairline. She held her glare for a tense few seconds before turning away with a toss of her head. A bit bewildered, we paid for the jacket and left.

"Good Lord," I said, when we were out on the sidewalk. "Give me some fresh air."

"You must look like somebody she hates," Helen remarked. "Some psychologist has probably filled her empty head with made-up memories of an abusing grandparent. Or maybe she really was abused. Who knows? Forget it. It's nothing to do with you."

I grouched a bit more about the crabby woman as we looked for a place to eat. Excellent hamburgers at a small restaurant helped my mood, at least to some degree, while Helen more serenely enjoyed the change from lunchmeat sandwiches and soft drinks.

An hour later we were back at walk's end, and I was putting on my pack and getting ready to start walking. Suddenly Helen said, "Philip, I don't think you're going to get very far. It looks like rain."

Maybe it was leftover annoyance with shop girl that kept me from paying more attention to the sky. In any case, a perfunctory glance showed me only a medium overcast merging down to an indistinct horizon about three miles to the west. Other than that, there was a slightly thicker patch to the north and a couple more to the south, from which hung wispy rain curtains. I dismissed these since we were forever seeing such showers; usually they missed, and even when they didn't, they rarely amounted to much.

I should have paid more attention.

"Phil, I'm telling you *it's gonna rain!*" Helen already considered the day a "washout," and she wanted to go back to the RV and nap the afternoon away. I was determined to walk, however; we had already lost two hours—right out of the middle of the day. "On we'll go," I said, "though the dogs are spent and the grub is gittin' low." That was close to a quote from "The Cremation of Sam McGee" by Robert Service, which I first heard at a scout jamboree in 1945.

Helen registered a few more protests, but I was all resolve and orders: "No problem! Just move out five or six miles; I'll see you in a couple of hours." She remembered my pre-deluge bravado back in Pennsylvania, and as she grudgingly eased the car away, I heard the expected mutterings: "Stubborn old man ... washed down a culvert ... serve 'em right ... old goat"—the usual.

I had walked only a few minutes when I noticed that the overcast, which seemed only moderate a few minutes before, had thickened toward the west and the thickness extended some distance north and south and clear down to the ground. Just then another car, westbound like Helen but a quarter mile ahead, suddenly vanished into the soup. Moments later the Toyota vanished too. It was obvious what was about to happen, and I wasted no time getting on the new jacket. It was about to have some serious water repelling to do.

A few drops arrived, not many at first but as big as small peas, and they came in almost horizontally on the wings of a whistling wind. They didn't stop either when they hit the "water-repellent" jacket. Underneath I wore a sleeveless shirt, and raindrops, hitting the jacket's sleeves with a thwack, burst through to wet my bare arms with a chilly spray. The full strength of the storm soon followed, and within a quarter mile I was soaking wet and shivering cold.

Helen, God love her, came back, although the car was less than a hundred feet away when it emerged from the downpour. No argument about continuing this time. Standing by the passenger door, I pulled out the jacket's elastic cuffs, and sure enough, water that had been trapped between my wrists and the raincoat's sleeves fell out over my hands and onto shoes that were already soaking wet.

I hesitated to get into the car knowing it would soak the seat, but Helen, in rare delight, just had to say, "I know you're un-dumb enough not to just stand there in the rain. Get in, m'Love. Now we'll go home, 'though the dogs are spent and the grub is gittin' low.'" She can be clever with words.

"My line," I said. "How come you remember my saying it?"

"You know why. Because you often say it, especially when you're sure you're right, close your eyes, and then just plow ahead … or in this case more or less wade."

I told her she was cruel, but she claimed I had always liked smokehouse poetry. She was quiet after that, except for an occasional chuckle as she drove us back to the campground.

*　　*　　*　　*

My first walk segment the following morning ended when I met Helen at the Illinois state line, and although we should have been in merry moods, we were both subdued. My knee was hurting, more than usual—of course it had been getting progressively worse for weeks. It was especially troublesome whenever I walked parallel to the road in the dirt margin of a field, or when I left the road entirely and crossed uneven ground to rest briefly under some rare tree. I would do that now and then. But most damaging to our morale was the knee's nighttime aching, which yielded only partially to aspirin or Advil. Pain, anxiety, and lack of sleep were contributing to a funk that we were both sliding into.

Tired and a bit discouraged, we decided to drive back up to Collegeville and return the water-repellent jacket that didn't repel water. The night before we had hung it up to dry, but it was still damp. "Just as well," Helen remarked. "It'll be more convincing when you tell that 'sweet' young woman it leaked like a sieve."

By the time we got there, I was primed and ready for Sweetie, but to our relief she was nowhere to be seen. Instead, a very different young woman approached and offered help as soon as we stepped through the door. "It's still wet," she said, declaring the obvious. "You must have nearly drowned—she resuscitate you?" She gestured toward Helen with a pleasant wave. She was definitely no relation of the girl who sold us the jacket.

"Yeah," I said with a smile. "It's especially wet *inside*, which is where I was when the rain started. But if you think it's wet now, you should have seen it yesterday afternoon. I got soaked!"

"Oh my, we can't have that, now can we? At least we can refund your money." Her accent, even her syntax, suggested British.

She returned our money and in ensuing conversation told us that she was in fact English, and a student at Saint Joseph's College in nearby Rensselaer. She was a pleasant soul—enthusiastic and full of fun; in fact, she made returning the jacket a pleasure. "Different person, different personality," Helen remarked, as we left the store and set out for the campground.

MY KNEE GETS REALLY SORE

That evening I decided to walk the following day, a Sunday. It would ordinarily have been a rest day, but thanks—or no thanks—to my sore knee and our being rained out, we had covered only fifty-seven miles in the preceding three days. Not enough! We would use Sunday to push into Illinois—try for another twenty miles before taking a day off. At least that was our plan when we went to bed. Come morning though, my knee hurt so bad I could not face walking, and even before breakfast we decided to stay put. We'd wash the car, or at least clean out the inside, but other than that we'd loaf around. Especially, I would rest that knee.

We went to work on the car as soon as the dishes were finished, and it could hardly have needed it more. Dust from dozens of gravel roads had penetrated every nook and cranny; even the glass covering the instrument panel showed an inside layer of grime. Whenever cleaning the car had come up, we put it out of mind, agreeing that the car's condition, or even the motor home's, didn't matter much. It only mattered that we kept the odyssey moving west.

But just working on the car became misery that morning. The knee pained constantly as with legs outside the car and torso inside, I tried to vacuum the interior. Clearly, something had to give.

Of course *something* had been coming for the past several weeks, and it finally arrived about nine-thirty when we grudgingly acknowledged we would have to break off the great walk. We would go home to Connecticut and get the knee checked out. The interruption would only be temporary; once it was examined and whatever had to be done was done, we would come right back to this very campground, and continue on from the present walk's end. We tacitly agreed not even to discuss the possibility that our adventure was ending for good, all because I had gone lame.

Helen thought we should call one of our daughters and ask her to let the rest of the family know we were starting home. "There's a pay phone in the shower building," she said. "After we finish the car, I'll go over and call Dianne."

But in the end, I was the one who went because my knee hurt so bad I had to quit working.

The phone, which was in a small room near the showers, turned out to be different from any I had ever seen. Rather than being mounted on the wall, it sat on a low table and looked like an old fashioned desk phone except for a small attached box with a slot for receiving coins. There was also a chair, and glad to sit down, I laid my notebook with phone numbers out flat, along with a calling card and a half dozen coins to feed the box. Nice arrangement, I thought—handy.

Then I tried to place the call.

When direct dialing didn't work, I dialed "O" to reach a local operator. That had always worked in other places; somebody nearby would connect me to a long-distance operator who would take my card numbers and complete the call. However, in this case, a local operator (if she was an operator) came on the line and said that she herself would put the call through. All she needed was the calling card number and my Personal Identification Number (PIN). I reluctantly obliged, but once she had the numbers, she went off the line. A moment later she was back: "Sorry. For technical reasons your call cannot be completed." Click. Silence. Dial tone!

Wary now, I tried again, but with the same result. A different voice murkily claimed connection to an obscure phone company, and then concluded with, "I can put your call through. Please give me your card and PIN numbers."

"Thanks but no thanks," I said this time. Then I gimped my way back to the campsite, and straight away we drove into town. There, at a legitimate-looking pay phone, I was able to get a legitimate long-distance operator who changed our calling card's PIN right on the spot. She said it was probably a good thing I called.

Relieved, we started back to the campground.

Maybe we were overreacting, but twice in the past Helen and I had had calling card numbers stolen. In one case, years before, a well-meaning relative had signed us up with a fledgling long-distance carrier. Although unrequested by us, the company quickly mailed calling cards that were followed within weeks by three successive letters in which they changed, re-changed, and then changed the PIN yet again. Each time, the company wrote that they had reason to believe our account had been compromised. Nevertheless, only days after the third letter, the first bill arrived, and it was more than any phone bill we had ever seen.

The thief had immediately begun using the account for numerous calls to Europe as well as to cities in the eastern U.S. Within weeks the charges were over nine hundred dollars as I almost daily called the company, telling them the account was indeed compromised and that not a single call had ever been made by Helen or me.

During the year it took to get the mess straightened out, I talked to a number of midlevel people in the company. In every case they were pleasant, understanding, and apologetic; several even declared they really believed me when I said we had never used their service. Almost invariably they would promise to straighten the matter out once and for all. And I'm sure at least some of them tried, because for a while the bills and nasty phone calls would stop. Then, just when we'd think the battle was over, another bill would come, another threatening letter, or a phone call from some human pit-bull in St. Louis. It was always the same. He would hotly say that he could prove we made the calls and we had better pay up or else. Eventually he sold the account to a collection agency, and for the first time in our lives we found out what those animals are like.

"Mister," I said to some thug who called one night at dinnertime, "I never signed up for phone service from that company, never used their calling cards, never billed a single phone call to them. That goes for my wife too. Does that matter to you?—even a little?"

"Not in the least," came the snarling reply. "My company bought and legally owns this account, so by law you owe, and we have a legal right to dun you to collect. So PAY UP!" I was surprised he actually used the word *dun*.

Eventually, far up in the phone company, I got hold of a powerful woman with an elongated title like "High Priestess Responsible for Solving Unsolvable Billing Problems in Northeastern United States." She said she not only could solve the problem but *would* solve it. "And immediately, Mr. Beam!" She even said there would be no "black mark" left on our credit record either—wherever the hell "they" keep credit records and black marks. Who cares?

But she did what she said she would do. We heard no more from the collection types; we received no more bills, no more nasty phone calls. Years later, when we checked it out, our credit *dossier* carried no reference to the affair—not that we cared then any more than we had earlier. Looking back, it's clear that we should have canceled the calling card account as soon as we received the company's first letter admitting the account was compromised. But how could we know that that particular spawn of deregulation would be at least a year getting its security and billing practices right?

The other time that we had card numbers stolen we were using a different phone company. It happened when Helen placed a call from a hotel lobby in Florida, and the first evidence that something was wrong came as a bill for over three hundred dollars. I called the company, dreading we might be in for another long struggle to get things straightened out. But different from the other carrier, this one's representative was able to settle the matter right on the spot. She took my word for the obviously fraudulent calls and re-billed us for our actual usage. That was the end of the matter. The two companies' handlings of the problem were as different as night and day.

But to return to the story.

It was just after we got back to the campground—after we changed the PIN number—that my sore knee took a nasty twist. We had finished breaking camp, and I was making sure the jacks were up when my shoe caught on a tree root and wrenched my whole leg sharply to the left. Good Lord, did it hurt! Down I went onto the other knee but fortunately onto soft soil. The pain was agonizing at first, but it quickly began to subside—and amazingly, it continued to subside. A few minutes later the knee felt better yet, and a half hour later it was hurting less than it had for weeks. We could hardly believe it, but what a break! "We better stay out here for a few more days," I said to Helen. "If this knee's going to be better, even for just a day or two, we ought to get in as many more miles as we can."

"All right," she reluctantly agreed. "But we're going to call this off—period!—if that knee kicks up again. And it will, mark my words."

So I started Lurch, and when we reached the highway, we turned west instead of east toward Connecticut and home. Our next stop was a campground near Kankakee, Illinois. Though sixteen miles north of our projected walk track, it would have to do since it was the only campground in the area. Inconvenient though it was, we would spend an interesting few days there, starting that evening when we met a retired couple, Mr. and Mrs. Donald Rightmyer of Dillon, South Carolina.

Our conversation with the Rightmyers was at first about national events and the weather, but it quickly got around to a great tourist attraction near their hometown. It's called South of the Border, and it is located off Interstate 95 just below the North Carolina-South Carolina line.

Everyone who uses I-95 for biannual migrations between the Northeast and Florida knows about the place. It is a collection of souvenir shops and other small businesses designed to extract tourist bucks from families passing through on the interstate. This is accomplished by grabbing the kids' attention with advertising signs that extend fifty or more miles north and south along the highway. Just below the complex there used to be a sign that read KEEP HOLLERING KIDS, THEY'LL TURN BACK! Helen says the advertising is a scream.

Indeed, it's a laugh just to drive by South of the Border, but it is a lot more fun to stop. They have a good RV park, and the ice cream is outstanding.

That night at the Kankakee campground, as it grew dark and slowly cooled off, I told our companions how for me South of the Border conjures up images of a great big money-separation machine.

"How's that?" Don asked.

"Listen to this," I said, and then sketched the following picture:

SUVs and minivans full of parents and children are sucked from the highway by tens of miles of enticing billboards. Out of their vehicles the good folk tumble, to pass with gleeful anticipation through one of two entries in the front of a wide, flat building. At the other entry, workers carry in sweets, trinkets, and tee shirts in unending supply, and these are distributed to myriad booths which offer all the fascinating things that children, teenagers, and young adults love to buy.

With X-ray vision one looks into the building and sees happy people moving from booth to booth, the younger children with their parents, the older ones adventuring on their own. At each station a goodie of some sort—a tee shirt, a piece of candy, a brief amusement—is enjoyed by the innocent, while a soft, tentacle-like hose eases down from above and gently sucks money from pocket or purse. To complete the picture, cash hoses from all the booths connect to an overhead system of pipes which speed the liberated money across the ceiling and out the back wall into a great big barrel!

Nearby, and also emerging from the back wall, jolly families tumble down people chutes on their way to their cars and vans. For them it is back to the highway and south toward Florida, or north toward New England, depending on the season. Everybody's happy. The kids have got their money spent, and their parents are relieved it is gone. Who knows? Being's their broke, maybe they'll be quiet for a while—even take a nap. Better yet, the whole family has had a break from the numbing boredom of I-95. And best of all is management's celebration around that barrel full of money. Long live South of the Border!

Truth is it's a great place to visit, and anybody who has ever been there will tell you so.

When I had completed this word picture for our South Carolinian acquaintances, Mrs. Rightmyer, in laughing rebuke, said, "Don't knock it, Phil. South Carolina's not a rich state, and income from The Border is a real boost to the economy."

No doubt it is.

*   *   *   *

The next morning, twenty miles of driving got us back to the Indiana-Illinois line where we had finished up two days before. I had covered only nine miles that day, and we had made the relatively easy move to the Kankakee campground the following morning. Consequently, I was starting into Illinois after essentially two days off, and I expected to cover lots of ground if my knee held out.

Indeed, shortly after I began walking, the knee hurt so little I forgot all about it, and soon I was thinking about the occasional abandoned right-of-ways I had noticed back East, and how dynamic the modern Midwest railroads seemed in contrast. Grade-crossing signals rise up in stark, tall prominence as you walk up to then on lonely gravel roads. I would see many such crossings as the walk across Illinois took me through or near Pittwood, Ashkum, Saunemin, Pontiac, El Paso, Peoria and finally to Galesburg west of the Illinois River.

The first tracks I came to belonged to the Kankakee, Beaverville and Southern Railroad—the longest railroad name I would see all the way across the country. They were four miles west of the border, and only five miles farther on I crossed tracks of the Union Pacific. From there a twelve-mile hike brought me to the first of several Illinois Central crossings—this one near Ashkum, and seventeen miles beyond Ashkum were more Illinois Central tracks, these passing through the town of Cullom.

A grade crossing of the Norfolk Southern lies six miles beyond Cullom; then it is only twelve more miles to tracks that run right through the center of Pontiac—these again belonging to the Illinois Central. And so it goes as you walk farther west, and so it is behind you to the east, back through Indiana and Ohio—all the way to the mountains of Pennsylvania. In all, there were fifteen grade crossings along our route through Illinois, which averages to a crossing every fourteen miles.

Of course, when you are walking from the East Coast to the West Coast, you are crossing only north-south tracks, but if you divert just a few miles from your route, you soon come to east-west tracks. In fact, only eight miles below Pittwood is a right-of-way of the Toledo, Peoria and Western, and eighteen miles to the north lie tracks of the Norfolk Southern. The Midwest is overlain by a vast network of tracks that were originally built to serve farming districts and supporting towns. Thus, almost every town, except for the smallest, lies along the tracks of one or another railroad.

The farm road I was walking that Monday was very dusty in the environs of Ashkum, and for mile after mile it was so flat that small elevations changes were barely noticeable. There were a few trees though: a small patch here, a lone willow there, and there were several acres of woodland near the Iroquois River. Other than that, it was just fields and fields of corn, beans, and occasionally oats. Of course there were a few farmhouses, and sometimes there would be an old wooden corncrib with ventilated sides and sharply peaked roof. But wooden cribs are infrequent nowadays. Modern methods dry corn with blowers in round, sheet-metal silos.

In early afternoon, a car startled me as it abruptly turned into a lane and stopped only feet in front of me. Its driver, an elderly man, wanted to know where I was going. I told him the usual—that I was walking across the U.S. and that Helen was waiting somewhere up ahead. His wife was immediately interested and asked a question; however, even as I began to answer, the man became suddenly annoyed and cut me off in mid-sentence. Why? Who knows. But he snorted a clearly audible "damned nonsense," before gunning his car down the lane toward a farmhouse in the trees.

Whoever he was, he was a downer to me, and I wished he had not asked where I was going if, moments later, he couldn't be civil as I tried to answer his *wife's* question. Still, what really bothered me was his use of the word *nonsense*. Was all this walking really just nonsense? Indeed, although Helen and I were enjoying the adventure, I had more than once wondered if it made sense. Even so, at those times I could honestly acknowledge to myself that it was an exciting break from working around the house, volunteering at a hospital, or sailing in a cruise ship to who-cares-where. And most important of all, the walk was proving an effective hedge between me and a sense of uselessness that had steadily worsened in the years since retirement. Maybe the fellow is depressed, I thought. I could sympathize with that.

But it was impossible to stay disconcerted by a chance encounter with an grouchy stranger. There were interesting wildflowers all along the road, and twice I met friendly dogs.

Helen too had a good day and she recorded how she took a small walk a couple of miles south from where she was parked. She often took such excursions, and occasionally she would walk east to meet me. I would first see her far ahead, a tiny figure in the vast openness; then we would close with surprising quickness and many waves of our hands. We would meet and talk and then continue to the car, where she would be apt to laugh and say, "Keep walking Dearie; I'll just ride. Don't you wish you could?" I would usually threaten to drag her out of the car and make her walk the next segment, but she never seemed too worried.

Thanks to plenty of clouds it stayed cool that day, thus contributing to my making good time. It had been getting so hot by midafternoons that we had begun thinking about starting the day's walks around 4 a.m. That way, we could quit about noon, before the hottest part of the day, and still cover maybe twenty miles. We had not done that yet, and we wouldn't during the remainder of the summer, but the following year, in the Idaho deserts, starting early and quitting early would be necessary in order to avoid the blazing heat.

By five that afternoon we had got in a respectable twenty-eight miles, and my knee was still feeling fine.

BUT MORE KNEE TROUBLE

It was when I was walking south of Cullom, Illinois, that I began daydreaming about a motorcycle trip that had taken me through the town many years before. I was on my way to the West Coast, and Helen was to fly out and meet me in San Francisco, where we would take a ten-day vacation.

I refueled in Cullom and everything was fine as I left town, but seven miles farther west the gas tank sprang a leak. As quickly as possible I pulled off the road, leaned the bike on its kickstand, and scampered a few steps away. Already there was a wet spot of gasoline on my left pant leg near the knee.

A couple of minutes later it was obvious that if there had been a fire in the offing, it would have already begun, for by then the muffler and exhaust pipe were cooling. So I stepped forward, before more gas could leak away, and put my finger over a new-sprung pinhole near the bottom of the tank.

Standing there, it struck me as ironic that I could diagnose any electrical problem the bike might have and replace any component that might have failed. I had the spare parts. Also, I could remove, clean, and reassemble the carburetors if I had to. I could repair a punctured tire; I had tire plugs and knew how to use them. I even had a spare tube and a heavy rubber boot to put inside a tire, in case it were somehow torn. A number of long, lone rides, including ones through Canada, Alaska, California, and the southern U.S. had prepared me to be ready for almost any mechanical or electrical problem. But there I stood on an Illinois farm road with a finger on a gas-tank leak and no chewing gum to plug the hole—as if gum would work, which of course it would not.

In the next few minutes I worked out a plan: Keeping a finger on the leak, I would ride into Pontiac which was fifteen miles ahead. Approaching town, hopefully I would come to a motorcycle dealership that could help; if not, I would stop at the first hardware store and lay the bike on its side—the side opposite the leak. That way no more gas would leak out. Then I would rush in and buy a funnel, a bucket, and a tube of epoxy filler. With the bike still on its side, I would take off the tank, pour the gas into the bucket, and patch the leak with epoxy. With a bit of luck I would be back on the road in a couple of hours.

It was a good thing no cop saw me riding into Pontiac that afternoon, because I was twisted like a pretzel, my left arm stretched way down between bike and leg, my finger just barely covering the leak. Worse, a motorcycle's clutch is on the left handlebar, so every shift of gears required a tricky maneuver in which I would bring up my hand, work the clutch, and then grope with my finger to re-cover the leak. Every time I shifted, gas would jet out, and I had a well-soaked pant leg by the time I came to a motorcycle dealership just east of town.

Now, it happened that a young man with a pickup truck pulled into the dealership the same time I did. I gestured for him to come over, and as I sat there, finger on leak, I asked him to go inside and try to get me some help. Minutes later he came out with somebody from the service department, but that worthy took one look at me with the gas-soaked leg, muttered an apologetic "sorry, can't help you," and disappeared back inside.

Disappointed with that response, I asked the young man for directions to a hardware store, but he briefly ignored the question and stood there seemingly thinking. "Tell you what," he finally said. "My brother-in-law's got a little automotive shop. Maybe he could solder your tank. How 'bout you follow me and I'll lead you over there?"

Just his offer was a big morale boost, and I was quick to accept. A short ride brought us to a small garage where Byron (I soon learned his name) went in and got his brother-in-law, who came out with two other men. They walked over with smiling faces, and I had no more than begun my tale of woe than one went back inside and brought out a bucket to hold gasoline. He replaced me as finger-on-leak man, and for the first time in an hour, I had no "pressing" use for my left index finger—which by then was so soaked with gasoline I was sure it would eventually fall off.

With my hands freed up, I had the tank off in a couple of minutes; then somebody poured the remaining gas into the bucket and took it inside.

I got fresh pants and socks out of a saddlebag and went into the garage to wash my hands and leg with soap and water at an old sink back there. When I came out, to my surprise, Byron was still there talking to the garage men. Brother-in-law told me he could not fix the tank, but that he had a buddy on the other side of town who had a radiator repair business. "Buddy" did lots of soldering and he could definitely do the job. Furthermore, Byron would drive me over, wait until it was finished, and then bring me back.

So off we went, the gas tank bouncing around in the back of the pickup and the motorcycle being wheeled into the garage, where everyone agreed it would be safer than if left outside.

Things went so smoothly at the radiator shop that in less than two hours we were able to leave and return to brother-in-law's with the soldered tank. Ten minutes after that, I had the motorcycle together again with the remaining gas poured back into its now-fixed tank. I was ready to go.

Talk about getting out of a bind quick and cheap!

The fellow who soldered the tank would take only fifteen dollars for the job, and Byron wouldn't take a dime, although I pressed him hard to accept something—anything. Neither would brother-in-law nor his crew, who had been so helpful.

After all of those kindnesses, I was in a love-for-humanity mood as I said goodbye to my benefactors and rode away. Of course by then it was late afternoon, and having had enough for one day, I determined to put in at the first motel I could find. And what a place I stumbled onto! Borderline dirty and with paper-thin walls, it fronted a large parking lot that also served a number of other lowbrow businesses, including a sleazy nightclub. The cleanliness of my room, i.e., the cleanliness of sheets, rug, and bathroom floor, suggested I douse myself with flea powder, and I would have if I'd had some, although I saw no vermin other than flies.

There might have been a symbioses between the nightclub and the motel, because the room next to mine was rented twice that night for ninety-minute sessions of groaning, giggling, and erotic push-ups that rocked the bed with squeaks and thumps. The racket was impossible to ignore; in fact it became so funny at one point that I accidentally laughed out loud. Hearing me, the loving couple instantly froze, but minutes later they were at it again in a reckless abandon that swept them to a climax of squeals and gasps and drawn-out moans.

Sometime before dawn I gave up trying to sleep, took a shower, and went out and had breakfast at an all-night café a block down the street. Then it was back on the motorcycle for another leg of the long ride to California.

And that's when my daydream ended—as the motorcycle faded from under me and I was walking again, in the present and somewhere southwest of Cullom, Illinois.

Helen and I finished the day at a dusty crossroads about four o'clock. We had tallied another twenty-eight miles, but my knee was hurting again, more than ever. Nevertheless, I was determined to continue the walk if the pain would just let up. And it did— at least enough that I was back on the road by eight the next morning and entering Pontiac by eleven.

$$*\quad *\quad *\quad *$$

I had long been aware of Pontiac, Michigan, but had only known about Pontiac, Illinois, since the day of the leaking motorcycle. I assumed, of course, that both towns had been named after the Ottawa Indian chief, and a year later, after we had finished the cross-America walk, I looked into the towns' names.

As expected, Pontiac, Illinois (founded 1837), like Pontiac, Michigan (founded 1818), was indeed named after the legendary chief, who had been a fearful figure on the frontier in the early 1760s. After participating by some accounts in the defeat of Braddock at Fort Duquesne in 1755 (Washington was there), he went on to organize resistance to the British throughout the rest of the decade. His influence grew to where he was able to send emissaries to most tribes from Lake Superior to the lower Mississippi Valley, and ensuing diplomacy resulted in the most united Indian front to white expansion heretofore seen on the continent. In 1762, when the Peace of Paris ended the French and Indian War, the way was open for further western settlement by permitting Colonials to build and occupy western forts. In response, Pontiac led the combined tribes in what came to be called the Pontiac Conspiracy or Pontiac's War.

Focal points of the conflict were a dozen or so fortified posts in the Great Lakes area, including Fort Edward at present day Green Bay, Wisconsin; Forts St. Joseph, Michilimackinac, and Detroit in Michigan; Fort Sandusky at Sandusky, Ohio; Forts Presque Isle, Venango, and Pitt in Pennsylvania; and Forts Schlosser and Niagara in present day western New York. Other fortified posts were Pelee and LeBoeuf, both in Ontario.

Most of the forts fell to lightning Indian attacks during the summer of 1763, and in at least one case an entire garrison was massacred. However a few forts did hold out, in particular Fort Detroit, and after a six month siege, support by the allied tribes for Pontiac's cause began to wane. Peace was re-established in 1765 after two more years of sporadic hostilities, but by then the Indians had failed once again to halt the inexorable advance of the white man.

But why, I asked myself, had settlers chosen twice to name towns after an Indian who had terrorized the entire frontier sixty years before? Was it Pontiac's leadership skills in assembling the Indian coalition that engendered the respect of a later generation of whites? Surely it was not his bloody albeit spectacular generalship. There are other examples of this curious popularity that can accrue to military leaders of defeated enemies, after a war in which they loom as threats but are admired for their skill and character. Several Civil War generals come to mind as well as others, like the German, Erwin Rommel.

Nevertheless, it remains strange to me that white settlers would admire Pontiac enough to name towns after him. And it is stranger still that the Oakland Motor Car Company of Pontiac, Michigan, when merging with General Motors in 1909, chose to rename its car line Pontiac, and to assume for its logo the profile of an Indian who had fought the white man a brutal war.

*   *   *   *

That afternoon, as I walked west from Pontiac, I noted how different bird behavior had become, as compared to how it had been a few months before. Back then, aside from families of ducks, I saw mainly adults birds—usually blackbirds, swallows, and killdeer. The blackbirds would often fly just above me, almost at a hover, while the swallows would peel off and buzz by only a few feet overhead. Killdeers would land in the road and run half dozen yards before taking off again. It seemed likely that all three species were trying to warn me away from their roadside nests and young.

But things had changed. There were still plenty of blackbirds and swallows, but they no longer bothered to harass me. Perhaps the young had hatched and matured to where their defense was no long a concern of their elders. As for the killdeer, I was seeing whole families trooping along the edge of the road, mom in the lead, chicks trailed out behind. Upon my approach to these processions, the birds would typically stay together until I was almost to them; then they would break into darting confusion before disappearing into roadside weeds. Helen was forever worrying that she might run over one of those "darling little creatures" with the car.

But thoughts about history and birds aside, that day, Wednesday, June 30, was truly a prolonged ache in the knee, and although we didn't know it yet, it would be our last walking day until mid-September. I caught up with Helen about half past four and took a picture of her in the shade of a two-story corncrib. She leans on the car with her right hand just above the driver's door, and she is

We'll Soon be Heading Home

looking toward the east. Maybe she subconsciously knows that we are about to head home. Even so, our spoken plan that afternoon was to move Lurch still farther west, rest a day, and then continue the walk. And the following morning, still unaware that walking was temporarily over, we moved Lurch sixty-five miles to Hickory Hill Campground near El Paso, Illinois.

We spent an enjoyable afternoon exploring and driving around town—past Jefferson Park, past Franklin Park, and finally down town to Front Street. It was easy to find where the east-west tracks of the Toledo, Peoria and Western intersect the abandoned right-of-way of the Illinois Central. Of course the town grew up around the railroad junction, and on Front Street there is an old railroad hotel where Ulysses Grant once spoke while running for president in 1872.

That evening, as we sat down for dinner at The Elms Restaurant near the center of town, I mused to Helen: "*El Paso*. That's Spanish for *the pass*, isn't it?"

"Yes, but where's the pass?" she replied. "There are no mountains within hundreds of miles. How do you suppose they came up with that name?"

Earlier in the day while touring the historic district, we had learned that Mexicans by the hundreds had come to the area to work on railroad construction. "But Mexicans? El Paso, Illinois? El Paso, Texas?" I wondered aloud if there could be a connection.

"It can't be what you're thinking," Helen declared. "It might have been Mexican muscle that built the railroads, but no way could they have been influential enough to have anything to do with naming this town—even if they did come from El Paso, Texas!"

Dinner came and we busied ourselves eating, yet if the walls could have talked, they may have told us all about El Paso, how it was started and how it got its name. For The Elms, where we sat eating, was once the home of George Gibson, who with his partner, James Wathen, actually founded the town.

The year was 1852, and Gibson and Wathen, two thirty-something businessmen, had picked up three hundred and twenty acres of unclaimed land lying twenty-six miles east of Peoria. The land straddled the newly built, north-south tracks of the Illinois Central Railroad, and the partners bought it from the government on a tip that a brand-new railroad, the Peoria and Oquawka (P&O), intended to lay tracks from Peoria east toward Indiana.

Sensing a business coup, the partners immediately offered P&O free right-of-way over their land. All the railroad would have to do was lay its tracks just a little north of where it intended to run them anyway. Knowing a good deal when they saw it, the company quickly accepted, and thus the junction of the Illinois Central and the Peoria and Oquawka railroads was built entirely within the partners' land. Overnight it changed from low-value, prairie acreage to high-value, near-junction building lots, on which would quickly rise the town of El Paso. The young men prospered, and Gibson built and lived in The Elms, the fine house-turned-restaurant in which Helen and I sat wondering about the town's name. And indeed, the town's name *is* the rest of the story.

It developed that each founding partner as well as George Bester, chairman of P&O, wanted the town named after himself. George even offered the founders 250 dollars if they would name the town Bester. The partners declined however—Wathen wanting Wathener, Gibson wanting Gibson City. In a draw of straws Gibson won the right to pick a *neutral* name, and he chose El Paso.

But why El Paso? It is hard to know. Gibson had passed through El Paso, Texas, on his way home from the California Gold Rush, but of course he passed through dozens of other towns as well. Maybe he just liked the sound of the name, or maybe something special happened to him there. Then too, maybe he was just tired of the drug-out task of picking a name. Maybe he just flipped a coin and El Paso came to mind....

Sometime near the end of dinner, as we sat there in Gibson's one-time parlor, I announced that we would have to suspend the great walk and go home to Connecticut. Much as I hated giving in, fears for the knee finally outweighed compulsions to go on. Helen agreed it was the sensible thing to do. The decision had been a long time coming, for the pain would wax and wane: one day I would be happy to keep going, another I'd be ready to quit.

This particular day the knee had hurt badly, and I had to admit that trend-wise, the problem was becoming worse. So the next morning, even if it felt better, we would start the long drive home. Once there, I would have it examined by MRI and find out if there really was something seriously wrong.

My resolve was not tested the following morning, because it hurt so bad I couldn't walk without limping.

We had decamped and were heading east by ten o'clock.

SECTION III

El Paso, Illinois, to Hastings, Nebraska

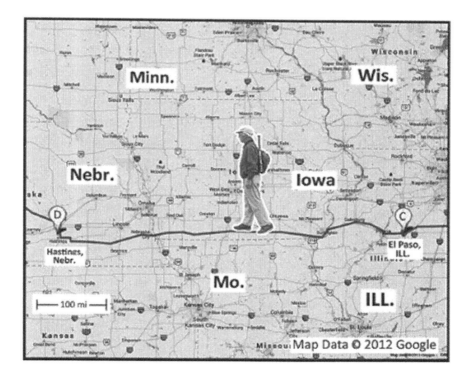

Third Walk Segment: September 5 Until October 22, 1999

RETURNING TO ILLINOIS

Back home, Helen and I spent the hot months of July and August doing home projects rather than volunteer work, which can be hard to disengage from once you become involved. Of course our big concern was getting my knee checked to find out why it had hurt so much when I was walking.

A late July examination including an MRI gave reassuring results. The doctor said the knee did indeed show some "wear and tear," that it was clear I had not lived a "sedentary life," but that lucky for me, there was neither arthritis nor torn cartilage. However, he pretended to think Helen and I were a bit eccentric. Can't imagine why.

The news that there was nothing obviously wrong with the knee was a welcome relief, but it did not answer the question of why it had hurt so much to begin with. Although the good doctor could give no definite answer, we began to suspect the pricey walking shoes I'd been wearing. Their heels were only an inch thick, and I often thought they didn't absorb much shock.

So began a search that introduced us to the current brands of *gotta-have* shoes—the trendy kinds you're supposed to wear if you *wanna-be* in style. One fresh-faced clerk warned me to stay away from "entry-level" shoes if I planned to do "serious walking."

"How much is 'serious walking'?" I asked.

"Some people," he said, proud to report what real people do, "walk as many as five or six miles a day!"

Several types of shoes looked as if they would be okay, but they cost up to a hundred dollars a pair. I had already spent sixty-some each for the three pairs I bought in Binghamton, New York, when we visited the Herrmanns. Why not try something less expensive?

"How about Wal-Mart?" Helen suggested. "Their shoes are reasonable."

So off we went to Wal-Mart's where we found a pair of Dr. Scholl's shoes with special shock absorbers built into soft heels that were fully an inch and a half thick. The shock absorbers were flat pads containing some kind of soft material, much like similar pads in the cool, high-priced shoes. In addition, instead of laces, these shoes had Velcro straps, which are a real convenience (easy off, easy on) when you have a stone digging into a foot. Of course you often pick up stones when you walk gravel roads.

The Dr. Scholl's shoes looked just right, and the price was right too—only twenty-six dollars a pair. I bought a pair size nine and a half, which was perfect for my left foot and only a half size too big for my right. But a slightly loose shoe is not much of a problem. After a few blisters your skin toughens and you hardly notice the rubbing; anyway, I was in no mood to buy two pairs a half size different just to get a perfect fit for both feet. Later though, at a Wal-Mart in the West, I would do exactly that, convinced by then that this particular brand and type was the best I would get for "serious walking."

*   *   *   *

With the knee checked out, new shoes, and plenty of enthusiasm, Helen and I left home on September 9 and headed back to El Paso, Illinois, and nearby Hickory Hill Campground, where we had called off walking, the last day of June.

Arriving there three days later, we quickly parked Lurch and then drove back to the lonely corncrib near Flanagan where the walk track actually ended. Just to be sure there would be no gap, Helen dropped me off a hundred yards east of our old stopping place. Then, gravel flying, she literally dug out down the road heading west, almost as if her flying start would hustle me along faster.

I caught up with her four and a half miles farther along in the next county, and for some reason that first day back, we felt that merely crossing a county line was something special. What a high we were on! We joked around and speculated about how far we would get before cold weather—surely we would reach the halfway point, the middle of Nebraska, by late October. I almost did more walking that afternoon, but it was getting late, and in our rush to get back on the road we had parked the motor home without leveling it or even connecting the electricity."Best we get back and finish setting up before dark," Helen said. "We'll get an early start tomorrow."

Come morning, we were still full of excitement and eager to go. Of course the terrain was unchanged from two months before; it was still a flat patchwork of cornfields and beanfields within the usual grid of farm roads. But colors were noticeably different. The weeks we had been home spanned the end of the growing season; it was nearing harvest time; the ubiquitous greenness had faded, and there were hints of amber in the crops and in the weeds along the road.

Once, toward the middle of the afternoon, I turned around, and walking backwards for a few paces, I gazed out over the vast landscape. Far off was an approaching eighteen-wheeler, its dust cloud rising tens of feet before drifting off towards the north. It slowly grew larger, and when it was still some distance away, I crossed to the south side of the road in order to avoid the dust. Minutes later the monster pulled alongside, and its grinning driver called down a cheery "Good afternoon."

"Good afternoon yourself," I said and smiled.

"I'm on my way to Chillicothe, over on the Illinois River. Give you a lift?" He was fair complexioned, sandy haired, and very neat. His truck was neat too—spotless except for a thin coat of dust.

"Thanks but no thanks. My next town is Metamora. From there I'll walk on down to the river at Peoria—not that I'll get that far today. Should get there tomorrow sometime."

"Do you have any idea," he exclaimed, "how far it is from here to Metamora? If you don't, I can tell you. It's fourteen miles!"

So I told him about the great walk, and obliging me with surprise and congratulations, he climbed down from his huge truck to shake hands. He was full of questions as I sketched how we had begun walking in the fall of '98, had continued the past spring, and how we had taken off because of my sore knee. I concluded with, "We started in again just yesterday, and hope to get to the middle of Nebraska by late October."

He became thoughtful for a moment, and then said, "I wish you'd do something for me. Down here on your left about three miles is a little schoolhouse, and I happen to be on the school board. Now, would you mind stopping there and telling the kids what you're doing? I think it would be good for 'em to hear your story if you don't mind takin' the time."

I told him I would be glad to—but how? I didn't know if it would work for me just to walk up, knock on the schoolhouse door and say, "Hello, I'm John Beam. I'm walking across the United States and maybe you'd like to hear all about it."

"Nah," he said, "don't worry. I'm gonna to be passing that way; I'll stop and let 'em know you're coming."

"Sounds good," I allowed. "But I hope you're right about the kids being interested in an old man's crazy walk."

"They will be," he replied with a laugh.

We shook hands again, and soon the truck was growing smaller and smaller as it moved west—a diminishing image eventually hidden by its own churned-up dust.

I walked on then, wondering what in the world I, a product of the East and sixty-seven years old, could possibly say to a group of Illinois farm kids, who, he had told me, ranged in age from seven to fourteen.

An hour passed before I began to make out a small, white building standing by itself in a sea of corn, and as I came closer, the image sharpened into a one-story schoolhouse. The front door was in a gable-end beneath a low porch facing the road, and the far roofline supported a small steeple which made me wonder if the place doubled as a church on Sundays. Several trees graced a playground which had swings, a ball diamond, fifteen or twenty children, and a tire that hung on a rope from a high wooden frame. The place looked austere except for the kids, who, as I came up, bounded over with smiles and hellos that would have made anyone feel welcome.

The biggest girl tried to introduce herself, but I smiled and politely put her off while scanning the schoolyard and looking toward the front door, expecting the teacher to appear any moment. Twice more the girl tried to get my attention by saying "Sir" and tugging at my sleeve, and only on her fourth try did I realized she was not a girl at all, but rather a young woman, indeed, she was "Ms. Schoolmarm" herself!

Petite, pretty, and obviously in her early twenties, she laughed good-naturedly at my blunder. I had been expected, of course, and after we introduced ourselves, she introduced me to the children.

Then, formalities behind, I began to talk.

"Well," I ventured, "I see the gentleman with the truck stopped and told you I was coming … ah … and I suppose you want to hear all about the different places I've been, how far I walk in a day, when I started, where I stay at night … ah … all sorts of things like that. Right?"

"Yes," came murmured replies and shy nods of heads. So with teacher's encouragement I plunged ahead.

"Have any of you kids ever been to the East Coast?" I asked. None had. "How about the West Coast, anybody been there?" Again, nobody had. "Well," I said, "who's been farthest from home and where'd you go? Hold up your hand. Let me see."

Mennonite Schoolhouse

One little girl had been to Colorado with her family. Few of the others had been very far, and that seemed to include the teacher. Nevertheless, I went on to tell them how Helen and I had left from home the year before and how we managed to walk to the Hudson River in New York by late November. Clearly, for them New York was as distant as China; even so, as I described the continuing walk across Pennsylvania, Ohio and Indiana, their expressions ranged from fascination to amazement.

One little girl was especially charmed when I talked about the carousel museum Helen and I had visited in Connecticut, and moments later, when I mentioned my annoyance with loud motorcycles, a boy asked a number of questions about them. He pretended to match my disapproval with disapproval of his own. I almost laughed. He was fascinated by motorcycles—especially loud ones— and clearly dreamed of owning one himself someday. (Later, I realized it would probably be taboo in his culture.) But overall, the kids were a smiling, sharp group, the kind anybody would enjoy talking to. More questions included "Any problems with dogs?" "How far can you walk in a day?" and "Where do you stay at night?"

I cautioned the children to avoid, as they grew older, the traps of smoking and drugs, and to be careful with alcohol. Some of them seemed to wince at mention of those worldly vices, but they remained polite and friendly. So I rushed on, telling them about all the opportunities available to young people in modern America. I reminded them that besides farming, which I assured them had my deepest respect, there were a hundred other occupations they could aspire to—like medicine, law, business. "And you girls: Listen up! You can reach for those jobs too. When I was kid, about the only careers open to women were nursing, teaching, and secretarial work. Things are different now. There are even women pilots!"

Here, the teacher, who had begun to appear a bit pained, spoke up and told me that Jimmy, who stood nearby, wanted to fly airplanes.

"Jimmy," I said, addressing a clear-eyed boy of maybe twelve, "if that's what you want, then be sure to take all the math and science courses you can as you go through school, because those in particular underlie the study of navigation and flight. If you can, learn to fly locally when you're seventeen or eighteen, or whenever you're old enough to get a license. Do school sports too, and be broad in your extracurricular activities."

I remembered that admission to West Point began with nomination by a member of congress, and I assumed it would be the same for the Air Force Academy. In any case, I told him to check that out because it was my understanding that many commercial pilots were former air force pilots. "And be sure and register to vote," I said, "when you turn eighteen."

I was on a roll.

Jimmy was a quite formal person, and he was forthright in asking a series of pertinent questions. When we paused, minutes later, he surprised me by initiating a handshake with the words, "Sir, I want to thank you for this … sounds helpful." As our palms touched and before I could firm my grip, he squeezed my hand in a positive way, and moments later, with a distinct release, he, not I, concluded the handshake. It was more as if he shook hands with me rather than we shook hands mutually. *This kid,* I thought to myself, *is the kind that naturally takes charge.*

Eventually, a few children began drifting away toward the ball field, and eager to get a group picture, I got out my camera and asked the teacher if it would be okay. This clearly made her and the remaining children uneasy. They did not want to flatly tell me "no," but neither did they want me to just start snapping away. Less yet were they inclined to pose.

Finally, it dawned on me that my audience were Mennonites. I had been aware that the teacher's clothes were slightly different from what you would expect in an ordinary suburban middle school. Still, this was farm country, and her long skirt and flowered blouse, together with the children's neat, everyday farm clothes, were hardly enough to alert me that they were not simply rural, public-school children. I should have been more perceptive.

For long moments they conferred about having their picture taken; then, clearly uncomfortable, the teacher told me it would be wrong for them to pose. I quickly apologized for putting them on the spot, and they were quick to accept.

Mutually relieved to be past the awkwardness, we talked for several more minutes. They told me that for them formal education normally ended with the eighth grade, but after that some children took advanced courses by correspondence, usually in agriculture. Of course their education is geared to the needs of their rural culture and the farming industry.

All too soon it was time to leave, but as we said good-byes and I was turning to go, Jimmy, the would-be pilot, again took my hand and shook it while thanking me for my advice about a flying career.

He'll succeed, I thought, as I walked away, if not as a pilot then in some other endeavor—indeed—whatever he chooses. Jimmy reminded me of the boy I had met three months before near Nicklin, Pa., the boy with the mechanically perfect bike and the ambition to become an engineer.

But exactly what kind of Mennonites are those people? I wondered as I walked along. I was beginning to realize there are many versions of Mennonitism, varying widely in religious doctrine and visible lifestyle. The most conservative (and most visible) groups speak German, drive horse and buggies, fasten their clothes with hooks and eyes, and participate no more than necessary in the community without. In these groups, which include the Amish, men wear beards, and a primitive Christian doctrine is enforced with the most heartless of all punishments— shunning, a.k.a. *the silent treatment*. The least conservative hardly differ in doctrine and lifestyle from conventional Protestants except they do not participate in military service. These folk embrace all occupations and interact seamlessly with mainstream society. Between the two extremes, conservative to liberal, old order to modern, are dozens of subgroups born of endless schisms, much like Protestantism itself.

But why, I thought, didn't I just ask the teacher what her Mennonite group was called and where it fit in with other more, or less, conservative groups? Often, after meeting people and talking to them, I would think of questions I *should* have asked.

WE SKIP THE ILLINOIS RIVER BRIDGE

We had heard that a famous old courthouse in which Lincoln practiced law was located in Metamora, Illinois. Evidently this and several other courthouses where he practiced have been preserved or restored, and are listed in the National Registry of Historic Places. Since our intended track would take us through town en route to Peoria, we decided to stop and visit the courthouse, if it was within a few blocks of where I would be walking.

However, when I got to Metamora the following morning and talked with Helen at the corner of Niles and Mount Vernon Streets, neither of us wanted to digress from the walk for even an hour. The urgency bug was biting again. After all, it was already mid-September, and fully eleven months had passed since we started from home the year before. We had come nine hundred miles, which sounded like a lot but was actually less than a third of the way across the country. We would have to keep moving, we agreed, if we were to get to Nebraska before November. So I walked right through Metamora without even inquiring where the courthouse was, although we later learned it was only a block or two north from where we stood and talked.

Southwest of town I was soon passing the usual fields of corn and beans while getting a workout stepping around potholes and heaped gravel on the unusually rough road. Eventually my thoughts drifted to the Mennonite schoolchildren of the day before. *How briefly kids are young,* I mused, *so quickly they pass through adolescence to young adulthood, while gradually receding from their families in distance and outlook. Ultimately, they relate to their parents in ways that range from less than acquaintances to more than friends. But you, John Beam, can count yourself lucky; fate smiled on you and Helen. Your family remains as close as can be. True enough,* my pleasant thoughts continued, but then they took an unhappy turn: *Fate may have smiled on you, Beam, but she certainly didn't smile on the Cowdright or DeArros families.*

Art Cowdright and Jean DeArros were old friends, and in their families parent-child bonds stretched and finally parted, leading into years of unhappy estrangement for parents and children alike. The memory sobered me until I determinedly took charge of myself, and I was getting out the camera when I reached U.S. 24 east of Peoria. After turning left, I took two or three pictures before meeting Helen where she was waiting near an abandoned nursery. We ate a quiet, almost pensive lunch (Helen too seemed subdued—anticlimax after yesterday's high?) and then it was back to the road for the afternoon walk.

*   *   *   *

McClugage Bridge, which crosses the Illinois River in north Peoria, is really two side-by-side spans where the northern span has three lanes and the southern two. I met Helen at the eastern approach about four o'clock, and standing by the car, we could see that for me to walk the bridge would be about as sensible as walking a runway at JFK. The southern lanes were closed for construction, and the three northern lanes, carrying all the traffic, were only about forty feet wide. Were I to cross during next morning's rush, cars would be whipping by only five feet away—much too close for comfort!

"You're going to have to skip this bridge," Helen suddenly declared. "We want this walk to be unbroken, but your risking suicide's no go. We'll come this way when we're returning east. Walk it then, if construction's finished and the lanes are open. I don't want you run over. End of discussion! ... *Period!"*

"Hear you, Boss Lady," I answered, and then made some noises about leaving options open till we saw how traffic was the next morning. But I could tell that for the time being there would be no point arguing. Helen is rarely so firm, more rarely so blunt.

The next morning, extremely heavy traffic put walking the bridge out of the question. We would skip it and pick up the walk from the other side, i.e., from the western approach. But even there, there was hardly a safe place for Helen to stop the car and let me off. Eventually, she swerved onto a small grassy area among a tangle of off-ramps, where she paused, I jumped out, and she roared away.

From McClugage I followed the highway up a steep hill away from the river. Fortunately, a sidewalk on the north side made for safe walking, and there were interesting views. The ground in places dropped off into undeveloped ravines and hillocks— welcome patches of green in otherwise urban Peoria. Near the top, I passed an attractive residential area with streets named Harvard, Cornell, Princeton, and Purdue. Three Ivy League and one Hoosier! And in Peoria, Illinois, of all places!

An hour later, I caught up with Helen where she had parked in a convenience store lot on War Memorial Drive. Cars, trucks and motorcycles, moving and parked, were so thick we nearly missed each other. Indeed, we probably would have if she hadn't stationed herself on the sidewalk and yelled as I was passing on the other side of the street. Then, foolishly, we stood by the car and drank coffee, even as we agreed we hardly needed it. Wired already, the coffee would only wind us up more.

But the morning, which began with much tension, soon turned peaceful as I turned onto Sheridan Road and walked north under a deep-blue sky. On my left passed the wide grounds of the Lakeview Museum of Art; then, on my right, Proctor Hospital and the Leo Donovan Golf Course. A jog, first west then north, put me on University Street, and soon I was passing Exposition Gardens.

Land development changed along University Street as I continued out of town. Large institutions (hospitals, community colleges, etc.) ended, and small businesses (welding shops, garages, cement plants) began, and these, in turn, became increasingly separated by vacant lots as I walked on toward the first of the farms.

Helen was waiting near a grain elevator beside a spur of the Chicago Rock Island Railroad. It was lunchtime, and lunchmeat sandwiches washed down with soft drink still tasted fairly good.

It would not be long, however, when thoroughly sick of cola and sandwiches, we would pack bite-sized pieces of chicken, beef or pork, and water would become our drink of choice.

That afternoon Helen repeatedly became confused while trying to find roads and crossroads that were labeled one thing on the map but something else by county or township road signs. The computer program frequently gave more than one name for a road, and Helen would look for corresponding signs, but with no luck. Worst yet, there would be a road here or there that would not show up on the map at all.

Overall, it was a difficult afternoon for Helen, and some of her frustration spread to me. She would drive off toward the west, and I would expect to meet her in eight or ten miles, but invariably, maybe a half hour later, she would reappear up ahead—coming back. I would know then that we were about to have another discussion trying to figure out where we were and where we were going. Navigation problems had been infrequent before this; all the way from Connecticut the map program had most of the time been quite reliable. Things would get better farther west, but for a few more days we would battle these nagging confusions.

Toward five o'clock we came to the only campground for horses that we would see during the entire trip. It was in the James Spurgeon State Park twenty miles northwest of Peoria, and it was indeed an interesting place. Such campgrounds make plenty of sense. After all, if you're traveling long distances with a horse, you have to find some place to put *him* or *her* at night—unless you can sneak *her* or *him* into your motel room like people do with dogs and cats. Besides, *Mr.* or *Ms.* Horse needs to get out of *her* or *his* trailer now and then, just as people need to get out of their cars. So if you are ever traveling near Peoria and need a place to put your horse for the night, I would definitely recommend the Spurgeon campground rather than a motel room—easier to get *him* or *her* (or *her* or *him*), in to and out of.

Once more I frolic with gender and style.

Anyway, people use different rigs when traveling long distances with horses. As we walked through the campground, we saw men with large horse trailers which they pulled behind powerful pickup trucks. Three youngish couples had small motor homes, and they were using much smaller trailers, the one-horse size. There was even a custom-built monster that was essentially a motor home in the front and a three-place horse stall in the back—all on the same chassis. The owners told us they kept their kids back there when they weren't hauling horses, but we didn't believe them.

Several women were walking horses the way people usually walk their dogs, and one woman was walking a horse and a dog at the same time—leash in one hand, bridle in the other. Twice, the dog, a lively little mutt, crossed over and got his leash tangled between the horse's front legs, but both times the patient horse merely stopped while the woman sorted things out. The third time, mom lost patience and picked the dog up, whereupon Mr. Horse nuzzled him and received a lick on the nose in return. Helen and I watched—fascinated, amused.

So our brief visit to Spurgeon Park was a gratifying break. It had been a long, hard day, and wandering through that unusual place lightened our spirits, as we talked to friendly people and a lively colt named Matilda.

That evening we ate at Delaney's, a new restaurant on the west side of El Paso. We had ordered and were sitting quietly when Helen suddenly said, "Phil, your knee—" whereupon I interrupted with "doesn't hurt anymore."

"That's exactly what I was going to say," she exclaimed as we both laughed. Indeed we were pleased. My going lame had loomed as a threatening showstopper ever since we had given up walking and gone home in July. But now we were back, and I had walked three consecutive days with no knee problems at all. Maybe it was the new walking shoes; maybe it was the muscle rub I was lathering on each morning, or maybe it was both. Whatever the reason, the pain was gone, and although we didn't know it then, I would have no further knee trouble all the way to the West Coast.

We were eating dessert when I drew a wonderful response from Helen by declaring we would break camp and move Lurch to

Galesburg, Illinois, that very evening. "After all," I said, "walk's end is already well beyond where we're camped, and another day's hike will leave us a seventy-five-mile drive home in the evening. Too far. We'll move tonight."

"Great idea, Honey! You'll be driving Lurch and I'll be asleep in the back. By the time we get there and get parked, the sun will be up and you'll be all ready for another twenty-five mile walk. No use wastin' time sleeping—you won't even have to change your clothes. You can even skip breakfast."

Buzzing along, she happily picked up on my "break camp," by saying the expression suggested preparations like pulling up tent pegs. "Phil, Lurch compares no more to a tent than a motel does, and we don't say we 'break camp' when we move out of a motel. And certainly we never do it in the deep, dark, middle of the night, now do we, m'Love? By the way, how are you going to get the car to Galesburg if I'm asleep in the back of Lurch?"

Then she finally took a breath.

"Helen," I came back, "you shouldn't be so timid about speakin' your mind. Think we oughtta wait till tomorrow to move?"

*　　*　　*　　*

We were up early the next morning, intending to complete the move to Galesburg by midmorning, but it didn't work out that way. First, we drove into El Paso and did a wash; then later we made an unplanned stop in Eureka, Illinois, after only a half hour on the road. President Reagan's alma mater, Eureka College, is there, and suddenly interested, we wondered if they would have memorabilia of their famous alumnus.

Of course they do. The college keeps a large collection of pictures and mementos from the President's life. He attended college on scholarships, majored in economics, and was head of the student body. Active in sports, he played football and was captain of the swim team.

The collection, which is housed in dedicated rooms, covers not only the President's college life. but also his early careers as sportscaster and actor prior to his emergence in California politics and eventually on the national scene. The whole time we were browsing the collection, first Helen and then I would declare that we just had to get moving. We would agree but invariably linger on, and fifteen minutes later one of us would again announce the importance of getting back on the road. Eventually, sometime after twelve, I said, "You know, Helen, there's no use leaving here till we've had something to eat."

We had noticed an adjacent student area with a small lounge and a galley, so we went there and had grilled ham and cheese sandwiches. That set us back another three quarters of an hour until finally, about two o'clock, I climbed into Lurch, Helen got into the Toyota, and after the usual radio check, we once again continued west.

We settled down that evening at Holiday Campground, which is just east of Galesburg and about fifty miles west of Peoria. Our plan was to take the next day off—really off. We would stay at the campground, lay around, be bored, and get rested up. Truth was that of the preceding eight days, we had spent three and a half driving out from the East, three and a half walking, and this day moving Lurch. We were tired out and determined to take a rest.

But come morning, predictably, we both felt better, and before long I wanted to head for town.

Helen challanged: "What about our resolution to rest today?"

"Look," I said, "the only resolution we really have to keep is the one we tacitly made never to give up on this walk. We'll keep that resolution; we'll be on the road again tomorrow. But this business about resting today is like a New Year's resolution—meant when made, kinda, but not to be taken too seriously. Anyway, Galesburg's a good-sized town. Let's go have a look."

Helen began to show some interest, but not quickly. She knew that Knox College, which is in Galesburg, had been the scene of the Lincoln-Douglas Debates, and also that it was attended by the poets Carl Sandburg and Edgar Lee Masters—the latter a favorite of hers and author of the *Spoon River Anthology*. East of Galesburg we had crossed the Spoon River, which flows southeast and passes only a few miles from Lewistown where Masters lived as a child. Somehow, seeing the river stirred Helen's interest, and now she was saying she might like to visit the college. She was poky, though, about getting started, and soon she was musing about the anthology. "I wonder," she murmured, "why Masters named his town Spoon River … you know, the town with the graveyard full of ghosts."

"Who knows," I grumbled. "He was here, the river was nearby, he needed a name for his town. Let's go or we'll be here all day." It crossed my mind that Masters probably had good reasons for naming his fictitious town Spoon River, but it might be that he never told anybody what they were.

We never did visit Knox College, but we did have a good time. Galesburg is a commercial and distribution center for the surrounding agricultural region, but beyond that it's a great place for downtown sightseeing. Helen's diary gives the flavor of our touristy day:

Beautiful historic district. Had coffee and cinnamon rolls at a bakery. Looked at guns, antique and modern. Gawked at a steam locomotive that's part of a train museum; wish the museum wasn't closed for the season. Ate lunch at an old meatpacking plant that's nowadays a restaurant. Visited an antique mall with four full floors of things from yesteryear (a nostalgic return to earlier times). Stopped at a Hi Vee grocery store on the way back to the campground; wonder what *Hi Vee* stands for? Nice dinner tonight: Cleo's chicken, mashed potatoes, corn, salad, and cranberry sauce. Phil bought a bottle of Chardonnay—very good. Wonderful day. Wonderful time.

APPLE DUMPLINGS AND
A CORNHUSKING CHAMP

A 250-foot climb had brought me out of the Illinois River Valley, and since then I had been encountering less plain-like countryside than had been the norm east of the river. A series of valleys and ravines, including one requiring a fifty-foot climb, was making walking much more interesting. Shallower valleys included those of the Spoon River and the Kickapoo, French, Haw, and Brush creeks.

As I walked between those uneven areas, I passed a number of hog farms where the animals rooted about in fenced, grassy fields instead of muddy barnyards. That seemed strange, for a livestock farmer had told me that hogs, though omnivorous, were generally fattened on cereal grains and soybeans. Maybe so, but these fellows were getting none of that. They would snuff along the ground for a few feet and then drive their snouts into the grass and dirt for whatever they could find. One of my pictures shows twenty of the rotund critters in a broad field, all with their heads down and routing aimlessly about. And another thing: Although I had heard that hogs were unusually smart, these showed almost no curiosity, although they *were* skittish. Several times, as I carefully maneuvered to compose that perfect picture of some small, sedate group, they would suddenly bolt and ruin my composition. Inconsiderate beasts!

The day wore on. Tassels atop a million cornstalks glowed yellow in late-summer sun. But tree leaves, when there was a rare tree, were still green, although dull and worn looking from a hundred days of sun and wind and very little rain. I looked in vain for that occasional branch of brilliant red or yellow that always signaled the coming of fall back home. The dull leaf colors in the Midwest were a disappointment to Helen and me, who have always enjoyed New England's brilliant autumns.

About four o'clock that afternoon, Helen was "no-show" at a crossroads where we had agreed to meet. I waited for ten or fifteen minutes and then continued west, but I soon heard her coming fast, from behind me, from the east. She had been shopping in Abingdon and trying to telephone the children. Her phoning hadn't worked out, but she was happy to report she had a pre-roasted chicken for dinner.

*   *   *   *

One day, west of Gilson, Illinois, I came upon Mrs. Marie Leeder cleaning flowerbeds beside her front porch. She had seen me coming, and when I called *hello*, she happily stood up, declaring herself delighted to take a break, and *why hadn't I come along sooner?* We talked for a fifteen or twenty minutes about the walk, the weather, and the coming end of summer; then, just as we were winding down, Helen came along. Bored with waiting at the car, she had begun walking east to meet me, and now Marie was eager to hear about her role in the walk project.

Easing myself out of the conversation, I sat down on the ground. "Been on my feet for hours," I muttered. "Need to get off 'em." Almost immediately I dozed.

When I roused a short while later, the women were still talking, but now the conversation was about raising children. They said I had been asleep so long they talked out the walk subject.

"So what'd she tell you?" I asked Marie, "that she's the boss and my step lacks spring?"

"Not exactly.... That she's the boss and all you do is eat, walk, and sleep along the road."

"I can see you two get along just fine."

"Sure do," Helen said with a laugh.

A few minutes later I remarked that it was lunchtime and that we all probably needed something to eat, especially me. "After all," I said, "I still have an afternoon's walk ahead ... don't have the luxury of cleaning flower beds or dozing away in a car."

That got little response, but before long they obligingly finished their conversation and Helen and I started on to the car. Of course we didn't expect to see Marie again, but an hour later, just as we were finishing lunch, here she came, lickety-split, down the road in a maroon Buick. She pulled up with a puff of dust and happily told us that she had had apple dumplings in the oven even as we were talking. They'd turned out just fine, thank you, and would we like some? "I've got four right here on a paper plate. If I'd had more food in the house, I'd of asked you in for lunch."

I hopped out of the car and walked around to take the plate from Marie's outstretched hands, but then I fumbled and nearly dropped it on the way back. That drew laughs from both women and mutual agreement that overeager "young" men tend to be clumsy, whatever that was supposed to mean. The women seemed to think alike—it was uncanny, they could have been psychological twins.

The cars were sitting driver's-door to driver's-door with Helen behind our car's wheel; consequently, the women were able to sit there and talk to each other from five feet apart. And talk they did—for another twenty minutes—during which no car or truck or anything else came along to oblige Marie to move and let it pass. The farm roads were often that untraveled.

Eventually their conversation wound down, but by then I had begun reading and would have happily stayed in the car. Helen thought I should. "Rest a while, Philip. You sure you feel all right?"

"I'm fine," I told her as I screwed up my resolve and got out to begin walking. Back on the road, however, the drowsiness returned, and it wasn't long before I was ready for another nap, if I could just find an inviting place to lay down. Of course the longer I walked the sleepier I became and the less inviting the place had to look. Eventually, a weedy flat spot beside a raggedy cornfield looked just fine as I stepped off the road and eased myself to the ground.

I hadn't been lying there long before my dozing mind had me walking a cool mountain road between colorful outcroppings and endless wildflowers. And the sun was behind me and not in my eyes, and the wind was a breeze that pushed me along—the whole world couldn't have been a pleasanter place in which to be. Then a ghostly truck faded into view, far away at first, but ever closer and ever louder, and now it was slowing, its driver having seen me and wanting to talk. I vaguely resented the growing racket, but even as I struggled to stay asleep, a real-life truck door slammed and woke me with a BANG!

I jumped up mildly embarrassed as a man walked toward me from a huge pickup truck. The expression on his ruddy face quickly changed from frowning concern to a big broad smile. "I thought you was dead," he blurted with obvious relief. "Thank God you're not. I woulda had to drive clear into town and tell 'em I found a corpse. Don't have time for that … gotta work this afternoon."

This was going to be good.

After we traded names (his was Kibel), we began to talk, tentatively at first but soon with ease. He was from a hundred miles farther west, somewhere on the other side of Burlington, Iowa, and he had come over to Illinois to help a relative harvest several fields. Behind his truck was a trailer with a huge combine, and that led our conversation first to harvesting, then to the cost of farming, and finally to what kind of living a farmer could make nowadays.

"Farming's no way to get rich," Kibel declared. "A lot of guys do a lot of borrowing: for machinery and insurance, for seeds and fertilizer—all part of the cost of doing business." "Like other people," he continued, "they also borrow for cars and houses. Some get in too deep, and a few, like nonfarmers, even get themselves buried in credit card debt. Farming's a tricky business. You can make money one year and lose it all the next, but the fixed costs stay pretty much the same. Either you put money aside for the lean years or you eventually get wiped out. Working the dirt's not easy, but at least you're your own boss. I like it that way."

We talked about credit card debt, and I told him I knew somebody who was tens of thousands of dollars in hock to that kind of borrowing. Kibel said he used "plastic" for travel and sometimes for convenience, but he never carried a balance; rather he paid off his one-and-only card every month.

Eventually we drifted away from credit card talk and the economics of farming, and he got around to telling me he had been a state corn-husking champion.

"What do you mean?—corn-husking champ? You mean whoever's got the biggest combine wins?" I pointed toward the monster he was towing behind the truck.

"Nah," he said, "I'm talking about a fun thing. Guys get together at harvest time and 'contest up' to see who can take corn by hand the fastest."

"How do you do the actual husking?" I asked. "I do it back home sometimes. There's this place where you can pay a farmer for a dozen ears and then go out and pick 'em yourself. I get the ears off the stalks easy enough, but getting the husks off the ears is another story."

"Keep talkin'," Kibel said with a laugh.

"Okay. Well, I pull the husk loose on both sides at the ear's silk end, and then yank. One side always tears right down while the other side sticks to the kernels and hardly comes down at all. Next, I grab the stalk end with my right hand and yank the stuck side with my left. Both halves of the husk are now hanging onto the end of the ear tight as can be—got me?—and after another twenty seconds of battlin' and grouchin', I finally get the whole thing wrenched free." "I'm even better at shuckin' oysters," I went on. "I use a hammer and chisel."

By now we were both laughing, but eventually we became serious again as he told me all about husking corn by hand. "First of all," he began, "you wear a special kind of hand gear. It's a leather affair—a partially fingerless glove with a hook attached to the palm. It doesn't help you gettin' the ear off the stalk, but it's great guns for gettin' the husk off the ear. It's awkward at first, but once you get the hang of it, you can go really quick. It's like learning to milk a cow."

"I've done that," I injected. "Learned it when I was a kid."

"I knew you was a dairyman," Kibel said with a laugh. "Anyway, the contestants line up, and on a signal they begin racing down their assigned rows. They pull the ears off the stalks, husk them with the hooked glove, and throw the cobs, kernels still attached, into horse-drawn carts. After an agreed upon time, the contest is stopped and judges decide the winner. Criteria include not only how many ears are taken, but how clean they've been husked and how many have been missed and left behind."

It sounded like fun to me, and apparently it's also something of a social event with lots of eating, singing, and square dancing. There's probably plenty of beer drinking too, but I didn't think to ask about that.

We talked and laughed for another few minutes—Kibel was a talkative, light-hearted person. But eventually he had to go on about his business, and I was soon back walking and thinking about the last time I had been caught sleeping along a road. That was back in Indiana, and I had come awake after a car stopped and the driver, a small elderly woman, had already got out. She was standing by the front bumper on the driver's side, staring at me with an expression of dread and anxiety.

I smiled and said, "I'm okay, no problem," and then I started to get up, grabbing as usual at any chance to talk to somebody—anybody. But just my moving thoroughly spooked the poor woman. She quickly turned, stepped back to the driver's door, jumped into her car, and took off in a cloud of dust. She didn't smile, she didn't look back, she just went! For the next hour I half expected a sheriff to come along and accuse me of trying to mug the little old lady by lying down and playing hurt along the road.

SIGHTSEEING ALONG THE MISSISSIPPI

After camping four days near Galesburg, we moved Lurch to Mount Pleasant, Iowa. There were railroad tracks only a few blocks from the campground, and a couple of times during the first night both Helen and I were wakened by the sounds of passing trains. Still, the occasional whistles, squeals, and diesel-engine roars were not really a problem. It would be the following spring, while camping farther west, that nighttime trains would at first keep us awake, until eventually we would become used to the noise and hardly notice it.

Mount Pleasant was another town whose name somehow called for an explanation, and here again we thought about getting into it, i.e., inquiring at City Hall, the public library, or even the Chamber of Commerce. The town does not sit on high ground; in fact, for three miles northwest to southeast elevations change by less than maybe thirty feet. Only to the southwest, a mile or two from town square, is the flatness broken by the beginnings of a gentle downslope that leads first to Big Creek and then to Skunk River, a major stream that eventually drains to the Mississippi. However, the entire drop in four and a half miles is only a hundred and fifty feet—hardly enough to inspire its founders to name the town "Mount Anything." "We've got to come back here someday," Helen said. "There's a story behind this 'Mount' name, and I'd like to know what it is."

I agreed, though thinking at the same time that we'd probably never make it back. Becoming interested in places or things and then forcing ourselves to quell our interest and move on was becoming routine. We had recently done it with the Lincoln courthouse at Metamora—we had to, we told ourselves, if we were to keep making progress on the walk. So this time we suppressed delving into Mount Pleasant's name; we didn't even come close to admitting that maybe we were just too lazy. Instead, we resolved to relax for the day, be tourists, see the sights. And almost immediately we found something interesting right there at the campground.

It happened that the campground owner's hobby was refurbishing old cars, and we had no sooner checked in than he was proudly showing us his extensive collection, including a car he was working on at the time. Before long, I was enthusing about rebuilding a car myself. "Helen," I said, "I'm gonna find me an old Studebaker and rebuild it."

We had had a fifty-one Studebaker the first nine years of our marriage; in fact we brought all of our newborns home in it. Of course, as soon as I started talking about rebuilding one, Helen immediately wanted to know when I would find the time, given I was walking across the country and had vowed to rebuild the back deck as soon as we got home. "Not only that," she said, "you'll be back doing volunteer work."

But seeing the antique cars got me thinking about an old man we had met at a Florida car show years before, and I determined to tell the proprietor the story. The old man in question was displaying a mid-fifties Rambler sedan, but his car was not for sale like other cars in the show. No-sir-ee! This one held special nostalgic memories for him and his wife, who stood demurely nearby.

Seems as newlyweds, they bought the car used about 1960, and for the first three years of their marriage they lived with her parents in a small bungalow in Florida. The house had paper-thin walls, so the young people would avoid their bedroom upon the "onset of affections." Instead, Jack, the husband, would casually announce he was going out to work on the car. His self-conscious young wife would wait a few minutes, say she was bored, and then tell her parents she was going out to help Jack. Maybe they'd go for a ride.

"Both our kids was conceived while I was givin' her rides in that hard-buckin' Rambler," the old man said with a grin and gleeful emphasis on *rides* and especially *buckin'*. "That's why it's not for sale."

His now blushing wife landed a playful but hard punch on his tattooed right arm. "One of these days I'm gonna wring his damned neck," she declared with happy menace.

The proprietor got a good laugh from that story, but then another camper, who had come in while I was telling it, delivered one that was so risqué as to be unrelatable in this narrative—it made Helen blush and put me in stitches. Helen, suddenly anxious to leave, said, "Phil, let's walk down town while there's still time before dinner."

So off we went. We would have driven except that having just driven over from Galesburg, neither of us felt like getting into the car.

As we walked down U.S. 34 toward town, we noted the usual small businesses and here and there a modest house, but what mostly drew our attention were big yellow school buses. "There are buses everywhere," Helen remarked, and she was right. Two, both apparently brand-new, were parked at a service garage near the campground entrance, and several more were in nearby parking lots. They too appeared to be new.

The buses looked so heavily built they reminded us—especially me—of army tanks; and as high as they were, it seemed as if their occupants would be safe during any collision, except maybe one with a good-sized truck. A car hitting from behind would hardly more than jolt the occupants, and in a broadside collision, even a pickup truck would impact well below floor level. Children in bolted down seats should be perfectly safe.

Upon getting to town and asking somebody, we learned that the buses' manufacturer, the Bluebird Company, had a plant a couple miles west of town.

We wandered around downtown Mount Pleasant that afternoon, gawking like other tourists at city hall and at a huge steam tractor that dominated one corner of the town square. I was impressed enough to tell Helen how much old steam tractors reminded me of yesteryear's steam locomotives. Of course they were parallel applications of the same nineteenth-century technology.

The next day, needing another day off and still in the mood for sightseeing, we drove down to Keokuk, which is an Iowa town near the Missouri border. There, navigation lock nineteen of the Mississippi Navigation System lifts or lowers shipping thirty-six feet between the river below Keokuk Dam and the river above the dam.

While we were there, a "push boat" approaching from downriver nudged a group of barges, five long and three wide, slowly, ever so slowly, into the lock. When the downriver gate had closed, water slowly rose to the level above the dam, and before long, with many a whistle and toot, push boat and barge train continued upriver. Whatever Helen or I had imagined a navigation lock to look like, we certainly did not picture anything that huge, nor did we expect anything as long as five end-for-end barges and their pushing tug. The lock is 110 feet wide by 1200 feet long—nearly a quarter mile—and the barges together with the push boat filled it up. (Panama Canal locks are also 110 feet wide but only 1050 feet long, thus significantly smaller.)

Full of anticipation for the next new thing we might see, we headed for the docking place of a stern-wheeler showboat called the *George M. Verity*. No luck there. It had been closed since Labor Day, and so was a nearby river museum which we would also have visited.

Well, we'd go north—follow the river—something interesting was bound to turn up. So leaving Keokuk, we drove to Fort Madison, which originated around a fort of the same name built in 1808. The fort itself was reconstructed in the 1990s, and we would have visited, except that it too was closed for the season. "Everything in this part of the whole darned country is locked up tight," Helen complained.

But not quite everything was. Eventually we came to the Catfish Bend Riverboat Casino, and stopping there, we found the usual casino combination of gambling together with good, low-priced food. We avoided the gambling but they had a great buffet, and afterwards we headed back to Mount Pleasant for dinner at home—followed by an unpleasant evening battling the computer.

For some reason the computer suddenly refused to *print* maps that it exhibited perfectly on its screen. The images would be there, looking just fine, but nothing I tried would produce a hardcopy. About ten o'clock I quit in disgust, deciding to take the laptop along in the car the following day. Whenever necessary, I would generate a map on the screen, and we would decide as we looked at it where I would walk and where our next rendezvous would be.

*   *   *   *

Well rested the next morning, I maintained a lively pace until about eleven o'clock, when I paused on a low bluff. Below me the road dropped away through scattered trees to lowlands through which flowed a picturesque creek; and six miles beyond lay Burlington, Iowa, on the west bank of the Mississippi River. Completing the picture was beautiful, cable-stayed MacArthur Bridge, strikingly framed against a series of low hills. I hurried on with growing anticipation; crossing the Mississippi would be a major milestone.

Helen was waiting three miles east of town, and after a quick lunch I was at it again and soon walking the bridge. MacArthur was the first main highway bridge we had come to since McClugage over the Illinois River weeks before. However, different from McClugage, no construction was in progress here, and although there was no walkway, at least traffic was light and slow. Crossing was easy despite a buffeting wind.

Once across the river, I walked through the heart of Burlington, then nine miles south, to a place labeled Wever on the map but which Helen simply logged as the *Amoco station where U.S. 61 meets CR J48.*

So much for our crossing the Mississippi and entering Iowa. The distance walked that day was only twenty-four miles, but it had been increasingly interesting as the scenery changed from endless fields to beautiful bridge to Burlington itself, with its attractive buildings and busy pedestrians. I even managed to coax a few sentences from an ancient Burlingtonite, whom I met at the corner of Main and Angular Streets, and from whom I had asked directions.

"Yes sir," the old man wheezed, "to get to sixty-one, all you gotta do is walk ten blocks west on Angular Street there." He gestured over his shoulder with a thumb.

"Then what?" I asked. I'd been lost for fifteen minutes and knew that Iowa 61 wasn't anywhere near that close.

"Well, that'll meet Summer Street. There you wanna turn left and walk about five miles due south. Sixty-one comes in there from your right."

"Thanks," I said. That made more sense. "You retired?"

"Yep, but it's hell. Don't have enough money, and this Social Security thing's gonna go down the tubes."

At the time there was talk in the media about the fund going bankrupt in 2020. I told the old gentleman I didn't think there was much to worry about. However, he thought there was and that he could end up without benefits in his "old age." He must have been at least eighty-five. I didn't tell him I doubted either of us would live to see many changes, unless they happened in the very near future.

I ACQUIRE A BICYCLING BUDDY

The Mississippi from Burlington to south of Fort Madison is about a mile wide and bounded on the west by highlands that reach a hundred feet above the valley floor. Burlington sits on high ground above the river, but Fort Madison lies down low where the river once flowed, and where it will someday likely flow again. We intended to follow U.S. 61 along the crest of the bluffs from Wever to Fort Madison. It was only twenty-four miles, and we were anxious to complete the necessary southern jog before turning west again, across the hills and farther into Iowa.

However, the next morning U.S. 61 was so busy that we quickly changed plans. Instead of following the highway, I started from Wever and took a crescent-shaped "longcut" through less-trafficked, hillier country to rejoin the main road just above town. From there it was an easy walk down off the bluffs and past the Iowa State Penitentiary—which must be one of the most depressing sights on earth. There should be a sign over the front gate reading "All hope abandon, ye who enter here!" or better yet, "Arbeit Macht Frei." The mere sight of the place should scare a body straight.

A half hour beyond the penitentiary, I found myself talking to a handsome woman holding a yard sale. She was very pleasant as she asked question after question about the walk, and she smilingly commented on my answers with phrases like *I'm really impressed, Not many people could do what you're doing, You should write a book, You're very articulate you know.* And more and more. She might even have said, "Bet nobody can con or flatter you," and I would doubtless have agreed.

In any case, I bought three old math texts that had belonged to her sons when they were in college. She let me have them for five dollars apiece, and I thought she was throwing in a used can opener gratis until she told me it would be two dollars more. I ponied up anyway and got back on the road.

I had been bugging Helen about buying things along the way that we wouldn't use during the rest of the trip—not that she bought much, but it was fun to kid her about it. Now, knowing my buying the books would make her day, I determined to sneak them into the spare-tire well when I got to the car. Later, back at camp, I would hide them permanently in the motor home's under-floor storage space.

She was parked in downtown Fort Madison on Avenue G off route 61, and as I walked up behind the car, I could see her head bent forward as if she were reading or doing a cross-word puzzle. So far so good. I didn't even greet her, just quietly opened the trunk and oh-so-gently began to move things around to get the tire-well cover off. Maybe she heard something or felt the car move, or maybe it was just her keen antenna for intrigue, but she sensed right away that something was going on. Out of the car she bounced, and as I enthused about the fantastic buy the books had been, she happily interrupted with just the right question: "A pretty woman sold 'em to you—right?"

I didn't mention the can opener.

After lunch, during which Helen twice mentioned how people should practice what they preach, I walked through the center of Fort Madison, past the Shaffer ballpoint-pen factory, past Riverview Park, and finally past the Casino where we had lunched a few days before. Near 4th Street, I met a Latino boy on a bicycle, and he accompanied me most of the way through town. "I'm twelve," he announced, and he would have told me his life story and his family's too, if I had let him.

I asked the kid why he wasn't in school, and back came a long-winded reply that mentioned sickness in the family, a neighbor's kitchen fire, teachers away at institute (that's an old one), and finally a broken bike. His bike looked okay to me, and he rode it well enough as long as he didn't try to go too slow. However, reduced to essentials, his long-winded explanation told me he was playing hooky.

"You cut school," I challenged, one eye squinted down, the other glaring at him from under an arched brow. "You're wasting your time trying to con me. I raised two boys!"

He grinned and jumped off his bike. "I had a broken rib," he said, changing the subject.

"How'd you get that? No, don't tell me; you fell off your bike."

"How'd you know that?"

"Because I was a kid like you sixty years ago. It was a long time gettin' better, right?"

A two-time veteran of broken ribs, I figured I could tell from his answer whether he really had one or only thought he had.

"More than a month," he said. "Ached real bad too. Every time I took a breath it throbbed, and whenever I coughed it hurt like hell!"

He clearly had had the real thing, earthy kid that he was, and with that painful bond between us, I asked if he wanted to hear how I got my first broken rib.

"Yeah, fall off your bike?"

"Nope, got it lifting a dog out of the ocean into a boat."

"Nuh-uh," he quickly countered. (It seems as if kids everywhere combine *no* and *uh-uh* to get that grunting *nuh-uh*, which clearly translates into a *no way*.)

"Don't believe me? Suit yourself," I said, and we walked along without talking for a while, him still pushing his bike.

Presently we stopped at a street corner, and when traffic had cleared and we crossed, he said, "You really break your rib lifting a dog into a boat?"

"You wanna hear about it?"

"Yeah," he conceded, as he got back on his bike and tried to ride along beside me. But the pace was too slow and he only wobbled along, meandering first onto the grass then back onto the sidewalk where he shortly banged into me. We both nearly went down as I grabbed him and the bike, and steadied the combination while he got off. Then I checked where the bike's pedal had gouged skin off my left ankle, and once that was done and we were walking again, I told him the story.

"When I was a young man," I began, "I lived with my family in Bermuda, which is a small island in the Atlantic Ocean...."

Continuing, I told him how one Sunday morning, the boys and I were boating in a small bay when we spotted Helen, the girls, and Gina, our seventy-pound Alsatian, on a nearby beach. Thoughtlessly, we hailed the group from offshore, and Helen and the girls called back greetings. Gina however—predictably if we had used our heads before we yelled—jumped into the water and began swimming out toward the boat.

No end of shouts and calls were enough to get the old dog to swim back, and soon she was in deep water fifty yards out. I eased the boat first beside her and then past her, trying to lead her back to shore. That didn't work, and before long she was tiring and starting to sink. Fortunately, the boat was low enough in the water that with the boys holding my feet, I was able to lean sideways over the gunnel and get my arms around her. Then, pivoting on my rib cage, I hauled her out of the water and up over me into the boat. A rib gave way with a felt but not heard pop, although surprisingly, it hardly hurt at the time.

That night though was a different story. Sometime after dinner the misery began with a dull ache, and by bedtime every breath hurt and any coughing was enough to prompt a groan. To make matters worse, I had got a fresh dose of sunburn that day. So began five weeks of diminishing aching punctuated now and then by a stab of pain seemingly brought on by anything: a sudden cough, a thoughtless twist, a hiccup, or even just a longed-for deep breath.

The boy listened patiently to this woeful tale and then declared: "You had a broken rib all right."

Spoken like a man who knew—someone who'd "been there and had it."

By now we had come to another corner along U.S. 61, and I was starting to worry about how far the kid was getting from home. "I've been farther than this," he assured me. "I broke my collarbone too."

"Yeah, well, I had another broken rib I haven't told you about." I wasn't about to let this twelve-year-old outdo me.

"Okay, but you must have got *that one* riding a bike."

"Nope, one of my sons and I were wrestling over who was going to sit in an overstuffed chair. It was fun until he got his head against my chest and pushed so hard he broke my rib."

"You get mad?"

"Ah … well … yes … but not very."

Truth was I considered my sixteen-year-old flagrantly guilty of unnecessary roughness—even his mother did. But he had only recently become strong enough to give me a really rough time, and I shouldn't have been surprised when he went all out. Immediately afterward, while I was still nursing my aching chest, the "armchair battle" didn't seem very funny, but as weeks passed and the soreness wore off, I began to see the episode in at least slightly humorous terms. Nowadays, forty years later, we laugh about it at family gatherings if it happens to come up.

"So who got to sit in the chair?" The kid was still with me.

"Me, of course, who do you think?"

That held him for a minute as we crossed 23rd Street, each of us busy with our own thoughts. The next thing he said was, "My sister's gonna get married."

"That's nice. When'll that be?"

"Real soon. She's gonna have a baby too, and mom hollered like—"

I cut him off right there and turned the conversation to the weather. I didn't need to hear about that particular family crisis; anyway, by that time we were coming up on the next corner and I was determined to go into a store or something—anything to get rid of the kid. He had been with me for a good half mile.

There was a drugstore across the street in the middle of the next block, and grabbing the opportunity, I fixed him with a stern look and said, "I need to get something from that store down there. Now, you turn around and go back. I'm worried 'cause you're too far from home." I held out my hand, which he shook with a grin.

"That's where I live," he said, "over near that drugstore," and as I started across the street, he came right along.

When we reached the store, I turned and said, "GOOD-BYE! Now you take care of yourself—no more broken bones. Hear? And quit cuttin' school!" I half shouted the last because he had suddenly jumped on his bike and was pedaling back the way we'd come, his skinny legs pumping up and down like piston rods.

276

What spooked him was a cop who had pulled up and parked on the street just behind us. I'd barely noticed, but the kid must have thought he was the truant officer.

The cop got out of his car and paused for me to walk into the store just ahead of him. Inside, he branched away and went back toward the prescription counter while I busied myself looking for muscle rub. Sure enough, the timing worked out so that five minutes later, I ended up right behind him in the checkout line.

While we stood there, I kept thinking about the boy and how many people might have noticed us walking together through town. A heck of a nice kid, I thought to myself, but he's a boy's boy and a wide-ranger besides. If he goes missing in the next few days, God forbid, the cops will be combing Iowa for a white-haired gringo with a backpack. For a moment, images of the penitentiary came to mind; then I told myself to knock it off, pay for the muscle rub, and leave off the paranoia.

When I walked outside a few minutes later, the cop had just got into his cruiser—from which he looked over and said, "Nice morning."

"The best," I managed, feeling silly by then.

Walking on, I followed U.S. 61 out of Fort Madison to higher ground beyond bluffs to the west. After that, the road descended into Sugar Creek Valley, where I met Helen about four o'clock. She enjoyed hearing about my Latino-kid buddy, and she laughed about how he raced away at sight of the cop. "But I don't think you need to worry about being seen with him," she said. "You don't look dangerous to anybody."

"Thanks, m'Love. I'm not dangerous, but I don't think you appreciate how dangerous some people can be. Anyway, no stranger will con that kid into getting into a car with him. He's pleasant enough, but he's streetwise and definitely his own person. They'd have to kidnap him by force, which would be a darn noisy event!"

Kidnap? Force? Put off by the implications of my own words, I changed the subject and asked Helen what she had been doing all day besides eating bonbons and catching me hiding books in the car trunk. She too was happy to leave the kidnapping subject, and soon we were talking about her day.

Besides browsing Fort Madison's shopping district, Helen had briefly visited a beautifully restored schoolhouse called Brush College, which was northeast of town. The one-room building was closed for the season, but peering through a window, she could see authentically restored teachers' and students' desks, a log stove, and many books neatly arranged on shelves. She wondered if there weren't a few too many books, considering their likely availability during the period when the school was actually in use. That was from the 1870s to the 1930s. Unfortunately, there were no posted abstracts giving a history of the building, at least none that she could read through the window. She said the old schoolhouse was another fascinating treasure of Americana that we would definitely have to revisit someday.

DID TODD LINCOLN
LIVE NEAR HERE?

The following morning we were again ready for a break from walking; also, it was time to do a wash and buy groceries.

A small shopping center with a Laundromat and food store worked for Helen to wash and get groceries; meanwhile, I had a productive morning making computer maps. The maps still wouldn't print directly from the map program, but I had found a way to print them, though awkwardly, through a program called Paint—after hours of "try-and-fuss" as Helen likes to put it.

That afternoon we turned lazy and read some, but mainly we just wandered around the campground. A fellow camper told us that land thereabouts had once belonged to Robert Todd Lincoln, the President's son. I checked it out, and although Todd Lincoln might have owned land near the campground, it was doubtless the holdings of his wife's family, the Harlans, that our acquaintance had in mind. They owned plenty of land in Mount Pleasant, but a mile across town near Iowa Wesleyan College.

Nevertheless, the Lincoln story is interesting: Todd Lincoln met his wife, Mary Eunice, through the friendship of his father and Mary's father, who was Iowa Senator James Harlan of Mount Pleasant. The two were married in 1868, and throughout Todd's varied career (politics, diplomacy, business, and law), the Lincolns lived mainly in Chicago and Washington DC. Mary Eunice and the couple's three children did spend summers at the Harlan's house in Mount Pleasant, but Todd himself seems to have only occasionally visited there, except for a few months in 1890. That was shortly after their son Jack had died in Europe. Senator Harlan died in 1899, and Mary Eunice eventually gave the family home to Wesleyan College in 1907.

*　　*　　*　　*

Lakeside Campground near Bloomfield became our next camping destination, which we started for early on September 22. Along the way we stopped at a computer service business near Fort Madison. I was determined to have the laptop checked out—being unable to print maps directly from the map program was an annoying inconvenience.

The staff at Keyboard Computers were helpful and would take no money when they determined that nothing was wrong with the computer itself. The problem, they found, lay with something in the software called a printer-driver, and they recommended I have that upgraded when I got back East. Why the driver would let the printer make maps for areas east of the Mississippi, but not west, seemed a mystery to me, but the important thing was that the laptop itself was okay. Meanwhile, I could continue to print hardcopy maps by first transferring them to the Paint program, which, thankfully, remained on good terms with the printer.

Leaving Keyboard, we arrived at Lakeside about noon in a driving rain, and by the time we leveled Lurch and connected utilities, I was chilled and soaked. Helen, no more in a mood to hit the road than I was, was equally ready to stay inside the rest of the day. The next morning we even broke our rule always to go out to walk's end regardless of conditions. (Although it was still drizzling, it was definitely clearing up.) Instead, a bit guiltily, we drove back to Mount Pleasant to visit the grounds and museums of the Midwest Old Settlers and Threshers Association. We had heard it was a don't-miss attraction.

The Old Settlers' complex takes in about ten square blocks on the south side of town, and it includes several museums as well as the Midwest Central Railroad, whose mile and a quarter track girdles the grounds. The Heritage Museum contains many antique steam tractors, an antique school bus, and even a horse-drawn hearse. There is also a buckwheat mill, various examples of

Steam Tractor at the Heritage Museum

evolving farm machinery, and an extensive display showing the development of modern gas-powered tractors.

Another Old Threshers' museum houses theatrical memorabilia from the 1850s to 1950s, when troops of traveling actors moved around the country staging productions in small opera houses, town halls, and even tents. Plays included farce and comedies, some of them Broadway hits. There were also Chautauquas and minstrel shows. Museum exhibits include programs, costumes, and playbills. Scenery and stage drops are also on display, along with a notable collection of scripts and music scores.

While we were visiting the museums, we learned about The Old Threshers Reunion, which is held on association grounds each year during the five days before Labor Day. Thousands of people attend. Some come to see craft displays or to watch farm-product competitions. For others, main attractions are harvesting demonstrations, horses at work or tractor pulls. Still others enjoy vintage car shows, and probably everybody enjoys the parades. Riding the Midwest Central Railroad is popular, and nightly entertainments include bluegrass concerts as well as variety, gospel, and children's shows.

Not surprisingly, there is unlimited food at the Old Threshers Reunion, as befits a yearly celebration "Dedicated to Preserving Our Agricultural Heritage in a Modern World." Numerous tents and booths provide a wide variety: meatloaf, baked potatoes, drum sticks, beef and noodles, funnel cakes, pancakes, pies, and ice cream—not gourmet food, but rather foods that can power a man who does real work like farming or bricklaying (especially bricklaying), or a woman who cooks, cleans, sews, and raises children.

On our way back to camp, we stopped at a small general store in Fairfield on Iowa 34. Helen bought peanut brittle and a jar of sorghum syrup, both made locally by Mennonites. She thought the sorghum would go good on pancakes—like Aunt Jemima's syrup. However, after tasting some we agreed it would be better for cooking since, though sweet, it had a faint tang of bitterness. The peanut brittle was a different story. That was supposed to be a treat for our sweet tooths during the next few days of walking, but alas, there would be no point in taking it walking if we didn't like it. We'd sample a piece or two—maybe three or four—on the way back to the campground. Of course, by the time we got there it was all gone but the crumbs.

*   *   *   *

Helen likes to tell about three great pictures she almost got the following day. We had gone back to walking that morning, and her first "almost got" happened about 10 a.m. while she was sitting in the car. Three raccoons emerged from a ditch only a dozen yards away, and of course Helen reached for her camera which was on the seat beside her. Trouble was, by the time she got hold of it and aimed, the raccoons were too close. She snapped a picture any-way, even though she expected it to be sun-struck by glare from the hood of the car. And indeed it was. When developed, the pic-ture looked as if it had been taken by an antique bellows camera with a serious light leak. All it showed was a big white foreground with a couple of washed-out blobs in the middle distance, which, Helen swore, were raccoons. Raccoon number three was "under the white," i.e., so close to the car the camera couldn't see it for glare.

Her second "almost-got" happened an hour later while she was still sitting in the car. This time she was doing a crossword puzzle when she looked up to see three deer wandering out of an adjacent wooded streambed. For ten minutes Helen sat in motionless fascination as the deer nibbled grass shoots and slowly meandered toward the car. They were still a hundred yards away when it occurred to her to get out the camera, but after the raccoon bungle, she had put it in the glove compartment. She would have to reach for it.

Slowly, ever so slowly, she placed her left hand on the front edge of the passenger seat, and then began to stretch—far, farther, still farther with her right hand toward the glove compartment door. She was almost there when her hand slipped off the seat and she sprawled out with her buttocks (she nixed a better word) half off the driver's seat and her torso and head on the floor beneath the dash. By the time she got straightened up and found her bent glasses, the deer were gone. She claims she said *Fiddlesticks*. I don't believe it—never heard her say *Fiddlesticks* in fifty years—hate to think what she might have said. But even if she had got a deer picture, the prize-winner would have been her sprawled across the front of the car.

Her third near miss came that afternoon. After driving a dozen miles farther west, she had got out of the car and was walking when she sighted a small group Mennonite children near a white frame schoolhouse. She paused. The children would be great candidates for human-interest shots, but could she take their pictures in good conscience?—either individually or as a group? She knew that Mennonites were not fond of being photographed, and she knew that the teacher whom I had talked to in Illinois had demurred when I asked to take pictures of her and her students. But maybe the teacher at this school would be less conservative.

Deciding to give it a try, Helen continued on with camera in hand, hoping to meet "teach" and get permission for a snapshot or two. She had greeted the children and walked past them en route to the schoolhouse door, when a woman in homespuns opened it, stepped onto the stoop, and called for the children to come inside. She smiled and nodded to Helen as the children filed past, and she continued to smile as she turned and followed the last child in while meaningfully pulling the door closed behind her!

Helen says she deserved the rebuff just for thinking about taking pictures.

In the meantime, while Helen was missing prize-winning pictures, I was walking the countryside of southeast Iowa near Donnellson and Farmington. At times I had feelings that the terrain was quite high ground, until I realized it only seemed high because of the bluffs I had recently climbed while leaving the Mississippi floodplain. Every mile or so the ground would gently slope to a streambed that was often but not always dry. Steeper grades led down to Little Sugar Creek, Sugar Creek, and the Des Moines River.

It was by no means rugged country, but the slight hilliness made for interesting walking. Overall, I had a pleasant day, especially when passing through Shimek State Forrest, a dozen square miles of deciduous woodlands that provided plenty of shade and cool, refreshing airs.

*   *   *   *

The following days took me along a series of back roads that were just above the Missouri border and a few miles below Iowa 2. To the north and just out of sight lay first Milton, then Pulaski and then Steuben, but the broad farmlands through which I was passing gave no hint that there were nearby towns and people. I saw little wildlife beyond pheasants, although I often saw animal prints beside creeks or near muddy puddles along the road. Helen saw a distant flock of turkeys, but she got no opportunities for wildlife pictures that were anywhere near as good as those she had missed on "picture fiasco" day. Her phrase.

One afternoon I was passing a small woods on the north side of the road, while to the south, beyond a weedy ditch, lay an already-harvested wheat field. I was thinking of it as perfect place for pheasants when suddenly three flew up not twenty feet in front of me. After the initial flurry, they settled into long shallow glides toward a patch of low brush a quarter mile away.

The birds' startling departure returned me to childhood, to 1936, and to the depths of the depression. My father had received a soldier's bonus of fifteen hundred dollars with which he bought a two-bedroom house in Hatboro, Pennsylvania. It had a tarpaper roof and mud cellar, a kitchen pump and no bathroom. It badly needed paint, but to my depression-ridden parents it must have seemed wonderful after years of rented apartments and tiny row houses.

Near our "new house" lay a field of tall grass beyond a shallow creek, and one day, soon after we moved there, I crossed the creek and ventured deep into the field. The grass was so tall I could barely see over it, yet I was not so courageous as to let myself lose sight of a chimney that rose above the gray roofline of our house. Suddenly, even as I rejoiced in imagined bravery, a pheasant burst out of the grass only yards away scaring me half out of my wits. I squealed as I blundered back toward the creek, falling down on the way and nearly wetting my pants. For days afterward I avoided the field, but eventually I did go back, and as time passed I probed deeper and deeper into the tall grass, for it became a game to flush the birds and watch them fly away....

With a start I was back in Iowa and walking, walking, walking. It was late afternoon, and though I had come nearly thirty miles, I was still feeling fine, thanks in part to continuing fascination with the countryside. There were low hills in the area that sloped perhaps sixty feet into shallow valleys, occasionally with slow-moving streams. Sixty feet is easily enough height difference to allow interesting panoramic changes as you crest successive rises. Meanwhile, it had become quite cool, and I paused once to put on a jacket.

That day I left the road a number of times to explore creek banks and muddy floodplains. Always there were deer and raccoon tracks, but there were coyote tracks as well, and once, south of Steuben, I saw the tracks of a bobcat. Later, I met a man who told me there were even a few panthers in southern Iowa. That surprised me, for I thought they only lived in the mountains much farther west.

TWO VERY DIFFERENT BROTHERS

Southeast of Leon, Iowa, there is a commune of people who have branched off from the Mormon faith to embrace a simple agrarian lifestyle. As I was approaching an entrance to their lands, a commune member drove up and got out of her car to open the gate. She paused when I waved, and she quickly returned my greeting when I called *good-morning.*

Myra Kovaciny, who appeared to be in her early fifties, was small and wiry, and she wore a flowered housedress that was faded and not especially clean. Nor was Myra. Nevertheless, she was friendly and eager to talk, and after tentative comments about the weather and harvest time, she began to tell me about herself and her zealous commitment to her sect.

Myra had been a secretary in Portland, Oregon, before hearing the call, and listening to her touching ramblings, I learned that an apocalypse is coming that will destroy the infrastructure of society as we know it. Organized government will fail, public services will be no more, bridges will collapse, municipal reservoirs will be destroyed, and electric power will be a thing of the past. Since transportation and transport systems will be gone, provisioning urban society, even with food, will become impossible. Survivors will be only those who, like her group, are rural, self-sufficient, and able to live off the land.

After the apocalypse, Jesus will return to earth, and this, of course, will be the Second Coming. But just what His role will be in this strange new world, Myra did not seem to know. I suggested that from my early religious indoctrination, He would come back as King of the World. I thought she would immediately agree, but she held back and seemed troubled. Was she, I wondered, this Portland woman from a world of money and cars, central heat and telephones, really prepared to live in a world of barter, buggies, dug wells, and fireplaces? Would not singing praises all day long, even to a fatherly God, become tiresome, indeed deadly boring?

I asked if I could look around the reservation. "No," she said, "nonmembers are often welcome, but today isn't a visitation day because we're harvesting sorghum." I think she began to see me as a possible convert, since she enthusiastically encouraged me to come back another day. She said I could even meet the group's leader.

As we talked, a girl of perhaps seventeen came up walking a horse. The horse had fallen and bloodied its knee; the girl had got by with slightly scraped hands. I spoke to the girl, but she was shy, avoided eye contact and would not respond.

Myra finished opening the gate, and when girl and horse had passed, she turned back to me and said, "A lot of people say bad things about us … all untrue … we really are harmless."

"What kind of bad things?"

"Like we have to sign over all of our property to the sect when we become members. They call us 'Wannabes' too—they don't like us very much."

I said something that I hoped would encourage her to keep talking; I wanted to hear more about how she felt the outside world viewed her group. But she would not be drawn out, and perhaps thinking she had already talked too much, she smiled, offered her hand, and said, "I gotta go. I've been to town for the mail and was supposed be back an hour ago."

With that she turned, almost abruptly, and walked a few steps back to her car where she paused for a moment as if to say something else. Then, apparently thinking better of it, she got in and drove past me into the compound, still smiling, though, as she went by.

After talking to Myra, I had walked only a mile or two when I met a farmer who knew some of the cult members and had had dealings with them. "They're good neighbors," he told me without reservation, "helpful and pleasant to live near—couldn't ask for better."

Conversely, other people, whom I would overhear in a café a few days later, seemed to subscribe to a local belief that sex orgies and other debaucheries were a way of life in Wannabe land. As far as I could tell, however, none of those people had ever dealt with a Wannabe, ever been on Wannabe land, or had ever met a member of the sect.

*   *   *   *

Within hours of talking to Myra, I met two boys who also made lasting impressions, one bad and one good. They had been sitting on straight-back chairs on a farmhouse porch—sentenced there for bickering, the smaller one later told me. But when they noticed me approaching, they went on the lam and sauntered down the front lawn to wait just off the road. *These kids look bored,* I thought, *wonder what they want?*

The shorter boy toyed with a small, bright object that he held in his hands; the taller fellow kept flipping a ball in the air and catching it as it came down. Between flips he would look my way, and as I drew abreast, I was surprised to see he was scowling. "Where *you* goin'?" he abruptly demanded in a voice that was high pitched and a shade too loud.

"I'm walking to Oregon."

"Where from? You from Allerton?"

Allerton was a small town a few miles to the east. But again, the kid's manner was challenging, and he showed no smile, just an insolent stare. He looked to be twelve or thirteen; the little guy, who continued fiddling with his whatever, was probably eight or nine.

I stared back at the older one for a moment and then answered, "I'm from Connecticut. Walked here from there. Know where Connecticut is?"

"Sure. It's over by New York. You claim you're walking to Oregon?"

"I don't claim anything. You asked me, I told you. You don't have to believe it."

I was in no mood to humor the little jerk. In spite of his looking twelve, it dawned on me that he was a lot older, probably a sixteen-year-old still stuck with a pre-pubertal body. Maybe that's what had him ticked. Other boys his age would be enjoying deep voices, face hair, and wet dreams. I started to walk on, but he almost growled, "Hold on!"

Pausing, I turned toward him again, and darned if he didn't continue in the same skeptical vein: "You say you're walking to Oregon. If you really walked here from Connecticut, that means you're trying to walk clean across the country. Right?"

"You got it."

"No way," he scoffed, as he turned, and with a toss of his head started up the lawn toward the porch. I walked on, thoroughly annoyed now and glad to get away from the snotty whelp.

I had walked only a short distance when I was startled by quick footsteps coming up from behind, and spinning around, I was surprised to look down into the face of the younger boy. "Want to see my secret coin?" he asked.

"Yeah, let's see it," I answered—not too pleasantly either. Then, "Who's that guy you were with back there? Not your brother, I hope."

"Yes," was his reply, which came out quietly and with seeming resignation. I was taken aback, but not surprised by the cheerlessness of his answer; it crossed my mind that he probably took a lot of bullying.

I took the coin from his outstretched hand and looked it over, at first with forced patience but soon with genuine interest. It was a bit thicker than a silver dollar and consisted of threaded halves that screwed together like a high-priced watchcase. When the coin was assembled, the seam between its halves lay around the edge and was invisible between parallel decorative groves in the metal. One face of the coin was embossed with a dog's image, the other with the outline of a cat, and both were so poorly struck that the coin looked exactly, and no doubt intentionally, like something a kid might win at a carnival. Inside the coin (the boy opened it for me) was a tiny slip of paper—which in another time and place may well have been microfilm. Whatever its history, right now the secret coin was the prized possession of a small boy with a cherubic face and an urge to talk to a passing stranger.

"Any secrets in there?" I asked, as I handed back the coin while ignoring the fragment of paper. I assumed there would be markings on it, maybe a few letters or a tiny picture—the stuff of an eight-year-old's make-believe world.

"Yeah, but I can't tell *you* what they are."

"Why not?" I asked, as I started walking again. He fell in beside me.

"Because Jimmy Wales might find out. That's who the secrets are from."

"Who's Jimmy Wales?"

"Kid lives down there." He pointed down the road in the direction we were walking. "It's about a club. We're making a club."

"But you can't tell *me* about it?"

"No, 'cause then it wouldn't be a secret."

We walked on for a few minutes, neither of us saying much. Then from me: "What do you need a club for? Will it look like a baseball bat?"

"Not that kind of club." He laughed and slapped his leg. "It's gonna be a secret club with just four of us guys. We don't want Jimmy in it. No girls either."

"How long have you been mad at Jimmy?"

"Since yesterday. He wouldn't go fishing."

"You often go fishing with Jimmy?"

"Yeah, couple times a week."

"Think you'll ever go fishing with 'em again?"

"Nope."

"Ever had a fight with Jimmy before?"

"Yep, plenty of times."

"Ever hit each other?"

"Nah, we just wrestle."

"This club you're talking about: Is it gonna to be a fishing club?"

"Yep. We're gonna catch plenty of fish too. At a secret spot. Lots of big ones there."

"Where?"

"By the mill on Butternut Creek. We'll use worms."

"Well," I said, "I better keep walking and you better go home. I've got to walk clear to Oregon before dark. You tell that to your brother. And don't worry about me spillin' your secrets; we didn't talk secrets anyway—right?"

"No ... well ... er ... not much.... You won't tell anybody, will you?" He shuffled his feet and looked at the ground.

"Course not. Whatever you told me I've forgotten already. Besides, I'll be in Oregon."

That satisfied him and he soon started home.

I continued walking then, but in a far better mood having talked to the little guy. He was entirely different from his brother— so much so that I wondered if they really were brothers or if one or both were adopted. They didn't look much alike.

NEW TIRES AND
A MOTEL INVASION

For weeks the Toyota's tires had been getting steadily noisier. Not that it was a problem when we were driving the gravel roads I usually walked. Rather it was on paved roads to and from the campgrounds that we kept hearing the ever-louder wamp wamp of scalloped tires. It seemed as if they were wearing out too soon, given they had been regularly rotated and were fairly expensive to begin with. Even so, it was time to give in and buy new ones; the noise was becoming too much.

Just before closing time on a Thursday afternoon we found a small tire dealership with a big jolly owner. "Tires for a 1990 Corolla? Hell yes! All different grades—cheapies through standards to the best tires money can buy. Anything you want! Come back in the morning! Fix you right up, ha-ha!" The man just naturally talked loud. Next morning, we were there bright and early and bought the only four tires he had that would fit the car. The price was reasonable though and he was fun to talk to—he had an endless supply of anecdotes, one of which went more or less as follows:

It seems he sold a woman a set of tires, and she immediately set out for "Yankee Land" on a cross-country sightseeing tour. When she returned from "Out East," she hurried into his dealership and told him she had enjoyed the trip so much that she brought him a special treat. "So what'd you git me?" he asked, thinking he was about to dig into some special junk food. He weighed a good three hundred pounds.

"Over two hundred pictures that I took on my trip," she happily told him. "I've got 'em all right here." And with that she plopped a shoebox full of snapshots right in the middle of his service desk—it being ten in the morning and him having four or five customers "milling around" waiting for service.

He told her he couldn't possibly look at the pictures just then, whereupon she got "madder 'n hell." He placated her, he claimed, by saying he would like to see them all, but the following Sunday after church, on a table in the rec-room below the sanctuary.

Continuing, he said that true to his word he did indeed sit in the rec-room below the sanctuary for "two full hours" while she showed him "every dammed picture she took clear across the U.S. of A., and a hundred others of her kids, grandkids, and two dogs besides."

But Church? Sanctuary? No way, I thought to myself. Those words don't fit this guy and neither does rec-room—unless "rec" relates to "wreak" or "wreck" instead of "recreation."

But Helen didn't just stand there thinking. She fixed the man with a gimlet-eyed glare and demanded: "Did you really?"

"Did I really what?"

"Did you really look at every one of her pictures?—the way you just said you did."

"Certainly," he answered with a smile. "God's honest truth!"

I jumped in: "What about all those different kinds of tires you said you had that would fit my car last night? You only had one set when we got here this morning. Where's the God's honest truth there?"

"OK, so a shade less than God's truth," he allowed, "but it would be blasphemous to overstate His truth, now wouldn't it?"

Shaking our heads, we walked out to the car, and by ten o'clock we were back on the road south of Centerville. That part of Iowa has many parks and wildlife areas. There are the state parks, namely, Bob White, Sharon Bluffs, Lake Wapello, and Red Hawk Lake, as well as the Wildlife Management Areas Rathbun and Colyn—all within a radius of twenty miles. I was not surprised to see plenty of wildlife, including several flocks of turkeys.

Helen picked me up at four o'clock that afternoon, and on our way back to camp we detoured a couple of miles north in order to pick up a long stretch of paved road. We wanted to check out the new tires. Sure enough, the noise was minimal; indeed, the tires were unusually quiet and they would serve us well for years. The "Honest Truth" man had sold us good tires.

*   *   *   *

On October 2 we moved Lurch seventy miles to Clemmons, Iowa, to a combination motel and campground. Our campsite was about a hundred feet from the motel office, and during check-in the owner gave us a key to the building's back door. That way we could come inside anytime and take showers in restrooms back there.

We were set up and comfortable by five o'clock when I noticed four men and two women standing in front of the office door. I thought little of it at the time, but they were still there a half hour later, and when I started over to take a shower, the women broke away and hurried over to intercept me.

"Excuse me, but do you know where the owner is?" one of them asked. She was an attractive redhead, probably in her early forties.

"Couldn't tell you," I said. "He was here an hour ago when I checked in."

"We called ahead and reserved rooms. He knew we'd be coming in about now, but the office is shut up tight."

"Wish I could help—don't know where he is."

I unlocked the door and, nodding politely, went inside. When I came out a quarter hour later, they were still there, and one of the men had come back to join them. "I gotta pee somethin' awful," the redhead blurted. "Will you please, please unlock this door so I can use the ladies room?" She was fidgeting about in obvious misery, and her woman companion suddenly exclaimed, "If you don't let her in, she's gonna to have an accident."

I hesitated for a moment but then said, "Go ahead, I'll wait and lock the door when you come out."

Trouble was, when I opened the door to let *her* in, the other woman and the man beckoned to the others who were still out front. They trotted right back, and before I knew it, they were all inside, my protests good-naturedly brushed off. One of the men headed for the men's room; the others walked up the hall to the office.

They were a jovial enough bunch, if slightly drunk, and they paid no attention to me as two of them took chairs, one just stood, and the woman companion took a seat on the manager's desk.

I came to a quick boil about their invading the place when all I meant to do was let the redhead use the ladies room. "You realize," I hotly told them, "that you're putting me in an awkward spot just walking in here and taking over like this? If any of you has to go to the bathroom, let's do it; then how 'bout going back outside so I can lock the place up."

They didn't like that very much, but after a minute or two of face-saving stalling, they filed back down the hall and out the door. I waited for the remaining two; then I quickly locked up.

A half hour later, I looked out the motor-home window, and since they were still standing by the office door, I decided to go on a good-deed mission.

Back among the campsites, a half dozen Mexicans, who lived there and worked in the area, were cooking their suppers over a barbecue grill. I walked over, and although they couldn't speak English and I couldn't speak Spanish, I eventually got them to understand that I was looking for the owner. Laughing hard and with many gestures, the Mexicans let me know that the owner was probably downtown somewhere in a beer joint. Then they offered me tortillas and a Sol, the "Pabst Blue Ribbon of Mexican Beers." But I told them no thanks, knowing that if I didn't leave right away, I'd probably take them up on the beer and forget about my mission.

So I went back to the would-be guests and volunteered to drive into town and look for the owner—I said I had a pretty good idea where he might be. Ah, did that make me a great guy in their books! "Thank you sir, thank you!" Nevertheless, one of the men threw me a cockeyed glance and said, "Where's he at? In some beer joint someplace?"

"Don't know—see if I can find 'im."

But indeed, that's exactly where he was, bellied up to a bar debriefing some buddies about a pheasant shoot they had recently returned from. He too invited me to join the gang and have a beer, but when I thought about the high-and-dry guests, I told him I'd go back to the motel and do them a song-and-dance if he'd spot me a week's free camping. That brought him around—somewhat—and after more leisurely minutes of pheasant talk he began ... to prepare ... to get ready ... to begin ... to walk out the door and eventually—very eventually—head back to the motel.

He dragged his feet so long I couldn't stand it any longer and finally blurted, "You want me to go back and tell 'em to go away, or are you gonna go back and check 'em in?" I wanted to get back myself; Helen was getting dinner ready. "Motel Man" finally left, but I hung around for another ten minutes with his friends. I was surprised they would talk with me, a walk-in stranger, but no doubt my brief acceptance was thanks to the banter I had just had with their motel-owning crony.

The guests were gone when I got back to the motel, and it wasn't until the following day that we learned they had checked in and hadn't just given up and gone away. Late that afternoon, the redhead came down to the camper and thanked me for letting her into the motel and for chasing down the owner. Clearly sober now, she apologized for her "earthiness" in telling me she had to use the ladies room. I didn't remind her that she actually used the word *pee*.

She went on: "And you shouldn't have had to chase us out of the motel after bein' kind enough to let us in. Where you from, Honey?"

"Connecticut," I said. "We're out here walking across the country."

Helen came out and joined in as I told about the walk, and since it was still fresh in my mind, I also told her about the pleasant little boy with the contemptuous big brother—the kid who had pointedly doubted I was walking across the country. Even after several days, the older boy remained an irritating, albeit fading, memory.

The woman turned out to be from Philadelphia, not far from where Helen and I were raised.

THE LOUDEST CRICKET IN IOWA

It rained most of the next day, so we took a twelve-mile trip to Lamoni, Iowa, to visit Graceland College. I had heard of the college sometime in the past, but at first I couldn't remember when. Then it dawned on me. Sure enough, it was during the 1976 Olympics, and Bruce Jenner, the decathlon gold medalist, had been a student there. That tidbit was confirmed for us by a well-meaning freshman, who seemed to find it hard to believe that everyone was not simply born knowing all about Graceland College, and especially about Bruce.

During our visit we also learned that the college was affiliated with the Reorganized Church of Jesus Christ of Latter Day Saints. The Reorganized Church is different from the Church of Jesus Christ of Latter Day Saints (the Mormons), the distinguishing word being *Reorganized*. A group of secessionists from the Mormons formed the Reorganized Church in 1852, when they rejected the name *Mormon* along with the leadership of Brigham Young and some of his doctrines, including plural marriage. The Reorganized Saints hold that theirs is the legitimate continuation of the original church, as founded by Joseph Smith in 1830.

Now the Wannabes, those back-to-basics folk southeast of Leon, originated as quiet secessionists from the Reorganized Church—thus second-remove separatists from the original Mormons. Myra Kovaciny, whom I met near their commune, was a Wannabe.

Helen and I speculated about whether the Wannabes themselves would become a large group with many adherents in years to come. She thought they might, but I wasn't so sure. My impression was that they were probably a collection of modest, well-meaning people who would be held together only temporarily by a charismatic leader (hopefully no Jim Jones), whose eventual passing would begin the movement's decline. There seemed something pathetic yet endearing about their humble sincerity, at least as I perceived it while talking to Myra.

*   *   *   *

That night, just as we were going to bed, a cricket crawled under the engine cover, which humps up into the motor home's living quarters between the driver and passenger seats. There would be no sleeping with the loudest cricket in Iowa only eight feet away.

So what to do?

I imagined two scenarios: First, I would open the engine cover and the cricket would jump down to the ground. There it would take a few hops, disappear, and be heard no more. Second, I would open the engine cover and it would jump inside with Helen and me. There it would take a few hops, disappear, and be heard all night.

Wanting no part of scenario number two, I left the engine cover in place and went outside with a can of bug spray. Then, crawling under the front axle, I reached up and gassed the motor area thoroughly, the cricket hopefully, and myself definitely. With aching head and tight throat I was soon back in bed, but at least Jiminy Cricket was silenced.

It was in the morning, as we sat drinking coffee, that Helen said, "Honey, what's that smear on your pajama sleeve?"

"Don't know, don't see a thing," I pretended. It was grease, of course, and I had already noticed some on the bedclothes. There was even some on Helen although she didn't know it yet.

*   *   *   *

"It's too muddy, you'll get stuck." That bald statement came from a roofer who had paused from nailing shingles onto the roof of a new house. A gas-powered compressor droned away as I stood on the ground and shouted up to him, trying to find out what the road to the west was like. However, the man said no more, and I assumed he could hardly hear above the noise. He would grab a shingle, hold it in place, and then nail it with four quick shots from a nail gun. Then he would grab another and nail it, and another, and another.... It reminded me of laying bricks: pick up a brick, skim on a joint, lay it to the line, catch the mortar; pick up a brick, skim on a joint, lay it to the line, catch the mortar. And so on *ad infinitum*. Of course it wasn't really *ad infinitum*—more like *ad nauseam*, but sometimes it seemed that way when you'd been stooping and straightening for hours on end.

Anyway, the house sat on a corner lot that was bordered on the north by a west-going road leading to Leon. Helen had parked at the corner in full view of the house, and I had walked over to talk to the roofer. It had rained hard during the night, and the broad cow path, which when paved would become the home's driveway, was at that point a "mudway" of sticky black ooze. I was scraping it off my shoes and still trying to talk to the roofer when an electrician, who had been inside, came out and said, "You can get through easy enough. Mike up there's just chicken."

"The hell I am!" Mike exploded. "Iffen he goes out that there road, he's gonna be back here on foot after while wantin' somebody to go pull him out of a ditch. He needs to go north from that there corner. That'll take him into Leon—the long way round maybe, but he'll not make it goin' west."

Until he said all that, I had been thinking he could hardly hear over the compressor; now I decided he could hear anything he wanted to but didn't feel like talking to me—this stranger who had just walked up from out of nowhere.

The electrician again: "To hell you say, Mike. You came out that road this morning. If you can do it, anybody can—lousy as you drive."

"I got a four-wheeler, you dope. That bullshit rice bucket of hizzen won't be worth shit on mud." He waved toward the Toyota out by the corner. Helen thought he was waving to her, so she smiled real nice and waved back. I seethed.

Besides finding out about the road, I had come over hoping for some conversation, but these characters paid no attention to me at all. Mouthing off at each other was obviously a game to them, and I had just given them something to get started with.

Meanwhile, the compressor droned on, and every time one of them said something he would yell a little louder. Soon it was as if they were the only two people around while I stood there ignored. Half laughing but definitely annoyed, I muttered "thanks for nothing" and walked back toward the car. Helen watched me coming and got ready for the complaining: "Pair of windbags over there can't agree whether this road can be driven or not. Here they had a chance to talk to a genuine cross-America thru-walker, and they wouldn't shut up long enough to find out who they were talkin' to—make that in front of. I would a given 'em my autograph—let 'em share a bit in the glory. It's a tough world."

"I'm with you, Dearie, you're underappreciated. Now what about this road? It looks too muddy to me."

Helen hates mud or snow when she is driving, but the road didn't look too bad to me. "It's a trifle mushy," I allowed, "but it shouldn't be a problem." She was still reluctant, but after five minutes of my cajoling and minimizing the chances of a spinout, she finally agreed to try it.

So off she went, and I watched the car grow smaller in the distance, tracking straight at first, fishtailing some as it got farther away, and finally turning almost broadside before lurching into a curve to the north.

Having seen her skid, I was pretty sure what lay ahead. Ten minutes later, lugging a pound of mud on each shoe, I followed the road around to where Helen was standing beside the car. It was still on the road, but oblique to a ditch with its right rear wheel no more than a foot from the edge. She had been lucky to get that far. The track of the roofer's SUV showed that it too had slalomed from one side of the road to the other; even with four-wheel drive he'd had a hard time not spinning out.

"Sorry m'Love," I said, "I shouldn't have pushed you into this."

"No problem, Dearie," she happily replied. "But you're going to have to get it out of here!"

With Helen's kind though gleeful direction (along with a bit of luck), I got the car turned around and we headed back to the corner by the new house. When we arrived, I couldn't help sneaking a glance in the direction of the roofer. Sure enough, there he was, up near the chimney and grinning from ear to ear as he yelled, "Told you, dint I?" I threw him a wave; then we started up the north-going road, with Helen driving to the next rendezvous and me walking—of course.

A few hours later I reached Leon, passed through without stopping, and eventually met Helen at a crossroads west of town. We had lunch there; then, all too soon I was walking again. An overcast and fading colors made the countryside seem stark and austere, but there were plenty of pheasants to break the monotony. I would look ahead and try to predict which patch of corn or tangle of undergrowth they might fly up from. Once, a covey of probably five burst out of weeds along the edge of the road. I jumped and was doubly surprised—surprised at the number of birds, surprised by my own jumping.

In spite of becoming lost several times, we managed twenty-eight miles that day. Throughout the afternoon it grew steadily colder, and Helen declared that really chilly weather would come that night. She was wrong as it turned out, but only by days; a week later came the first autumn cold snap.

*   *   *   *

Somewhere southeast of Kellerton, there appeared a man up ahead carrying a milk can down a curved lane toward the road. He was Amish, by his dress, and we met where the lane and road joined; then we walked together for a mile—to a farmhouse where he and some friends were gathering to make apple cider. "That's what the milk can's for," he said with a laugh, "to put cider in."

He was a big fellow, thirty-something and pleasant, but very private, and what little I coaxed (wheedled?) from him came in slow, carefully chosen words. His family was one of a dozen that had emigrated up from Missouri to establish themselves in southern Iowa. Although he declined to tell me why they emigrated, he politely emphasized that they were self-sufficient people who farmed with horses not tractors, and drove buggies not cars. Socializing was with themselves not the "English," he said, softening that detail with a disarming smile.

After some additional stop-and-go small talk and some comments about the weather, I came back to their immigration: "Well, you picked a beautiful part of the country to settle in."

"Yes," he said in that methodical voice of his, "but it's a little hilly ... a bit hard on the horses, you know."

Well I didn't know, of course, and I certainly wouldn't have thought of it. Still, it was delightful to hear him say it that way.

I asked if his group missed their extended families, most of whom were still in Missouri. He answered that they didn't, that although the distance was too great for other than infrequent visits, they nevertheless kept in touch. End of response.

Although we walked together for another ten or fifteen minutes, comfortable in each other's presence—at least I was in his—the cultural difference was plainly too great, and neither of us found much more to say. Eventually, we came to the farm where he and his friends would make cider, and after a warm handshake and mutual good wishes, we went our separate ways.

It wasn't long, however, before I was wondering *how* his group kept in touch with their relatives in Missouri. In the culture without, that is, in the culture of we "English," one communicates by telephone, conventional mail, or e-mail. What kinds of communication, I wondered, did his culture allow? But driven to keep moving, I suppressed curiosity as usual, only to wish later that I had simply gone back and asked. He probably wouldn't have told me much, but I might have learned something about cider making.

Toward the end of the day I came to a self-service road stand which offered apples and jars of honey for sale by an honor system. I bought apples, put money in an old cigar box, and journeyed on—lugging the apples and looking forward to surprising Helen. I might have known. When I caught up to her, she was eager to show me the honey and apples she had bought at this "nifty fruit stand where you put your money in a cigar box."

That night we ate at the Sale Barn Café near Mount Ayr, Iowa. As the name suggests, the Café is attached to a large barn, one part of which is used for auctioning livestock. In another part you can buy almost anything from work clothes to saddles to children's toys. Much of the inventory was locally made; all of it was interesting to Helen and me. In fact, we became stuck browsing, until Helen declared we were not there to Christmas shop but rather to eat dinner. And with that she led the way into the café proper. We had barbecue beef sandwiches and homemade pie for dessert.

The sandwiches were excellent, but we especially enjoyed the pie—so much so that we tried to buy a couple to take with us. "Sorry, we're running out," the friendly waitress told us, "can't sell pies right now. Come back about eleven tomorrow when they're hot out of the oven. We sell a few then."

Of course we didn't get back the next morning, it being a walking day; however, we made a special trip three days later and bought two, one peach and one cherry. We would be glad we made the drive.

BATTLING RADIO PROBLEMS

In the second week of October we moved to Lake of Three Fires State Park near Bedford, Iowa. Three Fires, being only ten miles beyond walk's end, would mean relatively short drives the first day back walking, but unusually long ones the second and third days. We would have to accept the longer drives or else move again after only two days. Camping thirty miles farther on, somewhere in the vicinity of Clarinda, would have been much better, but Helen's book listing RV parks showed nothing in that area.

On our way to Three Fires we decided to stop in Leon and try to solve a long-standing CB radio problem. We had two radios: one permanently mounted in the RV and another, hand-held unit, that Helen kept in the car. We only needed them on moving days, but they were important then. As we drove along, we would use them for airy gossip or for assigning blame in the event of a wrong turn. Helen said the latter was a no-brainer since I was always in the lead driving the RV.

Helen's was the radio causing trouble. It seemed to quit working whenever we really needed it, for example, when we were discussing the implications of some unexpected detour. Since it drew power from the car's cigarette-lighter socket, I thought maybe the socket was faulty, and indeed, my voltmeter showed that sometimes there was power there and sometimes there wasn't. That alone could account for the problem.

Upon arriving in Leon, we quickly found a back-street garage where a slow-talking mechanic said he could bypass the socket by installing a separate power outlet for the radio. "Perfect, let's do it," I said, not even asking how long it would take or how much it might cost. And was he ever slow! It took him a couple of hours to run two wires and install the socket, and another ten minutes to verify there was power there. He had done a good job, however, and when we plugged in the radio, it came up loud and clear. And his bill? Indeed, it was so modest that I insisted he take an extra ten dollars.

By then it was already after twelve o'clock, so we had lunch in a restaurant there in Leon. On the road, finally, about two o'clock, we had not gone far when Helen reminded me that the propane tank was almost empty. Good Lord, running out of propane could mean a cold dinner or, worse yet, no morning wake-up coffee! We'd need to get filled up along the way, but would we ever get to Three Fires?

The first gas dealership we came to was staffed only by an elderly woman who said she was the office manager. There was nobody else around, but if I could wait until five o'clock, "somebody who can fill you up *might* stop by here on his way home."

Might stop? I wanted the tank filled *for sure*, and long before five o'clock. I thanked the pleasant lady, and Helen and I got back on the road.

Before long we came to another dealership, but this one was locked up tight—on Friday if you will—at two in the afternoon! Tired and frustrated, I walked away from the front door and back to the motor home, where I tried to radio Helen. She was sitting in the car on the far side of the parking lot. "H.B. this is J.B. We've probably got enough propane to last till tomorrow. Let's keep going and get camped—bring this day to an end. Over."

"H.B. to J.B.," came her reply, and nothing after that but fragmented words, dropouts, and intermittent static. And her only "spittin' distance" away! Why the *heck* couldn't we get to the bottom of this radio problem? I turned off my CB's squelch because nobody within miles was using that frequency; then I walked over to the car and arranged with Helen to try another radio check. No luck. She could hear me loud and clear, but everything from her came through my radio broken up and garbled.

Next, we put batteries into her radio and tried it that way— we'd never used it with batteries before. Same result. She could receive just fine, but she couldn't transmit.

At that point it finally dawned on me. We had had two problems: the Toyota's lighter socket had worked only part-time, and the radio's transmitter had an intermittent fault of its own. The mechanic had fixed the socket problem, but the intermittent was still with us, just waiting to scotch communications at least opportune times.

Thoroughly frustrated, we began driving again, but within a few miles our luck changed when we came to a propane dealership with an on-site staff. The jolly fellow who filled the tank gave me lots of free advice about how to drain a motor home's black-water tank. "Gotta be careful," he said with a grin, "or your crap'll come flyin' right back atcha." As if I didn't know all about that!

We arrived at Three Fires sometime after six o'clock, and too tired to cook anything elaborate, we made poached eggs for dinner. Later, Helen caught up on her log: *"Hectic day—one thing after another—although it's ending up pretty well. Phil's interrupting me ... as I try ... to write. Says he hears coyotes far away. I don't hear anything but he hears better than I do."*

Indeed, I did hear coyotes that night at Three Fires. It sounded like a number of them by their nonstop yips and yaps, but I had heard plenty of coyotes by then and knew that two or three can sound like a dozen.

*   *   *   *

The next morning we slept in; then, after breakfast, I took time to print a new set of computer maps while Helen telephoned our daughters. By the time we got on the road, it was nearly nine-thirty.

Through the remainder of the morning the walk paralleled state route 2, taking us south of Bedford along empty dirt roads. Once, a warning sign said that a bridge farther along had been washed out. Helen waited near the sign, and when I arrived, we drove forward to check it out. The road narrowed at first but eventually widened again, and finding no bridge problem, we returned to the warning sign, from whence I resumed my solitary march. There was hardly any traffic; I saw only three or four cars although a number of times I heard rumblings from tractors or combines in distant fields.

By midafternoon, sunlight had warmed the near-ground air, so that man-made noises were refracting upward and no longer masking the rustle of leaves or occasional birdsong. Sometimes it was so quiet that I was reminded of deep-ocean silence, a silence I had often struggled to "listen through" toward some faint and far-off target.

I had always imagined Iowa to be pool-table flat from east to west and north to south. However, across the state and just above the Missouri border, the land slowly rises from Fort Madison on the Mississippi River to high ground near Bedford, and continuing west, it slowly descends to the Missouri River at Nebraska City. Over the 180 miles from the Mississippi to Bedford, the change in elevation is about 700 feet—far too gradual to notice while walking, yet somehow I imagined I could sense the increasing altitude. In addition, in some areas, like where I was walking that day, the country is hilly in a local sense, that is, there are brief, moderate grades between shallow valleys and low rises. I remembered my Amish friend's phrase: "a bit hard on the horses, you know."

By four o'clock we had covered twenty-five miles under nearly cloudless skies; then it was back to Three Fires, but we would stop on the way for dinner.

On state route 2 just west of Bedford, there is a place called the Starlight Café, which features a band on Saturday nights. Most of the music is out of the fifties, and many of the clientele were born in the thirties. They're a friendly crowd, and we fit right in that Saturday night, October 9, 1999—especially age-wise.

After dinner when everybody was having a good time, Helen took a notion to dance. I thought it was a great idea until I tried to get up, and that's when I found that neither bones nor muscles were willing to do one more bit of work that day. Maybe it was the twenty-five miles they had already carried me. In any case, it was a tonic just to sit there and enjoy, if only vicariously, the camaraderie between these locals, who had known each other most of their lives.

It was more than an hour until we had had enough and started up the road to Three Fires.

THE DANGERS OF BLASPHEMY

It sounded like a far-away motorcycle when I first heard its rumble in the distance toward the east. Well, it's a motorcycle's third cousin, I thought, when it was finally close enough and I could see it was a quad bike. (Quad Bikes, a.k.a. All-Terrain Vehicles or ATVs, are small, noisy, four-wheeled, off-road machines that evolved years ago from motorcycles through a larva stage of fat-wheeled, motorized tricycles.) As it drew near, the driver began to slow down, and I could tell from his expression that he would want to know what this lone figure was doing marching across the countryside—maybe his countryside.

Carl Nadok was old and mostly curious, but he was also suspicious—as if he thought I might be up to something "vandalish," as he subsequently put it. He came around quickly, however, upon learning that I was only walking across the country, and he apologetically explained his suspicions by telling me how vandals had been burning hay bales awaiting collection from the fields. I was reminded of Dianne Fencer's concerns about similar vandalisms back in Ohio months before.

"But you're obviously not the vandalish kind," he allowed, now smiling, and that being settled, he was delighted to tell me what I could expect farther west. The roads, he assured me, would be just like the ones I had been walking: dusty, windy, cold, and endless.

Thanks Carl, I needed that!

He would have gone on a good while about my upcoming hardships as he saw them, except that I politely interrupted and asked if he was retired. He had to be, he looked at least eighty years old.

"Partly, I still do some farming," he answered.

"You always been a farmer?"

"No."

He didn't volunteer what he had done as a career, but my guess was that he had been military or law enforcement, or maybe a successful businessman. When serious, which he obviously could be, he spoke well and with authority.

And then we somehow began talking about grown children. Older people, whatever their backgrounds and age, can usually relate to each other's interests in their children, and Carl had a middle-aged son with an unusual job.

An ordained minister in one of the major Protestant denominations, this son had had at least two churches before becoming a roving troubleshooting peacemaker for church government. He would travel to a congregation that was having major difficulties of one kind or another—sometimes financial problems, sometimes intra-congregational squabbles—or sometimes, believe it or not, harassment problems, where the minister was being bullied by his hostile flock. As troubleshooter, Carl's son would spend a few months at the church, do his best to put out the fire, and then move on to another church with another problem.

It struck me that this kind of firefighting could be depressing, not so much when finances were involved, but when the parishioners were battling each other or badgering the poor minister. The peacemaker would need the Wisdom of Solomon and the Patience of Job! Or just maybe, it crossed my mind, he would do better with the jawbone of an ass to beat the fools over the head with. But I didn't say that to Carl; I just told him that he must have raised a mentally tough son, and that he was probably an apple that hadn't fallen far from the tree. I meant it as a compliment; there was something solid about the old man—no nonsense but fair minded.

Carl and I parted with smiles and handshakes, and five minutes later I was hoofing along complacently thinking, *And these are supposed to be Christians—Love thy neighbor!* I felt a twinge of remorse, however, that's doubtless rooted in a lonely ambivalence toward organized religion along with a genuine respect for religious people of any persuasion. That's provided, of course, that they respect other people's religions, do not refer to agnostics as atheists, and agree with Saint Paul that faith and hope are important but that charity matters most of all.

But mild remorse didn't get me off the hook with God, for just then a bug flew into my left ear—all the way down till he hit the eardrum.

For "Mr. Bug" it must have been like happily flying through space and then suddenly plunging down a black hole. For me, it was like being punched inside the head. At first I could feel his feet scratching against my ear canal as he tried to get out, but he was in headfirst and too dumb to back up. Next, he tried to fly out, and what a noise that made! For some reason it reminded me of somebody trying to get a stuck car out of a muddy ditch. The screech of tires rises to crescendo, only to recede to quietness followed by another try a few moments later. Mr. Bug would vibrate his wings, slowly at first but then right up to full throttle. The buzz would continue for five or six seconds after which he would get tired and there would be quiet again—the quiet of a plugged-up ear. Of course he got nowhere trying to fly out, but his wings oscillating against my eardrum make a racket unlike anything I had ever heard before.

I scotched an impulse to pull and twiddle the ear in hopes of helping him work his way out. Wax had been forming in there lately, probably from the cold, and I was afraid twiddling might get him mixed up in the wax. Didn't need that. That could end up with somebody at a hospital digging out both him and the wax, at my inconvenience and expense. Then, thoughts of working him out with a car key were briefly entertained—and resolutely dismissed!

Meanwhile, I tried by telepathy to will him simply to turn around and walk toward the light. After all, if telepathy works better the closer the subjects, it ought to work well in this case. Our brains, the bug's and mine, were no more than inches apart, albeit different in size, I like to think.

Five minutes of scratching and buzzing were followed by sudden silence. I hadn't felt him leaving, so I walked along for some time continuing to wish him out but expecting the noise to restart any second. Five, ten, fifteen minutes passed in welcome silence before I was distracted by a deserted car that was partly off the road and in a ditch. That was unusual. Then it was back to worrying about the bug: Why no more buzzing? Has he come out? He doesn't seem to be in there. At least I can't feel him anymore.

Helen's car appeared up ahead, and I began to think about how good a granola bar would taste. Then it was back to worrying about the bug, but less now as concern began mixing with growing relief. *He's gone,* I began to think. *Thank God, I'm home free.*

Was their irony in my unspoken *Thank God,* I wondered? No, I assured myself, it's only a figure of speech.

Things learned that afternoon along a dusty road in southwestern Iowa: One, don't blaspheme if there is a bug around that can fly down your ear. Two, telepathy is real, at least between bugs and people.

*　　*　　*　　*

It was Helen's birthday and I thought it would be nice to celebrate at good old Starlight Café, which we would pass on our way back to Three Fires. Besides, we expected to reach the Missouri River the following day, and we could celebrate that too, even if a day in advance.

Our dinners were again excellent, and afterwards café staff brought Helen a piece of strawberry shortcake with a candle on top. Then we all clapped hands and sang "Happy Birthday."

THE TRANSIENT IOWA INDIANS

Thirty miles east of Nebraska City the countryside is drained by the Nishnabotna River, which joins the Missouri fifty miles to the south. Between the two rivers lies the crumpled, wooded terrain of Waubonsie State Park, which borders the eastern edge of the Missouri floodplain. I followed Iowa 2 across the Waubonsie hills, and then a side road across the plain, which in that area is fully six miles wide. The road passed a number of modest farms before bearing north along a high dike, which I climbed at one place for a look-see. You can see great distances from twenty feet when the surrounding country is flat for miles.

To the west lay the Missouri River, meandering for miles along the boundary of the floodplain, and across the river, beyond the far shore, bordering bluffs stretched north and south. Nebraska City's buildings marched downslope toward the water, while south of a highway bridge (which I would soon walk), I could see train cars on a spur of the Union Pacific Railroad. Not far from the cars was a striking cleft in the hills where South Table Creek flowed down to the Missouri.

It was quiet, almost silent, as I turned and gazed eastward over another vast plain. Three miles away and squarely in its center lay north-south I-29, which was paralleled by a main line of the Burlington Northern Railroad. A long freight train moved slowly southward toward Kansas City, 170 miles downriver.

But it was the northeastern highlands that were most intriguing and which impart a poignant sense of history. On those hills, forty miles upstream, lies Council Bluffs, the scene of great meetings between surviving Iowa Indians and the Lewis and Clark expedition in 1804. By that time the Iowa, a tribe of hunters and farmers, had been decimated by smallpox.

Whatever understandings were reached during those meetings, the Indians, twenty years later, ended up ceding their lands to the government and were relocated to southeastern Kansas and Oklahoma. In a mere twenty years their way of life ended, and I, flesh and blood and ever so transient, could not help marveling how human affairs change so quickly while geologic changes take eons. The bluffs were there and looked the same before humans lived in North America. How different would they someday be, when the last human beings were gone?

The sun was low and I shivered a bit—partly from the growing chill but partly from a turn of thought that in the stillness included a keen awareness of the grass, the river, the dusty road, and my very mortal self.

Time to move on, time to come back to the moment, I thought, as I clambered off the dike and continued north to rejoin route 2 where it crosses the river. A strip of jerky and a drink of water helped me back to real life, and shortly I spotted Helen, waiting at the end of the bridge. We took some pictures and then I walked "across the wide Missouri." We had celebrated that milestone in advance the night before, but we would do it again when we got back to Bedford, seventy miles to the east. We needed people, lights, and music that afternoon, and that was exactly what we would get.

On the east side of Bedford we found a place that was notably different from the Starlight Café, where we had celebrated with seniors the night before. The other end of the age spectrum hangs out there, and instead of fifties ballads and instrumentals, you hear the music young people love—jackhammer loud. Personable youngsters hang out there; if you catch their eye, they'll smile and nod, but you cannot talk to anybody because nobody can hear over the noise.

With gestures and loud voices we ordered pizza and soft drinks to re-celebrate our crossing the Missouri. The Sprite and pizza might have been okay, but you could hardly tell because of a blue fog of cigarette smoke. Part of the taste process, I've read, is olfactory, and the concentrations of smoke and pizza aroma must have been about the same. "They cancel each other out," I laughingly told Helen. "That's why we can't taste anything." She was tired. I could tell, because all I got was a faint smile, which meant she was played out and anxious to head home to Three Fires.

The following morning we set out to solve our nagging CB radio problem. Helen's hand-held unit had always been awkward to use while driving; with its intermittent malfunction it was now almost useless. Clarinda was only twenty miles away, so we would leave Lurch at the campground and drive over in the car. With a little luck, we'd be able to buy a dash mounted radio there. It would be easier and safer to use than the hand-held unit.

Arriving early in town, we quickly found an auto parts dealership that sold and installed CBs. Fortunately, they had a brand-name radio for a reasonable price, and even better, the manager said they could install it that afternoon if we would come back after lunch. That was fine with us. We'd wander around town and be back by one o'clock.

Touring the main streets, we noted Clarinda Municipal Hospital, drove past Iowa Western College, even followed signs to the birthplace of Glen Miller, the famous bandleader, who, though born in Clarinda, seems to have grown up in Colorado.

Sometime late in the morning, I caved in to a worry that had been nagging me for several days—ever since the bug flew down my ear. The ear didn't feel quite right. Was part of him still in there? Soon after it happened, I was pretty sure he crawled out, but had he left a leg or wing or something else behind? Every once in a while I would get two or three quick twinges deep down near the eardrum, not intense, but enough to be noticeable. Maybe Mr. Bug was actually a Ms. Bug, and maybe she had laid eggs down there; maybe they had hatched and the young were getting ready to eat their way out. As long as we couldn't get the radio installed until afternoon, why not use the time to drop by Clarinda Municipal and get somebody to look down there?—see what was what.

As soon as we arrived at the hospital, it was "déjà vu all over again." The woman at the reception desk took insurance information and then called for a volunteer with a wheelchair—just like back in Indiana when I had my knee X-rayed. And just like then I protested: "But I'm walking across America ... don't need a wheelchair." And just like then I got nowhere. "Sorry," said the firm, reception-desk lady, "but tell me all about this walk before you leave the hospital. You must have some story." She really was a pleasant soul—just doing her job.

Before long I was being pushed along by a young woman, maybe a volunteer, who happily joined Helen in rapid-fire repartee about helpless old men, "this specimen in particular." I listened quietly until we were almost to the examining room; then I laughingly declared it should be every man's birthright to have a woman at beck and call to earn his living, cook his dinner, push his wheelchair; in short, to minister to his every wish, whim, desire, or lust—day or night. Especially night.

Helen was ecstatic as she punched my left arm and hissed, "You'll pay for that!" but "Wheelchair Girl" turned out to be better at *give* than *take*. She stiffened, I could feel it by the way she pushed the wheelchair, and when we got to the examining room she shoved me through the door with a brusque "He's all yours" to the waiting staff inside. Then she disappeared.

"Done it again," I said to Helen.

A nurse and a nurse's aide checked my blood pressure and temperature, and told us the doctor would arrive shortly—he had to come in from home. Indeed, he was a while getting there, but when he did he took a long look in the ear and told me the bug was gone, all of it, and that everything looked fine. Wind and cold, he said, were probably causing the aching.

Both the doctor and hospital staff were not only thorough and professional but congenial and fun to talk to. The nurse's aide thought she ought to be able to "look into one of this guy's ears and see out the other." I asked how that could be and wasn't disappointed. "Didn't somebody say he was walking across the country?" she quipped.

After that happy exchange, Helen and I took leave of Clarinda Hospital with our thanks for the medical attention and for the many good wishes. I would have liked to spot Wheelchair Girl to tell her I was only kidding about the birthright thing, but she was nowhere to be seen. She was so annoyed she might have quit volunteering.

We had just enough time for a snack at a local café; then it was back to the auto parts dealership. They let me stand in the garage part of the dealership and watch two men install the radio. The pair worked well together, but one fellow did all the talking while the other said nothing. And I mean nothing. The talker, however, was not really the boss; more often than not the men would attach a bracket or run a wire according to the gestured directions of the quiet one. Curious, several times I tried to get "Mr. Taciturn" to say something, anything. No luck. He wouldn't even make eye contact. I'd almost given up, when just as the job was finishing, he suddenly looked my way and said, "Now Mister, just why did you set out to walk clear the hell and gone across the country?"

I was so surprised I stared at the man—right into a smiling face with a missing front tooth. "I thought you couldn't talk," I growled.

"Which would you rather have?" he came right back, "a quiet first rate job on your radio, or a boot's job and a lotta chitchat." Then, turning serious, he wanted to know all about the walk: Had any problems with dogs? How many miles do you walk in a day? What's your wife do while she's waitin' for you? Any problems with people?

They were the usual questions, but I jumped on the last one. I told him I had had no problems with people who could talk. "But once in a while," I was pleased to tell him, "you meet some character who *can* talk but pretty much *won't*." I was thinking of the roofer back near Leon, the fellow who called our beloved Toyota a *rice bucket*. Mr. Taciturn hardly batted an eye as he laughed and extended his arm to shake hands.

After that we did small talk until things wound down; then Helen and I headed back to Lake of Three Fires. As soon as we arrived, we got on the radios and began talking between the one in the motor home and the new one in the car. At a range of a hundred feet they worked fine. "Good Lord," Helen said, "let's hope so!" As we continued nonstop chatter, she drove the car out of the campground and down the road toward Bedford. At a distance of two miles we could still hear each other loud and clear. Thank goodness, the new radio was working fine, and it looked as if our CB problems were over.

And they were—almost.

PHOTOGRAPHER OR CARPENTER?

Since it was approaching mid October and already quite cool, only a few people were still camping at Three Fires. In fact, after dinner one evening, Helen said she doubted there was anyone within miles. I agreed, but only minutes later, when I was outside closing the car windows, I noticed a pickup truck facing north and parked along the edge of a clearing about two hundred yards away. Only the hood and cab were actually in the clearing; the driver had backed up so as to force the truck's bed and rear wheels deep into some bushes. We had passed the spot when driving in an hour before, and I was sure there was nobody there then. Curious, I watched for several minutes and then turned to go back inside. Just as I did, there was motion inside the truck's cab.

Five minutes later the truck had moved to the other side of the clearing, but now the hood was pushed into the bushes and the cab and bed jutted into the clearing. "What's going on?" I said to Helen. "It can't be somebody likely to make trouble; whoever it is surely knows we've seen him." I agonized for a few minutes and then decided to walk over and find out what was going on. I knew that if I didn't we would be wondering after dark if he was still there, far away, or right outside.

"Shh, hello," a young man softly hissed while I was still several paces from the driver's door. "There's a couple of deer up there, and I'm hoping they'll come down so I can get a picture. Move real slow, will you, maybe you won't scare 'em … any more than you already have." He gestured up the clearing. Indeed there were two deer about three hundred yards away, but they were doubtless aware of him and his truck, and now I had shown up. They wouldn't likely come closer.

However, respecting young man's concerns, I very slowly stepped the remaining distance to the truck's cab and then looked in. Sure enough, there was a camera with a telephoto lens pointing out the passenger window and up the clearing toward the deer, but more interesting, it was mounted atop a unique wooden cabinet.

"You make the cabinet?" I whispered.

"Yes," he said. "I do a some carpentry, but photography's my real passion."

If he was inclined to downplay his woodworking, I was nevertheless impressed. The cabinet's body sat on the passenger seat, but its front edge was steadied by detachable legs that rested on the truck's floor, and a polished crossbar with ingenious brackets held it firmly against the seatback. In addition to the camera mount, the cabinet had little drawers for storing lenses along with all those extra gadgets serious photographers seem to carry. It was a striking piece of work, cleverly designed and skillfully made.

By now the deer were gone, probably thanks to me, but the young man's good nature got the better of his annoyance, as he introduced himself as Alben Barkley. Would he know, I wondered, that his name was the same as Truman's Vice President? I guessed he would, although he would not have been born until long after the Truman era. I took him to be in his late twenties.

But how much of a photographer was this fellow? I wondered, as I drifted into reflections. No one would doubt he was a skilled woodworker, but it struck me that he might be more intrigued by cameras and gadgets than by picture taking itself. I thought of myself as a young man, when I still aspired to be first-rate photographer. I read books on both photographic art and darkroom technique, but expertise in the latter was my real forte. No finger marks detracted from my pictures; negatives were perfectly exposed and enlargements were skillfully cropped, blocked, or burned-in. Technically, the finished pictures were quite respectable; artistically, they were never more than mediocre, although I had trouble admitting it in those days.

I had been taking and developing pictures for several years when a cousin, Neal Welliver, showed me a number of photos he had taken. Neal was en route to becoming a successful landscape artist, and he regarded his photos as preliminary work in support of his paintings. Unconcerned that they might be stained or smudged, he never meant them to be finished products. To him, they were rough working pictures that would eventually relate to a finished painting as rough drafts might relate to a finished essay. He was only interested in artistic composition, and from the pictures he considered his poorest to the ones he considered his best, every one was better than any I produced. That was the end of my youthful illusion that with experience and a great deal of practice, I could become a really good photographer. To be an successful artist of any kind, you must first have *substantial* natural talent....

"You okay sir?" The young man suddenly asked.

"Yea, sure ... thanks," I said, recovering. Then, "That's a nifty cabinet and a good steady camera support, but you can only take pictures through the passenger window. What'll you do if a deer stands out there in some other direction?" He grinned as I asked the obvious.

"Get out and hold the camera by hand," he said. "Actually, I rarely sit in the truck; guess I'm a bit lazy tonight. Usually, I work down by the lake with the camera on a tripod."

Using a tripod for pictures of wildlife didn't seem quite right to me. In order to point and shoot quickly, I thought a person might do better hand-holding. But I didn't venture the unasked-for opinion, and in any case, it was time to leave. I had checked the fellow out and somehow he reminded me of a youthful me: photographer, tradesman, naïve, and harmless. He had to be all right, I decided, especially since he even looked a little like me—a forty-years-younger me.

I walked back to the motor home, and when I looked out a few minutes later, Alben was just leaving. Five minutes after that, two deer (the same two?) sauntered across the near-dark clearing only yards from where he had been parked.

THE PRAIRIE AS IT ONCE WAS

Walk's end was now west of the Missouri River and far from our campground at Three Fires. It was time to move again, and on the evening of October 15 we selected Pawnee State Park near Lincoln, Nebraska, as our next home base. Dawdling the next morning, we got a late start; still later we chose a wrong road and consequently had a hard time with traffic in Lincoln. It was a long drive—130 miles—so it was nearly five o'clock when we finally got the motor home parked and set up.

At that point we might have stayed put and fixed a leisurely dinner. But we had been told that nearby was a section of natural prairie maintained by a wildlife club in association with the Nebraska Game and Park Commission. Late as it was, we set out to find it, and it proved well worth the effort.

The last rays of sun were glowing on original prairie grass when we pulled off the road and got out of the car. "Hurry up and get the camera ready," Helen said, "or it'll be too dark." And even as I worked the camera, the shadow of a low hill slowly replaced the sunlight with pre-dusk shade. My two film pictures, which were developed later, show a golden field of clumpy, coarse grass standing waist high on smiling Helen. She's wearing her pink-red jacket, and the smile is one I often see just after I've done something she's told me to do—something she knew I was going to do anyway. Beyond her, and stretching on to a distant hill, the vast grasslands gave a modern view of how the plains must have looked for hundreds of miles and thousands of years.

"You can see why the pioneers talked about 'sod busting.'" Helen remarked. "It's obvious they didn't break this ground with flimsy plows.

"No, they didn't," I answered, "and it's obvious there was little erosion before they started plowing."

Original prairie grasses held the soil in place in an undisturbed mesh of tough roots, but nowadays, with the root mesh gone and fields regularly plowed, loosened soil is much more easily washed or blown away. We had already seen plenty of signs of erosion, especially as evidenced by muddy streams back in Ohio. Average topsoil thickness all across the heartland is much less now than it was a hundred years ago. It is something the farming community grapples with continuously. Crop rotation and modern plowing methods minimize the loss, and farming associations and state governments support programs to assist farmers in managing the problem. As troublesome as topsoil loss has been, there is at least some consolation in knowing that responsible people consider its avoidance something owed future generations.

It was dark by the time we got back to camp, and too tired for serious cooking, we threw together a simple dinner. Then it was off to bed with resolutions to take it easier the next day and get rested up.

In the morning, resolutions forgotten as usual, we headed for the University of Nebraska's museum at Lincoln. Entering the lobby, we were immediately attracted to a set of display cabinets that housed souvenirs and pictures from a local couple's auto odyssey. They had driven from Lincoln to the Rocky Mountains and back in a vintage Buick sedan. It was the 1920s; roads were unpaved, and cars were far less reliable than they are today. They became stuck, they blew tires, they even had engine problems. But through it all the wife kept a journal in which she described event after event in fast-moving, lucid narrative.

You could tell from the woman's writings that they enjoyed their adventure, and you could also tell why they were able to do it. Simply put, they were mentally resilient and knew how to persevere. Once, after the Buick became mired in mud and had to be pulled out with much struggling, she wrote how gloomy they became. But she made tea and it revived their spirits, and then she noted how one's moods, attitudes, and emotions are affected by food or by the stimulation of coffee or tea. For Helen and me, many of her observations were easy to relate to.

We left the museum in early afternoon to go shopping for walking shoes and groceries. The shoes I had bought two months before were becoming ragged, and I was determined to replace them with proper fits for both feet. That meant I needed two pairs because of that one foot being shorter than the other.

After twenty minutes of blindly scouting for a Wal-Mart, I caved in and asked a pedestrian for directions. Sure enough, there was a Wal-Mart about four miles away, thus a quarter mile from where we'd begun looking to begin with. Helen smiled. Twenty minutes later we were buying two pairs of Dr. Scholl's twenty-six-dollar shoes, the same kind I was in the process of wearing out.

Back out in the parking lot, I took a size nine shoe from one box, a nine and a half from the other, and behold: I finally had a pair that fit both feet. From then on my shorter right foot would not be loose and scuffing up and down in a too-long shoe. "Perfect," Helen happily enthused. "Now you'll be able to do some real long-distance walking 'stead of just skimpy twenty-some-mile days."

After Wal-Mart's we found a grocery store where we bought food for a special dinner that night. We were both tired of eggs and TV fare. And what a dinner Helen turned out! The roast chicken was perfect with all the right extras; it was like Thanksgiving in October, but with chicken, which I like even better than turkey. I awarded the dinner a well-deserved A-plus, according to my Generic Dinner-Grading Scale. In addition, I gave Helen a kiss and an extra A-plus for effort, which prompted the remark, "Keep at it, Buddy, and you'll be eating TV dinners for the next month."

We finished the day with a movie followed by the last of the Sale Barn pie.

ZIGZAGS, DUST, AND A GRIM
RIVER FLOODPLAIN

The next day we drove back to the west side of the Missouri River bridge at Nebraska City, where we had finished walking three days before. Well rested and glad to be on the road again, I quickly covered two miles along a detour south of Nebraska 2; then it was west on a gravel farm road, unmarked on my map but labeled K-2 by a road sign along the way. After a few miles, I turned south for another half mile, then west onto soft dirt, this road simply marked L.

Many zigzags and choking dust characterized the midmorning walk. There had been no rain for a week and the air was still; consequently, I would first become aware of a far off vehicle just by its kicked-up dust. Dense, roiling, and undispersed by breezes, it would trail out behind for a quarter mile—a long, approaching tube of grime that would be at least a minute drifting south after car or truck had passed. Always, before it arrived, I would cross to the north side of the road and cover my nose with a handkerchief, wishing all the while for a mild breeze to clear the air and make walking easier, or at least less dirty.

Eventually I got more than I wished for, for the wind began to blow, gently at first but then with increasing strength, and not as the gentle breezes I had hoped for, but rather as malevolent gusts that whipped up the dust and blew it about in swirling abandon. By late morning my pants, shirt—even my hair—had a gritty feel, and my saliva was tinged with brown.

Helen hardly fared better. One minute the wind would be from the northwest, next from the south, moments later it might swing around to the east. She would park the car and open a window on the side away from the currently approaching wind. But sure enough, before long it would change direction again; there would be an especially strong gust, and she would get another dose of choking dust. When I met her at lunchtime, there was a layer of grit on the dashboard, the windowsills, the seat tops—all through the car. Not that the car was ever very clean; we usually ate lunch sitting in it, and occasionally one of us spilled something. This grime, though, was something else....

After eating, we sat for over an hour waiting for the wind to die down, and toward two o'clock it did, until it was almost as still as it had been hours before.

Back walking again and far more comfortable, I recalled leaving the Mississippi River Valley, and how I appreciated the higher terrain west of Fort Madison. Now I was noticing similar topography west of the Missouri as the ground rose into similar hills blanketed by similar fields, similar pastures, and similar wood plots. Vistas were beautiful and my awareness of the elevation added to the appeal.

According to my map, the road I was walking would dead-end at a T-junction a half mile east of the Nemaha River near the town of Syracuse. Helen and I had agreed to meet there, after which I would detour north through town, west a little and then south again to get back on track.

However, when we met, thoughts of the five-mile detour soon had us wondering if I couldn't simply push on cross country and avoid the extra walking. I had done it before. Looking west from where we stood, a footpath ran several hundred yards before fading out along a cornfield which was bounded on the north by a stretch of trees and brush.

"It's up to you," Helen said, "but watch out for snakes."

"If a snake bites me, it'll get sick and die," I declared, as I made up my mind to continue straight through. I would walk along the cornfield and look for a place to wade the river when I got there. I didn't expect it to be wide; in fact, on the map it looked too narrow even to be called a river. If I missed joining up with Helen somewhere on the other side, I would hitchhike to camp or find someone to drive me. One way or another, we would meet back at Pawnee Campground.

Then we were off, Helen driving north along an old right-of-way and me walking west along the field. A half-mile hike brought me to a steep bank that sloped down to the river, which in that place was narrow but deep. Though unfordable there, it appeared wider and shallower a hundred yards to the north. I started that way, and after twisting and wiggling through leafy undergrowth, I was eventually able to slide down the embankment of a dry streambed that gave on to the river's floodplain.

But how stark that muddy place was! Its surface was pock-marked with recent tracks—bobcat, coyote, raccoon, and fox—but the dead were there too. The body of a rat lay feet-up and bloated to three inches across; a partially eaten fish lay in shallows nearby. Something had killed a large bird and its strewn wreckage looked like a plane crash—feathers here, a foot there, a single eyeball staring skyward, as if regretting a lost opportunity for airborne escape. Nearby, its eyeless, severed head, beak still attached, lay on its side like the forlorn nose cone of Pan Am 107. The floodplain was a lonely and macabre place, a place where animals were either quick or dead.

Put off by the sights and smells, I became anxious to move on. Crossing would be easy, for the stream was slow and no more than a foot deep. Taking off my shoes and socks I stuffed them into the pack; then, holding it high in my left hand (in hopes of keeping it dry should I fall), I waded across the slippery bottom with no more risk than a good soaking.

But if the stream was easy to cross, the far bank was high, steep, and comprised of claylike mud that stuck to my feet and legs like glue. Worse yet, the ground on top was covered by clumps of crabgrass interspersed with coarse sand that glued itself to my muddy legs like sprinkles on an ice cream cone. I spent as much time wiping off mud and sand as I had walking from the road to the river. Then it was back on with shoes and socks, and west again through chest-high brush and right into a blackberry patch! I took the usual scratches on arms and legs, and there weren't even any berries in compensation, it now being so late in the season.

Fifty more yards of thick undergrowth and low trees brought me to a west-going path that eventually became a farm road. And suddenly, there was Helen, only a hundred yards ahead. I had crossed a field, slid down a bank, waded a stream, climbed another bank, and plowed through thorny undergrowth—all in exchange for five miles of walking and an hour and a half's time. It had been a questionable trade off, but worth it or not, I was on a high and ready to keep charging.

"Don't do it Philip," Helen said. "Give it up for the day. You're bleeding like a panther gotcha."

But I was in no mood to quit. "I'm good for six more miles," I announced in a tone meant to fend off objections.

"OK, six it is. But it's late in the day and you're gonna to be one sorry unit!" And with that she drove away and I went back to walking.

Fifteen minutes later I was so tired I hated the thought of even another hundred yards, let alone five more miles. Fifteen more minutes and I was approaching a crossroads where there was a short row of low trees, and behind them, thank goodness, was the Toyota. Helen was standing by the driver's door with a cup of water in one hand and car keys in the other. Both water and keys were just for me. She was tired too and wanted me to drive back to Lincoln.

Approaching the city, we caught Friday rush-hour traffic, which, Helen pointed out, we would have missed had we started home when she wanted to. "Ah yes," I replied, now much recovered, "but you wouldn't be witnessing my matchless driving skills."

"Could have lived without it, Sweets, and your modesty too.… Phil, pay attention! There's a boy on a bicycle."

"Helen, the kid's clear up on the sidewalk!"

THE VIETNAM VET

He had been changing a wheel on a farm wagon when he seemingly sensed my approach and rose to look in my direction. Although I was still some distance away, I waved, and he answered the greeting before turning back to the wagon, which was down a short driveway from the road. Coming closer, I glanced toward him several times and was actually passing, when, impulsively, I stopped and called, "Nice day."

In reality it wasn't that nice. A light breeze was coming in from the west, and the sky was a lumpy, gray layer of fast-moving clouds. Dreary was how I had been thinking of it, and a light drizzle added to the gloom.

He nodded—tentatively I thought—but I'd talked to no one so far that morning, so I started down the drive, hoping for a little conversation.

"Does farm equipment always give trouble when you need it most?—like during harvest time?" I tried for starters.

"You're no farmer," came his disconcerting reply. "I can see that.... Yeah, about harvest time's when it'll quit ... if it's gonna. Where you walkin' to?" In spite of the direct words, his manner was detached, preoccupied, as he threaded lug nuts to remount the wheel. Then, before I could answer he continued, "Don't see many people with packs walking these roads. Saw you near Syracuse the other day; you walk all the way over from there?" He picked up a wrench and began tightening the nuts.

"Yep, all the way from there, and before that from Nebraska City, and before that from Clarinda, Iowa, and before that from a dozen other places all the way back to Connecticut. I'm walking to the West Coast."

That kind of declaration usually brought a quick response, but for some moments the man said nothing. Was he going to talk, or would that be the end of the conversation? More moments passed; then, just as I was getting out, "Gotta go, take care—" he interrupted with, "How far do you think you'll get before winter?"

It was asked as if he simply accepted that I had walked a third of the way across the country and would eventually walk the rest. There was almost no expression on that enigmatic face; in fact he seemed subdued, mildly depressed. Still, he was not unfriendly, and I sensed he was less intrigued that I was walking across the country than that I was doing it as a not young man. Came the inevitable question: "Mind if I ask how old you are?"

"No problem … sixty-seven. I've surprised myself. Turns out I can walk twenty-five or thirty miles a day. When I was in the army, we thought fourteen was a long haul."

When had I been in the army? he wanted to know, and I told him: "From fifty-three to fifty-five—after the Korean War, at least after the shooting stopped. I didn't go overseas, spent two years at Fort Lewis, Washington."

"I was in Nam."

He said it softly, almost in a whisper, and I sensed right away that I was about to hear a tragic story in a very private life.

"You weren't young then when you were over there, were you?" I took him to be in his mid-sixties, just a few years younger than myself. He was warming now, but I still hadn't seen a trace of smile and I never would.

"Not young at all," he answered. "Most of the guys were a lot younger. I was thirty-eight."

The sky became darker and drizzle turned to rain, as he told me a bleak tale of war. I remember it now as a surreal horror of images, sounds, and smells that begins with a wet morning in far-off Vietnam. There is the roar of a helicopter skimming low over rice fields, the crew tense, purposeful, and on their way to provide fire support for a platoon of pinned-down infantry.

Eventually the fields give way to low wooded hills, and as the helicopter thunders over a village, it is hit by ground fire from a mix of scrambling figures, a few with guns, most without. The crew fires back, and in seconds the chopper is past and over trees, only to take more fire from a hill just east of the embattled GIs. In trouble now, the pilot banks to the south, dropping low over the treetops in a desperate attempt to get at least a visual screen between the crippled helicopter and the deadly fire. But there is no escape; the Vietcong are below them too. They've descended into a hornet's nest of invisible enemy, and direct fire pours in from all sides.

It's over in less than a minute. Severely damaged, the helicopter slues about and slowly settles until its rotors flail the treetops. Then the ground lurches up and there is a grinding, drawn-out crash followed by silence.

The old veteran paused as wisps of fog rose from fields behind the barn. His shoulders were wet and I could see his breath in the chilly air. Suddenly I was shivering myself. Was it the cold? Was it the demeanor of this stolid soul? Or was it the sorry tale he was telling with words, phrases, and broken sentences that I strained to hear?

When he continued, he told how the brief silence after the crash ended in a bedlam of shooting and screaming along with a stench of jet fuel, guts, and cordite. He said that during the melee a crew member was shot dead, torn half apart, and it wasn't until then that the survivors, battered and hopelessly outnumbered, tried to give up. Surprisingly, they were not shot on the spot but were allowed to surrender. After that, however, it was a brutal march into two years of hellish captivity. "They were tough on us," he said in his strange flat voice, "but we were the lucky ones; we got through it alive."

I wondered, given the mood I was seeing, if he really was that lucky.

Whoever he was—I didn't ask his name—he seemed less scarred by that last horrific firefight or by his years as a prisoner of war, than he had been by the daily nature of duty in Vietnam. "The only time you were sure the VC weren't right behind you," he said, "was when you were in that cursed helicopter roaring around the countryside. You fired away at an enemy that appeared out of nowhere then disappeared like smoke. Most of the time you knew you were shooting at Vietcong, but there were other times, too, when you knew damned well they weren't all guerrillas you shot.

There wasn't time to sort out who was who. Delay for a second and you'd surely be dead. You detach yourself from all that stuff; you force it out of mind."

He allowed that he had no regrets for any *particular* thing he had done while in Vietnam. "You fought for your buddies," was how he put it. "You fought for your life." And he was proud of his own good fight: he'd done his duty. But the experience had left him with a faint sadness, a mild depression that would go away for months, only to return now and then when he was alone in the fields or awake in the small hours of night.

Winding down, he said he still kept appointments at a veteran's hospital in Omaha, Nebraska, for some sort of treatments. It sounded as if they gave him drugs and counseling for depression.

I was chilled to the bone by now and not just from the rain. I spoke of the cold and wetness, and said that I had better be on my way. "Good luck," he said, and then, incongruously, "Think there's any hope for me?"

Taken aback, I awkwardly, haltingly, said I hoped he would someday find peace—some escape from memories that people like me were lucky enough not to have. But even as I spoke, I sensed I was making a mistake. He became embarrassed and said, "Ah, sorry I laid all that on you; it's been a lousy morning. Half the junk around this damned farm is on the fritz."

We shook hands then and I walked out to the road and west into the rain. A hundred yards farther on, I glanced back intending to wave, but he had knelt down and gone back to work.

Walking along, I wished I had said more to the man. I should have told him that to me he was a hero, that if he had regrets about things that had happened in Vietnam, he should remember that he had been sent there to fight an enemy that mixed freely with a sympathetic civilian population. The tragedy of civilian deaths was inevitable. Although he may, in some cases, have been the involuntary agent of such deaths, he was no more to blame than millions of Americans who at first supported the war, but in the end turned their backs on the men they sent to fight it.

It rained off and on the rest of the afternoon, but toward evening, the sky cleared into a particularly beautiful sunset. I told Helen about the vet, and as we watched the sun disappear, she suddenly said, "Let's hope he's watching this tonight; maybe he'll find some sort of solace."

"Maybe so," I said, as I pondered the willingness of people to reveal deeply personal parts of their lives to a casual stranger they will never meet again. The Vietnam vet had not been the first person to talk so freely; it had happened in Ohio with Dianne Fencer, the woman who had cancer, and it would happen again only a few days hence. In a way, it made me feel good that I inspired such trust that a troubled person might feel safe bearing his or her soul to me. On the other hand, the stories themselves were invariably depressing and it bothered me that I had no real help to offer—unless my mere listening could provide temporary comfort. Beam, I thought, you definitely lack the makings of priest or psychologist.

"FOREIGN HUNTERS"

Maybe I was daydreaming when I took a one-mile jog south instead of north and consequently arrived at a crossroads where I expected to meet Helen, and where, of course, she wasn't. I stood around for a half hour thinking up witty things to say to her for being late. Then, suddenly realizing my mistake, I began walking again but now devising witty answers for what she might toss at me—when I met her where I should have gone to begin with.

Double-quicking along, I soon spotted a man in a wheelchair, sitting beside a truck in the side yard of a dilapidated farmhouse. He motioned for me to come over, but being in a hurry, I just called "nice day" and kept walking.

He wouldn't settle for that, however, and instead called back, "How's 'bout takin' a break and havin' a cigar?"

So I walked over, but had hardly arrived before he began talking about "foreign hunters." "They come in here, buy a big chunk a land, let it go fallow, and then just use it for hunting," he complained. "Course they post it, and if anybody tries to hunt there, they have 'im arrested.... Hey good buddy, could you reach in that there pickup truck and get me a cigar. There's three of 'em on the seat."

I found the cigars; actually, they were under an old sweater, and when he had lit one and taken a puff, I said, "What do you mean 'foreign hunters?' Who are they and what do they hunt?"

"Deer," he answered, which told me what they hunted, but the rest of his answer went vague. I couldn't tell, though I gingerly probed, whether they were from nearby Omaha or Lincoln, or from some more distant city like Chicago or even Detroit. In any case, they loomed to him as rich, faceless outsiders who, individually or in groups, were a growing threat to local hunters. "They buy up parcels of land," he repeated at least three times, "and they post 'em off limits to everybody but themselves."

Eventually he got around to telling me he had been hurt in a heavy equipment accident. "Thirty-nine and paraplegic," he lamented. "What the hell's a man got to live for?" He was far overweight and he coughed a smoker's hack.

I struggled to think of something upbeat to say, but I knew nothing about the man's personal life. I couldn't remind him that he was fortunate to have a good wife—didn't even know if he had one—and I hardly knew how to ask. And who helped him in and out of that wheelchair? Could he drive? Did he have a specially equipped car? The truck had no handicap controls; it wasn't drivable by a man with no use of his legs, and there were no cars around. Did he have anything—or could he expect anything—more pleasurable in life than food and cigars? He was obviously poor.

Talking with that broken man, I couldn't help being aware of the gulf that separates people of vastly different physical circumstances. *Consider yourself,* I thought, *well-off, sixty-seven, and able to walk twenty-five miles a day. And then there's this fellow: poor, thirty-nine, and unable to take a single step. How could he not feel resentment, and me not chagrin?*

I retreated to the notion that neither he nor I should have such feelings, that it's a world of chance and people have to accept what they're served up in life—you know, British style: stiff upper lip, bite the bullet, make the best of things. But even as I rationalized, some cerebral voice kept whispering, "Easy for you to think that way, Beam. After all, you're the lucky one, and when don't you whine if things aren't going well for you—even temporarily?"

I mumbled a few encouragements to the man, but quickly found myself hamstrung by the banality of my own words. They seemed no more uplifting than those I had offered the Vietnam Vet a few days before. Finally, I lamely said, "I suppose the best thing a person can do is just try to be brave."

To which he replied:"Thanks for saying that, good buddy. Usually all I hear is a lot of bullshit about how things'll be gettin' better."

Walking again, I was grateful the weather was not dreary, as it had been when I talked to the Vietnam Vet. Even so, the Wheelchair Man's gloom lay upon me like a lead blanket, until I finally spotted the Toyota up ahead. It was chilly by then, but the warm car and Helen's cheerful needling about "people late for rendezvous" were welcome lifts to my spirits.

WHO LOST THE PICNIC COOLER?

There came a chilly morning when I was wearing a baseball cap beneath a knitted hat that I'd rolled down to keep my ears warm. Heavy pants felt good, and so did a terry-cloth coat worn over a light windbreaker. Along the horizon low sunlight broke through layered clouds, and here and there fence posts or lone corn shocks caught the rays and cast long, sharp shadows toward the west. Keep walking, I thought to myself; those shadows are pointing your way.

I rejoiced as the sun rose higher, and by nine o'clock my back was deliciously warm and pleasantly contrasting with a still cold nose, cold fingers, and a chilled but warming torso. Hours passed and presently the sun was beaming down through irregular holes in a thick overcast, so that the strange dark sky appeared oddly supported by a dozen white pillars of misty light. Middle-distance fields of oats and winter wheat caught brilliant sunbeams and glowed as vivid islands of green and yellow. And on and on I walked as the sun passed zenith and started down the western sky. New shadows appeared, but pointing eastward now and growing ever longer as the temperature began to fall. A gusty wind sprang up, and soon I was tiring and chilling as I careened about, working hard just to keep my balance.

I had covered twenty-five miles that interesting day when I reached the car about five o'clock. Helen, meanwhile, had been touring. Her first stop was Douglas, Nebraska, where she took pictures of the Farmer's Bank, saw a school, a post office, a church, a bar. There were few stores however—only where stores *had* been. Just as in countless other towns, clear back through Ohio, the automobile had relegated Douglas to a bedroom farm community. Presumably the townsfolk do their serious shopping at supermarkets and chain stores around Lincoln.

Quickly tiring of Douglas, Helen drove six miles farther west until she came to Panama, a town of about two hundred souls who were once served by a main line of the Missouri Pacific Railroad. The railroad is long gone, but northeast of town the abandoned right-of-way can still be seen. It appears again near Hickman, seven miles still farther west, where it briefly parallels modern tracks of the Burlington Northern en route to Lincoln.

Nowadays, anything entering or leaving Panama does so over state routes 43 or S55D, the latter also known as Panama Road. Like Douglas, serious shopping is done near Lincoln, and like Douglas, Panama has a school and a café, a fire house and a hardware store—and little else except for a very special fabric shop. Housed in what was once a one-room school, it had, according to Helen, "the largest selection of materials" she had ever seen. "If I'd been home," she said that evening, "I might have bought some."

"Might have my foot!" I exclaimed. "No doubt you would have." She loves to sew and can hardly resist an eye-catching piece of material.

The next day we were parked and eating lunch when a truck pulled in and the driver got out. He studied us and the car for a long moment; then, curiosity driven, he came over and asked if we were maybe having "trouble with the car or something?" We assured him we were fine, and with that and little preamble, lonely Frank Mottes, ex-military and nowadays farmer, began to tell us all about himself. We quickly learned that he had been in the navy for twenty-five years, was now retired, and had no close relatives. Duty tours had posted him to Rota, Spain; later to Subic Bay, the Philippines; then lastly to the Pentagon—which assignment he had not particularly liked since it involved some kind of intelligence work. He talked about his military career for probably ten minutes before abruptly changing the subject to pig farming. "You raise a pig in this part of the country, and you're lucky to make any money at all," he declared.

According to Frank, there were only two or three large meat packers to whom a farmer could sell his animals, and the packers, of course, set the price. He said that one outfit not far from there had facilities for slaughtering up to five thousand hogs per day. I put that down to shear exaggeration, but later, while looking into the subject of meat production in the U.S., I learned that Nebraska's hog population was in the neighborhood of four million. Obviously, thousands of animals are processed at different plants every day, and looking back, his claim didn't seem so far out after all.

Frank grumbled a bit more about the cost of raising a pig— said three quarters of what he got from the packer was about equal to what feed cost to raise the animal to begin with. Then, with another quick change of subject, he asked if Helen or I had ever eaten turnips that taste like radishes.

We said we hadn't.

"Wanna try one?"

"I would," Helen said, after a moment's hesitation.

"Well that's great. I've got some right here in the truck." And with that, Frank headed for his truck with me, by now out of the car, following a few steps behind.

There were all kinds of things in the back of the truck: old pop bottles, a car battery, some burlap bags, two tires (one with a hole in it), and a twenty-year-old dog. At least she looked that old. She didn't bother to get up—just lay there, wagged her tail a few times, and went back to sleep.

Near the front of the truck bed, behind the cab and amongst the trash, were a half dozen turnips and about twice as many ears of corn. Frank grabbed a turnip, and after cutting off a slice and quartering it, he offered me a piece. Sure enough, it tasted like a mild radish. I wondered how many people other than turnip growers and food connoisseurs would know about turnips that taste like radishes.

"Great," Helen enthused, when she tried a piece. "They'd be good in a vegetable platter at Christmas." That was all it took to get Frank to present her with three more turnips and four ears of corn. We had grilled corn the following two nights, and in addition, from time to time over the following weeks, we would boil part of a turnip and cut it into small squares for mixing with mashed potatoes. My mother used them that way when I was a kid, and I still liked the dish, although Helen wasn't particularly fond of it.

But back to our newfound friend.

Frank was wanting to know exactly why "two people your age would be walking across the country?" In addition, he wanted to know what Helen did each day—exactly what she did—and he wanted to hear it from her, not me.

As soon as she recited her short answer, he said, "Good Lord, you can't spend all your time knitting, reading, taking pictures, doing crosswords, writing in a journal—can you?"

That prompted the long answer: "Nope, I also shop, cook, clean, wash dishes, wash clothes, wash the car, and take care of the money. I take care of Phil, too, when he can't take care of himself."

"When can't I take care of myself?"

"Anytime you're hungry, or you can't find your socks or your clothes are torn. Or you've lost your watch, or your backpack, or your canteen, or your car keys, or your dog spray, or some science journal you're wading around in. Or your this, that, or whatever else. Should I keep going?"

Frank blurted: "Good Lord, lady, divorce him and marry me. You're one in a million!"

I jumped in: "Believe me Frank, she knows, she knows; you don't have to tell her; she's tough enough to live with! By the way, aren't you supposed to be somewhere else about now?—like over around Lincoln, sixty or seventy miles from here?"

"Nope. Got all day to just stand here and talk. So your wife works. What do you do besides walk?"

And so the banter went. He might have stayed and talked all afternoon, and I probably would have too if Helen hadn't been eager to get going.

Unable to break it off any other way, she finally got into the car and began easing away, all the while politely talking and smiling toward Frank and me. Once she twisted around and looked back, just to make sure some once-in-an-hour car wasn't about to rear-end her. Soon she was far enough away to pay full attention to the road, and Frank and I were left watching the car grow smaller in the distance.

He turned to me and said, "When do you figure you'll get to Oregon?"

"Next September."

"You'll get there," he assured me, "with her behind you."

Always, it seemed, people were encouraging.

We shook hands then and I started down the road. A few minutes later Frank eased past in the truck, and looking over, he grinned and said, "I'll spare you eatin' the dust." The old dog raised her head and gave a sleepy woof.

*　　*　　*　　*

Helen had driven over six miles, and consequently nearly two hours passed before I caught sight of the car up ahead. She saw me coming in the rear-view mirror, and as I walked up to the trunk, she unlatched it from inside so I could get the water jug. A long, cool drink was refreshing, as usual, but gradually I sensed that something was wrong, something was missing … sure enough: the picnic cooler!—left behind and sitting in the pull-off where we talked with Frank.

Seizing the opportunity, Helen was quick to reconstruct how I, not she, had left it behind. According to her, I took the cooler out of the car trunk and put it on the ground beside the driver's door. Then I handed the sandwiches to her through the driver's window, after which I went around and sat in the passenger seat to eat. Frank pulled in and parked "forty feet" from my side of the car, and although she too had been out of the car and talking, Frank and I had "milled around out there" and "talked and talked" long after she got back into the car to leave. Finally, after she had been kept waiting for quite some time (not really so), I closed the trunk lid neglecting to put the cooler back in. That's why she didn't know it was not aboard when she drove away; otherwise it would have been in there. Obviously, leaving the cooler behind was entirely my fault. So there!

We had done little recreational squabbling that day, so I was quick on the comeback: "You're darn right you didn't know it wasn't aboard. You never even thought about it. You were right there by it when you opened the driver's door, and all you had to do, once you got in, was look out your window and down toward the ground and you would have seen it. You were in too big a hurry to get out of there."

"The two of you were too busy talking about the navy, turnips, and me; that cooler was no more than ten feet away when you closed the trunk. If it'd been a snake it would have bit you—both of you."

"You never know about a thing like this," I said, but then, instead of finishing with my oft used "I could be as wrong as you or you could be as right as me," I accidentally reversed it saying, "I could be as right as you or you could be as wrong as me."

"Thanks for the admission," Helen answered with delight. "Now how's 'bout you start the car, turn it around, and we go back and get the cooler ... if it's still there."

So back we went, and of course the cooler was right where we left it, as we were sure it would be. Frank could not have seen it as he pulled out, or he would have told me when he drove slowly past, thoughtfully sparing me the dust. And it was unlikely anybody else had passed that way since noon.

Hours after the picnic cooler episode, my light-hearted mood had changed with a darkening sky and increasing chill. To the north lay Halstead, another farm town seemingly in the middle of nowhere. The place looked forlorn amid the fields, but I knew, even as I thought about it, that Halstead would not be "nowhere" to the good people who lived there. For the fortunate ones it would be home sweet home; neighbors would be nearby to lend a hand, provide company, give solace in times of bereavement. Old roots would connect people through church, school, community involvements, and long traditions of farming the prairie. I imagined warm, well-lit houses, and I witnessed in my mind's eye warm greetings between family members arriving home at day's end—all pleasant thoughts, but rendered bittersweet by a sense of isolation that was brought on, no doubt, by the lonely country-side, and the now gusting wind.

My right ear was hurting again—a steady dull ache punctuated now and then by more sharp twinges. Occasionally, the eardrum would bulge in or out, and I would try for relief by gaping and swallowing. A particularly strong gust shoved me sideways until I caught my balance, and it was then, as if on cue, that a thought sprang to mind, one that I'd been suppressing for several days yet one which nevertheless had been quietly hovering in the background. Now, unbidden, it took form in words: *We're going home soon!*

There, I had said it, albeit to myself, but we would not leave the next day or even the day after that. We would hang on out there for a while longer, but there would come a moment, and it wouldn't be far off, when either Helen or I would say, "Let's just get out of here—go home." We'd know then that within hours, certainly within days, we would begin the long drive east.

Tired and cold as I was, my spirits rose and I began walking faster. It would be good to finish up the day's walk; I was eager for the warm car and Helen's company.

WINDING DOWN

The next day I walked due west along a single road—no jogs north or south—for nineteen dusty miles. During the afternoon it warmed up, but not enough to be really comfortable in spite of all-day sun. In the evening we had the campground to ourselves, except for a single deer that kept appearing, disappearing, and reappearing among a group of nearby trees. She was unusually tame. Once she let us approach to forty or so feet before she slowly moved away, only to return after we went back to the motor home.

Walk's end was now sixty miles from of our campsite near Lincoln; it was time to decamp and move farther west, but time too for a day off from walking. Neither of us felt like breaking camp the following morning, and consequently we spent the day dawdling around Lincoln, where we had pictures developed and shopped for groceries. In the afternoon I cleaned the car, which was grimy again, inside and out.

It was October 24 before we finally moved to a campground near Hastings, Nebraska. Upon arriving, I was still not ready to walk, so after lunch we visited the Hastings Museum on Burlington Avenue. The museum has an outstanding collection of mounted animals from all over the world, and the individual exhibits, along with their write-ups, are valuable educational displays for adults and children alike.

We continued to put off walking, and the next day drove to Minden, about thirty miles southwest of Hastings, to visit the Harold Warp Pioneer Village. Here a visitor sees thousands of arti-facts of early rural life, as well as three-dimensional room displays exhibiting progressive changes in rural homes since the 1830s. The developing kitchens are especially interesting. In addition, the museum houses antique car, airplane, and motorcycle exhibits.

At noontime, we had outstanding chili at a nearby café; then it was back to the Mary Lanning Hospital in Hastings to have my aching ear checked out again. The doctor had little to say—could see nothing wrong. "It's likely the cold wind you've been walking in," he allowed.

Another day passed and still no walking. We were stalled. Then, on Friday morning, October 27, we sat at breakfast and briefly talked about hanging around Hastings for yet another day. "There's plenty more to see around here," I said. "We don't have to start walking yet. We could visit—"

But Helen interrupted: "Phil, we've got to stop this. Let's either get on with the walk or else start home."

"Then we'll get on with the walk," I said, "at least for a few more days."

We got up then and with shaky resolve drove out to walk's end.

Cold, cold, cold. I wore the knit hat pulled down over my ears as I trudged along all morning, never really getting warm. Sometime around noon, I wandered into a roadside graveyard to escape the wind by crouching behind some evergreens.

There was a child's grave nearby, which I managed to ignore for a while. Presently however, perhaps impelled by some vague sense of tragedy, I got up and walked over to the resting place of Jessica Stahl, who had lived from April 9, 1989 until April 27 of the same year—a very short life indeed. Somebody had recently tended the grave, and around the low mound were fresh baskets of flowers—purple, white and lavender—and guarding the tiny headstone was a cherub and a toy dog.

It was 1999, Jessica had lived only eighteen days and been dead for ten long years, yet the neatness of the burial place vouched for her cherished place in somebody's memory. That thought briefly cheered me, but the smallness of the tiny grave amid the surrounding much larger headstones was unignorable. After a minute or two, I shivered and walked back to the evergreens, sat down, and fought back an encroaching loneliness.

For another four hours I plodded west into that everlasting wind until finally, about five o'clock, I saw the car up ahead. Helen was parked at the corner of roads 1 and D, Clay County, Nebraska, and about a hundred feet from the corner stood a metal silo with a faded sign near the roof.

"This'll be a good place to start next spring," I said when I got to the car. "Let's go home."

"Sounds good to me," she quickly replied. "But why have we waited so long?"

ON THE WAY HOME

On our first night coming east, we stayed at a campground near Durant, Iowa, which was reasonably quiet thanks to a low hill between the campground and the nearby highway. Better yet, the campsites were cleaner and better kept than those usually found in RV parks; and best of all, the owner, a woman, had a small dining room adjacent to the office. There she served home cooked meals—perfect after a long day on the road when you are too tired to prepare dinner yourself. Meatloaf and mashed potatoes would be the special that night, and it would be served at five o'clock sharp. "Better be here!" the pleasant lady told us.

We had hooked up Lurch and were walking back to the office for dinner when Helen noticed a familiar van parked on a remote campsite among some trees.

"Doesn't that belong to Mr. Religion, the man who's afraid of dogs?" she mused.

A glance was all I needed to confirm what Helen already suspected. There couldn't be two chartreuse campervans with JESUS-SAVES stickers, owned by two different handymen who were afraid of dogs and looking to save souls.

We had met the fellow two months before near Galesburg, Illinois. That time he was parked far away from other campers on probably the least desirable campsite in five acres. I asked the manager why anyone would want to park beside an industrial-size trash bin next to a thousand-watt floodlight. "Afraid of dogs," he replied. "Must be some kind of a phobia with the man. Ordinary guy, though."

Well he wasn't ordinary, and besides a phobia (if he even had one), he was obsessed with religion. Every summer, his calling was to travel from one campground to another doing odd jobs and spreading Jesus' word to whomsoever would listen. I had met him, his name was Dave, and we began a conversation, but the conversation was "with him" for only the first two minutes. After that it was a monolog from him to me as he gave in to a compulsion to save souls—mine that day. For the next ten minutes I smiled, nodded, mumbled, and finally had to turn and walk away.

He buttonholed me a day later but stopped promoting Jesus when I said, "No offence, Dave, but I just don't do your kind of religion." The following day I met him a third time. This time we talked for probably fifteen minutes before Jesus came up, whereupon I closed my eyes and shook my head. "Sorry," he said, and after that he never mentioned the Galilean again, although I talked with him two more times. It was like there were two parts to the man's mind. One part was permeated with religious zeal while the other part was free to talk intelligently about anything: the environment, the weather, the traffic, or the "gol-darned" government as he euphemistically put it.

Strangely, although Helen talked with him twice, Dave never mentioned Jesus to her, and she was pleased to tell me that that showed her to be a woman already possessed of Grace. I said it more likely showed her beyond redemption, a comment she took in stride.

Anyway, we had not seen Dave for two months, and tonight, tired and hungry, we were not looking forward to seeing him again. Of course, moments later, when we stepped through the office door, there he was, big as life and sitting by himself at a table set for four. He grinned from ear to ear and beckoned for us to join him.

It was too late to turn and run, so squelching misgivings, we walked over and sat down for what would be a pleasant dinner—especially the conversation part. Dave's recall was impressive. He remembered things he and I had talked about two months before, and he laughingly touched on my reluctance to talk religion. Eventually, he began to tell us what to look for in western Nebraska where we would be walking the following spring. "Be sure and visit Carhenge if you go anywhere near Alliance," he said.

"What do you mean, *Car Hinge*?" I asked. I thought he was kidding.

"Not *Car Hinge*, it's *Carhenge*. It's a take-off from *Stonehenge*, you know, that prehistoric monument in England—the one they claim was used to predict seasons and stuff in ancient times."

Yes, we knew about Stonehenge.

On he went: "Historians say that pagan rituals were practiced there. Well, Carhenge is a spoof on Stonehenge, you see; at least its makers claim it's a spoof. But some of us think they were devil-inspired spoofers. They planted cars, upright and sticking half out of the ground, to imitate the stones at Stonehenge. Go see the place. You'll never forget it. They used to do human sacrifices there too"

"Where? Car Hinge or Stonehenge?" I asked.

Helen hit me under the table but Dave just grinned.

"Just levitizing," I said. "We'll be sure to visit the place. Glad to know about it."

Eventually our companion began to ask about people we might have met since we last talked. He was mildly interested in the Amish man who had been on his way to make cider; he was very interested in the man in the wheelchair—the paraplegic who couldn't walk and was worried about "foreign hunters." When Dave asked *exactly* where that man lived, I pretended to forget, sensing he might pay the poor fellow a visit and try to save his soul.

An hour later we had finished eating and conversation was winding down. The food had been disappointing. The meatloaf and mashed potatoes were tasty and homemade, but made at home a bit too soon—they were warm, not hot, by the time they got to us. On the other hand, the proprietress had meant well and we had had an unexpectedly pleasant time with our re-met acquaintance.

Outside, Helen and I too quickly exchanged handshakes with Dave, so that our subsequent walking together down the service road seemed awkward after the parting gestures. Trying hard, we exchanged halting small talk along the way until we came to the path that branched away toward Dave's van. Here we shook again, self-consciously this time, but suddenly Dave perked up and said, "Hope you finish your walk to the Pacific. But wish me luck; I've got lots more of the Lord's work to do." Then, after a pause and a broad smile, he continued: "Promise you—that'll be the last plug for Jesus you'll hear from me."

That re-broke the ice, and we laughed and exchanged waves as he started down to his campsite. He was a strange man: worldly on the one hand, religious on the other. And neither Helen nor I thought he was really afraid of dogs; he mentioned no such fear to us. "He probably always tells park management a dog-phobia story," Helen remarked, "and that he needs a campsite far from other campers who might have one." Privacy, we agreed, was what that was all about—he certainly didn't mind bright lights.

*   *   *   *

Our next day's drive brought us to the environs of Milan, Ohio, where we found a campground just west of town. We fixed a quick dinner; then, as Helen began the dishes, I carried out the trash and began looking for the campground Dumpster. Hoping to get directions from somebody, I walked toward a campfire where I met three people, a father and mother, and their twenty-year-old daughter. They were en route east from California where daughter attended college, and though they could not help about the Dumpster, they were more than ready for conversation.

"Where you from?" the man led off.

"Connecticut," I answered. "You?"

"Connecticut too; actually we're from near Willimantic. That's in the southeastern part of the state."

"So are we."

"Oh, hear this!" exclaimed the woman, and suddenly we were all anticipating a coincidence.

"We live on Tobacco Road," the man continued, "near Uncle D's restaurant, just off route 87."

I knew the road, knew the restaurant. So I told him the name of my road, and was telling him where it was when he cut in: "I *know* where it is; my attorney lives there and I've been to his house."

In another minute we had established that his attorney was Helen's and my next door neighbor. These unlikely acquaintances, met at a campfire in an Ohio trailer park, were even familiar with our house; they had walked through it one evening in 1997 when it was still under construction.

We chatted for another ten minutes, and then I carried the trash back to the motor home, having completely forgotten why I went out in the first place.

"Why'd you bring the trash back?" Helen asked, motioning toward the bag.

I told her about meeting the people from Connecticut, and that led to speculations about the chances that strangers from the same town in Connecticut would be in the same campground in Ohio on the same night. Not real high, we agreed, but far better than the chances of winning a lottery. Of course this begged further speculation about the chances that such people would discover each other in the dark. "Oh," Helen said, "those chances would be a lot less than the chances you'd forget and come back here with the garbage."

"Are you implying, m'Love, that I'd be more likely to find people to talk to than a Dumpster to put trash in?—or the other way around?"

"Suit yourself," she said, but she probably had the odds right.

I found the Dumpster at six-thirty the following morning, just before we got back on the road.

It would be a long drive on I-80 that day, but we were determined to be home by day's end. Pressing along, hour after hour, we worked our way across eastern Ohio and then into the Appalachians north of Pittsburgh.

Sometime in early afternoon a woman's voice burst out of the CB. "Honey Dear, I gotta go to the bathroom." It sounded as if she was right outside, and just then, as an eighteen-wheeler was passing, I noticed a sign on the road's shoulder saying REST STOP TWO MILES.

"I gotta go too," the man replied. "Sign here says there's a rest stop a couple miles ahead. They sell good brownies; I've been there before. We'll swing in, Babe."

"That'll work for me," Babe replied, as she whipped by in a white Ford sedan, no more than thirty feet behind the truck. Then she said, "Honey, what time do you think we'll get home. I've got that feeling."

"Now don't start that," he laughingly answered. "We'll be too tired, time we get there."

"You'll manage," she replied, "Once I get you turned on, you always *rise* to the occasion."

I cut in with a quick "H.B., up one," which meant for Helen and me to switch up one CB channel.

A moment later we were in the clear, away, we thought, from that merry couple. "J.B., how do you copy?" came Helen's giggling voice. "Did you hear that pair? They're a scream!"

But the other couple had switched up too, and before I could answer, Honey Dear's deep-southern drawl came over the air: "Y'all Yankees can probably be a scream yourselves; anyway, y'all have yourselves a good day." Babe too was pressing her CB's transmit button, and we could hear her laughing in the background. I swung out and was passing the Ford as it slowed to enter the off ramp to the brownie stop. Babe looked over and grinned and waved as I tooted and threw her a smiling salute.

That lighthearted exchange kept Helen and me laughing for the next hour as we chatted back and forth on the CBs. By six in the evening, however, we had long since become serious as driving seemed to go on forever. Overdue for a break, we stopped at a restaurant near the Connecticut-New York border. The food and rest were helpful, which was a good thing, because it had grown dark and from there on traffic would be fast and heavy toward Hartford. Several times we talked about finding a motel and staying over till morning, but neither of us would give in to being *that* tired. We were headed for the barn and in no mood to spend another night on the road. So we pressed on.

Sometime after ten o'clock, we turned into our lane, drove slowly through the trees, then onto the fallows and around the last bend. And there was home!—just as we'd left it two months before.

We had walked half way across America.

Hastings, Nebraska, to Teton Hole, Wyoming

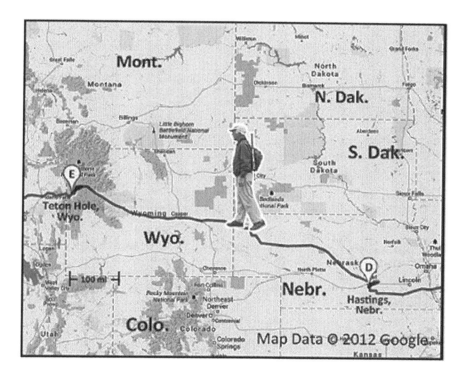

Fourth Walk Segment: April 12 Until June 22, 2000

AN IMPATIENT WINTER
IN FLORIDA

Helen's and my intention was to spend the winter of 1999/2000 near Naples, Florida, just as the year before, but before we could go down, there was much to do in Connecticut. When we arrived home from the walk, we found that mice had invaded the house. They had to be expelled (preferably) or exterminated (if unavoidable); also, the lawn was a foot high and needed mowing. Two cartons of junk mail waited to be sorted; Lurch and the Toyota needed servicing; storm windows would have to be installed, and so on. Besides those things and the usual chores of daily life, we had a Christmas party to prepare for—that year we were hosting one for old friends and work colleagues.

Autumn raced by, sped up, it seemed, by the breakneck pace, and almost before we knew it, it was Christmas night and our family of twenty—children, children-in-law and grandchildren—were milling around the house in various stages of post-Christmas-dinner exhaustion. It had been a wonderful day and everybody had had a good time. Even so, the kids were suffering from too many presents, too little sleep, and too much candy, while their parents were likewise suffering, but from too much driving, too much eating, and too much noise. Helen and I were just plain sated and secretly yearning to start for Florida.

Our original plan was to leave a few days after Christmas. We would use those days to recover from the holiday and secure the house for the remainder of the winter. However, the morning after Christmas, indeed, even as we prepared breakfast, the urge to get going came over us again. We were just sitting down when Helen said, "What say we just—"

"Leave this afternoon," I finished for her.

"You betcha, my Dear."

So there followed a confused morning of unloading the motorhome of things we *had* needed while walking in the West, and reloading it with things we *would* need in Florida. As frantic as the pace was, we were on the road by early afternoon. The house still looked like Christmas, but Helen said taking down decorations would give us something to do between our return from Florida and our departure for the West, come April.

That night, content to be on our way, we stayed at a hotel in northern New Jersey—there being no RV parks open that time of year. The room was certainly okay, but checking out the following morning turned into an unexpected hassle. It was five-thirty when I handed the desk clerk eighty-nine dollars to settle the account, and politely asked for a receipt and the credit card impression I had provided when we checked in.

"Here you go," he said, handing me an sheet of paper that began with the hotel's letterhead, below which were several lines that were empty except for the date and a couple of indecipherable codes. Next came a line listing the eighty-nine dollars; below that was a curious looking sentence in legalese, and at the bottom was a place for a signature. "Sign here," the man said, thrusting out a ballpoint pen and gesturing toward the paper.

The eighty-nine-dollar entry made the "whatever-it-was" look like a receipt, but why would I be signing my own receipt? And if I did sign it, what would it mean? The more I squinted the more it appeared that once I signed my name, the dollar-amount line would become nothing more than a declaration by me, the guest, that I had paid the bill. It was not an acknowledgement by the hotel that it had received a penny. Worse yet, the legalese sentence clearly empowered the hotel to bill for any charges that might dribble down to the desk after we left: charges for unauthorized phone calls, charges for soft drinks taken from the honor-system refrigerator, charges for special TV services, indeed, charges incurred for anything by anybody—the maids or even this guy who was now, for a second time, telling me to sign. "No thanks," I said. "I'm not signing this."

"Well, you have to sign but you do get a copy," he said.

"I won't sign and I don't need a copy; I'm not committing to this thing. All we did was sleep in the room, didn't use any other offered services. I signed all I'm going to sign when we registered last night; nobody told me there'd be more stuff to sign this morning. Now's the time for you to give me a signed, straightforward receipt clearly acknowledging that I've paid the bill in full, with cash, and don't owe any more money. Period. You can keep a copy of that if you want."

"Can't do that."

"Then give me back that money I just gave you."

We bickered back and forth for a few more rounds, but eventually I got him to write on the "whatever-it-was" a barely legible *paid in full*, which he affirmed with a squiggle he claimed was his signature. A big, stubborn man, he was obviously unused to being challenged by a mere guest—said he was only trying to do his job and didn't make hotel policy. True, no doubt, but though I asked twice, he would not return my credit card impression—just angrily tore up something he *said* was the impression and threw it into a wastebasket. Surely that can't be hotel policy, I thought, but who knows, it's obviously policy to issue ambiguous receipts.

Ten minutes later Helen and I were driving dark and traffic-free streets looking for someplace, anyplace, to get something to eat. Food should help me out of a post-argument mood that at one point had me demand:"Why the devil does just checking out of a hotel have to end up in an argument?"

After a short search we found an all-night diner, and eating there became another interesting experience.

Breakfast for me was two eggs, two pieces of toast, and one small orange juice; Helen's was one egg, one slice of toast, and also an orange juice. In addition, we each had coffee from one of those "bottomless" vacuum carafes they put on your table and supposedly keep refilling.

The over-easy eggs turned out to be hard as rocks; the toast was dark brown on one side and virtually untoasted on the other. No matter. It was food and the waitress was amiable—if half asleep. We'd just eat and be on our way.

Helen had brought the Thermos in from the car, and as we were finishing up, she asked the waitress to fill it with coffee. Right in front of us she poured in the coffee that was still in the carafe, and then she went back to top it off, we assumed, with hot coffee from the urn. She returned a minute later with the Thermos but without the check. That would be over at the register, she said.

"That'll be twenty-four dollars and forty-nine cents with tax," said the thirty-something woman at the cash register.

"Must be a mistake," I said. "We didn't have cocktails."

"Well, that's eighteen fifty-five for the breakfasts and four fifty-five to fill the Thermos—not counting tax."

"Four fifty-five to fill the Thermos?"

"Certainly. Says here it took three and a half cups. It's a dollar thirty a cup. There's tax too, you know; this is New Jersey."

"Well," I said, "half the coffee in that Thermos is what we didn't drink from that bottomless carafe. That should count as mine to begin with."

"It's not yours till you drink it," she said with a smile.

Whatever I answered made the woman laugh, and that was all I needed to keep going. "Another thing: Don't I get a break for buying the coffee in bulk? That's a big Thermos."

"No."

"Well, do I have to pay New Jersey sales tax? After all, we live in Connecticut."

"I'm not even answering that."

"Well, can't you at least give me a senior discount?"

"We don't give senior discounts, but if we did, I'd give *you* one, no questions asked." Then she smiled toward Helen and said, "She your daughter?"

Helen nearly cracked up.

The gall of the woman! I gave up and paid the bill—she definitely knew how to handle early-morning grouches; she even had me laughing.

Later, as Helen and I caravanned south on I-95, we talked back and forth on the CBs and laughed about "Cashier Lady" and her unanswerable comebacks. She'd been fun in a left-handed way, and in spite of the high price, we were pleased to have coffee for the road.

Two hours later, our breakfast pick-me-ups having worn off, we pulled into a rest stop for a much-needed break. Helen got out the Thermos, but instead of the coffee being hot and strong it was lukewarm and weak—so weak that she poured it out on the ground. That launched me into another round of grousing about chain hotels and second-rate breakfasts, until Helen got sick of listening and said, "Relax, Phil, you're still wound up and tired out from Christmas. We'll be in South Carolina tonight; it'll be warm there and you'll forget all about weak coffee and tricky receipts."

Eventually the world did get straightened out. Not only that, it was warm that night when we arrived at good old South of the Border, that landmark we had admired with the Carolinian couple the summer before. Just as we remembered, the campground was excellent: nicely laid out, well maintained, and reasonably priced. And we were already below the heavy Northeast traffic. Things were looking up.

*   *   *   *

For Helen and me, the rest of the winter became little more than an impatient wait for spring. Nothing seemed particularly interesting after our months of walking across America. Dreaded Y2K came and went; the Super Bowl came and went though I can't remember who played. I tried to learn golf but didn't really care where the ball went or if I even hit it. Helen worked at crafts—painting and bottle decorating—but her heart wasn't in it any more than mine was in golf.

Nevertheless, using the computer mapping program, we explored no end of back roads east of Naples on the edge of the Everglades. Sometimes we would park the car and I would walk for miles; sometimes we would find footpaths leading to off-road swamps and lagoons. It would be quiet in those places, and we'd be imbued with a pleasant uneasiness, as if there might be something lurking here or there. Cameras ready, we took dozens of pictures of birds and alligators, and even a few of snakes. But it was all just a protracted wait. Winter would end, we told ourselves, and then we'd get on with the great walk west.

Sometime around Valentine's Day, I began talking about going home to Connecticut in the middle of March. Helen, on the other hand, repeatedly said we should wait until later. Her argument was essentially, *Why go home early? It'll still be winter up there and there'll be nothing to do. We'll not be going west, you know, until the middle of April.*

She sang that same tune until the second week of March when over just a few days her refrain changed to, *Let's go home now. It'll still be winter up there but there'll be more than enough to do. We'll be going west, you know, come the middle of April.*

I called her on the turnabout. "This sounds like your usual theme except that now you're ready to go."

"Ingenious, huh?" she replied.

But I was more than ready myself by March 18, and abruptly, as we have often done things, we checked out of Club Naples RV Resort and started north the same afternoon.

We arrived home three days later, and from then until our departure for Nebraska, there was no end of things to do. Most importantly, the bills and taxes had to be paid, and Lurch and the car had to be serviced. In addition, arrangements had to be made for handling the mail, and the house needed securing again. Of course, like the previous summer, I forgot to hire someone to mow the grass; consequently it would be two feet high when we returned home in September.

Nevertheless, all the maddening and detailed preparations were complete by Wednesday, April 12, according to Helen's ever-precise notes; then we said good-bye to family and neighbors and began the long drive back to Nebraska. Our precise destination was Traveler's Rest Campground at Hastings, where we had been staying when we quit walking the autumn before.

Three days later and just sixty-five miles from Hastings, we pulled into a campground near Waco. It was only midafternoon, but gusting winds and snow squalls had forced us off the road.

Still, what a pleasant evening we had! Motor home camping can be especially pleasant when the weather is cold and raw. You sit inside—warm and perhaps mellowed by a glass of wine—and you thank God you are not outside in a tent!

We completed the drive to Travelers Rest about eleven o'clock the next day, and we were very glad to be off the road. The highways had been cleared by then, but the weather was still occasional flurries, and gusty winds had trees and bushes dropping shards of ice.

"Shall we start walking this afternoon?" Helen wondered, even before we had leveled Lurch and plugged in the power. She was more than ready and so was I; still, it seemed unlikely that the dirt roads we would be using would be free of snow or mud. In the end, we decided to wait till the next day, and it was just as well we did. There would be more than enough mud.

ON THE ROAD AGAIN

By six-thirty the next morning we were driving back to where we had finished walking the autumn before—to the intersection of Clay County Roads 1 and D, twenty miles east of Hastings. We talked about the silo we remembered being near the corner, and we began looking for it while we were still many miles to the south. Time seemed to drag, but eventually Helen spotted it far ahead and barely rising above the surrounding fields. It grew slowly taller … then taller … then taller still … until suddenly, at long last, we were there! Our long winter's wait was over and finally, indeed finally, we could get on with the walk.

Helen had no more than stopped the car than she turned to me and said, "Time to get your feet in the mud, Dearie."

And mud there was, plenty of it. West-going Road D, which I had planned to walk, was overlain with a half-inch of the gooey stuff—not enough to capture the car, but enough to make walking difficult. Maybe if I walked a mile north I would find the next road freer of mud. If not, I could always come back and wade into D.

So off I went.

During the winter, we had bought walkie-talkies, and now, eager to try them, we chatted back and forth as Helen drove out ahead. Before long she came to Road C. "You'll be able to slog along on this one," she happily radioed. "It's dryer than D. I'm turning west, you keep walking. I bet we get twenty miles today!"

I stopped and scraped a layer of mud off my shoes.

A few minutes later my walkie-talkie crackled again: "I'm down here at the next crossroads. Can you still hear me?" By then we were about a mile and a quarter apart.

"Loud and clear, m'Love. Keep driving."

About three and a half miles was the maximum range the radios would give us that day, but we were consistently able to talk over distances of two to three miles, provided there were no buildings between us, especially metal ones. Of course the land was billiard-table flat. Two months later, in the Rocky Mountains, radio ranges could be as short as a quarter mile if there was high ground in the way.

It stayed brisk and breezy during the early hours that first morning back, and occasionally there would be a brief shower—just enough to keep the road from drying. Once, a youngish woman pulled alongside and began to question what I was doing out there by myself—"you being from the East and all." The first thing she had asked was where I was from. And how in the world did I stand the wind?

"Not easily," I told her, "but maybe it'll dry the road. Mud's my biggest problem."

"Oh," she said, "the wind'll dry the mud if these showers ever stop. Couple hours and mud'll be no problem at all. Wanna ride for a mile or two?"

She was a good-hearted person, but I didn't think she believed I really intended to walk every step to the West Coast. Again she offered a ride, and again I declined. Presently she drove on, shaking her head in wonder at "you crazy Eastern types." Had she met others?—sometime? somewhere?

Toward eleven o'clock the breeze and showers let up, and I could hear the drone of a crop-dusting plane somewhere to the northwest, near a distant line of trees. Although too far away to be seen, the plane was easily heard as its sound moved first to the right, then to the left, then to the right, then to the left.… During reversals, its engine noise would rise in pitch and loudness, only to quiet again as the pilot swung round for another pass above the distant fields.

A half hour went by as I continued on, and the droning grew louder while the back-and-forth swings lengthened and moved as a whole toward my right. Finally, now and then, I would glimpse the far-away plane as it appeared and disappeared against the sky. At the end of each run it would swing high in a beautiful arching curve, its wings nearly vertical in the tightness of its turn. Then forward and down it would plunge—surely to crash—but always, at the last second, to level off and skim safely along above the ground. Once or twice I caught whiffs of pesticide.

Eventually I passed about a mile south of where the plane was working, so that toward one o'clock it was well behind me. Still the pilot kept making his endless passes. Sooner or later, I thought, he's going to run out of spray, get low on gas, get hungry for lunch, or just get tired and need a break. And sure enough, there came a moment when the sound changed, and I turned to see him bank sharply and head off toward the southwest.

He'll eat and gas up, I said to myself, and then he'll come back and begin spraying again.

And he did. About two o'clock I heard him again, now far behind me and well to the south, but heading toward where I first saw him—toward that tree line, which was now low on the horizon and many miles away.

An hour later I was slogging along in an exhausted daze when a farmer pulled alongside in an SUV. "You've only got another quarter mile of this," he informed me. "It'll be easier walking after that."

"This" was mud, and it clung like—well, like mud. I must have been carrying a pound on each shoe. It had cleared in early afternoon and the breeze had picked up again—not strong, but enough to dry the road except for short stretches. Unfortunately, the stretch I was on (I had been on it for several hundred yards) had little or no crown and very shallow roadside ditches. Broad puddles and soupy mud lay everywhere; in several places sheets of water were almost the width of the road. I was grateful not to have come upon Helen stuck—at least so far.

I thanked the farmer, who wished me luck and then drove on. *Either I'll get through this mess or I won't*, I thought. *If I have to, I'll radio Helen and have her come back and rescue me*. I was played out from having walked eighteen miles, thus farther than on any day during the winter. Every muscle cried foul at the unaccustomed exertion. Nevertheless, although I had to scrape my shoes twice more, I eventually got past the muddy area and back to dryer road.

But where was Helen?

Answer: She was still two miles ahead, and when I finally reached the car about four o'clock, she, with great enthusiasm, wanted to "get in another three or four before dark." I balked loudly and told her I would try it only if she would leave the car where it was and walk along with me. Should I go down somewhere, it would be up to her to walk back, get the car, drive forward, and "gather me up." I made it clear that "gather me up" meant for her to physically lift me into the car.

"Well honey," she said, "you've been lying around for months. Thought you'd want to do it right today. Grand Island's only fifteen miles. How's about one more mile?"

She was in a playful, teasing mood, and tired as I was, I enjoyed it. Even so, I had had enough walking for the first day back— certainly the physical part of me had. Minutes later we headed for Travelers Rest, with her driving and me on my way to sleep.

*　　*　　*　　*

The countryside northeast of Hastings was quiet the morning of Tuesday, April 18, 2000. As yet no machinery worked the spring planting. Cornfields, still unplowed, stretched on and on, and scattered about lay fragments of last year's crop—a bent stalk, a stripped ear, dull kernels lying here and there upon the ground.

Still, there seemed a gathering energy in the land, as if it were poised for the soon-to-come growing season. I passed a farm, and among the outbuildings a dozen sheep forlornly watched as I walked by. Aside from them, the place appeared deserted, but suddenly an engine revved behind the barn and a man's voice shouted something about hurrying. Almost immediately another motor started and a truck lurched out of a shed, swung quickly around, and disappeared behind the house. Then the motors stopped and quiet closed in again. I walked on and saw no one during the next hour. It seemed as if most people were in late-winter hibernation, still resting up for the demanding tasks of approaching spring. The pace of farm-country Nebraska in April is nothing like southern New England, which seems perpetually frenetic.

362

But if the people were not yet out and about, the wild creatures were. Deer prints seemed to be everywhere in muddy places along the road, and late in the morning, near an I-80 overpass, two deer broke from a thicket and bounded away. I held my breath lest they veer toward the highway, but to my relief they turned away and raced out across an empty field.

There were also signs of coyote and fox, and now and then the prints of a bobcat. Twice I passed places where misguided groundhogs had dug burrows in the middle of the dirt road—such was the volume of traffic. Hawks sat on favorite poles or posts, and other birds, probably with newly built nests, would fly along overhead, often emitting their nagging cries. *Go away, go away*, they seemed to say.

Helen and I were weary that second day back. No doubt it was due to both the long drive out from home and our overdoing ourselves the day before. We kept at it though, until about two o'clock; then we called it off and drove back to Traveler's Rest to relax and read away the afternoon.

The following morning brought us to the Platte River about 10 a.m. Somebody once said that William Jennings Bryan's mind was like the Platte—a mile wide and an inch deep. Where I crossed it, on a U.S. 34 bridge, it was closer to a quarter mile wide, although in places it really was only a few inches deep. A half mile downstream, it tightened into a braided network of narrow creeks that carried its flow through swamplands to another, wider section farther along. Upstream to the south, it remained wide for miles.

Grand Island was now only three miles ahead, and I looked in vain for the large island that presumably inspired its name. No island of that name showed on my map. Maybe it is not there anymore, lost over the years since the 1860s, a consequence of the ever changing shapes and courses of the river. However, downstream to this day are prominent named islands, among them Guendel, Bush, Parker and Hurley—all within thirty miles of the city.

From the river it was a quick walk to the southeast edge of town, and it was a relief to arrive there. The wind had risen, but tall, attractive houses broke it somewhat, thus allowing for more comfortable walking as I turned uptown. Before long I met elderly Muriel Chasse working in her garden. We exchanged tentative hellos and comments about the weather; then I complimented her on her multicolored tulips. That broke the ice, and it wasn't long before Muriel was telling me that she was the widow of a state trooper who had passed away fourteen years earlier. Obviously they had been close, for she spoke of his kindness toward her, of far-away places they had visited, and of the many things they had done together. About him, professionally, she said, "He liked to help people." Soon Muriel was telling me antidotes from the couple's younger years, but among them was an incongruous if humorous tale about one of her husband's colleagues, and how he'd arrested his own brother-in-law.

Seems that brother-in-law became drunk one Christmas Eve, and then was foolish enough to take off in his car. "Trooper" stopped him; however, brother-in-law, seeing's the cop was mere family, gave him a "full ration of lip" (the old lady's words), in consequence of which he found himself an overnight guest of the state. (It must have been some ration!) Still, the law was not without heart. Trooper went to his sister's house, got a few of the man's presents, and gave them to him in the lockup. Muriel said the family got over it—eventually—but it made for a "somewhat strained holiday."

Leaving Mrs. Chasse, I continued north up town. I was aware that Grand Island's origin was closely associated with the Union Pacific Railroad, and later I read about it in Stephen Ambrose's *Nothing Like it in the World*. The essential story goes as follows:

By 1857 a settlement had been established on the Platte River opposite now vanished *La Grande Isle*, which had been named years before by early French trappers. During construction of the first transcontinental railroad, the Central Pacific company built east from Sacramento, California, while the Union Pacific built west from Omaha, Nebraska. The Union Pacific's tracks reached a point six miles north of *La Grande Isle* in the summer of 1866, whereupon the adjacent river-front settlement was moved north to the tracks and given the name Grand Island Station. It kept that name until 1873, at which point *Station* was dropped and the town was incorporated as *Grand Island*.

Grand Island was a lively enough town during the years of railroad construction. But the place that really hopped was a tracks-end settlement called Hell on Wheels, which materialized in 1867 about a hundred miles to the west. Hell on Wheels was nothing more than a group of shanties, tents, and human vermin that followed the work crews as they laid the tracks, and it provided everything from prostitution to gambling to almost daily gunfights. At one point, squatting on Union Pacific turf and draining off work-crew energy—not to say testosterone—the town became the target of a railroad-sponsored cleanup that left several roughnecks buried on a nearby boot hill.

Nowadays the Union Pacific is not the only railroad at Grand Island, although with tracks running through center city it was obviously the first. Nebraska Central joins the Union Pacific on the eastern edge of town, while the Burlington Northern comes in through north Grand Island and continues east toward Lincoln.

From the northwest corner of town, I branched west onto Nebraska 2, which leads into the countryside past Ashley Park and then along tracks of the Burlington Northern. The last protective buildings fell away behind me, and for the next two hours the landscape stretched out to an indistinct horizon seen through hazy, wind-driven dust.

Wind always made for noisy walking. If it came from left or right, it was not too bad, but when it came from directly ahead, its flow past my ears made for a steady whooshing that could drown out everything else. And that afternoon it was indeed coming straight at me. Masked by noise, every car approaching from behind would burst unexpectedly into the edge of my vision, whip past in a split second, and then recede into the haze ahead. I would think to myself, *Keep walking Beam; your chances of being hit by one of these cars are a lot less than being bit by a dog.* I ignored the reality that being bit by a dog could be a painful nuisance while being hit by a car would likely end the walk.

Danger from traffic ceased six miles west of Grand Island when I branched from route 2 onto Hall County 39, a gravel section divider that would parallel 2 for twenty-one miles. Within fifteen minutes I came to Helen, waiting by the car and ready to call it a day.

For some reason that evening I took a notion to walk the following day. Helen quickly objected. "Phil, you've just walked three consecutive days; you need a rest."

"Well," I came back, "we did all right the first two days, but today was a short one; we got only seven miles beyond Grand Island. Why don't I walk tomorrow?—make up for it."

Every once in a while I would decide to walk a fourth day, but it rarely paid off. I would be too tired to cover much ground, and invariably I would get sore and grouchy. Helen would say she didn't feel like "listening" to me walk a fourth day.

"What do you mean, *listen* to me walk?" I'd come back. "You don't hear me; you're always up ahead somewhere sleeping or doing crossword puzzles."

"You know what I mean. You're grouchy—not your usual sweet, sunny self."

"Hear yuh, m'Love—hear yuh, hear yuh, hear yuh."

In any case, walking was out of the question the following morning, since it was raining and blowing so hard it threatened to shake poor Lurch off his jacks. Nevertheless, instead of just lying around, we would use the day for doing necessities. We needed groceries and there were clothes to wash. In addition, we both needed new underwear and socks to replace ones inadvertently left behind in Connecticut.

So we declared it a shopping day, and finishing early, we returned to Lurch and stayed inside to read and watch movies during the afternoon. Rain continued well into evening, pleasing us with its gentle patter but at the same time promising more mud. We were content, though, like that last night coming out from the East—the night wind and snow drove us off the road and forced us to camp near Waco.

THE NOISE OF
NIGHTTIME TRAINS

The next day, rather than facing for-certain mud, we moved to the Wagon Wheel Motel and RV Park at Broken Bow, Nebraska, seventy-five miles northwest of Grand Island. A row of campsites lay directly behind the motel building, which was long and narrow and faced the street. The proprietor told us to set up anywhere we wanted to, since all the campsites were empty.

Now, if there had been only one vacant site, we would have gladly put Lurch there and that would have been the end of it, but all those choices resulted in a ten-minute debate about which identical campsite might be best. Finally, we picked one directly behind the middle of the motel, thinking the building itself would block any street noise. What we did not know was that the Burlington Northern Railroad ran through town only three blocks to the north.

That night I lay awake feverish of brain and suffering from the rumblings of passing coal trains. We had passed a parked train the day before, and using the car's odometer, we measured it to be a mile and four tenths long. That figured, because at forty miles per hour the trains were taking roughly two minutes to pass the campground. Bad enough, but you could hear the locomotive from a minute before it got there until a minute after it passed, and adding to the din were warning bells on crossing gates at 6th, 9th, 10th, and 14th avenues. Thus twice per hour there would come a clanging, rumbling railroad racket that would last a good four minutes—even longer than that advertising break before *Final Jeopardy*.

I passed the hours in a restless funk while tossing, turning, and fighting unwanted memories of insults endured or imagined, and acts regretted. There was contemptuous Professor Galbraith whom I would have liked to put down—as in ridicule, of course, not as in slay. Freudian Slip? There was our beloved dog Gina whom I did put down—to be an aching memory till the end of my days.

However, other recollections gave humorous relief in that endless and struggling night. In one I was a kid again, and three of us boys had gone plinking, i.e., shooting tin cans and bottles. We normally did it with 22s, but this particular day I brought along a short-barreled deer rifle that had the blast of a cannon. The racket had us half deaf and shouting at each other by the time we finished, but had anybody so much as put a finger in an ear to save it from the noise? Of course not. Nowadays, no sensible person shoots benchrest or skeet or even 22s without some kind of ear protection. But we were young and immortal, and to admit that the crack of a rifle hurt our ears would have been to admit to being "chicken," which was definitely not the thing to be in 1947.

After we finished shooting, we went to a local greasy spoon for hamburgers, and while we were talking to each other, some dried up old stick (probably twenty years younger than I am now) called over from another booth and said, "How's about you squirts keep it down. People can hear you all over the restaurant!"

The man was half smiling. But squirts? We were sixteen whole years old, by gosh. Up until then we had not been intentionally loud; it was just that we were still half deaf from shooting and were unknowingly talking loud to make up for it. But after he told us to pipe down, we naturally got louder. A few minutes later, "Puppy," the owner of the place, who knew us well and whom we considered our bosom pal, came over and ordered us out of the restaurant. He told us not to set foot in his place again for three weeks, and we told him we wouldn't be setting foot in his place again *ever!* But we were back in two or three days, and all Puppy made us do was promise to keep our mouths shut.

Then there was the business of swimming. Every spring, somebody would get an idea to go swimming while it was still only June. The water would be in the sixties, thus turning skinny adolescents blue in fifteen minutes. But did anybody ever admit to being cold? Of course not. That would have been a sign of weakness—definitely to be avoided if girls were around. A kid would stay in the water until he was one step away from hypothermia; then he would come out with the excuse that he needed to lie in the sun and get a tan. He'd die before he'd admit he was cold and couldn't take it any longer.

Sometime around 1 a.m., after a particularly loud train, I stoked myself into a climactic lather for having a lifelong low tolerance for noise while other people can stand no end of din—or pretend they can. "You should be able to tune it out," they tell me—like they do and like anybody else can who's not a wimp.

God, what a night.

How do people live with this racket? I wondered. On the other hand, the good folk of Broken Bow evidently learn to do just that, at least enough to sleep at night. People are no different here, I thought, than anywhere else. They're personable enough, not the irritable insomniacs they'd be if trains kept them awake the way they do me.

I finally passed out around 2 a.m., exhaustion overriding concerns that I would get little sleep while we were camped at Broken Bow. Of course it was needless concern, for a day or two later it seemed that Burlington Northern was running less trains at night. They might even have begun equipping them with rubber wheels, because the ones I did hear seemed quieter. By the time we had been there four days, I no longer noticed the trains at all. Helen, who had been less bothered by the noise, said, "You've become used to them, Phil. It's like when you were a kid and could hear the Pennsylvania Railroad at night. The trains would give you a comfy-purr sense of security. You would lie in bed, listen to them, and know the stars were still shining; and above all, you'd know that mom and dad were nearby to make sure all stayed well in your world."

"Thank you, Dear Psychologist. Shouldn't such security be every kid's birthright?"

"Should be. 'Course it often isn't. You know as well as I do that we were among the lucky ones."

*   *   *   *

We had planned to head out to walk's end early in the morning after moving to Broken Bow, but we were no sooner on the road than I noticed the car pulling to the right. Sure enough, the right front tire was going soft; we would have to go back to town and get it fixed.

We found a garage but it was an hour until it opened, and then a mechanic spent a good half hour trying to find the problem. No luck. He put soapy water on the tire—as they always do—and he and I looked it over inch by inch. Not a bubble formed anywhere to indicate a leak. In the end, we just gave it more air, put it back on the car, and agreed to hope for the best. In particular, I hoped for the best since I was the one heading out of town. "Mr. Mechanic," on the other hand, allowed that although he too hoped it wouldn't leak, he would be happy to come out and tow me in if it "went back flat." "Good money in it," he concluded with a grin.

Since we were already late en route to walk's end, Helen insisted we go to the local hospital and have a toe of mine treated that had been sore for the last few days. The problem was obvious: The nail, broken off beneath the cuticle, was cocked up at the front so that every step forced it back and down into the nail bed. As wretched as that sounds, it didn't hurt much, even when I was walking. Still, it was becoming red, and Helen, ever the nurse, wanted it checked out.

At the Jennie M. Melham Medical Center we received the same first-class treatment we had received at Clarinda Municipal the autumn before—the time I blasphemed and the bug flew down my ear.

The minute the doctor glanced at it, he said, "That nail needs to come off." I was ready for that, but I wasn't ready when he added, "I'll shoot a little painkiller in the base of your toe. That'll numb things up and you won't feel a thing."

Now, the mere thought of a needle being stuck into the base of the toe made me shudder, nor did I relish the prospect of a partially numb foot for the next four hours.

"Why don't you just yank it off?" I said, the bravado for the benefit of Helen, the doctor, and in particular for two pretty young nurses who had just walked in. "It'll be over in a split second, and it shouldn't hurt much, especially if one of these young ladies holds my hand." I gestured toward the nurses.

They laughed and oohed, but Helen just smiled and said, "No need for one of you girls to hold his hand; I'll do that. And Doctor, wouldn't it be better just to pull that nail off real nice and slow? Better yet, how-z-bout I do it?"

In the end, the plan became no anesthesia and a quick pull. That worked fine, and a few minutes later the nail was gone—the doctor had jerked it out so quickly I hardly felt it. One of the young women applied a dressing, and after good-byes and good-lucks all around, Helen and I were off to a pharmacy for an antibiotic.

It was eleven-thirty by the time I began walking that day. The toe didn't hurt at all, but flexing the foot with each step eventually worked the dressing into a wad at the front of my shoe. It was like walking with a rolled up Kleenex in there. After half an hour I took the shoe off, wrapped the gooey dressing in tissue paper and stuck it in my backpack to be trash-caned later.

"You can't go without a bandage," Helen said when I arrived to the car. "Calvin Coolidge's son got a blister playing tennis. He didn't take care of it and ended up dying."

I had heard that story probably twenty times in the near half century I had known Helen, and before that I used to hear it from my mother, who was also a nurse. "Well," I said, "young Coolidge's father was the President of the United States, so it couldn't happen to me."

Helen muttered something I couldn't hear.

During the next few days I kept salve on the toe and often changed my socks—only that sock, I would tell Helen. "Don't want you havin' to wash 'em both." But the toe was no further problem. Within days it was healing well, and as the weeks passed the nail began to grow back.

A ROADSIDE CREMATORIUM

It was a morning of warm sun and gentle breezes as the countryside seemed to awaken all around me. Along the roads, farmers were moving plows, harrows, and seeders in preparation for spring planting, although as yet little actual fieldwork was being done. I was humming as I walked toward a group of cattle in a dirt holding pen on the north side of the road. They were fat, healthy-looking animals—most were black or brown but two were gray with white faces.

Cattle passively grazing in vast fields usually did not look up, but here, confined, they seemed more curious. A number of them stopped milling around and stared at this "something different" that was briefly breaking the monotony of corral life. I began patting one; however, it suddenly spooked and lurched away. Was it aware that it was living out its last few days and would soon be going to market? Had it been seized by some premonition that my kind would soon bring its end?

I stared at the cattle. Well, that's just the way it is, I thought. Animals and people inherited their roles of feeders and fed; they're certainly not roles I invented. They've been in place for a million years, and they'll be around long after I'm gone. Even today, I mused, chemistry cannot start with a pound of anything and synthesize a single molecule of digestible protein. So like it or not, we're stuck with eating animal flesh or else tons of vegetables and grains. And with that I firmly suppressed all thoughts of the cattle's fate and determinedly marched on.

Nevertheless, whatever complacency I garnered vanished fifteen minutes later, when I half gagged at the sight of two partially burned calves lying in a ditch near a dilapidated house. Somebody was using the ditch for both household burn pile and makeshift crematorium. Scattered around the gruesome carcasses were bits of garbage, broken bottles, blackened cans, and fragments of dishes. Farther out lay some half-burned boxes, along with charred newspapers and two or three old shoes.

Why didn't they just bury the calves, I wondered, or were they diseased and had to be burned for health reasons? But if that were the case, why didn't they burn them far from the house and all the way to ashes? Why leave half-burned, rotting carcasses across the road from where you live? They stank even when they were not burning; when they were smoldering away in step-by-step cremation, the stench must have been awful.

I was momentarily tempted to go over to the house and ask questions—satisfy my curiosity. Ordinarily, I had few qualms about approaching houses, but here and there I would see one which instinct would tell me to avoid. It might have a posted warning like PREMISES PROTECTED BY SMITH AND WESSON or TRESPASSERS WILL BE SHOT, SURVIVORS SHOT AGAIN. I actually saw signs with those very words. Or maybe a place would be especially trashy and poorly cared for, or maybe there would be a tied-out dog—the mean, half-starved kind. But this house, the house of half-burned calves, had no warning signs; it was simply austere and forbidding, and immersed like the whole area in that sickening burned-flesh smell.

I stifled my curiosity and quickly walked on—to come, within miles, to another depressing place.

This time "Bleak House" was set into a hillside at the end of a long, gravel drive. On the rear elevation, turf met the back wall just below a flat roof, and along the sides, packed soil reached to within inches of blue-painted eaves. The long, brown-shingled front facade was joined at both ends by concrete retaining walls that extended right and left, bounding the turf and defining a stark, grassless yard that contained a large, noisy heat exchanger. In the front wall, four barred windows and two heavy doors provided the only openings to the outside.

No flowers, no bushes, no trees softened the starkness of this bunker, which was clearly designed for function alone. Recessed into the hillside, it would be invulnerable to storms, even tornadoes, and it would be easy to maintain and heat. However, survivalist defense was obviously the builder's first priority, judging by razor wire atop an eight-foot, chain-link fence. This surrounded the property and was interrupted only by the driveway gate, which bore the sign: TRESPASS AT YOUR OWN PERIL.

No stopping there!

An hour later I approached a third house, but this one appeared the exact opposite of the house of defense or the house of burned calves. A low brick ranch, it sat invitingly in a grove of shade trees and was set off by well-kept plantings and neatly trimmed lawns. Hanging from a pole above the garage door, a decorative flag said WELCOME, while on the paved driveway were three parked cars—not new, but clean and well kept. A bag of golf clubs leaned against one car, as if someone had been about to put it in the trunk but suddenly remembered something left in the house, something they'd gone back to get.

While I was passing, a woman came out and waved a greeting as she walked toward the car. I called over and wished her luck. "Make par!" seemed a good thing to say.

"Not likely," she called back with a smile. "Anything near a hundred and twenty will make my day."

And then I was beyond that oasis of trees with its inviting home and pleasant golfer. Still, the warmth of the exchange lingered as a welcome antidote to the wretched places I had passed a little while before.

Meanwhile, a dozen miles southeast of Ravenna, Nebraska, Helen had come upon a white clapboard building with the evocative sign, SODTOWN, 1876. One end of the building was a blank wall facing the road; an adjacent west-wall had a door and only two small windows, although along its base were several stunted plantings. From its plainness, Helen thought it may have been a school or church, but a passing farmer told her it had once been the town hall of a farming settlement that was also a way station for oxen trains. The trains had carried potash, but he was unable to tell her where the potash came from or where it was being taken; nevertheless, he did tell her that there had been much more to Sodtown than the now aged town hall. "A church once stood there," the man said, gesturing with his arm, "and houses and a school and a blacksmith shop," he continued, pointing now in another direction.

"Were they originally sod buildings?" Helen asked.

"Yes," he replied. "The first buildings were sod. But as soon as people could bring in lumber they darn quick got outta the mud!"

"Did any of your ancestors live here?"

"No. But there's plenty of families whose people have been around here for a hundred years."

Helen tried to keep the conversation going, but the farmer had things to do and he was soon off about his business. When I passed the building a few hours later, several cows were browsing in the front yard.

Neither Helen nor I mentioned Sodtown after that morning, but it would come back to mind several weeks later, when we were learning about the potash industry in the western part of the state.

*   *   *   *

Lazy thoughts came and went as I walked Nebraska 2 on Easter Morning. Studying maps the night before, I had become interested in various rivers that drain the Missouri River's watershed between Omaha and Kansas City, 170 miles to the south. Included in the group was the South Loup River, which I would cross near Ravenna within the hour. That shallow, wide stream flows northeast, eventually to join the Middle Loop River which then joins the North Loup which eventually becomes simply the Loup. The Loop continues northeast to the Platte, which empties into the Missouri near Omaha.

South of the Platte, the Republican River, with its tributaries, flows into the Kansas River, and this, in turn, empties into the Missouri at Kansas City. It was fascinating to think how those meandering, slow waterways drain sixty thousand square miles of land surface. Rain falling anywhere within that vast area either evaporates, seeps into the water table, or slowly flows to the Missouri, thence to the Mississippi, and finally to the Gulf. Such global musings were hardly profound, but they kept me occupied until my attention withdrew to the terrain just around me, by which time I was past Ravenna and following route 2 along Mud Creek.

Mud Creek, a sluggish tributary of the South Loup, crosses and re-crosses beneath the road three times between Ravenna and Litchfield, seventeen miles farther on. There was no wind that morning, and consequently all along the south bank motionless trees cast perfect reflections in unrippled backwaters. Excellent! Soon picture taking had me occupied as I stopped a number of times trying to compose that perfect scene.

Once I noticed movement in a wide spot in the stream. Amid the marsh grass a muskrat was silently swimming between rotting branches and a fallen fence post. I quickly raised the camera—no time to aim—and punched hard on the save button. Then back to walking.

An hour later I met Helen for midmorning coffee, and after that, walking continued west on route 2 through a mere cross-roads called Sweetwater. Unbeknownst to me, somewhere near there I was noticed by a middle-aged woman dedicated to doing good, and two days later she would spot me again and try her best to do me some. Also, I was twice whistled at by coal trains trundling east along tracks that parallel the highway from Grand Island to Alliance, 270 miles farther on. Still later, I talked with a track-maintenance crew who wanted to know "what in hell" I was doing walking across Nebraska. They went on to tell me that a half dozen train crews were wondering the same thing. That explained the whistlings earlier in the day.

About noon, the town of Hazard broke the monotony of end-less miles. Helen was waiting, and we ate lunch near a large sign which positioned Hazard at the center of the state and proclaimed the importance of the cattle industry. Day's end—the walking end—was just west of Litchfield.

That evening, after downloading the day's pictures, I opened the one that I thought contained the muskrat. "Honey, you missed the critter," Helen said, and it did look that way at first. Even so, I enlarged the image, applied contrast, lightened it, sharpened it, and finally enlarged it again. Presto! There he was, a mosaic of coarse brown squares, but a muskrat, nonetheless, against a background of reflected sky and brown marsh grass. Hooray for digital cameras! Hooray for digital editing! Did Ansel Adams turn over in his grave?

Throughout the next day I continued west along route 2 as it followed Mud Creek upstream from Litchfield toward Broken Bow, where we were still camped. Over the intervening miles the terrain rose roughly three hundred feet—too gradual, as usual, to be noticed in itself, but the lazy flow of the stream, always toward me, kept me aware of the steady climb. Vast lands to the north and south were also slowly rising toward the Rocky Mountains, which were now only four hundred miles ahead.

I saw many horses along the way and even succeeded in making acquaintance with a few. They would see me coming, and after first staring, some would trot over to the inevitable roadside fence. The least shy would come right up and let me pat their noses and necks and shoulders. Occasionally however, when several were simultaneously vying for attention, they would become competitive, bicker, and try to shove each other aside.

Friendly Faces

At one point, I approached a corral defined by fences of wide-square mesh instead of the usual barbed wire. Nice, I thought; the horses can't cut themselves by brushing against barbs. But why were the fences bulged outward in places? The animals had doubtless done it, but why?

Even as I looked I got my answer. Two ponies meandered over to a relatively straight section, and once there they turned around, backed into the fence, and began rubbing their rear ends up and down and then right and left. The harder they pushed the more the fence gave, and no doubt the better their rumps felt. They were still going at it as I walked away, so I did not see how much the fence recovered when they finished. For some reason—can't imagine why—I began thinking about bulged screen doors and my blessed grandchildren.

LIKEABLE DO-GOODERS AND WELDER'S ART

A truck or maybe a van—some sort of vehicle—was slowing as it approached from behind, but I paid little attention. A weather front was moving in from the west, and I had put on my jacket and was fighting the zipper when a tentative, almost plaintive, voice called, "Sir, can I give you a lift?" Turning, I saw a woman of perhaps fifty pulling up in the opposite lane in a white and well-worn van.

"Thanks but no thanks," I answered. "I'm just passing through." I smiled for good measure but determinedly kept walking. Usually I welcomed any chance to talk, but this morning I wanted to get in as many miles as possible in case the front should bring rain.

"You look tired." Again that almost sad voice, and now, heaven help me, with a hint of pity.

I didn't feel tired; in fact I felt just fine, except that I was becoming frustrated with the darn zipper and distracted by this obviously well intentioned do-gooder. By now she was taxiing along beside me by matching her van's speed to my pace.

"I saw you near Sweetwater," she continued, "the day before yesterday. You know, sir, you don't have to walk; I'd be glad to take you wherever you're going."

I put on a sunny smile and began to angle toward the middle of the road, thus toward the van. I half hoped, half expected her to gun the van and dash away, but instead she pulled ahead and off the road while beckoning me to come right up to the driver's window. Clearly, she was unafraid and determined to talk, and even before I got there, she began telling me that she was a member of a church group that provided transportation for very senior citizens. To the grocery store, to the pharmacy, to the doctor, to church: she would take them anywhere they wanted to go—especially to church.

Three of her beneficiaries were in the van with her, two on the seat directly behind and another in the passenger seat. Although the ones in the back appeared somewhat out of it (actually she did too), the one in the passenger seat looked wire-sharp and worldly, though well into her eighties. She had snow-white hair, and her finely lined face was set off by mischievous dark eyes bordered by laugh wrinkles. Her name, she quickly told me, was Alice, and "her," she said, grinning and tossing her head toward the driver—"that's none other than our beloved Nancy! But you should take a ride with us queens. You'll never feel like walking again." She laughed with delight as embarrassed Nancy snapped her eyes away from me and stared straight ahead.

"Really, ladies," I said, "I don't need a ride. My wife's waiting just up the road. She wouldn't like it if I eloped with you four."

Nancy and the two in the back remained inert, but Alice grinned and said she guessed that was probably true. "But what in hell are you doing?" she went on, "out here in the middle of nowhere walking by yourself."

So I began to tell them how I had walked all the way from Connecticut and how Helen and I were trying to do some good works ourselves. Our good works, I told them, amounted to having invited people back home to pledge a few cents to their favorite charities for every mile I would walk. We had already written home several times so that the local paper could report our progress for readers who had made pledges. However, I told the ladies, we didn't know how much money, if any, had actually found its way to the Salvation Army, Red Cross, United Way, etc.

All four women liked the idea of our doing good by getting pledges, but except for Alice, the walking part of the story went right over their heads. Alice was right with me, however, and she came on with two quick questions. The first was standard: "Where do you stay at night?" The second stopped me cold: "What do you do when you gotta go?"

Recovering, I managed, "What we all do when we gotta go. We look for the nearest privacy—in my case, usually the *backside* of a tree!"

She burst into laughter. "You must have said *back … side*, but it sure sounded like *backside*!"

"You heard me," I rejoined with a grin. Her companions missed it all.

Nancy presently declared that my trying to get people to make charitable contributions gave the two of us something in common: we were both doing God's work. But just how far she came from appreciating my commitment to an unbroken walk was evident by the next thing she said. "Sir, you still ought to let us give you a ride."

That took me back, and I was taken back still further when the two old folks in the rear inexplicably came alive with loud *amens*. The charity part of the story they easily appreciated; they were the kind of people who think a great deal about doing good. On the other hand, I couldn't convince Nancy that I was not a poverty stricken old man—a drifter—down on my luck and in need of a handout. I gave up, and with smiles and small hand-waves I began to back away, determined to break free and get walking again.

But the woman would not let go. "Can't you just accept this?" she suddenly asked. "Maybe it will help you along your way." She was holding out a five-dollar bill!

"He doesn't need the *damned* money; can't you see that?" Alice snapped in a voice that finally betrayed the patience *she* needed to put up with her companions. Nancy, however, still didn't get it, and again tried to give me the money.

"You don't understand," I said, beginning to have a patience problem myself. "I'm here because my wife and I are on a project to walk clear across the United States. We are not poor and I do not *have* to be here; we are doing it because it's fun, exciting, and because we *want* to do it. When we finish in Oregon, we'll go home and resume living like millions of other retired people. We'll do volunteer work, spend winters in Florida, travel a little, spoil grandchildren a lot. You keep your five dollars and use it for gas, so you can keep helping people get around—like you're helping these good folk right here." I gestured toward the women in the back seat.

If I was being overly firm, it didn't bother Alice, who smiled in sympathy.

Nancy was starting to say something else when I suddenly had an inspiration. In the most reverential voice I could muster, I interrupted with, "May God bless you in all that you do."

A kindly smile spread over her face, and more amens issued from the back seat. But Alice's eyes met mine—just for a second—as her face took a knowing grin and she rolled her eyes toward the sky.

I walked on then, amused by Alice's earthiness but humbled by Nancy's sweetness, her obvious decency, her commitment to doing charitable things. This one, I thought, trusting and vulnerable as she is, definitely lives her religion.

*   *   *   *

Although there had been no rain, it was still blustery as I entered Mason City a few hours later. My intention was to walk right through town without stopping, but off the main street behind a gas station I spotted a 1951 Studebaker, and that was a good excuse to get behind the building and out of the wind.

I was quickly fascinated by the old car, which appeared to be in excellent condition except for fading paint and light rust. Viewed from the rear and a little to one side, the Studebakers of 1951 were boxy and ugly; viewed from the front and a little to one side, they were streamlined and beautiful. The rooflines slanted in, just as they should

1951 Studebaker

in order to emphasize a sloping hood adorned at the front with a big chrome jet plane—of course. Beneath the jet the hood continued its downward incline to a bullet nose that was set off by foreword-leading fenders guarded by a big chrome bumper. Thems were the good old days—when they knew how to make a car look really good!

Recalling the Studebaker that Helen and I had owned way back in the fifties, I began to think about maybe buying this one and taking it back to Connecticut to restore. I checked in the gas station, and although the attendant did not think the car was for sale, a woman customer, who happened to know the owner, gave me his phone number. "Call him," she said. "Maybe you can make a deal." Then, changing the subject, she went on: "Now if you really want to see something interesting, go to the corner of Reed and Jenkins Streets.

"What's there?"

"Sculptures. A man lives there who welds up pieces of old farm equipment and junkyard stuff to make artworks. Some are human figures, some are animals. They're all over his lawn. Some stand by themselves, some are on carts or pedestals. He makes the pedestals too—also from salvage. Go see the place, you'll never forget it."

She was talking too promotionally to suit me, so I begged off by telling her I had to keep walking if I was to get in a twenty-five-mile day. That impressed her not at all, and several more times she said I ought to see those "awesome" sculptures. "Missing them'll be a big mistake!"

Finally, I pretended to have gone deaf, whereupon we smilingly shook hands and I left—with no yen to see back-street art but plenty of enthusiasm about getting my hands on the Studebaker.

On the road again, I had not gone far before the idea of encumbering the walk project with a forty-nine-year-old car seemed completely at odds with ever getting to the West Coast. Two hours later, when I caught up with Helen, she, like me, at first became excited about how we could restore the car and drive it in parades, or visit the kids, or just go for Sunday-afternoon rides. She enthused for several minutes until her excitement began to fade and she gradually quieted. I waited, knowing what would come next.

"Phil, this in nonsense," she suddenly said. Then she plunged on with essentially following: We have to get it out of our heads. We'd be weeks getting that car home and more weeks getting back out here to walk. You've never rebuilt an old car, and it would be letting us both in for a great-big, long-term project. Remember that twenty-foot boat you built back in the seventies? You said you could do it in three months; in the end it took two years. This would be the same thing!

Here she ran out of breath and was again briefly quiet. Then, "Not only that, Philip, there'll be other things you'd rather do—like write a book about this walk. You already mentioned that. It's up to you, Dearie, but if it was me, I wouldn't take it on!"

"*Were me*, Helen—your English is slippin'. You're right though; we won't take it home. Issue decided! But you look funny when you're talkin' and turnin' blue. And why so timid? When you've got something to say, just spit it out."

Minutes later it crossed my mind that at that precise moment I should have hopped out of the car and begun walking. Instead, I continued to sit there and tell Helen about the sculptures and how the gas station customer had hyped them up. She appeared thoughtful as she listened, but then she said, "It would be nice to see the sculptures … or you could take one more look at the Studebaker—you never know."

"Good Lord! Helen, we've already agreed not to take on the Studebaker. Remember? Can't we just stick with that?" Her insinuation that buying the old car was still an option threw the issue from decided right back to undecided, and it threw me off balance— as she no doubt intended.

"Do you want to go back and see the sculptures or not?" I growled. "Forget the car!"

"I have forgotten it, but you've got to make up *your* mind. I can't do it for you."

It was obvious she was stringing me along, and again I should have got out of the car. Instead, I said, "Darn it, I have made up my mind—you're the one who's reopening the issue. I wanna get on with the walk; now what'll it be?—sculptures or no sculptures."

"It's up to you."

"You."

"You."

"Oh Lord! Look out sculptures, here we come. Darn woman!"

Helen, triumphantly: "Gotcha m'Love. That'll teach you to correct my English and make fun of my breathing! How 'bout a kiss?"

"I'd give you more than that," I told her as I grabbed her and said, "No car!—agreed?"

"You got it."

And with that we started back to Mason City....

We had seen welder's art before at fairs and specialty shops. Typically, the pieces were small chickens and ducks made from old shovels, screwdrivers, garden trowels, etc. Nothing we had seen impressed us much, but the sculptures at Mason City were different.

The first thing we noticed, upon approaching the corner of Reed and Jenkins Streets, was a neatly kept house in front of a two-story building with a red roof and white walls. The walls were painted with large phoenixes as well as a long gun and a bow and arrow; and as striking as these were, even more impressive were metal sculptures that sat at various places in the front and back lawns. The shape of an Indian, complete with headdress, occupied a spot near the sidewalk, and nearby was a black-painted pedestal made from nine wagon wheels. On the pedestal, and constructed of red-painted hoops, was a form that we first took to be human. But it held a pitchfork in one hand and bolt cutters in the other, and the more we stared at it the more it seemed to be the artist's rendition of a devil.

Then there was a skeletal soldier wearing a doughboy helmet and aiming a rifle, while around the house near a picket fence, a low-wheeled platform held another skeleton. This one, however, wore a German helmet and was firing a pedestal-mounted machine gun!

Aside from those disquieting pieces, most of the sculptures were relatively lighthearted. There was a ladybug about four feet long—squat, fat, and red with black spots. There was a five-foot penguin in formal attire, all dressed up for a night on the town. There was a white stork with a bright orange beak, cocking its head to gobble down a grasshopper. Other denizens of that fascinating place were a roadrunner, a crow, and a monstrous beetle made from the hood of an old car.

All the figures were artistically painted, but the roadrunner's finish was best of all. His yellow beak and crest, together with white legs and tail feathers, achieved pleasing contrasts with tan wings and body as he raced across the yard at break-neck speed—BEEP-BEEP! Wily Coyote was nowhere to be seen; evidently he'd been left completely behind.

Where's Wily Coyote?

Helen enjoyed the sculptures, but she eventually became restless. "Come on, Phil. We need to get going. We've been here a half hour."

I was not quite ready to go, since I had begun writing down a few of the different pieces and parts the artist had used in his creations. These included old grass shears, scythe blades, plowshares, railroad spikes, sickle blades, tractor seats and an endless assortment of nuts and bolts. Besides these, there were dozens of unidentifiable pieces, large and small, that could have come from people's attics or workshops or even the town dump.

Eventually we did break away, and twenty minutes later Helen dropped me off at our last rendezvous—the place we talked Studebaker an hour before.

Most of the animals I saw the rest of the afternoon were road kill victims rather than metal sculptures. There were plenty of pheasants in the area, and cars had hit three of the slow-flying birds. Twice I saw squashed skunks and once a dead coyote. Two bull snakes had also "bought the farm"—it's hard to miss a five-foot snake when you're driving along and it's stretched across the road sunning itself. I knew that from experience; by the time you see the unlucky serpent it is usually too late to swerve.

Walking ended about five o'clock when I met Helen near a grade crossing of the Burlington Northern. She had had a pleasant day, having especially enjoyed the sculptures. I had enjoyed them too, and I told Helen I was glad I insisted we go back and look at the car—told her I was still thinking about buying it.

She kindly asked me not to mention car again.

A TOO PROFESSIONAL YOUNG COP

By the time we reached central Nebraska that spring, Helen and I had both been taking many pictures. Sometimes I would take two, three, or four adjacent, overlapping digital snapshots and later use the computer to stitch them into wide panoramas. These never turned out well, because I invariably had trouble aligning the snapshots while holding the camera. I needed a tripod.

So it was tripod hunting that took us into downtown Broken Bow one morning, but finding nothing there, we continued on to Grand Island. It was a seventy-five-mile drive, but it paid off when we found a good tripod at a small photo shop. We also bought groceries, a heating pad, and several other items that we had been meaning to buy but hadn't got around to. Then it was back to Broken Bow that afternoon, but stopping on the way at Mason City for one last look at the Studebaker. Thoughts of buying it, however, had long since been laid to rest.

We could have walked the following morning, but the 150-mile, round-trip drive the day before had tired us out. We'd just do a few chores, hang around the campground, and maybe take a walk around Broken Bow. That would rest us up, and we'd be ready to go the following morning.

Indeed, that second day off was a good idea, for by the following morning we were eager to get back on the road.

It was chilly as we drove out of town—only forty degrees by a thermometer on a downtown bank— but once I was walking and the sun was rising, it was not long before I was comfortable. Alas, that lasted only a few hours, for as the morning wore on, clouds developed and the wind became strong out of the west, thus right into my face. By lunchtime it was another noisy, hard-walking day.

While we were eating, Helen got an idea to measure the speed of clouds that were racing by overhead. She started the car, did a U-turn, and minutes later we were cruising along at thirty miles per hour, and just keeping pace with a particularly prominent cloud. Of course, at ground level the wind was considerably weaker. Nevertheless, when I got back to walking, it felt as if I was walking into a gale. If it suddenly stops, I complained to myself, I'll probably fall on my face.

The only person I talked to that day (besides Helen, of course) was a young highway patrolman somewhere beyond of Broken Bow. He too was traveling west, and he slowed way down and held pace beside me for twenty or thirty yards before pulling ahead and parking on my side of the road. After sitting there for a long moment, he got out, walked around the cruiser and assumed a posture with legs spread and arms folded. Then he smilelessly stared at me through mirrored sunglasses as I walked up to him.

Irritated by his forbidding demeanor, my first thought was that somebody had complained about an old man trespassing on railroad property. The Burlington right-of-way ran parallel to the road, and NO TRESPASSING signs were posted at regular intervals along the tracks. Only fifteen minutes earlier I had crossed to find a private place for duties, and a train had been coming. I knew the engineer saw me because he waved and blew his whistle. But maybe he wasn't just being friendly; maybe he was warning me off of railroad property.

Just in case the cop wanted to talk trespassing, I rushed some candidate excuses to mind: Couldn't wait any longer. When you gotta go, you gotta go. Nature called. I've got a gimpy prostate—something a "yout" like you wouldn't know about.

I would try the last one only if I could get him smiling with one or more of the first three.

I needn't have worried because he didn't mention the railroad. And he wasn't about to smile. He was only interested in questioning me about what I was doing walking by myself in the "middle of Custer County." Once I was sure he was satisfied,

I ventured a comment on the weather. But he'd have none of it. Squeaky clean and perfectly groomed, he left with a crisp departing courtesy.

I was glad to see him go.

*   *   *   *

The terrain was changing now. Since leaving Grand Island the week before, we had been passing through a relatively flat countryside of wheat fields, sorghum, and cornfields—the farmlands of southeastern Nebraska. Now, beyond Broken Bow and nearing Anselmo, ranches were taking over from farms, and the terrain was becoming a vast grass-covered area of dunes. These are the famous Sand Hills and they extend almost to Alliance, in the western part of the state.

Most people know about the Gobi and Sahara deserts. Significant portions of those deserts have dunes, and most Americans are probably aware of the gypsum dunes at White Sands, New Mexico. However, to this Easterner sand dunes were always associated with ocean coasts, where they were always shifting and sometimes covered by yard-high beach grass. The Sand Hills' dunes, which cover about a quarter of Nebraska, are different from the ten- to twenty-foot mounds I was used to; some are two hundred feet high. At one point, I climbed one and looked north over a landscape that once again reminded me of a seascape.

There are six north-south bands of higher dunes between Anselmo and Antioch, 160 miles to the west, and between the bands, which are like low uplands, lie five valleys—troughs one might say—in which local dunes are somewhat lower. Wind, of course, shapes both sea and land; it develops ocean waves in hours and sand dunes in eons, but the surfaces have distinct similarities.

Thin grasses overlay the dunes almost everywhere, except in widely separated places where there are small bare spots known as *blowouts*. These too are caused by the wind, which has also given the lower dunes their direction. They are generally longer east to west than north to south.

As dry as the Sand Hills appear, rocks beneath the surface hold abundant water, thus making them suitable for cattle ranching. Spreads are huge, ranging from a few thousand acres to two-, five-, or even ten-times that size. Consequently ranch houses and support buildings are widely separated; one can walk for miles and not see a house or barn or outbuilding of any kind, although occasionally there may be a windmill pumping water for a small herd of cattle. People are scarce and walking can be lonely.

One day, ready for a change from the endless dunes, I detoured north into the town of Linscott. Hardly a soul was on the streets; the good folk must all have been working in Broken Bow or Anselmo or out on the range. Probably the kids were in school. Lonely and slightly gloomy, I wandered along Baxter Street until I came to an old auto dealership. And behold, behind a dirty showroom window was another Studebaker—not a '51, to be sure, but a Studebaker nonetheless.

My spirits rallied, but not for long. The car was in bad shape— dirty, fenders dented, bumpers gone to rust; its better days were decades behind it. But these were the cars of my youth, I lamented, and now they're old and past their time. In that deserted street, under a brilliant sun, I felt like a lonely holdover from another era. Where the heck are all the people? I wondered, when you really need somebody to talk to.

I hurried back to the highway and soon spotted Helen up ahead, smiling and waving as she stood by the car. I was overdue and she had been looking for me with binoculars. She was in an upbeat mood at first, but after five minutes of my funk she too began to come down. Suddenly however, she put a stop to it: "Phil, why don't you get out your camera and start looking for things to take pictures of. This is silly. You need to get your mind out of itself—you'll feel better."

"All right, all right," was the best I could manage, as I got out of the car and began walking.

It was not long until a half dozen ducks burst from a roadside marsh, and although I had begun to think about taking pictures, the camera was still in my pants pocket—unreachable in time for that shot. But it was in my hands a few minutes later when two more ducks took wing. I snapped a picture, only to realize that in the background a string of wooden telephone poles marched across the hills like crucifixion crosses. My eyes followed them to the horizon from where imagination took me up into space, and presently I was looking down and envisioning the poles and wires of the world's great power grids thickened and covering the continents like vast wire nets.

Beam, I thought, come down to earth and consider this: In wooded parts of the country, like the Northeast, if you notice wires at all, they are usually following the roads. Out here, in this land of dunes and ranches, what you mostly notice are high-tension wires cutting cross-country, and much of the time, except for roads, they are the only man-made things you see. They spring up out of nowhere, you know, whenever you go to take a picture.

Amusing myself with more such thoughts, I gradually began to feel better, especially when farther along there came an opportunity for close-up photos of a bull snake. He was crawling along in the grass beside the road. Unafraid, he hardly minded my walking right up to him, nor did he mind the lecture I delivered about staying off the road. Eventually though, tiring of my repeatedly trying to scare him farther into the grass, he assumed a belligerent stance and made grunting sounds.

I walked on.

An hour later I was watching a smoke column develop to the northeast. I had seen such columns before, but this one was becoming especially huge. In the space of an hour, its stem, which must have been a quarter mile across, rose thousands of feet before spreading into that familiar, disquieting, mushroom-shaped cloud. It was probably a controlled burn, but later, in Idaho, we would see similar clouds from both prairie and forest fires that definitely were not controlled. The year 2000 would be bad for fires in the west.

I took a picture of the smoke; then, tiring of photography, I put the camera away and began walking in earnest—only to shortly come upon my first cactus plant. It was in the berm beside the road, and it looked like a dozen small, yellow-green pancakes with pins sticking out. I brought the camera out again, and as I carefully focused, I thought, *Okay, Beam, this must really be the beginnings of the West!*

The picture turned out fine and it came cheap and pain free too. A month later, while squatting to take pictures of a bug, I accidentally tipped backwards and sat right down on a similar cactus. Funny enough in retrospect—not so funny at the time.

WAS THE OLD RANCHER LYING?

At Dunning, Nebraska, a Burlington Northern railroad bridge spans the highway bridge which in turn spans the Dismal River. It's an unusual double-decker construction, and pausing on the roadway, I stood with fingers to ears as an empty coal train thundered overhead. The racket was deafening. With disquieting thoughts of a rail disaster, I moved close to a massive concrete support, which trembled in response to the pounding wheels.

Well, I thought to myself, if it jumps the track, it shouldn't take out this bridge. Nevertheless, I was soon picturing the train flying off the rails and through the air, but with its crew happily parachuting to safety. (They would have ejection seats like fighter pilots.) The crew clear and safe, I further envisioned a dozen empty coal cars landing with spectacular splashes in the Dismal River. Be a "dismal" scene for Burlington management, I thought, and a miserable mess to clean up. On the other hand, it would be a boredom-breaking event for the good folk of Dunning—give 'em something to talk about for years.

Wake up, Beam! You're becoming warped up by monotony! You've been alone too long!

The train safely past—thank God for that—I was soon through Dunning and walking along the Middle Loup River just west of its junction with the Dismal. Toward noon the wind began to blow as usual, slowly at first, but within an hour it was strong and directly out of the east. Fairly pushing me along, it made for easy walking except for the noise. Meanwhile, the air, which had been clear earlier, became hazy with dust, and my normally weathered face became hotter and dryer than ever. Cracked skin, especially around lips and fingernails, comes with the territory when you walk forever in the rain and wind and sun....

Day's end came about four o'clock when I met Helen in the middle of nowhere. I was punchy, but we were twenty-four miles still farther along the way.

*   *   *   *

Somewhere on the north side of the road near Halsey, Nebraska, there is a long-deserted, block building where many a bitter adolescent has applied graffiti. The building probably started out as a gas station called RILEY (not RILEY'S). There is a faded sign saying RILEY over two rotting six-paned window frames, which are themselves adjacent to a door big enough for a small truck. But if it started out a garage, plenty of random additions and oddball walls have made it something only a paleontologist would try to identify. I used to kid a paleontology student by telling him that if his professor found a single fifty-million-year-old bone fragment, he would proceed to describe the donor beast right down to the color of its eyeballs.

In any case, local kids have decorated this wrecked building with paint and words. Patches of red, green, violet, and blue are splashed on the walls in psychedelic abandon, often as backgrounds for words or phrases, many obscene. Brian's name appears and so does Tanya's, Konni's and Angie's, although probably not with their permission. Two phrases stand out: *'98 nilz* and *Ass Kickin Time for FHS*. What would *nilz* stand for? *FHS* is probably a high school.

The outline of a hand, three feet across, suggests some secret gang, and so does a cloud-like symbol painted high on a second level wall. *Love* appears in numerous places and so does the *F* word. In one place it's painted in broad white letters on a red background, which also contains the *U* and *C* of a still larger version of the same expletive.

I wondered how many of the artists, no longer young, drive by from time to time and wince at the artwork of their adolescence. Strangely, for me the building and its "decorations" were both an upper and a downer. The obscene graffiti was depressing, as usual, but the old building itself, standing alone in the open, was a refreshing point of interest in the endless, hilly landscape.

*   *   *   *

On the last Sunday of April Helen and I attended an arts and crafts show at Melbourne, Nebraska. Local artists were display-ing paintings, mostly of prairie or ranch scenes; however, a few had portraits, and one or two had paintings of groups of people, mostly ranchers and business types. A particularly amusing water-color showed a smiling politician holding a campaign poster of his own smiling likeness.

Soon after we arrived, Helen began talking to a wood carver, and I met a rancher, the grandfather of one of the artists. An octogenarian with worn out knees and a lively sense of humor, he regaled me rapid-fire anecdotes about ranch life in the "good old days"—he grinned as he used the phrase. Eventually he came to his masterpiece.

"And then there was this bull snake," he said.

By then we were on casual enough terms, so I came right back with a skeptical, "This should really be good."

"You wanna hear the story or not?" he demanded with cocked eyebrow and meaningful glare.

"I can tell I'm gonna hear it if I stay in this gallery. I can't go anywhere; my wife's over there talking to the wood carver."

"Okay, okay," he said. "Well then, when I was a kid about nine years old, mom kept this here bull snake—"

"What do you mean 'kept a bull snake'?" I interrupted. "Sounds like *bull-something-else* to me."

He grinned, waited a minute, and then started over word for word: "Well then, when I was a kid about nine years old, mom kept this here bull snake. He was a good-sized fellow, maybe five feet long and thick as a pick handle in the middle—"

I broke in again. "Which part of a pick handle? A pick handle's thicker at the ends than it is in the middle. At least a Connecticut pick handle is."

But he rolled right on, and I kept quiet, figuring another interruption might be one too many.

"Bull snakes never bother anybody," he said. "In fact, they're a help if your business is raising chickens. They eat rats and mice that otherwise eat lots of chicken feed."

He paused for a minute while he shifted his weight from a leg that was bowed four inches at the knee. "Leg's plain wore out," he muttered. Pretty soon though he was comfortable enough to continue.

"As I was saying, mom kept this here bull snake. She'd made a house for 'im; it was an old slatted wooden crate that she'd piled sticks on top of, maybe so's it would seem homier. He'd crawl in and out between the slats when he was around. I say 'when he was around,' because sometimes he'd disappear for days or weeks and we'd think he was gone for good, but then one day he'd be back and mom would be glad to see him. Them times she'd usually give 'im a bowl of milk."

There's no way this is true, I thought to myself. *But at least it's a good story.*

He continued: "The only problem with having a bull snake around a chicken coop is that every once in a while he'll eat an egg—if you can say bull snakes eat eggs; actually they swallow 'em whole.

"Now our chickens laid their eggs in what we called a *gang nest,* a long cabinet-like thing my dad built and nailed to the inside of the chicken-coup wall. It was waist high above the floor so's the rats couldn't get in and bite the hen's legs when they was straining away laying eggs. Nowadays, that gang nest would remind people of a row of motel rooms. 'Course, back then there was no motels, you know. That was in … let's see … if I was nine, that would be 1922. Do you realize that were only four years after the First World War?"

He was beginning to ramble, and I wondered if he would ever get to the end of the story. In 1922 the Great War had indeed been over only four years; I did know that, and I now knew the old man was eighty-seven. He stood there with a distant look in his eyes, as if he'd left the summer of 2000 and was a kid again in far off 1922 and his mother had sent him out to collect eggs. Still, as abruptly as he drifted away, he came back and went on with the story.

"Each nest in that there chicken motel was a foot and a half wide and a foot and a half deep, and separated from the nest beside it by a wooden partition. The floor of each nest had straw so's when an egg dropped out of a hen it wouldn't hit the bare wood and break—hens drop eggs, you know, they don't really lay 'em. Now, dad had thrown the whole motel together with scrap boards that had splits here and there, and there was plenty of knotholes.

"Well, one day I was collecting eggs and had gathered almost a basketful, when I looked in one of them nests and there was the tail-half of the bull snake with a big bulge in it. His head-half was in the next nest over, and it had a bulge too. That snake, glutton that he was, had eaten two eggs. After swallowing one, he'd slithered his front-half through a knothole into the next nest and there he'd swallowed another one. He was like a rope with two knots, one on either side of that wooden partition—a hell of a fix he was in. He waren't goin' nowhere!"

"What'd you do?" I asked. I was looking hard at the old man's eyes, trying to tell if he was lying.

"What'd I do?" he came back, as if the question was silly. "Why I just stuck my hand in where his head wasn't and his tail was, grabbed the bulge, turned him a tad, and broke the egg with my thumb, just the way you'd shoot a marble. You know, you curl your finger around the marble, cock your thumbnail, and when you got your aim just right you let 'er go. You can ping another kid's head that way too—then you say you plucked his melon. Anyway, by turning Bully (that's what Mom called 'im), and plucking 'im a goodin underneath, I broke the egg without breaking his ribs. Can you imagine what it'd be like to have a hundred ribs and ten of 'em busted?" He grinned from ear to ear.

"No I can't," I told him with a scowl. "Is this the truth?"

"Do I look like a man who'd tell a lie?"

Truth was he looked like a man who'd return your wallet if he found it in the street, a man from whom you could safely buy a used car. He also looked like a man who would happily convince you the ocean was boiling hot, that pigs could fly, and that he himself had roped a streak of lightning.

Not about to ask him for the rest of the story, I began talking about the weather. "Dry year so far, right?" No answer. "Is it usually this windy out here this time of year?" Still no answer. He had drifted away again, maybe back to the twenties. Then I switched to politics. "Think President Clinton'll get out of this latest scrape he's in?"

"What scrape?" His eyes lit up and back he came. "What's he done now?"

"Who knows?" I said, "but he must be in some kind of mess; he usually is."

That got the old Republican started on a rambling denunciation of Democrats in general and Clintons in particular. "They're typical eastern politicians," he said, "can't believe anything they say."

"They're from Arkansas and that's closer to Nebraska than Connecticut is, which is where I'm from."

"You wanna hear the rest of this snake story, or don't cha?"

"Yep, let's hear it." I'd out waited him.

"Well, I ran up to the house and told mom about the snake, and 'course she came rushin' down. The broke egg was still a good-sized bulge, but mom thought that if he was smart enough to wait till nightfall, it oughtta be small enough to fit through the knothole and he could slither forward and get free. He was in no hurry though. I guess he'd gorged himself full and maybe was sleepy. He laid there all day, half in one nest and half in the other. Come dinnertime, I thought both bulges looked smaller, as if the eggshells was meltin', you know, from stomach juice. Mom said she s'posed he had indigestion in two different nests, and she warned me about bein' a glutton. Nowadays people laugh about eatin' too much; that's why they're all pleasingly plump"—he grinned and shook his head—"but in them days a glutton was a glutton, and pleasingly plump meant *fat*."

He paused then—for a good half minute. He'd left me again, but I was hooked and had to hear the rest of the story. "How many days did he lay there?" I asked.

"Huh?"

"How many days did he lay there?"

"Just that day. Next morning he was gone. We didn't see him for about a week and a half, but then one day there he was again, front half sticking out of the house mom made for him. She got him a bowl of milk, which he soon began to drink. He hung around our place for a couple years after that before he finally disappeared for good. We never did see him in the hen house again. Maybe he learned something."

A few minutes later we shook hands and the old rancher wished me safe walking. I didn't know what to make of his story—still don't. But two weeks later I talked to a restaurateur in Alliance, Nebraska, 180 miles farther west. When I told him about the old man and his bull snake, he laughed and said, "Hell, they're notorious liars in that part of the country. That's where the original Liars Club started."

Maybe so, maybe not. I wasn't even sure I believed the restaurateur.

After leaving the rancher, I drifted over to where Helen was still talking to the wood carver. A local man, he had begun carving only three years before and had had no formal instruction—said he simply bought books and learned from them. That seemed incredible, for to Helen and me his carvings of Indians appeared as skillfully done as any we had seen—granted ours were untrained eyes.

Out on the street I said to Helen, "He couldn't have learned to carve like that just by reading books; that man has followed some self-imposed regimen where he's read about carving technique, practiced carving, read technique, practiced carving.... I mean lots and lots of hands-on carving—couldn't be otherwise."

Presently, our speculations progressed to the possibly different natures of people according to where they might live or have come from. "Shouldn't talent of almost any kind," Helen ventured, "be more often present in adventurous subgroups of people than in, say, larger ancestral populations as a whole? For example, people of the modern American West are the progeny, only a few generations removed, of those gutsy people who left the safer East to risk all homesteading the prairies. Cannot they, on the whole, be expected to provide more than their share of overachievers in all walks of life?"

I wasn't so sure. I granted her that compared to historically stationary populations, the intrepid pioneer's descendants might provide more than their share of audacious people: generals and explorers, for example, or astronauts and entrepreneurs. But I thought they might provide fewer cerebral types like artists, writers, philosophers—people like that.

"Phil," Helen came right back, "that's close to the old stereotype that Midwesterners are less intellectually sophisticated than Easterners, and that's almost a corollary to the notion that Americans have always been less sophisticated than Europeans."

"It's not the same," I said. "Stereotypes are held by people who don't think much, and I've been thinking about this for the last two minutes—about as long as you have. And another thing, m'Love, I've just thought of a brand new word for this notion of different personalities associating with different localities. Want to know what it is?"

"Only if you insist."

"It's geopersonalityism."

"Heaven help us."

We left the subject right there, agreeing it would make a good thesis topic for some masters candidate in sociology.

Helen hoped it would never be studied under a government grant.

MOUNTAIN OYSTERS AND A VERY SORE LEG

One evening while we were still camping at Broken Bow, we went to eat at a particularly nice restaurant. When we saw "mountain oysters" on the menu, we both thought we knew what they were, but just to be sure I asked the waitress. She was not a young woman; in fact she looked to be in her forties, and neither Helen nor I expected the mortification my question would cause her. She turned red, dropped her eyes and barely stammered, "male parts ... ah ... privates—you know ... un-talked-abouts ... from young bulls."

It struck me that she might have been cruelly teased by people who were well aware of her sensitivity, or maybe she was just overly sensitive by nature. In any case I somewhat recklessly remarked, "Sorry. I wouldn't have asked the question if I'd known it would distress you so." Then, plunging on, "Please don't let yourself be embarrassed like this ... now ... ever ... or by anybody. It's just not worth it."

Even as I spoke, I feared I was going too far, maybe crossing some blurry line to impropriety. Nevertheless, she recovered slightly and mumbled appreciation for my "consideration." Then she left to get us wine.

When she came back, she was accompanied by the cook, who personally discussed our steak orders with us. He told us how thick and big around they would be, and he asked how well done we wanted them. "I'll get 'em right, believe me," he said, "or she'll have my scalp." He grinned and gestured toward the waitress who, obviously feeling better, clearly enjoyed the attention.

And he did get them right; in fact the entire meal was excellent. His discussing steak orders with the diners was evidentially something taken for granted at that restaurant. He did it with everyone ordering steaks; in particular he spent a good five minutes with a group of cattlemen at a nearby table. Maybe there are other places where they do that sort of thing, but for Helen and me it was a first. We were so pleased with everything that when the waitress brought the check, we asked her to tell the cook he could keep his scalp. "Oh," she assured us, "he'll be glad to hear that. He's a great cook but an even nicer guy." Then she smiled my way and added, "So's he."

"Oh, he's one in a bunch!" Helen declared. "I know, I've been putting up with him for fifty years." Then more seriously, and softly, "Indeed he *is* one in a million."

I loved that.

*   *   *   *

It was time to break camp and move on from Wagon Wheel Park, but first we had a couple of things to take care of. Most importantly, Helen needed dental work because she had recently lost a filling. At first she hoped she could put off replacing it until we got back to Connecticut, where she could have our regular dentist do it. However, the tooth was beginning to hurt, and clearly it would have to be treated there at Broken Bow.

As usual, whenever we needed help we were quickly able to find accommodating people. In this case a local dentist worked Helen into his morning schedule and refilled the tooth. We were very grateful for that, and grateful too to be out of his office in less than an hour. Our luck continued at a local Ben Franklin where we found colored yarns that Helen wanted—the exact colors. In fact, things moved so smoothly that morning that by ten o'clock we had decamped and were en route to a national forest campground fifty-eight miles farther west.

We arrived there in early afternoon, and since there were few people around, we easily found an isolated campsite near a wide section of the Middle Loup River. Not surprisingly, the ubiquitous tracks of the Burlington Northern passed nearby, and when we checked in, the park host said the trains might keep us awake the first few nights. "Don't worry, though," he said, "you'll get used to them."

"We're already used to them," Helen said, and for conversation's sake she asked what the trains carried, although she already knew. "Coal," our host replied, "from coal fields in Wyoming—millions of tons of it for power generation around the Great Lakes and all down the Mississippi Valley."

Aside from trains, nights were quiet around the campground except for the occasional cry of a night bird. It was an odd sound that began with a rattling stutter and ended with a sound like a honking goose. At dusk one evening we crept along the riverbank trying to spot one of the nightly noise makers. No luck. We never did see one, although several times in the gloom before dark, we were sure that one or several were only tens of yards away.

During our first day at the campground, we met a friendly ranger who was in charge of Scott Lookout Tower, a fire spotting post about three miles to the south. "Go take a look," she said as she handed me a key. "There's a gate that secures steps leading to the observation platform; this'll open the lock. Be careful though; it's a long way up ... and down."

Upon arriving at the tower, I asked Helen if she wanted to climb up with me, but she opted out saying, "Honey, I'm in nowhere near as good shape as you, and we don't need another Pennsylvania episode." She was referring to her last day of walking the year before, and how sick she had become.

So I started up, and after thirteen flights of steps I reached a square platform which was about twenty-five feet on an edge and which contained in its center the observation room. Various antennae sprouted from the room's flat roof, and peering inside I could see maps and telephones, as well as a plotting table and a short wave radio. There was also a compact refrigerator and a small television set. The place struck me as the site of deadly boring jobs, albeit with great views.

The weather was so dry and windy that I passingly wondered when the ranger would staff the place for fire season. Then pushing aside such thoughts, I addressed myself to taking pictures. The view was spectacular—small islands of evergreens in a sea of grass, as far as the eye could see.

The observation room was bordered by a four-foot walkway on which I set up my recently bought tripod. Gusts were jostling me as I mounted the camera and took fifteen or twenty of what I thought would be great pictures—even in themselves. Surely the computer would combine these side-by-side snapshots into outstanding panoramas.

Then it was back down some two hundred steps in grateful retreat from the wind.

That night I booted up the computer naively hoping to make a first-rate panorama. I worked and worked, but in the end the effort was pretty much a flop. The individual pictures came out fine, but in the panorama the tower railing sagged like an overloaded bookshelf.

"There ain't no justice," I told Helen. "A body oughtta be able to offset lack of talent with fancy equipment. We'd better get back to walking, where no talent's required, just tough feet and strong legs."

What I didn't know was that my lower left leg would be far from strong enough to take the punishment I would inflict upon it the very next day—punishment that would arise from my wearing too tight socks.

The year before I had found it important to cut the cuffs off of walking socks; otherwise they made deep dents in the skin— obvious harbingers of circulation problems. But a long time had passed since our early days of walking in Pennsylvania, so much time that the morning after the fire-tower visit I pulled on new socks without noticing they were unusually tight. Then we drove out to walk's end, and soon I was on the road, happily unaware that I had made a serious mistake and would soon pay for it.

West of Seneca, Nebraska, route 2 and the Burlington Northern railroad both closely follow the Middle Loop River. Eventually however, route 2 swings south a mile or so, and an older road, the Potash Highway, branches away and stays with the river. I chose the older road, which I soon found to be a walker's dream. Narrow but traffic free, it offered a continuous sequence of changing views—distant dunes, river wide-spots, groups of cattle against light brown hills.

My Black Angus Shadow

Once, an Angus bull stood in perfect profile on a nearby knoll and impassively watched me approach; then he fell in to accompany me, walking along behind the roadside fence. After a quarter mile, I was tired of his stolid presence (as well as a bit unnerved), and hoping to drive him away, I took a *few quick steps in his direction* while throwing up my arms and letting out a loud *whoop*. What in the world was I thinking? He hesitated for only a second before angrily shaking his head and taking a *few quick steps in my direction*; then he stopped and fixed me with an unblinking, stony-eyed stare. I had tempted fate, but at least he didn't come through the fence as I retreated across the road and hastily put distance between me and him. As a parting shot, I yelled, "See you at McDonald's." Meant in fun—sorta—it nevertheless did my conscience mild offense.

But overall, it was a pleasant morning's walk. Several times I came to stretches where modern route 2 temporarily re-joined then re-separated from the older road, which invariably followed the Burlington Northern right-of-way. I would always stay with the old road. My only concern was for tall clumps of grass that grew here and there from cracks in the ancient, oil-sand surface. I had been warned that rattlesnakes liked such places. They sun themselves on the road until they became too hot; then they crawl into the grass to cool off, or so a rancher told me.

Toward eleven o'clock I met another railroad maintenance crew, this one bossed by a rawboned, Viking-looking figure in a yellow hard hat. "So you're the guy!" he boomed in a parade-ground voice. "Crews've been talking about you for days. Word has it your walkin' across the country!"

"You got it!—walking across the country; didn't know I was a celebrity."

"And that's your wife, ain't it? waitin' up there along the road—in the white Toyota." He gestured over his shoulder with a thumb.

"That'd be her," I confirmed, "couldn't be another like 'er."

"My dad likes to walk too," he said uninhibitedly, "but not like you. He does more like four miles a couple mornings a week."

"Retired is he?"

"Semi-retired. Has his own business, but my brother's taking over—iffen he can ever get the old man completely out." He grinned. "One day he swears he's through and 'll never come round the shop again. Next day, he's not only back, he's out on the floor bugging the mechanics. Jack thinks the world of the old man but hates the micromanaging."

"Sounds like you're talking about a car dealership."

"Trucks and heavy equipment. But why the hell are you walkin' across the country?"

So I gave him the usual short story, ending with how far I walked in a typical day. Then I said, "If your dad likes to walk, maybe he'd like long-distance walking. 'Course he'd need somebody to drive support. If my wife wasn't dropping me off and picking me up, I wouldn't be going anywhere."

By then the rest of the gang had walked over, some of them eating sandwiches. They too told me that "people" had been noticing me, and that everybody was fascinated by what I was doing. The maintenance crew were a good-humored bunch—they reminded me of my early years on construction jobs.

Ten minutes later, after a round robin of handshakes, I was back on the road newly provisioned with a Mars Bar and two apples. For the umpteenth time I had been warned to watch out for snakes.

I met Helen an hour later and we had lunch; then, determined to get in a long day's walk, I asked her to drive at least six miles ahead. Back walking, I noticed no problem for the first half hour, but eventually my lower left leg began to ache. By two o'clock, I was thinking to myself, *Just keep going, Beam, and never mind the leg. It's the too-tight socks; you'll definitely have to cut the elastic off tonight.*

A break in the pavement made me stumble and catch my breath from a throb that radiated up from just above the ankle.

The old road had plenty of rough spots. More conversation with myself: *Tonight might be too late, Beam. Better get rid of those cuffs right now—use your knife.*

Now? Heck no! You took too long for lunch and you wasted time gabbin' with that maintenance crew. Keep walking!

It wasn't wasted. Gabfests with people are some of the best parts of this ... this ... whatever it is you're doing. Just keep walking.

And keep walking I did, while determinedly ignoring the growing pain.

I met Helen again about four o'clock, and had I been wise I would have quit right then. Instead, I took three aspirin, ate the train-crew Mars Bar, and walked four more miles—more than enough to put an end to walking for over a week.

The next morning I crawled out of bed onto a hot, swollen, and very sore leg. Helen and I discussed whether we should stay put there at the national forest, or break camp and move to Alliance, 130 miles farther west. I wanted to stay where we were, lay off walking for a few days, and let the leg get better by itself. "Besides," I argued, "if we move to Alliance, we'll have a seventy-five-mile drive back to walk's end once I can walk again."

But Helen, ever the nurse, worried about a "lower extremity blood clot," and she doggedly held out for moving "not this afternoon, not in two hours, but right now—DARN IT! There'll be a hospital in Alliance, and we're going to get that leg checked out!" She was so stubbornly insistent that by seven o'clock we had broken camp, and three hours later we were arriving at Sunset Campground on the outskirts of Alliance.

I thought maybe I'd get a break once the RV was set up, but she maintained the pressure till I agreed to go straight to Box Butte General Hospital near the northern edge of town. There, hospital staff did blood work and took X-rays, but neither showed a clot. The doctor, however, was a conservative fellow, and much to Helen's approval he contacted Regional West Hospital in Scottsbluff and sent us down there for an ultrasonic vein-flow test. That, he said, would check circulation and determine for sure if there were any serious problems.

Upon arriving at Regional West, I was introduced to a forty-something technician who checked my circulation with an impressive assortment of rack-mounted medical equipment. The results were gratifying. "Ah," said the young man, "wish I had circulation like yours." I feigned deafness and asked him to repeat himself, but louder.

He did, and then he called in a doctor who confirmed there was nothing wrong with the leg beyond tendinitis, which, he said, would be painful but would take care of itself with time and rest.

In fact, it would be eight days before I would attempt cross-country walking again.

CONVALESCING AND TOURING NEAR SCOTTSBLUFF

I stayed in bed most of my first three days of convalescence. The leg hurt continuously except for occasional short periods, when, propped up, it would temporarily improve. At those times I would invariably get up and try walking, but the pain would come right back and I would soon lay down again. One afternoon it hurt so bad I took a pain pill that was left over from surgery Helen had undergone the summer before. Good-bye pain, hello nirvana! It was like an exquisite, twenty-minute high—a delightful, billowy, blissful trip to the moon. Talk about dangerous! No wonder people get hooked on drugs.

By the fourth day, the pain was tapering off and we began to get out now and then. Once we drove from Alliance a few miles north to Carhenge, that tongue-in-cheek replica of Stonehenge, England. Mr. Religion's worries notwithstanding, we saw no signs of human sacrifice.

Another time we visited a small museum in Alliance, and still another time we spent several hours fiddling with the CB radios in the car and motor home. Helen would stay with Lurch and I would drive off in the car, both of us talking and twiddling knobs—trying to get that extra half mile of range.

The business of adjusting radios came after I mistakenly diagnosed a new problem as coming from a damaged microphone cable. Acting on that, I had gone to a local electronics store to buy a new cable, but the only one the store offered came in combination with an attached microphone. The price was more than I wanted to pay, and standing by the cash register, I told the cheerful manager that I wasn't sure I actually needed the cable, let alone the attached microphone. If I didn't need either, could I return them for a refund?

"Tell you what," the young man said. "Take the whole works, and if that solves your problem, then come back and pay me; otherwise, just bring it back. I won't bother ringing it up."

I was amazed he would let me take it without paying. "But I'm just passing through," I objected, "don't even live here. Why don't I just pay you?—so your receipts stay in line with your inventory … just in case I can't get back."

"Don't worry about it; you look honest to me," he said with an open-faced smile, "and if you can't use it, it'll be easier for me to just plop it back on the shelf rather than ring it up now and refund your money later."

It turned out that we needed neither cable nor microphone, and the following morning I promptly took them back. I was unused to that kind of transaction, and I knew I would get no peace of mind until I either paid for the items or returned them.

I had rarely met a person as trusting as that manager. Hope his trust is never betrayed, I thought to myself. Then confidently, cynically, perhaps a little sadly, I thought, *But of course it will be!*

In truth, although I appreciated the fellow's willingness to accommodate my needs as a customer, it struck me that slightly lazy and a bit over trusting were not qualities that would do his business career much good. On the other hand, *aside* from his work, *slightly* over trusting would hardly hurt. Better that than overly wary—in which case he'd doubtless miss out on many gratifying interactions with honest people, even strangers.

*　　*　　*　　*

After five days of convalescence I felt well enough that we went exploring back roads south of Alliance, and toward "restaurant time" we were in the environs Scottsbluff.

The place we found to eat looked inviting from the outside, but inside it was cool and we'd hardly been seated when we realized we were under a large air-conditioning vent. Cool air dropped down on us while loud music from a nearby speaker made it difficult to talk. After a long time a waitress showed up, at which point I stage-whispered, "What say we sit at a different table?" It's a bit cool here."

"Can't hear yuh, talk louder." She neither smiled nor said please; it was simply a bald order coupled with a neutral stare.

"Can we sit somewhere else?" I repeated. "Not under an air vent." To back me up, Helen grinned and pretended to shiver.

"It won't be warmer anywhere else," the woman said, staring now at Helen. Then back to me: "I still can't hear you." End of discussion. And there she stood—staring, unsmiling, and nearly six feet tall.

"Well, how 'bout turning down the music so you *can* hear? I'm not shouting." I smiled but gestured with a palms-up hand.

"That's how loud we always keep it. You wanna order?" She didn't add "or don't cha," but she arched a brow, pursed her lips and definitely hardened her eyes. Helen said later that somebody could have fried a lemon on her face.

Trying to break the tension, Helen politely suggested that we would need menus and a few minutes to make up our minds.

Away stalked our waitress; then back she came with a pair of menus which she airmailed to the table from two feet away. That statement made, she strode over to join two other women, who were smoking and talking beside a counter near the kitchen door.

It was early and there were few other customers; clearly, the help were in no mood to be bothered by a couple of undisciplined early birds. Our waitress, her back toward us, talked to her companions in low tones, while occasionally gesturing in our direction with subtle tosses of her head. Now and then one of the other women would glance our way.

For some reason, the absurdity of it all struck me as funny. Ordinarily, I would have been fuming, but there I was, chuckling toward Helen and with a hand covering my face so the shrews by the counter wouldn't catch me laughing. But Helen, of course, was not laughing; as always, she was thinking. "Do you suppose," she whispered, "that one of those Soup Nazis might work in the kitchen? ... you know ... put who-knows-what in our food?"

So much for funny.

"Don't know," I answered, "but we'll not hang around to find out."

With that, and with thoughts of who-knows-what in our dinners, we quietly got up and headed for the door. Out on the sidewalk Helen said, "Let's go to some fast-food place where we'll just be numbers. I've had all the personal attention I need for one day."

That rare bad-restaurant experience turned out to be a good deal for me, because Helen declared that we would stay home the following night and she would cook a roast pork dinner.

"Perfect," I said, and then continued when I should have kept my mouth shut. "Dearie, I'm really glad that during your student-nurse days—back during the Truman Administration—they warned you about the dangers of undercooked pork. By the way you've cooked it ever since, there's no way we could ever have got trichinosis."

"Phil, Eisenhower was president, and I don't overcook pork. Another thing: I've changed my mind. I'm having salad tomorrow night; you get a cold-pork TV dinner. They're mass-produced so it'll be just the way you like it. Not only that, you won't burn your clever mouth. What do you say to that?"

"You're getting prettier the older you get."

"Too late—it's still cold pork."

And with that we headed home.

*   *   *   *

The next day we visited Scotts Bluff National Monument, which is just a few miles southwest of Scotts Bluff City. From the monument's north side you can look out across the town and beyond toward a thousand square miles of farmland. Then, turning around, you can view the south side of the bluff's base, where a footpath leads to ruts left by wagon trains on the Oregon Trail. Although weaker folk often rode in wagons during the great migrations, many pioneers literally walked across the country, at least from Saint Louis on. But what an exhausting trek it must have been, what with rough trails, poor food, and frequent sickness—to say nothing of fears of Indians.

For us, the wagon ruts were a humbling sight, as was a replica Conestoga wagon parked near the visitor center. "Whatever we do," Helen said, "let's not mention to anyone around here that we, meaning you, are walking across the country. Our journey compared to the pioneers' is like a reality show compared to a war—one risk free and insignificant, the other a matter of life and death."

A woman at the visitor center recommended a coffee shop in nearby Gering as a good place for lunch. She said they knew her over there and appreciated her sending tourists their way. We took her advice, and the little restaurant, which we found after considerable searching, was indeed a good place to eat. Helen tried chicken salad, and I had rolls and two kinds of soup—bean and vegetable. Everything was excellent. Then it was back to the bluff for another hour, and then off to Wal-Mart's for two more pairs of walking shoes, again sizes nine and nine and a half. "Helen," I said, "this having different size feet can be expensive when shoes cost twenty-six bucks a pair."

"You know," she replied, "if you really wanna go cheap, you could buy ten-dollar shoes—like the kind you wear at home.... And another thing: it's only one toe that's too long, so instead of buying two pairs, why don't you just have some quack doctor amputate—"

"I hear yuh."

*　　*　　*　　*

A number of prominent rock formations lie along the Oregon Trail southeast of Scottsbluff, and the most spectacular of these is Chimney Rock, an ancient spire jutting three hundred feet above the surrounding plain. A half mile to the east is a modern visitor's center which houses artifacts from the surrounding area, write-ups about local geology, and letters written by pioneers upon first seeing the Rock. Visible from thirty miles, it was a portent to pioneers that the dreaded Rockies were not far ahead.

For some travelers the strangeness of Chimney Rock, so alien to Eastern eyes, elicited both longings for home and worries about the future; to others, it was simply a curious geologic feature—something upon which to scratch one's initials. Thousands of people climbed part way up to do just that. Looking at pictures of those scratchings, we again marveled at the similarity between the human urge to mark trees or rocks or pavements with initials, and the animal urge to mark their territories with urine or feces or claw marks. And that begged the corollary: If the urge to mark did not first appear in some common ancestor of man and animal, could such an imperative have occurred twice, by chance, in both kinds of life—if indeed they were separate creations?

To which speculations Helen remarked: "Only if a creating God wished that to be the case," and then she added, "Phil, this reminds me of our talks about pyramids and whether that concept could have happened more than once by coincidence. We talked about that last fall … when we visited the Indian mound back in Ohio … remember?"

We wandered out of the visitor center and looked around at the surrounding fields and hills. It was late afternoon and very quiet. Take away a building, a fence, an idle tractor, and the moment could have been anytime—the time of the pioneer, the time of the Indian, the time of the saber-toothed tiger. On a nearby historical marker we read how in 1932 a group of paleontologists recovered bone remains of two saber tooths from a nearby excavation. The animals had died in a mortal combat that left the saber of one buried in the shoulder of the other. Obviously their deadly fight had been the last event of both their lives, and they had lain there conjoined and fossilized for forty million years.

Loren Eiseley, a student member of the discovery crew, was deeply impressed by the find, and years later in "The Innocent Assassins," a dark and beautiful poem, he deftly related the way of the long extinct saber tooth to the way of modern man. He wrote how the tiger, perfected in fang and claw for combat, lived out its species' destiny in "brutal unreflecting innocence." Eons later, self-aware man, physically defenseless yet inventively armed, still follows the tiger's savage path—likewise in a kind of innocence but not without misgivings: "Sometimes we seem wrapped in wild innocence like saber tooths, as if we still might see a road unchosen yet, another dream."

The sun was low and a distinct chill was setting in as we lingered a while longer. Presently we walked behind the museum and stood mesmerized by the stillness, the shadows, the needle's profile against the darkening sky. Suddenly Helen shivered and said, "Phil, this is a lonely place, let's get out of here. I'm feeling a bit too transient."

And so we left.

It was late when we arrived back in Alliance.

BACK ON THE ROAD

Eight days after my leg became sore, we were more than ready to get back on the road. We would leave the motor home parked at Alliance—wouldn't bother moving it back toward walk's end which was eighty miles to the east, beyond the town of Whitman. The long car drive went quickly enough, but as I got out to walk, I was still hurting above the ankle and the leg still showed residual swelling. Nevertheless, I would walk a mile while being mindful of how it felt, and I would quit, if necessary, at any sign of trouble. If the first mile went well, I'd continue for a second. That should be enough for the first day back; no point overdoing it and being laid up for another week.

We needn't have worried. During the first five or ten minutes I felt the usual morning aches and pains, but they quickly faded along with the last of the pain above my ankle. Things were going to be better than expected.

"Great," Helen said, when I got to the car and told her I would keep walking. "But you better take it easy and not do yourself in again. I'll drive ahead another mile and wait."

"Drive out five more miles, there'll be no problem."

And so I continued, but every half mile or so Helen would be waiting with joking questions and comments that were really a veneer over her determination to protect me, if necessary, even from myself. "You sure you're okay, Honey?"

"Yes m'Love."

"Phil, you say you're okay, but I remember when you wouldn't admit you were getting sick, and you ended up with walking pneumonia."

"Yes, m'Love."

"I'd hate to see you laid up for another week; you weren't always the sweetest, you know."

"Yes, m'Love."

"I can tell you're all right or I wouldn't be hearing all these smart alecky 'Yes m'Loves'; you'd be honeying up and looking for a ride back to camp."

"Yes, m'Love."

"Phil, stop saying, 'Yes, m'Love' and be serious!"

"Yes, m'Love."

Eventually she got so used to my being okay that she drove three or four miles before stopping to wait. When I got there, she was sound asleep against the steering wheel, a crossword puzzle on her lap, her pencil on the floor. I was tempted to walk right by just for the fun of it. She'd eventually wake up and wouldn't know whether to drive east or west to find me—have a megaton fit. Prudence, however, overcame temptation; I woke her up and we had coffee and rejoiced in being back on the road.

About twelve o'clock we met again, this time at a small cemetery just past the town of Whitman. I had walked ten miles, and elated by a feeling that the leg problem was over, I decided to push my luck and continue walking, at least for a few more hours. When Helen objected, I promised I would walk part of the time on the right hand side of the road, so as to even out stresses on my knees.

"Even out stresses on your knees?" she exclaimed. "Bologna! That's a red herring; it's your tendon we're worried about."

"You're worried, m'Love. I'm not." And off I went, down the right side of the road.

Actually, before starting the Great Walk, I had never thought of a road's crown as inducing side-stresses in a walker's knees. It happens though, and although I usually walked facing traffic, sometimes, to even up the wear and tear, I would cross over and walk on the other side. I only did it when traffic was rare, but even then I would be ill at ease since anything traveling west like me would approach unseen from behind.

So that afternoon I was walking on the right hand shoulder when I sensed that a car had eased off the road, and was quietly rolling up behind me. Reflexively stepping into the grass, I turned as a police car stopped about forty feet away. Clearly the cop wanted to talk, so I hooked both thumbs in my backpack's straps (up real high so he would see my hands were empty); then, smile on face, I walked back to the cruiser and around to the driver's door.

He stayed seated and continued talking on his radio, but he gestured for me to wait behind the car until he finished. A minute or two later he got out and came back, but before he could say anything, I preempted him with "I'm walking across the country, believe it or not."

"You're what?" came his response in half disbelief.

"Walking across the United States. I've walked here from Connecticut, over on the East Coast."

"I know where Connecticut is, but how are you doing that? You look like you're out for a day-hike.… That's not much of a pack you're wearing."

I told him I didn't need a big pack because, one, I never camped along the road, two, Helen was never far away with the car, and three, we spent our nights in a motor home. His concerns, suspicions—whatever—soon satisfied, he became increasingly curious about the walk itself. I was the first person he had met who was actually walking across the country, although he had talked to a number of people who were bicycling across. He had even talked to a man who was crossing Nebraska on horseback.

Soon, I had told him how Helen and I began walking in 1998, continued in 1999, and how we expected to reach the Pacific by fall. Fascinated with the details, he wanted to know how many pictures we had taken, how we found places to park the motor home, and how far past the motor home I usually walked before we decamped and moved still farther west. Especially, he had to know:"What made you decide to take this walk in the first place— why are you doing it?"He had become an engaging personality—a pleasure to talk to, and one of the relatively few people to ask me the "why" question as if he had some unmentioned reason for being so interested. At first I just put it down to his being a cop.

I told him that my post-career boredom had had a lot to do with our starting the walk, but that the project had quickly become a tonic for Helen too. Except for rare, brief intervals of blues or blahs, almost all of our days were interesting and adventurous, our spirits often close to mild elation. "It's been a long gentle high," I said, "captivating and different—really fun too." I was on a roll and starting to enthuse.

Eventually, our conversation left the walk itself and returned to western Nebraska, to cattle ranching and in particular to the damaging effects of overgrazing on the Sand Hills. He said that overgrazing had been a serious problem in the past, but grass cover in general was better now than it had been fifty years before. Running cattle on the hills, he said, actually improves the grass, provided it's not overgrazed. "It's a like mowing your lawn—makes it grow thicker. But don't let it get cropped too close on the dunes or you'll end up with blowouts—you know—areas blown bare by the wind. Takes forever for grass to grow back on them."

We talked about deer that live in the Sand Hills and how dangerous they made driving. Helen had seen a dozen or so, but had had no close calls. "It's not bad in the daytime," the trooper said, "but when people drive seventy out here at night, it's usually not long till they hit one."

I asked him when I could expect to see antelope, and he said not for another hundred miles, over toward the Wyoming border. He had grown up there. "Beautiful country—remote though," he allowed.

"Even more remote than this?"

"Different remote. Around here there are towns every so often; you see a few people, and I bet you get to talk to somebody probably every day. Out there it's just endless open country with a few back roads, so you rarely see anybody, and when you do, they're apt to be in a pickup going eighty miles an hour. Not likely you'll get to talk to many people … except maybe a bored cop once in a while, who's pulled over wondering what you're doing."

I marveled that it could be more remote than the country I had been walking through. In fact, he was the first person I'd met to talk to in days.

Eventually he came back to the *why* of Helen's and my trek. It turned out that he was interested in getting his own father involved in something to keep him busy. "Dad needs some sort of big project like yours," he said. "He's younger than you, but he retired a year ago and he just lays around the house. Too much television and he's driving mom nuts. They've got a little money—enough to travel some—but he doesn't seem interested in anything right now, although he used to take lots of pictures. I'm gonna to tell him what you're doing; maybe that'll get him started with walking, picture taking … anything. Something's gotta give."

I thought about the track-crew foreman whom I had met the day my leg got sore, and also about the strange young man we met in Ohio the year before—the fellow Helen thought was an undercover narcotics agent. Both their fathers were in retirement and having sundry problems; now here was another young man grappling with how to help his parents. It must be my age, I thought; these young people see me in my late sixties hiking across America, and it gets them thinking that something adventurous, or even just different, might be good for their own parents. Maybe I'm a bit of an inspiration; maybe I *should* write that book when I get home. That could be the best thing of all to come out of this, this—boondoggle?

The cop and I talked for another ten or fifteen minutes. He was familiar with Sodtown and its blurry association with potash, and he knew about defunct potash-reclaiming facilities near Antioch, through which, he told me, I would be walking a few days hence. Some of what I write below about the potash industry and the Potash Highway, I learned from him. He was an interesting, knowledgeable person, and we might have talked for another hour except that he suddenly brought things to a close. "Whoo," he exclaimed, looking at his watch. "I've been standing here way too long—gotta get back on the road."

With that we shook hands, exchanged so-longs, and he went back to his endless patrol. When I met Helen an hour later, she said he had stopped and said hello.

*   *   *   *

During the following days I walked from near Whitman, Nebraska, through Hyannis, Ashby, Bingham, Ellsworth, Lakeside, and finally to Antioch, which Helen and I had already come to associate with potash. The town lies in vast barren lands just west of the Sand Hills, and the area could well be called the *Land of Lakes*. There are hundreds of them ranging in size from a few acres to a few square miles. Indeed, the lakes had been the source of potash that made possible Antioch's economic boom eighty-five years before. After the walk, I looked into the potash story and found it to go as follows:

Before the First World War the United States imported large quantities of potash from France and Germany, mainly for the manufacture of fertilizers. With the beginning of hostilities in 1914, that source was cut off, and necessity inspired two University of Nebraska graduates to develop methods for extracting potash from the lakes. Pumping stations were built at Antioch, and pipelines brought the mineral-rich water to plants along a railroad right-of-way. There, by evaporation methods, potash was recovered and shipped east for use in the Midwest and Deep South.

The bonanza, however, did not last long. With the coming of peace in 1918, the importation of potash resumed, and Antioch's potash, being more expensive to produce, was in decreasing demand throughout 1919. By the early twenties the pumps and plants were in decay, and an industry that had briefly flourished was fast disappearing. Antioch too went into decline. Today, near the remains of the town, you can still see crumbling leftovers of pumping stations and reduction plants—relics of a transient prosperity.

But the ruins at Antioch were not the only legacy of the potash industry. Toward the end of 1917, not anticipating potash's demise, people began thinking about a continuous highway that would follow the railroad from Alliance (sixteen miles west of Antioch) to Grand Island, a distance of 260 miles. Besides benefiting the potash industry, they felt the highway would help farmers and cattlemen as well—probably by giving the railroad competition. They even imagined it opening northwestern Nebraska to tourism via the new-fangled automobile, and in their wildest dreams they saw the road extending from Alliance north to the Black Hills, and maybe even west to Yellowstone Park.

Short sections of road already existed between certain towns along the proposed route, and others sections were quickly being built. A planning meeting was held at Mullen, Nebraska, in February 1918, to promote the project of connecting segments and completing the road. At that point the attendees still did not sense the impending collapse of potash, and they enthusiastically chose to name their hoped-for road the Potash Highway. The project was eventually undertaken and roadwork begun in 1919, the through road being completed in 1922. By then, of course, the potash industry was well in decline, and when, in 1926, the state incorporated the new road, it was not as the Potash Highway but simply as Nebraska state 2. To its original planners, however, and to history buffs alike, it would always be the Potash Highway.

Upon researching Antioch potash, Helen and I found ourselves confused by what she had heard from the farmer she talked to at Sodtown. He told her that potash had been hauled down the main street in oxen trains. Now Sodtown was founded in 1880, had briefly flourished, and had pretty much disappeared by 1900; while at Antioch, 244 miles to the west, the potash industry didn't get started until fifteen years later, and was defunct by 1920. In addition, potash from Antioch was hauled away in trains, while the Potash Highway, its name notwithstanding, was not completed until 1922—thus two years after the Antioch industry went under, and over twenty years after Sodtown's decline.

So if Sodtown had come and gone before the potash industry at Antioch, we reasoned, then where did the potash come from that was hauled through Sodtown by oxcart? Of course there was an easy, no doubt clear, answer to that question; we just didn't know what it was. Still don't. Helen laughs nowadays and says that that mystery is just one more reason we need "to go back west."

*   *   *   *

As barren as the countryside was around Antioch, it was nevertheless an area of many birds. There were hundreds of them in the myriad lakes. Blackbirds were everywhere: some were completely black, some had red heads, some had wings trimmed in red or in both red and yellow. Here and there I would see wading birds, standing like statues and focused with unblinking concentration on fish or tadpole. And there were always ducks, often alone but occasionally in small groups. Birds never ceased to be a welcome sight. Sometimes I would walk for days and see few animals, but birds were omnipresent and often I could anticipate where I would see them and what kinds they might be.

The barren Land of Lakes ends about six miles west of Antioch, and there begins a broad fertile area that lies between the lakes to the east and more arid lands near the Wyoming border. For the remaining ten miles to Alliance there is plenty of agriculture. Once again, local roads gird the land in one-mile squares and the countryside and farms look almost like the Midwest. Corn, wheat, alfalfa, potatoes, and soybeans are all important crops.

I arrived at a Burlington Northern overpass on the outskirts of Alliance late in the afternoon of May 13. To the west and a mile down the tracks lay great railroad yards, while to my right and a quarter mile away, I could see good old Sunset Campground. I could even see Lurch, and through binoculars I picked out Helen standing by a picnic table talking to a neighbor. It was another of those rare but appreciated days when walking ended at the motor home's door.

A DOOMED COMMUNICATION TOWER

We took a day off to rest; then it was back to walking, starting from the campground, passing through downtown Alliance, and finally entering farmlands to the west. Three miles from town, I branched west off of Nebraska 2 onto Madison Road.

For a while Madison was gravel, but eventually it became dirt, and with the ground dry and the fields newly plowed, it was not long before I was grimy with dust. Helen fared even worse. In the afternoon there was a brief, local windstorm where she was waiting. She still declares that the dust was "so thick you couldn't see a hundred yards," and I still kid her and say she's exaggerating. Nevertheless, when we met that afternoon, the car was permeated with grime. I could even see it on her clothes.

"How'd you get so much dust in the car?" I asked for needling's sake, "go for a walk and leave the windows open?"

"Not a chance!" she growled to keep up the game. "Had 'em closed the whole time—except for maybe a minute when I took a picture. I'm telling you, Phil, you couldn't see a hundred yards, and I've got a picture to prove it."

Helen admits there is a hazard in showing a picture if it is supposed to support a story that's hard to believe to begin with. Nowadays, even years after the walk, we still laugh about an elderly German woman who showed us a picture to back up a bear story. We met Ursula Gweiss at an RV park about a month after Helen took her dust-storm picture. The gutsy eighty-year-old had flown in from Germany, rented a camper, and was touring the National Parks—all by herself! She told us that at Yellowstone she had seen two bear cubs and had "a picture to prove it." I noticed that the old lady said she had "a picture to prove it," not "a picture *of the cubs* to prove it." But she went to her camper and soon came back with the "proof." Trouble was, there was nothing in the picture except a medium sized bush in the middle of a small, grassy clearing. Beyond that was a wall of trees. "Where're the cubs?" Helen asked.

"Well, you can't see them because they're behind the bush, except for one little fellow's paw. That's it sticking out right here." She pointed to a small brown spot near the base of the bush. It could have been a paw, it could have been a rock, it could have been anything. Suddenly Ursula laughed and said, "I guess this picture doesn't help my story much. Next time I don't think I'll bring it out."

"Wasn't momma bear around?" I asked. "I've always heard it's the mother you better look out for."

"She was beyond the clearing in the trees. I didn't see her, but some of the other tourists did. There were probably a dozen of us."

I suddenly wondered if the old lady was telling the truth. There was a good-natured wily quality in the way she talked and smiled. Could she, I wondered, be a German cousin of that art-show rancher?—the octogenarian with the gimpy leg and the bull-snake story?

But back to Helen's photo—the one that "proves" she couldn't see a hundred yards. Indeed, her picture *does* show a dim scene. There is no horizon; it's invisible beyond a diffuse layer of wind-blown dust. However, starting beside the car and marching into the murk is a column of power-line poles, the most distant one visible maybe two hundred yards away. It was very dusty, her picture proves that. But it also proves that at the moment she took it, she could see far more than a hundred yards, not less as she enthusiastically declared.

Helen pretends to get defensive when I tell her it's a good thing she has a picture to prove her hundred-yard claim. "You think I'd have a window open when the dust was blowing around the worst?" she demands. "I took it when the storm was almost over. There was a minute or two when you really couldn't see a hundred yards!"

Probably so, but it's fun to yank her chain now and then.

*　　*　　*　　*

The next morning, on our way to walk's end, Helen spotted a large female hawk sitting on a pile of sod beneath a telephone pole. (We assumed it was a female because they are usually larger than males.)

I stopped the car well past the bird, not really expecting her to stay around for long. We were used to seeing hawks on the tops of poles or fence posts rather than on the ground, and they would usually fly if we even slowed down. However, this bird did not fly; instead she sat motionless and watching as Helen took a hurried snapshot from the car window. After a brief wait, I slowly backed up until we were directly opposite her and no more than fifteen feet away. This was closer than any hawk had ever let us come, and now, to our surprise, she turned her back toward us as if we were not even there.

"This *is* strange," Helen mused. "Do you suppose she's sick?"

I got out and stood by the driver's door. She didn't move. I walked around the car in order to get closer. She still didn't move. Then, just as we were concluding that something was definitely wrong, she took off and climbed a few hundred feet above the field where she circled twice before gliding down to land *on top* of the pole.

"Let's get moving." Helen said. "We've bothered her enough. I bet she's hunting mice in the grass around that sod pile.

"You're probably right," I agreed. "If one comes out now, she'll have to drop clear down from the pole to get it, 'stead of just down from the pile."

We drove on for a few minutes; then Helen said, "Think you'll reach it this morning?" She was referring to a tower we had both seen the afternoon before. I first noticed it when it seemed to simply materialize, tall but pale, above the western horizon. It had doubtless been growing more visible for some time, during which I subconsciously took it to be an ordinary five-hundred-foot communication tower. They're all over the country—could be the national tree. Twenty minutes later and a good mile closer, it dawned on me that it was far from ordinary; indeed, it was gigantic, and its paleness came from seeing it through miles and miles of dusty air.

Through another hour and three more miles I marched steadily closer, marveling all the while as the enormous structure grew even taller against the sky. It was clearer and better defined, though still far away, when I met Helen about five o'clock. Now, the following morning, she wanted to bet about how far I would walk before reaching it. "I've got five dollars that says it's four miles from where you'll be starting."

"More like six," I answered. But in the end, our bet was that she would win if the distance was less than four and a half miles and I would win if it was more.

When we arrived at walk's end, I parked the car and we reaffirmed the bet. Then I was off and walking toward the tower, which appeared much clearer now with the sun lighting it from the east.

Helen won. After just over four miles, I reached the site and stood across a dirt road from the tallest man-made structure I had ever seen.

Fascinated by its height, I had been standing there for several minutes when I gave in to a long postponed need to relieve myself. Unfortunately, there were small hills and dips in the area—just enough to hide a pickup truck—and thanks to my up-gazing fixation, one managed to sneak right up on me. My first awareness of it came when it burst over a knoll not sixty yards away, catching me by surprise as I stood gawking and watering the road. Spinning away, I struggled to zip up and was walking with awkward dignity when the truck went roaring by. I couldn't resist a furtive glance, and sure enough, I glimpsed the driver's grinning profile through the truck's rear window, and just then he sounded his horn in the cadence of "shave and a haircut … two bits." As the truck receded into the distance, my embarrassment receded with it, but it would be revived soon enough.

Two hours later Helen and I were parked and finishing lunch when a man came along driving a thirty-foot road grader. I had seen him earlier, working a section of road where loose dirt lay four inches deep. But what was he doing here, three miles farther west, and why was he stopping, and why was he grinning so?

After hellos and pleasantries that told me nothing about why he had stopped, I asked how people managed way out there when the weather became bad in wintertime.

"Sometimes people get snowed in for days," he said, "but you can get in trouble around here anytime." Still the grin.

"How's that?"

"Well, rain's predicted for tomorrow—plenty of it—and some of these roads'll turn to muck. Take that place back there where I was scrapin'. By tomorrow night you won't be able to get through without you got four-wheel drive."

"But it must be worse in winter."

"It's really bad then. I drive snow plow, and you know them stretches where the road cuts through little knolls?"

"Yep," I said, "I know all about knolls, dips, and cuts along roads. A truck can come over one of those knolls and be on you before you know it."

Instantly I knew I'd said too much.

"Yeah," he came back, his grin giving way to a belly laugh. "Like the one caught you, ha-ha, over by the tower a while ago."

"How'd you know about that?" I blurted, again quicker than I should have.

"Shayne told me. He was the guy in the truck. Pulled up 'longside my grader laughin' like hell. Said there was this here Q-tip standing over by the tower with his face pointin' up in the air, his hands on his hips, and his pecker wettin' the road"

"Thanks for telling me. What's a Q-tip?"

"A skinny old man with white hair!" More laughs.

"Let's change the subject," I said with a reserved chuckle as Helen faintly smiled. "How long have you known Shayne?" At the moment, that was all I could think to say.

"All my life. Went to school with 'im; then he became a part-time cop. Your goof made his day!"

"Made yours too, didn't it?" I growled, determined to move on to something else and feeling he was doing too much laughing, being's we'd just met.

When I finally got him away from my *faux pas* at the tower, he got back to talking about terrain features along dirt range-roads. The gist of it was that a road will normally be laid out to run along on top of minor surface irregularities, although sometimes it may have to be cut into a higher than usual knoll. During dry periods, soft dust blows into such cuts, and over time it accumulates to where it has to be pushed aside with a grader. Otherwise, it turns into mud during rainstorms, as he had already said. The trouble is that bulldozing the dust steadily heightens the bordering embankments, and consequently the cut becomes deeper as the years go by.

"It's them deep cuts," Grader-Man said, "that cause trouble in the winter. In a blizzard, blowing snow fills 'em up level, and some are six feet deep. That's higher than my plow blade. It can take a couple days to clear a long one out."

"Does anybody ever die out here?—in the winter I mean, snowed in."

"Not often anymore. Used to happen now and then, back before the sixties and mostly to old people. They'd get caught low on fuel and sometimes freeze; you couldn't get to 'em soon enough. It wasn't they starved."

Eventually I steeled myself to ask if he knew how tall the tower was, though I dreaded taking the conversation back to that. I was sure it would get him laughing again, and it did, but not as long this time.

"I've heard it stands twenty-six hundred feet," he said when he finished chuckling. "Round here, they say it's the tallest tower in the world. Couple of Wyoming types jumped offen it wit chutes— got arrested."

Twenty-six hundred sounded far too tall to me, but the man seemed on the level, even though he could be annoying. He walked back to his grader then, and after laboriously turning it around he started back toward where I had passed him working on the road. It dawned on Helen and me that he had made a special trip of several miles just to talk to us. But how, we puzzled, would he have known that we were at that particular crossroads, rather than miles still farther west, or even north or south?

Suddenly Helen had an idea. "Phil, remember that pickup that passed just as we started eating, you know, the driver stared and waved as he passed. I bet he stopped and told him where we were."

"Probably so," I agreed.

*   *   *   *

Late that afternoon while I was paused taking a drink, I happened to look east and notice a trace of dust and then motion in the road. Far away but coming toward me was a medium-sized dog that ran with a looping, effortless gait similar to what one sees in videos of wolves.

Minutes later the animal's long run slowed to a walk that brought her to a few paces from where I stood. And there she stopped—to gaze in puzzlement as I slowly

Ms. Grace

raised my camera. Even as I took the picture, I realized that a lucky orientation of her body toward the sun was casting her shadow as the silhouette of a coyote. Sometimes I got lucky with the camera.

I talked to her then—man to dog: "Where do you live? What's your name? Do you always check out strangers who happen to be walking your roads?" She cocked her head and smiled a wolfish grin.

"You know," I continued, "you look to be part coyote. Granted you're way too heavy, but you've got a coyote's tail and a coyote's white underbelly—still, where'd you get that reddish-blonde coat, and how come's your face so wide? Was mom or pop the coyote?—or do you favor more distant kin? Can I call you Graceful Runner? Because you are, you know ... or maybe I'll call you Grace for short."

By now I had got a Milk-Bone from my pocket and was slowly edging toward her, my hand extended with the treat. She took a few steps back and stood motionless, watching. I edged forward again; she moved still farther and sat down, faced away, and looked back over her shoulder. "Be antisocial, if you want," I muttered, "but remember, you came to me, I didn't come to you." And with that I turned and began walking again. She jumped up and came along with me.

For half a mile we stayed together as if she were mine (or I hers), and we were out for an afternoon walk. Sometimes she would be behind me, but mostly she would trot alongside— in parallel but not too close. Once she trotted ahead but then suddenly stopped, her face jerked close to a clump of sage, her nose held fast by some enticing smell. But never did she approach to take the bone from my fingers, let alone so close that I should touch her.

When we got to the car, Helen had no trouble getting in good with Ms. Grace. Within minutes she came right up and gently took a piece of jerky from her hand—no coaxing required. Helen laughingly declared it a gender thing, but I said it was because the offering was meat instead of dust-dry dog biscuit.

Still, Grace didn't eat the jerky; instead, she buried it in soft dirt along the edge of the road. Helen gave her another piece and she buried that too, but not before carrying it some distance back along the way we had just walked. With the third piece she started east at a trot that soon broke into that effortless, long-legged lope I had watched as she first come toward me an hour before. She grew smaller in the distance, and finally disappeared into a low dip in the road.

"Think we'll ever see her again?" Helen wondered.

"We will," I said, "if by luck she lives on one of the ranches I passed about six miles back. We'll see if we can find her place in the morning; I'd like to know if she really is part coyote." By now it was five o'clock and too late, we decided, to do more walking. Besides, another segment would put us farther west, thus farther from where the dog might live.

The following morning we were unexpectedly lucky when the first ranch we stopped at proved to be the right one. We had no sooner pulled in than Grace stepped out of a nearby shed, and as if remembering us from the night before, she trotted right over wagging her tail and, surprisingly, wanting to be patted.

A man and a boy were standing on the ranch-house porch, keeping out of a chilly drizzle that was the start of an off-and-on, two-day rain. "Come on inside," the man called. "I'm Mike Brandis. What can we do for you?" He gestured for Helen to come too, but she opted to stay in the car. "It's about to rain hard any minute," she said, as I started toward the house. "I'm staying here in the dry."

The boy was Amos, Mike's son, and you couldn't miss that: they looked alike and moved alike; their voices even sounded alike, except that dad's speech was slow and measured while the boy's came out in tumbling eagerness. Amos was almost as tall as his father, and from a distance you could easily mistake him for an adult. Up close, however, you would see that he was at most fifteen.

For the first five or ten minutes, I told them about the walk, about when we started, where we had been, and when we thought we would get to the West Coast. Then I said to Mike, "Your dog followed me yesterday for a good mile along the road out there. She doesn't run like any dog I've seen. Do you know if she's part coyote?"

"Can't say for sure," he answered, "but everybody sees her asks the same question. She was a drop-off; somebody left her at Doc's place a few miles from here. Doc's my brother-in-law."

"Is Doc a veterinarian?" I asked.

"No, everybody just calls him Doc—ever since we were kids. Anyway, Doc had her for a while and then we took her. But she still spends time over at his place, when she's not off who knows where." He laughed and went on: "People notice that run, and somebody's always wantin' to know if there's coyote in 'er."

Here Amos cut in. "I'll tell you this," he enthused, "she never gets tired. Once when Doc—"

"Uncle Doc," his father corrected.

"Once, when Uncle Doc decided to drive over here, Brit"— so that was her real name—"happened to be at his place, and I guess by coincidence she decided to start for here at the same time. Well, Uncle Doc drove his pickup over and she cut across the fields, and by gosh, you know what? She got here about the same time he did!"

"How far was that?" I asked.

"About a mile."

"Fast dog," I said, though I was more impressed with her loping gait than with how fast she could actually run. "I've met lots of dogs," I went on, "but she runs differently from any I've seen. She's dainty too." I told them how she had carefully buried the two pieces of jerky and how she ran off with the third.

"Well that explains the jerky," Mike said. "She came in here late yesterday still carrying it in her mouth. It was a mess by then—all over drool. Amos took it off her. We was worried about what she'd got into; she'll eat anything."

"Hope we didn't cause you concern. We wouldn't have—"

I was going to say 'given it to her,' but Mike interrupted: "No problem at all. It's just that she'd eat poison if she found some. It's good to know she hasn't stumbled onto some place where they've put out scraps—some poisoned, some not—and that yesterday she was just dumb-lucky enough to get a clean piece."

Ten minutes later, the conversation was winding down and I was getting ready to leave. "My wife's waiting in the car," I said, "and I've got walking to do. Besides, I've held you up long enough."

"Not at all," Mike countered. "We were draggin' our feet, figured it'd start pourin' any minute."

As we were stepping onto the porch, I paused to ask how old the dog was; but before either father or son could answer, I thought of another, more urgent, question: "By the way, how high is that communication tower over west of here?"

"I've heard twenty-four hundred feet," dad said.

"Three thousand," blurted the boy.

Dad ignored the contradiction but winked at me and said, "Younger than you'd think—"

Thinking his father's "younger than you'd think" referred to the dog, the kid cut in again: "Well, she's not that young; she's at least four years old. We've had her for three years, and she was probably a year old when Doc got her." He'd slipped back into "Doc."

I smiled as the boy's father, with a roll of his eyes, said, "Couple of years are going to make for a lot of growing."

He was referring to the kid, of course, and he meant growing up, but the innocent still didn't catch on. "What do you mean 'growing,' Dad? Brit won't grow anymore; she's as big as she's gonna get."

Dad smiled and shook his head, which irritated Amos who glared and demanded, "What?"

"*About this tower,*" I hastily put in, hoping to head off a father-son "event." "Yesterday I met a man with a road grader, and he told me it was twenty-six hundred feet high. He also said that two guys from Wyoming climbed up and jumped off with parachutes a couple of years ago."

"That would be Aaberg," Mike said, his smile vanishing. "I went to school with him, and if he says twenty-six hundred, it's probably five hundred feet less. He knows all there is to know … or thinks he does. Yeah, two guys did jump off with parachutes, got fined for it."

Following that, Amos mentioned Mary Aaberg, the roadman's daughter, on whom he obviously had a crush. His father just uh-huhed as I drifted into my own musings: *Sure enough, I thought, Brandis here, the rancher, knows Aaberg the road worker who knows Shayne the cop. No doubt just about all the men and women for miles around know each other well. For the most part they've grown up together, and they meet and re-meet at church, sporting events, festivals, fairs. But they wouldn't always like each other. There's probably something between Brandis here and Aaberg. Maybe Aaberg is too much the wise guy; he was darned sure overdoing it when he kept needling me about pissin' at the tower.*

But it was time to get moving. Mike had asked me to sit down ten minutes earlier, but I'd begged off, saying I hoped to get at least a twenty-mile day. Now, rain was steadily drumming on the porch roof. "You'll do no walking today," the rancher said. "Why don't you call your wife in; we're gonna be rained out too, so we'll all just sit here in the kitchen and visit."

But the must-walk imperative was plaguing me as usual, so I begged off. As I trotted out to the car, Mike called, "By the way, your dog friend doesn't like rain." Sure enough, Brit was nowhere to be seen.

Back on the road it was muddy driving. Helen wanted to call it off and go back to Alliance, maybe use the rest of the day to move Lurch farther west. But I was in the driver's seat and determined to "skid on out to walk's end" and wait for a while. "It'll stop raining," I declared with more confidence than I felt, "and then we'll get in a few more miles."

Subdued then, perhaps by the grayness and the rain, we quietly rode along, each in our own world and slightly mesmerized by the droning rain and the clatter of gravel thrown up by the tires. Suddenly, stark and gray, the tower appeared in the mist, its upper reaches vanishing into the overcast. Then just as quickly we were past, and Helen, twisting and looking back, broke the silence with a muttered "going, going, gone."

There was something sadly prophetic about her "going, going, gone," although we couldn't know it then. The day would come, however, when Helen and I would be startled to read that the tower collapsed on September 25, 2002, two years and four months after we were there. Two workmen, who were installing new equipment near the top, rode it down to their deaths. The newspaper article said it had stood 1965 feet high—a bit shorter than the locals had thought but almost six hundred feet taller than the World Trade Towers, which themselves had been destroyed only twelve months before.

Twenty minutes after passing the tower we arrived at walk's end, but the rain would not let up until noon, and then only temporarily. We hung around until nine o'clock before giving up and driving back to the RV park, where we spent the rest of the day doing little other than lying around. When it was still raining the following morning, we didn't even try to walk. Instead, we moved Lurch to Harrison, a small town in the extreme northwest corner of Nebraska, only nine miles from the Wyoming border.

THE LONELY RANCHER

County names in central and northwest Nebraska tell a thought-provoking story. As you travel across the state from Grand Island through Broken Bow and eventually to Alliance in the northwest, the road goes through Sherman, Custer, Thomas, Hooker, Grant, and Sheridan counties—all Civil War generals and Union, of course. Easy to tell who won that war. Easy too, to gauge the sentiments of the people who settled the region and named the counties. By singular irony, Sheridan County's northern border abuts the Pine Ridge Indian Reservation in southern South Dakota. Presumably it was fate that compassionately placed Box Butte and Dawes Counties between Sheridan County on the east and Sioux County on the west.

But did General Sheridan in the 1870s really say, as Captain Charles Nordstrom reported, "The only good Indians I ever saw were dead"? or did he say, "The only good Indian is a dead Indian"? as he is popularly believed to have said. Who knows? Either way they were callous words reflecting little sympathy for a desperate people in the final decades of subjugation. Of course, by the Doctrine of Manifest Destiny, many nineteenth-century Americans felt they had a God-given right to expand across the continent to the Pacific Ocean.

While we were camped at Harrison, we took two car excursions: a short one to Fort Robinson which is twenty-five miles to the east, and longer one into Sowbelly Canyon which lies north-northwest of Robinson. Helen was particularly interested in the fort because of her general interest in Indian history.

In 1877, Chief Crazy Horse, who had led warriors against Custer at Little Bighorn, was mortally wounded at Robinson while resisting imprisonment. Later, in January 1879, the fort was the site of the Cheyenne Outbreak, a bloody running battle in which a band of Indians, resisting return to reservation life, broke out of confinement for twelve brief days of hardship, starvation, and freedom. For many, those were last days, and I resolutely suspended my imagination rather than picture, even for a moment, the horrors of that chase.

But Fort Robinson's history is not entirely about Indian conflicts. During the Second World War, German and Italian POWs were held there. There is a small museum, and judging from the exhibits, which are mainly handicrafts, the captives had it good. They often put on concerts and plays, and not surprisingly, many of the men were quite talented. For work, the government trusteed them to local farms and ranches, and paid them according to Geneva Convention guidelines. Clearly, they fared far better than Allied soldiers held in Axis prison camps.

Our second excursion took us east-northeast from Harrison into rugged highlands of pine forests and deep grassy ravines. Eventually we entered Sowbelly Canyon and followed it out onto flatter lands north of where the Cheyenne escapees had been killed or captured those many years before. There were intermittent showers, but later the skies cleared into a golden evening of long shadows and constantly changing landscapes. Once we stopped, and through binoculars watched a hunting coyote. He would stand motionless in the grass for long moments before springing high into the air, to come down, he obviously hoped, on some "unsuspecting bunny." Helen's phrase. Several times he missed, but finally things worked out and he caught himself a luckless-rabbit dinner. Helen gasped.

We drove on, and on and on. In three different places we saw grazing deer; on a lone ranch we saw a dozen elk, and once we saw a coyote that had come to the end of its days. It had been shot and hung upside-down from a barbed wire fence. The message was clear: Stay away coyotes, or die!

Night was approaching when we realized we had no idea where we were, except about forty miles from Harrison and somewhere north of U.S. 20. We would bear south then at every opportunity; surely we would reach the highway in a half hour or so. Thirty minutes passed, forty, then an hour. We were resigning ourselves to a night in the car, when in a last attempt to find our way, we paused on high ground and got out to look. Almost immediately, Helen thought she glimpsed far-off car lights. Hoping upon hope, we watched for several minutes; then, sure enough, there were more lights, definitely headlights, and then the running lights of a truck.

Ten minutes later we came out to 20, turned west, and headed for Harrison under a hard rain shower. Helen said she wouldn't have minded sleeping in the car, but she hated going to bed without brushing her teeth. "What bed?" I asked.

*　　*　　*　　*

I began walking the next morning under clear skies which soon gave way to clouds followed by cool off-and-on drizzles. The moisture softened the road slightly which felt good in my knees, especially since no mud stuck to my shoes. With cool air and easy walking I made unusually good time.

Toward late morning the Toyota appeared up ahead, and parked beside it was a white pickup truck. Helen and a rancher were talking it up, driver's window to driver's window, and they were so engrossed that I was almost to them before either noticed me.

Moments later, Helen introduced me to Wilfred Lummis, an elderly man whose home of residence was Scottsbluff, thirty miles to the south. Will owned the ranch lands through which we were passing, and he was up working his "small spread of three thousand acres." He had inherited the ranch from his father, and he often stayed there for weeks at a time in order to tend the cattle.

Obviously lonely, Will had been talking with Helen for fifteen or twenty minutes, and now he wanted both of us to follow him to the ranch house, which sat on a low knoll a hundred yards to the north. "I brew good coffee," he said, "and besides, you'll never get to Oregon today."

We declined with thanks-anyways, for it was early, and as usual we wanted to get in a many-mile day. I turned and began sidling away as Helen started the Toyota and eased it into drive.

But it was hard to withdraw from Will, who was clearly reluctant to see the conversation end. Even as we tried, he kept talking, his voice at first hurried but then slowing and finally halting as the distance between us opened. We gave in. Feigning new interest, I stepped back to the truck while Helen backed up and pretended that something he had said—right there at the end—had rekindled her interest. Will was surely not fooled, but he was in need of listeners, and before we knew it we were hearing his life story.

Will was born on the ranch in 1931, the first of four boys, the last of whom died at birth, his mother nearly dying with him. Although she survived, she never fully recovered, and she too passed on in the spring of 1941, leaving behind a husband, ten-year-old Will, and the remaining boys, ages eight and five.

Life was hardscrabble after that. Will Sr. worked for the railroad out of Alliance when he wasn't running cattle, but neither way did he make much money. He would have continued living at the ranch, but the boys were too young to be left alone. Helping out, a maternal uncle who dealt in real estate, loaned Will Sr. money to buy a house in town.

So the Lummises moved to Alliance and lived there throughout the Second World War. Although Will remembered those as happy years, he allowed the family was dirt poor. It must have been a strange life for the children. Working for the railroad, their father would be away for days at a time, while the boys, Will in the lead, would fend for themselves with the help of a neighbor woman. When home, Will Sr. often took the boys back out to the ranch. They loved it there, but their educations suffered; in particular, Will's did. In 1945, at age fourteen, he quit school over his father's objections and went to work for a local rancher.

Will's earnings during the next four years added to the household income so that life became a bit easier for the family. But in 1949, perhaps as some act of passage to adulthood, Will joined the army—just in time to catch the Korean War, which began the following year. Surviving the brutal fighting of 1951/1952, he eventually returned stateside and was stationed at Fort Lewis, Washington, where he met a local girl and was married after a three-week courtship. Discharged from the army in 1954, he went home to Alliance. He was twenty-two and lucky to be alive, but he was also restless, discontent, and the father of a new-born baby girl.

Will said that after the service he would have liked to had more education, but with no high school diploma and a second child on the way (it would be another girl), working for the railroad was inevitable. His life became routine and much like his father's: frequent, indeed welcome periods away from home; periods at home working for the railroad at Alliance; and, as ever, periods at the ranch where he would join his father whenever he could. Always close, their relationship had long since changed from child to father, to man to man. Probably they were both lonely. Will Sr. never remarried, and Will Jr.'s marriage, though stable, provided neither him nor his wife much happiness.

By 1980 Will's daughters were long grown-up and had left Alliance. The older, a scholarship recipient, had gone to the University of Nebraska at Lincoln, eventually marrying and taking a job as a school teacher in Grand Island. The younger girl, after a series of minimum-wage jobs and ill-advised relationships, had also gone to Lincoln, but she to hairdressing school. A natural at the trade, she excelled during her training program and graduated with several job offers in the Lincoln area. Accepting one, she worked there for two years and then moved on to Los Angeles—much to Will's disappointment. He obviously loved her dearly and had hoped she would settle in Alliance.

With the girls gone, a marriage that had never really worked sputtered on through 1985. By then Will was spending most of his time at the ranch; his wife had taken a job and worked evening hours in a drug store. She had acquired a wide circle of friends, and when not working or participating in church or social activities, she did volunteer work at a local hospital. The marriage finally ended in the summer of 1986. They had clearly both tried through thirty-four long years, but it was time to call it off. In the amicable parting, Mrs. Will kept the house and Will took an apartment. Strangely, for a while thereafter they would meet from time to time, eat at a restaurant, go to a movie. However, this too dried up within a few years. In Will's words, "We were just too different, and right from the start."

Retirement from the railroad came in 1990, and once again Will moved back to the ranch. His father lived there now—had lived there for a number of years. But his time was running out, and he would pass away in the summer of 1994, quietly, during an afternoon nap on the back porch.

After that, Will's younger brother, a petroleum engineer living in Scottsbluff, talked Will into moving down there, no doubt feeling it would be better for him than living alone at the ranch. It was a well-meant gesture, and it seems that Will, though a loner by nature, tried to develop a social life that centered on his brother's church. He became a member and then a deacon; he participated in church activities and also worked as a volunteer at a local museum. But his participation in such things had gradually diminished in recent years, so that nowadays he spent most of his time by himself at the ranch—a lot more, he admitted, than was necessary to run the few cattle required for a "ranch to be a ranch."

And with "ranch to be a ranch," Will brought us to the present. I shifted about to relieve my stiffening legs, and Helen rubbed the back of her neck. Neither of us could think of much to say.

It was Will who eventually broke the quiet. "I've kept you people too long," he said, "I need to get up to the house."

We wished each other luck, and I had taken just a few steps when I heard Helen say, "Your life, Will: It always keeps coming back to this ranch, doesn't it?"

"You're right," he said. "It was the ranch when I was a kid; it was the ranch through my middle years, and it'll be the ranch, here, when I finally hang it up."

I began walking again and Helen drove on, to meet me a half dozen miles farther west. Our lunchtime rendezvous came around one o'clock, a bit later than usual thanks to our long stopover with Will. We had eaten and were lost in separate thoughts when Helen suddenly said, "Phil, one of these days they're going to find him at that ranch—alone, you know, and dead."

"You're probably right," I answered. "He intends that. His words, 'it'll be the ranch, here, when I finally hang it up,' were not just figurative. He might even have his exit planned."

The weather remained unsettled the rest of the afternoon; several times it showered and once there was hail a half mile from where I was walking. That brought Helen hurrying back to rescue me, but by the time she got there the storm had veered away. Meanwhile, we both saw many animals. Helen saw her first antelope (she would see hundreds in Wyoming), and once she spotted a herd of twenty deer. Of course there were always cattle, and once a cow and calf cautiously approached where she was parked. When they were still many feet away, the calf suddenly trotted ahead toward the car, whereupon its mother hurried forward and roughly shoved it around behind her. Then she lingered a few feet from the car, gazing at Helen with that familiar mixture of curiosity, unease, innocence....

*   *   *   *

A few days later, we crossed the Niobrara River near Agate Fossil Beds. This national monument comprises about six square miles and extends roughly four miles east to west and a mile and a half north to south. The river runs through monument grounds from the west, and it was among outcroppings overlooking the river that rancher James Cook and his wife Kate discovered fossils in the summer 1884. At the time the Cook's home was Agate Springs Ranch, which still stands on the west side of state route 29 opposite the monument grounds.

Cook, who was earlier a professional hunter and army scout, seems to have associated easily with people from all walks of life. Indians and ex-generals were among his acquaintances, and so too were paleontologists, some of whom he had met several years before. At the time he helped convince skeptical Sioux Chiefs that would-be fossil hunters were, as they claimed, really interested in finding not gold, but merely fossils on tribal lands.

Paleontologists were therefore the people to whom Cook turned to announce his discoveries at Agate Springs, and resulting expeditions from the American Museum of Natural History, the Carnegie Museum, and the University of Nebraska eventually found thousands of remains. Collectively, they neatly outline the area's animal life millions of years ago. There were giant hogs, rhinoceroses, turtles, fish, mammoths, saber-toothed tigers, tiny deer, and even a three-toed horse. Fossil remains of many of these animals are on display in a small museum inside the monument's visitor center.

There was a picnic table near a footpath winding up to the outcroppings, and we had eaten there and were resting when a thirty-something couple came down. She would have gone directly to the visitor center, but he motioned for her to hold up as he paused, uninvited, to talk to Helen and me.

Talk, however, was hardly the word for it. What came out of the man was a long-winded, bad-tempered grumble: There were eight, no seven, anyway, too many people up there. Somebody threw candy wrappers on the ground—Babe Ruth and Snickers; there were even M&Ms lying on the ground! Can you imagine that? People are really pigs, don't you think? It's at least a hundred and ten degrees up there; almost made me sick. I'm out of shape, overweight, and too old for this crap. They oughtta have an escalator.

The escalator remark was a jaw-dropper because he could hardly have been serious; nevertheless, instead of smiling he went right on complaining. We wondered how his companion, who was as good-looking as he was the opposite, put up with it. She must have been thoroughly bored. At any rate, he made the mistake of stopping for a second, whereupon she grimaced and jumped right in: "You guys should walk up there, you'll enjoy it. It's an easy climb and the views are spectacular; we even saw a snake. Trouble was, before I could take a picture it crawled under some rocks. Maybe you'd be luckier, but if you do go up, have your cameras ready because you'll need to be quick!"

Helen said that even before the woman finished her sentences, which she delivered without pausing, she, Helen, almost asked her to slow down. Obviously, the woman was embarrassed and trying to put a lid on her whining other's complaining.

It didn't work. The word *snake* got him going about how dangerous snakes could be. "I"—not *she* or *we*—"could have been bitten, and it would have been the park's fault."

The woman, finally getting her fill, suddenly interrupted with real annoyance. "The snakes weren't anywhere near us," she snapped. "All they wanted was to be left alone … like me!" And with that she turned and stalked off toward the visitor center.

Appearing puzzled, the man pulled at his mustache and said, "She's turning out to be a real witch. This is the first time we've traveled together. We drove out from Portland last week to tour the area, and after we leave here we're going to Yellowstone. Imagine her just walking away like that! We've gone to movies and dinner before, but this is the first time we've been together this long. Maybe we're just getting on each other's nerves."

He turned and walked off a few steps to look down toward the visitor center, and as he did, Helen nudged me and whispered, "Well, *he's* definitely getting on *her* nerves, and you can bet this'll be the last time they're together for long."

We hoped he would just go away, or maybe go find his companion—poor soul. But to our dismay he came right back and started complaining all over again. This time the parking lot was too far from the visitor's center. "Lousy planning," he declared, "courtesy your Park Service."

Neither Helen nor I said a word as we collected our sandwich wrappers and began walking away. A few minutes later Helen said, "Wonder if he even knows we're gone? He might still be there talking to himself."

"Well, before long 'himself' is the only person he'll be talking to," I answered. "Unless I miss my guess, she won't be around much longer."

*   *   *   *

I crossed the Niobrara River two more times the following day, once while walking west and crossing where the river flows south, and later, while walking north and crossing where the river flows east. For twenty miles the river valley continued to be defined by bluffs that were similar to those at Agate Springs. Helen and I thought the upstream bluffs should also yield fossils, but if so, there was no reference to them at the visitor center, at least none that we remembered.

About four o'clock we tried to make a celebratory event out of crossing the Nebraska-Wyoming border. We hugged and exchanged hi-fives, but with only lukewarm enthusiasm. Crossing a state boundary was old hat, and within minutes we gave up trying to make something out of what we'd so often done before. Then Helen left to drive three miles north, to the intersection of C.R. 51 and U.S. 18, where, an hour later, we met and quit for the day.

Overall, we were feeling good that afternoon as we drove back to our campground at Harrison. We had come sixty-some miles in the preceding three days, and by tomorrow night we would be at least twenty miles into Wyoming. Lots of progress!

We couldn't know that next day would be the toughest of the entire coast-to-coast walk.

PRAIRIE DOG HUNTERS

Things started out pleasantly enough. There were gentle breezes, traffic was light, and the road's shoulder was wide and even. Within miles, however, the shoulder became progressively narrow and eroded, so that for long stretches its rutted bottom would be three or four inches *below* the road surface. Walking in such places became a twisting workout for hips and lower back, since my right foot would tread lightly on the roadway while the other pounded hard into the washed-out gutter. Meanwhile, the gentle breezes changed to frequent gusts that occasionally shoved me a step into the road.

The wind and rough pavement would have made walking hard enough, but to top it off, heavy truck traffic developed soon after eight o'clock. The Burlington Northern was building a raised right-of-way all along the north side of the highway, and trucks were coming and going to a dozen worksites. One after another they would arrive at their destinations, dump their gravel loads, and then leave again—passing sore-backed, wind-blown, noise-harassed, self-pitying me (whew) at a rate of one every few minutes, or so it seemed.

Late in the morning, I met Helen where she had parked in a turnout near one of the worksites. Eeven as I stood there grouching, a particularly noisy truck lurched in from the west and sent a cloud of dust over us and the car. In a ballistic outburst I hurled my walkie-talkie against the side of the car. Batteries flew one way, the battery cover another; the radio itself rebounded past me so fast I never saw where it landed.

Helen found the radio several minutes later behind a clump of sage, and amazingly, when I put the batteries back in and the cover on, it still worked. The only consequence of the tantrum was a slight dent in the car's rear door and my lingering chagrin at the loss of self-control. Helen, of course, was helpful and calming, as she always is when I really need help. "Sorry, that'll never happen again" I apologized, minutes later, as I began to calm down. Even so, a familiar small voice in my head whispered, "Don't bet on it, Beam—you've been a baby like this before."

But nothing was easy that day. In the last half hour, Helen and I managed to miss each other at an agreed-upon corner in eastern Lusk, Wyoming. As we struggled to reconnect, trucks and buildings constantly broke up our walkie-talkie transmissions. Eventually, through the static, we agreed to head for the southwest corner of town; surely we would spot one another somewhere down there. And we did—an hour later—at the corner of Linn and Eighth Streets, where U.S. 18 starts west out of town.

We were glad to see the day end, and it was good to know we wouldn't be "in the field" the next day. It was time to decamp from Harrison and move Lurch farther west.

*　　*　　*　　*

Buffalo Campground lies a few miles west of Douglas, Wyoming. A spacious, pleasant place, it proved to be typical of several campgrounds we stayed at that have a core of permanent residents as well as short timers who stay for a few days or a few weeks. Most of the latter are either vacationers traveling through with motor homes, or railroad workers who stay a bit longer while their ever-moving jobs happen to be in the area.

One evening, however, I talked to two men who were none of the above. I met them when I was walking to the campground office to buy grocery items. "Hello ... beautiful weather," I said, as they prepared their dinners on the tailgate of a truck.

They returned the greeting—pleasant enough fellows.

"You work for the railroad?" I asked, even as I took note of backpacks and scoped rifles lying on their picnic table.

"No, we're just out here to kill prairie dogs," one of them said. "We come for a week every year if we can get off."

"... Uh-huh," I managed, freezing for a second but trying not to show it. "What do you do with the ones you kill? Eat 'em?" I knew they didn't.

"Nah, nobody eats prairie dogs; they're varmints. We just leave 'em lay. Hawks and coyotes clean 'em up."

"How do you know where to hunt? I thought prairie dogs were scarce anymore."

"There's plenty of 'em out there, but you need to hire an outfitter to take you to 'em. Costs two hundred bucks a day, but your outfitter takes care of everything."

"What's everything?"

"Well, you hunt on private land, see, which means you pay a 'trespass fee'—part of the two hundred's for that. Beyond that your get a guide and transportation to the dog colony; also, they provide a shooting bench, soft drinks, and lunch. It's a good deal; all you gotta do is just sit there and blow 'em away."

"Obviously," I said. "You bring your own guns and ammo?" I nodded toward the rifles.

"Yeah, and we find our own lodging and meals too, 'cept for lunch. The outfitter covers everything else. We stay here at Buffalo, but you can stay anywhere."

I left them then and walked on to the office to get the bread or milk or whatever it was. They seemed a decent enough pair—albeit from a different planet. And though I was turned off by their "sport," I was troubled by memories that I too had been a hunter back in my "innocent" youth, and I too had let "varmints" lay where they fell—or were thrown by the impact of my bullets. Unpleasant memories, those, and calling for rationalization: *Come off it, Beam; you were young and naïve.... You were acting within the norms of the culture you grew up in.... You grew away from all of that.... You've done secular penance for those deeds—over and over again—you've earned atonement....*

But alas, I have never felt atoned—don't expect to—and there remain these faint regrets.

When I got back to Lurch and told Helen about the prairie dog hunters, she pulled a face and called then *murdering skunks*! She didn't say much through dinner and early evening, but toward nine o'clock she began rambling about despicable "fun-and-money-trails."

I couldn't imagine what she was talking about. "What do you mean?—'fun-and-money-trails'? Where's that come from?"

"I'll tell you where," she growled. "Those prairie dog killers are clients of outfitters who in turn are agents for ranchers. The killers pay for the fun of the hunt, and the outfitter takes his profit and passes the rest along to the rancher—it's a fun-money-money deal. It's like any kind of entertainment, except it's the next thing to contract murder."

"Bushwhacking prairie dogs makes me sick too, but where's your trail? This really bugs you, doesn't it?"

"You're darn right. It's sort of like when people go to a movie only sickeningly different. The moviegoer pays to watch the show. His or her money goes immediately to theater management and from there it's ultimately distributed to the producer, director, actors, camera operators, extras and so on. That's your trail—the path of money passing from hands to hands. And it's a good deal. The customer enjoys the show and everyone else has created value—decent entertainment, not murdered prairie dogs."

"Helen, it's interesting to hear your 'decent entertainment'; usually you say that ninety percent of what Hollywood makes is junk. Anyway, those hunters enjoy shooting prairie dogs, so I guess you could call that entertainment—at least for them." I was trying for a tongue-in-cheek exit from the subject; things were getting too intense.

"Phil, you can't breezily talk as if going out to a movie is *in any way* like going out to shoot prairie dogs!" She was really getting frustrated.

"So who's saying shooting prairie dogs is the same as going to a movie?"

"You just came close. We're talking, you know, about the morality of hunting when people don't use what they kill. If those ranchers have too many prairie dogs, then they oughtta get busy and thin 'em out themselves, or hire professionals if they don't have the guts to do it themselves. But these ghouls who come out from the city, kill 'em for fun, and then leave 'em lay—they make me sick!"

At that point, I determinedly changed the subject, because I had begun to think about all the decent people I knew or had known who never questioned the hunting premise. Years before, I even knew a barber who believed that God created animals to be used for man's food and hunted for his pleasure—convenient beliefs if you like to hunt.

*　　*　　*　　*

Helen and I rested the next day except for a trip to Douglas. There we visited the Wyoming Pioneer Memorial Museum, a must-see place for anyone touring the area. Several galleries are dedicated to everything from pioneer and military history to nineteenth-century artifacts, which range from clothing to tools to medical equipment and more.

After leaving the museum, Helen went shopping while I went looking for a barbershop with an honest-to-God barber's pole. It didn't take long to find one, but a half dozen men ahead of me meant a fairly long wait. The gossip, however, was wonderful. Somebody had been in a fight, and somebody else had wrecked his car; some rancher had three or four cattle down, i.e., sick, and a big, rugged twenty-something had been bucked off his horse. He sat there with his leg in a knee-to-ankle cast. It was just the kind of chitchat you would expect to hear in a real-man's barbershop— not what you would expect in some unisex hair salon where dainty *coiffeurs* "sculpt" lesser men hairstyles.

Enjoy it though I did, I was becoming bored with he-man talk when a clean-cut young fellow walked in and took the only empty seat, which happened to be next to me. He was only seventeen years old, but before long we were having a fascinating conversation. No scatterbrain, this fellow was, by his own modest admission, at the top of his high school class. That was easy to believe. We talked economics, then politics, then finally even religion (Christianity versus Islam), not as superior to but simply as different from—in origins as well as geographic spread. Not surprisingly, his ambition was to become a history professor and eventually to do serious historical research.

Then he surprised me still further by mentioning that he was a hunter. Every year, he and his father would drive up to Montana to hunt elk. When I mentioned the prairie-dog killers, he grimaced and said that to him and his father, those people were "low-class." He saw stalking and shooting an elk as light-years away from sitting under an umbrella, guzzling beer, and shooting prairie dogs "just for the hell of it." In addition, he and his father always butchered the game they took, and used the meat—every last bit of it. They didn't just "leave it rot in the sun."

After the prairie-dog killers, it was refreshing to talk to a hunter with scruples.

That evening Helen and I talked about taking another day off; we were not ready to go back to walking although we had just had a good break. We were even less enthused the following morning. By then, however, that "monkey on our backs" defied ignoring, and soon we were driving fifty miles east from Douglass back to Lusk, where we had finished walking two days before. We were feeling a bit down and I suggested it was because over the next two days we would be heading right back to Douglas, mostly over roads we were presently driving—it all seemed anticlimactic. Helen said the problem lay in our subconsciously thinking of our present campsite near Douglas as where walk's end actually was. According to her, as we drove along, we were suffering a mile-by-mile downsizing of our sense of how far west we had come since entering Wyoming four days before.

In truth, the real root of our worries, and we both knew it though it wasn't mentioned, was that the last day we were on the road had been miserable. Between wind, noise, rough road, my radio tantrum, and our loosing each other at the end of the day, we had been mentally pummeled and we dreaded another day that might be anything like it.

450

When we finally arrived in southwestern Lusk about 7 a.m., I hopped right out of the car, skipped coffee, and immediately started walking on U.S. 18. We had already agreed not to sit and talk and stoke each other into additional caffeine-fueled angst.

And so began a surprisingly pleasant day. Traffic was light; the heavy trucks that had been my nemesis only days before branched onto U.S. 85 and traveled south from town, not west the way we were going. What a relief! I saw deer and dozens of antelope that day. Sometimes I would look across a vast field only to see nothing. Then presently a distant snort would tell me that if I looked long enough and hard enough, I would eventually spot an antelope. Standing still in the endless sage, they were always hard to see; nevertheless, their inclination to sound off often gave them away.

We finished the day about five o'clock, by which time I had got in an unexpectedly easy nineteen miles, and Helen had caught up on her notes and completed an afghan. What a change in our moods since early morning! Things were definitely looking up.

The next day we left U.S. 18 and took dirt connecting roads along a circuitous route toward Douglas, which was now only twenty-three miles ahead. We did well, finishing about six miles east of town, but that afternoon I paid a price for not taking enough time for lunch. For some reason I ate only a half sandwich and an apple before rushing on into a brutal headwind. When I met Helen only three miles farther on, I had not yet begun to fade; in fact, I felt fine, though a bit windblown. "Drive on six more miles," I told her. "See you in a couple of hours."

"You better eat something or you'll be sorry."

"Nah, I'm okay. Let's just go!"

I would pay for that. Within a few miles I began to play out, and the more tired and hungry I became the harder the wind seemed to blow. Every small hill became a mountain, every step an ordeal. I would have radioed Helen to come pick me up but I knew that would make her day. *Old man,* I would hear, *didn't I tell you not to try to walk on an empty stomach? Maybe next time you'll listen, ha-ha. You look like you're gonna fall over. Get in the car sweetie and gimmie me a kiss.*

To myself: Screw up your resolve, Beam, and keep walking. And when you get to the car, act as if you're not tired at all. Suggest another couple or three miles—put her on the spot. She'll wanna head back to camp; it's been a long day for her too, and she's got a book going back there.... But wait! What if she takes you up on it?—challenges you to another three miles? You'd be lucky to make another hundred yards. Better just keep your mouth shut. Crawl in car and call it a day.

It was nearing five o'clock when I finally spotted the car out ahead. But behold, beyond it and approaching was an SUV that slowed, passed Helen, and then abruptly stopped and began backing up. My fatigue vanished, as if with a shot of adrenalin.

The two vehicles sat side by side for a dozen seconds; then, even as I hurried toward them, the SUV's driver got out and Helen got out to meet her. That relaxed me, for I knew that Helen would have stayed in the car or left in a hurry if she'd sensed any danger. Of course, by the time I got there, all out of breath, the women were in animated conversation.

Sue McKee was a schoolteacher who had, of all things, grown up only twenty miles from Lebanon, our hometown in Connecticut. She had spotted the Toyota's license plate, and just *had* to find out what a lone woman in a grimy Connecticut car was doing near a sheep farm in eastern Wyoming.

Sue McKee

We marveled at the chance encounter. Not only had Sue grown up near Lebanon, she had graduated from Eastern Connecticut University, which is only eight miles north of town. She knew Lebanon well, knew the roads, the grocery store, the town hall—even the green where Helen and I were walking the night we decided to start west.

Sensing a chance for good conversation, we explored possibilities of meeting for dinner, but our schedules could not be adjusted to fit. Sue would be busy for the next few evenings, and after that Helen and I would be gone from the area. We talked on for a few more minutes, enjoying the pleasantries but fascinated by the unlikelihood that we were standing there at all. Finally we exchanged good-byes and Sue returned to her SUV as we walked over to the car. Helen volunteered to drive, so I hoisted myself into the passenger seat, where I remained awake just long enough to become touchy.

"Helen," I said, "don't you feel a little guilty about having been sitting in the car eating bonbons while I was walking into the wind on an empty stomach?" I was actually kidding at the moment and not anticipating an imminent shift of mood.

"Told you to eat more lunch, didn't I?" she happily countered. "Maybe you'll listen next time."

"Yes, Helen," I replied—suddenly mildly annoyed, although I had started the exchange myself. "From now on I'll always listen and do everything you say, whenever you say it. Your wish will be my command, and if you want, I'll put that in writing and sign it. Anything else I'm gonna have to listen to?"

"Sure is, Grouchy. I've got a great idea; wanna hear it now or later? Won't cost all that much! I just need you to promise we'll do it."

"Later. Let's find a restaurant; then tell me after we've eaten."

I had no excuse for the grouchiness, although I knew that lack of food was the problem. I also knew that just for fun she was trying to maneuver me into some promise she wouldn't care if I kept or not—some small thing I'd try to sidle out of later and she could kid me about.

Say no more, I thought to myself as I drifted off to sleep.

*   *   *   *

I walked through Douglas about midmorning on Memorial Day; then it was west out of town on state 96. Ninety-six carried little traffic and was easy walking; presumably most people were using I-25 a mile or so to the north. I met a Canadian bicyclist about eleven and invited him to join Helen and me for lunch at the motor home. It would be our usual lunchtime fare of sandwiches and soft drinks, but we would be eating at a table—instead of Helen and me in the car, and him along the road somewhere. But the young man thanked me and declined. He said he never ate in the middle of the day—just "used" great big breakfasts and dinners when riding cross-country.

In early afternoon I came to where 96 joins I-25 about six miles west of town, but determined to avoid the interstate, I branched onto a parallel gravel road. It took me yet another four miles—to an underpass where I crossed from south to north of the highway.

Using the gravel road was fortunate, for in the underpass I got to see fascinating swallows' nests wedged between the ceiling and a side wall. It was a community of row houses stretching the length of the tunnel. The nests were made of mud and had foot-across bases with cone-like sides that extended out to small, round openings. I could see residents in two or three nests; however, most of the birds were flying about in great excitement just outside the ends of the tunnel. Occasionally, a particularly nervy fellow would break out of the crowd and buzz right through just above my head. I took several pictures before quickly moving on. Later, Helen said that when she *drove* through the tunnel, the birds were not bothered at all. Evidently they were used to the passage of an occasional car, while a person on foot could put them in a frenzy.

There was a small creek a hundred yards west of the tunnel, and there on a mud flat squatted another dozen little birds, all lined up along the water's edge. *So that's where they got their mud!* I paused, wanting to see exactly how they did it. But no luck. Suddenly, as a group they flew away, presumably alarmed, as in the tunnel, by the unusual nearness of a person.

A mile farther on, my gravel road petered out, and for the first time I was forced to walk an interstate. Misgivings aside, it proved safe enough. The wide, paved shoulder meant that cars coming toward me from the west passed at least fifteen feet away, while traffic from the east was safely on the other side of the median. Consequently, I had no worries about being hit from behind, even though the wind was noisy and I could hear almost nothing.

I hadn't gone far when I came to another back road, and since it looked promising, I was quick to clamber down off the interstate and begin following it. Again gravel, the new road led a mile or two along an old railroad track before branching north for a couple miles then west again through unfenced rangelands. Meanwhile, it changed to dirt and gradually narrowed. Along the way, I accumulated an entourage of Black Angus cattle, and eventually, cresting a low hill, I spotted Helen parked a quarter mile ahead and surrounded by still more of the jet-black animals. One particularly bold fellow was standing by the driver's window getting his head scratched.

As I walked down toward the car, my gang trailed along thirty feet behind, spanning out across the road onto grass on either side. Twice I stopped and turned around, and each time they would pull up and stare in that quiet, uneasy way of cattle; then I would move on and they would casually fall in behind. When I arrived at the car, Helen

My Black Angus Entourage

got out, and for five minutes we stood talking within an encircling company of forty or fifty cattle that watched or browsed on the nearby grass.

We decided to stay with the road, although we half expected it to eventually peter out and force us to return to the interstate. Sure enough, just a mile farther on, I again caught up to Helen, but this time she was standing in front of a ranch house talking to another woman.

And that's where the road ended—right in front of the Jillian Ravenshaw's front porch. According to our map it should have continued for miles, and Jillian said that it had many years before. However, that was then and this was now, and the once-through road had long since reverted to private ownership and was disappearing in a slow return to rangeland. All we could see of it, beyond a barbed wire fence, were several faint ruts on an otherwise grassy slope.

We would see a few other roads that showed on the map as public but would prove to be blocked off and private. We speculated with Jillian about whether such roads had always been private or had earlier been public and later *became* private. She didn't know, but she did remark the obvious: that some back roads become almost unused when new highways alter traffic patterns, and that it consequently makes sense to return them to private ownership—if only to save county maintenance costs. In any case, I walked seven extra miles that afternoon with nothing to show for it but a half dozen pictures of Black Angus cattle.

We said good-bye to Jillian, and Helen drove me back to where I had come down off the interstate three hours before. Walking west again, I soon decided that the interstate would be as uninteresting to drive as it was to walk, not that I expected otherwise. There were no houses, no people, no interesting middle distance scenes—just far-view vistas invariably spoiled by boring foregrounds of concrete pavement and off-road gravel. But why, I asked myself, would you expect anything different? The interstate system was conceived as working highway for the military's deployment of troops and supplies; only later did it become an arterial system for commercial freight distribution and passenger travel. Least of all was it intended for cross-country hikers. *Keep walking, Beam, and get off this thing as soon as you can.*

*   *   *   *

The following morning eleven miles of walking got me off of I-25 and onto U.S. 20, which in that area lies between the interstate to the south and the Platte River to the north. There was hardly any traffic thanks to the nearness of the interstate, but the few drivers who came along seemed unusually disposed to smile and wave. I'd smile and wave right back, thereby working myself into a what's-the-hurry mood that slowed down walking and soon had me stopping too often to take pictures.

One picture shows a vast meadow with two antelope that let me come unusually close. In another, an ominous sign inquires, HAVE YOU READ MY NUMBER 1 BEST SELLER? THERE WILL BE A TEST—GOD. There was a third picture, lost now, but which I dubbed PRESCHOOL 2000. It showed a corral-like enclosure containing eight young children and two jolly women. Two sides of the enclosure were four-foot fences while a third side was a ridge of loose dirt, too steep for any preschooler to climb. The area was the exercise yard of a day-care facility that connected to the basement of a ranch-style house.

The women were all smiles, and the children seemed happy as they played their organized games. Nevertheless, the scene bothered me. Granted the kids would benefit (some more, some less) from their sessions of collective play, but were those highly supervised sessions being balanced by relatively unsupervised periods around home? I believed (still believe) that children need a great deal of time in which to exercise their imaginations in the absence of on-looking adults. They need to create and play their own games or, with minimal guidance, plan little projects like making doll clothes, building models, or collecting snakes and bugs. Doesn't hurt if they get dirty either, as long as they're scrubbed up later.

Overall, however, it was pleasant to behold the day-care scene, but there would be a downer a few miles ahead.

Somewhere near the outskirts of Glenrock, I clambered down under a road bridge beneath which flowed a stream. There, on a broad supporting wall was a tangle of lurid graffiti. Swastikas, devil's faces, and images of penises besmirched the concrete, along with the words *death, fuck, pigs, kill, shit, bitch, hocker,* and *pot.* It was more of that bitter, high school hatred I had seen several times before. But why do these kids hate? I wondered, as I struggled to grasp a reality that has always troubled me.

It is common knowledge, my thinking ran, that members of any high school population are unequally gifted with such qualities as beauty and personality, let alone leadership, verbal, athletic, or artistic skills. Additionally, they come from families that range from poor to rich, from socially invisible to prominent.

Children more richly endowed with advantages are often likely to find themselves respected by teachers and accepted and esteemed by exclusive subgroups of peers. Such acceptance provides a reinforcing sense of "I'm-doing-all-right," along with increased self-confidence for facing swiftly approaching adulthood. A few will remember those years as the best of their lives.

However, the majority of adolescents, often though not always less gifted, neither seek nor are welcomed to such coteries, and instead have independent lives, identities, and friends of their own. Some view the in-groups as clannish cliques, but most are relatively unmindful of them, being focused instead upon activities and events outside the high school experience. A few of the majority may wistfully yearn to belong to the elite, but generally they resign themselves to being mildly unhappy peripherals. At least to some degree, both kinds of people, the chosen and the majority, tend to mature and mellow as the years go by. To be sure, the defined social stratification that develops early remains intact through future years, but boundaries become more diffuse. At class reunions, many people mix, mingle, and speak to each other, while they would have shunned one another as adolescents.

However, the graffiti I saw on the road-bridge wall doubtless reflected the attitudes of a few who were neither high school nobility nor run-of-the-mill majority nor even peripheral wannabes. Columbine showed that some student killers can not only be talented and bright, but can come from achieving, wealthy families. Nowadays, few doubt that early environment plays a major role in an individual's adolescent attitudes, but Herman Melville was probably right when he attributed Claggart's implacable malevolence to a "depravity according to nature." Two sentences of the graffiti showed hatred directed not only toward high school classmates but far beyond. One said, "Fuck all jocks in

Glenrock." Ominous enough, but the other went much further. It said, "Fuck the world."

Back up on the road the world seemed light-years away from that under-bridge place of hate. A mile of stately cottonwoods followed the meandering Platte, and nearby were green fields and pastures with many horses. An unusual fence caught my attention. Rather than the usual strands of barbed wire, this one was a matrix of coarse wire mesh, and it reminded me of the rump-scratching ponies I had seen in Nebraska the month before. Suddenly, I laughed out loud at images of them undulating their backsides in equestrian bliss, the fence giving way behind them.

Many thanks little horses; I needed the laugh.

BRAVE CASPER COLLINS AND POISON SPIDER ROAD

On the first of June we moved Lurch to the vicinity of Casper, Wyoming, and then spent a day doing household chores and exploring the area. Near the campground and nestled in a loop of the North Platt River is Izaak Walton State Park—shades of Walton's *Complete Angler*. On the other side, to the east, is the Fort Casper Museum. The fort, as well as the city itself, was named after Lieutenant Casper Collins, son of Colonel William O. Collins of the Eleventh Ohio Cavalry. The colonel's namesake city is Fort Collins, Colorado, 180 miles to the south.

The Eleventh Ohio was in the Platt area in 1865 defending settlers against Cheyenne Indians who were trying to block white expansion. On July 26 of that year young Collins was killed in a skirmish with a war party. One account holds that he was a "wild and heedless young man," and implies that it was those qualities that cost him his life. I don't like the smirch. Whatever else he may have been, Collins was incredibly brave as he rode out from a military post to die fighting for wagon-train soldiers, who were themselves already trapped and doomed.

Two days after we moved to Casper we were back on the road, and toward noon I walked into town and met Helen at the corner of Curtis and Iron Streets. From there we drove to the motor home for lunch, after which we spent an inconclusive hour peering at maps trying to decide what route to use beyond Casper. Our next big destination was Riverton, 130 miles farther on, and the most obvious thing would be to continue walking U.S. 20. Unfortunately, 20 passed through the towns of Mountain View, Natrono, Moneta and Shoshoni, and since it was the only main road west, we were sure there would be plenty of traffic.

But we did spot an alternative route. It ran more or less parallel to the U.S. highway but generally thirty or forty miles to the south, and on the map it appeared as a connecting set of thin black lines. Road names along the way were Poison Spider, Dry Creek, Gas Hills, and eventually Wyoming route 24, the latter ending in the Wind River Valley only a few miles from Riverton. Doubtless this back-road route would be shorter than U.S. 20, and there would certainly be little traffic. On the down side, we would be letting ourselves in for a very isolated walk.

We left the motor home without having decided which route to use, and before long I was back on 20 with the branch-off to Poison Spider only a few miles ahead. I found an excuse for delaying the decision still longer when I spotted an antique oil rig where Rancho Road comes up from the south. Great! I would stop and look it over; this was oil country, after all, and I'd be looking at industry history.

Antique Oil Rig

The rig was maintained in excellent condition by the Petroleum Association of Wyoming, and with its components all in place it was easy to see how ingenious yet simple the great machine was. Its derrick, a wooden tower about one hundred feet high, was obviously used for raising and lowering well casings, drills, and other equipment. Its other main component was a steam engine that was still connected by belt to a large wooden crank wheel. Through a vertical connecting rod, the crank wheel drove an overhead beam for supplying up-down motion to the drill-bit assembly. In the broadest sense, that is all that such machines were. But indeed, how they changed the world!

The oil rig was striking, but just as striking was the fact that it had to be transported to the drilling site and assembled in place. Moving the steam engine, in particular, must have been a herculean task, considering that it was before the days of modern roads or trucks. It was probably brought to Casper by rail, I decided, and from there to the well site by wagons pulled by oxen or horses. I was as intrigued by how it was moved as I was by how it worked, and I pleasantly loafed away another ten minutes before breaking away and getting back to walking.

Inevitably I came to the Poison Spider turnoff, where procrastinations finally had to end. U.S. 20 had been busy with traffic all along the way, but when I looked down Poison Spider, there was nothing in sight except a single distant car. There's probably nothing on this road from here to Riverton, I thought, as I turned the corner and began walking past an area of worker housing. This was followed by a trucking depot on the right, an oil rigging yard on the left, a few business facades on both sides, and then nothing but widely scattered oil fields along with supporting equipment and storage tanks. For mile after mile the country was more desolate than any I had ever seen. Side roads with names like Oil Camp and Forest Oil bespoke the reason there were roads at all in this baron land of alkaline pools and scrub grasslands. Eventually, there were no longer even oil fields, and for the rest of that day and all the next, I saw only two vehicles in the course of forty miles.

But as lonely as Poison Spider was, I frequently saw antelope or heard their distant snorts, and around rare water holes there would occasionally be mule deer. Once, during the morning of the second day, a doe appeared near a marshy area that angled toward the road some distance ahead. As I continued walking, she tried to stay in front of me but was forced by the marsh to edge ever closer to the road, thus closer to me as well. It seemed odd that she did not simply bound away as deer usually did, and odder still when she stepped onto the road and stamped her hooves in agitation.

I paused—uncertain of her odd behavior. A moment passed, another; then, to my surprise, a spotted fawn emerged from the grass and stood close beside her.

So that's why she hadn't bounded away!

Although the doe and fawn were too distant for good pictures, I nevertheless raised my camera and took aim. But just then a second fawn stepped onto the road directly across from where I was standing, and pausing only briefly, it folded its ears like a trusting puppy, walked over, and thrust itself between my legs!

Amazed, I reached down with my left hand, and was even more surprised when the tiny deer raised its head and tried to suckle my fingers. For several seconds neither of us moved; then, very slowly, I crouched slightly and began stroking its back with my right hand, in which I still, awkwardly, held the camera. After a stroke or two the camera slipped away and fell to the ground, but that didn't bother the infant in the least. It simply folded its legs and sank to the road asleep.

The Fawn on Poison Spider Road

Probably a full minute passed as I stood contorted and unmoving; then I painfully crouched still more, picked up the camera and re-aimed it at mother deer and *her* fawn, neither of whom had moved. That picture taken, the question became what to do with *my* fawn. Traffic was nonexistent; there had been none so far that morning, but if I moved, would this little one, fast asleep at my feet, wake up? become frightened? perhaps to become lost from its mother? I had become the object of an innocent's trust, and thus felt a sense of responsibility on the one hand yet helplessness on the other. Of course reason soon took over. This fawn did not need me; it needed its mother, and if I simply moved on, she would surely come back to claim it.

I slowly straightened up while carefully pulling my right foot from under the fawn's haunch; then, stepping back, I took its picture before crossing the road and resolutely walking on. Twice I paused and looked to see if it had got up, but it hadn't stirred. Meanwhile, mother deer crossed the road only yards ahead and walked some distance into the grass. She paused there, but soon began a long circular track back toward her sleeping offspring. To my relief, when I looked back a third time, the fawn was just entering the roadside grass, about to be reunited with its mother, I was sure.

About three that afternoon and thirty miles from Casper, a dusty pickup approached from the west—the only vehicle I saw that day.

The driver, who appeared to be in his seventies, stopped and told me he had already met Helen and that she was only a couple of miles ahead. Helen later told me he had found it hard to believe when she said he would shortly come upon me walking along by myself. Incredulous, he'd blurted, "You mean he's all to hell and gone walking across this *goddamned* desert by hisself?" He stressed everything he said about the out-backness of the country with a John-Wayne-like drawl and a hearty *goddamned*. Helen said it seemed as if the only adjective he knew was *goddamned*, and that he believed the Almighty had already laid a curse on just about everything.

The man told me he was a scrap metal dealer and that he'd been farther west that day closing a deal on some "obsolete *goddamned* gas-well equipment." Before we parted he made me promise to call him that evening when I arrived back in Casper— just so he'd know Helen and I weren't "out there sleeping on the *goddamned* ground somewhere." He said we could be bitten by "a *goddamned* scorpion or maybe even a *goddamned* rattlesnake."

On our way back to Casper that evening, Helen and I looked hard for my favorite fawn and its sibling and mother, but of course they were nowhere to be seen. I asked Helen how she would have liked it if I had come walking up to the car with the fawn in my arms.

"Let's not even think about it," she said with a laugh. "It would have been worse than if you'd taken that monster pup the woman tried to give you. We could be driving all over Wyoming tonight looking for somebody to adopt an infant mule deer."

The following morning I came to the end of Poison Spider Road, and after a series of deserted connectors, I reached the beginning of Wyoming 136. It was a good place to quit until we moved Lurch to Riverton. As it was, the drive back to Casper would be over sixty miles, and another day's walk would make it nearly ninety.

*   *   *   *

Cottonwoods RV Park north of Riverton became our next base camp. Getting Lurch there required driving busy U.S. 20, which, of course, we had avoided walking by using the Poison Spider route. We considered but discarded the idea of driving Lurch over Poison Spider; we had too little confidence in the old lemon's mechanics.

Cottonwoods turned out to have gravel, shade, and full hook-ups. Its only negative was more of those showers where you feed a coin slot to get water. The trouble starts when your first quarter's worth of water runs out and you are still covered with soap. Another quarter gets the soap off, but of course you'd like to stand under the hot water for another few minutes, spend a few more quarters—luxuriate. Alas, the hot water is not really hot; it's only lukewarm, and the only thing more quarters gets you is more frustration. Leaving those showers, we invariably felt clean but "calorifically shortchanged" as Helen put it, and the second night we were there I headed for the office to complain.

The owner himself, Philip Lanyon, was on the desk, and I later concluded that I would probably have got what I wanted quicker if I had started off with more honey and less vinegar. "Evening Sir," I said without preamble. "I'm one of your campers, and I hate to tell you, but the water in your bathhouse is barely lukewarm. How's about heatin' it up a little? … I mean a lot!"

Actually, my blunt demand came out louder than intended.

He stood there a moment—didn't glare, didn't growl—just smiled unhurriedly and said, "Nah, can't make it hotter. It's the way it's supposed to be, and I've got three good reasons for keeping it that way. Wanna hear em? You'll be cooled off … ha-ha … make that warmed up, by the time I'm done tellin' you."

That stopped me cold. Flippancy, I seethed to myself, on top of cold water—that's insult piled on injury! He's playing the amiable joker, this guy; figures he knows exactly how to handle complainers: mollify 'em with left-handed charm, then don't fix the problem. Business must be darn good or he wouldn't be talkin' like this.

I drew myself up: "No I don't need to hear three good reasons why it can't be hotter. I'm paying you plenty to camp here, and I'll be lookin' to take a shower tomorrow night. The least you can do is make sure it's hot."

Maybe it was the absurdity of the situation, but all of a sudden I couldn't keep my face straight. He saw it and widened his smile as I demanded just one—"that's one!"—good reason why it couldn't be hot.

"Well first," he said, clearing his throat with a couple of unnecessary *harrumphs*, "and you gotta hear this ... 'cause I'm serious ... ahh ..." Here I nearly told him to quit stalling, but eventually he continued: "ahh ... if I make the water hotter ... ahh ... people will spend more time in the showers and less time touring. They'll leave here feeling unfulfilled ... you know, like they haven't seen it all. There's a lot of touristy things to see in this part of the country, and you don't wanna miss 'em."

"You're changing the subject!"

"Second reason—"

"The first reason was no reason. How can there be a second?"

He acted as if he hadn't heard me. "Second reason: If they spend less time tourin', they'll spend less money down town and the merchants'll be down on me."

"You really look worried. I suppose your third reason makes even more sense?"

"Sure does. Campers like you might get scalded and never come back, might even sue me." He was almost laughing.

"You've got the never-come-back part right." I gave him a toothy, mocking glare, but I couldn't manage spite and he knew it; in fact, our exchange was becoming a half-friendly game. Then I said, "You're worried about making less money yourself, not about the merchants making less. That's why the water's not hot."

"How'd you guess? Bet it's hot tomorrow night."

"What'd you say?—just then—after you said, 'How'd you guess?'"

"I said the water'll be hot tomorrow night!"

"Well.... Okay.... Thanks.... Why the devil didn't you say that to begin with?"

Smiles now and no hard feelings, and from there, after a few more friendly jabs, we drifted into normal conversation about the area's economy. At a local grocery store I had seen a number of people paying for food with certificates that looked like money. I remarked on that and asked Lanyon what they were. When he told me they were food stamps, I recalled that most of the people using them were poor-looking Indians. I would see many more such people in the weeks just ahead.

Moving on, Lanyon told me that the local economy depended heavily on tourism, ranching, wheat farming, and natural resources. Helen and I had seen no farming or ranching while approaching from the east; that was more to the north, he said, but the importance of natural resources was hardly news. We had passed widely scattered oil and gas fields, and walk's end was presently in an area of uranium mines.

Eventually I realized that the conversation had moved far away from the hot water issue, and I wanted to be sure he wouldn't forget. "Whoa, wait a minute," I said, holding up a hand. "Are you sure that water's gonna be hot tomorrow night?'

"Never fear," he answered with a smile. "Time you're ready for it, it'll be plenty hot."

I hoped so, and sure enough, the next evening it was fine.

*   *   *   *

The day after we moved to Cottonwoods, we drove thirty-five miles back east to resume walking along Wyoming 136. The road was paved but without shoulders, and it would have been hard going if there was much wind. Fortunately, there was almost none, and cars and trucks were rare except for a few coming or going to the mines. Those drivers almost flew across those wide-open spaces; probably most were going well over eighty.

Along the eastern approaches to Riverton, I began seeing the ramshackle homes of poverty stricken Indians. Once, a couple pulled up in a car and offered to drive me into town. I thanked them but said I wanted to walk, and to satisfy their curiosity, I told them I was walking across America. That brought the usual expressions of astonishment and the usual *how's* and *why's*.

I had to be almost rude in order to disengage and start walking again, and even then they idled along beside me for many yards, repeatedly wishing me good luck and urging me to be careful and not be hit by a car.

Five minutes later another Indian tried to give me a ride, this time a middle-age man.

It was good to be back where people lived, and away from the empty wastelands to the east. Poison Spider had been the loneliest stretch of road Helen or I had ever traveled, walking or otherwise, and we would encounter nothing like it the rest of the way across the country.

The day's walk ended where state 136 crosses the Wind River, about three miles south of Riverton.

Next morning I finished the short stretch into town. It was something of an impatient walk, for we were anxious to get on with another task, namely, preparations for hosting grandchildren beginning ten days hence. We would be meeting them at Salt Lake City Airport, and they would be spending two weeks with us in the Yellowstone area. We needed to make reservations at a campground near the park, and in addition, we needed to shop at a local supermarket for supplies. There wouldn't be much time for that once the children arrived. From dawn till dark we would be touring, rafting, flying or else browsing the gift shops of West Yellowstone, a small town on the park's border.

Things went so smoothly that by late afternoon we had made telephone reservations at a campground near the park, and had got in all the food we could that was not perishable. We even bought an electric ice-cream maker which we were sure the kids would like.

It was outside of the supermarket that we met an interesting retired couple from Washington State. They traveled not in a van or motor home, but on a motorized trike that looked like a cross between a car and a motorcycle. I had noticed a few such machines before, but they were commercially manufactured and sold through regular motorcycle dealerships. This one was homemade. Its owner was a machinist by trade, and before that he had spent many years as a chief in the navy. In my mind, his beautifully made cycle-car went right along with his having been a submariner. During my working years, I had spent much time at sea in submarines, and I knew firsthand the remarkable resourcefulness of that kind of sailor.

WALKING INDIANS AND
A CHEERFUL SWISS NATIONAL

Helen and I felt we were entering a new phase of our journey as I resumed walking from 8th and Main Street in Riverton. We were now entering the Rocky Mountains, and leaving town the road would climb steadily for about seven miles. After that, it would briefly descend before beginning a seemingly endless repetition of local hills and valleys where each hill, each valley, would be higher than the one before. This general climb would end a hundred miles to the west, at the Continental Divide, and beyond would come a twenty mile descent to the Snake River in the shadow of the Teton Mountains.

I had not been walking long when I began to pass a house with a large front yard bounded along the sidewalk by waist-high fencing. Unbeknownst to me a Pit Bull had been silently watching my approach, and as I walked quietly along, it suddenly charged out from low bushes to burst into a snarling ruckus just feet away. I jumped and grabbed the bat. After its initial charge the powerful animal matched my pace along the entire hundred-foot fence, snarling and threatening all the way.

That was the second home in Riverton where I had encountered big, aggressive dogs in large yards with fences running along the sidewalk. I wondered if the property owners had had problems with trespassers or burglars—there were plenty of poor in the area, mostly Indians but some Whites. Or were these dog owners just western versions of eastern faint-hearts—men and women hyped up by Eyewitness News, security-system ads, or even just each other into seeing their own neighborhoods and the whole country as far more dangerous than they really are. What's wrong with these chickens? I wondered. It seems as if half the people in the U.S. are afraid to go to bed without bright lights outside.

But I couldn't stay upset for long. Cool and without wind, the morning was perfect for walking; the upgrade warmed me, sped up my heart, gave me a glowing sense of well-being. Snarling dogs aside, the day was off to a good start and it would only get better. Toward midmorning I met Helen for coffee and cinnamon buns, and two hours later we thoroughly enjoyed watching a horse play games with a flock of geese.

Mr. Horse—more about gender later—was in a fenced pasture across from a turnout where we had parked to eat lunch. He was not alone however. Sharing the pasture were a dozen geese, which were minding their own business and quietly grazing on meadow grass. This peaceful coexistence had been going on for ten or fifteen minutes when suddenly the horse began charging the birds. Every few minutes, he would inexplicably race toward them as they fussed and ran helter-skelter to get out of his way. After scattering them a few times, he would let up and the geese would re-form into the semblance of a flock, only to be charged again a few minutes later. Eventually, the birds abruptly split and five or six flew over the fence into an adjacent pasture. This seemed to satisfy Mr. Horse, and for several minutes he stood there leaving the remaining birds alone. Before long, though, he was at it again—to their dismay and our amazement, not to say delight.

Watching this drama, Helen and I became convinced that the horse was not trying to trample the geese, although he could easily have accidentally squashed one. This was sport to him, not malice; we were watching an animal at play—he had a sense of humor, although not one his quarry appreciated. The game continued as one by one the remaining birds flew over the fence until a single holdout remained as sole object of the playful horse's attention. That fellow allowed himself to be chased for another few minutes; then even he became fed up, and with a loud, squawking flight went over to join his companions. Seemingly satisfied, the horse returned to browsing. We continued with our lunches.

Helen and I laughed about the horse-and-goose show for days after that. Once she demanded to know why I kept referring to the horse as *Mister*. "It," she asserted, "could just as well have been a lady horse, a girl—you know, a mare. You need a course in gender awareness."

My heart leaped with joy because this time she'd really set herself up. "I am gender-aware," I shot right back. "That horse had a dick, and although he may have been a gelding, he certainly wasn't a mare! I could see that through my fifteen-dollar field glasses, Dearie, and if your three-hundred-dollar glasses had been at your eyes instead of under your car seat, you too would have known that horse was a stallion—like me. How do you like that?"

"Sometimes you make me tired."

"I'm tired too, Honey; what say we go back to Lurch and take a nap?—spend a little time in bed together."

"Sometimes you're a *little* too smart-alecky for your own good. For that you're taking me out to dinner tonight, right?"

"You bet, m'Love, absolutely; then we'll go to bed."

Once in a while I would get the verbal better of her, and that time it was worth the price of a dinner. By day's end, however, we were too tired to look for a restaurant, although a few days later we found a good one in Dubois, seventy miles farther along.

*　　*　　*　　*

It was a couple of hours after the horse-and-goose show that I spotted two Indians up ahead, walking west like me but on the other side of the road. I quickly gained on them, and coming abreast I called greetings, which they duly answered with friendly nods and smiles. That was enough for me to cross the road, and after we exchanged remarks about the hilly terrain, they told me they were sister and brother, and on their way to Jackson, Wyoming, 110 miles away.

"You don't plan to walk clear to Jackson, do you?" I asked.

"Yes," the man replied, "but only if we don't get a ride. We've made this trip before … many times. Never had to walk far, probably won't this time."

"Where will you sleep tonight?"

"Oh, wherever we are," his sister cut in, then, "We're Shoshone"— as if that explained why they had no idea where they might stay the night.

We talked for five or ten minutes, partly about the weather but mostly about what I was doing—this unexpected white man all alone on the road. They said little about themselves.

Presently I told them I had to get moving, that my wife was waiting somewhere up ahead. "We'll walk with you," the man declared as he fell in beside me. His sister briefly objected, but then began following along behind.

"I walk pretty fast," I warned. "That's how it is when you've been doing this for weeks on end."

"No problem, we'll keep up," he determinedly replied.

As we began walking, he told me that he was forty-four and she was thirty-seven, although they appeared older to me. Well over six feet tall, he looked as if he could have been an NFL linebacker years before, but now he was fat in the midriff and long gone soft. She too was tall and heavy, and she looked even less in shape. Within a quarter mile they were both huffing and puffing, and she had fallen several yards back. Then he too began losing ground, so that after another five minutes he was a dozen paces behind while she was trailing by fifty yards.

I paused and waited for him to catch up. "You know," I said, "this won't work. You're pushing yourself too hard and your sister can't even keep up with you. You two should walk by yourselves … at your own pace." He agreed, and after his sister finally got there, we said good-byes and started off again, this time not trying to stay together. Within minutes they'd fallen well behind.

But I was bothered as I walked along. Obviously these people had little money, and the question remained: Where would they spend the night? They both wore small, cheap knapsacks, but did they have any food in them, and if not, would they have anything to buy food with?

Well, who knows, I thought, as on impulse I turned and started back. Approaching them, I tried to think of some tactful way to ask if they were broke, but in the end the direct route seemed best.

"It's none of my business," I began, while still some feet away, "but do you people need money?"

"Oh no, we're okay," he replied, but not without hesitation. He was a proud person and clearly reluctant to admit they were hard up. I gently pressed, and he soon conceded they could use "maybe two or three bucks." Meanwhile, his sister stood behind him nodding a vigorous *yes*.

Feeling more self-conscious than ever, I got out my wallet and offered a bill while trying to be as inconspicuous as possible since a car was approaching from the east. Briefly distracted as the car whooshed by, he never got to see the money. Her hand shot out in an instant, and just as quickly the bill disappeared into the breast pocket of her shirt. With a sweet smile she said, "God bless you, sir," and resumed walking, turning momentarily to gesture another *thank-you* to me and a sign for him to fall in behind.

He and I stood there astonished. The woman couldn't walk two miles an hour, but she must have had the quickest hand in the West. And now she had definitely become the leader of the two.

Her puzzled brother, still wondering what happened, leaned toward me, and in a confidential voice asked how much I had given her. When I told him, tears, indeed tears, came to his eyes as he thanked me and said they would eat well and sleep in a motel that night.

A minute or two later, after reciprocal expressions of best wishes, I extended my hand to shake good-bye. But to my surprise, instead of completing a *conventional* handshake, the huge man lifted my hand and arm high above my head, put his other arm around my waist, and pulled me to his chest in a gentle, bear-like hug that lifted me to my tiptoes. It was like nothing I had ever experienced before. With his mouth close to my ear, he thanked me again in a voice husky with emotion. Choked up myself, I told him he was very welcome....

An hour passed and I had stopped to look at one of those roadside memorials with which people mark where a loved one or friend has been killed in an auto crash. This one was different from the crosses that bereaved Christians put up all over the country. Obviously

Indian, its base was a low pyramid of piled-up rocks, and surrounding these was a triangular structure of three bare branches tied at the top and decorated with tuffs of horsehair. Small bouquets poked out from spaces between the stones, and several deflated balloons completed what was probably the memorial to a child.

Indian Memorial

I raised the camera to take a picture. To my left lay two small bunches of flowers tossed off the pyramid by the eternal winds, and farther away, beyond a grassy field, was a stand of low trees, all bowed toward the east. The Wind River Valley is indeed appropriately named. I braced myself against the restless air—steady, steady, now trip the shutter! Take another, Beam, you moved! I was crouching for a last picture when a lone pickup sped by heading west. In the back, my Indian friends, brother and sister, waved and shouted thank-yous that whipped away on the wind.

I spent a few more minutes tidying up the little marker; I put the blown-about flowers back where they belonged and reattached a wisp or two of horsehair. Then it was back to walking for the last few miles of the day.

*   *   *   *

The next morning we moved to Riverside Park, which is three miles east of Dubois, Wyoming, a town I would walk through the following day. From the highway, a road led down between corrals where campground management kept horses for summer recreations. The park itself was quiet, and many of the campsites were in shady groves of stately trees. An ancient reaper was parked near a trail along a creek bounding the property, and walking the trail, it was easy to imagine you were living in another century.

We had Lurch set up by eleven-thirty, and after a good lunch I was back on the road by early afternoon. The wind was brutal, so noisy I could hear almost nothing as I climbed steadily to elevations above six thousand feet—more than a thousand feet higher than Riverton. Even so, tiring was no problem, nor did I expect it to be. For days the terrain had been steadily rising, and I was confident I could easily handle the still higher altitudes that lay just ahead. However, I did notice that the air seemed clearer and thinner. It was cooler too; that morning there had been fresh snow on high peaks ten miles to the north.

As I climbed and climbed, the hills became ever choppier and a different flora gradually replaced the deciduous trees and vast grasslands of lower altitudes. Smaller, localized, grassy areas still appeared on the hillsides, but scattered stands of leafy trees gave way to more numerous groups of conifers. Here and there were yellow, white, or blue wild flowers, and yellow-green lichens clung to rocks along the road.

I stopped to take pictures of a ground squirrel that lived in a roadside culvert. A fearless little fellow, he allowed me to approach to within fifteen feet before he dove for cover with much scolding. I moved closer and stood very still. Sure enough, minutes later, out he came and I got a picture. Again I moved in, whereupon he ducked back but soon came out again. Presto, another picture. One more time we played our game of me-advance, him-duck, him-reappear, me-take-picture. My third snapshot was from only five feet away.

We covered over fourteen miles that afternoon, finishing three miles east of the campground and glad to stop for the day. The wind had been relentless.

It was time for a break from walking, but we were scheduled to meet the grandchildren in only eight days so resting would have to wait. Pressing on the following morning, I was early through Dubois, which proved to be an interesting tourist town of shops and restaurants. On the western outskirts, I met Helen at the Bighorn Sheep Museum. We had agreed to meet there since we were both interested in whatever displays they might have, but we especially wanted to ask about my surprising experience with the mule deer fawn two weeks before. Was that common? occasional? rare? And why had it happened?

Fortunately, a woman attendant had time to talk, and she told us that although my fawn encounter had indeed been a "rare and beautiful event," it was not unheard of for a very young deer to attempt to bond with a "fortuitously available human." She said that when first born, fawns are predisposed to quickly attach themselves to any protective animal which, of course, is normally their mother. "Your fawn," she continued, "was extremely young and became separated from its mother before bonding was complete; you just happened to be in the right place at the right time. It's unlikely you'll ever be so *blest* again." Indeed.

We would have spent more time at the museum, but duty called and I was soon back on the road. The Continental Divide was only twenty miles ahead, and crossing it had become a special objective for Helen and me. Of course we knew differently, but we had made a game of declaring the walk from there to the Pacific as "all downhill," thereby conveniently ignoring the looming Tetons, let alone the numerous mountains of Idaho and Oregon.

Hours later I was paused and looking out over a striking mountain vista when a soft voice, almost beside me, said, "Good morning sir." Surprised, I swung around to face a bicyclist who had pulled up behind me, his approach so quiet it was masked by the wind. Actually, I was doubly surprised: surprised by the sudden nearness of the man and surprised that a cyclist would even stop. Usually they were properly dressed, head-down, and studiously pumping along about their business. But this fellow seemed different. Smiling broadly, he straddled a bike that towed a small trailer with a fiberglass flagpole and a small Swiss flag. Now who, I wondered, can this be?

Chris Brienne, it turned out, was a Swiss national who worked for an import-export firm in Baltimore, Maryland. On vacation and riding to Yellowstone Park, he was using a route that had taken him through eastern Arkansas and then northwest across the plains into Wyoming. Brienne said he was no purist, by which he meant he did not have to ride every last mile to feel he had "properly accomplished" a bicycle tour across the country. The frankly honest man even admitted using a bus to spare himself long, flat stretches in Kansas.

We discussed the weather (which happened to be cold as well as windy), and we easily agreed that prevailing winds always come directly at you—no matter in what direction you happen to be riding or walking. But dogs were what we talked about most. "They oughtta be shot on sight," Brienne hotly declared. "They're a damned nuisance. Worse than that, they're dangerous!"

He had had a particularly close call somewhere in Arkansas when a farm dog—an unusual one in my experience—had chased him for a good quarter mile. He had to pedal "like fury"; even so, the big dog nearly got him.

"How big was he?" I asked. I had met plenty of dogs, but most were medium-sized, friendly mongrels.

"I'd say he weighed a hundred pounds," he replied with a grimace, "big enough to really do some damage."

I had to agree. Even so, I couldn't help smiling at the image of this powerful man furiously pedaling along with his trailer holding him back, the Swiss flag flapping in the breeze, and a snarling dog trying to catch him and take a piece out of him.

Brienne himself was soon smiling. "Can't blame you for seein' it funny," he said. "Must have been a hell of a sight."

We were standing about a hundred feet from a small café, and since our conversation was going well, we decided to continue over coffee. Entering the café, we were joined by two college-age bicyclists, a boy and girl who were headed east, and we had no more than found seats than the Swiss asked the kids to confirm what he and I had already agreed about. "Is it true?" he asked, "that the wind always blows from the direction you're heading, whether you're walking, biking, or whatever?"

The kids laughed, but then the young lady took a serious face and matter-of-factly said, "Everybody jokes about that, but it's been proved, you know, that if two bicyclists pass while going in opposite directions, the wind *can* actually blow toward each at the same time—in other words, it can simultaneously blow, say, east on one side of the road and west on the other side."

"Come on," I said, "not for more than a second or two—never heard this before."

"Well it can, and a lot longer than a second or two … sometimes twenty or thirty seconds, even up to two or three minutes. I mean a steady strong wind, not gusts. That's taught in Meteorology 101; it's called *Protracted Ground-Level Wind Shear*, P-G-W-S"—she spelled it out—"but I knew about it when I was twelve years old—everybody does who's grown up in Kansas."

"You're joking," said her young companion, more question than declaration.

"Never more serious in my life."

The Swiss cleared his throat—cleared it again.

Nobody wanted to baldly contradict the girl, but her apparent seriousness *was* mildly disconcerting—like when someone declares belief in spirits or telepathy. Seemed spooky and fishy at the same time.

As we men became quieter, she smilingly looked from one of us to another—directly into our eyes—the picture of sincerity, cajoling us to believe. And we, in turn, turned our eyes away; even our murmurs were fading into embarrassment when she suddenly laughed and gave out with a delighted "Got you guys, didn't I? All three of you!"

"You did, you did," conceded the Swiss with a laugh. Her boyfriend simply grabbed her with both arms and gave her a squeeze and a kiss, which she clearly enjoyed in spite of struggling protestations.

However, it crossed my mind that she had played this happy hoax before. She herself had said "everybody jokes about it," meaning, presumably, that bicyclists joke about it—which joking could well inspire a two-way wind story for bamboozling the unwary. When I asked if the story was making the rounds or if she had made it up on the fly, she replied, "Why I'm always concerned with the truth, Sir, criminology is my major in college."

Which, of course, was no answer at all.

For another half hour we laughed and chatted—an odd group: an older man (me), a man in his prime (the Swiss), and two twenty-year-olds brimming with excitement and on the edge of adulthood. The Swiss told the kids they would have it downhill all the way to Riverton, which they appreciated although they said they would not be going that far. They intended to branch south near Dubois. From there they would ride through Rawlins and Laramie to their final destination, Cheyenne. Friends with a van would be waiting there to take them back to Corvallis, Oregon, where they were students at Oregon State.

Eventually I announced that I had better be going, that Helen would come back looking for me if I was too long overdue at the car. She would drive by heading east, and maybe go a couple of miles before surmising I had found people to talk to and was probably "hanging out in that café back there shootin' the breeze."

The Swiss insisted on paying for everybody's coffee; then we were off and going our separate ways. It had been a pleasant break meeting those friendly, interesting people and getting to talk to them. *And they were bicyclists!* I thought. After the Canadian I had met near Douglas and the two lawyers back in Ohio, they were the fourth, fifth and sixth of that species who were undercutting my impression that most bicyclists tend to be snobs. I had been forced to a similar attitude change in Ohio the year before, when the helpful Harley-type stopped to offer Helen assistance. That time I had had to admit that even some of "them kind" can be gentlemen or ladies.

Later, thinking about the girl's wind story, I was again reminded of the old rancher at the art show in Nebraska—he of the bull snake tale—and that, in turn, led to the old German woman who said she had a pictures to prove she had seen bear cubs. *Well, I thought, at least the girl admitted her story was a hoax. But the old rancher?— maybe a germ of truth there; the German?—probably true, but you never know.... Wonder if I just look gullible?*

Contemplating those pleasant uncertainties, I continued west, climbing as ever until about eleven-thirty when I crossed the Continental Divide at the crest of Togwotee Pass. Helen was waiting with lunch at a nearby turnout. She told me the car lacked power at that altitude, which was 9600 feet above sea level. It was cold there, probably below forty degrees; however, the turnout was a perfect place to eat lunch and enjoy the scenery. Clouds passed in billowy bunches against an azure sky, which in turn arched over green meadows, deep valleys, and isolated stands of evergreens—beautiful. There were flowers everywhere: blue, white, orange, and red and yellow. Once a group of elk ambled across a distant hillside, and still later, just as I began walking again, two mule deer broke cover along a roadside brook.

The rest of the day was a downhill trek—twelve miles on a grade so steep that with each step my leading foot pounded forward in its shoe. I half expected blisters by quitting time. None developed however, but only because the road was cool so that my feet stayed dry and tough. The pounding, however, was definitely having an effect. That night the nail on the second toe of my left foot was turning blue and obviously doomed. Pity. It was young and only partially grown in, being a replacement for the one yanked out by the doctor back in Broken Bow.

LONELY TETON HOLE

Eight more miles of downhill walking brought me out of the Wind River Range and down to Moran Junction, where we had agreed to meet for lunch. The junction lies at the north end of Jackson Hole, which, its name notwithstanding, is really a fifty-mile-long valley just east of the towering Teton Mountains. Almost flat and six miles wide, the valley is home to many animals including buffalo, and I was looking forward to seeing some.

There was little at the junction except a ranger station and a post office, and by the time I arrived, Helen was bored and wanting to go somewhere else to eat. Consequently, we backtracked a few miles and parked in a shady grove of evergreens where Lava Creek passes under U.S. 26.

Lucky us! A hundred yards down the creek, Helen spotted a huge eagle's nest complete with a chick whose head and stubby body jutted up like a big brown thumb. Through binoculars we could see it flapping its wings, impatiently waiting, we assumed, for a parent to return with food.

Just fine. We'd hang around and witness the event.

So we waited and waited, but if it was lunch the chick looked forward to, it was in for a disappointment and so were we. Though we watched for nearly two hours, no adult bird came, although "Flapper" hardly stopped moving his wings in all that time. Frustrated, we eventually gave up and returned to Moran Junction.

From the junction, U.S. 89 leads north to Yellowstone Park, while 26, which I began walking, turns south and goes down the valley past the Tetons to Jackson, Wyoming. Twenty-six is therefore the route of choice for people touring the valley or simply en route to Yellowstone. Traffic was heavy, and of the dozens of people using the road, two drivers stopped to offer lifts. Less than a mile from the junction my first would-be benefactor came up from behind, slowed, and paused in the travel lane. "A ride you need?" called the middle-aged, brown-faced driver in questionable English and strange accent.

"Thanks but no thanks," I replied, "it's not far to where my wife's waiting. I'm okay." With that I thought he would drive on, but he was curious.

"Your car broke someplace?" he asked. "Maybe we take you garage someplace?" Inside the van were two women, two more men (one young one old), a boy about ten, and a large black dog sitting beside the driver. By then he was pulling onto the road's far shoulder, so I crossed and told them that I was walking across America and couldn't accept rides.

Immediately there was a burst of strange chatter as they all piled out of the van to talk and shake hands with this "very interesting fellow"—or at least ordinary fellow embarked on what to them seemed an amazing project. The driver asked about logistics, and responding, I told them how Helen and I leapfrogged Lurch in eighty-mile jumps farther and farther west, and that on a typical walking day she would drop me off from the car, drive ahead, wait till I caught up, drive ahead, wait, drive, wait, and so on. This puzzled them for a few moments while they exchanged rapid-fire dialogue in Hindi, I assumed, since they were clearly from India. Then came a pair of truly great questions: "Be Lurch an American woman, sir?" and "How you ever get her sit in car and wait you come walkin' along?"

How indeed? I smiled and said that Lurch was the motor home and Helen was my wife—and very definitely American! I told them that at first I had tried to get Lurch—no Helen—to drop me off and pick me up by promising to share with her the proceeds of any book I might write. When that didn't work, I just turned on the charm—at least that's what I told them, since Helen wasn't there to contradict. The driver was right with me and gave out with a good laugh, and so did the young man. Even the boy laughed, but he was probably just following the men and didn't really know what was going on.

The two women definitely did not laugh. Maybe it was the bright sun that made them frown slightly, or maybe they understood no English; then again, maybe they didn't like my sense of humor. It's happened before. In any case, trying to lighten the scene, I told them that Helen was really the boss and that she would drop me off each morning and tell me to be sure my step didn't lack spring—or else. That got them laughing again, but they seemed more confused than ever.

Presently the driver smilingly changed the subject to the *how, when, where* and *why* of the walk, and all in his fractured sentences of maybe ninety percent English and whatever the rest was.

I answered his questions and, in between, slid in a few of my own. They told me they were members of a religious organization that was headquartered, or at least had a branch, in Seattle, Washington. Good works were a major part of their religious commitment, and that struck a resonant chord with me. They were all eager to take part in answering my questions, including the women, who it was now clear *could* speak a *little* English. They spoke their broken phrases with warm smiles. The young man spoke haltingly, the boy somewhat better, but the old man, who seemed to have clerical status back in India, spoke only a few words. Mainly he just smiled and nodded. But overall, we had a good time trying to make each other understand.

The pleasantries had been going on for five or ten minutes when the dog suddenly broke free from the boy and made a heart-stopping move toward the road. One of the men and I made reflexive grabs for her collar, and by luck, we both got good holds. Captured, the powerful animal made a quick turn, forcing us into klutzy scramblings to keep from falling. A good laugh about that marked *time-to-go,* but first they had to have a picture of all of them with me—as if I were some sort of celebrity.

But who would take the picture?

While they were debating in their language, a car pulled in a hundred feet away and an elderly white couple got out to change drivers. To my surprise, the old Indian cleric broke away from the group and half trotted back toward the new arrivals, who, surprisingly, did not bolt but rather paused and waited as he came up. It was easy to interpret the Indian's sign-language request for the old White Man to take pictures, and as they walked back together, they moved on to cross-garbled introductions, again with much gesturing and smiling. The old White Man seemed as gregarious as the Indian, and presently his wife, who had got back into the car, got out again and came hobbling along to join the crowd.

After pictures, I stayed long enough to hear the White Man tell the Indians that he was a retired Methodist minister, and to hear the Indians begin explaining their old man's religious status. Within minutes they were all happily engrossed, thus giving me an opportunity to say quiet good-byes and return to walking. They must have talked for some time, for it was at least twenty minutes before the Indians caught up to me and passed with tooting horn, followed shortly by the minister and his wife.

Less than a mile farther on a second vehicle pulled up, but this time it was a new Mercedes sport car driven by a strikingly beautiful woman. "Can I give you a lift?" she asked.

"Of course," I nearly said, momentarily forgetting my cross-America mission. Then, amazed, I got hold of myself and declined. Of all the different kinds of people I might have guessed would stop and offer a ride, a thirty-something Venus in a fancy sport car would be among the last. On the other hand, I'm an uncommonly good looking man when seen from my better side, even now at eighty years old. I must have looked even better that day in Teton Valley—might even have looked modest.

I began walking again. If people keep stopping, I thought, I'll hardly get anywhere this afternoon. Alas, I needn't have worried. The Indians and the thirty-something beauty would be the only people aside from Helen that I would talk to all day. As I walked south along route 26, more conventional tourists—couples, groups, and parents with children—passed in droves with car windows closed and air conditioners on, although it was not really warm. Rarely did anybody wave. It was not like the farm roads of the Midwest where almost everyone would acknowledge me walking along by myself, or would stop and talk with Helen waiting in the car. These valley tourists (I would meet a few but not along the road) were usually from urban areas and often on short vacations; they were living on holiday as they lived their daily lives—intense, focused, and relatively unaware of strangers.

Not that these urban folk were not, in some settings, friendly. Two different times, while we sat in ersatz teepees at touristy barbecues, friendly young professionals talked easily with Helen and me about the weather, the scenery, or about animal life in the valley. Nevertheless, along the road at developed turnouts, where you can park and take pictures, few people talked. Tourists would stand near each other to take in the view or read posted scene descriptions, but rarely did they acknowledge one another. Nor did they speak as they passed going to and from their cars.

On the whole, I found Jackson Hole a lonely place in spite of all the people. However, when I complained about it to Helen, she casually remarked, "Phil, you've got to remember that we've been immersed for months in this walk, which is a different way of life from anything these people have ever experienced." She went on: "It's different, too, from anything we've done before. We'd be the same as them if we were forty years younger and out touring with the kids."

I partly agreed. Nevertheless, there were times when I felt mildly resentful toward people when I was lonely and couldn't connect, or felt unwelcome even to try. Helen had less of a problem; she's more self-sufficient than I am—emotionally less dependent on others.

*   *   *   *

The hours dragged on as I gradually worked my way down the valley, cars whizzing past by the hundreds. At one point, to break the monotony, I walked parallel to the road along the edge of a field from where I would view the spectacular Tetons six miles to the west. Later, up ahead, I saw a number of people standing behind their cars and pointing into a field at something that was not yet visible from where I was. Coming closer, I saw that three buffalo were the attraction, and two were meandering toward the road. As they came nearer, a number of people got into their vehicles and a few drove away.

What to do? With nothing to get into, I crossed the road to be on the side away from the buffalo, and once there, I hurried along, keeping each successive car between me and them. Soon I was past. The animals, of course, paid no attention—no doubt they didn't notice me quick-stepping from car to car as apart from the cautious tourists. In fact, they gave no sign of noticing anything other than the grass they were browsing on.

By four o'clock, clouds were rolling up from the south and threatening our goal of reaching Moose by the end of the day. Moose was essentially a small group of eateries and souvenir shops across the Snake River from the road to Jackson; thus it was an inviting place to stop. But it was still six miles away, and I was reluctant to get wet. After all, there was no pressing need to get there by day's end; we were not scheduled to pick up the grandchildren for two more days. A couple hours of walking would get us there in the morning, and there would still be time to move Lurch to Yellowstone. The day after that we would drive down and meet the kids at Salt Lake City.

So we quit for the day, but it turned out that it didn't rain after all. It was the following morning, as we drove to walk's end, that the weather really went bad. The clouds of the previous afternoon had been the leading edge of a strong weather front, and as I got out of the car to begin walking, it looked as if it was about to pour. "Phil, you better stay right here," Helen advised, her tone implying the imminence of a deluge. "Within a mile you'll be soaked."

"It's not raining yet," I answered. "If I sat in the car every time it looked like rain, we'd still be in Pennsylvania."

"This is déjà vu all over again! You've been soaked before, and you're gonna be soaked again. You've done this three times already!"

But off I went, leaving her sitting there shaking her head and pretending to think I was out of my mind. She sat for a good two minutes before she finally started the car and drove past me, looking straight ahead and smiling in anticipation of what she was sure would happen next.

Only minutes later the rain arrived—not much at first but steadily more as the minutes passed. *Why'd Helen leave?* I got out my raincoat and began the usual struggle to put it on in a driving wind. By the time it was on and snapped, the weather was a mixture of rain and spray so thick you could hardly see across the road. Two cars stopped nearby, their drivers obviously unable to see and waiting for it to let up.

Meanwhile, Helen was creeping down the road, blinded by rain and afraid to turn around for fear of being T-boned in the milky downpour. Eventually she found a parking area where she pulled in and stopped. Unbeknownst to me she had planned ahead, and now she opened a plastic garbage bag in which she had packed me a change of clothes complete with underwear. There was even a light jacket.

It seemed like ages until the Toyota emerged from the downpour. Helen had put the garbage bag on the seat to keep it dry, and as I got in she smiled and said, "Glad to see you, Dearie. Think it'll rain?" Then she drove a mile north before pulling into Glacier View turnout where, with much struggling, I managed a complete change of clothes.

We sat in the car for what seemed like ages—until the sky began to lighten and the rain slackened off. "Time for you to get on with walking," Helen finally said with a laugh.

But dry now and deliciously warm, I was content to stay right there. Not only that, the slackening didn't look as if it would last, and anyway, off-and-on rain was predicted for the rest of the day. It was June 21, and not too soon, I decided, to quit walking until after we had the grandchildren.

Helen became impatient: "You gonna try it or not?"

"Nope, I've had enough. Let's just drive on down to Moose and get some pancakes at that teepee—you know, where we talked to the Yuppie tourists the other day."

"They weren't Yuppies. They were Dinks."

"If they were Dinks, then they had to be Yuppies."

"What do you mean?"

"Well, all Dinks are Yuppies, but not all Yuppies are Dinks."

"Don't getcha."

"A Dink couple are young urban professionals with a double income and no kids. A Yuppie couple are young urban professionals with a double income and maybe, maybe not, kids. So a couple can be Yuppies and at the same time Dinks—or Yuppies and not Dinks. But if they're Dinks, then they gotta be Yuppies too."

"They were still nice people; I liked all of them."

"Me too. Just because they were Dinks or Yuppies, doesn't mean they weren't nice. Helen, did you know that young couples with single incomes and no kids are Sinks?"

"Phil, it's too early for nonsense. Let's just get some pancakes."

And so we did. Then we drove back to Riverside Campground to spend the rest of the day house-cleaning Lurch and resting up for our coming "vacation" with the kids. By the time that was over, we would indeed need resting up again.

The following morning we set out for West Yellowstone and the nearby KOA where we had made reservations. KOA stands for Kampgrounds of America, and yes, they spell it with a *K*. The 140-mile drive through Grand Teton and Yellowstone Parks was beautiful, but traffic was nearly bumper-to-bumper in places and it moved at a snail's pace. It was early evening when we finally got there.

The first campsite to which we were assigned had water and electricity, but no provision for draining an RV's holding tanks. That deficiency meant that every other day we would have to disconnect the water and electricity, raise the leveling jacks, drive Lurch to the park's dump station, empty the tanks, drive back to the campsite, lower the jacks, and reconnect water and electricity. Not a convenient situation when you're hosting ten- and thirteen-year-old girls. Even so, the campground manager, a particularly helpful man, said that a campsite with full hookup would become available in just a few days. Great! When it did, we would be sure to move there.

Meanwhile, we settled in early for a good night's sleep, because the following morning we would be driving to Salt Lake City.

SECTION V

Teton Hole, Wyoming, to the Pacific Ocean

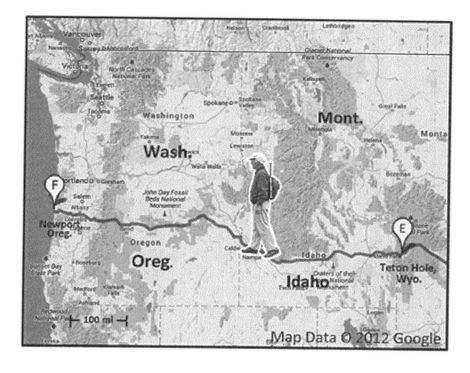

Fifth Walk Segment: July 6 Until September 4, 2000

HOSTING GRANDCHILDREN AT YELLOWSTONE PARK

As we drove south on June 23 to collect the grandchildren, we bemoaned our meeting them in Salt Lake City, Utah, rather than Jackson, Wyoming, which would have meant only one third as long a drive. However, Helen and I had been immersed in our walking world and hadn't participated in out-sourced, back-East planning that was now causing the too-long drive. "Out-sourced planning" would become a phrase with which we would kid Ed, the children's father, who had had his office staff make the travel arrangements. Still, as the long miles passed, we acquiesced to reality and began looking forward to visiting the city, since neither of us had been there before. There wouldn't be much time for touring, but we would make sure to drive down town and see the Mormon Temple lit up at night, as we had often seen it in pictures.

Brittany and Kate were coming first, and they would be arriving in the benevolent custody of their Uncle Jon, Ed's older brother. They would spend the following week with us; then the week after that we would have their sister and brother, Christina and Ian.

By four o'clock we had met the threesome at Salt Lake City Airport, and by five-thirty we were ensconced in a nearby motel, the adults weary from

Helen, Brit, Kate, and Uncle Jon

the long day's travel, the kids hungry and wanting to eat. Uncle Jon, a steak lover, somehow knew about a downtown restaurant reputed to serve a great New York strip, and by seven o'clock we had found the place, after working our way through rush-hour traffic. Although the food was excellent, it was clear, even before we finished eating, that we would do little sightseeing that night.

The kids, played out at last, were half dozing over their plates, and Helen was interested in nothing but ending the day.

Nevertheless, on our way back to the motel we did manage to drive by the temple, which was beautifully lit by dozens of floodlights. But that was all we saw of the city, because early the next morning we dropped Jon off at the airport and immediately started back to Yellowstone.

Our plan for the return trip was to avoid interstates by using an indirect route east into Wyoming, then ultimately north to Jackson. From there it would be up past the Teton Mountains to West Yellowstone and the campground.

Of course, using the indirect route made the otherwise six-hour drive last ten, but it turned out to be worth it. Early in the trip we stopped in Montpelier, Idaho, for lunch at a pizza café on Washington Avenue. Across the street and a half block down is a bank that is old and vacant now, but it was serving customers on Thursday, August 13, 1896, when Butch Cassidy and the Wild Bunch walked in. Butch made an "unauthorized withdrawal" of $16,500, after which the gang rode east out of town and up Montpelier Canyon, where they eventually disappeared into what is now Caribou National Forest. A single, remarkably brave deputy borrowed a bicycle and tried to catch the robbers, but he was easily outdistanced—probably lucky for him. As folklore and the movie have it, Cassidy was never caught but seems to have disappeared in Bolivia, along with his sidekick, the Sundance Kid.

For our grandchildren, the best part of the long drive was spectacular views of white-water rafters on the Snake River, where it flows through canyons south of Jackson. We also saw a moose that day, and once, just outside of a small town, the oldest or sickest deer in the west stepped onto the shoulder of the road. His coat was a mottled brownish gray rather than the glossy tan of a younger, healthier animal, and around his neck the skin hung like a sick old man's. Skeletal ribs were clearly visible, and he narrowed beyond the rib cage to a shrunken abdomen that gave on to bony, oversized hips. Somebody said he looked like a hide-covered skeleton.

Yet for all his apparent poor health, the old deer was growing a huge set of antlers. They were in velvet, very thick, and at least two feet across; already they showed eight points. One of the kids remarked that his horns were as thick as his legs, a remark that was actually understatement. Later, looking at a picture Helen had taken, it was clear that the bases of his antlers were actually *thicker* than his lower legs.

Kate, the Author, and Brit

But how, we asked each other, did this deer with such huge antlers live to grow old near town? The residents were bound to be aware of him, and many were no doubt hunters. In deer season, they would be looking for a buck with a mammoth rack and he would be easy to spot. In idle chitchat we tossed the question back and forth, but nobody had any suggestions beyond "He knows when hunting season is, and that's when he heads for the mountains," or "He's somebody's pet, and they pen him up during hunting season," or "He's become an institution around here, and even the hunters leave him alone." The latter seemed unlikely.

Eventually our conversation turned to what we would be doing for the next week. Helen and I had made reservations to take the kids flying, rafting, horseback riding—even to attend a rodeo. Beyond that, each day we would tour a different part of Yellowstone Park, making sure to see the buffalo and elk. Of course, we would always be on the lookout for bears, although we never would see any. Visiting Old Faithful was a given.

During the next six days, we managed to do everything we planned. The kids clearly enjoyed the sporting and adventuring, and when not that, the gift shops of West Yellowstone. God bless 'em, they loved those places. Almost before we knew it the week was ending, and on June 30 we took Brit and Kate back to Salt Lake City to meet their father, who would arrive with Christina and Ian, ages fourteen and eight. We would swap our two for his two and then drive back to Yellowstone for a second week of touring with grandchildren. We were beginning to feel like parents again!

We followed the same one-week agenda with Christina and Ian as we had with Brittany and Kate—minus a 10,500-foot climb up Mount Washburn in Yellowstone Park. Instead of that, we drove into downtown West Yellowstone to visit Grizzly and Wolf Land, a modern zoo where bears and wolves live in well-kept natural surroundings. We watched as one bear pushed and hauled till he downed a four-inch tree. He was lightning quick and agile as a cat.

Christina and Ian at Yellowstone

Notorious for wrecking trees, he had a total of twenty-three to his credit when we were there. The zookeepers—if one can justly call that natural place a zoo—try to maintain pleasant surroundings for the bears by constantly replanting the trees. The bears, in turn, apparently enjoy knocking them down.

Across from the bear corral was a fenced-in half acre that was home to a pack of wolves. During the days before we were there, a dissension had occurred in the pack and the target of the group's ire became the smallest and weakest female. She was a pitiful sight; she had been bullied and bitten, and was obviously being shunned by the rest of the wolves. But what was her sin? we wondered. A keeper told Helen that staff were watching the situation and hoping that "Hester"—as we found ourselves calling her—would eventually be reaccepted by the rest of the pack. Otherwise, they would have to remove her for her own safety.

Ian, at eight years old, wanted to know why Helen and I referred to the tragic little wolf as Hester, and our answer was that we didn't really know, that it just seemed to fit.

Ironically, Helen and I and the children would ourselves be involved in a wildlife tragedy that very afternoon.

We left Grizzly and Wolf Land in late morning, shopped for a few hours in West Yellowstone, and were on our way back to camp about three o'clock—surely not the time of day you would expect to see much wildlife. Nevertheless, a full-grown cow moose suddenly trotted out of the woods to our right, and on a perfect collision course with the car! Helen, who happened to be looking that way, saw her first and shouted, "Phil, watch out!" and reacting as quickly as possible, I swerved to the right in a desperate attempt to pass behind her.

Alas, it was not to be. With a sickening thud the bumper below the left headlight clipped her back legs so that her huge dark body hurtled past my side-view mirror, to land with a sickening whop upon the asphalt. Fighting the wheel, I plowed into tall grass along the road's edge, careened back onto the pavement, got straightened out, and finally pulled over and stopped. The entire tragedy, from impact to car-stop, had occurred in less than ten seconds.

Long moments passed as we sat in shocked disbelief. The children seemed hopeful—as if they thought the animal would somehow be all right—although Helen and I were sure her legs were broken. A number of cars had already stopped, and more were stopping. Presently, the shock lessening, Helen and I got out and walked slowly back to join a group of people who were gathering by the side of the road. By now, in an appalling caricature of walking, the moose had struggled across the road and several yards into the trees. And there she lay—head up, fully alert, and terribly afraid.

Somebody with a cell phone had called 911, so police and game wardens were on their way. I thanked the caller and was grateful for the sympathy of several people who had actually witnessed the collision. They assured me it had been unavoidable and not my fault—that I should not blame myself. They were right, of course, and I appreciated what they said, but it was far too soon for it to help. Turning to Helen, I muttered, "Heck of a thing to come here to show your grandchildren the animals and end up killing one right in front of their eyes." But overhearing me, a young woman quickly spoke up. "Mister," she said, "nobody could have missed that moose."

When the officials arrived, they soon determined that nothing could be done for the animal; she would have to be put down.

Helen and I hurried back to the car and waited with the children in breathless dread of the gunshot—which seemed forever in coming. Afterward, the officer in charge came over to talk. Like the people who had seen the accident, he assured me it was not my fault; however, he was amazed there was no damage at all to the Toyota. Often, in moose-car crashes people were hurt or even killed, and the cars were almost always badly damaged. We had been very lucky, he said.

But we didn't feel very lucky that dismal afternoon as we drove the remaining few miles to the campground. Everyone was subdued, indeed saddened, although the kids appeared to handle it better than Helen and I. Unless it involves a pet or someone especially close, perhaps death seems less real to children than to older people. An awareness of the *life-struggle,* shared by all creatures, may be the basis of an empathy for living things that grows through the years, at least in some people. It becomes easy to identify with an animal's sufferings, and easy to sorrow when one meets a tragic end.

We were approaching the campground when Helen suddenly said, "We've got to snap out of this and start doing things. It'll make us feel better—get our minds off that moose." The children and I agreed, and as soon as we arrived, Ian and I drained the black water while Christina helped Helen fix dinner. None of us could eat much, but at least we tried. Afterwards, to get ourselves into better spirits, the kids rode

Riding a Pedal Car

bikes around the campground while Helen and I browsed the gift shop. Still later, we rented a gaily painted pedal car, and that was a good idea because we briefly found ourselves laughing. Then sobriety settled in again as we returned to the motorhome, to our beds, and hopefully to sleep. But Good Lord, what a grim memory the day would always be.

*　　*　　*　　*

Our week with Christina and Ian was soon over, and on Saturday we headed back to Salt Lake City. On the way we stopped at a visitor center on the eastern edge of Hell's Half Acre Lava Field, which is a National Landmark bordering I-15 below Idaho Falls. In spite of *Half Acre* in the landmark's name, it is actually 160 square miles of barren, beautiful wasteland. Behind the visitor center are paved footpaths that one can follow through several acres of lava fields. It's a walk through a devil's landscape of sinkholes and jutting cones, all dormant now but once a field of fire. Over the eons since lava flowed, flora have gained footholds in this incredibly harsh environment. There are ferns, sparse grasses, bush-like junipers, and even a red-berried tree with leaves that look vaguely like a maple's. Ground squirrels live in burrows and cracks in the rocks, and so do rabbits. I took a picture of a rabbit who probably poses for tourists every day.

It would have been easy to spend hours at Hell's Half Acre, but the need to keep moving soon had us back on the road. By four o'clock we had arrived at our motel in Salt Lake City and had met Meg Cowdright, a friend of the children's father. She had flown out from the East to escort the children home.

After dinner that evening, we went for a ride through a quiet industrial park not far from the airport. No smokestack industries there, the place was home to businesses engaged in law, insurance, financial services—white-collar things. Buildings were low and beautifully designed, and many were set off by well-kept gardens and lawns.

There was almost no traffic that evening, and as we drove the park roads in relaxed good humors, I allowed no hint that I was pursuing a sly agenda of my own. Eventually, I pulled up by a stop sign on a street that was itself crossed by a divided avenue with a narrow grassy island. To my right and a hundred feet from the corner was just what I was looking for. A lawn sprinkler had been positioned to wet the grass, but it was actually throwing most of its water out over the roadway. I casually cranked up my window, distracted the gang with suggestions of ice cream, and then gunned the car around the corner and right through the spraying water. Perfect! Treated Meg and the kids to a brief unexpected shower. The next thing I knew I was being told in no uncertain terms that I had better deliver on the ice cream—or else.

Luckily, I found them ice-cream sandwiches at a nearby convenience store; then it was back to the park for one last drive-through since there was nothing else to do. Dusk was approaching; we were all bored, and to break the monotony, I told them about an Air Force major I had met years before at a tracking station in the Bahamas.

The major and I had just been to the station's airstrip about the unexpected arrival of a twin-engine private plane. He had told the pilot there would be a fifty-dollar fine for the unauthorized landing, which the middle-aged man expansively declared was perfectly reasonable—he'd be more than happy to pay up. The major later admitted that at that point he should have collected the fine or "put the tricky bastard in irons"; instead, he turned the matter over to his young-looking duty officer, the idea being to give the "youngster" some experience. "Lieutenant Fuzz," in a post event debriefing, reported that the dissembling "scumbag of a pilot" immediately went into "stall-around mode," artfully dodging all questions about where he had come from, where he was going to, or even what cargo he was carrying. Meanwhile, the major and I had left the scene and were in the staff car following the runway's service road back to the highway.

It developed that while the lieutenant was talking to the pilot, the copilot was refueling the plane, and when that worthy finished, he walked over and offered the lieutenant a hundred-dollar bill against ninety-some dollars' worth of aviation gas. The lieutenant didn't immediately take the bill, but rather went into the office to get change. Of course, by the time he came back out, the two flyboys had jumped into their plane and were taxiing to the end of the runway, from which, moments later, they headed back to the sky—no fine paid, no gas paid for. They roared right over the major and me, and just then the lieutenant's chagrined voice came over the radio to report he'd been taken. The smiling major ambiguously declared that it was the most entertaining thing to happen around there since the big hurricane. Underneath though, I could tell he was thoroughly embarrassed and fighting mad. He admitted he should never have left his duty officer to deal with those "sky hustlers" by himself.

Anyway, we were back on the highway when I asked the major what people based at that lonely outpost normally did for entertainment. "Well," he said, after a rueful pause, "there are three things you can do. First, you can get together with your wife and order something from a Sears Catalogue; second, if it's raining, you can go down to the catch basin and watch a whirlpool that forms near the take-away pipe; or third, you can ride out to the airport and hope a plane lands." He paused for a moment before adding, "Thrilling, don't you think?" We road along in silence after that, for what he had said was an implicit commentary on the numbing boredom of his assignment out there. I felt sorry for the man; that lonely tracking station was clearly the last posting of his expiring career.

I finished the major's story and we had been back in the industrial park for five or ten minutes when we came to a snake lying on the road. He was stretched out four feet long on the warm macadam near the law firm of Hiss, Coyle and Strike. Of course that was not the firm's real name, but it'll do for this story—through which slithers the snake as a serpentine element of truth.

Mr. Snake did not appear to be squashed, and he was not afraid as I eased the car past him only yards away. However, he wouldn't remain *unsquashed*, as Ian put it, if he didn't get off the road.

Although I had got the kids wet, I had somewhat redeemed myself with the ice cream; even so, for good measure I decided to do a conspicuous good deed. But first I would have to listen to a mini-lecture from Christina, who had begun to bug me about referring to the snake as *he*. "Don't you know, Paw, that *he* or *she* is not acceptable English in reference to animals. You should be using *it* when talking about Mr. Snake."

Pesky endearing fourteen-year-old.

I came right back: "I hear you my Dear, and I'll be more careful from now on. But you know, the word *it* sometimes seems too inexpressive, too wooden—depends of course on the context—right? After all, you wouldn't refer to Isabel, that little dog of yours, as an *it*. The name Isabel itself connotes femininity and sweetness; that's why you speak of her as *her*, and I bet if you were writing about her, you'd rather use *her* than *it*. Nevertheless, I'll mind my grammar and try to use pronouns correctly from now on—whether I'm talking to you or just writing."

Suddenly Ian spoke up: "Isabel *is* an *it*. Mommy had her fixed."

I was surprised he knew what fixed meant, but eight-year-olds know a lot more nowadays than they did when I was young. They fix more dogs too.

In any case I parked the car, walked back to the snake, and began making a legal-sounding case for why *it* should get off the road. But did *it/he* rush away? Not at all. He acted as if he had a duly registered quitclaim to the whole street. For a couple of minutes I postured, argued, and lunged in his direction. No luck. He stood his ground. Finally I told him I'd have him arrested for blocking the street; whereupon, he lazily crawled into the grass and with unerring instinct headed straight for the law office. He coiled up once or twice to hiss objections, but firmly overruled, he continued winding along until he reached some bushes beside the front steps. Somebody, it might have been Helen, said he probably fit right in around there, that maybe he was the firm's mascot.

It was getting late. I made a few more lawyer jokes—nothing mean-spirited, certainly nothing intended to be. In fact I told the kids that some of my best friends were lawyers, although I always made sure the homeowners insurance was paid up before I let them on the property.

Christina started in again: "Paw, now you're being two-faced. You should stop making jokes about lawyers. We have several in the family, you know, and they really are nice people. You're nice when you talk to them face to face, but out here you're making jokes behind their backs."

"I'm joking about lawyers in general, Honey, not our lawyers. Our lawyers are nice ... you know that. We love 'em and want them to go to heaven. That's why you and Ian need to pray hard for them every single night—in the morning too, and maybe three or four times a day wouldn't hurt either."

I started the car and we rode along quietly for two or three minutes. Then I heard Ian whisper, "I don't get it. Sometimes he doesn't make sense."

The next morning, Helen and I took Meg and the kids to the airport for their flight back East. We had spent two good weeks with the children, weeks that except for the moose tragedy would always be pleasant memories. It had been nice to share time with them, but now, more than anything else, we wanted to get back to West Yellowstone and on with the walk.

But we wouldn't leave the airport until our gang were airborne; we wouldn't risk their being stranded by the flight's being delayed and our premature departure. So we walked them down to the boarding area and, after hugs and best wishes, watched them pass through the door leading to the plane. Remaining passengers boarded and we waited for the plane to leave, waited, waited....

Eventually it drew back from the gate and trundled across the apron onto a taxiway to the end of the runway. And there it stopped again. Ten, fifteen, twenty minutes passed while it seemed to sit there forever. But finally it did begin to move, and then faster and faster until it was racing down the runway and into the air, and higher and higher and smaller and smaller and ... gone!

We hurried out to the car—mission complete—now we could begin the long drive to West Yellowstone with peace of mind. There would be no using secondary roads this time; we'd go straight up the interstate with no stops except for restrooms and gas.

Even so, the sun was setting when we arrived at the campground and parked beside good old Lurch.

WE RETURN TO CROSS-COUNTRY WALKING

Upon returning from Salt Lake City, Helen and I should have stayed put at West Yellowstone for a few days. We were far more tired than either of us realized. Predictably however, the urge to get back to walking trumped our need to rest, and the next morning we packed up and moved south to a tiny campground near Irwin, Idaho.

Actually the move was a bad one, for it put us seventy-five miles and two mountain passes southwest of where we had quit walking two weeks before. Thoughts of crossing and re-crossing the mountains especially discouraged us as we obsessed over their appearance on a new topographic map. We blamed our sloppy planning on over eagerness to get back to walking.

But if the Irwin campground was too far from walk's end, it was still a nice place to stay. The office people were pleasant, and Helen and I enjoyed the kids, of whom there were many. Most of the residents were semipermanent and poor, yet surprisingly friendly. They lived in old trailers not new motor homes, and their children, who seemed to be everywhere, wore clothes from yard sales not suburban malls. One ten-year-old wore threadbare khaki pants with a hole in one knee and a blue patch on the other. His left shirtsleeve was ripped to the armpit and his shoes did not match. Both were old sneakers, but they had started out as members of different pairs, one tan, the other blue and white. Between Helen and me he became affectionately known as "Mr. Mismatch."

Now Mismatch was an innovator of considerable imagination. There were few store-bought toys around the decrepit trailers; on the whole the kids either did without or made their own from whatever they could find. When I first met Mismatch, he was working on a modified metal wagon that was attached by a dog chain to an older plastic wagon with fat black wheels—the rumbling, loud kind that preschoolers like so well.

The metal wagon was especially interesting. A lidless Crock-Pot sat near the back of its bed, while up front was a small, wooden box the kid had made himself. Several chunks of nut coal lay on top of the box, and these were surrounded by strips of wooden lath held by nails that were only partly pounded down. Several stuck an inch above the laths they were intended to hold. Hanging from the wagon's low sides were dirty white squares of cloth about the size of handkerchiefs, and two were attached to the second wagon as well. The whole rig (wagon, box, and Crock-Pot) was painted shiny black except for a dull blue area. Mismatch had scrounged a spray can of gloss black but ran out before he finished. He'd solved that problem by brushing on flat blue.

"Why didn't you pound the nails down flush?" I asked the boy while pointing at the box.

"Hammer handle's busted," he replied. "Had to pound 'em in with just the head."

"Well, what are the pieces of cloth for? … those hanging on the wagons."

"Steam," was all the kid said, and before I could ask what that meant, he hurried off along a gravel path toward the back of the campground.

The following morning Helen and I drove over to walk's end, and after a slow start, I managed a dozen miles. But that was all it took to play me out, and Helen was not much better off. No doubt our weariness came from the flat-out pace we had kept during our weeks with the grandchildren. We had driven over 2500 miles to and from Salt Lake City, and every day at Yellowstone we had been busy doing one thing or another. In any case, I finished walking about one o'clock that first day back, and by two-thirty we were back at the campground ready to relax and watch a movie.

Trouble was that throughout the rest of the afternoon and even after dinner, Mismatch would periodically peddle his bike through camp, towing the wagons and yelling "Woooooo, Woooooo" at the top of his ten-year-old lungs. About seven o'clock I determined to find out what he was doing, or imagined he was, and before long I caught up with him in a small clearing behind the park. It was where camp residents left their non-garbage trash and where Mismatch scavenged raw materials for his innovations. "Lemme guess," I said, when I got him to hold up. "You're a steam train."

"Nope, a train engineer."

"Gotcha," I said. "So you're the engineer, your bike's the locomotive, and these wagons are just plain train cars.

"Nah, I'm the engineer, bike's the locomotive, and that metal wagon's a coal car. My grandpa's dad used to drive a train."

"What's that plastic wagon?" I pointedly asked, "the one that makes all the racket."

"That's the rest of the train; it's *supposed* to make noise." I could tell from his look that this was not the first time somebody had mentioned *racket*.

"Got a schedule to keep!" he suddenly announced, as he began to work his way around me. I had him sort of boxed in.

"Wait a minute, I said. "How many more runs will you make tonight?"

He paused. "Only one."

"What time?"

"Eight o'clock."

"From where to where?"

"From the office up front back here to the dump. One stop at Ned's, then down by your place."

"What's this wooden box and Crock Pot doing on your wagon?"

"This?" he said, pointing to the box.

"Yeah, that."

"That's my coal pile. Fireman shovels it into the engine. Gotta keep steam up."

"What about the Crock Pot?"

"Boiler water. Need lots and lots of water for steam. That's steam—I mean them rags hanging down from the wagons. Gotta go."

With that he went back to driving his train and I walked back to the motor home, where Helen and I, after a fitful discussion, decided that another day of lying around might help us get over the tiredness.

So we stayed put the next day; however, toward late afternoon I went outside and stopped the train again. "Yo, Pablo," I called (I'd found out his real name), "it was ten after eight when you came through last night; you were runnin' late."

"Overheated a bearing," he said, "slowed me down. Can't talk now—need t' finish me run."

Helen had come out and we watched the boy head for the back of the campground. He wore the same clothes as on the first day we saw him, same torn shirt, same patched pants. But he was a train engineer, by gosh, a man with a mission, and he'd make sure the train got through on time.

Twenty minutes later he came over to the motor home—without the train, thank God. "Gracias," he said, when Helen offered him a cookie. While he munched, I gently quizzed him and was not surprised to learn that his dad was a railroad worker. Inspiration for the train came from his father's telling him about his own grandfather (the boy's great-grandfather), who had been an engineer on a Mexican railroad.

*   *   *   *

It was after Mismatch left that Helen and I really slid into the dumps. Before our weeks at Yellowstone, getting up, fixing breakfast, packing the knapsack, loading the car—all were chores we had accomplished with an efficiency developed by months of repetition. Now we were overtired and everything required conscious thought; to get anything right seemed hard, and the simplest routines were a drag to our weary minds and bodies. I, especially, bemoaned those upcoming mountain passes that somehow loomed like Everests.

Eventually, as the evening wore on we bottomed out, and little by little our agonizing gave way to the beginnings of resolve. Were we dissatisfied with where we were camped? Yes! We had come much too far south. Well then, we would do something about it!

Driving to walk's end two days before, we had passed Wayside Campground, which lies outside of Driggs near the western foot of Teton Pass. We agreed that had we camped there to begin with, the drive from there to walk's end would have been much shorter, and so would drives in the days just ahead. Okay! We would move there tomorrow morning; then we would get on with the walk—patiently, methodically, one day at a time.

Towards midnight we finally relaxed enough to fall into fitful sleeps.

Breaking camp the next morning went reasonably well, and we had crossed the mountains and arrived in Driggs by eight-thirty. Feeling somewhat better by then, thanks to our new resolve and a half-night's sleep, we set about getting several things done that we had put off in our haste to leave Yellowstone. Lurch needed minor repairs: the stove's spark-lighter was broken, and the convertible bed was sagging—thanks to being jumped upon by a beloved ten-year-old granddaughter. Beyond that, I needed a haircut and Helen wanted to get her hair washed and set. Also, we would have to find someplace to buy Propane.

Things went so well that we had everything done by noon, and, after checking into the campground and eating lunch, we drove over Teton Pass to Teton Village, where we had quit walking two days before. From there I started south on Moose Road, toward its junction with Wyoming 22 near Wilson. Traffic was light, and even better, I met someone to talk to—a bicyclist who had already met Helen where she was waiting up ahead.

Bill Sevard was a cameraman for WBGR, a TV station in Oakland, California. He had arrived with his family in Teton Village the night before and they had spent the morning touring by car. Getting their fill of "that kind of togetherness," as he laughingly put it, the family had "amicably parted," his wife and daughters going souvenir hunting, Bill renting a bicycle. He had peddled south at first, but even the few cars he met in that direction were too many for his mood, so now he was heading north toward Moose. I told him I had already walked the partially paved road and that it might be too hard on his bike. He just laughed again and said he would carry the "rented junker" if he had to.

I talked with Sevard for ten or fifteen minutes, and he was intrigued by our walk, as people almost always were. And as people frequently did, he eventually maneuvered the conversation to where he could gracefully ask my age. Fifty-eight I told him, giving myself ten years. He stared for a moment before saying, "No way, you're older than that!" So I told him the truth, but that brought the flattering response, "Negatory, you're younger than that!"

When we had finished the age game, we talked weather, wildlife, and politics (the election was only months away), until the conversation began to slow. Then we took each other's leave and he continued on toward Moose.

It had been refreshing to talk with Sevard, and although I didn't know it then, it would be a long time before I would have another friendly, along-the-way chat. In a few hours I would turn west onto Wyoming 22, and for several days walking would again be on relatively main roads. Cars would be buttoned up and traffic would be fast to and from the Jackson Hole tourist areas. A few times people would pull over up ahead to change drivers, to take a kid behind a bush, or maybe just to rummage the trunk or back seat—for a snack, for a toy, for who knows what. Invariably, however, they would manage to be back in their cars and pulling away by the time I got there.

Just north of Wyoming 22, I began to pass houses, and once I paused in fascination before a homestead that simultaneously projected both warm welcome and icy rebuff. The house itself sat well back from the road, but I could see it down the driveway through an overgrowth of trees. To the right was a charming outbuilding, apparently a child's stand-up playhouse, while to the left was a picket fence and what looked like a lawn ornament in the form of a running goose. Above the front door, a pennant said WELCOME, and from the front of the garage a two-foot smiley face beamed out on the world. There seemed a warmth about the house and grounds, a certain friendliness. But barring access to this otherwise inviting place was a metal-art humanoid on guard beside a post only yards from where I stood.

I had already seen excellent metal sculptures, especially in Mason City, Nebraska, where the artist had displayed those fascinating pieces around his house and lawns. The figure I stared at now was just as creatively conceived, but it appeared hostile and out of place in front of the tranquil grounds beyond. Its upper and lower leg bones were narrow metal cylinders connected by universal joints that formed knobby knees. The torso was an ellipse of scrap metal with holes like an old tractor seat, while its arms were pipes that ended not with hands, but with spindly fingers clutching a five-foot gun.

The figure's head sprouted white-metal spikes, presumably hair—or had this monster's creator simply spiked its head to torture it, to drive it out of its mind, to make it appear terrible to the casual passerby? Just as intimidating was its long, narrow face, which had widely separated eyes and a spring-like nose sloping to flaring nostrils and a frowning mouth. It was the head and face, more than the gun that conveyed an impression of implacable malevolence. Was this wretched thing the artist's substitute for a NO TRESPASSING sign? To me, at least, it was far more repelling.

There was another sculpture on the south side of the same driveway. Just as striking and only a shade less bleak, it was a three-foot bird standing atop a reinforced mailbox post. Heavy bodied and with drooping tail and outstretched wings, it was bending foreword and holding a writhing snake in its parrot-like beak. The bird was made from strips of sheet metal welded with great skill and painted bronze. The workmanship in this piece was even better than that in the monster, but why couldn't the artist have created something with a more uplifting even humorous tone?

Put off by the macabre art work, I hurried on and before long turned right onto Wyoming 22. A mile west would be Wilson, and Helen would be waiting on the far edge of town. It would be good to finish the day. The afternoon had become brutally hot.

That evening, guests at the campground moaned and groaned about a power shortage. Probably ninety percent of them kept trying to run their air conditioners, and consequently the campground voltage was so low you couldn't even use a microwave. I got around the problem by using the propane stove to heat TV dinners, which Helen happily judged edible but not the "culinary delights" they would have been if "nuked." "They'd come in about D-minus on your *very own* dinner-grading scale," she declared, with special emphasis on *very own*.

Frustrated by the power shortage, a fellow with a forty-foot RV moved from the campsite next to ours to the back of the park, where the manager had told him the voltage would be higher. As far as we were concerned, the trouble was that nobody was willing to conserve power by just opening windows and using fans. The air conditioners were not working anyway, and some people, who had larger motor homes, were even trying to run two. They wheezed and rattled on the too-low voltage. One man complained loudly about paying "too damned much" for a campsite to begin with, and then not having enough "juice to keep cool with."

The situation became even more tense as the evening wore on, especially when a couple camped near us set up a portable outdoor dog pen. Soon two constantly yapping mini-mutts provided "music" for the whole campground, until there was some loud shouting about "#@!%!# barkin' dogs."

Eventually darkness fell, and the campground quieted as tempers cooled, probably thanks to the cooling air.

ENTERING IDAHO

The morning after the #@!%!# dogs, we left Wilson and I began a steep climb over the southern end of the Teton Mountains. It's a 2200-foot rise along curvy Wyoming 22 from Wilson to the high point of the pass, and although there are no pull-offs big enough for cars, there are smaller places where a walker can rest and enjoy spectacular views. Pausing at one, I looked eastward toward a distant, sloping terrain through which ran a road—a convolved section of the one I was walking—and below that was the switchback of an older, narrower road that was once the only way across the mountains. To my left and right, the view was framed by old evergreens, and far off lay the Snake River, and beyond, the rumpled peaks of the Gros Ventre Mountains. A foreground of many-colored flowers completed a breathtaking panorama.

Minutes passed as I postponed and re-postponed the uphill trudge. It was early though, only eight-thirty—too early for a nap. *Get up, Beam! Sitting here in the flowers will never get you over this mountain.* And presently I did get up and began walking again, aches and pains and all.

At the top of the pass there was an especially broad turnout where tourists were standing about and taking pictures of the view. Helen was waiting, and after hugs we drank coffee and declared it a celebration for crossing the Rockies, or at least for reaching the summit of Teton Pass. Then she headed down toward Victor with a list of things to do.

I went back to walking.

At first the long downgrade was very steep, in places as much as ten percent, but eventually the grade lessened and the road broke out of dense tree cover and onto the farmlands of Teton Basin. The basin bounds the Teton Mountains on the west just as Teton Hole does on the east, and it intrigued me that as spectacular as the famous mountains are, they extend only thirty miles north to south and a dozen miles east to west.

Soon after entering the farmlands, I came to a broad fallow field sloping off to a creek, and since my feet were hot and sweaty, I was glad for a chance to soak them. I had just crossed the guard fence when I noticed a narrow dirt road running along the creek's bank and winding in and out among some bordering trees. Three tourists were on the road, a man and two women, and they were fifty or so feet from a parked minivan. He was busy taking pictures, so the women were first to notice me coming toward them down the field.

I smiled and threw a casual wave—who knows, maybe I'd get some conversation. I could use some. But getting uneasy returned glances instead of tentative smiles, I abruptly angled away so as to come no closer to them than thirty or forty yards.

Even so, that would be too close for them. It seemed as if my mere changing direction startled the women, for in twittering alarm they alerted their companion, who fixed me with an appraising stare. Obviously not liking what he saw, that worthy gestured the women to hurry to the van. He, of course, stood fast—as if defending their withdrawal—although I was still fifty yards away. As soon as the women were safely inside, "Brave Heart" stalked to the van, got in, and quickly backed away along the dusty road. He must have backed two hundred feet before turning around and driving away.

What's wrong with that clown? I wondered. *He didn't have to leave backwards; he could have turned around right where he was. It's flat and dry there.*

Despite the rebuff the detour down to the creek soon seemed worth it—certainly as far as my feet were concerned. I sat on a rock as the cool water did its reviving magic, and before long I began to think about where we were in our cross-country walk and how far we still had to go.

Within the hour I would cross into Idaho. There would be plenty of desert walking in that state; then it would be on to mountainous Oregon with its Cascade and Costal ranges. But there would come a day when all that walking would be behind us and we would look out over the vast Pacific. We would make it—I was suddenly sure—where even of late I would often refuse to acknowledge the likelihood. Better just to keep walking, I would tell myself. Do that and you'll get there automatically someday.

So there I sat with my feet in the water, but well aware that that vague someday was just around the corner about eight weeks away. For two years the great walk had been the focus of our lives, but it wouldn't be much longer. And after that, what could we possibly do that would seem anywhere near as interesting?

My thoughts took a sudden downturn: Well, there'd better be something to replace this walk, something to give a new sense of *becoming*. Either that or the rest of these fool's-gold retirement years are going to be nothing but lead.

I fought back: But wait! There'll always be volunteer work, cruising holidays, birthday celebrations, things like that to fill your time, yours and Helen's.

Still no recovery: And long boring days with Helen having to listen to me relive the past. Maybe we'll get lucky, Helen and I … check out with bangs instead of whimpers!

That thought jolted me into a rally: *Enough of this poison, Beam. Get up, put on your shoes, and get walking. Now! You're due in Victor in a couple of hours. Miss that rendezvous and you'll have more than gutless tourists to be bothered about.*

Helen was waiting at the corner of Main and Center Streets, and just up the block she had found an emporium where she thought the ice cream would be "just delicious." She was right, and several dozen tourists thought so too. I had a root beer float and she had a sundae (world famous the Emporium claimed). President Reagan had been there years before, and he certainly liked whatever he had. From a picture on the wall, he beamed his famous smile out over the crowd.

I nursed and nursed the float, but there came a moment when Helen refused to let me sit there any longer.

"Why are you buggin' me?" I demanded. "Thought you'd like to stay here all afternoon and eat 'just delicious' ice cream."

"Sure would, Honey. Once I get you moving, I'm coming right back here."

After that she wouldn't even argue—just maintained low-level pressure till she pestered me back to the road.

Only a mile or two of walking brought me to a deep roadside ditch in which lay the body of a half-grown moose—a sight I didn't need, given my recent moodiness. She had been hit by a car, probably the night before, and skid marks, broken glass, and fragments of car trim gave evidence of the tragedy. I hoped no people had been hurt, that they had been as lucky as we had been when I hit the cow moose near Yellowstone. Until then, I would have maintained that anybody who couldn't miss a full-grown moose in broad daylight shouldn't be allowed on the road. Since then, however, I had changed my mind. It's easy to adjust your opinion when the moose hit (or ox gored) is in fact your very own!

Of course Helen had not gone back to the Emporium; rather she had driven ahead, and a few hours later, at the end of the day, I met her near a wide driveway leading to a handsome log building. An attractive yellow sign labeled the place a "Wildlife Art Gallery."

"Another place to visit someday," I said to Helen. She made a face, however, and said it was probably nothing but a taxidermy studio.

*　　*　　*　　*

The next morning took me over the Big Hole Mountains, the second of those not-so-high passes we had dreaded the week before. Actually, it was borderline boring—too many cars and nobody to talk to—although the scenery, as usual, was beautiful. About two o'clock I came down onto flatlands at the junction of Idaho 31 and U.S. 33, only four miles from where we had camped before moving to Driggs. We had reached Swan Valley, which leads west onto the vast Snake River Plain, and it would be relatively flat walking for the next 350 miles, all the way to Boise, Idaho.

But before going farther, Helen and I would take another breather. We were almost recovered from our two weeks with the grandchildren, so a few days of no walking, leisurely touring, eating out, and early-to-beds should bring us back to *full rest,* as we liked to put it. Also, we would stay no longer at Wayside Campground with its low voltage and barking dogs. Using her RV catalog, Helen located Sunrise Campground in Idaho Falls, and that would be our next home on the road.

Upon arriving at Sunrise, we were again glad we had a small motor home, for we were assigned to a shady campsite that was too small for a big rig to fit into. Typically, big motor homes are assigned to long, pull-through campsites—campsites that lie between specially constructed parallel entry and exit roads. To park a behemoth, the driver pulls forward from the entry road into the campsite, and upon breaking camp, he or she continues forward out of the campsite and onto the exit road. No backing or maneuvering required! Nevertheless, as convenient as such sites are, they frequently have no shade. This is because their construction requires considerable site preparation, including road building, and in the process trees are cleared, if the site was not a field and had trees to begin with. In any case, big, luxurious motor homes often end up parked in the sunniest, hottest, least private locations; while their small, inexpensive counterparts get the shadiest, coolest, most secluded places among the trees.

How's that for a twist?

ONE WOMAN'S VIEWS ON OVEREATING

On our first evening in Idaho Falls, Helen and I went to a downtown restaurant and overheard a remarkable conversation about dieting. Arriving early, we were shortly joined by three or four other couples whom the hostess seated at tables scattered around a good-sized dining room. Minutes later she seated still another couple, but this time at a table next to us. Service was slow and it wasn't long before our table neighbors got into an argument that was heard all over the room.

"You weigh too much because you eat too much."

It was the woman who said it, and that was just for starters. Her companion didn't look overweight to me. I would have guessed he was five-eleven and weighed maybe 200 pounds.

"I don't eat too much," he came right back. "I eat less than you; I just move once in a while. By God, I hustle around all day!" He looked like a construction worker or maybe a rancher—ruddy complexion, rough hands.

Although they had been the last people seated, a waitress suddenly appeared from nowhere to take their orders; then she headed straight for the bar. She was soon back, delivered drinks to the glowering pair, and only then did she take one or two orders from the other tables. The arguers quieted briefly, but they were soon at it again.

"Honey, if you eat a balanced diet and keep putting on weight, then you're eating too much."

"The diet I'm on is supposed to let you eat all you want ... without gaining weight!"

"If you're gaining weight, then you're eating too much."

He mumbled something else after which there was another welcome lull. Trouble was, a couple minutes later she said, "Look Jack, suppose you keep living just as you're living now—same job, same hunting, same endless TV, same doin' nothing around the house. Now, say the only thing you do different is eat ten percent less ... same food, only ten percent less. If you live like that for three months, what do you think will happen?"

"I'll gain weight," he replied, sullen now.

"Okay. Now suppose for another three months you keep things the same—same inactivity regimen, same everything except that you eat another ten percent less. What then?"

"I'll still gain weight." Quiet but definitely ominous.

For God's sake lady, I thought to myself, why don't you quit while we're all still ahead?

"Okay. Now suppose for—"

"I hear you, goddamn it, and I know where you're headed. Gimmie a break." They heard that all over the dining room.

"Well, you started this, Jack!"

"No he didn't," I mouthed to Helen. "She did."

Somebody at another table glanced up as Helen leaned toward me and whispered that the waitress had better hurry up and get then fed or else call the cops.

The battlers quieted for a little while; then—wouldn't you know?—she started in again. "Jack, some people can eat all they want, whenever they want to. They can live active lives, sedentary lives ... any kind of lives and never gain an ounce of fat. Obviously, for them it doesn't matter how many calories go in. Their bodies metabolize what's needed to maintain their weight and support the way they live, and the rest goes out their you-know-whats."

A woman three tables away yucked softly in disgust. Nobody else had been served yet, not even a drink.

Jack chimed in, and surprisingly, he seemed to further her point. "People like that do all right nowadays since there's plenty of food. They'd been goners, though, way back when there was famines all the time."

"That's right," she said. "There the winners would have been fat people who could get even fatter during fat times. During less fat times, those fat people would live off their fat while less fat people would starve. Those surviving fatties would be the ones who'd reproduce, and they'd no doubt have fat babies too." The woman managed to work *fat* or *fatties* into every phrase she spoke, and his neck turned as red as a lobster.

Back he came: "Now you're going to tell me that people's tendencies to put on too much weight are because of some bullshit evolution thing. I can hear it already: 'Jack, in earlier times natural selection culled out the skinny types—I mean the ones nowadays considered fortunate for their tendency to stay thin. But Jack, you're just naturally fat. That's why you've got to eat less. You'd be okay in a famine.'"

"Yep," she said.

"Yep what? So what's your advice, Ms. Know-it-all? Tell me how to eat." Sarcastic now and loud.

"Less."

He muttered something that ended with "never had a weight problem in your whole damned life."

Would they never stop?

But she had still more: "I read somewhere that since the nineteen-forties there have been over twenty-five thousand diets published in the United States alone—every one of 'em somebody's bright idea for turnin' a fast buck. Fortunes have been made, but people are still fat because they eat too much."

"Ah, shut up."

"You know those pictures you still see of people coming out of concentration camps? Ever see any fat types among *them?*"

"Hell, they're usually half starved: fat bellies and all that. They don't count!"

"They darned sure do count! They're proof that if you get a lot less to eat, you don't get fat; in fact, you turn into an emaciated stick—like a super model."

That came out so loud that everybody in the place looked over. Helen and I were about to get up and leave when out rushed the waitress with the battlers' dinners. A number of people already in the restaurant when they walked in were still waiting for their drinks. Still, nobody complained; it was smart management to get the "Lockhorns" fed as quickly as possible, because they quieted to occasional mutterings once they began eating. Helen whispered that that was proof of the calming effects of food on hunger-shortened tempers, but I said they quieted only because they stuffed their mouths and could only mumble—her at him, in particular.

We had been served and were about half way through eating when the Lockhorns finished and immediately went back to bickering. Politics was the subject this time, and it seemed inevitable that she would be Republican and he a Democrat. Within minutes they were getting noisy again, and presto, another waitress appeared with their deserts—which were mountainous.

Helen and I had heard enough, and when the waitress turned to take our desert orders, we thanked her kindly but asked her to quickly bring the check. She smiled and whispered, "Wish I could go with you."

*   *   *   *

The three days we spent at Sunrise was a time to renew contacts with family, do some sightseeing, and meet—or at least observe—a few more interesting people. Helen used a calling card to touch base with family; then we took a short trip around town. My one picture from that excursion was of the local Mormon Temple. Snow white, like the one in Salt Lake City, it rises above a line of trees near a waterfall on the Snake River. The building, broad at ground level, consists of an impressive series of narrowing layers leading to a spire which supports a statue of the angel Gabriel. As usual, I afterward wished I had taken more pictures.

At the campground, we, along with several neighbors, could not help noticing a couple who traveled with surely the biggest load of stuff-and-a-dog that was ever crammed into a Volkswagen camper. When they were actually driving, there must have been just exactly enough room for them, the dog, and their cargo, but certainly none to spare. If they wanted anything, they obviously had to park and dig for it, and when at the campground, they seemed to spend half their daylight hours doing either of two things: standing and talking to some pleasant passerby (they were pleasant people themselves), or else arranging and rearranging the infinitude of things they carted with them.

And what all did they have? Well, there were gallon jugs of water, two different camp stoves, one electric oven, one foam cooler, one pair of binoculars, and three cowboy hats. Why three? Who knows. Why any? In addition, there was a coffee pot, Thermos bottle, laundry bag, and a small set of storage drawers in a flimsy plastic frame—something you would expect to find taking up room on a bathroom counter.

Several piles of clothes, mostly blue, were stacked on top the storage drawers, and everywhere were towels, more towels, and just as many washcloths. Four boxes of dog bones and a dozen jars of people-food mixed at random with seven rubber children's toys—Helen counted them. It was some time before we realized that the toys belonged to the dog, who was usually asleep under the table when she wasn't barking at somebody.

Blue and white seemed to be the couple's favorite colors; their van was blue and so were the storage drawers, while most of the towels were white. The dog's toys provided bright contrasts in yellow, red, and green. A big pail sometimes sat beside the couple's picnic table, and several times Helen speculated about what that might be for. When it was not under the table, it could be seen on the floor of the van, in front of the passenger seat if the door was open—which it usually was.

In the evenings, neighboring campers discreetly enjoyed watching the Volkswagen couple transfer everything out of their camper and onto the picnic table in order to make room to go to bed. One amused woman suggested it would be easier if they left the stuff inside and slept on the table themselves.

Once, as I was walking past, the man smiled my way and volunteered, "Our problem is we forgot and left too much at home."

I couldn't resist asking what the pail was for. "Oh, no reason in particular," he said with a sheepish grin. "Hilda just thought it made sense to always have a pail."

I still think it was an on-the-road chamber pot.

*   *   *   *

Another person whom we met at Sunrise was more obnoxious than interesting. He was camped directly across the service road from us, and one evening he moseyed over as Helen and I sat outside reading. We thought we might be in for some pleasant visiting, but the man no sooner arrived than he launched into a querulous monologue about economics. *Induced want*, he loudly proclaimed, was the prime mover of the American economic system. Pervasive advertising, particularly on television and coupled with easy though expensive credit, kept people buying and constantly in debt. Keeping people in hock up to their ears, he said, was the intention of that powerful, small percentage of people who own or control most of the country's wealth. That way *even children,* as well as men and women, strive like "busy little beavers," creating more and more wealth, most of which—you guessed it— ends up controlled or consumed by the top two or three percent of the population.

We sat and listened, and soon hoped he'd go away. But suddenly he glared at me and growled, "That's the way it's s'posed to be, right?"

I grunted something about the weather, but he wouldn't be deflected from economics. This time it was about how everything was being made overseas nowadays and how wonderful that was. "Hell, this shirt I'm wearing only cost ten bucks. Made in Sri Lanka where they work for nothin'. Outsourcing pal! Can't beat it."

Helen nudged me to keep quiet, but I eventually gave in and engaged. I asked him what would happen if too many skilled jobs moved to other countries where labor was cheaper. Wouldn't the average American, earning less, gradually become less able to pay for consumer goods in general? In fact, with the approaching global economy, would not developed nations see slight (hopefully only), temporary (hopefully only) declines in their standards of living until the standards of poorer countries came abreast? After that, I thought we could hope for the world standard to move upward again, if only slowly and spottily.

He ignored those comments, and said that a steady influx of immigrants would take care of almost all the country's service jobs.

We hadn't been talking about immigrants and service jobs!

"Service jobs," I said, "aren't the issue. It's skilled jobs: high-tech tool design and hands-on manufacturing. That's where outsourcing's going to cause real trouble."

Suddenly, out of the blue, he said, "You're a damned arguer, probably a Northeast Liberal."

I was stunned. What in the world, I thought, could be considered political, let alone Liberal, about concern for outsourcing? By now, of course, he was getting under my skin. He had come over to our campsite, started the conversation, and done most of the talking. Helen had said nothing and I'd said little. Worse yet, he was getting louder and beginning to bend toward me—closing the distance between me and him from normal conversational separation to an in-your-face ten inches. I backed up a foot along the picnic table bench.

Two campsites over, a couple of dogs lunged at each other and the racket briefly drew his attention. He stood up, and while he gawked I whispered to Helen, "Stand by for the name-calling. He thinks he's some two-bit news-talk type."

But the man did have me confused. When he first began talking, I thought he was leading into a complaint about some Americans being better off than others—he didn't appear to be wealthy; in fact his motor home was small and shabby, and parked beside it was a five-year-old Saturn.

I began pumping our uninvited guest, and it was soon clear that he was actually a little cheerleader for those he considered the movers and shakers of the world. He had been an assembly line worker for most of his career, but near the end he advanced a notch to become some sort of straw boss. Not surprisingly, he never moved higher, but his new status went straight to his head. To him, fellow workers who remained "on the line" stayed there because they were borderline lazy, not conscientious, or else a bit stupid—especially if they were black. Becoming a mere straw boss was all he needed to convince himself that he was above the herd, and he quickly identified with management all the way to the top. It became "we" and "us" in relation to company management; rank and file workers were clearly "them." Unions became refuges for weaklings or would-be slackers, not for company-men like him.

Of course he had been a union worker himself, although he retained no respect for unions per se. A lucky little opportunist, he had ridden the swell of four decades of cold-war prosperity, and retired on a pension won for him by the organized labor he now badmouthed. Everything about the man seemed small. Helen refers to the type—and we have known a few—as traitors to their working-class heritage.

To our relief, as abruptly as he had come, the "Tycoon" went back to his own camper, and it wasn't long before we began to hear more of his rantings, but mixed now with angry rejoinders from a woman. It waxed hot and heavy, although we couldn't hear what they were saying until he suddenly yelled, "Close this f'ing place up; the air conditioner's on." There was the thud of a slamming window, and after that—finally—welcome quiet.

It was a hot night, and soon after the window slammed, the couple next door came out to chat. Sarah and Howard Martin had heard our noisy, unwelcome guest, and had stayed inside until he went home. Howard, whom I had met and joked with before, was now happy to inform me that he would be my second should I get into a duel with the man.

"Like where were you when I needed you?" I demanded. Then, "I know; you were keepin' low—afraid to come out till he went away."

"You got that right," he said with a laugh.

We spent a relaxing hour with our pleasant neighbors, which was just the kind of socializing we had been hoping for when the tycoon came along. The Martins were happy, outgoing people who had been married forty-five years and clearly enjoyed each other's company.

Later, after we had gone to bed, Helen sleepily romanticized: "They're still in love … isn't that sweet?" Then, incongruously, "I pity his poor wife."

"You mean Howard's?"

"You know who I mean," she mumbled, on her way to sleep.

PANTHERA-LEOS DUAL AND QUAD

We were determined to make Monday, July 17, another rest day. The campground held a pancake breakfast which we made sure to attend, and after relaxing and eating we went grocery shopping. The rest of the day we lay around except for cooking a roast beef dinner. Helen declared that we were getting lazy and would have to hit it hard tomorrow, but the next day we still did not go out to walk's end. At least I printed maps of the roads ahead—in case we ever got going again—and I heard an interesting story from a fellow camper.

Jacob and Ida Bonald were from Ottawa, and they had a son who had been with Canadian peacekeeping forces under UN command in Slovenia in 1991. That was after Slovenian irregulars had clashed with federal militia as Slovenia seceded from Yugoslavia.

As Jacob told it, his son's unit was billeted in a house that was so badly run down the steps to the second floor were collapsing. Resourceful young men, the troops immediately set out to make repairs. They petitioned their regiment, whose office was at a nearby UN command center, to buy the necessary materials. But alas, Slovenians worked at the command center, and when they got wind of the project, they informed a local union. The union, in turn, raised such a howl about lost work that the troops were told to leave the steps alone. According to Jacob, they had to sit around and watch six union men take a whole day to do a two-man, three-hour job.

The old Canadian became steadily more agitated as he told the story. Part of the time he laughed, but on the whole he kept getting louder, and before long he was word whipping the "friggin' unions" with all the gusto of the straw-boss tycoon a couple of nights before. Eventually he calmed down, but then he suddenly said, "Well, maybe they had a right to be mad; the troops was only there to save their asses from the Serbs!"

"Huh?" I replied, after an involuntary double take. "Am I missing something?"

"No, you heard me right," he said, and from there he began talking about the nearby Mormon Temple that I had taken a picture of, but suddenly, for him, the temple had moved to Bountiful, British Columbia, where he said people were practicing polygamy—had been for years.

Realizing the old man was "age compromised," I went back into the motor home and told Helen I had just heard several things that made no sense at all: Slovenians?—right to be mad while Canadians were protecting them from the Serbs? Mormon Temples?—suddenly moving from Idaho Falls to British Columbia? I must have been hearing things, I said.

To which Helen replied: "Philip Dear, sometimes I think *you're* age compromised when I try to talk to you—I mean when you're thinking about something else and pretend you can't hear."

*   *   *   *

By Wednesday we had had enough rest and were ready to get back to serious walking. Helen drove me to the intersection of Idaho 31 and U.S. 33, the current walk's end, and after overlapping the old track by twenty yards, I began walking west. Healthy fields of corn, potatoes, and wheat bordered the road, and there were infrequent fields of timothy or alfalfa grown for fodder. The neat rows and different colors were attractive, but I was tiring of the scenery when I rendezvoused with Helen at a tourist pavilion near the Snake River. It was a scenic place, and as we looked down toward the water, Helen spotted a pair of bald eagles in the uppermost branches of an ancient spruce. One was fully grown; the other was a slightly smaller juvenile, still lacking the distinctive white head and tail feathers of an adult. These were the first eagles we had seen since the chick in the oversized nest near Moran Junction the month before.

Moments later a trucker pulled in, and we were quick to call his attention to the birds. To him, however, they were a familiar sight, one he had seen many times before. He told us there were many more eagles at American Falls Reservoir, fifty miles to the south. "You really ought to go down there and see 'em," he said. A pleasant fellow, he would have preferred to stay and talk with us rather than go back to driving the truck. But we all had our things to do, and before long he drove away while Helen departed for Idaho Falls to buy groceries and film for her camera. She was going window-shopping too, although she wouldn't admit it.

An hour passed—almost another; then presently I was entering a small town, and up ahead was a hitchhiker whom I could see was an Indian.

The fellow appeared to be skeptical about getting a ride, for he sat slouched on an odd-looking box most of the time, and only moved when the occasional vehicle came along. Then he would drag himself up and stick out his thumb, only to drop his arm and sit back down when the car or truck or whatever invariably passed him up. This guy looks like a human wreck, I thought. No wonder nobody stops.

He gave no sign of noticing me as I approached, but when I paused directly in front of him and said hello, he quickly answered with, "Nice day, y' think?"

He was not old, but he was gaunt and tired looking, and it was actually a portable shoeshine stool he was sitting on. Nearby lay a shabby suitcase, partly sprung at one end but held together near the middle by rope and a pair of old belts. In spite of the heat he wore an old sport jacket, which was tattered and dirty and far too big. Poking above its right side pocket was the top of a flask. "Gonna be warm," I said. "Been sitting here long?" They were the first words that came to mind.

"About an hour. I'm headin' for Driggs … if I ever get a ride…. Been watching you for the last five minutes. How old are you? Thought you was eighteen by the way you walk."

"Come on," I scoffed. "You didn't know I was coming till I was almost here beside you."

"You stopped along the road down there and got your camera out"—he gestured with a nod—"down by that little store. Then you walked a couple hundred feet and took a picture ... stuffed your shirt in too."

He'd been watching all right, and he had stoked my vanity with the eighteen-year-old comment. Setting me up for the touch, I thought.

"What tribe you from?" I asked. I'd talked to enough Indians to be comfortable asking.

"Arapaho.... Spare a few bucks?"

And there *was* the touch.

The twenty I gave him lit him right up and made me the greatest guy in the world for the next few minutes. Becoming embarrassed by more flattery, I tried to change the subject, and that's when I yielded to a truly irrational impulse. "How 'bout a taste of that stuff you got there in your bottle?" I said.

Even as the words were leaving my mouth, I was taken aback by my own recklessness. The man was visibly unhealthy. *Wise up, Beam,* I thought. *Talk about leaping without looking! You just leaped even as you were staring into the face of who knows what kind of disease. For all you know, the man could have tuberculosis— or worse.*

But I needn't have worried, because he wasn't so grateful for the twenty as to be willing to part with a swallow of whisky, Kenny Rogers and "The Gambler" notwithstanding.

Trying to get past denying me a nip, he complimented me again on how fit I looked; then, changing the subject, he said that when he got to Driggs he hoped to get farm work. "But hitchin' a ride's tough nowadays," he declared. "When I was growin' up, you just stuck out your thumb and the first car along picked you up."

"Well, then things were different out here from how they were where I was raised," I told him with a smile. "Back East, it was never easy to get a ride. And you sure couldn't sit on a box; you had to stand up and work for it."

That was definitely the wrong thing to say. I was kidding, but he immediately took offence—took it that I was chiding him for appearing lazy while thumbing a ride. He stiffened and abruptly asked "where the hell" I was walking to, and when I told him Oregon, he curtly replied, "You'll never make it; you better start stickin' out your thumb!"

Annoyed by his glare, as well as what he said, I politely withdrew and got on with walking. When I glanced back a few minutes later, he was head-back and bottle-to-lips, doubtless ministering to an unquenchable thirst. I felt like asking for the twenty back.

Later, I regretted having become annoyed with the hitchhiker, but I was confident I hadn't shown it. Two years before, when deciding to carry a gun, I had resolved "never to show irritation, never to speak a cross word, never to allow a confrontation of any kind." I had mentally reviewed the phrases so often I knew them by heart. Now I was thinking, *Beam, you did all right with that guy. But be more careful; you never know who you're talking to, and an initially innocent exchange can turn sour in the blink of an eye.*

*   *   *   *

I had been fascinated by welder's art, most recently near Wilson in Teton Hole Valley. Now, on the outskirts of Idaho Falls, I was seeing more examples of that kind of handiwork. Generally, these were small pieces, usually animals, dispersed here and there on the lawns and grounds of houses, but presently I came to an example that was property-wide. It was comprised of a footbridge, a fence and an archway, which in combination graced a two-story house with a broad lawn sloping to the inevitable roadside ditch.

To walk from the road to the house, one crossed the ditch via the bridge, passed through the fence via the arch and then up across the lawn to the house. The fence extended perhaps a hundred feet to the right and left, and effectively bounded the lawn.

But it was the design and workmanship of the three pieces that was particularly striking. The fence was constructed of old wagon-wheel tires that were actually steel rings about four feet in diameter, each separated from its neighbor by lace-like ornamental work. Railings made the bridge safe for walking, and these were made from smaller wagon tires welded together and bounded on the ends by rings that distinctly resembled Olympic logos. But the archway's rounded top was the most impressive of all. It contained cloverleaf shapes fashioned from short iron rods, and these alternated with metal disks patterned with concentric circles of holes. Fence, railing, and arch were all painted bright white, and they stood out against the green lawn which suggested inviting, cool relief.

It was hot, and through the arch, indeed framed by the arch, I could see a hammock slung in the shade of two evergreen trees. How pleasant that looked! But something in my head kept saying, *Only a fool would go there, Beam; there'll be a Rottweiler in there somewhere. He's probably watching right now, and waiting, waiting....*

By midafternoon I was west of Idaho Falls and entering a nearly flat agricultural area that was still part of the Snake River Plain. For the first six miles there were the usual roads at one mile intervals, and along these were farms with fields of potatoes and corn. Farming there is only possible because of irrigation systems that take water from the Snake and distribute it via ditches to the crops.

Beyond the farmlands was unreclaimed desert and presently I came to the Russet Lions Noise Park Raceway, about which I fabricated an outrageous fib for later telling to my grandchildren.

"Kids," I would begin, "an Idaho man told me about a zoo-park where lions live that are ferociously competitive—really dangerous—and that I should stop by and see 'em for myself."

Continuing, I would say that two varieties of powerful lion frequent that inferno of sage and bunchgrass, but they are not there all the time. One variety, Latin name Panthera-Leo-Quad, had been seen there two days before, and another variety, Panthera-Leo-Dual, was due on July 22—several days hence. Both varieties are known to bound along at forty to sixty miles per hour, and both are notorious for mind-numbing whines and snarls and roars that can be heard for miles. Crazy young men walk up to these lions, boldly mount and then race them, one against another. Often however, the beasts manage to throw their riders, and although they've never been known to actually eat a body, they often give them big scratches and gouges, and nasty brush burns called road rash.

Going even further, I would say that I listened to the Idaho man and then decided to do more than just see the lions; I'd catch one and ride him myself when I got to the park. "But listen up, kids" (this to be accompanied by a meaningful wink) "when I finally got there, I was in too big a hurry to mess around catching and riding lions; I could do that anytime—and twice on Sunday if I wanted to. What I really needed was to keep walking if I was ever to get to the West Coast. So with deep regrets, I marched right past the Russet Lions Noise Park Raceway, glancing into the sage now and then and fingering my pepper spray, just in case a noisy lion showed up with an attitude."

All of this I would feed my grandchildren, knowing full well they would gesture secretly among themselves and whisper things like "Pay no attention t' him; he's forever trying to fool somebody," or, worse yet, "Call Grandma, he's tellin' lies again!"

*   *   *   *

We were now crossing desert that was essentially flat except for isolated prominences with names like Kettle Butte, Table Legs Butte, Firestone Butte, and Saint Marie's Nipple—the latter undeniable well named. Forty miles still farther on rose the southernmost mountains of the Sawtooth Range, and to the south lay vast lava fields.

Walking through that area the third week of July was like walking through an oven. Images of approaching cars would float down as low mirages to alight upon the road two miles ahead. Then they would slowly grow as they hurtled closer, eventually to whoosh by with a blast of wind.

Late one afternoon, clouds began to form several miles to the west. It cooled a bit, and a half hour later there was a brief, light shower just as I spotted Helen and the Toyota up ahead. "Could have used that deluge two hours earlier," I said, as I slid into the passenger seat for the ride home.

"I'm just glad we got it," she answered. "It's probably the only rain there's been for months. My gosh, it's dry out here."

That brief shower may have been why it was so pleasant walking the following morning, although not a drop of moisture was left on sage or occasional flower. It had cooled some, but by noon the temperature was again ninety-five and rising, and by midafternoon it was well over a hundred. Helen insisted on posting herself no farther than three or four miles ahead, arguing that if I became dehydrated, I would be in trouble within a mile. In fact I was having no trouble at all. As long as you wear a hat and drink plenty of water, it's possible to walk safely, even comfortably, in a great deal of heat. *Just don't run out of water.*

But though I was having no problems that afternoon, several motorists near the Idaho National Laboratory became quite worried about an "old man walking alone in the desert." Nobody stopped to offer a ride, but three people dialed 911 with the result that a uniformed sheriff, or maybe he was lab security, stopped near Helen's car about four o'clock. The cop, or whatever he was, walked over and asked Helen if that *"elderly gentleman"* walking out there in the boonies *"belonged"* to her, and if he was *"all right."* He said there had been several concerned calls from people who had "sighted him along the road."

The man, a bit of a wise guy, had no interest in our walk across America, and he let Helen know how he felt by the sardonic way he asked if I was all right. He was suggesting that I might not be right in the head. Helen was tempted to tell him she'd been wondering the same thing; however, the man walked and talked like a "Dudley DoRight," so she thought it safer to bore him with dull answers than try to humor him with lighthearted wit.

Two weeks later, near Boise, we would meet an entirely different kind of lawman. Laughing and outgoing, that fellow would tell us that National Lab security had a reputation for being stuffy and paranoid "what with the nuclear work they do over there."

The day of Dudley DoRight was the last day I walked very far into the afternoon. The heat was too much after one o'clock, and consequently we decided to change our daily routine. From then on, we would get up at two-thirty in the morning and be on the road an hour later. That way we could get in a good twenty-mile day and still finish up by lunchtime. Meanwhile, before I walked again, we would move Lurch farther west, this time to Mountain View Campground beyond Arco, Idaho.

*   *   *   *

While at Mountain View we took two more interesting car excursions, our first being to Experimental Breeder Reactor-1 (EBR-1), which is located in the desert about twenty miles southeast of Arco. On December 20, 1951, EBR-1 became the first nuclear reactor to generate electricity. To be sure it was a tiny amount—just enough to light four two-hundred-watt light bulbs. Still, that's where it all began. Today, the ancient reactor is a National Monument; you can tour it and see one of the famous bulbs on display. A second bulb, our pretty guide told us, is at the Smithsonian, and a third is at the University of Chicago. Nobody knows what happened to bulb number four. One story has it that a technician took it home and used it for a cellar light.

Aside from being the first reactor to generate electricity, there was more history to be made by EBR-1. Five years later, in 1956, the reactor's generators were temporarily connected to the local power grid; thus Arco became the first city in the world to be powered by fission. This, of course, was the precursor of the nuclear power industry.

A second car trip took us to Craters of the Moon National Monument, which lies twenty miles southwest of Arco. Aptly named, the monument consists of eleven hundred square miles of lava flows and cinder cones, some two or three hundred feet high. Pathways allow people to walk up a few of the lower cones, and looking down into their tubes, you can see old snow which remains unmelted in the summer, thanks to the remarkable insulating properties of porous lava rock. In some areas of the monument there is absolutely no vegetation, and the vast landscape, rocky and harsh, truly looks like the moon. However, in other places there are pine trees, sparse grasses, lichens, and junipers shaped vaguely like Christmas trees—all of which struggle along, sometimes in 130-degree heat.

We had been visiting the monument for several hours when at lunchtime we found a picnic table shaded by scraggly pine trees. Perfect, we thought, for a nice quiet lunch. Unfortunately, the place was home to a colony of tourist-wise wasps, which we naively thought could be decoyed away by peanut butter. Helen wasted dabs of the wonderful stuff on small pieces of napkin and laid them on the far end of the table. "Let's hope that holds 'em," she said.

Of course it didn't. The wasps knew there was better food to be had, and they began landing on our sandwiches the minute we tried to eat. There were not many at first but more came within minutes, and Helen's initial "cute little bees" became "darn pesky wasps"; her gentle shoos became frustrated flails. I finally swore and took a smack at one, which promptly began buzzing around with a sting-the-bastard attitude—at least it looked that way. Moments later, fussing and shooing, we grabbed our lunches and headed for the car, whereupon Helen stumbled and dropped her Sprite. That got us both laughing, until she tripped getting into the car and scattered sandwich all over the floor. That left only me laughing—diminishingly—in the absence of her usual smiles.

We finished eating with the motor running, the air conditioner on high, and the bees enjoying a peanut-butter lunch complete with napkins. I had given Helen the other half of my sandwich along with what was left of the Sprite. She said I was sweet, so I told her she was too when she wasn't madder than a hornet—which comparison she objected to, so I changed it to *old wet hen*. For some reason that made her laugh.

Back at the campground that afternoon, there came an unexpected knock on the door. Helen opened it and there stood elderly Harriet Shaw, who had seen our Connecticut license plate and wanted to explore our "mutual roots." With little preamble she announced that she had been raised in California "in ancient times" and then moved to Fairfield, Connecticut, where she met her husband before moving on to New York.

So that was the Connecticut connection! Our "mutual roots" were somehow through our car's Connecticut license plate and her having lived in Connecticut sixty years before. God bless you, you desperate, lonely old lady. What a stretch!

Once past our mutual roots, Harriet launched into a long story about her family, first about her grouchy husband who was asleep in their motorhome two campsites over. Then it was her manic-depressive son who lived in Virginia, then an unhappy daughter who lived in Germany.

Talking to—no—listening to Harriett was tedious and depressing. Helen and I tried hard to cheer her up, to get her to tell us where she and her husband had last camped, where they were going, whether they had seen Craters of the Moon, EBR-1, or the Half Acre Lava Fields. No luck. For Harriet, life was deep blue that unhappy afternoon. She said so herself. She was obsessed with family problems and living entirely in the past.

WOLFDOGS? A SUBMARINE IN THE DESERT?

I had been walking since an hour before dawn, and was now looking forward to that rise in spirits that almost always came with first light. Twice I had stumbled, and once an animal startled me as it dashed off into the brush. Probably a badger, I thought, stepping off the road and shining my flashlight left and right, trying to glimpse whatever it was. No luck, just purple-gray sage fading clump by clump beyond my light and into the darkness. But though I missed seeing that animal, during the soon-to-come dawn I would meet three others in the most harrowing moments of the cross-country walk.

A half hour passed, and my mind was in idle as I gradually became aware of a bulky white vehicle in the gloom just ahead. It was on the north side of the road—a van, I shortly decided— broken down, deserted, and left for dead. Nothing unusual about that.

Moments later, however, and a dozen steps closer, I noticed three shadowy forms near the *maybe-not* deserted van. Alert now but still unconcerned, I continued walking and was quite close before it struck me that the shadowy forms were actually animals; indeed, they looked a bit like wolves, and they were staring my way in motionless concentration. *Come on, Beam. They've got to be dogs—who ever heard of wolves in this part of the country?*

I paused. Should I keep walking?—or should I backtrack and wait for Helen to return and escort me past what increasingly appeared to be a dangerous place. She could drive three or four miles per hour, and I would walk along keeping the car between me and the—wolfdogs? Indeed, that's what I should have done, but instead I steeled myself and continued forward.

The animals quickly became restless and started moving toward me, although slowly at first and beyond a roadside gully.

After fifty or sixty feet they paused, and several seconds passed as they hesitated near a patch of tall grass. I relaxed slightly, but only briefly, for suddenly, all inhibitions gone, they burst into a dash along the gully, crossed in single bounds, and came racing toward me. "My God, they *do* look like wolves," I muttered as I grabbed for the pepper spray in my right shirt pocket. Also, for the only time in the two-year walk, I drew the thirty-eight, cocked it, and held it low and away behind me.

With snarling menace the creatures, each weighing probably eighty pounds, stopped a dozen feet away—again bringing brief relief. But not for long. Seconds later, two of them began to fan out, one to the left one to the right, margining me on either side, while the third, with continuous growls and a stiff-legged walk, resumed its menacing approach straight toward me. I let it come in to about six feet before I pressed hard on the pepper-spray's button—no short bursts this time, just one long prayerful jet. Most of it went over the animal's head, but enough struck it in the face that it instantly broke off its attack and made off toward the far side of the road. To my relief the others immediately followed, leaving me with pounding heart and sweating hands—along with silent curses for the people who had let the brutes run loose to begin with.

I could hear them circling deep into the sage then back toward the van, as I stood there angry and sweating. Had the lead dog not turned away, I would have shot it within seconds, but would I have had time to deal with the others if they'd closed in from both sides? Or might I have gone down under a quick, combined assault?

Moments passed, but presently I began walking again, and then I was closing on the van, closing, closing, and finally passing on the opposite side of the road. Suddenly, beyond the van, a man shouted into the brush: "Buck! ... Spooner! ... Wolf! ... Get the hell back here!" and shortly a woman joined in with anxious calls of her own. I quickened my pace, almost to a trot, and soon the van, the people, and the dogs or wolfdogs or whatever they were, were far behind.

I would think a lot about that encounter during the next few days: *Were those animals really part wolf?... They sure looked it.... Couldn't be ... Bet they were!* Two weeks later I would learn that they were almost certainly crosses between German shepherds and light colored Canadian wolves.

Sunrise was most welcome after the wolfdog encounter, but what calmness I regained was soon suspended when I came upon a still-live owl that had been hit by a car. Of course my distress at seeing it lying in the road was a minor thing compared to the disaster it had suffered. Indeed, I was half sickened by the sight. It had brown- and black-striped feathers, a hooked beak, and tuffs on its head that looked like ears. Tan feathers splayed out from yellow eyes that stared at me—alert, unblinking, seemingly unafraid. Its obvious fate was to die in the heat as the sun rose higher, and it crossed my mind that putting it out of its misery would be an act of compassion. I was approaching Arco, however, and too near to use the gun, while thoughts of doing the job with a stone or the heel of my shoe were appalling even in contemplation.

So I hurried on, complaining to myself about having the bad luck to encounter first wolfdogs and then a dying bird. Eventually, tiring of those unworthy whinings and trying to get into a better mood, I told myself to be grateful I didn't have a face full of pepper spray or hadn't been hit by a car.

Neither thought helped much.

Relief finally came as I entered town. Cars and streets and people, instead of open prairie, engaged my mind and provided welcome new focus. Things improved even more a half hour later when, approaching town center, I caught sight of a black monolith-like structure some distance ahead. As tall as a two story building, it was sitting in an open area beside the road, and it looked strangely—but that's impossible!—like the superstructure of a submarine!

What in the world could it be? Increasingly puzzled, I continued walking and was quite close before it dawned on me that it *really was* a submarine's superstructure, a.k.a. conning tower, or *sail* as it is sometimes called.

Then suddenly it all made sense! The National Engineering Laboratory, which I had passed a few days before, built dozens of nuclear reactors for the Navy. Arco, only twenty miles from the lab, would understandably be interested in displaying a conning tower as a symbol of the town's support for the Navy's submarine program. It must have been a great economic boost for the town. Still, how odd that tower looked, five hundred miles from the ocean! I was used to seeing submarines at Groton, Connecticut, twenty miles from where we lived and two miles up the Thames River from Long Island Sound.

In downtown Arco I was fortunate to meet a woman who told me all about the "submarine in the desert." She had been unlocking the door of a Front Street business when I approached on the pretext of asking directions. Actually, I knew exactly where I was going; what I really wanted, indeed needed, was someone to talk to.

The woman told me a local civic group was establishing a small science and engineering museum, and that the museum's theme would be nuclear reactors built at the Engineering Lab, especially ones built for submarines. So what better centerpiece for the museum than a submarine's conning tower? With that in mind the group petitioned the Naval Historical Society, which eventually donated the conning tower of USS Hawkbill (SSN 666) upon its decommissioning at Puget Sound Naval Shipyard. Bringing the tower from Puget Sound to Arco was also part of the story, but the nub of it was that volunteer truckers did it for just the cost of diesel fuel.

Leaving the submarine topic, the pleasant woman exchanged opinions with me on a number of topics ranging from crop insurance, to farm-product advertising, to farm-product TV advertising. Probably I was still troubled by the wolfdog and owl incidents, for in spite of her cheerfulness I sank into a gloomy monologue about TV advertising in general, and its effect on society in particular. The windstorm went something as follows:

> Television ads spew from the family TV at a rate of at least fifteen minutes per hour, and it goes without saying that they influence people to buy products. If they didn't, no business would pay to have them run, and the television industry would not be what it is today. Ads are obviously effective at getting people to buy stuff, stuff, and more stuff, and that keeps the economy humming along. But ads make people do stupid things too.

She seemed to agree, so I kept going.

> For example, when some hotshot thirty-something sees a flashy new sport car ad and goes out and buys his current dream wheels, he might drive it like a sane person. But if he drives it as wildly as cars are often driven in car ads, then he'll probably kill himself and Lord knows who else besides. Of course the advertiser typically fakes social responsibility by offsetting twenty seconds of reckless driving with a three-second, half-inch, barely-visible, bottom-of-the-screen notice saying CLOSED COURSE, PROFESSIONAL DRIVER.

Bummer!

> And the influencing power of TV doesn't stop between ads, when sponsored programming is grudgingly squeezed back in. Education programs, nature programs, how-to programs, etc., can all be worthwhile by inspiring young people toward worthy careers. And sports events and dramas can be good recreational entertainment—unarguably valuable in themselves. On the other hand, what producer would acknowledge that his blasé treatment of a powerful woman's out-of-wedlock parenthood might influence some dream-world teenager to be careless about getting pregnant? Dan Quayle had the Murphy Brown thing right, even if he couldn't spel potatoe. But who am I to fault a body's speling?

After *that* monologue I got ready to move on; however, the long-suffering woman suddenly surprised me by switching the conversation back to the conning tower. "How come you didn't see the tower the other day when you were moving your motor home to Mountain View? You must have driven right by it on your way through town."

"Good question," I answered. "When I'm driving that thing, I hardly notice anything except the road directly ahead, along with enemy traffic." I'd been groaningly negative and wanted the remark to be light cover for my departure. And it did make her laugh as we shook hands and told each other we had enjoyed the conversation. Maybe she was just being kind.

A few hours after talking to the woman in Arco, I met a farmer and his wife who were working in a particularly beautiful flower garden. They were about my age and appeared to be quite well off, judging by their large, well-kept house and a late model Cadillac that sat in the driveway. Still, he was worried. For forty years he had farmed his three hundred acres, but this year, for the first time, there had been too little rain to fill the reservoir that supplied his ag-water (agricultural water). The dearth of rain coupled with hotter than normal temperatures had brought the reservoir down to where there was a declared water shortage. For him, the shortage would mean stopping irrigation on one of his fields, and this weighed heavily on his mind. It was not that it would cost him that much money; it was just that loosing part of his crop smacked of incompleteness. "If you plant, you gotta *harvest*," he declared. "That's all there is to it. You *gotta* have the closure."

Now, if the farmer was worried about losing a field, his loquacious wife was anything but. Presently he wandered off toward a tool shed to get something, and as soon as he was out of earshot, she began telling me how he was a congenital worrier. "He's got nothing to be worried about," she said. "We've had much-blessed lives—Jesus has been good to us."

"I'm sure he *has*," I replied. "But it's been plenty dry, and I've talked with several other farmers who are worried about their crops."

"Well, don't get me wrong; I can sympathize with Hiram. Nevertheless, he could have retired ten years ago; we have plenty of money and a winter place in Arizona. No way, though. Every spring he has to plant—the whole darn farm—and if the crops are anything but perfect, he gets all uptight."

Her husband was soon returning with a rake, whereupon she adroitly glided from him as her subject to a digital camera she had recently bought. She was clearly used to his worrying and not much bothered by it. Anyway, she had bought a scanner too, one that could handle 35-mm slides as well as black and white prints—of which she had thousands. Her big project was scanning and organizing everything she had which included pictures of their four children going all the way back to when they were born. She had hundreds of pictures of their firstborn, less of number two, still less of number three, and maybe a dozen pictures of Mr. Four, who was currently city manager for some town in Texas. When finished, she would have all those pictures on CDs and backed up twice. Then her plan was to show them as continuous slide shows at family gatherings. "That'll fix 'em," she said with a twinkle in her eye. "Heaven help the relatives!"

"I'd do it to 'em too," I said, as her husband, finally brightening, joined in the laughing.

*　　*　　*　　*

Hours passed as the countryside changed from farmland to rangeland, and now there were lava fields to the south while far ahead rose broad highlands with more buttes and cones.

I was looking forward to day's end when a vehicle began to slow down behind me, prompting me to pause and turn. Would this be a brief, welcome exchange with a curious farmer or rancher?—or maybe a cop bored stiff by his endless patrol?

Not to be. Three stony faces stared out from a stake-body truck that was olive drab with brown camouflage patterns. Must be the army, I thought, but that idea quickly passed. I had never seen a stake-body army truck, and besides, there were no white stars or unit insignias on this truck's doors or hood. Nor could those hard-looking characters ever pass for soldiers—street thugs maybe, but not soldiers.

For several moments the two passengers held their stares; then suddenly, surprisingly, they grinned, shaped their hands like pistols, and pretended to shoot—bang! bang!—straight up into the air.

Willing the driver to keep moving, I threw a casual wave and attentively resumed walking, but he responded by slowing still more and taxiing beside me for an uncomfortable few seconds. Then suddenly, with a grin and loud gunnings of his motor, he continued west.

Big relief! Probably they were harmless—at least to me— but fairly or not, I imagined them at best lowbred rednecks or at worst ragtag militia. They'd be dedicated to saving the country, I decided, from the government, from immigrants, from minorities, from who knows who else.

Whatever those men were, they left me uneasy, and presently I was comparing them to other people I had met and talked to along the way. There was the happy clan of "Indian Indians" back in Teton Hole, then the beautiful woman in the Mercedes sport car. And even today there had been the Arco businesswoman, and the farmer and his wife who liked to take pictures. All were pleasant, nonthreatening people—the kind I was comfortable talking to and unafraid of being surrounded by. The militiamen, however, had been something quite different.

So ended a mixed-day of dangerous dogs and hard-looking men, but balanced, thankfully, by pleasant exchanges with agreeable, friendly people.

*   *   *   *

Streaks of dawn were showing, as I stood beneath a still starry sky contentedly watering the road. Suddenly, my relief was interrupted when a large owl whooshed by as a ghostly passing presence, unseen and hardly audible yet very real. Startled, I ducked away, sprinkling a pant leg with a few warm drops. Then I stood very still.

You can hear a flying owl, believe it or not, if you are especially quiet and it passes within feet of you. But will it come back? I wondered, as several coyotes yipped nearby.

Be quiet little wolves; I'm listening for an owl!

A minute passed, another ... three ... four. Suddenly it came over again; then shortly a third pass marked its departure as I glimpsed it against the lightening sky. As quickly as it had come, it was gone, and I was walking again, grateful for the bird's brief visit yet wondering what had impelled it to fly so close. Had I violated its territory? Or was it mere animal curiosity? Did it have chicks nearby? Thus went my random thoughts as I trudged along, waiting for the sunrise.

The dirt road I was walking carried along, twisting and turning, but generally parallel to Idaho 20. A covey of grouse exploded from the roadside as I descended a grade onto flats from which rose foothills of the Sawtooth Mountains. Along the valley floor and between clumps of sage, fingers of rocky lava reached north toward the highlands like spent breakers on an ocean coast.

Negotiating these strips of lava was a forced necessity for pioneers migrating west. Farther south, the lava fields were continuous and impossible to cross; to the north lay the daunting Sawtooths. Between lava and mountains ran a northern bypass of the Oregon Trail called Goodale's Cutoff, which, according to pioneer J. C. Merrill in 1864, was so narrow in one place that "...we were obliged to drive over a huge rock just a little wider than the wagon. Had we gone a foot to the right or to the left the wagon would have rolled over."

It's doubtful the pioneers had time to appreciate the scenery along Goodale's Cutoff, but for me even the lava and sage had stark beauty as foregrounds for buttes and cones that seemed to be everywhere. Presently I crossed into Blaine County. Lava, lava, and more lava, and flitting among the tossed up cinders were hundreds of blue jays. That night Helen and I searched for tiny blue images in a dozen futile pictures I had taken. Is that one? No! How about there? Not a chance.... Birds at a hundred feet were a waste of film—or in this case digital camera memory.

Several days later: Another dark and starry morning—just a sliver of moon and pleasantly cool. In the darkness I'm fascinated by a stillness broken only by the shh, shh, shh of crop irrigators throwing water first this way then that. In the absence of wind, local temperatures differ in adjacent layers of the morning air, so as I walk down a hill I feel increasing coolness, first on my ankles, then my hands, and finally on my face. The change is striking—probably six or eight degrees over a height difference of no more than eighty feet.

Dawn comes and then midmorning as the road takes me through wastelands of sage. The cool is gone and a hint of approaching heat reminds me of why we started so early in the morning. The day wears on, much as the day before, and presently it's one o'clock and there's Helen out ahead, waiting to quit for the day.

*   *   *   *

The next morning we continued the walk from the intersection of U.S. 20 and Idaho 75, which leads north to Sun Valley and Ketchum. It was cool, as usual—thus welcome relief after the noontime heat of the day before. Lonely and bored, I began recording an aimless monolog that soon ended with "think I'll do this later—maybe I'll feel more like it."

Eventually recording resumes: "A dry creek bed meanders along the road to my left, but other than that the landscape's almost featureless—just sage and distant buttes under a high-overcast sky. Neither sunlight nor shadows to make things less boring. There're no animals either, no birdsong; there's not even the sound of a breeze. Thank God for an occasional car; otherwise I could be in a closed room except for the sound of my footsteps. Good Lord, it's desolate out here."

That morning I was indeed a solitary soul, and close to talking to myself when the monotony was relieved by two small airplanes passing a half mile away and heading west. One was a Piper Cub, that "air Model A" of yesteryear. I waved and waved but got no response. *They probably don't even see me,* I lamented, *although they could if they happened to glance my way. This white shirt and hat would stand right out against gray road and green sage.*

However, an hour later, sure enough, here came the Piper Cub back from wherever. It was about a quarter mile north of the road and flying low and slow, maybe two hundred feet above the ground. Then its pilot spotted me and abruptly veered my way. On he came until he was passing directly overhead and banking into a tight, right circle with me at its center—close enough that I could see his smiling face and waving hand.

Be careful, Good Buddy, and don't stall out, I breathed as I grinned and waved back. Upon completing the circle, the friendly pilot resumed his eastward course with a final wave and a dip of his wings. It had been a tonic of a greeting, one that left me with such warm feelings that for the next hour I waved at almost every car that came along. A couple of times it crossed my mind that had I just waved to a few drivers earlier in the morning, I would have got enough returns to keep from feeling so isolated.

Traffic increased as the morning wore on. Several people were trailering boats behind cars or pickup trucks, the boats no doubt for use on Magic Reservoir which lay a mile to the south. The reservoir was built in 1912 and has always been popular for boating and fishing, but recreational uses aside, its primary purpose was to supply water for agricultural areas to the west below the Sawtooths.

I passed through those areas that afternoon, and all along the road were fields of wheat, alfalfa, barley, corn, and occasionally even onions. Most of the time, between the fields and the road, there was the usual ditch or narrow wetlands, and these were invariably home to many kinds of birds and small animals. Among the usual road carnage was a dead beaver, probably a stray from nearby Camas Creek, the reservoir's principle feeder from the west.

ONCE YOU SEND 'EM OFF
TO COLLEGE....

Our next move brought us to Quiet Retreat campground, which is a dozen miles south of Fairfield, Idaho, and seventy-five miles east of Boise. Fairfield has a tourist information center at the corner of U.S. 20 and Soldier Road, and while visiting there, we met a woman who was a distant relative of the Sioux chief Red Cloud. Helen was delighted to talk to her, and the two found common interest in the remarkable chief and his valiant though futile efforts to forestall the Wounded Knee Massacre.

During our stay in the Fairfield area, we also visited a senior center which we hit just right for an excellent lunch. While eating, I managed fifteen minutes of fascinating conversation with a retired rancher who had come over from Nebraska to visit family. I was glad for the talk, because except with Helen I had had no conversation with anybody since the drought-worried farmer and his picture-minded wife.

"Keeping busy?" I tried for starters.

I was sitting next to him, half on half off the end of a picnic-table bench. Four men had scrunched over to make room for me, but now, little by little, they were "expanding" and I was struggling to hang on to my seat.

"Not like I oughtta be," the rancher replied. "What about you?"

I gave him the usual rundown on the walk, which prompted the usual questions. Then the conversation took an interesting turn. There had been an auto crash where he lived which had cost the area two young people. It was the usual sad story: a number of drinks, several friends, one car race, two dead teenagers.

"Twice as bad when you lose kids that way," the rancher remarked. "Usual way is they go off to college and never come back."

"What do you mean, 'never come back'? You can't mean they just disappear."

He started to answer, but just then I began to slip off the end of the bench, and throwing out a leg to steady myself, I tripped a woman carrying an apple pie. She nearly went down but somehow managed to save herself and the pie too—to everyone's relief, especially mine and Helen's. I was grateful the woman was good humored; she went out of her way to put me at ease, even as she joined the laughter of everybody in the room. Eventually, things settled down as my fellow eaters shoved over and I reseated myself on the bench. That done and everything orderly again, the patient rancher resumed his story.

"Well, I don't really mean they never come back," he said. "They come back all right, but only for visits. They don't stay. See, before they leave home, kids that live on farms and ranches get to see each other a good bit when they're in school. But during Christmas vacation, spring break, and all summer long, days go by when they don't see their friends at all. It's a long way between spreads, so unless somebody hauls 'em around, or until they can drive, they're most of the time stuck at home. There's only family there, and for teenagers that's not like friends. They get the lonelies."

"See the problem," I mumbled around a mouthful of potatoes.

"That's only the beginning of the story. The rest comes when they graduate from high school and go off to college. There they live on campus or maybe in town, but always around lots of other young people. And there's plenty of what they consider interesting stuff to do. They study everything but agriculture, by the way, and when they graduate, they head for the big city 'stead of coming home to ranch ... or farm." He was a rancher and he added *farm* after a pause, almost as an afterthought.

"Sounds as if you've got a brain drain on your hands."

"That's right. Let 'em take up engineering, computer science, business, communications—anything like that—and see if you ever get 'em back on the ranch."

"You have grown kids?" I asked on a sudden hunch.

His face morphed into a grin.

"Two boys."

"Yeah," said a skinny man a couple of seats over. "They're his kids and my nephews. He sent the older one to the Air Force Academy and now he flies for U.S. Air. The younger one went to the University of Nebraska. He did computer science and now he lives in California. The pilot's the one that brother Jeff here thought was gonna come home and take over the ranch."

Uncle was obviously proud of his nephews and Jeff was proud of his sons, although he leaned way back and gave his brother a playful whack on the head. After that the conversation returned to Helen and me, and what it was like to walk across America.

*   *   *   *

An elderly couple named Vizcarra owned Quiet Retreat (our current address), and their house was located across a wooden bridge and up a short driveway from the campsites. I walked up one afternoon to pay for extra days we planned to stay over, and Mrs. Vizcarra, who was clearly the mainspring of the family business, invited me in. There I was greeted by a big, friendly German shepherd who was a fixture around the campground. He would make rounds to the various campsites each evening, exchanging sociability for treats. We found he especially liked Reese's Peanut Butter Cups.

After I paid Mrs. Vizcarra, she took me back to the kitchen to see a rattlesnake she had run over on the road. It had happened a couple of hours before, and she had stopped, picked up the luckless serpent, and put it in the trunk. Now she had it nailed to a plank lying on the kitchen counter by the sink, and she had just finished taking its skin, which she planned to have made into a belt. She told me to stand by; then she proceeded to gut the thing and crosscut it into five sections one of which was flatter where the car tire got it. Next she said, "Watch how you cook a rattlesnake! No, I'm not trying to shock you; I just get a kick out of enlightening Easterners."

She flipped three of the tubes into a cast iron skillet, and before long the whole kitchen smelled like overripe fish. "Gotta go," I half croaked, as she apologized for not inviting Helen and me to dinner. "I would," she said, "'cept there wouldn't be enough for you, Helen, me, Fletch, and Viz." Fletch was the dog. Viz was her husband, whom she seemed to rate just below Fletch in deserving fresh-cooked snake.

I left Mrs. Viz to her cooking and headed home with mixed feelings of nausea and relief; after all, it's not every day you're threatened with home-cooked rattlesnake. On the other hand, who needs it? But then my thinking began to change, and just as I was crossing the bridge it occurred to me how wonderful it would have been if she *had* invited us. I would tell Helen, who's always eager to go out to eat, that we'd been "invited to dine with the Vizcarras."

"That's great," she'd enthuse, "I didn't feel like cooking anyway. What's she having, Honey?"

"Oh, some local dish," I'd say. "Nothing fancy ... just something she picked up when she went to town a while ago."

*   *   *   *

As I walked west out of Fairfield an hour before dawn, it seemed as if a car would no sooner approach and pass than another would emerge from the darkness out ahead. It would always seem a long time coming, and unless another car happened to be approaching from the east (from behind me), the oncoming driver would naturally be using his high beams. Dazzled by the light, I would sometimes doggedly keep walking, although slowly, tentatively, and keenly aware that any roughness in the pavement could cause a stumble. Occasionally, if the lights were particularly bright, I would step off the road and wait with half-closed eyes, grouchily wondering what I was doing in the middle of an Idaho desert at four in the morning. It was almost more annoying once a car *passed*, for it would be several minutes until night vision returned and I could see reasonably well, thanks to a third-quarter moon.

Such was walking the morning of July 31, 2000, until dawn came, headlights dimmed, and the world began to improve. An hour later it improved still further, when I met a middle-aged woman who would all but insist on giving me a ride.

Eleanor (she told me her name) had been coming east, thus toward me, but after passing she had turned around and come back to offer me a ride!

"No thanks," I replied. "I'm a cross-country walker and I do this for fun. Anyway, you're going east and it wouldn't be right for you to drive me clear to the West Coast; it'd take you out of your way— you wouldn't get to work on time." I was assuming she worked in Fairfield or maybe up north in Ketchum.

"Well, I couldn't take you that far," she laughingly answered. "But I just hate to see you walking alone out here in the desert. It'll be blazin' hot in a couple of hours. Why don't I just drive you to Mountain Home? Seriously, where *are* you going?"

"I told you," I said, trying to keep a straight face. "I'm headed for the West Coast—started walking from Connecticut yesterday morning ... northeast of New York City ... should get there tomorrow afternoon."

"You won't be serious, I can see that. But you should at least let me drive you to Mountain Home."

Mountain Home was forty-five miles farther west, so taking me there would have meant a ninety-mile, round-trip drive for her. I was amazed and touched by the offer—then sobered by a fleeting suspicion: *Could this sweet-seeming woman actually be a predator who would rob me if given a chance?* But that's unlikely, I quickly concluded, even as I wondered if her car could even make the trip. Indeed, there was an innocence, a sincerity, about the woman that reminded me of Nancy, the endearing do-gooder who offered me a ride and five dollars back in Nebraska.

After I thanked this latest would-be benefactor and convinced her I could get along without help, she pulled ahead a hundred yards, did a U-turn, and came back by me on her way east. By the way she smiled and waved, one would have thought we were family. I hadn't needed the ride, but her stopping was a lift to the spirits.

A short time later, I branched onto Harrison Road which is a gravel divider overlying more remnants of Goodale's Cutoff.

Harrison runs north of U.S. 20, skirts the southern edge of several ridges, and eventually connects to a series of remote roads barely passable by car. These, in turn, continue beyond the mountains and lead eventually to Boise.

Along the first few miles of Harrison, walking was through irrigated farmlands. Once a hawk, perched on his favorite fence post, complained with piercing cries as I gradually came toward him. When I drew so near that he could stand it no longer, he flew ahead to the next post, there to scream some more at my steady approach. Two more times the frustrated bird retreated, before, tired of giving ground, he flew out over the fields and back to the post he started from.

Beyond the farmlands, Harrison became suggestively-named Wild Horse Road, which took me into a scrubby rangeland of rolling hills covered by little more than bunch grass and dwarf sage. I saw a few cattle—but *only* a few—and perhaps for that reason the country was unfenced. Occasionally there were lush little ponds with marsh grass and reeds where muskrats and wading birds live out their brief lives. Once I took pictures of a low hillside where a variety of sages, splendid in fresh new growth, grew tall against highlands that were pockmarked with blowouts.

By late morning the country had changed even more. Now the hills were lower and almost grassless, and between them were dry ravines with occasional stands of lonely cedars. Bare rocks were everywhere. There were outcroppings of small, rough rocks, and in some places there were broad flat boulders twenty feet across. Still others were the size of houses! Some lay flat, some were on end, some were by themselves, and some were in groups—as if a giant's child had used them for playing blocks.

It was brutally hot, and just after twelve o'clock I came to Helen parked in a ravine under a lone, small cedar. I moved the car so that we ourselves could sit in the shade to eat our lunches.

In that windless heat, not an animal or bird or even an insect broke the utter stillness.

"PLAY DUMB," THE GOOD SHERIFF ADVISED

Early the next morning, I walked through an area called Castle Rocks, which is a famous pioneer's landmark of more tossed-up boulders, some forty feet high. Beyond the rocks my route came down onto U.S. 20 for a few miles, before branching west onto aptly named Lonely Road. Several times I was startled by distant explosions, until I checked my map and saw that Mountain Home Gunnery Range was only twenty miles to the south. The gunnery range! Of course! That would explain the explosions.

The distant rumblings no longer a concern, I began paying more attention to strange, carnivorous bugs that seemed to be everywhere along the road. Ugly black grotesqueries, they crawled about singly and in groups, usually on the road but sometimes in the roadside ditches and adjacent grounds beyond. An inch and a half long, they resembled heavy-bodied grasshoppers with inch-long swords jutting out from the backs of their abdomens. They were cannibalistic too; several times I watched as one stalked another on the dusty road, and once I saw two of them devouring an unlucky fellow. Nearby, four others feasted on the carcass of a snake.

*Cannibalistic
Mormon Crickets*

Toward noon I walked down a slight grade, stepping around still more of the repulsive bugs. Mostly I had been keeping to the south side of the road, because sometimes there would be shade there from a rare roadside tree. Several times, however, I crossed to look into a ravine that fell off beyond the road's north shoulder.

Near the bottom I sat down to rest near a corner-like bend, and had been there for several minutes when I heard a truck slowly approaching from the west. It stopped abruptly, without quite coming into view, and a man said something that was indistinguishable above the idling motor. Then he paused as if waiting for an answer. I was all ears, but then surprised and relieved upon hearing Helen laugh and say, "I'm just fine, thanks."

I got up and walked around to meet retired sheriff Richard Twynam. He had stopped to check on Helen's wellbeing, and the first thing he asked me, after we told him what we were doing, was, "How many pairs of shoes have you worn out?"

I told him I had bought several pairs because of my different sized feet, but that if I had started out with a pair that fit, and replaced them only when they wore out, and replaced that second pair only when it wore out, then I would be walking on pair number three and they would still be in pretty good shape. "Let's see," I said, "I have only Oregon still to walk across, so it looks as if I'll have used up about three pairs of shoes by the time I get to the coast! That make sense?"

"It does, it does," Twynam said with a laugh. "I've heard bullshit about people wearing out a dozen pairs of shoes on walks nowhere near as long as yours."

So began a conversation that lasted a good half hour as we paused several times to watch a hawk that kept circling overhead. At one point I asked Twynam about the black bugs, and he told us they were Mormon Crickets. In short, the story goes as follows:

In July of 1847, Brigham Young led a group of Mormons over the Wasatch Mountains of Utah and into the eastern edge of a great basin, where they founded what ultimately became Salt Lake City. Shortly afterward, another group of over a thousand souls joined Young, upon which settlement and farming began in earnest. Things seemed off to a good start until the following spring, when swarms of black crickets appeared and began devouring the new plantings. But lo and behold, there came unexpected relief. Just when disaster seemed inevitable, flocks of seagulls arrived to eat the crickets and save the crops.

Thus the Miracle of the Gulls in Mormon tradition, and that, Twynam told us, was the origin of the phrase Mormon Crickets. (*Crickets*, however, seems to be a misnomer, since the insects are technically grasshoppers according to entomologists.)

Eventually we got back to the cross-America walk. I told him about the three dogs I had encountered near Arco, and how I backed up as they charged, and how I was lucky to have driven them off with pepper spray. (I didn't mention the gun.) When I said the dogs looked to be half wolf, he immediately confirmed my suspicions, saying that there were many such animals in the area and they were a cross between a light colored Canadian wolf and a dog, usually Alsatian or Siberian Husky. He said that in Oregon they were the dog of choice for "types you wouldn't normally associate with."

"We've got them in the East, too."

"They're probably everywhere," Twynam allowed, then, "Any gaps in your walk?"

"Two," I said, "an Illinois River bridge at Peoria, and another over the Hudson near Kingston, New York. That's Rhinecliff Bridge."

"How come you didn't walk 'em?"

"The Illinois bridge was being worked on when we got there, but it should be finished when we head back east. We'll stop for a day or two in Peoria, and I'll walk it then."

"Sounds good. What about the other one?—what's it called?—Rhinecliff?"

"It has NO PEDESTRIAN signs at both ends, but I'll walk it one way or another."

"Cross it at night when nobody's around."

"What if I'm stopped? What'll I do? ... plead insanity?"

"Nah," said the lawman. "Play *dumb*. Act like you're an old man hard a hearin'. Make the cop repeat himself a couple times. Then smile and say, 'OK, thanks,' give a slight wave of your hand, and start walking again."

"He'll just stop me again."

"Smile and do the same thing you did the first time, but cup your hand behind an ear. That'll be a nice touch. You might have to play the game two or three times, but eventually he'll just give up and follow you off the bridge. No problem."

"Here we are," I said, "twenty-five hundred miles from the great state of New York and plotting to break its laws!"

"Ain't it fun?" the sheriff said with a laugh. "But I gotta go. Wife and I been staying at Quiet Retreat down below Fairfield. Should've been back an hour ago."

"That's where we're staying!" I exclaimed. "Maybe we can get together tonight."

"Love to," he said, "but it won't work. We're pullin' out this afternoon and headin' for Riverton. Anyway, it's been good talking to you."

So we said goodbye to the friendly sheriff and continued the morning's walk.

For over an hour I met no one else along the road, but eventually I came to a ranch, with the usual outbuildings, and not far beyond was another ranch. I approached this second ranch with special caution while keeping a wary eye out for dogs. I had been forewarned. Their personable owner had stopped and talked with Helen, and when he learned that I would be passing his place, he said he would go there "posthaste" and lock up his dogs. "They're a bit vicious," he allowed, "so I'll make sure they're inside."

Helen immediately radioed the word to me, and now I was on lookout for the beasts and fingering my pepper spray.

The dogs knew when I was passing and they certainly sounded dangerous. They were in a garage-sized shed, but I could see two of them through a heavy mesh door and they carried on as if they were thinking *Kill, Kill, Kill!* Not meeting them was fine with me, but I would have liked to meet their owner. His stopping and offering help to Helen did not fit with vicious dogs; it would have been more in keeping with good-natured mutts, as almost all ranch dogs were. On the other hand, he told Helen that he was having trouble with predators, the "two-legged stealin' kind."

We finished walking that day in downtown Boise, fully eighty miles from our campground near Fairfield. Getting to Boise had become a special goal the last few hours of the day, simply because the eastern approaches were dusty and boring, and I wanted to get into the city. Aside from that, we had walked one day too many without moving Lurch. So we would move the next morning, to River Bend campground southwest of town.

*   *   *   *

Surprise, surprise! Within minutes of arriving at River Bend we met a wolfdog like the kind I now dreaded meeting along the road. Her name was Shana, and she belonged to a couple from Alberta who happened to be camped next door. Ironically, Shana was benign to the point of being a pleasant nuisance; they didn't bother to leash her. When Helen and I were outside, she would invariably stroll over to be patted and talked to, and when we were inside

Shana at Our Door

the camper, she would often stand outside the open door hoping for treats—which she usually got. She especially liked bite-sized pieces of leftover beef.

During our first day in the Boise area we grocery shopped, Helen had prescriptions filled, and I ordered new glasses—something I had been putting off for much too long. In addition, I spent the following morning doing minor repairs to ever-ailing Lurch; then we scouted the walk track west to Ontario, Oregon, which was where we would be heading next. But sundry chores and scouting aside, we were glad to be off the road for a few days. It was time for a break, and temperatures had been over a hundred degrees in the afternoons.

WE CROSS INTO OREGON

Three days after arriving at River Bend, we were well rested and happy in the notion that it was only four hundred and sixty miles to Newport, Oregon, our now envisioned destination on the Pacific Coast. Only four hundred and sixty miles! We marveled that we could associate that many miles of walking with the word *only*. Our perspectives had come a long way in miles and outlook since we started walking two years before.

Long before dawn on August 11, Helen dropped me off in downtown Boise, and I began walking through four miles of mixed commercial and residential areas that eventually led into farmlands to the west. I was more diligent than usual about taping observations and impressions that morning—not to mention complaints and opinions. Consequently, instead of describing the morning's hike from paper notes and memory, I am including the following modified version of a tape-recording playback. "Modified" means expletives deleted and English formalized. In addition, it may be noticed that the world was out of sorts that morning, and it remained that way for hours.

I'm a half mile from downtown Boise where we started at four-fifteen this morning. This is residential area, and like many such areas, lots of houses have bright lights outside. Gives the impression that people are plenty security conscious, even fearful.

Saw a beautiful shooting star a while ago. Starting to pick up some noise. Traffic's building. At ten after five a back-up horn beeps away as somebody maneuvers an eighteen-wheeler.

Just passed a car parked beside a house. The driver's window is wide open and a two-way radio hisses away except for loud intermittent bursts of static or incoming voice traffic. Strange! Apparently somebody drove up last night, parked the car, left the window open, left the radio on, and went inside to bed. Sober? Who knows? No lights in the house. Hope the neighbors are sound sleepers.

Men are working on the roof of a McDonald's. There's lots of glare—street lights, security lights, etc., but the sky is barely showing light. They're friendly guys, brown skinned I think, although it's too dark to tell for sure. Probably Mexicans. We wave back and forth and call *good mornings* in muted voices. It's too early to be loud.

Twenty-five after six: More beeping back-up horns, and as usual, nobody anywhere near the forklift that's making the racket.

Seven o'clock and well west of Boise. Moving out into the country. Actually it's still kind of "sprawly" here. Farm lands to the right and left, but in the distance there's a large subdivision. It's a good ten degrees cooler here than it was in town. A thermometer at a bank near the campground said seventy-two degrees—big drop since yesterday—but it can't be more than sixty-five out here. Took off my flannel shirt a while ago, but when I get to the car I'll put it back on.

There are blackberry patches all along this road, and thousands of berries. It's tempting to eat some, but I've seen several signs saying NO SPRAYING. Presumably spraying is done at other places around here, but who knows for sure which patches have it and which don't. Better pass on the berries. Why the devil can't you even eat a blackberry without having to worry about being poisoned by insecticide?

West of Boise about eleven miles, and there's Helen's just up ahead. Gotta have more coffee; then I'll walk a mile north before continuing west. The map shows a narrower road up there, so traffic should be less. Fair number of commuters down here. Some look like they're still half asleep. They need coffee too—wake 'em up. People shouldn't be allowed on the road till they've had two cups. There oughtta to be a law.

Eight-thirty: Another barrage of noise from a backup horn. This time it's from earth-moving equipment, a grader off to the right. I've been hearing that darn thing for at least a mile, and its relentless beeps no doubt penetrate everything in the area, especially the nearby houses—even the people inside. It must get to the workmen too. Why's there so darned much noise in the world anyway?

Here the tape trails off into indecipherable grumblings, but eventually I get back on track and lecture myself:

Those loud, low-pitched beepers that sound off every time a truck or bulldozer or whatever backs up are definitely unnecessary. Low frequency sound is only slightly absorbed by air, so the infernal racket is a conscious or subconscious irritant to people hundreds of yards away—it nudges up the "public stress level." Worse yet, although the beeps may occasionally save a life, workers repeatedly bombarded by them doubtless tune them out, thus reducing their effectiveness as warning signals. Why can't we wise up?

A better warning system would use beeps and chirps of low amplitude, high frequency and varying pitch, together with rear-looking video cameras like they use on high-priced cars. The varying noise sequences would be unignorable by nearby workers, who would be visible to the machine operator on a dash-mounted TV monitor. Also, a supplemental rear-looking infrared sensor would probably work in cold-weather. People are hot, so a worker would be detected by the sensor which would cause a single loud honk like a car horn. That would alert both worker and operator that the immediate situation may be dangerous.

So why can't we get rid of these present-day loud beepers; they're neurological hazards to everyone within miles. OSHA should require quieter systems on moving machinery. Come on Government! Give up your hidebound, bureaucratic ways, and let's have systems that are safer for workers and easier for everybody else to live with. Too expensive you say? Bull! Make such systems mandatory and let the buyer pass the costs along to his clients and thence, ultimately, to the population at large. So it costs us all a few bucks a year—that's less than an overpriced cup of Starbuck coffee. Meanwhile, the payoff would be fewer hurt workers and more peace and quiet for everybody.

I quit taping here and begin wondering why Helen says I sometimes rant like Andy Rooney. I don't ramble on forever in a bitchy, nasal twang. Time passes and I began recording again:

I am interviewing the Wakeham family—mother, son, and grandson—whose business is growing mint plants and distilling the oil. Roger, the grandson, just gave me a tour of the distillery, and he outlined how they grow and harvest mint plants, and then extract the oil. Roger tells me the distilled oil is tested for quality before being accepted by buyers, who distribute it for use in confections, chewing gum, toothpaste, etc.

This is an interesting place, and the boy's tour, together with his mini-lecture on vapors and condensation, has been a real treat. *Roger is sharp and articulate, and he's grinning right now as I smile at him and suddenly* <u>*talk much louder into this recorder!*</u> *Bet he's some student! His father and grandmother are enjoying this too. Dare I say they are Beaming? But folks, I really must be getting back on the road.*

It's ten after twelve noon, and I'm twenty-two miles from downtown Boise and heading west through farmlands en route to Ontario, Oregon. The smell of peppermint is everywhere….

So much for the recording. The world, of course, finally righted itself, but it took until almost noon.

* * * *

A few mornings later I was walking through a sprawling commercial area on the outskirts of Caldwell, Idaho. Sodium lights gave jaundiced illumination, and threatening signs warned that guard dogs lurked in shadowy buildings or behind chain-link fences. The scene needed sunlight, people, traffic—anything to humanize it, render it less forbidding, ameliorate the eerie ambience of dark, lifeless streets.

I hurried on and an hour later was north of Caldwell, my route having taken me first to the Golden Gate Canal and then along the Boise River, which might better be called Mosquito Creek. Slapping and scratching, I eventually came to an old iron bridge near which was a sign saying IMMIGRANT'S CROSSING. It was a place where pioneers once forded the river, but only when they had to. Coming from the east but hemmed in by mountains, they would have preferred to cross thirty miles upstream. Up there, however, shifting channels and deep water sometimes made crossing too risky, and forced them to trek down the south bank, eventually to cross where I was standing. Years after the pioneer's brutal trek but years still before I stood there, settled locals recognized the shallow site as an ideal place to build a bridge.

Looking now at the decaying structure, I was almost saddened by its forsaken appearance. Before completion of nearby I-84, it had undoubtedly carried the main bulk of traffic from above town down into north Caldwell. Nowadays, almost everybody uses the interstate; only a local, now and then, uses the bridge, and it was this sparse traffic that I encountered after I crossed the river and continued north on Old Highway 30.

Far ahead, an approaching car momentarily kicked up dust along the edge of the road. Driver dozing? I wondered. The car recovered and moved back across the driving lane, onto the center line, back across the driving lane, and onto the shoulder again—all in slow motion from my point of view, but really going maybe forty miles per hour. It's time, I thought to myself, for a sensible walker to get off this road.

I hopped over a gully and onto a low bank as the car approached through another slow, scalloping trajectory. Finally it was close enough that I could see the driver holding a newspaper in front of his nose just below his eyes. For a third time the car hit the shoulder and threw up dust, whereupon the man glanced up and, with a practiced response, sent the car on another slow arc before returning to his paper. *Now that,* I thought to myself, *is truly efficient multitasking.*

An hour later, I paused to speak to an old man and a young girl who were working together along the edge of a field.

"You've got a good helper there," I called to the man.

"She's good all right," he answered with a laugh, "but she's beginning to think she's the boss."

The girl was his granddaughter, and the two were setting irrigation tubes—plastic pipes that led water from larger pipes to gullies between rows of plants. "For you know it," he continued, "she'll be telling me to hurry up. She's set three tubes already—not bad for a ten-year-old."

"Four, Gramps," came her sweet-sassy correction, "and I'll be eleven in December."

"Whatever you say, Honey, whatever you say."

*　　*　　*　　*

While I had been scowling at the multitasking driver and then talking to Gramps and Honey, Helen was touring a farm near Fruitland, which now lay just ahead. She had been parked and writing in her log when a hesitant tap on the window brought her face to face with Caroline Argote, who had come down from the farmhouse to satisfy her curiosity (although she didn't actually say that).

The two easily hit it off, and Caroline soon told Helen that she and her husband were retired airline workers, who had spent many years in California before coming to Fruitland to buy their dream farm. She was obviously proud of the farm, and she soon offered Helen a tour, which Helen was quick to accept. First they visited an orchard of golden delicious apples and next a stand of fast-growing poplars, which the Argots were growing as a lumber crop. Helen thoroughly enjoyed feeding Caroline's geese and later her arthritic old horse, who was clearly living the good life in his declining years. Lastly, they visited a pond near the end of the property, which bordered the Malheur River. Caroline's husband kept it stocked with trout, and Helen said it was a tranquil place that just begged to be fished—if you didn't have a good book to read.

Before they parted and Helen walked back down to the car, Caroline gave her a peck of Winesap apples, so that an hour later we had a good laugh when I arrived with a ten-pound melon. A farmer had given it to me, and with aching arms I had carried it for miles. People didn't often give Helen things, and items they gave me were usually small—like a bottle of water or a bar of candy. That was the only time we were both given really bulky items, but we were delighted nevertheless. We enjoyed melon and lots of apples the following week.

Walking ended that day near the Snake River Bridge in the eastern outskirts of Ontario, Oregon. We had crossed our last state boundary, the river, and our next goal would be the Pacific surf, four hundred miles to the west.

*   *   *   *

We were eating lunch under a roadside tree, when a man and woman came down from a nearby house and approached with smiles and gestured greetings.

"We're curious about what you're doing here," the man led off. "No offence intended, believe me, but not a half dozen cars pass here in a day—let alone park."

"Eating lunch," I answered, grinning so the answer didn't seem abrupt.

"See you're from Connecticut," he continued, nodding toward the Toyota's license plate.

"Lebanon, southeast of Hartford."

"We're from Jersey."

We were on an unpaved farm road west of Ontario—certainly a place where few tourists passed. This couple, who turned out to be brother and sister, seemed unusually inquisitive, and they were not shy about asking questions.

"Visiting somebody out here?" sister asked.

"He's walking across the country," Helen garbled, her mouth full of sandwich. "We started in ninety-eight, should finish next month. But I hear a North Joisey accent … right?" Then she grinned and added, "You people come straight to the point. Direct begets direct, you know!"

"You got it," sister answered with a laugh. "Sorry. We're from Weehawken, just across the Hudson from Manhattan."

God bless 'em, I thought to myself. They'd never admit it, but Weehawken may as well be part of New York City, and if a New Yorker wants to know something, he or she will just ask. They're not famous for shyness.

"We're out here visiting my daughter," brother continued. "That's her place." He gestured toward the house they had come down from, and just then a boy and girl burst out of the front door and started down the driveway at a run. When they got there, he introduced them as his grandchildren.

Both brother and sister were recently retired, and they had good reason for being interested in Helen and me. The night before, the whole family, including the children, had had a big discussion about how long it would take to walk across America.

"What a coincidence," he declared, "that the day after we talk about it, somebody walks past the house en route to the Pacific. How long do you think it would take us to do it?"

"Both of you?"

"No, him!" sister quickly put in.

I told them that if she would go along and drive support, he should be able to do it in about seven and a half months. "That assumes," I continued, "that he averages twenty-five miles a day for three days out of five. Figure thirty-four hundred miles coast to coast. So if he starts in the middle of March, he oughtta finish by the end of October."

They hadn't been far off the night before when they estimated it would take about six months; however, they assumed he could walk fifteen-minute miles, i.e., four miles per hour. I said *he* might be able to walk that fast, but it would be too fast for me.

Eighteen-minute miles were the best I could *sustain*. Faster than that was an exhausting half-walk-half-trot that invariably wore me out in hours.

The children heard all this with rounded eyes and questions of their own, and their mother, who had just arrived from the house, also joined the conversation. The idea of the walk especially intrigued her since she was the one who had brought it up the night before.

Eventually we began to talk about Helen's day-to-day role in the Great Beam Odyssey. Brother, in particular, asked detailed questions about how she kept busy while waiting for me, and how far ahead she would drive after dropping me off to walk. "Hell," he said, "it's her driving as much as your walking that's lettin' you get away with this!"

"You've got it wrong," I said. "She's driving to the West Coast and making me walk! Once, back in Pennsylvania, she even declared my step lacked spring—just because I'd only walked twenty-four miles that day. She's a dominatrix, sir; you don't know what I go through!"

Everybody laughed *except* Helen, who declared me in a jam and challenged me to talk my way out of it. So I continued: "If you're going to try something like this, then you'd better have somebody just like her to help you along. She's spoken for though. She's the greatest ... never gets mad ... still sweet at seventy years old. She's as comfortable as an old leather shoe. Get the picture?"

"The picture I get, mister, is that you is in big trouble!"

Everybody laughed *including* Helen, God bless her.

Ten minutes later our lunchtime visitors said good-bye and started back up the driveway. We rested a bit longer; then Helen drove on to the next rendezvous and I got back to walking. There were plenty of truck farms in the area, and there were scores of people in the blazing fields. Interestingly, they worked in groups rather than as individuals, which was obviously a matter of logistics. A single slowly towed wagon collected produce picked by nearby workers, and it also carried drinking water. Occasionally a worker would wave, but most of the time they attentively kept picking.

Day's end came opposite a one-story house behind a high board fence. No amenities made this place look homey. There were no curtains in the windows, no flowers outside. For that matter, there wasn't even grass—just a dirt front yard. I wondered if Mexicans lived there; if so, maybe they were still in the fields. Dust was everywhere: on the building, on the fence—piled high along the road. Things seemed to bake. The heat had the air shimmering as we looked toward Malheur Butte, a few miles to the northeast.

THE INDIAN FISHERMAN

Night was ending, but early brightness along the horizon still merged into blackness overhead. Suddenly a shooting star raced across the sky, burning out as I watched but leaving a smoky white track in the sunlight miles above. It seemed a perfect morning; the air was as cool and pleasant as it had been hot and stifling the afternoon before.

An hour after the shooting star, I branched onto U.S. 20 and soon met Helen at the corner of Glen and Morton Streets in downtown Vale, Oregon. She was all ready for an early morning snack. But why snack in the car when Lurch was at an RV park only three blocks away? Soon we were at table having doughnuts and coffee—actually, coffees one-to-many for both of us. Then it was back to the road.

North of Vale, I came upon a misguided snake who had chosen to sun himself in the middle of U.S. 20. There'd been few cars, but obviously Snake-o would not be alive long if he stayed where he was. But how to drive him into the weeds? I tried the usual: yelling, arm waving, gesturing my foot toward him—shoe sole first, of course, and well out of range. No go. He coiled up and stood his ground. Next, I stooped down, and holding the pack like a shield, I slowly advanced, crowding him until he could stand it no longer. After one half-hearted feint at the pack, he gave up and crawled to safety in the roadside grass. I walked on, and soon met Marvin Wately.

Marvin was busy loading a pickup truck beside a roadside barn, but being a pleasant, outgoing man, he was quick to stop and chat. When I told him I was from the East, he said he had an uncle living somewhere back there, maybe Philadelphia or Pittsburgh. He couldn't remember which, but he pronounced the uncle's name and hesitantly asked if I had ever heard of him. It was a shot in a million, as we both well knew, and of course the name meant nothing to me. But immediately Marvin became embarrassed—said he shouldn't even have mentioned his uncle let alone asked me if I had ever heard of him. "That was a six-year-old's question," he admitted. "I'm really not that naive about how big the East is, or how many millions of people live there ... or anywhere else for that matter."

I urged him to forget it, confessing that I was not immune to asking naive questions myself. "Less likely things have happened," I assured him, and went on to tell about an acquaintance who had experienced a truly once-in-a-million chance meeting. It happened in Morocco when this fellow, completely unexpectedly, bumped into an old high school buddy in the lobby of an out-of-the-way hotel in Tangier. It was not a case of geriatric retires meeting in some popular tourist destination; that happens often enough. These were middle-aged men in Morocco on business. They were unaware of each other's presence there; they worked for different companies in different U.S. cities, and they hadn't seen each other in years. Their meeting was pure coincidence—far less likely, probably, than winning a lottery.

That story got Marvin past his discomfort, but then he overcompensated by expressing too much concern about whether I was carrying enough water. "Don't get yourself dehydrated," he told me at least three times, and before we parted, he made me take three seventeen-ounce bottles of Poland Spring water. And me trying to travel light!

Hours passed as I slowly continued north along the windy, lonely road. The countryside was another farming area which, as usual, relied heavily on irrigation. High grasses lined the northern edge of the road, and beyond the inevitable swampy ditch lay the fields. Several times I scared up pheasants, the first I had seen since Nebraska, and once a hawk flew screaming from his roadside perch.

After six or eight miles, the road veered west, steepened, and climbed into low highlands from which it descended into a hot, dry basin. Then more, higher hills. Helen said it seemed as if everything west of the Rockies was an endless series of highlands and intervening valleys, some irrigated, most dry as deserts.

Sometime that afternoon I watched a cowboy herding cattle with a quad bike instead of a horse. His dog was right there with him, helping with the job by nipping the cattle's hocks. Still, something didn't seem right—cowboys are supposed to ride horses, not quad bikes. Even so, it made a fascinating picture: the man on his gasoline steed, the dog hard at work, the cattle out front—and all seen through a thin haze of dust. A newly mowed hayfield seemed an anomalous backdrop for this latter-day herding operation, and so did a segment of the Gellerman Froman Canal which ran nearby.

*   *   *   *

The town of Brogan, Oregon, was deserted when I arrived the morning of August 14, looking in vain for somebody, anybody, to talk to. There was a filling station on the left with an eighteen-wheeler parked beside it, and nearby was a pickup truck with a bumper sticker that warned all to LOVE AMERICA OR LEAVE HER. As if to drive the point home, a rifle was mounted behind the rear window. But I saw no people until I met Helen, waiting beside the car just north of town. Beyond her in a newly mowed field, two lazy deer barely looked up from browsing.

"I'm here to talk to you," I said, as we plopped into the car. "Thank goodness we have each other."

"Couldn't live without you, Dearie. Mean it. Here, have a doughnut."

We sat quietly then, holding hands and grateful to be together. I gazed absently at the deer as the moments passed; then, sensing a subtle shift of mood, I turned to see Helen faintly smiling, but with a tear trickling down her cheek.

"Penny for your thoughts," I whispered.

"Ah, they're worth millions, Phil … and thanks for so many good years."

"You're welcome, m'Love … and thank *you*…."

After while: "Phil, what do you suppose that is on top the telephone pole?—the one over there." She was pointing at a wooden cross-bar structure that stuck up above the pole's uppermost wires.

"It's a perch," I guessed, "to keep hawks up where they won't short out their wingtips on the power lines. Feathers are nonconductors, but there'd be enough voltage to drive juice through 'em ... enough to kill a bird."

"You serious?"

"Yep."

"No way."

"Helen, I'm telling you the truth! You wanna hear something even truer?"

Long pause, then, "You know, I bet you're right."

"Helen, we could have made TV commercials, you and me—like Garner and Hartley did for Polaroid cameras back in the seventies. He would explain how the camera worked; then she'd say she didn't think it worked that way. He'd ask how she thought it worked; then she'd say she didn't know—just that she didn't think it worked the way he said."

Helen laughed, and we agreed that the Garner/Hartley skit was innocently funny and shouldn't have bothered anybody very much, even people worked up over gender issues. On the other hand, we agreed that advertisements that consistently cast either gender or any race in stupid roles may sell products, but definitely with negative side effects.

I was soon going on: "Helen," I declared, "these days, if there is a dimwit in an advertisement, it is bound to be a white male. And watching that idiot will be thousands of white males. Most won't be bothered much, but some will be mildly annoyed, like me for instance."

"*Them* and *you* are not the problem, Dearie. It's the redneck types that must really get mad. They'd turn the clock back a century if they could. Women and minorities would be invisible—blacks would be subservient."

"Helen, There is more to it than that. Resentments engendered by such advertisements are surely, if only infrequently, contributing motivations for unkind acts carried out against others. Advertising people are smart enough; they know that. But if an edgy ad will sell a product, they'll air it and to heck with collateral social damage."

* * * *

Although I met no one besides Helen that morning, during the afternoon I had a brief but memorable chat with an Indian. He was fishing in a dammed-up lake just north of the road when I spotted him through a grove of evergreens. Anxious to talk, I called hello as I started down through the trees, and I was sure he heard me because he glanced my way. Nevertheless, he said nothing but suddenly stood up and began reeling in his line. Is he brushing me off? I wondered, as I slowed and pulled up only yards away from him.

Moments passed as he finished reeling in his line; then, very deliberately, he turned and with an appraising stare said, "Don't go 'way. I'm not leaving … just gonna try a spot over by those rocks.

The man had a striking, almost forbidding, demeanor. Tall, broad shouldered, big boned; his face was reminiscent of stern-faced chiefs with weathered skins, high cheekbones, and no smiles. But suddenly he did smile, albeit slightly, and with a toss of his head he beckoned me on: "Hurry up! Let's go! Maybe there'll be fish over there."

I still hesitated. *What'll it be?* I thought to myself. *Go with him or go the other way?* Long pause. Then, *Go with him, but stay alert.*

We were on our way to the rocks—nothing said so far—when I ventured, "What's the dam for? It's mostly mountains around here … not many fields to irrigate, is there?"

"There's a few—enough to need irrigation. Most of the farming is to the west and north. This here dam's called Murray."

"Any more?"

"Over by Unity City there's the Elms, Morfitt, Long Creek and Whited dams, and farther north there's Unity Reservoir. That's a big one. Actually they're all reservoirs, and they all supply ag-water from Unity in the west down the valley to Bridgeport, twenty miles that way." He pointed toward the east. "Lots of water around here." The man was articulate and he knew the country thereabouts.

"You fish all the dams?"

"All but Morfitt."

By now we had arrived where he was going to retry his luck, but just as he cast his line, somebody began crashing around in the woods along the bank, maybe fifty yards away.

"That'll be my son," the Indian allowed, not bothering to look. "He never fishes in one place more than five minutes—he's noisy and he's got no patience. He's like a White Man." Then he laughed and added, "His mother's White."

"Yeah," I said, a little taken back, "but you just moved yourself. I wonder how much of his moving around comes from the Indian side of the family."

"Some maybe, now you mention it. Anyway, fishing was better before the White Man came; you didn't have to move around. A man could just sit in one spot and catch all the fish he wanted in an hour. That's what the old people used to say."

"Well the old people didn't sit beside this reservoir 'cause there wouldn't have been a dam," I said, letting my hair down the way he was certainly doing.

"Can't argue with that. Anyway, what are you doing walking way out here? What's your story?"

He turned out to be friendly enough, although at first I thought he might have some cross-cultural tomahawk to grind, his wife and son notwithstanding. But I told him my story as a half hour slipped by and his half-white son kept moving and re-moving down the far shore of the lake. He was a good listener, although every time I tried to finish, thinking he might be getting bored, he would ask me to go on. Finally came the how-far, how-fast, how-long, and how-old questions, and lastly, he wanted to know if I had had any health problems.

"None so far," I told him as I stood up to leave.

"That's good," he said. "Hope you keep it that way."

We shook hands then, and I headed back up toward the road. The wind had picked up, and I'd walked about fifty yards when something, maybe curiosity, made me look back.

He was watching, and then he waved, and coming faintly on the wind, I heard, "You be safe, White Man … hear?"

"You too," I called back.

FUZZY-MINDED NORTHEASTERN ENVIRONMENTALISTS

We were still camped at Vale, Oregon, when one evening we took a ride east and visited a small town on the Idaho border. Our mission was to take pictures of a house we had seen that had a sign saying it was built from a Sears Roebuck kit. That's the nowadays department store chain; in yesteryear, Sears, like Montgomery Ward, sold many different kinds of buildings, including houses.

While I was taking pictures, I noticed an old woman sitting on a porch across the street, and when I finished, I walked over and introduced myself. *Lisa Harkins* was *her* name, and soon she was telling me what she knew about the old house and also the one beside it, which had also been bought from Sears by mail order. The houses had arrived in town during the 1920s on railroad flatcars, and her great uncle had helped put them up. He told Lisa they cost about fifteen hundred dollars each, and that as kits they came with everything—framing, precut molding, cabinet hardware, even nails. The houses had no bathrooms, however, when originally built, but they were added during the 1940s.

As willing as Lisa was to talk about the houses, she was even more willing, indeed eager, to tell me about herself. Maybe that was because she had buried her husband only three weeks before. Consoling family and friends had since returned to daily routines; Lisa was alone and lonely, and I evidently struck her as safe to confide in. Accordingly, in the following paragraphs I honor her confidence with omitted or changed town names, and "Lisa Harkins," of course, is a pseudonym.

Briefly, her story was as follows:

Lisa came from a family of two known branches: a small tight-knit religious group clustered near Bend, Oregon, two hundred miles to the west, and a larger, patently worldly crowd widely dispersed near San Diego, California. Lisa was of the latter group, and she had just turned eighteen when she met her wandering future husband on a Monday—and eloped with him the following Thursday! Brief as their courtship was, however, and as iffy their apparent chances, the young couple's instincts were right on. "We were made for each other," Lisa said with a catch in her voice. "Our marriage was made in heaven."

Thus began lives together which took them to many different towns along the Washington, Oregon, and California coasts. She often worked in fish canneries, including one in Monterey (shades of *Cannery Row*). Her husband, Jim, always found work as a handyman. It sounded as if he was especially skillful and would tackle any maintenance job he knew anything at all about—obviously a good man to know!

The Harkinses must have been prudent with their money, because somehow they managed to buy a sequence of houses that ranged progressively from "very very small to very small to just small," while along the way raising a boy and two girls.

And so the couple lived through their youth and middle years, and far beyond. Eventually, accommodating her parents' old age, the younger daughter and her husband renovated their own home in order to provide the old folks an apartment with an outdoor patio—the same patio I was standing on that evening as I listened to Lisa's story.

It was on their fifty-fifth wedding anniversary that Jim had his first "spell," which unfortunately proved to be a stroke. After that, life for him was a series of steadily more debilitated stable periods between ever more serious strokes, until, mostly paralyzed and deeply depressed, he began hinting to the children about checking himself out "to spare Lisa." He never did though. Perhaps he waited so long as to be physically incapable of doing it, or perhaps he lacked the resolve (don't most people?) or perhaps he felt his suicide would be harder on Lisa than if he just rode it down. In any case, he lived two more years, more vegetable than person.

The old lady admitted through brave sniffles that much as she loved Jim, she was glad his sufferings had ended and that he'd gone to his reward. Except for the last three years, their lives together had been "one long wonderful run." They had enjoyed it, and talking to the proud old lady, I didn't doubt it. Strong and pragmatic, she must have been born with one of those upbeat natures that require little of material things, can recover from almost anything, and yet somehow never lose enthusiasm.

Helen had come over from the car in time to hear the last of Lisa's story. Her "one long wonderful run" especially fascinated Helen, as it did me, and on the way back to the campground she said it must be wonderful to feel that way when looking back over one's married life. "But no need to feel too bad for Lisa," Helen went on. "She's going through a normal, natural process; and sad as she is right now, her life story is that of a strong person. She'll pull out of her grief and make the most of what she has left."

*   *   *   *

The next morning, I resumed walking near Unity, Oregon, at the beginning of a gradual nine-mile climb. Initially the road passed through pastures separated from the road's shoulders by fence lines and several yards of tall grass. Bluebirds flitted from stem to stem—at first ahead of me, but then out, around, and gradually back to wherever they began their noisy retreats. There were cattle too, occasionally a lone bull, but more frequently small groups of steers. Often they would watch me coming and pull back from the fence, only to fall in and briefly follow along after I passed. Cattle are touching animals. Look too long into those big gentle eyes and you might convert to vegetarianism—given you're in a weak moment and not in the cattle business.

Later, when I reached the car, Helen was eager to tell me about several cattle that had wandered onto the road not far from where she was waiting. She had walked down and shooed them back through a break in the poorly maintained fence. Still, although there was almost no traffic, she was afraid they might get out again and maybe cause an accident. We talked it over for a few minutes and then decided to try and find the cattle's owners—let them know about their fence problem, do our good deed for the day.

Not far from the car was a narrow dirt driveway that crossed a cattle guard into a field of sparse grass and occasional trees. We started down the driveway and within minutes came to a sign posting a family name between two symbolic Christian fishes. The fishes made a reassuring impression, but a hundred feet farther along was a weatherproof loudspeaker atop a twenty-foot pole. A thin wire ran down to a black, lens-equipped box which faced a matching box on the other side of the drive. Clearly we were standing in front of an electronic tripwire, and to determine if it was armed, I waved my hat in front of one of the boxes. Nothing happened—no wailing siren, no Klaxon-horn blast.

Satisfied that the system was unarmed, we screwed up our courage and walked right through, although with diminished enthusiasm for good-deed doing. Fifty more yards brought us to the crest of a low knoll and another sign, this one saying, NO TRESPASSING, PROPERTY PROTECTED BY SMITH AND WESSON!

From reassuring to unnerving to forbidding in a couple hundred yards!

We could see the house from beside the sign. Bleak, shaded windows stared like glowering eyes from beneath a sagging porch, while outside were a half dozen wrecked cars, a mountain of trash, and two big, chained dogs. They didn't bark; they just stared—we'd seen such stares before. "Enough of this good-deed nonsense," Helen whispered. "Let's get out of here."

So we hurried back to the car, but instead of beginning a new walk segment, we drove down to where the cattle had been on the road. None were in sight, but I spent twenty minutes and sacrificed six perfectly good bungee cords filling a three-foot gap in the long neglected fence. That quixotic repair might have lasted a day, provided no cattle showed up and wanted to walk through.

*　　*　　*　　*

The morning was beautiful but chilly in the Malheur Mountains thirty miles west of Unity, as I walked up a particularly steep hill. Once I stopped to look over a hollow, through which rushed a mountain stream bordered by evergreens. There were blue spruce as well as long- and short-needled pines—some were tall, some were dwarfed, all were backlit and highlighted by the rising sun. Once I paused and amused myself by scraping initials into frost on top of a guard-fence post. *Twenty minutes,* I thought, *and they'll be melted away.* Then I was off again and continuing up the grade, warmed up by then and comfortable.

Later that morning I met a road crew repairing guard fence a sleepy trucker had mangled the night before. "They knock 'em down, we put 'em up," the jovial foreman boomed. "A flat fence draws cars like slop draws coyotes."

I appreciated the comparison, but bear talk was what I really wanted to hear.

"Bears? Hell yes, we seen three of 'em just last week … well … not here, but within twenty miles of here. We even seen a mountain lion a couple weeks ago."

"Think there's much chance I'll see anything?"

"Not likely," the foreman declared. "They're used to crews like us; they see us all the time. We're like cars going by—nothing out of the ordinary far's a bear's concerned. A lone guy like you'd be different; a bear'd know about you long 'fore you'd see him. In fact you never would see 'im."

Of course that was just what I thought; I never had great expectations of seeing a bear, far less a mountain lion. Still, I hoped that Helen, waiting quietly in the car, might at least see *something.*

By ten forty-five I was down out of the mountains and had met Helen at Prairie City, where we snacked on cinnamon buns from a Front Street bakery. They were a pleasant change from the sugar doughnuts we had lately been buying in one-dozen boxes.

After the snack I had no excuse but to get on with walking, except that somebody had parked an antique Packard across from the bakery. Of course that needed to be inspected, but as

I started over Helen groaned and got on my case: "Philip, do we have to go through this again?"

"Through what?"

"Through you looking at a car for half an hour and then trying to decide whether to buy it and take it back East."

"It's not just a car; it's a Packard, and Packard merged with Studebaker way back in fifty-four. So you might say it's a surviving first cousin of our 1951 Studebaker, you know, the one—"

"Phil, never mind the foot-dragging; why don't you just start walking down the street so we get in some decent miles today? You're just putting off walking. If you're gonna spend twenty minutes salivating over that car, I'm going shopping for something big and expensive that I don't even want ... sweetheart."

"In that case, buy me the Packard."

Even so, I took only five or ten minutes to look over the car before starting out of town. The notion of buying and refurbishing an antique car had long since been laid to rest.

We finished the day about seven miles west of Prairie City along the John Day River. Helen said it would have been eight miles if I hadn't stopped to look at the car.

*   *   *   *

It was several days until we got back on the road, and during that time we moved Lurch to an RV park near Mount Vernon, Oregon. We did chores, rested, and visited local fossil beds; then it was back to walking on August 19, continuing along the John Day River. The terrain was almost flat, except for a barely perceptible slope to the south and some local knolls that were seldom more than a dozen feet high. To the north, however, and all along the way, there loomed a six-hundred-foot mountain front that bore gradually south before opening into hilly country to the west.

Upon reaching the *town* of John Day about 9 a.m., I turned south into still more hills; then I followed Canyon Creek for a dozen miles, to a place where the road veered west along the north side of a narrow valley. Walking the west-going road, I occasionally caught glimpses of another road on the valley's opposite slope—in some places it was less than a hundred yards away. *Now who, I puzzled, would build two side-by-side roads in the middle of nowhere when one would surely be enough.* Meanwhile, unnoticed by me, the valley floor was gradually rising toward road-level, and presently the two roads curved inward to meet in a U-turn bend at the base of a steep slope. Well, that explained the mystery! The two roads were one and the same, but laid out with a detour and a hairpin curve in order to avoid bridging the deeper, eastern end of the valley.

Having gone around the bend, I was walking in the opposite direction when I glanced across and noted of a car traveling west. *In a couple of minutes,* I thought, *it'll be coming at me from behind.* And sure enough, just over two minutes later (I timed it), it had come around the bend and was passing me going east.

Meanwhile, Helen was parked in a turnout about a mile away, and a man with a pickup truck had pulled in and stopped. Several minutes passed, during which he would look toward her now and then but look away whenever she returned his glance. Eventually he got out and walked over to the car. He was a logger, he explained, and he routinely stopped there to meet a partner whom he expected any minute. He hoped he hadn't been making her nervous. Helen thanked him for the consideration, and he had gone back to his truck when I arrived a few minutes later.

Tentative hellos between him and me easily progressed to conversation about the hairpin curve, then to the weather, and then to the presidential race—Bush versus Gore. We soon abandoned that and passed on to the *Kursk,* a Russian submarine that earlier that week had exploded and sunk in the Barents Sea. "Think anybody's still alive in that boat?" the logger idly wondered.

"Only if they were unlucky," I said. "If they were lucky, they all died when the thing blew up." Of course we couldn't know it, but even as we spoke, doomed men lay huddled in the stern of the stricken ship. The horror we had blundered into talking about subdued us both; conversation became awkward and briefly trailed off.

Suddenly rallying, the man began telling me about his early years as a rancher in the far-off 1950s.

"Why'd you quit ranching?" I asked, glad for the change of subject.

"Couldn't make enough," he said. "I sold the cattle business in fifty-eight and was lucky to get out sixty grand in the hole. After that I took up logging. It's been a lot better money."

I began to question him about the difficulties of making a living raising cattle, but presently another truck pulled in, this one driven by the man's partner, who appeared to be in his late thirties. Before long the younger man was telling me about the techniques of tree farming and how, by law, trees harvested in Oregon have to be replaced with saplings. "If they're not," he said, "the state comes in, replants, and assesses your property for costs. The assessments apply like property taxes, and they're nothing to sneeze at. You either replant," he continued, "or your property is confiscated and sold at auction to satisfy the state's costs for reforestation."

The reforestation laws, of course, are the reason you see so many replanted trees in Oregon. True, in some places there are still old patches of slash-and-run clear-cutting, but on the whole these reflect destructive practices of earlier times.

Conversation with the loggers eventually turned to forest fires, which were a big worry that summer. The younger man had a computer printout he had got via the Web, and it listed various fires burning at the time—where they were and how big they were. It even had listings of how many acres were considered threatened. "Not much you can do about the big ones," he said. "That takes organized fire-fighting. But at least you can know where they are and stay up on what else is going on—case a small one breaks out near you. Sometimes you can deal with them."

The loggers soon had to leave, but just before they got into their trucks, the younger fellow grinned and tapped his finger on my chest. "When you get home," he said, "you be sure and tell the good folk in Connecticut that there are still trees standing in Oregon—never mind what fuzzy-minded Northeastern liberal environmentalists think." I had mentioned I was from Connecticut, which made them think of Joe Lieberman and then Al Gore, who had just picked Lieberman as his running mate in the coming election. To the loggers, Gore was an environmental hot button.

My talk with the loggers was the last I would have with anybody apart from Helen for several days. Only a half hour later I turned onto Grant County Road 63, which would take me through the Malheur National Forest. From there, it would be eighty-five miles along deserted back roads to Paulina, Oregon, and then on to Prineville in the west-central part of the state.

WALKING IN WESTERN OREGON

In the Malheur Forest and farther west, we saw some of the most striking panoramas since the Rocky Mountains. Vistas were far, wide, and open; there was a rare cattle ranch, but mostly the scenes were vast woodlands that had been timbered and replanted to yield thinned stands of evergreens. During the day the sky was crystal clear so that in late afternoons the sun would backlight the trees, and now and then among their depths we would see deer, their near sides shadowed so they appeared as moving, almost ghostly, silhouettes. There was a fairyland quality to those ever changing scenes.

Finding our way through the forest, however, proved challenging. One day we were scouting by car, trying to validate our next day's route, when a friendly rancher gave us directions for the "best-of-all short cuts." His intensions were good, but did we ever get lost! For two long hours we milled around in the mountains southeast of Dayville, taking one wrong turn after another. Giving up in frustration, we began bearing south at every opportunity, so that eventually we came out about a quarter mile from where we started—on National Forest Route 2170 near Murderers Creek. We had gone in a great, big circle!

But the name Murderers Creek perked Helen right up. "Makes for an interesting thought," she said. "Wonder who got bumped off along this peaceful looking stream?" Other nearby and interesting place-names were Flagtail Mountain, Jackass Mountain, Shake Table Mountain, and Frenchy Butte.

Frenchy Butte! Shades of a dead French mountain man?—or some erotic couple's illicit interlude? Helen loves to speculate about the curious suggestions of place-names.

*   *   *   *

In Paulina one quiet Sunday morning, distant rumblings signaled the approach of a large group of motorcycles. I hardly noticed at first, but it wasn't long until the intensifying racket nudged me into grouchy reflections: *Darn bikers. They own America's roads on typical weekend mornings, and the cops ignore their noise no matter how loud it gets. They ignore ghetto blasters too, whether they're in cars or even at public beaches or parks. For that matter, a kid or woman or man can disrupt a high school or even a college commencement with uproarious celebrating, even including air horns, and no one in authority will do anything about it.*

The problem, I groused on, is that nowadays, many public officials of both genders came of age in the sixties and early seventies—the era of the hippy. Granted they helped end the Viet Nam War, freed us from stifling dress codes, and even promoted tolerance. But they also went in for drugs, free love, and the notion that they should arrogantly "do their thing," that is, practice "complete freedom" in their everyday behavior. This often meant ignoring traditional norms of common courtesy. Hell, those aging hippies are far beyond thirty now; they've made their money and become the establishment. It's time they stepped up and passed—and enforced—noise laws, even though doing so would tacitly acknowledge their boorish behavior as youths. After all, few would hold that against them (we were all young once), and most people would just be grateful for the quiet.

What musings I had fallen into! Lost in such thoughts, I had tuned out the growing motorcycle racket and was passing a convenience store when suddenly bikers were pulling up and stopping all around me! I paused, unnerved by their sudden presence as well as by their huge machines and loud talk. To their credit, however, they were immediately aware they had startled me, and a number went out of their way to put me at ease. Several even apologized for having surrounded me—said it wasn't intentional, that they had come into town planning to stop at the store anyway; they couldn't know that I would just happen to be walking by. Others smiled or nodded or said good morning. They reminded me of bonded thirty-somethings in an old beer commercial—macho but harmless—perhaps even good-natured and likeable. Anyway, they were soon off their bikes and heading into the store for coffee. I fell in with them thinking I could maybe use a whisky more than coffee.

By the time I came out, two bikers were already back on their steeds and talking back and forth between ear splitting revs of their engines. A member of their group was supposed to have rendezvoused with them there at the store, but he was overdue. In a country-western voice, one fellow declared he would "go out and bring 'im in," whereupon he wheelied his bike onto the road and sped off toward the west at break-neck speed.

I began walking again, but hadn't gone a mile when I heard him coming back, alone, and when he burst into view he was leaning forward on his screaming bike—jockey posture—perhaps imagining himself returning from some vitally important mission. He must have been going sixty miles per hour on the very narrow road. "Damn it," I said to myself, "he'll kill himself and they'll call it an accident, but in fact the fool-killer will have got 'im." Then, bothered by that callus thought and recalling the bikers had been a pleasant bunch, I mused on in silence: Beam, you were young once yourself, remember?... Yeah, but I was smarter than that.... Not always—you did your share of stupid things.... Not that stupid.... OK—maybe once or twice.

Twenty minutes later, I heard the whole gang blasting east out of town, which by then was at least two miles away.

*   *   *   *

That afternoon I passed through Prineville, Oregon, on state 126; then, just west of town, I found gravelly Houston Lake Road. This road parallels 126 for a dozen miles before curving left to rejoin the highway three miles to the south. I was happy to use the lake road, because it promised to spare me fifteen miles of heavy traffic. Once back on 126, I would have only seven additional miles to Redman, Oregon, and beyond that traffic should lighten.

A great deal of trash was strewn along the Prineville end of Houston Lake Road. Just west of town, there were dozens of cans and bottles, and in one place there was an illegal mini-dump containing rusty appliances, old car parts, even some ancient shop tools. The dumpers' attitude must have been, Why drive all the way to the dump if you can drop your trash at the edge of town?

Gradually the litter thinned to an occasional bag of garbage left over from somebody's fast-food lunch. The land changed too. Near town it had been barren and covered by low scrub; farther west were irrigated farms and attractive pastures.

I passed a weathered threesome of memorial crosses, which struck me as unlikely along a remote back road carrying so little traffic. But a half hour later, even before I saw another car, I came upon a another, very recent, accident site, this one with the usual fragmented car parts along with fluids spilled on the road. Teenagers, alcohol and speed, I thought to myself, the unholy trinity of teenage tragedy. I had heard it all before—most recently the previous month from the old rancher at the senior center.

Less than a mile past the accident site, I met Helen where she was parked in the driveway of a small ranch house. The rancher, John Dubois, was sitting on his quad bike telling Helen about the accident, which had happened only the day before. While taking her dog to a veterinarian, a middle-aged woman, completely sober, had crashed and was killed; the dog apparently survived. It happened in the middle of the day too— so much for my youth-and-alcohol theory. I was right, though, about the speed.

I commented to Helen about parking in John's driveway since she was normally scrupulous about avoiding private property. However, before she could answer, John cut in to explain that he had noticed her parked out by the road, and still upset about yesterday's crash, he had come down from the house and urged her into the driveway. He said it would get her "out of the line of fire." While she was moving the car, he went back in and got two Mountain Dews, one for Helen and one for me when I got there.

We had been chatting with John for ten or fifteen minutes when I recalled being interviewed by a reporter from Prineville's *Central Oregonian* a few days before. An article about The Great Walk would soon be appearing in the paper, and I mentioned that to John. He was immediately interested and said he would be sure to buy a copy.

But soon it was time to say good-bye, and a few minutes later Helen was driving ahead and I had returned to walking.

Things moved quickly the rest of the morning. An hour after talking with Helen and Dubois, I was approaching the curve in Houston Lake Road that would send me down to busy 126. But how, I wondered, could I put off coping with the highway a little longer? Could I maybe walk cross-country to Redmond?—it was only seven miles due west.

According to my map, the cross-country route appeared to be over pancake-flat rangeland. But there was a hitch. Somehow I would have to cross the North Unit Main Canal, a wide irrigation ditch that started near Bend, Oregon, twenty miles to the south, passed three miles east of Redmond, and eventually petered out near Madras, forty miles to the north.

Such were my thoughts as I approached Mr. Dick Cain, who was sitting in his pickup truck near the entry arch to his ranch. He had just given directions to a lost trucker, and we watched as that hard-working fellow wrestled his eighteen-wheeler through a U-turn in a nearby gravel lot. He had finished and was starting back toward Prineville when I asked Dick if the canal was swimmable.

Mr. Cain and Katie

"Don't even think about it," was his quick though pleasant reply. I don't remember what else he said, but I got the impression of a waterway a hundred feet across in places and possibly with swift currents.

"You don't have to walk cross-country anyway," Dick said. "Just follow around this curve, walk about three miles, and you'll come to state 126. Turn west there and it'll take you right into Redmond."

Of course I knew that already although I didn't say so, and after I thanked him I asked if I could take his picture. "No problem," came his reply, but he would like it if his dog Katie got into the picture too. Katie was half asleep on the passenger seat, but dozing or not, upon hearing her name she pulled herself up and stood with her front paws on Dick's lap. I quickly stepped back and snapped a picture, which shows a grinning Dick Cain and a sleepy-eyed Katie leaning out the driver's window.

"Poor Katie," I said, patting the dog's head, "yours is obviously a tough life." To which Cain responded with a hardy laugh.

Dick and I talked for another fifteen or so minutes—casual talk, weather talk—nothing explicitly revealing of character or personality. Nevertheless, in the years since, when I have recalled that quarter hour, my instincts have invariably told me that talking to Dick Cain was talking to a gentleman.

*   *   *   *

Not far from where I talked to Dick Cain, I came to a ranch-style house where the front yard was covered almost entirely by a neat layer of crushed gray stones. Here and there the gray stones were interrupted by circles of red gravel about twenty feet across, and in the middle of each sat an odd piece of old farm equipment. One circle contained an ancient wagon; another, some kind of towed rake; a third had a home-built affair with the tires of a tractor, the sides of a wagon, and chains, levers, and pushrods galore. The front end of this home-built whatever-it-was rested on a low, welded support, out of which extended a heavy tow bar. Its purpose was beyond this Easterner, although it was obviously the product of a very innovative mind.

I was taking pictures of the yard pieces, when I noticed a man standing in the doorway of a nearby building that looked like a small manufacturing facility. Curious, first about the yard pieces and then about the building, I walked over and was greeted by Mr. Daniel F. Rohrer Sr., owner of the Rohrer Manufacturing Company. Rohrer was a pleasant man, and soon he was giving me a tour of his facility, where he primarily manufactured T-Post Drivers—pneumatic devices for installing steel posts during the construction of fences.

Inside the building, large, floor-mounted, metalworking machines stood in various places; one especially large unit was even computer controlled. In one area sat a small table; in another, a large rack of partly assembled drivers. The building was clean, airy, and quiet; it crossed my mind that it was probably a good place to work.

Dan Rohrer Jr. and the T-Post Driver

After we went back outside, Mr. Rohrer's son, Daniel Jr., gave me a demonstration of a T-Post Driver installing a fence post. A small inexpensive air compressor was sufficient to power the device, and no more than twenty seconds passed from the time it began its cycle until the post was firmly in the ground. Of course Rohrer held patents on the concept, and he sold the drivers for $450 apiece. I told Helen they looked like a bargain; if I had a fence to build, even a short one, I would buy one in an instant. For somebody with miles of fence to install, it would obviously be a Godsend.

Everything around the Rohrer facility and adjacent grounds suggested energy, imagination, and ingenuity. I was not surprised when Mr. Rohrer Sr. said that he had been a machinist in the Navy and had been in the submarine service. He was the second very inventive ex-submariner I met that summer. He reminded me of the "cycle-car man" whom Helen and I had met in Riverton, Wyoming. He too had seen service in the subs.

Twenty minutes after leaving Rohrer's plant, I finally got to route 126, where I "bit the bullet" and turned west toward Redmond. Traffic was heavy and fast, but at least the road had wide shoulders so that passing cars left plenty of room. It had been a varied and interesting day, thanks to my having met Messrs. Dubois, Cain, and Rohrer. Even so, I was played out when I met Helen—of all places—where the highway crossed the North Unit Main Canal. Indeed, the canal was a good eighty feet across and it had a noticeable northbound current.

* * * *

I walked through Redmond the following morning, and by the end of the day we had reached the eastern slopes of the Cascade Mountains near Sisters. From there it would be 110 miles over to Sweet Home on the western slopes. I recalled driving the Cascades while in the army years before, and I especially remembered beautiful scenery made all the lovelier by frequent, unpredictable showers. I would not be disappointed this time. Over the following days, I would see spectacular changing landscapes of mountains and valleys, the weather, as expected, unsettled. One minute there would be sun, the next gathering clouds, then clearing skies, or maybe not—always changing, never the same for long. Sometimes the sun would break through lingering showers to dazzle droplets into exquisite rainbows, while ghost-like mists would rise from the shiny road. Trees with soaked and dripping leaves looked more like spring than early fall.

Autumn was indeed approaching. On September 2, as we began the day's walk, the snow line in the mountains was noticeably lower than it had been the night before. Beyond the mountains the sky glowed morning-blue, but here and there were broad tinges of pink. Helen shivered and remarked, "Pink morning, Phil, sailors warning. That's a winter sky—the snows are coming, you know."

WE REACH THE PACIFIC

Tuesday after Labor Day we moved to McKay's RV service center near Albany, Oregon. Lurch, hardly an example of quality workmanship, needed everything from modification of its propane furnace to repair of its generator—not to mention a thoroughgoing tune-up.

Although McKay's couldn't do the work until Thursday, they said we could camp in their parking lot until they got to the job and finished it. Good deal! The lot even had water, electrical hookups, and a place to empty holding tanks. After establishing ourselves, we used the rest of the day for doing chores. I washed the car, housecleaned the RV, and printed a new set of maps; meanwhile, Helen spent the afternoon cooking and baking. Extra wine with dinner was our anniversary celebration; we had been married forty-seven years.

The next day took me through Willamette National Forrest and along U.S. 20 toward Sweet Home. Wild raspberries grew in many places along the road, and Helen, while waiting at a rendezvous, picked a cupful which we washed and had with lunch. In the afternoon the road led through dense forests that were mixtures of evergreens and deciduous trees, the latter already turning shades of red and yellow, although without the brilliance of New England's autumn leaf shows. There was a chill in the air that seemed to hint of approaching endings—the end of the season, of course, but also the end of our walk.

Near Sweet Home, I approached a manufacturing complex that appeared as vast and impersonal as the Rohrer factory had appeared modest and inviting. In a large open area, a truck unloaded logs beside what looked like square pipes of some kind—possibly terracotta. A forklift busied about near a pile of pallets, and off to the left was a vast field of water sprinklers. Piles of logs stood ready to be loaded onto conveyer belts that led to several buildings, and these, in turn, were connected to each other by a labyrinth of sloping pipes—some carrying steam, judging by plumes of vapor that wafted up here and there.

A hundred yards farther on were two silo-like structures adjacent to a building with a tall smokestack, and on the far right, beside still another building, were stacks of finished product, all covered by tarpaulins.

But what might the product be? I wondered. My guess became that the stacks were chipboard or particleboard or possibly plywood. Sure enough, when I reached the western end of the complex, I spotted a natural-wood sign with a familiar pine-tree logo and the inscription: Willamette Industries Inc., Foster Plywood.

Vast indeed, both locally and nationally! Willamette Industries is a huge producer of wood and paper products with over a hundred facilities around the country.

*   *   *   *

On Thursday we were up at four o'clock and I was walking by five. By eight we had rendezvoused and driven back to McKay's to confer with the service manager about the needed repairs on Lurch. That went smoothly, and I was soon on the road again, eventually getting a twenty-mile day and finishing near the town of Tangent. An eight-mile drive back to the service center was followed by news that the mechanics were not quite finished with repairs. "Things are going a tad slow, Mr. Beam; we'll need your rig another day." That was no surprise; we had been expecting something like that, indeed hoping for it. Tired from being on the go all day, we hardly felt like breaking camp and moving to some local RV park, especially during rush-hour traffic and oncoming darkness.

So we whiled away another evening at McKay's, comfortably aware that the following day, while the mechanics were finishing Lurch, we would be covering still more ground. Late in the afternoon, we would return, pay up, and stay at McKay's one more night. Then we would break camp and move on to Newport, Oregon, which was—hooray!—on the Pacific Coast. Newport had definitely become our final destination, and it was now only sixty miles away.

*   *   *   *

I was in a buoyant mood as I walked through farming districts east of Corvallis. Autumn-gold fields were bordered by rows of trees, their summer-worn leaves scarcely freshened by a mild drizzle. Later it rained hard for a few minutes; then it abruptly stopped, leaving a double rainbow across the sky.

Only two, quick, unpleasant events marred the day. The first happened when I unthinkingly crossed against a traffic light in downtown Corvallis, and, in consequence, caused an attractive young woman to mildly brake her car. It was far from a near miss, but she would have none of my signaled apology. She pulled up very close, showed me a middle finger, and in a clear, low voice hissed "jerk" from five feet away and right in my face!

"God help your old man!" I angrily shouted, as people stared at me and the departing car. Few could have heard what she said, but everyone within fifty feet heard me.

Still smoldering from that encounter, I had walked but a few blocks when I overtook two teen-age girls sashaying along the sidewalk. I could hear them from twenty feet away, and although it was not clear what they were talking about (I couldn't have cared less) their speech was sprinkled with obscenities spat with exaggerated inflections and many gestures.

I stole a glance as I passed, and sure enough, they were as pretty as their language was foul. I had spent plenty of time at sea, and before that I was a bricklayer—obscene language was nothing new to me. Still, it bothered me there in that college town, and probably more so since it came from three young women. It may be a generational thing, or even a matter of gender, but in truth, it would have bothered me less had they been young men with foul mouths instead of young women.

But only a few hours later there came a third chance meeting with young people, and this one was as agreeable as the others were disturbing. We were sitting in the car eating lunch, when a police car pulled off the road and stopped a few yards behind us.

"Cops are coming," Helen said, looking in the rear view mirror. "Two 'youts' ... tall and short ... you rob a bank?"

"Nope, a gas station. You watch. One of these guys'll be the finger-witch's husband. Married to her, he's bound to be in a bad mood."

Car doors slammed and soon they were approaching my side of the car, the passenger side, as I stuck out my head to say hello.

"Any problems, sir?" This from the taller one.

"We're fine, thanks. Just finishing lunch."

On impulse I started to get out of the car even as I envisioned them ordering me not to—as per some by-the-book procedure for approaching car passengers. Suddenly inhibited by that thought, I sat back down; then, seeing their smiles, I again began to get out. This time, however, I banged my head hard on the door frame.

Moments later, I was out of the car and standing with the shorter fellow steadying me by the elbow.

"You okay, sir?" he asked.

"Okay till I did that; I do it about once a week."

"Sure there's no problem?" asked the taller one again—hopefully, it seemed to me. Something about the pair reminded me of boy scouts on good-deed patrol.

"No, we're walking across the country. Started in Connecticut and we'll be finished when we get to Newport."

The cops were a friendly pair, which was a tonic for Helen and me—especially me.

Upon learning that the end of our walk would be Newport, the shorter fellow made us promise to visit Sam's, a restaurant on Bay Boulevard in the Old Town's historic district. "They're famous for their clam chowder," he was happy to tell us. "It's the best I've had anywhere."

We duly promised not to miss Sam's, and after some parting small talk they left. I hung around a while longer—until Helen suggested I might sprout roots and grow fast to the car seat. Then I got back to walking, but in a better mood thanks to the cops. They were welcome opposites of the cheap-talking girls of a few hours before.

In late afternoon I reached tiny Flynn on the eastern edge of the Costal Range. The skies had clouded again, and a hard, chilly rain was setting in as I ducked under a tree, a mere hundred yards from where Helen sat warm and dry in the car. Getting colder by the minute, I shouted three or four times hoping she would hear me or just happen to look back. No luck either way, and when I couldn't stand it any longer, I made a wet dash for the car.

"Where've you been, Honey?" she asked when I plunked into the passenger seat. "Why didn't you call on your walkie-talkie? I'd have come back and picked you up."

"I don't have my walkie-talkie."

"Where is it?"

"On the kitchen table."

Helen wanted to quit for the day and head back to Lurch, but I was determined to get in another few miles. "I can do three in an hour," I said. "Let's wait for twenty minutes. Maybe it'll stop."

So began a half hour of "it's letting up," "no it's not," "sun's comin' out," "not a chance"—until we eventually gave up and headed back to McKay's, and Lurch's welcome warmth. The mechanics had finished work on the propane furnace.

*   *   *   *

Strange ambivalent moods came over us that night. In the morning, we would break camp and move to Harbor Village Campground, which overlooks Yaquina Bay at Newport, Oregon. After that, only two more days of walking would bring us to the Pacific. We looked forward to returning to Connecticut and home, yet we were mildly sad that our golden-years odyssey was ending. Another chapter in life was closing, and Helen wondered aloud about what we could possibly do next that would seem anywhere near as interesting.

Luck was with us again when we got the only available campsite at Harbor Village, and it proved unusually nice. Helen said it seemed as if we had had a great deal of good luck during our long walk west. Here we were on the West Coast; we had crossed the country one step at a time, and except for that week in Alliance, Nebraska,—the week I was laid up with tendonitis—neither of us had had any serious health problems. In fact, we agreed we looked great, at least to each other.

We did not hurry back to walking after arriving at the Village; rather we spent an entire day searching for back roads south from Flynn and thence west through the coastal mountains. Our map showed such roads, and had we found them, they would have allowed me to walk ten or twelve miles south of U.S. 20, which can be busy in that part of the country. However, in spite of eight hours of probing unmarked byways, inquiring at rare houses, and even, at one point, climbing a hill to reconnoiter with binoculars, we never were able to find a way through. In late afternoon we gave up and returned to Newport, where, anticipating completion of the walk, we bought two wine glasses for drinking celebratory champagne upon stepping into the Pacific.

The following morning I was back on the road, and well rested and sensing the end, I fairly flew along. There was no stopping for lunch; instead, Helen handed me a sandwich as I briefly paused beside the car. By one o'clock I had covered nearly fifteen miles through woods that were almost like rain forests. Trees were tall and close together; the forest floor was dense with ferns and mosses—there was an aroma from those wet woodlands, a potpourri of delicate scents against a background of fragrant pine. When we quit about four o'clock, I had covered thirty-two miles, and it seemed unreal that the next day would bring us to the Pacific, which was now only sixteen miles ahead.

*   *   *   *

Neither Helen nor I slept much that last night. We tossed and turned, and one or other would check the time, it seemed, every few minutes. About four-thirty, I gave up and crawled out of bed to put on coffee while trying not to disturb her. "Make all the noise you want," she muttered. "I've been awake for hours."

We were driving out to walk's end by six o'clock, just as it was starting to get light. Over the preceding weeks, the ever-later dawns had been reminding us of the approach of autumn, but that seemed altogether fitting. Summer was over, our walk was ending, and the adventure that had become the focus of our lives was coming to its inevitable close. We were both subdued. For two years we had anticipated the moment, half dreaded it, happily foreseen it, and often wondered if

Newport Ahead by the Sea

it would ever come. Today it *would* come, but how would we feel tomorrow? and what would we do the day after that?

Walking began in a thick fog which seemed to confine my hyped-up mind to a special awareness of itself and nearby things along the road. The external world converged inward from fog-limiting paleness to the black-and-white contrasts of nearby trees, rocks, and the narrow road ahead. Except for an occasional car, noises were few and muted, and they came from nearby—a pair of sparrows, a roadside stream, the quiet cadence of my footsteps as I hurried on.

Later, the mist burned away to reveal a landscape awash in brilliant sunlight, and eventually I was cresting a hill and approaching a blue and gold sign that invited people to "Explore Newport," and declared the town to be the "Friendliest." I paused. Ahead, framed by trees and down a half-mile grade, lay Newport itself, and beyond, flat out to the horizon, the endless reaches of the Pacific.

Into the Pacific

I stood there for some moments, almost reluctant to go on. Did this adventure really have to end? Had we actually reached the Pacific Ocean? Was this maybe all a dream? I drank some water, carefully composed a picture, and then, getting hold of myself, I muttered, "Quit stalling, Beam. Come back to real life and walk on down through town."

The sun was high as Helen and I hurried down a beachfront hill and out onto sand near the water's edge. "Well Phil," Helen said, as we stood staring beyond the breakers, "we made it ... not bad for a pair of oldsters."

"We're not finished yet," I replied. "We still have to get our feet wet."

Two years before, she had not hesitated when I suggested we walk across the country; now, and again without hesitation, she laughed and squeezed my hand as we ran forward and splashed our feet in the surf.

BUT THERE WAS A LITTLE MORE WALKING TO DO

Helen and I were slow starting the long drive home to Connecticut. For two days we remained in Newport, during which we lazily explored the historic district which lies along Yaquina Bay. A little harbor off Bay Boulevard was filled with yachts and fishing boats, and farther along the street we came to canneries, gift shops, and restaurants. Sure enough, we eventually found Sam's, right where the young cop said it would be.

It turned out that Sam's was packed and we had to wait a half hour to be seated. In addition, the chowder, when it finally came, was only so-so. "Phil," Helen said, as we walked back into the street, "this just confirms my belief that you need to take a twenty-something's restaurant recommendations with a big grain of salt."

"Why?"

"Because at that age they're always hungry, and everything they eat tastes good."

After Sam's, we walked around town like ordinary tourists— visited a wax museum, saw "Ripley's Believe It or Not," even watched sea lions bark and cavort in quiet waters behind a cannery.

Another full day passed before we got around to starting for Connecticut, but we wouldn't simply rush home. We would definitely stop on the way and close those bothersome gaps in the walk, namely Rhinecliff Bridge at Kingston, New York, and McClugage Bridge at Peoria, Illinois.

We expected no problem at McClugage. The eastbound lanes that were closed on our way out would doubtless be open by now. Even if there was no pedestrian walk, there would surely be a breakdown lane. Walking it, I would be facing on-coming cars from the west, but they would be passing eight or ten feet away. It should be easy and reasonably safe, though plenty noisy.

*   *   *   *

We arrived in Peoria four days after leaving Newport, but lo and behold, the bridge work still wasn't finished! The same two lanes were still being worked on, and groups of men with heavy equipment were busy near the top and down the west side.

So what to do?—walk four miles south to a different bridge, even though it would mean a detour of eight miles?—or start across McClugage even though it was being worked on. If stopped, I could always go the long way, once I talked my way out of the ensuing jam, if any. Five minutes of "back-and-forth" followed, but in the end we decided to try McClugage. Helen would drop me off well east of my old stopping point just to be sure we didn't leave a gap.

And then I was on my way: Going good … going good … going good. Keep walking, Beam, you're a quarter of the way up.

Things were still going good when somewhere, about a hundred yards from the top, I passed two men standing beside a pickup truck and bending over blueprints laid out on the hood. They hardly looked up as I nodded, smiled as confidently as I could, and kept right on going—as if it were perfectly natural for a morning walker to be heading right into a bridge construction site. So far, so good.

For a few minutes I thought I was in the clear, but suddenly the pickup was coming up the hill *backwards*. It passed at a good clip and continued another twenty yards before almost screeching to a halt. One of the men I had just walked past hopped out (big as he was), and although he didn't actually block my way, he stood away from the truck with his legs apart and his hands on his hips. Clearly, we were going to talk.

"Good morning," I said and showed what I hoped was a disarming smile. "Nice morning for a walk."

"Good morning yourself," he answered. He wore a hard hat and had a sun-browned complexion; his size alone could have been intimidating, but there was something about his tone of voice, the inflection, the barely straight face.... I had seen the demeanor before, and my immediate take was that he would be a decent enough guy—even if he did order me off the bridge. *This'll be okay,* I thought.

Then he got down to business: "Sir, do you mind telling me just what *in hell* you're doing up on this here bridge?" He cocked an eyebrow and raised his hands palms up.

"Nothing much. Just trying to get across the river; it's too dangerous to walk over there." I gestured with a thumb toward the north-side lanes. "Anyway, I'll be off here in less than ten minutes. No harm done."

Not a good choice of words, those last three.

"'No harm done,' you say? 'Just trying to get across the river'? You gotta be kidding! Why don't you walk someplace where you won't get yourself killed?" He brought a hand up to his mouth, but too late to hide the beginnings of a smile.

"I'm walking across America," I hurriedly went on. "So I've *gotta* walk across here. Soon as I finish this bridge, I'll have only one more to go. That's Rhinecliff, and it crosses the Hudson near Kingston, New York. Once I've crossed that one, I'll have an absolutely unbroken walk track clear across the United States!"

"Well, you might get to walk across Rhinestone or whatever you call it, but you can't walk across my bridge. I got men workin' up there!"

Just then, to my delight, a driver in the roaring north-side lanes must have done something wrong because horns blared, brakes screeched, and traffic slowed to a crawl before speeding up again. A couple of people gestured and one guy rolled down his window and yelled the f-word. It sounded more like Manhattan than Peoria.

"See that?" I said. "That's why I'm over here. Walking over there I'd probably get run down or shot."

He groaned and raised his hand to his forehead before quickly dropping it again to cover his face. Next, he wanted to know where I stayed at night. And why wasn't I wearing a pack if I was walking across America? "Is this bullshit?" he suddenly demanded, but it didn't come out harsh.

"None at all," I said. "We have a motor home that we move along as the walk progresses. Right now it's parked down there in that Ford dealership parking lot." I pointed in the direction of the dealership, but it was below the bridge and so close you couldn't see it from where we stood. I plunged on: "And I don't need a pack today because my wife's waitin' for me on the other side of the bridge. Soon as I get across, we'll head on east—be home in three or four days."

"Well, how do you do this walking?—she drop you off and then drive ahead, park, and wait till you catch up? … and then do it over again? … and again and again?"

He caught on quick. Good sign. He was becoming interested, forgetting for a moment the absurdity of a skinny old man walking through a bridge construction site.

"That's how it goes," I said, "rain or shine … day in, day out."

Another half dozen questions followed as he got steadily more into it. Finally he said, "I never heard of anything like this in my life. Sir, can I ask how old you are?"

Gotcha! I thought to myself, and he knew it too as he dropped his hand—giving up on hiding the smile.

He did not actually say that I could walk across the bridge. What he said was, "Now, *if* you walk up through there, don't for God's sake stop and talk to anybody. Anybody tries to stop you, you tell 'im you're doing exactly what the super told you to do, namely, gettin' the hell off this bridge pronto. I could get in a lot of trouble over this. By the way, why didn't you just *ask* before you hauled off and charged up here?"

"Hell," I said, "I figured you'd never give me permission, but you'd probably let me go if I got most of the way up."

"Get on with you," he said. "I could still change my mind."

But we both knew he wouldn't, and we were actually laughing as we shook hands and he got back into his truck. How relaxed I felt as he started downhill going forward, as compared to how anxious I'd felt when he barreled past me going uphill and backward!

And what happened when I walked through the construction site? Surprisingly, not a thing. I threaded my way between compressors, jack hammers, concrete saws—even around a truck that was spraying water to keep the dust down. The people I passed either looked up and barely nodded, or ignored me completely and kept on working. It was almost as if I weren't there.

I found Helen waiting on the western approach exactly where she had swung in to drop me off the year before. Traffic was lighter this time, but I thought she took a chance stopping there. She said she didn't want me walking any farther than necessary along that speedway, didn't want me "run over this late in the game." Nevertheless, I walked past the car about fifty feet—just to be sure the new and old tracks overlapped. Then we drove back to Lurch and had coffee before continuing the trip east.

*   *   *   *

Two days later we pulled into a familiar gravel parking lot at Weys Corners, New York, three miles from Rhinecliff Bridge. We had stopped there the last day we walked in the autumn of 1998, and it was there that Helen found the dollar and forty-nine cents, and where she first mentioned the idea of collecting cans to pay for campground fees. Back then, NO PEDESTRIAN signs and a frowning cop had kept us from walking the bridge, but signs or no signs, I would walk it this time—absent the law.

Dusk was early that evening, and a light rain was falling as we heated TV dinners and made plans for a 3 a.m. cross-bridge dash. Where we were parked was private property, but we would stay there anyway and set the alarm for two o'clock. A quick breakfast of coffee and eggs would do; then Helen would drop me off at the east end of the bridge before driving across to wait on the other side.

Two o'clock came quickly, and while we were eating, we decided that our meeting place would be on Ulster Landing Road, just beyond the river. "I'll keep the motor running and the parking lights on," Helen said. "You'll see me." Then she broke into a mischievous laugh. "But wouldn't that Idaho lawman just love this? It's not only pitch dark, it's raining besides. He'd be coaching you on how to talk your way free in case a cop stopped you." She was referring to the sheriff we had met near Fairfield, Idaho—the fellow who told us about Mormon Crickets.

"His advice was to play dumb if stopped," I said. "If a cop stops me tonight, he'll think I'm in my dotage."

The rain slaked off slightly as I started across the bridge about quarter of three. There were no cars in sight, and progress was good for the first few hundred yards; then lights appeared as a pickup truck approached from the east. Fortunately, not far ahead was a group of Jersey barriers protecting a work area along the south side of the roadway. I trotted behind the nearest barrier and ducked onto my hands and knees—and right into a puddle. That car passed just in time for another to come from the west, then two more from the east, and still another from the west. Just as I began wondering if I would ever get out of the water, the traffic cleared, and for the rest of the way only four more cars came by. To my relief none was a police cruiser, although I needn't have worried as I would soon find out.

West of the river the bridge approach forms an overpass with Ulster Landing Road, and as I came down the off-ramp, I spotted Helen parked beside a closed gas station with the motor running and the lights turned *off*. And right beside her was a police car! I walked a ways farther just to get the overlap; then I returned and started down the ramp toward the cars. I was scarcely concerned about the cop After all, the cross-bridge mission was complete! What could he do? Fine Helen for trespassing? Fine me for crossing the bridge? Put us both in chains? At the moment I was on such a high that no matter what the law might have done, it would have been a while before I began worrying about it.

But even before I got to the cars, the cop, satisfied no mischief was afoot, drove away. Helen said he seemed barely awake and muttered only a sleepy "OK," when she told him she was waiting for her husband. He wasn't the least bit curious about where I was or what I might be doing around a closed gas station at three in the morning.

An hour after finishing at the bridge, we broke camp and started the 120-mile drive home, where we arrived midmorning in a steady rain. As we drove down the long driveway, it was immediately evident what six months of neglect had done to the lawn. I had again forgotten to hire someone to keep it mowed, and now it was two feet high and long gone to seed. "I'll start mowing tomorrow," I said as we went into the house.

"Well, first we'll have to get rid of the mice," Helen said. She was kidding, but within hours it was obvious the house was again infested. I would have the grass under control in a week, but it would be two additional weeks before we would declare victory in the War of the Rodents.

But long grass and a mouse invasion were only minor distractions. By the time we were home a mere week we had a bigger problem, namely, a nagging sense of incompleteness. Our comfortable feeling of having walked clear across America had quickly begun to fade. Of course we both knew what was happening. For two years, to finish the walk had simply meant getting to the Pacific. However, no sooner had we arrived there than to finish began to mean filling the gaps, i.e., walking the McClugage and Rhinecliff bridges. Thoughtlessly, we assumed that walking them would be enough, that we would then feel satisfied we had walked all the way across the country.

We should have known better. Even before we were home that rainy Sunday, indeed, soon after we crossed Rhinecliff Bridge, that annoying meaning of to finish had begun to change again. Clearly, we would feel the walk was truly complete only when we had an unbroken track from ocean to ocean. That meant there was a little more walking to do, specifically, from some nearby place on the Atlantic coast to our home in Lebanon, a distance of about fifty miles.

We put off the *to-finish* issue for another few days by telling each other there was really no hurry; after all, we were healthy, and nothing loomed that might make completing the walk impossible. We could do the remaining segment whenever the spirit moved us, maybe even the following spring.

Of course those rationalizations didn't help for long. Clearly, we had to get that last short segment walked, and soon; we would have no peace of mind till the thing was done.

So the following Sunday, exactly one week after we arrived home, we drove to Misquamicut Beach near Westerly, Rhode Island. I took off my shoes and socks, pulled up both pant legs, and watched the surf approach, recede, approach, recede.... A quick dash in and out—oops!—wet pants cuffs, and then I was walking up the beach and toward the road. We had begun what would truly be the last leg of our coast-to-coast walk.

The nine miles I walked that day took me through Westerly, across the Rhode Island-Connecticut border, and finally into Mystic, Connecticut. I felt as if I were almost home when we stopped for the day near famous Mystic Seaport, a place where I had worked as a volunteer and would soon be working again.

The following morning, I crossed a downtown drawbridge over the Mystic River and continued toward the town of Groton. I had driven the road dozens of times, but I had never walked it before. Again I was struck by the difference between seeing things from a car and seeing them while walking. Helen and I had noticed similar differences two years before, the day we began the walk.

Once a young woman pulled up and asked for directions to a cider mill which she was "very very sure" was in the immediate vicinity—"within a mile or so." In the back, strapped in her car seat, a little girl laughed and cooed even as I struggled with illusive memories: Yes, a cider mill, an apple press—steam driven of course. I could picture it, I'd been there, I'd bought cider there. But where was it?

"Can't help you," I finally had to say. "You'd best go back into Mystic; somebody there will give you directions."

Only after she had driven away did I remember where the mill was. It was not nearby as she had thought; rather it was three miles north of Mystic and thus six full miles from where we talked. It occurred to me that had she not been so "very very sure" the mill was close by, or if I had been quicker on the uptake, I might have remembered where the place was and been able to tell her the way. I consoled myself knowing that somebody in town would surely set her straight.

Later, I branched down into Groton City and walked past the Electric Boat shipyard on the Thames River. There was a submarine under construction, and its superstructure looked far more fitting there in the sea-level shipyard than the Hawkbill's had in the desert near Arco.

A mile north of Electric Boat I crossed the Thames on the Gold Star Memorial Bridge; then it was north through Quaker Hill and Oakdale to just west of Gillman. The leaves were dry, of course; autumn was well along, and people were getting ready for Halloween. On the outskirts of Montville, where Helen and I had once lived, I passed houses guarded by grinning jack-o'-lanterns, ghosts in sheets, and here and there a witch. However, one house was watched over by a beautiful angel with delicate blue wings. Could this angel, I wondered, be someone's answer to the ghosts and goblins of pagan Halloween? And why did everything seem so clear, so alive, so vibrant that autumn afternoon?

*   *   *   *

Came the last morning. Two years less a week had passed since we walked out our driveway and turned west toward Lebanon Green. We recalled the excitement, the unease, the sense of coming adventure. Five miles from home, while walking on Gallop Hill Road, we had passed through a junction where McCall Lane comes up from the south. Little did we know that two years later, at that very corner, I would intersect our outbound track and the coast-to-coast odyssey would be complete.

By eleven o'clock, I had only two miles to go, and soon after I was passing an old Congregational church where our daughter and family worship on Sundays. I double-timed on, as if some Halloween spirit were in hot pursuit, until presently I approached the west end of Church Street where it abuts McCall. *Turn right,* I said to myself, *and keep moving. You've only a mile to go!*

Fifteen minutes later, I could see Helen far ahead at the corner of, yes, hooray, Gallup Hill Road! Waving her arms like a cheerleader, she was urging me on; I could faintly hear her calling: "Keep walking, keep walking, Phil; you're almost there!"

The closer I came the more clearly I could see her smile— closer, closer, then suddenly I *was* there, the walk was complete, and I tagged her with a celebratory kiss. She liked that, although she immediately said, "Phil, keep going. Cross the road. Get the overlap. That way we'll always know there were no gaps in this walk anywhere—I mean anywhere!—from the Atlantic to the Pacific Ocean!"

"You're overdoing it," I grumbled as I crossed the road and walked well into grass on the other side. Then turning, I called, "We're finished, Helen, we did it!"

"Absolutely!" came her happy reply. "But Phil, didn't you say something about writing a book?"

Made in the USA
Lexington, KY
27 May 2014